WEST ACADEMIC PUBLISHING'S LAW SCHOOL ADVISORY BOARD

JESSE H. CHOPER
Professor of Law and Dean Emeritus
University of California, Berkeley

JOSHUA DRESSLER
Distinguished University Professor Emeritus, Frank R. Strong Chair in Law
Michael E. Moritz College of Law, The Ohio State University

YALE KAMISAR
Professor of Law Emeritus, University of San Diego
Professor of Law Emeritus, University of Michigan

MARY KAY KANE
Professor of Law, Chancellor and Dean Emeritus
University of California, Hastings College of the Law

LARRY D. KRAMER
President, William and Flora Hewlett Foundation

JONATHAN R. MACEY
Professor of Law, Yale Law School

ARTHUR R. MILLER
University Professor, New York University
Formerly Bruce Bromley Professor of Law, Harvard University

GRANT S. NELSON
Professor of Law Emeritus, Pepperdine University
Professor of Law Emeritus, University of California, Los Angeles

A. BENJAMIN SPENCER
Justice Thurgood Marshall Distinguished Professor of Law
University of Virginia School of Law

JAMES J. WHITE
Robert A. Sullivan Professor of Law Emeritus
University of Michigan

INTRODUCTION TO EUROPEAN UNION LAW

CASES AND MATERIALS

■ ■ ■

Jens C. Dammann
*Ben H. and Kitty King Powell Chair in Business
and Commercial Law*

AMERICAN CASEBOOK SERIES®

The publisher is not engaged in rendering legal or other professional advice, and this publication is not a substitute for the advice of an attorney. If you require legal or other expert advice, you should seek the services of a competent attorney or other professional.

American Casebook Series is a trademark registered in the U.S. Patent and Trademark Office.

© 2019 LEG, Inc. d/b/a West Academic
     444 Cedar Street, Suite 700
     St. Paul, MN 55101
     1-877-888-1330

West, West Academic Publishing, and West Academic are trademarks of West Publishing Corporation, used under license.

Printed in the United States of America

ISBN: 978-1-64242-921-3

PREFACE

This casebook is designed to be used in U.S.-style classes on European Union law. Hence, there are several ways in which it is different from many of the existing treatises and casebooks on European Union law.

To begin, this casebook presents a selection of cases to be discussed in depth rather than trying to provide an exhaustive survey of all areas of European Union law. This approach requires selectiveness. Therefore, this casebook focuses on foundational concepts such as the supremacy of EU law, the role of the Court of Justice, state liability, the fundamental freedoms, and topics of great political importance such as the euro crisis and Brexit. By contrast, other areas that are sometimes covered in treatises on European Union law, such as antitrust or social policy, are outside the scope of this volume.

Furthermore, this casebook goes beyond a study of legal doctrine. Because it would be a fool's errand to understand modern EU law without considering insights from other fields, it introduces the student to historical, political, and economic perspectives.

Great efforts were made to limit the book's length. For better or for worse, EU law is typically taught as a two or three credit course. Accordingly, most teachers will find it difficult to cover an entire casebook unless it is sufficiently concise.

The appendix of this volume contains central provisions of European Union law that this casebook relies on. Students who want to study additional norms of EU law or cases that are not reprinted in this casebook will find both at https://eur-lex.europa.eu/homepage.html.

Comments and suggestions are most welcome. Please send them to JDammann@law.utexas.edu.

Finally, I wish to thank the various individuals who have been involved in preparing this casebook for publication. They include, in alphabetical order, Rachel Crooks, Jael Dammann, Michael Davis, Samuel Krauss, Henry Schiller, and Andrew Van Osselaer.

JENS DAMMANN

March 3, 2019

SUMMARY OF CONTENTS

PREFACE III

TABLE OF CASES XVII

PART 1. BACKGROUND

Chapter 1. Historical Background 3
A. Early Efforts at European Integration 4
B. The First Steps Towards European Integration 12
C. Theories of European Integration 15

Chapter 2. The Founding of the European Communities 17
A. The European Coal and Steel Community 17
B. The Treaties of Rome 21
C. The Development of the European Economic Community 22
D. The Development of EEC/EC/EU Membership 25
E. How to Join the European Union 27

Chapter 3. The Basics of European Union Law 33
A. The Institutional Structure 33
B. The Legal Framework 45

PART 2. THE JUDICIARY

Chapter 4. The Court of Justice 53
A. Composition 53
B. The Role of the Advocates-General 54
C. The Law Governing the Court and Its Procedure 54
D. Jurisdiction 55
E. Interpretative Methodology 57
F. How Powerful Is the Court of Justice? 59

Chapter 5. The Preliminary Rulings Procedure 63
A. Interpretation and Validity 63
B. National Courts 64
C. The Necessity Rule 67
D. Limitations on the Duty to Refer 72

Chapter 6. Enforcement Actions 77
A. Overview of the Procedure 77
B. The Reasoned Opinion 78
C. Infringement 81
D. Defenses 88

PART 3. CHARACTERISTICS OF EU LAW

Chapter 7. The Direct Effect Principle 95
  A. Background: Monism v. Dualism 95
  B. Treaty Provisions 98
  C. Regulations 102
  D. Directives 103

Chapter 8. The Supremacy of EU Law 121
  A. Flaminio Costa v. E.N.E.L. 121
  B. Subsequent Cases 123
  C. Supremacy: Priority in Application 127
  D. The Supremacy of EU Law and the Member State Courts ... 129

Chapter 9. State Liability for Violations of EU Law 137
  A. The Origin of the State Liability Doctrine 138
  B. The Preconditions of State Liability 141

Chapter 10. The Legislative Process 151
  A. Competence 151
  B. Subsidiarity 153
  C. Necessity to Achieve Objectives of the Treaty 154
  D. Procedure 154

PART 4. THE INTERNAL MARKET

Chapter 11. Free Movement of Goods: The Customs Union 171
  A. Customs Duties and Charges Having Equivalent Effect 171
  B. Article 110 TFEU 180

Chapter 12. Free Movement of Goods: Quantitative Restrictions ... 191
  A. Quantitative Restrictions 191
  B. Measures Having Equivalent Effect 191
  C. Justifications 199
  D. Practice Questions 223

Chapter 13. Free Movement of Workers: Personal Scope of Application 227
  A. Worker 227
  B. The Public Service Exception 239
  C. Discriminatory and Non-Discriminatory Obstacles 245
  D. Justifications 249
  E. Employers 249
  F. Practice Questions 254

Chapter 14. Directive 2004/38/EC and Regulation 1612/68/EEC 257
A. Directive 2004/38/EC 257
B. Regulation 1612/68/EEC 267
C. Practice Questions 268

Chapter 15. Freedom of Establishment 273
A. Discriminatory and Non-Discriminatory Obstacles 273
B. Justifications 273
C. Companies 274
D. Practice Questions 298

Chapter 16. Freedom to Provide Services 301
A. Services 301
B. Personal Scope of Protection 304
C. The Interstate Element 305
D. Discriminatory and Non-Discriminatory Obstacles 305
E. Justifications 308
F. Practice Questions 313

Chapter 17. Free Movement of Capital 317
A. Movement of Capital and Payments 317
B. Discriminatory and Non-Discriminatory Obstacles 325
C. Justifications 325
D. Practice Questions 325

Chapter 18. Fundamental Freedoms: Common Problems 327
A. Failure to Act 327
B. Private Parties 339
C. Practice Questions 343

PART 5. CURRENT CHALLENGES

Chapter 19. The Monetary Union 347
A. Historical Background 347
B. Joining and Leaving the Eurozone 350
C. The Monetary Union: An Economic Perspective 353
D. The State of Economic and Fiscal Integration 358

Chapter 20. Leaving the European Union 367
A. Historical Background 367
B. Can Withdrawing Member States Change Their Minds? 373
C. The European Union's International Treaties 383
D. International Agreements Following Withdrawal from the EU 389
E. EFTA 391
F. Expulsion from the European Union? 394

Annex 397
Part 1: Excerpts from the Treaty on European Union 397

Part 2:	Excerpts from the Treaty on the Functioning of the European Union	410
Part 3:	Directive 2004/38/EC	462
Part 4:	Regulation No. 1612/68/EEC	480

INDEX.. 485

TABLE OF CONTENTS

PREFACE III

TABLE OF CASES XVII

PART 1. BACKGROUND

Chapter 1. Historical Background 3
A. Early Efforts at European Integration 4
    1. The Briand Memorandum.. 4
    2. Rekindling the Idea of European Integration After World War II ... 6
        Sir Winston Churchill, A 'United States of Europe' Speech 19
            September 1946, Zurich, Switzerland 6
B. The First Steps Towards European Integration 12
    1. The Organisation for Economic Co-Operation and Development ... 12
    2. The Treaty of Brussels 13
    3. Council of Europe 13
C. Theories of European Integration 15

Chapter 2. The Founding of the European Communities 17
A. The European Coal and Steel Community 17
    Robert Schuman, Proposal Announced at the French Ministry of
        Foreign Affairs ("The Schuman Declaration"), Paris, March 9,
        1950 18
B. The Treaties of Rome 21
C. The Development of the European Economic Community 22
D. The Development of EEC/EC/EU Membership 25
E. How to Join the European Union 27

Chapter 3. The Basics of European Union Law 33
A. The Institutional Structure 33
    1. The European Council... 33
    2. The Council 34
    3. The European Parliament 35
    4. The European Commission 36
    5. The Court of Justice of the European Union 39
        a) The Court of Justice 40
        b) The General Court 40
        c) Specialized Courts: The Civil Service Tribunal 40
    6. The European Central Bank... 40
    7. The Court of Auditors... 42

8. The Economic and Social Committee and the Committee of the Regions 42
   Protecting Member State Autonomy in the European Union: Some Cautionary Tales From American Federalism 43
B. The Legal Framework 45
   1. European Union Law Versus Member State Law 45
   2. Primary Versus Secondary Law 45
   3. Regulations, Directives, and Decisions 46
      a) Regulations 46
      b) Directives 46
      c) Decisions 48
      d) Opinions and Recommendations 48

PART 2. THE JUDICIARY

Chapter 4. The Court of Justice 53
A. Composition 53
B. The Role of the Advocates-General 54
C. The Law Governing the Court and Its Procedure 54
D. Jurisdiction 55
E. Interpretative Methodology 57
   1. Wording 57
   2. Teleological Reasoning 57
   3. Dynamic Interpretation 58
   4. Systematic Arguments 58
   5. Legislative History 59
F. How Powerful Is the Court of Justice? 59

Chapter 5. The Preliminary Rulings Procedure 63
A. Interpretation and Validity 63
B. National Courts 64
   1. What Is a Court? 64
      RTL Belgium SA 65
   2. The Absence of Remedies Under Member State Law 66
C. The Necessity Rule 67
   Pasquale Foglia v. Mariella Novello ["Foglia I"] 68
   Pasquale Foglia v. Mariella Novello ["Foglia II"] 70
D. Limitations on the Duty to Refer 72
   1. Issues That Have Already Been Decided 72
   2. The *Acte Clair* Doctrine 73
      Srl CILFIT and Lanificio di Gavardo SpA v. Ministry of Health 74

Chapter 6. Enforcement Actions 77
A. Overview of the Procedure 77
B. The Reasoned Opinion 78
   Commission v. Grand Duchy of Luxembourg 80

C.	Infringement	81
	1. Administrative Practice	82
	Commission v. Ireland	82
	2. Enforcement Proceedings and Member State Courts	84
	Commission v. Italy	85
D.	Defenses	88
	1. Force Majeure	88
	Commission v. Hellenic Republic	88
	2. Internal Difficulties	89
	3. Reciprocity	89
	4. Other Excuses	90

PART 3. CHARACTERISTICS OF EU LAW

Chapter 7. The Direct Effect Principle 95
A. Background: Monism v. Dualism 95
   Commitment and Diffusion, How and Why National Constitutions Incorporate International Law 96
B. Treaty Provisions 98
   NV Algemene Transporten Expeditie Onderneming van Gend & Loos v. Netherlands Inland Revenue Administration 99
   The Transformation of Europe 102
C. Regulations 102
D. Directives 103
   1. Vertical Direct Effect 105
      a) Unconditional 106
      b) Sufficiently Precise 106
         Andrea Francovich & Danila Bonifaci et al. v. Italian Republic 107
   2. Quasi-Horizontal Effect 110
      Unilever Italia SpA v. Central Food SpA 111
   3. The Requirement to Interpret Member State Law in Conformity with EU Law 113
      Marleasing SA v. La Comercial Internacional de Alimentacion SA 113
      Konstantinos Adeneler et al. v. Ellinikos Organismos Galaktos (ELOG) 115

Chapter 8. The Supremacy of EU Law 121
A. Flaminio Costa v. E.N.E.L. 121
   Flaminio Costa v. E.N.E.L. 121
B. Subsequent Cases 123
   1. Member State Law Predating the Establishment of the European Economic Community 123
   2. Member State Constitutional Law 124
   3. Member State Administrative Acts 124

		4.	Member State Judicial Decisions 125
			Rosmarie Kapferer v. Schlank & Schick GmbH 125

C. Supremacy: Priority in Application.. 127
D. The Supremacy of EU Law and the Member State Courts 129
   "Solange I".. 129
   "Solange II".. 133

Chapter 9. State Liability for Violations of EU Law 137
A. The Origin of the State Liability Doctrine... 138
   Andrea Francovich & Danila Bonifaci et al. v. Italian Republic........... 138
B. The Preconditions of State Liability 141
   1. A Sufficiently Serious Violation of EU Law..................................... 141
      Brasserie du Pecheur SA v. Bundesrepublik Deutschland and
      The Queen v. Secretary of State for Transport, ex parte:
      Factortame Ltd and others 141
   2. State Liability for Court Decisions? 143
      Gerhard Köbler v. Republik Österreich 143

Chapter 10. The Legislative Process.. 151
A. Competence... 151
   1. Exclusive Competences 151
   2. Shared Competences 152
   3. Supplementary Competences 153
   4. Implied Powers and Article 352(1) TFEU.. 153
B. Subsidiarity 153
C. Necessity to Achieve Objectives of the Treaty...................................... 154
D. Procedure 154
   1. Commission Proposal 155
   2. First Reading in the European Parliament 155
   3. The Council's Response 155
   4. Second Reading in the European Parliament 156
   5. The Council's Response to Amendments Suggested by the
      Parliament 156
   6. The Conciliation Committee 156
   7. Approval by Parliament and Council... 157
   8. President's Signature and Publication.. 157
      Germany v. European Parliament and Commission 157

PART 4. THE INTERNAL MARKET

Chapter 11. Free Movement of Goods: The Customs Union............... 171
A. Customs Duties and Charges Having Equivalent Effect 171
   1. By Reason of the Fact That a Frontier Is Crossed 172
      Carbonati Apuani Srl v. Comune di Carrara 172
   2. Inspection Fees... 176
      Commission v. Germany 176

B. Article 110 TFEU 180
    1. Article 110(1) TFEU 180
        a) Similar Products 180
            Commission v. Germany 181
            John Walker & Sons Ltd. v. Ministeriet for Skatter og
                Afgifter 182
        b) Direct and Indirect Discrimination 183
            Chemical Farmaceutici SpA v. DAF SpA 184
    2. Article 110(2) TFEU 186
        a) Protective Effect 186
        b) Discriminatory Nature 187
            John Walker & Sons Ltd. v. Ministeriet for Skatter og
                Afgifter 187

Chapter 12. Free Movement of Goods: Quantitative Restrictions ... 191
A. Quantitative Restrictions 191
B. Measures Having Equivalent Effect 191
    1. Imports 192
        Procureur du Roi v. Benoît and Gustave Dassonville 192
        Criminal Proceedings Against Bernard Keck and Daniel
            Mithouard 194
    2. Exports 196
        New Valmar BVBA v. Global Pharmacies Partner Health Srl. 197
C. Justifications 199
    1. The Mandatory Requirements Doctrine 200
        a) Serving an Imperative Requirement of Community Law 200
        b) Proportionality 201
        c) Applicability Without Distinction 201
            Rewe-Zentral AG v. Bundesmonopolverwaltung für
                Branntwein 202
            Commission v. Germany 205
            Commission v. Hellenic Republic 211
            Konsumentombudsmannen v. Gourmet International
                Products AB 213
    2. Article 36 TFEU 217
        Campus Oil Limited et al. v. Minister for Industry and Energy
            et al. 219
D. Practice Questions 223

Chapter 13. Free Movement of Workers: Personal Scope of
Application 227
A. Worker 227
    D.M. Levin v. Staatssecretaris van Justitie 228
    Franca Ninni-Orasche v. Bundesminister für Wissenschaft, Verkehr
        und Kunst 231
    I. Bettray v. Staatssecretaris van Justitie 234
    Michel Trojani v. Centre public d'aide sociale de Bruxelles (CPAS) 236

B. The Public Service Exception 239
   Commission v. Grand Duchy of Luxemburg................................. 241
C. Discriminatory and Non-Discriminatory Obstacles......................... 245
   Volker Graf v. Filzmoser Maschinenbau GmbH 246
D. Justifications 249
E. Employers 249
   Clean Car Autoservice GesmbH v Landeshauptmann von Wien 250
F. Practice Questions... 254

Chapter 14. Directive 2004/38/EC and Regulation 1612/68/EEC 257
A. Directive 2004/38/EC 257
   1. Beneficiaries 258
      Shirley McCarthy v. Secretary of State for the Home
         Department 258
   2. Right of Residence 260
      a) Stays of up to Three Months.. 261
      b) Stays of More than Three Months................................... 261
         Blaise Baheten Metock v. Minister of Justice, Equality
            and Law Reform 262
   3. Right of Permanent Residence 264
   4. Restrictions on the Right of Entry and Residence 265
   5. Equal Treatment 266
B. Regulation 1612/68/EEC... 267
   1. Eligibility for Employment 267
   2. Equal Treatment in Employment 267
   3. Workers' Families 268
C. Practice Questions... 268

Chapter 15. Freedom of Establishment... 273
A. Discriminatory and Non-Discriminatory Obstacles....................... 273
B. Justifications 273
C. Companies 274
   1. Taxation 274
   2. Corporate Law 275
      Freedom of Choice in European Corporate Law.................... 275
      The Queen v. H. M. Treasury and Commissioners of Inland
         Revenue, ex parte Daily Mail and General Trust plc............ 277
      Reconceptualizing the Theory of the Firm—From Nature to
         Function 280
      Centros Ltd v. Erhvervs-og Selskabsstyrelsen....................... 284
      Überseering BV v. Nordic Construction Company
         Baumanagement GmbH (NCC).. 289
      Kamer van Koophandel en Fabrieken voor Amsterdam v.
         Inspire Art... 292
      Cartesio Oktató és Szolgáltató bt... 295
      Indeterminacy in Corporate Law: A Theoretical and
         Comparative Analysis 296

	Indeterminacy in Corporate Law: A Theoretical and Comparative Analysis 297
D.	Practice Questions 298

Chapter 16. Freedom to Provide Services 301
A.	Services 301
	Reinhard Gebhard v. Consiglio dell'Ordine degli Avvocati e Procuratori di Milano 302
B.	Personal Scope of Protection... 304
	Ian William Cowan v. Tresor public 304
C.	The Interstate Element.. 305
D.	Discriminatory and Non-Discriminatory Obstacles 305
	Alpine Investments BV v. Minister van Financien 305
E.	Justifications 308
	Omega Spielhallen- und Automatenaufstellungs-GmbH v. Oberbürgermeisterin der Stadt Bonn 308
F.	Practice Questions 313

Chapter 17. Free Movement of Capital 317
A.	Movement of Capital and Payments 317
	Regina v. Ernest George Thompson, Brian Albert Johnson and Colin Alex Norman Woodiwiss 318
	C. Baars v. Inspecteur der Belastingen Particulieren/Ondernemingen Gorinchem 319
	European Commission v. Portuguese Republic 319
B.	Discriminatory and Non-Discriminatory Obstacles 325
C.	Justifications 325
D.	Practice Questions 325

Chapter 18. Fundamental Freedoms: Common Problems 327
A.	Failure to Act 327
	Commission of the European Communities v French Republic 328
	Eugen Schmidberger, Internationale Transporte und Planzüge v. Republik Österreich 333
B.	Private Parties... 339
	Roman Angonese v. Cassa di Risparmio di Bolzano SpA 340
C.	Practice Questions 343

PART 5. CURRENT CHALLENGES

Chapter 19. The Monetary Union 347
A.	Historical Background 347
	Paradise Lost: Can the European Union Expel Countries from the Eurozone 347
B.	Joining and Leaving the Eurozone... 350
	1. Becoming Part of the Eurozone 350

	2.	Leaving the Eurozone 351
		Paradise Lost: Can the European Union Expel Countries from the Eurozone 351
C.		The Monetary Union: An Economic Perspective................................... 353
D.		The State of Economic and Fiscal Integration 358
	1.	Monetary Policy.. 358
		a) The European Central Bank's Organization 358
		b) Responsibility for Monetary Policy.. 359
		Peter Gauweiler et al. v. Deutscher Bundestag 361

Chapter 20. Leaving the European Union 367
A. Historical Background 367
   Revoking Brexit: Can Member States Rescind Their Declaration of Withdrawal From the European Union? 367
B. Can Withdrawing Member States Change Their Minds? 373
   Andy Wrightman et al. v. Secretary of State for Exiting the European Union.. 374
C. The European Union's International Treaties 383
   1. The Competence to Conclude International Treaties 384
   2. Different Types of Treaties 386
      A Little Bit Brexit? An Analysis of the Rules Governing Post-Withdrawal Treaties... 386
D. International Agreements Following Withdrawal from the EU 389
   A Little Bit Brexit? An Analysis of the Rules Governing Post-Withdrawal Treaties 390
E. EFTA.. 391
   Splendid Isolation or Continued Cooperation? Options for a State After Withdrawal from the European Union................................. 392
F. Expulsion from the European Union?... 394
   1. Article 7 TEU.. 394
   2. Lump Sum and Penalty Payments.. 395
   3. State Liability 395

Annex... 397
Part 1: Excerpts from the Treaty on European Union 397
Part 2: Excerpts from the Treaty on the Functioning of the European Union.. 410
Part 3: Directive 2004/38/EC... 462
Part 4: Regulation No. 1612/68/EEC 480

INDEX... 485

TABLE OF CASES

The principal cases are in bold type.

Agrover Srl v. Agenzia Dogane Circoscrizione Doganale di Genova, 58
Alpine Investments BV v. Minister van Financien, 305
Amministrazione delle Finanze dello Stato v. Denkavit italiana Srl., 63
Amministrazione delle Finanze dello Stato v. Simmenthal SpA, 124
Andrea Francovich & Danila Bonifaci et al. v. Italian Republic, 107, 138, 396
Andy Wrightman et al. v. Secretary of State for Exiting the European Union, 374, 394
Anton Feyrer v. Landkreis Rottal-Inn, 106
Asda Stores Ltd v. Commissioners of Her Majesty's Revenue and Custom, 95
Beate Weber v. European Parliament, 3
Blaise Baheten Metock v. Minister of Justice, Equality and Law Reform, 128, **262**
Brasserie du Pecheur SA v. Bundesrepublik Deutschland and The Queen v. Secretary of State for Transport, ex parte: Factortame Ltd and others, 141
C. Baars v. Inspecteur der Belastingen Particulieren/ Ondernemingen Gorinchem, 319
C P M Meeusen v. Hoofdirectie van de Informatie Beheer Groep, 227
Campus Oil Limited et al. v. Minister for Industry and Energy et al., 218, 219
Carbonati Apuani Srl v. Comune di Carrara, 172
Cartesio Oktató és Szolgáltató bt, 295
Centros Ltd v. Erhvervs-og Selskabsstyrelsen, 284
Charalampos Dounias v. Ypourgio Oikonomikon, 184
Chemical Farmaceutici SpA v. DAF SpA, 184
Clean Car Autoservice GesmbH v. Landeshauptmann von Wien, 250

Colegio de Oficiales de la Marina Mercante Española v. Administración del Estado, 240
Commission of the European Communities v. Federal Republic of Germany, 111
Commission of the European Communities v. French Republic, 328
Commission v. Belgium, 202, 239
Commission v. Denmark, 179, 181
Commission v. European Investment Bank, 3
Commission v. Germany, 87, **176, 181, 205**
Commission v. Grand Duchy of Luxembourg and Kingdom of Belgium, 90
Commission v. Grand Duchy of Luxemburg, 80, 239, **241**
Commission v. Hellenic Republic, 88, 211, 245
Commission v. Ireland, 81, 82, 84
Commission v. Italian Republic, 90
Commission v. Italy, 85, 87, 88, 89, 143
Commission v. Portugal, 195, 218
Commission v. Portuguese Republic, 79
Commission v. Republic of Austria, 59
Conceria Daniele Bresciani v. Amministrazione Italiana delle Finanze, 176
Conegate Limited v. HM Customs & Excise, 218
Criminal Proceedings Against Bernard Keck and Daniel Mithouard, 194
Criminal Proceedings Against Kenny Roland Lyckeskog, 67
Criminal Proceedings Against Tullio Ratti, 105
D.M. Levin v. Staatssecretaris van Justitie, 228
Da Costa en Schaake NV v. Netherlands Inland Revenue Admin., 66, 72
Deutsche Lufthansa AG v. Gertraud Kumpan, 105, 113
DHL International NV, formerly Express Line NV v. Belgisch

Instituut voor Postdiensten en Telecommunicatie, 273
Direktsia "Obzhalvane i upravlenie na izpalnenieto" Varna v. Auto Nikolovi OOD, 95
Dulaurans v. France, 147
ENU v. Comm'n, 57
Erich Ciola v. Land Vorarlberg, 202
Ernest George Thompson, Brian Albert Johnson and Colin Alex Norman Woodiwiss, Regina v., 318
Eugen Schmidberger, Internationale Transporte und Planzüge v. Republik Österreich, 333
European Commission v. Grand Duchy of Luxemburg, 273
European Commission v. Portuguese Republic, 319, 325
Flaminio Costa v. E.N.E.L., 121
Franca Ninni-Orasche v. Bundesminister für Wissenschaft, Verkehr und Kunst, 231
Franz Grad v. Finanzamt Traunstein, 48
Gabriel Simon v. Court of Justice, 59
Gerhard Köbler v. Republik Österreich, 143
Germany v. European Parliament and Commission, 157
Günter Fuß v. Stadt Halle, 95
H. M. Treasury and Commissioners of Inland Revenue, ex parte Daily Mail and General Trust plc., The Queen v., 277, 279
Hanns-Martin Bachmann v. Belgium, 202
Hans-Jürgen Ritter-Coulais and Monique Ritter-Coulais v. Finanzamt Germersheim, 301
I. Bettray v. Staatssecretaris van Justitie, 234
Ian William Cowan v. Tresor public, 304
Internationale Handelsgesellschaft mbH v. Einfuhr und Vorratsstelle für Getreide und Futtermittel, 124
John Walker & Sons Ltd. v. Ministeriet for Skatter og Afgifter, 182, 187
Kamer van Koophandel en Fabrieken voor Amsterdam v. Inspire Art, 292
Konstantinos Adeneler et al. v. Ellinikos Organismos Galaktos (ELOG), 115

Konsumentombudsmannen v. Gourmet International Products AB, 213
Les Verts v. European Parliament, 3
London Borough of Harrow v. Nimco Hassan Ibrahim and Secretary of State for the Home Department, 268
Manfred Trummer & Peter Mayer, 317
Marc Michel Josemans v. Burgemeester van Maastricht, 218
Marleasing SA v. La Comercial Internacional de Alimentacion SA, 113
Michel Trojani v. Centre public d'aide sociale de Bruxelles (CPAS), 236
Ministero delle Finanze v. IN.CO.GE.'90 Srl et al., 127
Ministerul Justiiei i Libertilor Ceteneti v. Stefan Agafiei, 67
New Valmar BVBA v. Global Pharmacies Partner Health Srl, 197
NV Algemene Transporten Expeditie Onderneming van Gend & Loos v. Netherlands Inland Revenue Administration, 99
Olympique Lyonnais SASP v. Olivier Bernard and Newcastle UFC, 246
Omega Spielhallen- und Automatenaufstellungs-GmbH v. Oberbürgermeisterin der Stadt Bonn, 308
Österreichischer Gewerkschaftsbund, 240
Pasquale Foglia v. Mariella Novello ["Foglia I"], 68
Pasquale Foglia v. Mariella Novello ["Foglia II"], 68, 70
Paul Miles v. Écoles européennes, 65
Peter Gauweiler et al. v. Deutscher Bundestag, 361
Philip Morris, 167
Pierre Corbiau v. Admin. des Contributions, 64, 65
Politi S.A.S. v. Ministry for Finance of the Italian Republic, 64
Printz v. United States, 47
Procureur du Roi v. Benoît and Gustave Dassonville, 192
R. H. Kempf v. Staatssecretaris van Justitie, 231
Radiosistemi Srl v. Prefetto di Genova, 200, 201
Reinhard Gebhard v. Consiglio dell'Ordine degli Avvocati e Procuratori di Milano, 302

Rewe-Zentral AG v. Bundesmonopolverwaltung für Branntwein, 143, 200, **202**
Rieser Internationale Transporte GmbH v. Autobahnen und Schnellstraßen-Finanzierungs-AG, 48
Riseria Luigi Geddo v. Ente Nazionale Risi, 191, 196
Roman Angonese v. Cassa di Risparmio di Bolzano SpA, **340**
Rosmarie Kapferer v. Schlank & Schick GmbH, **125**
RTL Belgium SA, **65**
Schutzverband gegen Unwesen in der Wirtschaft e.V. v. Yves Rocher GmbH, 199, 201
Secretary of State for the Environment, The Queen v., 201
Secretary of State for the Home Department v. Hacene Akrich, 262
Shirley McCarthy v. Secretary of State for the Home Department, **258**
Solange I, **129**
Solange II, **133**
Spijker Infrabouw-De Jonge Konstruktie v. Provincie Drenthe, 137
Srl CILFIT and Lanificio di Gavardo SpA v. Ministry of Health, 57, 58, **74**
Susanne Gassmayr v. Bundesminister für Wissenschaft und Forschung, 104, 105, 106
Überseering BV v. Nordic Construction Company Baumanagement GmbH (NCC), **289**
Unilever Italia SpA v. Central Food SpA, **111**
Union royale belge des sociétés de football association ASBL v. Jean-Marc Bosman, 245, 253, 254
Vlaamse federatie van verenigingen van Brood en Banketbakkers, Ijsbereiders en Chocoladebewerkers (VEBIC) VZW, 68
Volker Graf v. Filzmoser Maschinenbau GmbH, **246**
Walrave v. Union Cycliste Internationale, 253
Waypoint Aviation SA v. Belgian State—SPF Finances, 305

Introduction to European Union Law
Cases and Materials

PART 1

BACKGROUND
...

CHAPTER 1

HISTORICAL BACKGROUND

■ ■ ■

Today, the chief vehicle for European unification is the European Union (EU). The European Union rests on two main treaties, namely the Treaty on European Union and the Treaty on the Functioning of the European Union. Together, these two treaties can properly be viewed as the European Union's Constitution.[1]

The foundation of the European Union was created on March 25, 1957. Six European nations—Belgium, France, Germany, Italy, Luxembourg, and the Netherlands—signed the Treaty Establishing the European Economic Community (EEC), which became effective on January 1, 1958. Over the following decades, the Treaty Establishing the European Economic Community was expanded and amended repeatedly, as ever more countries joined the EEC. Soon it was clear that the Treaty had moved beyond its original focus on economic integration towards a more holistic concept of European social, political and economic integration, and effective January 1, 1993, the European Economic Community (EEC) was renamed the European Community (EC). That name did not survive long either because of the ever-progressing integration of Europe. On December 1, 2009, the European Community became the European Union. In this chapter, we will take a closer look at the history of the European Union.

Fig. 1: The Changing Names of the European Union

European Economic Community (1958-1992) → European Community (1993-2009) → European Union (2009-today)

---

[1] Case C-72/15, *Rosneft*, ECLI:EU:C:2017:236 ¶ 36 (referring to the treaties as the "basic constitutional charter"). Before the entry into force of the Treaty on European Union and the Treaty on the Functioning of the European Union, the Court of Justice referred to the EC Treaty as the "basic constitutional charter." *E.g.*, case C-314/91, Beate Weber v. European Parliament, 1993 E.C.R. I-1093 ¶ 8; Case 294/83, Les Verts v. European Parliament 1986 E.C.R. 1339 ¶ 23; Case C-15/00, Commission v. European Investment Bank, 2003 E.C.R. I-7281 ¶ 75. Note, however, that this view is by no means universally accepted. In fact, whether the European Union has a constitution is quite controversial. *See* Mattias Kumm, *Beyond Golf Clubs and the Judicialization of Politics: Why Europe Has a Constitution Properly so Called*, 54 AM. J. COMP. L. 505 (2006).

A. EARLY EFFORTS AT EUROPEAN INTEGRATION

Efforts to unite Europe in a peaceful fashion can be traced back much further than the European Union's founding. Proposals for European unity can be found throughout the centuries. For example, at the beginning of the fourteenth century, the French lawyer Pierre Dubois called upon Europe's monarchs to let their countries form a single nation.[2] In 1693, the English pacifist William Penn, best known for founding Pennsylvania, proposed European unity and a European parliament.[3] And in 1795, the German philosopher Immanuel Kant suggested the formation of a European federation of states.[4]

Not surprisingly, these early calls for European integration never came close to being implemented. To the extent that statesmen sought to unite Europe, their method of choice was armed conflict rather than voluntary association.

However, starting in the twentieth century, peaceful integration started to get more serious attention from European leaders. Given the history of Europe, this is hardly surprising. Both the desire to avoid a repetition of the terrible destruction wrought by the two World Wars and the relative decline of European power vis-à-vis the rest of the world provided powerful motives for Europeans to band more closely together.

1. THE BRIAND MEMORANDUM

In the first half of the twentieth century, French Prime Minister Aristide Briand initiated a serious political attempt at European integration. In a speech before the General Assembly of the League of Nations—the precursor of the United Nations—on September 5, 1929, Briand suggested the creation of an Association of European Nations with a particular focus on economic integration.[5] Moreover, Briand did not stop at vague suggestions. Rather, on May 17, 1930, he issued a famous memorandum to other leaders of European nations inviting them to commence formal talks regarding Europe's economic and political unification.[6]

---

[2] PIERRE DUBOIS, DE RECUPERATIONE TERRE SANCTE (BiblioLife 2009) (circa 1306).

[3] WILLIAM PENN, AN ESSAY TOWARDS THE PRESENT AND FUTURE PEACE OF EUROPE, BY THE ESTABLISHMENT OF A EUROPEAN DYET, PARLIAMENT, OR ESTATES (Georg Olms Publishers 1983) (1693).

[4] IMMANUEL KANT, ZUM EWIGEN FRIEDEN (Philipp Reclam Jun Verlag 1998) (1795).

[5] Aristide Briand, Speech Before the Tenth Ordinary Session of the Assembly (Sep. 5, 1929), *as reprinted in* LE PLAN BRIAND D'UNION FÉDÉRALE EUROPÉENNE 2–3 (Odile Keller & Lubor Jilek eds., 1991).

[6] Memorandum by Aristide Briand on the organization of a system of European federal union ("Mémorandum sur l'organisation d'un régime d'union fédérale européenne") (May 17, 1930).

It turned out, however, that Briand was ahead of his time. Although his suggestions were greeted with sympathy in countries such as France, Belgium, and Austria,[7] they met with rejection in most of the large countries of Western Europe including Italy, the United Kingdom, and Germany.[8]

The reasons for this lack of enthusiasm were manifold. The critics of European integration feared that such integration would entail an unacceptable loss of sovereignty[9]—a concern that to this day retains its political salience; others were concerned about alienating the Soviet Union, which Briand had excluded from his plans for European integration.[10] Germany feared that Briand's plan would perpetuate the existing map of Europe, thereby cementing the territorial losses that Germany had suffered as a result of World War I;[11] and Great Britain saw its own future in the Commonwealth rather than in European integration.[12]

Aristide Briand (1862–1932)

Aristide Briand was a French statesmen and member of the French Socialist Party. He repeatedly served as France's Prime minister, though, owing to the unstable political climate of the time, his terms in office were typically quite short, sometimes lasting only a few months.

In 1926, Briand, together with German statesman Gustav Stresemann, received the Nobel Peace Prize for his role in negotiating the so-called Locarno Treaties of 1925. These treaties were part of the reconciliation effort after WWI and were aimed at normalizing the relationship between the victorious allied countries of WWI, various Central and Eastern European nations, and Germany.

In 1927, a plan that the U.S. Secretary of State Frank B. Kellogg advanced together with Briand led to the so-called Kellogg-Briand Pact of 1928. The Kellogg-Briand Pact was an international treaty in which the participating nations pledged to abstain from using war to resolve

---

[7] UNDINE RUGE, DIE ERFINDUNG DES "EUROPA DER REGIONEN": KRITISCHE IDEENGESCHICHTE EINES KONSERVATIVEN KONZEPTS 54 (2003).

[8] *Id.*

[9] *See id.* at 56 (noting that Briand's memorandum sought to allay the concerns about a loss of national sovereignty by stressing that the planned association of European nations would respect the sovereignty of those nations).

[10] *Id.* at 58.

[11] *Id.*

[12] *Id.*

> their conflicts. The original signatories included France, Germany, and the United States, and numerous other countries acceded later. While unable to prevent WWII, the Kellogg-Briand Pact became an important model for the Charter of the United Nations of 1945. Moreover, during the Nuremburg trials following WWII, the Kellogg-Briand Pact, with its commitment to abstention from war, provided a basis for prosecuting Nazi war criminals for crimes against peace. In their influential book *The Internationalists*, Oona Hathaway and Scott Shapiro take the view that the Kellogg-Briand Pact was "among the most transformative events in human history." (Oona A. Hathaway & Scott J Shapiro, How A Radical Plan to Outlaw War Remade the World, xiii (2017)).

The lack of support among the major European countries would doom Briand's efforts.[13] In the following years, instead of Pan-European peace, Europe saw the rise to power of the Nazis in Germany in 1933, which led to World War II and the Holocaust.

2. REKINDLING THE IDEA OF EUROPEAN INTEGRATION AFTER WORLD WAR II

World War II had barely ended, when efforts to unite Europe resumed. On September 19, 1946, upon receiving an honorary doctorate at the University of Zurich, Winston Churchill gave a speech endorsing European integration. The speech is of lasting interest, not least because of what it reveals about some of the less savory motivations and attitudes behind the drive towards a united Europe.

Sir Winston Churchill, A 'United States of Europe' Speech 19 September 1946, Zurich, Switzerland[14]

This noble continent, comprising on the whole the fairest and the most cultivated regions of the earth; enjoying a temperate and equable climate, is the home of all the great parent races of the western world. It is the fountain of Christian faith and Christian ethics. It is the origin of most of the culture, arts, philosophy, and science both of ancient and modern times.

If Europe were once united in the sharing of its common inheritance, there would be no limit to the happiness, to the prosperity and glory which its three or four hundred million people would enjoy.

Yet, it is from Europe that have sprung that series of frightful nationalistic quarrels, originated by the Teutonic nations, which we have

---

[13] *See id.* at 58–60 (describing the failure of Briand's efforts).

[14] Reproduced with permission of Curtis Brown, London on behalf of The Estate of Winston S Churchill. © the Estate of Winston Churchill.

seen even in this twentieth century and in our own lifetime, wreck the peace and mar the prospects of all mankind.

And what is the plight to which Europe has been reduced? Some of the smaller States have indeed made a good recovery, but over wide areas a vast, quivering mass of tormented, hungry, care-worn and bewildered human beings gape at the ruins of their cities and homes, and scan the dark horizons for the approach of some new peril, tyranny, or terror.

Among the victors there is a babel of voices; among the vanquished the sullen silence of despair. That is all that Europeans, grouped in so many ancient States and nations, that is all that the Germanic Powers have got by tearing each other to pieces and spreading havoc far and wide. Indeed, but for the fact that the Great Republic across the Atlantic Ocean has at length realised that the ruin or enslavement of Europe would involve their own fate as well, and has stretched out hands of succour and guidance, the Dark Ages would have returned in all their cruelty and squalor. They may still return.

Yet all the while there is a remedy which, if it were generally and spontaneously adopted, would as if by a miracle transform the whole scene, and would in a few years make all Europe, or the greater part of it, as free and as happy as Switzerland is today. What is this sovereign remedy? It is to re-create the European Family, or as much of it as we can, and provide it with a structure under which it can dwell in peace, in safety and in freedom.

We must build a kind of United States of Europe. In this way only will hundreds of millions of toilers be able to regain the simple joys and hopes which make life worth living. The process is simple. All that is needed is the resolve of hundreds of millions of men and women to do right instead of wrong, and gain as their reward, blessing instead of cursing. Much work has been done upon this task by the exertions of the Pan-European Union which owes so much to Count Coudenhove-Kalergi and which commanded the services of the famous French patriot and statesman, Aristide Briand.

There is also that immense body of doctrine and procedure, which was brought into being amid high hopes after the First World War, as the League of Nations. The League of Nations did not fail because of its principles or conceptions. It failed because these principles were deserted by those States who had brought it into being. It failed because the governments of those days feared to face the facts and act while time remained. This disaster must not be repeated. There is, therefore, much knowledge and material with which to build; and also bitter dear bought experience.

I was very glad to read in the newspapers two days ago that my friend President Truman had expressed his interest and sympathy with this Great Design. There is no reason why a regional organisation of Europe should in any way conflict with the world organization of the United Nations. On the contrary, I believe that the larger synthesis will only survive if it is founded upon coherent natural groupings. There is already a natural grouping in the Western Hemisphere. We British have our own Commonwealth of Nations. These do not weaken, on the contrary they strengthen, the world organisation. They are in fact its main support. And why should there not be a European group which could give a sense of enlarged patriotism and common citizenship to the distracted peoples of this turbulent and mighty continent and why should it not take its rightful place with other great groupings in shaping the destinies of men?

In order that this should be accomplished, there must be an act of faith in which millions of families speaking many languages must consciously take part. We all know that the two world wars through which we have passed arose out of the vain passion of a newly united Germany to play the dominating part in the world. In this last struggle crimes and massacres have been committed for which there is no parallel since the invasion of the Mongols in the fourteenth century and no equal at any time in human history.

The guilty must be punished. Germany must be deprived of the power to rearm and make another aggressive war. But when all this has been done, as it will be done, as it is being done, there must be an end to retribution. There must be what Mr. Gladstone many years ago called 'a blessed act of oblivion'. We must all turn our backs upon the horrors of the past. We must look to the future. We cannot afford to drag forward across the years that are to come the hatreds and revenges which have sprung from the injuries of the past. If Europe is to be saved from infinite misery, and indeed from final doom, there must be this act of faith in the European family and an act of oblivion against all the crimes and follies of the past.

Can the free peoples of Europe rise to the height of these resolves of the soul and instincts of the spirit of man? If they can, the wrongs and injuries which have been inflicted will have been washed away on all sides by the miseries which have been endured. Is there any need for further floods of agony? Is it the only lesson of history that mankind is unteachable? Let there be justice, mercy and freedom. The people have only to will it, and all will achieve their hearts' desire.

I am now going to say something that will astonish you. The first step in the re-creation of the European family must be a partnership between France and Germany. In this way only can France recover the moral leadership of Europe. There can be no revival of Europe without a spiritually great France and a spiritually great Germany. The structure of the United States of Europe, if well and truly built, will be such as to make the material strength of a single state less important. Small nations will count as much as large ones and gain their honour by their contribution to the common cause.

The ancient states and principalities of Germany, freely joined together for mutual convenience in a federal system, might each take their individual place among the United States of Europe. I shall not try to make a detailed programme for hundreds of millions of people who want to be happy and free, prosperous and safe, who wish to enjoy the four freedoms of which the great President Roosevelt spoke, and live in accordance with the principles embodied in the Atlantic Charter. If this is their wish, if this is their wish, they have only to say so, and means can certainly be found, and machinery erected, to carry that wish into full fruition.

But I must give you warning. Time may be short. At present, there is a breathing-space. The cannons have ceased firing. The fighting has stopped; but the dangers have not stopped. If we are to form the United States of Europe or whatever name or form it may take, we must begin now.

In these present days we dwell strangely and precariously under the shield and protection, of the atomic bomb. The atomic bomb is still only in the hands of a State and nation which we know will never use it except in the cause of right and freedom. But it may well be that in a few years this awful agency of destruction will be widespread and the catastrophe following from its use by several warring nations will not only bring to an end all that we call civilisation, but may possibly disintegrate the globe itself.

I must now sum up the propositions which are before you. Our constant aim must be to build and fortify the strength of the United Nations Organisation. Under and within that world concept, we must re-create the European family in a regional structure called, it may be, the United States of Europe.

The first step is to form a Council of Europe. If at first all the States of Europe are not willing or able to join the Union, we must nevertheless proceed to assemble and combine those who will and those who can. The salvation of the common people of every race and of every land from war or servitude must be established on solid foundations and must be guarded by the readiness of all men and women to die rather than submit to tyranny.

In all this urgent work, France and Germany must take the lead together. Great Britain, the British Commonwealth of Nations, mighty America, and, I trust, Soviet Russia—for then indeed all would be well—must be the friends and sponsors of the new Europe and must champion its right to live and shine. ∎

Winston Churchill (1874–1965)

Winston Churchill is, or ought to be, familiar to most readers. He was a conservative British politician who served as the United Kingdom's Prime Minister from 1951–55 and from 1940–45. His second term of office covered most of World War II, and Churchill is best remembered for his early opposition to the Nazis and the fact that he ultimately led the United Kingdom to victory over Nazi Germany. Churchill is widely thought to be one of the most important political figures of the 20th century.

Some modern historians have noted that some of Churchill's statements are profoundly racist. A summary of his most problematic remarks is available at https://www.bbc.com/news/magazine-29701767. Pointing out this issue is not meant to obscure the fact that he played a central and likely indispensable role in protecting the world against fascist and genocidal Nazi Germany, thereby preventing uncountable additional atrocities that might otherwise have occurred.

NOTES AND QUESTIONS

1. One of the characteristic features of the Treaty on European Union is that it explicitly names the aims it was created to pursue. According to Article 3 of the Treaty, "[t]he Union's aim is to promote peace, its values and the well-being of its peoples." How does this compare with the reasons that Churchill advanced in favor of European unity?

2. Article 2 of the Treaty on European Union summarizes the European Union's values. According to this provision, "[t]he Union is founded on the values of respect for human dignity, freedom, democracy, equality, the rule of law and respect for human rights, including the rights of persons belonging to minorities. These values are common to the Member States in a society in which pluralism, non-discrimination, tolerance, justice, solidarity and equality between women and men prevail." How does this compare to the ideas Churchill expresses in his Zurich address?

3. The United Kingdom was not among the founding members of the European Economic Community (EEC) in 1957. At the time, U.K. politicians saw little need to let the United Kingdom become part of a united Europe. After all, the United Kingdom had its ties with the Commonwealth countries and

enjoyed a close relationship with the United States, at whose side it had successfully fought the Axis powers in World War II. In addition, many in Britain expected the EEC to fail.[15] However, in the following years, it became increasingly clear that the EEC was highly successful in economic terms.[16] Also, the United Kingdom, traditionally committed to preserving a balance of powers on the European continent, grew increasingly concerned that France might use the EEC to acquire a leadership role in Europe. It even feared that the United States might give particular emphasis to its relationship with the EEC, condemning the special relationship between the United States and the United Kingdom to secondary importance.[17] Accordingly, the United Kingdom changed its stance towards the EEC. At first, this change of heart proved futile: Britain's first two applications to join the EEC, made in 1961 and in 1967, were vetoed by the French President Charles de Gaulle.[18] De Gaulle justified this veto by questioning the United Kingdom's commitment to the creation of a common market; according to the testimony of officials involved in the pertinent negotiations, he appears to have been particularly worried that the United Kingdom would function as a "Trojan Horse" that would allow the United States to gain access to the common market.[19] But, in 1969, Charles de Gaulle resigned as France's president, thereby opening the way for the United Kingdom to become a member of the EEC. Effective January 1, 1973, the United Kingdom, Denmark, and Ireland became members of the EEC in what is known as the first round of enlargement.[20]

4. What were Churchill's ideas regarding Britain's place in the "new Europe"? What is the United Kingdom's relationship with the European Union today?

5. In advancing the idea of European integration, Churchill was breaking with the so-called balance-of-powers theory that had dominated European political thinking for many centuries. At its core, balance-of-power theory had both a normative and a descriptive component. Normatively, balance-of-power theory held that no single country should be allowed to gain enough strength to dominate all others, lest that country would then start waging aggressive wars. Descriptively, balance of power theory held that any effort by one country to obtain dominance would be checked by the efforts of other countries, since weaker countries would start forming alliances to counterbalance the country aspiring to dominance. In British politics, the concept of a balance of power had also held a more specific meaning: the United Kingdom had long sought to prevent any of the great continental European powers—which at different times might have been France, the German Empire, Prussia, Spain, or Russia—from gaining or maintaining hegemony on

---

[15] MARTIN ROBERTS, BRITAIN 1846–1964: THE CHALLENGE OF CHANGE 18 (2001).

[16] H.S. CHOPRA, DE GAULLE AND EUROPEAN UNITY 190 (1974).

[17] *Id.* at 188–90.

[18] PHILIP THODY, AN HISTORICAL INTRODUCTION TO THE EUROPEAN UNION 16–17 (1997).

[19] ANDREW MORAVCSIK, THE CHOICE FOR EUROPE: SOCIAL PURPOSE AND STATE POWER FROM MESSINA TO MAASTRICHT 192 n.82 (1998).

[20] THODY, *supra* note 18, at 17.

the European continent. After World War I, however, balance-of-power theory was increasingly rejected. Why might the descriptive component of the balance-of-power theory be viewed with skepticism from today's perspective? Why might Churchill and others have doubted the theory's merits as a normative theory?

6. How did Churchill envision the role of the individual German states—now called the "Länder"—in the "new Europe"?

7. Do you think that European integration strengthens or weakens the role of the states, departments, or regions that constitute the political subdivisions of the Member States of the European Union?

8. Based on what we know now, to what extent did Churchill's plans and predictions prove to be accurate?

9. What relationship did Churchill envision between the "new Europe" on the one hand and "Soviet Russia" and the United States on the other hand?

10. Churchill makes a reference to "the four freedoms of which the great President Roosevelt spoke." In his 1941 State of the Union Address, President Roosevelt had declared that the United States would seek a world based on four essential freedoms: freedom of speech, freedom of worship, freedom from want, and freedom from fear.[21] To what extent do Articles 3 and 4 of the Treaty on European Union contain a commitment to these four freedoms?

B. THE FIRST STEPS TOWARDS EUROPEAN INTEGRATION

Efforts aimed at European integration after World War II, unlike those after World War I, soon proved fruitful in that the decades after the war saw a number of important developments. But, the integration of modern Europe did not progress in a straight line. It involved the creation of numerous treaties, organizations, and initiatives. Some of these proved crucial, and some did not. Some were eventually included in what is now the European Union, whereas others continue to exist outside of and complementary to the European Union.

1. THE ORGANISATION FOR ECONOMIC CO-OPERATION AND DEVELOPMENT

In 1947, the United States created its famous Marshall Plan to rebuild Europe. To help implement the Marshall Plan, the Organisation for European Economic Co-operation (OEEC) was formed in 1948.[22] Working

---

[21] Franklin D. Roosevelt, 1941 State Of The Union Address, January 6, 1941, available at https://fdrlibrary.org/four-freedoms (last visited Feb. 17, 2019).

[22] Michael Ruddy, *European Integration, the Neutrals, and U.S. Security Interests*, in DIE NEUTRALEN UND DIE EUROPÄISCHE INTEGRATION 1945–1995, at 16 (Michael Gehler & Rolf Steiniger eds., 2000). The relevant international treaty, the Convention for European Economic Co-operation, Apr. 16, 1948, 888 U.N.T.S. 142, was signed in Paris.

together within the framework of the OEEC, the governments of Europe gained practical experience in economic coordination. Indeed, even after the Marshall Plan had run its course, the OEEC was retained as an instrument for cooperation. Nor has it disappeared since. Rather, in 1961, it was transformed into the Organisation for Economic Co-operation and Development (OECD) and broadened its focus beyond Europe.[23]

2. THE TREATY OF BRUSSELS

1948 also saw the conclusion of the so-called Treaty of Brussels between Belgium, Luxembourg, the Netherlands, France, and the United Kingdom. One of its core provisions provided for mutual defense in case of an attack against one of the parties to the treaty. Accordingly, the Treaty of Brussels is widely thought to be a precursor to the North Atlantic Treaty Organization (NATO).

Incidentally, the Brussels Treaty did not predate NATO by much: NATO was created less than a year later, on April 4, 1949. NATO's creation did not render the Brussels Treaty obsolete. Rather, the Brussels Treaty remained in force parallel to the NATO agreement and would later prove crucial to the development of a European defense policy. In September 1948, some months after the Treaty of Brussels had been signed, the parties to that treaty set up a common military agency called the Western Union Defence Organization. In 1954, West Germany and Italy also became parties, and the organization was renamed the Western European Union (WEU). In 2009, the mutual defense clause was written into the Treaty on European Union and hence became part of EU law. Accordingly, the Treaty of Brussels was terminated on March 31, 2010.

NOTES AND QUESTIONS

1. Can you think of any reasons why Germany and Italy did not join the Brussels Treaty until 1954? And if these two nations did not join the Brussels Treaty earlier, why did they join in 1954?

2. Can you think of any reasons why the Brussels Treaty and with it the Western European Union survived the creation of NATO?

3. COUNCIL OF EUROPE

In his Zurich address, Churchill suggested that "the first practical step" towards a United States of Europe should "be to form a Council of Europe." This suggestion was taken seriously, and in 1948 hundreds of

---

[23] Convention on the Organisation for Economic Co-operation and Development, Dec. 14, 1960, 12 U.S.T. 1728, 888 U.N.T.S. 179.

delegates attended a congress in The Hague, the Netherlands, to discuss the future shape of such a council.[24]

From these talks resulted a new international treaty, the Statute of the Council of Europe,[25] which was signed in 1949.[26] Originally, only ten countries—Belgium, Denmark, France, Ireland, Italy, Luxembourg, the Netherlands, Norway, Sweden, and the United Kingdom—were party to the treaty,[27] but since the treaty was signed, almost all other European nations have acceded as well.

The Statute of the Council of Europe created a new international organization which, unsurprisingly, was called the Council of Europe. Its aim is broadly defined as achieving "a greater unity between its members for the purpose of safeguarding and realizing the ideals and principles which are their common heritage and facilitating their economic and social progress."[28] However, the treaty provided the new organization with precious few powers to achieve that aim.[29] In particular, the Council's decisions are not binding,[30] meaning that the Council has remained, in the words of one commentator, "a powerless talking shop."[31]

In practice, therefore, the main role of the Council of Europe has been to facilitate the negotiation of new international treaties between its members. In particular, its work led to the adoption of the European Convention on Human Rights (ECHR) in 1950.[32]

The weakness of the Council of Europe was disappointing to those European countries, particularly France and Belgium, which had hoped to see a stronger organization with more extensive powers.[33] However, the United Kingdom, whose postwar prestige allowed it to play a central role in shaping the structure of the Council of Europe, was anxious to preserve its sovereignty and would not consent to any agreement that would create more than a forum for intergovernmental coordination.[34]

---

[24] FLORENCE BENOÎT-ROHMER & HEINRICH KLEBES, COUNCIL OF EUROPE LAW: TOWARDS A PAN-EUROPEAN LEGAL AREA 12 (2005).

[25] Statute of the Council of Europe, May 5, 1949, 87 U.N.T.S. 103.

[26] BENOÎT-ROHMER & KLEBES, *supra* note 24.

[27] *Id.*

[28] Statute of the Council of Europe, *supra* note 25, art. 1(a).

[29] BENOÎT-ROHMER & KLEBES, *supra* note 24.

[30] Statute of the Council of Europe, *supra* note 25, art. 15.

[31] DUNCAN WATTS & COLIN PILKINGTON, BRITAIN IN THE EUROPEAN UNION TODAY 14 (2005).

[32] Convention for the Protection of Human Rights and Fundamental Freedoms, Apr. 11, 1950, 213 U.N.T.S. 221. The Convention did not enter into force until 1953.

[33] BENOÎT-ROHMER & KLEBES, *supra* note 24.

[34] *Id.*

C. THEORIES OF EUROPEAN INTEGRATION

While the main focus of this volume is on European Union *law*, European integration has been studied by political scientists, historians, and economists, to name just a few examples. Each offers a unique perspective.

Political scientists have sought to develop theories that capture the process of European integration. One such theory is intergovernmentalism, which argues that the national governments play a decisive role in the process of European integration. Representatives of this school of thought include Stanley Hoffmann[35] and Andrew Moravcsik.[36] According to Moravcsik, the European Union, even though it has certain federal elements, fundamentally remains a confederation of nation-states.[37]

By contrast, so-called "neofunctionalist" scholars such as Anne-Marie Slaughter,[38] Alec Stone Sweet and Wayne Sandholtz[39] favor a rather different view of European integration. They believe that the European Union's institutions play a central role in explaining the dynamics of European integration. According to this narrative, EU institutions are much more than simply a means for Member States to coordinate their own policies. Rather, EU institutions often adopt policies that the Member States would not have negotiated among themselves.[40] For example, EU institutions will generally favor policies aimed at greater integration, sometimes despite opposition from the most influential Member States.[41]

What explains the importance of EU institutions in European integration? According to neofunctionalists, part of the answer lies in the logic of the political process: Once an institutional structure at the European Union level has been created, interest groups seeking to influence political decisions can no longer afford to focus their lobbying efforts on national institutions alone. Instead, they also attempt to influence the decisions and policies adopted by EU institutions.[42]

---

[35] *See, e.g.*, Stanley Hoffmann, *Reflections on the Nation-State in Western Europe Today*, 21 J. COMMON MKT. STUD. 22, 35 (1982); Stanley Hoffmann, *Obstinate or Obsolete? The Fate of the Nation-State and the Case of Western Europe*, 95 DAEDELUS 863 (1966).

[36] *E.g.*, Andrew Moravcsik, *Conservative Idealism and International Institutions*, 1 CHI. J. INT'L L. 291, 309 (2000).

[37] Andrew Moravcsik, *The European Constitutional Settlement*, in MAKING HISTORY: EUROPEAN INTEGRATION AND INSTITUTIONAL CHANGE AT FIFTY 23, 24 (Sophie Meunier & Kathleen R. McNamara eds., 2007).

[38] Anne-Marie Burley & Walter Mattli, *Europe before the Court*, 47 INTERNATIONAL ORGANIZATION 41 (1993).

[39] Wayne Sandholtz & Alec Stone Sweet, *Neo-Functionalism and Supranational Governance*, OXFORD HANDBOOK OF THE EUROPEAN UNION (2012).

[40] *Id.*

[41] *Id.*

[42] *Id.*

Moreover, European integration creates its own peculiar feedback loop: Transnational economic activity leads to the creation of supranational governance in the form of EU institutions and EU legislation.[43] Such supranational governance contributes to a further expansion of transnational economic activity, which in turn increases the demand for supranational governance.[44]

NOTES AND QUESTIONS

1. According to the neofunctionalist theory of European integration, as described by Stone Sweet and Sandholtz, how and why do European institutions matter to the process of European integration?

2. In what sense, if any, is the neofunctionalist theory of European integration more dynamic than the intergovernmentalist theory?

3. On March 29, 2017, the United Kingdom notified the European Council of its intention to withdraw from the European Union under Article 50 TEU. Can this development be adduced as evidence of the intergovernmentalist approach of European integration or of the neofunctionalist approach, or does it support neither approach?

---

[43] *Id.*
[44] *Id.*

CHAPTER 2

THE FOUNDING OF THE EUROPEAN COMMUNITIES

■ ■ ■

The treaties discussed in the previous chapter—the Treaty of Brussels, the Convention for European Economic Co-operation, and the Statute on the Council of Europe—all constituted important steps towards increased cooperation between the nations of Western Europe. Yet at the same time, all of these treaties very much remained cast in the mold of traditional international treaties. They facilitated intergovernmental coordination, but imposed few restraints on the sovereignty of the participating countries. Accordingly, they did little to move the continent toward a United States of Europe. Nor was this particularly surprising: the United Kingdom, which played a crucial role in the creation of these treaties, was not, at the time, ready to be part of any organization that would unite Europe at the expense of national sovereignty.

A. THE EUROPEAN COAL AND STEEL COMMUNITY

On the European continent, many were disappointed with the limited integration brought about by the previously described treaties. In 1950, therefore, the French foreign minister Robert Schuman unveiled a proposal with a much greater potential for European integration. The core idea was to place French and German production of coal and steel under the authority of one common agency, with other European countries also invited to join.[1]

This proposal, which had been designed by Jean Monnet and is therefore commonly referred to as the Schuman-Monnet plan, was remarkable for at least two reasons. First, the creation of a common agency in charge of the relevant industries meant a real curtailment of national sovereignty, if only in the relevant economic sectors. And second, the Schuman-Monnet plan was explicitly designed to lead to further integration. The idea was that the European Coal and Steel Community

---

[1] Robert Schuman, Proposal Announced at the French Ministry of Foreign Affairs ("Schuman Declaration") (May 9, 1950), *reprinted in* LA MONDIALISATION: DOCUMENTS ESSENTIELS 253 (James D. Thwaites ed., 2004).

would provide a foundation for a more far-reaching economic unification of Europe.[2]

The Schuman-Monnet plan was enthusiastically received in several European countries, including Germany. And on April 18, 1951, six European nations—Belgium, France, Germany, Italy, Luxembourg, and the Netherlands—signed the Treaty Instituting the European Coal and Steel Community (ECSC Treaty).[3]

Among the more important features of the European Coal and Steel Community (ECSC) was its institutional framework. The ECSC had an executive organ, the High Authority, which had the task of ensuring that the goals set forth in the ECSC Treaty were in fact met.[4] The members of the executive organ were under a duty to "exercise their functions in complete independence, in the general interest of the Community."[5] Accordingly, the High Authority can be understood as the beginning of an independent European administration. In addition, the ECSC Treaty created a Court of Justice, a Common Assembly, which can be understood as a precursor of the European Parliament, and a Special Council, which was composed of representatives of the Member States.[6] This institutional design largely foreshadowed the structure of today's European Union.

Robert Schuman, Proposal Announced at the French Ministry of Foreign Affairs ("The Schuman Declaration"), Paris, March 9, 1950

The protection of world peace requires creative efforts that are proportionate to the dangers threatening it. The contributions that Europe, organized and alive, can make to civilization are indispensable for the preservation of peace. By championing a United Europe for more than twenty years, France has always sought to advance the cause of peace. European union was not achieved, and we have had war.

European union cannot be realized in a day, nor will it be the result of a single plan. It must be built by way of concrete achievements that prepare the ground by creating de facto solidarity. Uniting the nations of Europe can only succeed if the long-lasting conflict between France and Germany is resolved. Any attempt to unite Europe must first and foremost focus on these two countries. To this end, the French government proposes to take immediate action on a limited yet crucial issue.

---

[2] *Id.*, *reprinted in* LA MONDIALISATION, *supra* note 1, at 254 (arguing that the new community for coal and steel would provide a foundation for the economic unification of Europe).

[3] Treaty Instituting the European Coal and Steel Community, Apr. 18, 1951, 261 U.N.T.S. 140 [hereinafter ECSC Treaty].

[4] *Id.* art. 8.

[5] *Id.* art. 9.

[6] *Id.* art. 7.

The French government proposes that the entirety of the French and German production of coal and steel be placed under a common High Authority, as part of an organization that is open to the participation of other European countries as well. Pooling the production of coal and steel ensures the immediate creation of a common basis for economic development. It will be the first stage of a European federation and will change the destiny of those lands long dedicated to the production of the very weapons for which they themselves have been the chief victims. This unity of production will demonstrate that war between France and German will not just be unthinkable, but in fact physically impossible. This powerful union in production, open to all nations willing to join it and aimed at providing all of its members with the basic elements of industrial manufacturing on identical terms, shall create the real basis for their economic unification. [. . .]. ∎

NOTES AND QUESTIONS

1. Robert Schuman was the French foreign minister, and the Schuman declaration was given at the Salon d'Horloge at the French Foreign Ministry on March 9, 1950. It was the starting point for the creation of the Coal and Steel Community and, ultimately, for the establishment of the European Union. How could he claim, with some justification, that France had long been a champion of a united Europe?

2. The Schuman declaration views the envisaged pooling of the French and German coal and steel production as the "first stage of a European federation." What was special about the production of coal and steel?

3. Schuman stresses that any attempt to unite Europe must focus, first and foremost, on France and Germany. What seems to motivate this focus?

4. France and Germany have traditionally wielded disproportionate influence in the European Union. Substantial reforms typically occurred because and to the extent that both France and Germany supported them. What might explain this dominance? Moreover, is it realistic to expect this dynamic to continue? What are the downsides of the central role played by France and Germany?

5. While the Franco-German partnership has traditionally played a crucial role in the process of European integration, that partnership did not always function well. In particular, its success depended on how well the countries' leaders managed to work together.[7] The partnership between de Gaulle and Adenauer was crucial in that these two statesmen had both the will and the authority to form the European Coal and Steel Community, the European Economic Community, and the European Nuclear Energy

---

[7] *Cf.* Carine Germond, *Dynamic Franco-German Duos: Giscard-Schmidt and Mitterrand-Kohl*, in THE OXFORD HANDBOOK OF THE EUROPEAN UNION 193, 193–205 (Erik Jones et al. eds., 2012).

Community. Their immediate successors were less successful in advancing the process of European integration. However, when Helmut Schmidt was elected German Chancellor in 1974 and Valéry Giscard d'Estaing became President of France the same year, another crucial phase of cooperation began. For example, both leaders were instrumental in creating the European Monetary System, thereby beginning a process that would ultimately lead to the creation of the euro. Another phase of successful Franco-German occurred when Helmut Kohl was Chancellor of Germany (1982–98) and Francois Mitterrand was President of France (1981–95). Their partnership survived even Mitterrand's initial reservations regarding German reunification (1990). In fact, Germany's reunification ended up reinforcing both men's commitment to the process of European integration. Partially out of concern that a reunified Germany might once again strive for European dominance, Mitterrand was eager to accelerate the process of European integration and found a willing partner in Helmut Kohl.

Robert Schuman (1886–1963)

Robert Schuman was a French statesman who played a key role in the post-World War II movement towards European unification. Both Robert Schuman and his mother were born in Luxembourg. His father had originally been a French citizen from the region of Lorraine, but became a German citizen when Germany annexed that region in 1871. Accordingly, Robert Schuman grew up as a German citizen. He studied law as well as economics, statistics, and philosophy in Berlin, Bonn, Munich, and Strasbourg before becoming a lawyer in Metz. Due to health problems, he managed to avoid military service in WWI. As a result of that war, the region of Lorraine became French again, so Schuman became a French citizen. A long career in French and European politics followed.

In 1919, at age 33, he was first elected to the French parliament. During WWII, when Germany occupied much of France, he was, for some time, a member of the infamous Pétain government, known for its collaboration with the Third Reich. However, he soon quit the Pétain government and in 1940 was arrested for resisting the Nazis. He narrowly avoided being sent to Dachau, managed to escape in 1942, and joined the French resistance.

After WWII, Schuman was found guilty of *indignité nationale* (national unworthiness) because of his role in the Pétain government

> and the fact that, as a member of the French parliament, he had voted in favor of a constitutional amendment surrendering all government power ("tous pouvoirs") to Pétain, thereby allowing the latter to govern as an authoritarian ruler. As a result, Schuman was deprived of various civic rights, including passive election rights and the right to work for the state. However, due to an intervention by Charles de Gaulle—who had led the French government-in-exile ("France Libre"), who was chairing the provisional French government after the war, and would later become President of France—Schuman's civic rights were fully restored in 1945.
>
> From November 24, 1947 to July 26, 1947, and then again from September 5 to September 11, 1948, Schuman served as France's prime minister. Starting in 1948, he served as foreign minister in several French administrations. It was in this capacity that he made the famous Schuman declaration in 1950. From 1958 to 1960, he served as president of the European Parliamentary Assembly, which would later be renamed the European Parliament. To this day, he is considered one of the most important figures in the history of the European Union.

B. THE TREATIES OF ROME

Following the creation of the European Coal and Steel Community, the French executive proposed the creation of a European Defense Community, but the French parliament was unwilling to endorse this plan.[8] Against this background, the Member States of the ECSC decided to focus, not on defense, but on further economic integration. Starting in 1955, a commission headed by the Belgian foreign minister Paul-Henri Spaak explored the potential for the creation of a common market and a common nuclear energy policy. The result of the commission's work, presented on May 29, 1956, was the so-called *Spaak Report*. Based on that report, an intergovernmental conference in Brussels, which was also chaired by Spaak, negotiated two treaties—the Treaty Establishing the European Economic Community (EEC Treaty)[9] and the Treaty Establishing the European Atomic Energy Community (Euratom Treaty).[10] Both treaties were signed in Rome on March 25, 1957, and entered into force on January 1, 1958. They are collectively known as the Treaties of Rome.

Of the two treaties, the EEC Treaty proved far more important to European integration, and it will therefore be the focus of the following discussions. The core purpose of the European Economic Community (EEC)

---

[8] ALAN S. MILWARD, THE RISE AND FALL OF A NATIONAL STRATEGY, 1954–1963, at 78–125 (1991) (describing efforts to establish a European Defense Community).

[9] Treaty Establishing the European Economic Community, Mar. 25, 1957, 298 U.N.T.S. 3 [hereinafter EEC Treaty].

[10] Treaty Establishing the European Atomic Energy Community, Mar. 25, 1957, 298 U.N.T.S. 167.

was the creation of a common market, a goal that was to be reached in a transitional period of only twelve years.[11] On the institutional side, the EEC strongly resembled the ECSC: its institutions included the so-called Assembly, the Council, the Commission (which was the equivalent of the ECSC's High Authority), and the Court of Justice.

The Council, the main legislative body of the EEC, was composed of representatives of the Member States.[12] The Commission functioned as the EEC's executive. Unlike the members of the Council, who represented individual Member States, the members of the Commission were required to "perform their duties in the general interest of the EEC with complete independence."[13]

The Assembly would later become the European Parliament. When the EEC was formed, however, the Assembly had very limited powers, and its members were not directly elected by the people. Rather, the Assembly was composed of delegates appointed by the national parliaments.[14] France, Germany, and Italy each appointed 36 delegates, the Netherlands and Belgium 14, and Luxembourg 6.[15]

C. THE DEVELOPMENT OF THE EUROPEAN ECONOMIC COMMUNITY

In the decades that followed, more and more countries joined the European Communities. Moreover, as European integration progressed, the EEC Treaty underwent several fundamental changes. Because we have not yet discussed the institutional and substantive law of the European Union, it makes little sense, at this point, to provide a detailed account of these changes. However, the legal literature often references the treaties that brought about these amendments, and so it is helpful to have at least a broad idea of what they were about. Hence, a brief chronological account seems in order. It may not be useful, at this point, to start memorizing the various treaties, but it is helpful to have come across their names.

On April 8, 1965, the Members of the European Communities signed the *Merger Treaty*, which went into force on July 1, 1967.[16] The Merger Treaty provided for all three Communities (EEC, ECSC, Euratom) to share one institutional structure.[17] In other words, while there continued to be

---

[11] EEC Treaty art. 8.
[12] *Id.* art. 146.
[13] *Id.* art. 157(2).
[14] *Id.* art. 138(1).
[15] *Id.* art. 138(2).
[16] Treaty Establishing a Single Council and a Single Commission of the European Communities, Apr. 8, 1965, 1348 U.N.T.S. 81.
[17] *Id.*

three separate Communities, there was only one Court of Justice, one Commission, etc.

On February 17, 1986, the Member States signed a treaty known as the *Single European Act*, which entered into force on July 1, 1987.[18] At the core of the Single European Act was the commitment to complete the creation of the single market by the end of 1992.[19] The Single European Act also strengthened the roles of the Commission and the European Parliament.

On February 7, 1992, the *Treaty of Maastricht* was signed.[20] It went into effect on January 1, 1993. The Treaty of Maastricht brought many important changes, but some were particularly significant.

To begin, the EEC was renamed the European Community.[21] This change reflected the fact that the Community was no longer focused solely on economic matters. Thus, starting on January 1, 1993, the three Communities were: the European Community (EC), the European Coal and Steel Community (ECSC), and the European Atomic Energy Community (Euratom).

The Treaty of Maastricht also sought to bring a more universal and systematic approach to European integration by creating the European Union as a common "roof" for various elements of European integration. Confusingly, the European Union created by the Treaty of Maastricht was not the same as today's European Union. Under the system introduced by the Treaty of Maastricht, the European Union consisted of three pillars. The first pillar consisted of the three European Communities. The second pillar was constituted by the *Common Foreign and Security Policy* (CFSP). And the third pillar consisted of cooperation in matters of *Justice and Home Affairs* (JHA). Crucially, the second and third pillars were to be areas of intergovernmental cooperation and hence beyond the reach of the institutions of the European Communities.

Under this pillar structure, the European Community was now part of one pillar of the European Union. In practice, of course, this new structure did not change the fact that the European Community was much more important than the other two Communities, let alone the CFSP or JHA.

Finally, the Treaty of Maastricht paved the way for the future creation of a common currency (now known as the Euro).[22]

---

[18] Single European Act, signed at Luxembourg on Feb. 17, 1986, and at The Hague on Feb. 28, 1986, 1754 U.N.T.S. 3.

[19] *Id.* art. 13.

[20] Treaty on European Union, Feb. 7, 1992, 1757 U.N.T.S. 3 [hereinafter Treaty of Maastricht].

[21] *Id.* art. G, sec. 1.

[22] *Id.* art. G, sec. 25, ch. 2 ("Monetary Policy").

The next major reform was brought by the *Treaty of Amsterdam,* which was signed on October 2, 1997, and entered into force on May 1, 1999.[23] Among other things, the Treaty of Amsterdam strengthened the role of the European Parliament and facilitated sanctions against Member States that breached their obligations under the treaties.

Further changes were brought by the *Treaty of Nice*, which was signed on February 26, 2001, and went into effect on February 1, 2003.[24] The Treaty of Nice particularly brought certain institutional reforms designed to ensure the functioning of the Communities' institutions in light of the rapidly increasing number of Member States. Meanwhile, in 2002, the Treaty Establishing the European Coal and Steel Community expired—50 years after entering into force. The relevant areas thus became subject to the Treaty Establishing the European Community.

If all had gone smoothly, the next major change would have been the adoption of the *Treaty Establishing a Constitution for Europe.*[25] On March 1, 2003, the so-called European Convention chaired by the former French President Valéry Giscard d'Estaing commenced drafting this Treaty, which is commonly referred to as the European Constitution. It would have replaced the existing treaties. It was also designed to bring about important substantive changes. For example, the European Constitution incorporated a Charter of Fundamental Rights[26] and provided for the Council's increased ability to decide via qualified majority rather than unanimously.[27] The European Constitution was signed on October 29, 2004, but it never went into force. While 18 of the 25 Member States ratified the Treaty, it was rejected by referendum in both France and the Netherlands, which effectively doomed its fate.

The rejection of the European Constitution, however, did not mark the end of European integration. Rather, the Member States simply shelved the ambitious and symbolically fraught attempt at creating an explicit European Constitution. Instead, on December 13, 2007, they signed the *Treaty of Lisbon*, which went into effect on December 1, 2009.[28] The Treaty of Lisbon was marketed as a mere reform treaty without any of the grandiose pretensions inherent in the European Constitution. But in fact, the Treaty of Lisbon contained quite a few of the substantive changes that the European Constitution had striven to realize.

---

[23] Treaty of Amsterdam Amending the Treaty on European Union, the Treaties Establishing the European Communities and Certain Related Acts, Oct. 2, 1997, 1997 O.J. (C 340) 1.

[24] Treaty of Nice Amending the Treaty on European Union, the Treaties Establishing the European Communities and Certain Related Acts, Feb. 26, 2001, 2001 O.J. (C 80) 1.

[25] Treaty Establishing a Constitution for Europe, Oct. 29, 2004, 2004 O.J. (C 310) 1.

[26] *Id.* pt. II.

[27] *Id.* art. I-23(3).

[28] Treaty of Lisbon Amending the Treaty on European Union and the Treaty Establishing the European Community, Dec. 13, 2007, 2007 O.J. (C 306) 1 [hereinafter Treaty of Lisbon].

The Treaty of Lisbon changed the structure of the treaties on European integration. Before the Treaty of Lisbon, "European Union" was simply the name for an aggregate of the various Communities and certain areas of intergovernmental cooperation. The Treaty of Lisbon renamed the "European Community" the "European Union" and integrated the various areas of intergovernmental cooperation into the European Union.[29] Thus, there now exist only the European Union and the European Atomic Energy Community (Euratom). The European Union is now governed by two treaties,[30] namely the *Treaty on European Union*[31] and the *Treaty on the Functioning of the European Union*.[32] Both treaties have the same legal value.[33] Together, they can be thought of as Europe's Constitution[34] even though they do not bear that name.

D. THE DEVELOPMENT OF EEC/EC/EU MEMBERSHIP

Given the success of the European Economic Community, it is not surprising that more and more countries joined. In 1973, the United Kingdom, Ireland, and Denmark became members of the three European Communities (EEC, Euratom, and ECSC). Norway was also set to join, but the negative outcome of a popular referendum doomed the Norwegian government's efforts in that direction, and Norway has remained outside of the EU ever since. Greece joined the Communities next, in 1981. Portugal and Spain followed in 1986. With the reunification of West Germany and East Germany, areas that formerly constituted East Germany also became part of the Communities, though not as a new Member State, but simply as part of Germany. Austria, Finland, and Sweden joined in 1995. And in 2004, in what is known as the *Big Bang*, the EU gained no fewer than ten new Member States—Cyprus, the Czech Republic, Estonia, Hungary, Latvia, Lithuania, Malta, Poland, Slovakia, and Slovenia. Bulgaria and Romania followed in 2007, Croatia in 2013.

---

[29] Consolidated Version of the Treaty on European Union art. 1, para. 3, May 9, 2008, 2008 O.J. (C 115) 13 (as in effect after the Treaty of Lisbon) [hereinafter TEU].

[30] *Id*.

[31] Consolidated Version of the Treaty on European Union art. 1, para. 3, May 9, 2008, 2008 O.J. (C 115) 13 (as in effect after the Treaty of Lisbon).

[32] Consolidated Version of the Treaty on the Functioning of the European Union, May 9, 2008, 2008 O.J. (C 115) 47 (as in effect after the Treaty of Lisbon) [hereinafter TFEU]. The TFEU was renamed from the Treaty Establishing the European Community, which in turn had been renamed from the Treaty Establishing the European Economic Community (EEC Treaty) by the Treaty of Maastricht in 1992.

[33] TEU, art. 1, para. 3.

[34] See sources listed in Chapter 1 note 1.

European Union

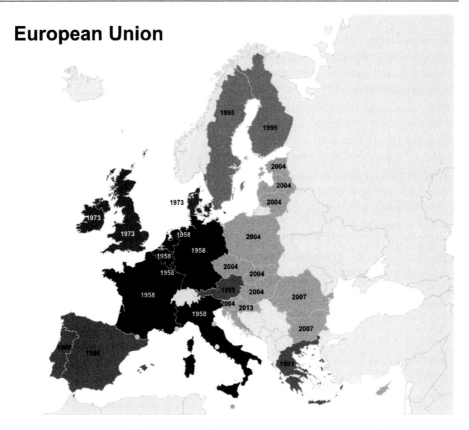

Accordingly, the EU now has 28 members, but that will likely change. On the one hand, the United Kingdom is on course to leave the European Union. On the other hand, some European countries that are not currently Member States may join the European Union.

Article 50 of the Treaty on European Union explicitly allows Member States to withdraw from the European Union. For a long time, this provision seemed to have little practical relevance. However, on June 23, 2016, the United Kingdom's voters surprised political observers by voting in favor of the United Kingdom's withdrawal from the European Union.[35] On March 29, 2017, the United Kingdom notified the European Council of its intention to withdraw, thereby setting in motion the withdrawal process under Article 50.[36]

Among those countries that may join the European Union, several groups can be distinguished.

---

[35] Jenny Gross, *U.K. Votes to Leave EU—Historic Election Sets Global Markets Reeling*, WALL ST. J., June 24, 2016, at A1.

[36] Stephen Castle, *Britain Initiates 'Brexit,' Wading Into Thorny Divorce From EU*, N.Y. TIMES, March 30, 2017, at A11.

First, there are so-called official candidates for joining the EU. These countries have formally applied for membership and meet certain membership requirements—the so-called Copenhagen criteria.[37] Currently, the list of official candidates consists of Turkey, Iceland, and Macedonia, though only Turkey is presently in negotiations. Moreover, many observers are skeptical that Turkey will be allowed to join the EU anytime soon.

Second, there are countries that have applied for EU membership but have not yet been accorded official candidate status. This group currently includes Albania, Montenegro, and Serbia.

Third, there are countries that would presumably be very welcome to join but for various reasons are not currently inclined to apply for membership. This group includes Switzerland, Norway, and Liechtenstein.

E. HOW TO JOIN THE EUROPEAN UNION

The European Communities and later the European Union steadily gained new members. However, the treaties provide only a very incomplete set of rules on the process by which new Member States are admitted. As a preliminary matter, it should be noted that the Treaty on European Union as well as the Treaty on the Functioning of the European Union are international treaties. And under the general default rules of international law, any change to an existing multilateral treaty requires a new multilateral treaty amending or replacing the old one.[38]

By default, a new multinational treaty must be signed and ratified by all parties. It follows that all Member States have to agree in order for new Member States to be admitted. Moreover, as with any treaty amending the European Treaties, each Member State can decide for itself which procedures have to be observed at the national level in order for the Member State to agree to an amendment. Many Member States deem it sufficient that, in addition to the Member State executive, the national parliament approve the amendment. However, some Member States have subjected amendments to a popular vote.

Article 49 of the Treaty on European Union governs the admission of new Member States, but it does not break with the unanimity principle described above.

---

[37] On June 22, 1993, the European Council adopted the so-called Copenhagen criteria defining the requirements that a country has to meet in order to be eligible for EU membership. *See* Presidency Conclusions, Copenhagen European Council (June 21–22, 1993), *available at* http://www.europarl.europa.eu/enlargement/ec/pdf/cop_en.pdf.

[38] Vienna Convention on the Law of Treaties art. 40(4), May 23, 1969, 1155 U.N.T.S. 331.

Article 49

Any European State which respects the values referred to in Article 2 and is committed to promoting them may apply to become a member of the Union. The European Parliament and national Parliaments shall be notified of this application. The applicant State shall address its application to the Council, which shall act unanimously after consulting the Commission and after receiving the consent of the European Parliament, which shall act by a majority of its component members. The conditions of eligibility agreed upon by the European Council shall be taken into account.

The conditions of admission and the adjustments to the Treaties on which the Union is founded, which such admission entails, shall be the subject of an agreement between the Member States and the applicant State. This agreement shall be submitted for ratification by all the contracting States in accordance with their respective constitutional requirements.

Article 49 of the Treaty on European Union is not the only relevant text on the admission process. Another important source of guidance lies in the so-called Copenhagen criteria that the European Council adopted in 1993 to set forth a basic understanding regarding the criteria for the admission of new members. Consider the following excerpt:

Membership requires that the candidate country has achieved stability of institutions guaranteeing democracy, the rule of law, human rights and respect for and protection of minorities, the existence of a functioning market economy as well as the capacity to cope with competitive pressure and market forces within the Union. Membership presupposes the candidate's ability to take on the obligations of membership including adherence to the aims of political, economic and monetary union.

The Union's capacity to absorb new members, while maintaining the momentum of European integration, is also an important consideration in the general interest of both the Union and the candidate countries.[39]

NOTES AND QUESTIONS

1. Article 49 of the Treaty on European Union sets forth certain requirements for the admission of new Member States. Suppose, however, that the existing Member States all agree that a certain country that does not fulfill the criteria set forth in Article 49—e.g. because it is located in South America—

---

[39] *See* Presidency Conclusions, Copenhagen European Council (June 21–22, 1993), *available at* http://www.europarl.europa.eu/enlargement/ec/pdf/cop_en.pdf.

should be admitted to the European Union. Can Article 49 prevent the existing Member States from admitting such a country into the European Union? And if not, what exactly is the function of the substantive criteria listed in Article 49?

2. Does Article 49 of the Treaty on European Union grant a right to be admitted to the European Union? In other words, can a country that meets all the criteria listed in Article 49 demand to be admitted to the European Union?

3. Turkey is a candidate country for joining the European Union. Turkey applied to become a member of the European Economic Community in 1987. Yet whereas numerous other countries have been allowed to join the European Union since 1987, Turkey's progress towards EU membership has been slow. Many observers, particularly in Turkey, have suggested that the European Union's reluctance to admit Turkey may in part be due to the fact that Turkey's population is predominantly Muslim. Given the values that the Treaty on European Union sets forth in its Article 2, would it be legal under EU law for a Member State to veto Turkey's admission to the European Union because Islam is the country's prevailing religion?

4. On November 24, 2016, the European Parliament formally voted to suspend talks on Turkey's EU membership. Assuming—hypothetically—that the Member States want to admit Turkey anyway, despite the European Parliament's vote, could they do so?

Valéry Giscard d'Estaing (born 1926) & Helmut Schmidt (1918–2015)

Valéry Giscard d'Estaing is a French statesman. Born in 1926, he was first elected to the French Parliament in 1956. After holding various other public offices, he was elected President of the French Republic in 1974 as the candidate of the conservative camp. His presidency ended when he lost the 1981 election to the candidate of the Socialist Party, Francois Mitterrand. This defeat was due in part to a split within the conservative ranks between Giscard d'Estaing and another future President of France, Jacques Chirac. During his presidency, France undertook a number of reforms such as legalizing abortion in 1974—a reform spearheaded by health minister Simone Weil—and reforming divorce law by introducing divorce by mutual consent (1975). When the Convention for the Future of Europe (or "European Convention") was formed in 2001 to draft a European Constitution, Giscard d'Estaing became its Chairman, and his views strongly influenced the draft Constitution.

Helmut Schmidt was a German statesman who served as Germany's Chancellor from 1974–82. As a member of Germany's social-democratic party (SPD), he was elected by a coalition of the SPD and the Free Democratic Party (FDP). His economic policy was guided, at least in his first years in office, by a Keynesian approach that relied on deficit spending to revive the economy and lower unemployment. These policies enjoyed some success in combatting the (worldwide) economic crisis that began in the early seventies, triggered in part by rising oil prices. By and large, the German economy was perceived to be doing better than many other Western economies. However, as deficits began to grow and the German economy stagnated in the late seventies and early eighties, differences over economic policies as well as on the issue of the stationing of U.S. nuclear weapons in Germany, which Schmidt favored, but much of his party disliked, caused a rift with the Free Democrats. In 1982, the Free Democrats left the coalition with the Social Democrats and instead entered into a coalition with the centre-right CDU, electing Helmut Kohl as Chancellor and thereby replacing Schmidt.

Konrad Adenauer (1876–1967) & Charles de Gaulle (1890–1970)

Konrad Adenauer (left) was a German statesman who became the first Chancellor, the German equivalent of prime minister, after WWII—an office that he held for a record 24 years (1959–63).

Adenauer had been a member of the Catholic Center party before WWII, and had served as the mayor of Cologne from 1917–33, until he was dismissed from this office when the Nazi party came to power in 1933.

Adenauer never joined the Nazi party NSDAP, though he had, in 1932, declared that the NSDAP party should join the national government in a leading role, given its success in elections. During the Nazi regime, he was arrested several times, but always eventually released. After WWII, the American forces reinstalled him as mayor of Cologne, but when Cologne was reallocated to the British zone he was dismissed for alleged incompetence. Once the Federal Republic of Germany was formed, Adenauer was elected as its first Chancellor in 1949 as a Member of the center-right Christian Democratic Union (CDU). As Chancellor, "der Alte" (the Elder), as Adenauer was nicknamed, he pursued a determined policy of integrating Germany with the West. In particular, he had Germany join NATO, steered Germany towards a market economy (as opposed to a more socialist approach then favored by much of Germany's political left), and recognized Germany's duty to compensate Israel.

Charles de Gaulle was a French statesman and general. He served as a distinguished officer in WWI, was wounded multiple times, and spent some time in German captivity as prisoner of war. Between the wars, he pursued a career in the military. In World War II, he had been appointed Undersecretary of War. However, he refused to accept the French government's 1940 armistice with Nazi Germany and instead led both a French government in exile ("France libre") and the Free French Forces ("Forces françaises libres"). Once France had been freed from German occupation, Charles de Gaulle led its provisional government (*Gouvernement provisoire de la République française*) from 1944 to 1946. Frustrated by what he viewed as political squabbling, de Gaulle resigned in 1946 and retired from politics some years later. However, the Algerian War of Independence (1954–62) and France's highly controversial efforts to hold on to Algeria as a French territory brought the French state—the so-called Fourth Republic—into a severe crisis. By 1958, the civilian government's control over the French Army seemed in question. That same year, the French president, with Parliament's approval, brought de Gaulle back as leader of the transition government, with the understanding that the transition government would introduce a new Constitution and that de Gaulle would be the next president. The new Constitution, approved by a 79.2% majority in a popular referendum in September 1958, created the so-called *Fifth Republic* and was characterized by a strong role for the President. De Gaulle was elected as the Fifth Republic's first president that same year and remained in office until 1969. As president, he oversaw part of a long period of economic growth, the so-called *trente glorieuses* (1945–1974). While embracing capitalism in principle, de Gaulle favored a strong dose of control by the state, an approach referred to as *dirigisme*. In matters of foreign and military policy, he sought reconciliation with Germany and found a willing partner in German Chancellor Konrad Adenauer. He also pursued a policy of national independence, taking France out of NATO and overseeing the creation of a nuclear arsenal for the French army.

CHAPTER 3

THE BASICS OF EUROPEAN UNION LAW

■ ■ ■

This chapter provides an overview over the basic features of European Union law. The various topics mentioned in this chapter will be discussed in more detail later on. However, because of the interconnected nature of European Union law, it is useful to begin with a brief summary in order to facilitate the understanding of later chapters.

A. THE INSTITUTIONAL STRUCTURE

The institutional framework of the European Union consists of seven main institutions: the European Council, the Council, the European Commission, the European Parliament, the Court of Justice of the European Union, the European Central Bank, and the Court of Auditors.[1] In addition, there exist two auxiliary institutions, namely the Economic and Social Committee and the Committee of the Regions, whose function it is to assist the European Parliament, the Council, and the European Commission.[2]

1. THE EUROPEAN COUNCIL

The European Council consists of "the Heads of State or Government of the Member States, together with its President and the President of the Commission."[3] In other words, the European Council is an institution that unites the top decision-maker from each Member State plus the head of the European Union's own executive apparatus (the Commission) plus the president of the European Council itself.

As befits the status of its members, the European Council's function is described in lofty terms. It is the European Council's responsibility to "provide the Union with the necessary impetus for its development and [to] define the general political directions and priorities" of the Union."[4] Because the European Council is not in charge of day-to-day decision-

---

[1] TEU, art. 13(1).
[2] *See id.* art. 13(4).
[3] *Id.* art. 15(2).
[4] *Id.* art. 15(1).

making, it meets only twice every six months.[5] As a general rule, the European Council has to make its decisions "by consensus," i.e., unanimously.[6]

Note that the European Council is not to be confused with the Council of Europe. The European Council is one of the institutions of the European Union. By contrast, the Council of Europe, which was briefly discussed in the first chapter of this casebook, is an international organization that is completely independent from the European Union.

2. THE COUNCIL

The Council—not to be confused with either the European Council or the Council of Europe—consists of one representative of each Member State.[7] These representatives are not, however, the Member States' heads of government or heads of state. Rather, they are representatives "at ministerial level."[8]

In earlier decades, the Council was the main legislative institution of what was then the European Community and also controlled its budget. Now, it shares these functions with the European Parliament. However, the Council still remains the slightly more powerful of the two institutions.

As a general rule, the Council decides by a qualified majority.[9] The threshold for that majority is of crucial importance to the allocation of power between the Member States. Because each Member State only has a single representative in the Council, a majority rule focusing solely on the number of representatives supporting a particular decision would favor small Member States at the expense of larger ones. By contrast, a majority rule focusing solely on the size of the different Member States would allow the large Member States such as France, Germany, Italy, Poland, and Spain to pay little attention to the concerns of smaller Member States. Therefore, the Treaty on European Union strikes a compromise between the interests of large Member States and smaller ones. Since November 1, 2014, a qualified majority requires "at least 55 % of the members of the Council, comprising at least fifteen of them and representing Member States comprising at least 65 % of the population of the Union."[10]

Note as well that the presidency in the council rotates among the Member States,[11] with each country's spell at the top lasting six months.

---

[5] *Id.* art. 15(3).
[6] *Id.* art. 15(4).
[7] *Id.* art. 16(2).
[8] *Id.*
[9] *Id.* art. 16(3).
[10] *Id.* art. 16(4).
[11] *Id.* art. 16(9).

NOTES AND QUESTIONS

1. The Council presidency's importance lies in the organizational responsibilities that come with it. Whichever Member State holds the presidency is in charge of meetings: organizing them, setting their agendas, and chairing them. These responsibilities may sound fairly technical, but the agenda-setter often influences the outcome of the decision-making process.

2. It is easy to see that the Council's rotating presidency comes with certain costs. For example, it can be difficult to maintain continuity if every six months a different Member State takes charge. Moreover, the administrative burden associated with holding the presidency can impose a disproportionate burden on the smaller Member States, such as Cyprus or Luxembourg. Can you think of other drawbacks?

3. Would it be reasonable to argue that the rotating presidency was more appropriate when the EU had fewer Member States? Or is the rotating presidency easier to defend now?

4. Can you think of any important reasons to retain the six-months rotations? For example, does it serve to protect the legitimate interests of smaller countries? Does it help prevent any particular country from accumulating too much power?

5. Read Article 15 of the Treaty on European Union to find out how often the President of the European Council changes. (Recall that the European Council is different from the Council.) Then read Article 17 to find out how often the President of the European Commission changes. What arguments, if any, might justify treating these institutions differently on this dimension?

6. Recall how the Article 16(4) of the Treaty European Union defines a qualified majority in the Council. Could the "old" Member States that joined the European Union before the "Big Bang" enlargement round of 2004 outvote the "new" Member States in the Council? Does that result surprise you? Could those Member States that are part of NATO outvote those that are not? How easy is it for Germany and France, acting in concert, to prevent a qualified majority? Could those Member States that border on the Mediterranean Sea block a qualified majority?

3. THE EUROPEAN PARLIAMENT

The European Parliament is "composed of representatives of the Union's citizens."[12] Its members are directly elected for a five-year term.[13] In practice, the decisive question is, of course, how the electoral weight is distributed among the Member States. To wit, how many representatives are elected by voters in Italy, how many by voters in Denmark, and so forth. The Treaty on European Union gives only a very general answer to that question by providing that the citizens' representation is "degressively

---

[12] *Id.* art. 14(2).
[13] *Id.* art. 14(3).

proportional."[14] In other words, the voters of more populous Member States elect more representatives than the voters of smaller Member States, but the latter must be given more than their proportional weight. The Treaty on European Union does not specify, however, the exact number of representatives that each Member State's electorate is entitled to elect. Rather, that question is to be resolved via a unanimous decision by the European Council, which also requires the consent of the European Parliament.[15] Such a decision was last adopted on June 18, 2013. Under that decision, the European Parliament has 751 members. Germany has the most representatives (96), Estonia, Luxemburg, Malta, and Cyprus the fewest (6 each).

As regards the European Parliament's functions, it is noteworthy that the European Parliament has grown ever more powerful over the decades. At least in part, this development is owed to criticism that the European Union lacked sufficient democratic legitimation.

Originally, when the Parliament was still called the European Assembly and its members were chosen by the Member State parliaments rather than directly elected by the citizens, the forum merely had an advisory function. Now, under the Treaty on European Union, the European Parliament shares control with the Council over the European Union's legislation and budget. Indeed, one can now speak with some justification of a bicameral legislature: the Council constitutes one chamber and the European Parliament the other.[16]

4. THE EUROPEAN COMMISSION

The European Commission essentially constitutes the executive body of the European Union, although it is also heavily involved in the legislative process.

To avoid confusion, it should be noted at the outset that the term "European Commission" has two different meanings. In its strict sense, it refers to the College of Commissioners. Since November 1, 2014, the number of members corresponds to "two thirds of the number of members states" unless the European Council unanimously chooses a different

---

[14] *Id.* art. 14(2).

[15] *Id.*

[16] *See, e.g.,* Steven G. Calabresi & Kyle Bady, *Is the Separation of Powers Exportable*, 33 HARV. J.L. & PUB. POL'Y 5, 14 (2010) (asserting that the European Union "in effect has a bicameral structure today"); Damien Geradin, *The Development of European Regulatory Agencies: What the EU Should Learn from American Experience*, 11 COLUM. J. EUR. L. 1, 7 (2004) ("[T]he EU system is moving towards a bicameral structure comparable to the US whereby the European Parliament represents the 'people' (like the House), whereas the Council represents the Member States (like the Senate)."). *But see* Armin von Bogdandy, *The European Union as a Supranational Federation: A Conceptual Attempt in the Light of the Amsterdam Treaty*, 6 COLUM. J. EUR. L. 27, 49 (2000) (arguing, albeit under prior law, that the Treaties do not provide a sufficient basis for such a categorization).

number.[17] In practice, of course, the term European Commission is frequently used in a much wider sense. In that wider sense, it refers not only to the College of Commissioners but also to the entire European administration headed by the College of Commissioners, which consists of about 25,000 civil servants. However, in this section, I use the term "European Commission" or "Commission" only in the strict sense as synonyms for the College of Commissioners.

A crucial characteristic of the European Commission is its responsibility to "promote the general interest of the Union."[18] This may seem obvious, but it has to be recalled that the Member States—and their representatives in the Council—will generally pursue their own interests. By contrast, the Commission is designed to act as the "guardian of the Treaties." Accordingly, the Commission is completely independent,[19] and its members are chosen "on the ground of their general competence and European commitment from persons whose independence is beyond doubt."[20]

Despite the Commission's independence, the Member States in practice are very much interested in having their nationals occupy important roles in the Commission. And the Treaty on European Union is not blind to that fact. To ensure proper balance, it provides that the Commission's members "shall be chosen from among the nationals of the Member States on the basis of a system of strictly equal rotation between the Member States, reflecting the demographic and geographical range of all the Member States."[21]

How exactly are the members of the Commission selected? The process is quite complicated. First, the European Council has to propose to the European Parliament a specific candidate for President of the Commission.[22] In order for this candidate to be successful, he then has to be formally elected by the European Parliament.[23] If he fails to be elected, the Commission has to come up with another candidate.[24] Once a President of the Commission has been elected by the Parliament, the Council and the President-elect have to settle on a list of candidates to fill the remaining slots on the Commission.[25] Crucially, these other members of the Commission have to be selected "on the basis of the suggestions made by

---

[17] TEU, art. 17(5).
[18] *Id.* art. 17(1).
[19] *Id.* art. 17(3).
[20] *Id.*
[21] *Id.* art. 17(5).
[22] *Id.* art. 17(7).
[23] *Id.*
[24] *Id.*
[25] *Id.*

the Member States."²⁶ In other words, the President-elect of the Commission enjoys very little discretion in choosing the other Commissioners. Finally, the Commission as a whole—including its President—is "subject as a body to a vote of consent by the European Parliament."²⁷ In other words, the European Parliament cannot reject individual Commissioners, but it can reject the Commission as a whole.

Once elected, the Commission serves for five years.²⁸ However, individual Commissioners have to resign before the end of the five year term "if the President so requests."²⁹ The European Parliament also has the power to end the Commission's term prematurely: The European Parliament "may vote on a motion of censure of the Commission," and if that motion is successful, the entire Commission has to resign.³⁰ Again, it should be noted that the European Parliament can only target the Commission as a whole—it cannot force the resignation of an individual Commissioner.

Individual Commissioners can serve more than one term. This creates at least a theoretical risk that they will be overly deferential to the interests of their home states in order to be nominated again for the next Commission. In practice, however, the Treaty's objective of ensuring the Commissioners' independence holds up remarkably well. Commissioners are frequently quick to put the interests of their home states behind them once they have left the arena of national politics. This may be partly because the job of Commissioner, instead of being a stepping stone for higher political offices, often comes at the dusk of a political career. For example, Édith Cresson was the prime minister of France before she had to step down from that office; she eventually became the European Commissioner for Science, Research and Development³¹ (1994–1999³²). Similarly, Martin Bangemann headed the German Department for Economic Affairs before he jumped ship and became the European Commissioner for Internal Market and Industrial Affairs (1989–1999).³³ However, there are exceptions. Romano Prodi, who had been Italy's Prime Minister (1996–1998), served as President of the European Commission (1999–2004), only later to become Italy's Prime Minister once more (2006–2008). Similarly, Prodi's fellow countryman Mario Monti served for many

---

[26] *Id.*

[27] *Id.*

[28] *Id.* art. 17(3).

[29] *Id.* art. 17(6).

[30] *Id.* art. 17(8).

[31] Wolfgang Munchau, *Female assault on power led by Cresson*, TIMES (London), Nov. 1, 1994, *available at* LEXIS.

[32] Stephen Bates, *European Parliament tells Cresson: quit now*, GUARDIAN (London), Nov. 20, 1999, at 2, *available at* LEXIS.

[33] Stephen Bates, *The Eurocrat with his own yacht sails into a storm*, TIMES (London), Apr. 15, 1999, *available at* LEXIS.

years as a European Commissioner (1995–2004) before eventually becoming Italy's Prime Minister (2011–2013).

Apart from the President of the Commission, one other Commissioner is particularly noteworthy, namely the High Representative of the Union for Foreign Affairs and Security Policy.[34] The High Representative is entrusted with the task of conducting the European Union's common foreign and security policy.[35] In other words, the office of the High Representative was designed as the EU equivalent of a national secretary of state. While the High Representative is part of the Commission[36] and as such is subject to the European Parliament's power to reject the Commission,[37] he is subject to somewhat different rules than the remaining members of the Commission. The basic idea is that the office of the High Representative is too important to be treated like any other position on the Commission. Thus, rather than being chosen on the basis of a suggestion made by a Member State, the High Representative is appointed directly by the European Council.[38]

5. THE COURT OF JUSTICE OF THE EUROPEAN UNION

The Court of Justice of the European Union, seated in Luxembourg, is the Union's judiciary. Its responsibility is "to ensure that in the interpretation and application of the Treaties, the law is observed."[39] In other words, the Court does not function as a general court of appeals for the courts of the Member States. Nor is there any equivalent to the diversity jurisdiction exercised by federal courts in the United States. The Court never ever applies the law of the Member States. Rather, it focuses solely on the application and interpretation of European Union law, the "federal law" of the European Union.

Like the Union's other institutions, the Court has evolved over the decades. In the beginning, there was really just one court consisting of one judge per Member State. However, as the caseload increased, it became clear that a more differentiated court structure was needed. Today, therefore, the Court of Justice of the European Union comprises several courts with different responsibilities: the Court of Justice, the General Court, and the Civil Service Tribunal.

---

[34] *See* TEU, art. 18.
[35] *Id.* art. 18(2).
[36] *Id.* art. 18(4).
[37] *Id.* art. 17(7).
[38] *Id.* art. 18(1).
[39] *Id.* art. 19(1).

a) The Court of Justice

At the top of the European Union's judicial hierarchy is the *Court of Justice*—not to be confused with the *Court of Justice of the European Union*, which is the name given to the judiciary as a whole. As in the old days, the Court of Justice consists of one judge from each Member State.[40] Since the Court of Justice will be discussed in detail in the following chapter, these few remarks shall suffice for now.

b) The General Court

Certain types of cases that are not important enough to be assigned to the Court of Justice are decided by the General Court.[41] The General Court consists of "at least one judge per Member State."[42] In other words, the Treaty on European Union leaves open the possibility of adding more judges to the General Court. However, the Statute of the Court of Justice, which, as explained above, also forms an integral part of the Treaty, is more specific and sets the number of General Court judges at 28.[43]

c) Specialized Courts: The Civil Service Tribunal

The Treaty on European Union also allows for the creation of specialized courts.[44] These specialized courts can be established by the European Parliament and the Council using the so-called ordinary legislative procedure.[45] The specialized courts thus created are meant to serve as courts of first instance for cases in specific areas.[46] In practice, however, only one such special court has been established.[47] The aptly named European Union Civil Service Tribunal hears cases in civil service disputes.[48] The European Union Civil Service Tribunal illustrates the need for specialized courts: Given the mundane nature of most employment-related lawsuits brought by the European Union's civil servants, it hardly makes sense that such lawsuits should be heard by the Court of Justice.

6. THE EUROPEAN CENTRAL BANK

The European Central Bank, seated in Frankfurt, Germany, is in charge of the European Union's monetary policy.[49] Together with the

---

[40] *Id.* art. 19(2).

[41] TFEU, art. 253(1).

[42] TEU, art. 19(2).

[43] Statute of the Court of Justice of the European Union art. 48.

[44] TEU, art. 19(1).

[45] TFEU, art. 257.

[46] *Id.*

[47] *See* Council Decision 2004/752, 2004 O.J. (L 333) 7 (EC, Euratom) ("Establishing the European Union Civil Service Tribunal").

[48] Statute of the Court of Justice of the European Union annex I, art. 1.

[49] TFEU, art. 282(1).

central banks of the Member States, the European Central Bank (ECB) forms the European System of Central Banks (ESCB).[50]

To understand the law governing the European Central Banking System, one has to be aware of its history: When the Member States first moved towards a common currency and monetary policy, those Member States with stable currencies—particularly Germany with its *Deutsche Mark*—were extremely reluctant to give up their national currencies unless the new European currency was guaranteed to be just as stable.

This reluctance is not difficult to explain. Having seen their savings wiped out in two periods of extreme inflation—first in the 1920s and then again after WWII—Germans had long come to place a very high value on monetary stability. But not all Member States were as focused on monetary stability as Germany was. Other countries such as Italy have traditionally tolerated much higher inflation rates. Accordingly, Germany and other adherents of monetary stability were worried that a European Central Bank might sooner or later sacrifice monetary stability for the sake of short-term economic growth.

Additionally, there was concern that the Central Bank might be susceptible to political pressure. This concern was not entirely unfounded. While the U.S. central bank—the Federal Reserve—has been independent since 1913, some European countries have been much slower to insulate their central banks from executive pressure. For example, even the Bank of England did not acquire its independence until 1997.

Against this background, the "hardliners" among the Member States—particularly Germany—insisted on strong legal guarantees of both the European Central Bank's independence and its commitment to monetary stability. Accordingly, the Treaty on the Functioning of the European Union explicitly provides that the European Central Bank shall be independent and that this independence has to be respected by both the institutions of the European Union and by the governments of the Member States.[51]

Moreover, the Treaty makes it clear that the "primary objective" of the European System of Central Banks is to "maintain price stability."[52] And while the ECBS also has the task of supporting "the general economic policies in the Union," that task comes strictly second: it can only be pursued "without prejudice" to the primary objective of maintaining price stability.[53] In other words, the ECBS can pursue economic aims such as growth, but not at the expense of monetary stability.

---

[50] *Id.*
[51] *Id.* art. 282(3).
[52] *Id.* art. 282(2).
[53] *Id.*

7. THE COURT OF AUDITORS

The Court of Auditors is easily the most obscure of the European Union's seven main institutions. Indeed, it is fair to say that the general public is, for the most part, unaware of its existence. As its name suggests, the Court of Auditors undertakes the European Union's audit.[54] Given the size of the European Union's budget and bureaucracy, that task is of considerable importance.

The Court of Auditors is composed of one national from each Member State.[55] As one would expect, its members are completely independent in how they perform their duties.[56]

8. THE ECONOMIC AND SOCIAL COMMITTEE AND THE COMMITTEE OF THE REGIONS

The Economic and Social Committee and the Committee of the Regions are auxiliary institutions whose function is to assist the European Parliament, the Council, and the Commission.[57] Their function is merely an advisory one.[58]

The Economic and Social Committee is composed of representatives of employer associations, trade unions, and "other parties representative of civil society, notably in socioeconomic, civic, professional and cultural areas."[59] The exact composition is left to the determination of the Council.[60]

The Committee of the Regions is composed of representatives of "regional and local bodies who either hold a regional or local authority electoral mandate or are politically accountable to an elected assembly."[61] This description is somewhat labored because regional and local bodies are organized quite varyingly across the European Union. In some Member States, their members are elected. In others, they are appointed.

It is noteworthy that both the members of the Economic and Social Committee and the members of the Committee of Regions are under a duty to act in the interest of the European Union.[62] Accordingly, they are not beholden to instructions from the organizations to which they belong.[63]

---

[54] *Id.* art. 285(1).
[55] *Id.*
[56] *Id.*
[57] *See* TEU, art. 13(4).
[58] TFEU, art. 300(1).
[59] *Id.* art. 300(2).
[60] *Id.* art. 301(5).
[61] TFEU, art. 300(3).
[62] TFEU, art. 300(4).
[63] *Id.*

PROTECTING MEMBER STATE AUTONOMY IN THE EUROPEAN UNION: SOME CAUTIONARY TALES FROM AMERICAN FEDERALISM

Ernest A. Young
77 N.Y.U.L. Rev. 1612, 1638–39 (2002)

"[One] set of challenges involves the EU's "democratic deficit"—that is, the exercise of considerable governmental power by the EU institutions without any direct grounding (except for the Parliament) in the electorate. The problem reflects the EU's diplomatic and technocratic—and not populist—origins; the initial institutional impetus, after all, was an attempt to rationalize particular industrial sectors (coal and steel) by establishing a coordinating bureaucracy. As David Calleo has observed, "[e]arly Brussels federalists tended to be benevolent technocrats who disliked the mass democracy of the modern nation state. They deplored its complications for rational policymaking and feared the opportunities it offered for evil manipulation." The European political tradition probably reflects a greater belief in and tolerance for "apolitical" technocratic decisionmaking than one generally sees in America; nonetheless, the EU's technocratic structure has come under increasing pressure as its responsibilities have ventured further into the inevitably political core functions of government. The "democratic deficit" problem may take a number of forms. Some critics have focused on the relative weakness of the European Parliament—the only directly elected body in the EU structure. Others seek democratic legitimation in the Council of Ministers on the European Council, which is at least made up of delegates from directly elected national governments. On this view, the problem is the comparative strength of the Commission vis-à-vis the Council or, with the advent of qualified majority voting in the Council, the prospect that a given Member State will be outvoted and subjected to policies never consented to by the State's own voters. Finally, as Giandomenico Majone has pointed out, the "democratic deficit" sometimes refers to "a set of problems—technocratic decision making, lack of transparency, insufficient public participation, excessive use of administrative discretion, inadequate mechanisms of control and accountability—[arising] whenever important policy-making powers are delegated to bodies operating at arm's length from government, such as independent central banks and regulatory authorities." From this perspective, the problem is not so much one of electoral control as it is the procedures by which government operates. ∎

QUESTIONS

1. The above excerpt mentions the "relative weakness of the European Parliament—the only directly elected body in the EU structure." Is it reasonable to argue that indirectly elected/appointed representatives have less democratic legitimacy? What would this imply about, say, U.S. presidential

elections? What about the election of the German chancellor, who is elected by the German parliament?

2. Can you think of any arguments against giving the European Parliament greater powers than it now has?

3. The excerpt mentions "technocratic decision-making, lack of transparency, insufficient public participation, excessive use of administrative discretion, inadequate mechanisms of control and accountability." Do these problems arise only in cases where "policy-making powers are delegated to bodies operating at arm's length from government"? If so, why? If not, when else do they arise and why?

4. How might issues such as "technocratic decision-making, lack of transparency, insufficient public participation, excessive use of administrative discretion, inadequate mechanisms of control and accountability" pose a problem for democratic legitimacy?

5. In his influential article *What if Europe Held an Election and No One Cared?*, 52 Harv. Int. L. J. 109 (2011), David Schleicher also points out an additional challenge for the European Parliament: The same political parties that represent parties at the Member State level also tend to gain the lion share of the votes cast in elections for the European Parliament. Moreover, European voters tend to cast their votes in the elections for the European Parliament based on how the relevant parties have performed at the national level. In other words, the relevant parties are not held to account for their actions in the European Parliament, but for their role in national politics.

6. Do you think that the problem highlighted by Schleicher undercuts the democratic legitimacy of the European Parliament?

7. Schleicher puts forth a specific suggestion for fixing the problem he identifies. Specifically, he suggests that in order for candidates to be elected to the European Parliament, the candidate's party should have to win both a minimum percentage of votes in the Member State where the candidate is elected and a minimum percentage of votes in the European Union as a whole.[64] The intuition behind this approach can be summarized as follows: Under the current system, candidates for the European Parliament generally run as members of the political parties organized at the Member State level.[65] For example, a moderate left-wing candidate in Germany seeking to be elected to the European Parliament might run as a member of the German Social Democratic Party, and that party affiliation will be displayed on the ballot. As a result, voters may perceive the candidate primarily as a member of the relevant national party, and voters might then try to punish or reward that party based on how it has performed at the Member State level. By requiring parties to gain a minimum percentage of votes at the level of the European Union as a whole, the law might incentivize candidates to run as members of

---

[64] David Schleicher, *What if Europe Held an Election and No One Cared?*, 52 HARV. INTL. L.J. 109, 116 (2011).

[65] *Id.* at 142.

pan-European parties, that is, as members of parties that operate at the EU level. As a result, voters might no longer identify these candidates with national political parties. Instead, they may start identifying candidates with EU level political parties and start evaluating them based on EU-level politics. Do you think that this suggestion would solve the problem?

8. Can you think of any problems that might arise if the reform proposed by Schleicher were in fact adopted?

B. THE LEGAL FRAMEWORK

A few short remarks on the legal framework of the European Union are also in order.

1. EUROPEAN UNION LAW VERSUS MEMBER STATE LAW

Historically, one of the most contentious questions of European Union law concerns the relationship between European Union law and Member State law.

The relationship between EU law and Member State law is governed by two core principles: the direct effect doctrine and the supremacy of EU law. The direct effect doctrine holds that EU law can have "direct effect" in that it can create rights and duties for individuals that these individuals can invoke before national courts.

The direct effect principle thus creates room for EU law to clash with national law: Given that both EU law and national law can create rights and duties for individuals, the question is which legal system enjoys priority in case of a conflict between the different rules. This is where the supremacy principle comes into play. According to the case law of the Court of Justice, EU law enjoys priority over Member State law. However, Member State law violating EU law is not void. Rather, the Court of Justice has made it clear that Member State law that is incompatible with EU law simply must not be applied in those cases where it conflicts with EU law. In other words, the relevant national law may still be applied in cases where it does not come into conflict with the EU legal system. But if, in a given case, EU law and Member State law clash, both the European Union's institutions and the Member States have to apply EU law.

2. PRIMARY VERSUS SECONDARY LAW

EU law can be divided into two categories: primary EU law and secondary EU law. The term primary EU law refers to the Treaty on European Union and the Treaty on the Functioning of the European Union.

The protocols and annexes of the Treaty are also part of EU primary law because they constitute an "integral part" of the Treaties.[66]

By contrast, the term secondary law refers to legal acts (regulations, directives, decisions, etc.) of the institutions of the European Union. For example, whereas the Statute of the Court of Justice of the European Union is part of primary EU law because it was enacted as Protocol No. 3 annexed to the Treaties, the Rules of Procedure of the Court of Justice constitute secondary law because they were adopted by the Court of Justice.[67]

The distinction between primary and secondary EU law matters because primary law ranks higher than secondary law. Secondary law has to comply with primary law. As a general rule, acts of secondary law that violate the EU's primary law are void.

3. REGULATIONS, DIRECTIVES, AND DECISIONS

The secondary law of the European Union generally, though not always, comes in one of five flavors: regulations, directives, decisions, recommendations, and opinions.[68]

a) Regulations

Regulations are the EU equivalent of federal statutes. They are directly applicable in all Member States. In other words, no action on the part of the Member States is necessary in order for regulations to become binding on the European Union's citizens.[69]

b) Directives

Directives are a different matter. According to the Treaty on the Functioning of the European Union, "[a] directive shall be binding, as to the result to be achieved, upon each Member State to which it is addressed, but shall leave to the national authorities the choice of form and methods."[70]

To better understand the meaning of this provision, it is helpful to consider the basic idea behind the concept of directives: Given that the Member States have vastly different legal traditions, it can be difficult for

---

[66] TEU, art. 51.

[67] *See* JENS DAMMANN, MATERIELLES RECHT UND BEWEISRECHT IM SYSTEM DER GRUNDFREIHEITEN 17 (2007).

[68] *See* TFEU, art. 288 ("To exercise the Union's competences, the institutions shall adopt regulations, directives, decisions, recommendations and opinions."). Note, however, that not all acts of EU secondary law fall into one of these five categories. For example, the Rules of Procedure of the Court of Justice are deemed to be an act sui generis. Bernhard Wegener, EGV art. 223, ¶ 7, *in* KOMMENTAR DES VERTRAGES ÜBER DIE EUROPÄISCHE UNION UND DES VERTRAGES ZUR GRÜNDUNG DER EUROPÄISCHEN GEMEINSCHAFT (Christian Calliess & Matthias Ruffert eds., 5th ed. 2016).

[69] TFEU, art. 288.

[70] *Id.*

the European Union to enact legislation that fits in with all the various legal systems. In other words, sometimes one size does not fit all. Accordingly, the idea underlying directives was that the European Union would specify only particular legislative objectives in a directive. It would then be up to the Member States to *transpose* (or *implement*) the directive by enacting legislation that would accomplish the relevant objectives. This arrangement would give each Member State the necessary flexibility to design the relevant legislation in the way best suited to its local needs and peculiarities.

This explains why the TFEU provides that directives should only be binding regarding "the results to be achieved"[71] and why the directives are declared to be binding "on the member states"[72] rather than on the citizens of the European Union.

In practice, however, the law has moved beyond this somewhat simplistic model. Perhaps most importantly, directives are now often very detailed, leaving the Member States very little leeway in implementing them. The legality of such detailed directives is now universally recognized. Doctrinally, this can be justified on the ground that it is up to the EU institutions to decide in how much detail they wish to define "the result to be achieved" by the directive.

At its core, the directive is a command issued by the European Union to the Member States that tells the latter to enact legislation to a certain effect. The fact that the Treaty on the Functioning of the European Union explicitly allows for this type of command stands in interesting contrast with U.S. Constitutional law, where a federal statute instructing states to adopt a particular state statute would be considered illegal commandeering.[73]

QUESTIONS

1. Are there any reasons why Member States might prefer directives to regulations? Can you think of any reasons why Member States might prefer regulations?

2. Can you think of any reasons why directives might be more useful in the European Union than they would be in the United States? In other words, can you think of any features of the European Union that might make reliance on directives rather than regulations particularly desirable as a matter of legal policy?

---

[71] *Id.*
[72] *Id.*
[73] *Printz v. United States*, 521 U.S. 898, 924–933 (1997).

As noted above, directives are, in essence, commands addressed to the Member States to modify their own national law. For example, a directive might require the Member States to amend their own law so as to prohibit age-based employment discrimination. The basic rule is that directives only bind the Member States but do not have any direct effects on the Member States' citizens. However, over time, the Court of Justice has recognized various exceptions to this rule. The relevant case law is quite complicated, and we will discuss it in detail in a later chapter. For now, some brief remarks will suffice.

As a general rule, it remains true that directives that have not been implemented cannot be invoked in a dispute between two private citizens. For example, assume that an EU directive calls upon the Member States to provide consumers with certain warranties vis-à-vis sellers. If a Member State has failed to implement the directive, and a consumer in that Member State sues a seller, the consumer will not be able to invoke the warranties envisioned in the directive. In technical terms, we say that directives do not have *horizontal direct effect*. By contrast, citizens are able to invoke a directive against the Member State that has failed to implement it, thus giving it a *vertical direct effect*, under certain conditions.[74] Such a vertical effect requires that the relevant provision of the directive is both unconditional and sufficiently precise.[75] Moreover, directives can only have a vertical direct effect if the deadline, by which the Member States were required to transpose the directive into national law, has passed.

c) Decisions

Like a regulation, a decision is directly binding. However, if a decision specifies to whom it is addressed, then the decision binds only those whom it addresses.[76] Decisions can be addressed to natural persons, but they can also be addressed to legal entities such as corporations or even Member States. Decisions are the most common legal acts used by the EU administration.

d) Opinions and Recommendations

Recommendations and opinions are not binding.[77] They simply propose a certain course of action to the addressee. That does not mean,

---

[74] Case 9/70, Franz Grad v. Finanzamt Traunstein, 1970 E.C.R. 825 ¶ 5.

[75] *See, e.g.,* Case C-157/02, Rieser Internationale Transporte GmbH v. Autobahnen und Schnellstraßen-Finanzierungs-AG, 2004 E.C.R. I-1477 ¶ 22 ("[W]herever the provisions of a directive appear, as far as their subject-matter is concerned, to be unconditional and sufficiently precise, those provisions may, in the absence of implementing measures adopted within the prescribed period, be relied upon as against any national provision which is incompatible with the directive or in so far as the provisions define rights which individuals are able to assert against the State.").

[76] TFEU, art. 288.

[77] *Id.*

however, that they are entirely without legal significance. For example, the Treaty on European Union imposes a general duty of loyalty on the Member States, obliging them to adhere to the principle of sincere cooperation.[78] This general duty of loyalty also requires Member States to give due consideration to opinions and recommendations issued by EU institutions.[79]

---

[78] TEU, art. 4(3) ("Pursuant to the principle of sincere cooperation, the Union and the Member States shall, in full mutual respect, assist each other in carrying out tasks which flow from the Treaties.").

[79] *See, e.g.*, ANDREAS HARATSCH, CHRISTIAN KOENIG & MATTHIAS PECHSTEIN, EUROPARECHT ¶ 412 (11th ed. 2018).

PART 2

THE JUDICIARY

■ ■ ■

That the integration of the European Union has come as far as it has is in no small part due to the work of the Court of Justice. Often named the "motor of European integration,"[1] the Court of Justice can be credited with taking many of the steps that allowed the Community and later the Union to move beyond the many obstacles that have doomed other efforts at European unity.

Indeed, the Court of Justice has developed much of EU law. Accordingly, much of this course is dedicated to the Court's jurisprudence. It is helpful, therefore, to consider in some detail the rules governing the work of the Court of Justice as well as the methodology that it employs.

---

[1] *E.g.*, Miriam Aziz, *Integration as the Test Case of European Union Citizenship*, 15 COLUM. J. EUR. L. 281, 291 (2009); David J. Gerber, *The Transformation of European Community Competition Law?*, 35 HARV. INT'L L.J. 97, 116 (1994); Clemens Rieder, *Protecting Human Rights Within the European Union: Who Is Better Qualified to Do the Job—the European Court of Justice or the European Court of Human Rights?*, 20 TUL. EUR. & CIV. L.F. 73, 99 (2005).

CHAPTER 4

THE COURT OF JUSTICE

■ ■ ■

As discussed in the previous chapter, the Court of Justice of the European Union currently consists of three separate courts: the Court of Justice, the General Court, and the Civil Service Tribunal. However, not all of these courts are equally important. The Civil Service Tribunal has jurisdiction to hear civil service disputes, an area that is of little general interest. The General Court has a more diverse jurisdiction,[1] but a disproportionate number of its cases arise in specialized areas such as antitrust law—an area that European law refers to as *competition law*—and intellectual property law.[2] However, these two areas of EU law are beyond the scope of this casebook. Accordingly, this casebook will largely ignore the Civil Service Tribunal and the General Court and instead concentrate on the Court of Justice.

A. COMPOSITION

Given the central role that the Court of Justice has in the institutional framework of the European Union, it is not surprising that the Court's composition reflects the multinational character of the European Union: The Court of Justice consists of one judge from each Member State.[3] Each judge must be appointed by unanimous decision of the Member States.[4] A judge serves for a term of six years, but can be reappointed. The heterogeneity resulting from the judges' different legal and cultural backgrounds may sometimes make it difficult for the judges to find common positions. But it also has important benefits. Because the Court is composed of judges from all over the European Union, its expertise extends to different Member States' legal traditions. In addition, the inability of the large Member States to dominate the Court presumably contributes to the Court's high degree of acceptance across the European Union.

---

[1] The General Court has "jurisdiction to hear and determine at first instance actions or proceedings referred to in Articles 263, 265, 268, 270, and 272, with the exception of those assigned to a specialized court . . . and those reserved in the Statute for the Court of Justice," TFEU, art. 256.

[2] *See* COURT OF JUSTICE OF THE EUROPEAN UNION, ANNUAL REPORT 2010, 176 (2011), available at https://curia.europa.eu/jcms/upload/docs/application/pdf/2011-05/ra2010_version_integrale_en.pdf (showing that of the new cases filed in the General Court in 2010, 79 arose in the area of competition law and 207 arose in the area of intellectual property law).

[3] TEU, art. 19(2).

[4] TFEU, art. 253(1).

B. THE ROLE OF THE ADVOCATES-GENERAL

The Court of Justice is assisted by Advocates-General.[5] The office of the Advocate-General is a very peculiar one and has nothing in common with that of the Attorney General as it exists in the United States. There are eight Advocates-General. Like the judges, they are required to be completely independent and impartial.[6] Their main responsibility is to prepare the work of the judges by making "reasoned submissions on cases" requiring their involvement.[7] Therefore, each judgment by the European Court of Justice is preceded by an opinion written by an Advocate-General.

The importance of these opinions cannot be overestimated. In part, this is because the Court's judgment often follows the path laid out by the Advocate-General. But there is another reason why the Advocate-General's opinion is quite important: Following the French legal tradition, the judgments rendered by the Court of Justice—particularly in older cases—are often very brief, containing only very short explanations for why the Court has adopted particular positions. In contrast, the Advocate-General's opinion is often very detailed and frequently contains elaborate discussions of the pertinent cases and scholarship. Thus, those seeking to understand the Court's legal reasoning will often gain valuable information from the opinion of the Advocate-General.

C. THE LAW GOVERNING THE COURT AND ITS PROCEDURE

While some of the fundamental rules governing the Court can be found in the Treaty on European Union and the Treaty on the Functioning of the European Union, there are two other important sources, the Statute of the Court of Justice of the European Union[8] and the Court's own Rules of Procedure.[9]

The Statute of the Court of Justice of the European Union is annexed to the Treaties as Protocol No. 3. It therefore enjoys the same rank as the provisions of the Treaties themselves because the Treaty on European Union expressly provides that the protocols form an integral part of the Treaties.[10]

---

[5] TEU, art. 19(2).

[6] TFEU, art. 252.

[7] *Id.*

[8] TEU & TFEU protocol 3 ("On the Statute of the Court of Justice of the European Union") [hereinafter Statute of the Court of Justice].

[9] RULES OF PROCEDURE OF THE COURT OF JUSTICE, 1991 O.J. (L 176) 7 (as amended), *consolidated at* 2010 O.J. (C 177) 1; RULES OF PROCEDURE OF THE GENERAL COURT, 1991 O.J. (L 136) 1 (as amended), *consolidated at* 2010 O.J. (C 177) 37.

[10] TEU, art. 51.

The Rules of Procedure, promulgated by the Court itself,[11] complement the Statute.[12] They rank below the Treaties and have to comply with the provisions set forth in the Treaties and the Protocols—including the Statute of the Court of Justice.

D. JURISDICTION

Generally, the responsibility of the Court of Justice of the European Union is "to ensure that in the interpretation and application of the Treaties, the law is observed."[13]

A more specific description of the Court's jurisdiction can be found in various provisions of the Treaty on the Functioning of the European Union. Before addressing the relevant rules, however, it is helpful to start with two caveats regarding the Court's role.

First, EU law does not recognize any type of diversity jurisdiction. One private party can never file suit against another private party before the European Court of Justice, and this remains true even if the parties are residents of different Member States.

Second, it is important to keep in mind that the Court of Justice and the other courts that form the Court of Justice of the European Union are not the only courts that can apply EU law. Rather, the national courts of the Member States also routinely hear cases that hinge on EU law.[14] Indeed, only a tiny fraction of cases involving EU law ever lead to the involvement of the Court of Justice of the European Union, let alone the Court of Justice itself. Of course, this is hardly surprising given that the Court of Justice, like the General Court, has only 28 judges.[15]

So when exactly does the Court of Justice have jurisdiction? The Treaty on the Functioning of the European Union defines the Court's jurisdiction in connection with the various types of proceedings before the Court. The most important proceedings are the preliminary rulings procedure, the infringement procedure, actions for annulment, and actions for failure to act.

The *preliminary rulings procedure* involves both the courts of the Member States and the Court of Justice: When a national court is confronted with a novel question regarding the interpretation or validity of

---

[11] That is, the Court of Justice and the General Court each adopt their own Rules of Procedure. *See* RULES OF PROCEDURE OF THE COURT OF JUSTICE pmbl.; RULES OF PROCEDURE OF THE GENERAL COURT pmbl.

[12] Statute of the Court of Justice art. 63.

[13] TEU, art. 19(1).

[14] Indeed, the Member States are required to provide a legal forum in which cases involving EU law can be heard. *See* TFEU, art. 19(1) ("Member States shall provide remedies sufficient to ensure effective legal protection in the fields covered by Union law.").

[15] Statute of the Court of Justice art. 48.

EU law, the national court may—and sometimes even must—refer that question to the Court of Justice.[16] The Court of Justice will answer the relevant question, and the national court then has to decide the case before it on the basis of the answer given by the Court of Justice. Crucially, the Court of Justice does not decide the case itself. The Court of Justice does not even decide how EU law is to be applied to the facts of the case. Rather, the Court of Justice is solely concerned with the validity or interpretation of EU law.[17]

Another procedure of major importance is the so-called *enforcement procedure*, alternatively referred to as the *infringement procedure*. The purpose of this procedure is to ensure that the Member States abide by EU law. If a Member State is in breach of EU law, the Commission as well as other Member States can bring suit against the breaching state. If the Court of Justice rules that EU law has in fact been violated and if the defendant state fails to comply with the Court's judgment, the Court can eventually impose a financial penalty on the state in question.

Of course, the institutions of the EU may also sometimes breach EU law. For that reason, the Treaty on the Functioning of the European Union allows so-called *actions for annulment* in which the Court reviews the legality of a measure taken by an EU institution. If the relevant measure is found to violate EU law, then the Court of Justice will generally declare the relevant measure to be void.[18] Actions for annulment can be brought by the Commission, the Council, the European Parliament, or a Member State.[19] In addition, such actions can be initiated by any natural or legal person, but only if the contested measure is addressed to or otherwise of direct concern to the applicant.[20]

The above-described *actions for annulment* allow the applicant to seek judicial help against measures adopted by EU institutions that violate EU law. Sometimes the institutions of the EU violate EU law by not acting all. In other words, sometimes the violation of EU law lies in a failure to act. Therefore, the Treaty on the Functioning of the European Union allows an action to be brought where "the European Parliament, the European Council, the Council, the Commission or the European Central Bank, in infringement of the Treaties, fail to act."[21] Such an action can be brought by another EU institution or by a Member State. Moreover, any legal or natural person can initiate an *action for failure to act* as long as the desired

---

[16] TFEU, art. 267.
[17] TFEU, art. 267.
[18] TFEU, art. 264(1).
[19] TFEU, art. 263(3).
[20] TFEU, art. 263(4).
[21] TFEU, art. 265(1).

action, if it were taken, would be of direct and individual concern to the applicant.[22]

E. INTERPRETATIVE METHODOLOGY

In interpreting EU law, the Court of Justice has developed its very own methodological approach, which is tailored specifically to the idiosyncratic characteristics of the European Union legal system.

1. WORDING

The importance of a provision's wording lies in the fact that the text is usually the obvious point of departure for any interpretation. This said, the Court of Justice does not accord text-based arguments priority over other criteria of interpretation. Rather, the Court will often conclude that the wording of a provision has to yield to other considerations, such as the purpose of the particular provision or the broader aims of EU law.

In addition to the lack of a normative primacy of text-based arguments, there is also a practical reason why text-based arguments often do not prove decisive. It has to be kept in mind that European law is written in many different languages—at this point no fewer than 23. These different language versions "are all equally authentic,"[23] forcing the interpreter to undertake "a comparison of the different language versions."[24] In practice, of course, the different language versions of a particular provision often have subtly different meanings, a factor that greatly reduces the relevance of text-based arguments.

Moreover, the Court has made it clear that "even where the different language versions are entirely in accord with one another, . . . [European] law uses terminology which is peculiar to it" and that "legal concepts do not necessarily have the same meaning in [European law] and in the law of the various member states."[25] This principle, often referred to as the *autonomous interpretation* of EU law, further erodes the importance of text-based arguments.

2. TELEOLOGICAL REASONING

In light of the limited role of text-based arguments, the greatest weight is typically given to teleological reasoning, i.e., reasoning based on the aims of European law. Importantly, the aims to be considered include both the aims of the specific provision to be interpreted and the broader aims of

---

[22] Case C-107/91, ENU v. Comm'n, 1993 E.C.R. I-599 ¶¶ 17–18.
[23] Case 283/81, Srl CILFIT & Lanificio di Gavardo SpA v. Ministry of Health, 1982 E.C.R. 3415 ¶ 18.
[24] *Id.*
[25] *Id.* ¶ 19.

European Union law as a whole.[26] And, as indicated before, the Court has no qualms in disregarding what may appear to be an unambiguous wording if the Court believes that a textual interpretation does not do justice to the goals of the particular provision or the goals of European Union law more generally.[27]

3. DYNAMIC INTERPRETATION

Closely related to the dominant position given to teleological arguments is the concept of dynamic interpretation. While the legitimacy of adjusting the interpretation of law over time remains controversial in the United States,[28] the European Court of Justice has made it very clear that its interpretations are contingent on the relevant state of development of European law. In other words, as European Union law evolves the Court may conclude that a meaning previously ascribed to a particular provision no longer adequately serves the goals of European law and that a different interpretation of the same provision is therefore called for. In the words of the Court of Justice,

> "[E]very provision of Community law must be . . . interpreted in the light of the provisions of Community law as a whole, regard being had to the objectives thereof and its state of evolution at the date on which the provision in question is to be applied."[29]

The basic idea underlying this approach is that that the European Union is—and was conceived as—a work in progress, such that EU law continually evolves towards a more perfect state. And indeed, the Preamble to the Treaty on European Union expressly incorporates the idea of progressive integration by stressing Member States' commitment "to continue the process of creating an ever closer union among the peoples of Europe."[30]

4. SYSTEMATIC ARGUMENTS

Another important factor in interpreting European Law is the relationship between the provision to be interpreted and other provisions

---

[26] *See* Case 283/81, Srl CILFIT & Lanificio di Gavardo SpA v. Ministry of Health, 1982 E.C.R. 3415 ¶ 20 (stressing the need to consider "the objectives" of European law as a whole in interpreting individual provisions).

[27] *See, e.g.*, Case C-173/06, Agrover Srl v. Agenzia Dogane Circoscrizione Doganale di Genova, 2007 E.C.R. I-8783 ¶¶ 21–22 (concluding that "[t]he literal interpretation of [a particular provision of the Customs Code] cannot . . . be accepted," *id.* ¶ 22, after noting that whereas the wording of the provision in question "expressly" applies only to certain goods, the relevant provision, "the light of the purpose and general scheme of that provision," "must be considered" to be intended to apply in other cases as well, *id.* ¶ 21.)

[28] *Cf.* William N. Eskridge Jr., DYNAMIC STATUTORY INTERPRETATION (1994) (making a compelling case for the legitimacy of interpreting statutes dynamically).

[29] Case 283/81, Srl CILFIT & Lanificio di Gavardo SpA v. Ministry of Health, 1982 E.C.R. 3415 ¶ 20.

[30] TEU pmbl.

of the Treaties or, more generally, the Treaties as a whole. Essentially, the Court will try to interpret each provision such that contradictions between different provisions are avoided and European Union law as a whole remains coherent.

5. LEGISLATIVE HISTORY

Arguments based on the legislative history of EU law—often referred to as *genealogical* or *historical* reasoning—tend to be of more limited importance. In particular, this is true for the interpretation of the Treaties themselves where the Court of Justice rarely makes use of such arguments. As a matter of constitutional theory, this reluctance to use historical reasoning is justifiable not least on the grounds that until relatively recently, the travaux préparatoires for the Treaty of Rome was not even publicly accessible.

Regarding the interpretation of secondary EU law such as directives or regulations, the Court of Justice makes more frequent use of the legislative history.[31] In particular, the Court may take into account how the wording of a particular provision has changed over time. For example, the Court has argued that "the difference in wording between [an older provision and the newer provision that replaced it] is itself an argument capable of leading to the presumption that the authors of the new provision intended to amend the former criterion, since in the absence of evidence to the contrary, it must be assumed that any difference in wording involves a difference in the scope if the new wording leads to a different interpretation."[32]

NOTES AND QUESTIONS

1. Setting aside the Treaty's reference to the ever closer union of the peoples of Europe, can you think of any other factors that make EU law inherently dynamic? Differently put, can you think of any factors that render the benefits of dynamic interpretation greater in the European Union than elsewhere?

2. Similarly, can you think of any reasons that make the extensive use of the *travaux préparatoires*—the documents recording the negotiation and drafting of the Treaties—in interpreting the Treaties particularly problematic?

F. HOW POWERFUL IS THE COURT OF JUSTICE?

Changing the Treaty on European Union can be very difficult, especially now that the European Union has 28 Member States. Changing EU regulations and directives can also be challenging. For example, doing

---

[31] *See, e.g.*, Case C-53/08, Comm'n v. Republic of Austria, 2011 E.C.R. I-4309 ¶ 144 (justifying a particular interpretation of Directive 2005/36 by reference to the directive's legislative history).

[32] Case 15/60, Gabriel Simon v. Court of Justice, 1961 E.C.R. 121, 124.

so typically requires a qualified majority in the Council, and the cultural and political heterogeneity can make it difficult to achieve that majority.

Arguably, the difficulty of changing EU primary and secondary law has increased the relative influence of the Court of Justice. Two factors are crucial in this context.

To begin, the difficulties that the Member States face in changing EU law may have made them more willing to accept the Court's role as a motor of integration. If the Member States want EU law to be adjusted to changing socio-economic realities, but are unable to bring about the necessary reforms themselves, then they have no alternative but to rely on the Court to play a very active role in the process of European integration.[33]

Furthermore, the harder to it is for the Member States to adjust EU primary and secondary law, the more difficult it is for them to "override" the Court's decisions.[34] In other words, the harder it is for the Member States to change EU law, the less the Court has to worry that the Member States will make such a change in reaction to a judicial decision that they do not like. This matters because if the Court had to worry about the Member States overriding its decisions, the Court might avoid adopting "unpopular" decisions in the first place.

Of course, despite the difficulty of Treaty amendments, if enough Member States dislike the Court's rulings, they can change the European Union's secondary law or even amend the Treaties and thereby "override" the Court's rulings. However, the question is whether this "threat" is realistic enough to motivate the Court of Justice to abstain from adopting positions that the Member States dislike. A number of empirical studies have sought to shed light on this question.[35] Most of them come to the conclusion that the threat of override is typically not credible and that the available evidence does not support the claim that this threat influences the Court's decisions.[36]

---

[33] *E.g.*, R. Daniel Kelemen, *The Court of Justice of the European Union in the Twenty-First Century*, 79 L. & CONTEMP. PROBS. 117, 120 (2016) (noting that Member States understand the necessity of relying on the Court of Justice to overcome collective action problems faced by the Member States).

[34] *E.g.*, *id.* at 120–21.

[35] *E.g.*, Clifford Carrubba et al., *Judicial Behavior under Political Constraints: Evidence from the European Court of Justice*, 102 AM. POL. SCI. REV. 435 (2008); Alec Stone Sweet et al., *Constructing a Supranational Constitution: Dispute Resolution and Governance in the European Community*. 92 AM. POL. SCI. REV. 63 (1998). For a summary of the relevant literature *cf.* Alec Stone Sweet & Thomas Brunell, *The European Court of Justice, State Noncompliance, and the Politics of Override*, 106 AM. POL. SC. REV. 204–13 (2012).

[36] But see Clifford Carrubba et al., *Judicial Behavior under Political Constraints: Evidence from the European Court of Justice*, 102 AM. POL. SCI. REV. 435 (2008) (coming to the opposite conclusion).

NOTES AND QUESTIONS

1. A collective action problem exists where, collectively, a group of actors would benefit if an action were taken, but, individually, no actor finds it in his interest to act. For example, imagine that 100 persons live in a village. Fixing the village's decrepit roads would cost a total amount of $200. Each of the villagers would reap benefits worth $10 if the village's roads were fixed because better roads would result in fewer traffic delays and less damage to cars. It is easy to see that the total benefits to all the villagers (100 times $10 = $1,000) would outweigh the cost of repairing the roads ($200). Hence, fixing the roads is clearly within the collective interest of the villagers. However, no individual villager will find it in his interest to fix the roads by himself since the cost of doing so ($200) exceed the individual benefit ($10). Can one argue that the Member States face certain collective action problems in the context of European integration and that the active role played by the Court of Justice helps to overcome those collective action problems? Explain?

2. Can one argue that the active role played by the Court of Justice creates certain risks for European integration? If so, what are those risks and why have they failed to deter the Court of Justice from playing an active role in the process of European integration?

CHAPTER 5

THE PRELIMINARY RULINGS PROCEDURE

■ ■ ■

Given the slender structure of the European Union's judiciary, it is unsurprising that most cases involving questions of EU law are litigated in the courts of the Member States. In fact, if one private party wishes to file suit against another private party, she necessarily has to bring her case in a Member State court since the European Court of Justice has no jurisdiction in cases between two private parties.

Of course, this decentralized approach to adjudication in which the Member State courts carry the bulk of the caseload bears an obvious risk: Different Member States' courts may interpret EU law differently, thus preventing any uniform application of EU law. This scenario is all the more plausible given that language differences frequently prevent national courts from reading one another's opinions. For example, few German judges will have access to or be able to understand opinions by Portuguese or Latvian courts.

Against this background, the Treaty on the Functioning of the European Union contains a special procedure designed to ensure the uniform application and interpretation of EU law—the so-called preliminary rulings procedure. The purpose behind the preliminary rulings procedure is thus to secure the "uniform interpretation and application" of EU law.[1] A Member State court confronted with a question pertaining to the validity or interpretation of EU law may—and sometimes must—refer the question to the Court of Justice. Based on the Court of Justice's answers, the Member State court will then decide the case. For those seeking an analogue procedure in the U.S. legal system, the preliminary rulings procedure is best compared to certification.

A. INTERPRETATION AND VALIDITY

Art. 267(1) TFEU provides that the Court of Justice "shall have jurisdiction to give preliminary rulings concerning: (a) the interpretation of the Treaties; [and] (b) the validity and interpretation of acts of the institutions, bodies, offices or agencies of the Union." In other words, there

---

[1] Case 61/79, Amministrazione delle finanze dello Stato v. Denkavit italiana Srl., 1980 E.C.R. 1205 ¶ 15.

are two types of questions that national courts can refer to the Court of Justice—questions of interpretation and validity questions.

Note that when it comes to validity questions, the Court of Justice only has jurisdiction to give rulings on the validity of "acts of the institutions, bodies, offices or agencies of the Union." The Treaties themselves are not mentioned in this context, which means that the Court of Justice can only address the validity of secondary—as opposed to primary—EU law. By contrast, when it comes to questions of interpretation, the Court's jurisdiction is broader: the court can rule not only on the interpretation of secondary law but also on the interpretation of the Treaties.[2]

B. NATIONAL COURTS

Where a question of interpretation or validity is "raised before any court or tribunal of a Member State, that court or tribunal may, if it considers that a decision on the question is necessary to enable it to give judgment, request the Court to give a ruling thereon," Art. 267(2) TFEU. In other words, Member State courts generally have the option—but no duty—to refer questions to the Court of Justice. However, under Article 267(3), the national court must ("shall") refer the question to the Court of Justice if "there is no judicial remedy under national law" against the decisions of the Member State court in question.

In practice, there are two questions that arise in this context. First, because both the option and the duty to refer questions to the Court of Justice apply only to a "court or tribunal" of a Member State, it becomes necessary to define which national institutions are courts or tribunals. Second, because the duty to refer questions to the Court of Justice—as opposed to a mere option to do so—exists only where "there is no judicial remedy" against the decision of the Member State court, one must know what constitutes a lack of judicial remedy.

1. WHAT IS A COURT?

The Court of Justice has made it clear that Member State law is not dispositive regarding whether a body qualifies as a court for the purpose of Article 267 TFEU.[3] This makes sense: the principle of autonomous interpretation dictates that EU law terms have meanings independent of those ascribed to them by the legal systems of the Member States.

---

[2] TFEU, art. 267(1)(a).

[3] Case C-24/92, Pierre Corbiau v. Admin. des Contributions, 1993 E.C.R. I-1277 ¶ 15 ("It must be remembered that the expression 'court or tribunal' is a concept of Community law, which, by its very nature, can only mean an authority acting as a third party in relation to the authority which adopted the decision forming the subject-matter of the proceedings.). *Cf.* Case 43/71, Politi S.A.S. v. Ministry for Finance of the Italian Republic, 1971 E.C.R. 1039 ¶ 5 (concluding that "the president of the tribunale di torino is performing a judicial function within the meaning of article 177 [now Article 267]").

But what exactly does it take for an institution to qualify as a court? In a 1993 case, *Pierre Corbiau*, the Court noted that the "expression 'court or tribunal' . . ., by its very nature, can only mean an authority acting as a third party in relation to the authority which adopted the decision forming the subject-matter of the proceedings."[4] In other words, both the ability to make decisions and the status as a third-party are indispensable attributes of a court. Soon, however, this rudimentary definition proved inadequate. Today, to determine whether or not a body qualifies as a court, "the Court takes account of a number of factors, such as whether the body is established by law, whether it is permanent, whether its jurisdiction is compulsory, whether its procedure is *inter partes*, whether it applies rules of law and whether it is independent."[5]

RTL BELGIUM SA
ECJ, Case C-517/09, Dec. 22, 2010, 2010 E.C.R. 14093

36. According to settled case-law, in order to determine whether a body making a reference is a court or tribunal for the purposes of Article 267 TFEU, which is a question governed by EU law alone, the Court takes account of a number of factors, such as whether the body is established by law, whether it is permanent, whether its jurisdiction is compulsory, whether its procedure is inter partes, whether it applies rules of law and whether it is independent. [. . .]

38. According to the case-law of the Court, the concept of independence, which is inherent in the task of adjudication, implies above all that the body in question acts as a third party in relation to the authority which adopted the contested decision.

39. There are two aspects to that concept. The first aspect, which is external, entails that the body is protected against external intervention or pressure liable to jeopardise the independent judgment of its members as regards proceedings before them.

40. The second aspect, which is internal, is linked to impartiality and seeks to ensure a level playing field for the parties to the proceedings and their respective interests in relation to the subject-matter of those proceedings. ∎

---

[4] Case C-24/92, Pierre Corbiau v. Admin. des Contributions, 1993 E.C.R. I-1277 ¶ 15.
[5] Case C-196/09, Paul Miles v. Écoles européennes, 2011 E.C.R. I-5105 ¶ 37.

NOTES AND QUESTIONS

1. As previously noted, the purpose of the preliminary rulings procedure is to secure the "uniform interpretation and application" of EU law.[6] In light of this purpose, do the various factors make sense from a legal policy perspective?

2. As part of the criterion of independence, the Court of Justice requires that "the body is protected against external intervention or pressure liable to jeopardise the independent judgment of its members," paragraph 39. Does this criterion strike you as convincing? Does the Court of Justice confuse the questions of what constitutes a court and how the Member States should ideally treat their courts? How about the argument that decision-making bodies that are not sufficiently protected against external pressure are all the more in need of being able to make references to the Court of Justice so as to strengthen their own position?

2. THE ABSENCE OF REMEDIES UNDER MEMBER STATE LAW

Whether a Member State court has a duty to refer a question to the ECJ or merely an option to do so depends on whether "there is no judicial remedy under national law" against the court's decision. Over time, two theories have developed on how to determine when there is no judicial remedy. Under the so-called abstract approach, only those courts against whose decisions the parties never have any remedies have a duty to refer questions to the ECJ. By contrast, under the concrete approach, the decisive question is whether, in the case at hand, the court's decision is subject to appeal under national law.

It is sometimes said that the ECJ has committed to the concrete theory.[7] In support of that view, one can adduce the Court's judgment in *Costa*.[8] There, the Court of Justice categorized the Dutch court at issue, the so-called *Tarifcommissie* (tax court), as a court against whose decision there was no judicial remedy under national law[9]—despite the fact that this was true only in the specific case since in some situations the decisions of the *Tarifcommissie* are subject to appeal.[10] However, it is not clear from the Court's opinion whether it was aware of this fact. In particular, the judgment refers to the *Tarifcommissie* as "the Dutch administrative court of last instance in taxation matters"—suggesting that the *Costa* judgment is also compatible with the abstract theory.

---

[6] Case 61/79, Amministrazione delle finanze dello Stato v. Denkavit italiana Srl., 1980 E.C.R. 1205 ¶ 15.

[7] *E.g.*, PAUL CRAIG & GRAINNE DE BURCA, EU LAW 469 (6th ed. 2015).

[8] Joined Cases 28 to 30–62, Da Costa en Schaake NV v. Netherlands Inland Revenue Admin., 1963 E.C.R. 31.

[9] *Id.*

[10] *E.g.*, PAUL CRAIG & GRAINNE DE BURCA, EU LAW 469 (6th ed. 2015).

Nor does the Court's decision in the 2002 *Lyckeskog*[11] decision resolve the question.[12] There, the Court made it clear that "[d]ecisions of a national appellate court which can be challenged by the parties before a supreme court are not decisions of a court or tribunal of a Member State against whose decisions there is no judicial remedy under national law. . . ."[13] Furthermore, the Court noted that "[t]he fact that examination of the merits of such appeals is subject to a prior declaration of admissibility by the supreme court does not have the effect of depriving the parties of a judicial remedy."[14] Thus, the ECJ decided that the existence of a remedy in the case at hand meant that there was no duty to refer the question to the ECJ. It cannot be deduced from this decision, however, whether the absence of remedy under national law has to be judged on an abstract or concrete basis.

NOTES AND QUESTIONS

1. Can you think of any policy or doctrinal arguments supporting either the abstract approach or the concrete one?

2. Should the national court or the Court of Justice be the final arbiter on whether there exists a remedy under national law?

3. Might it be useful to limit the *right* to refer questions to the Court of Justice to Member State courts against whose decisions no remedy exists under national law?

C. THE NECESSITY RULE

The right as well as the duty to refer questions to the Court of Justice presuppose that the referring court "considers that a decision on the question is necessary to enable it to give judgment," Art. 267(2) TFEU. In other words, the question to be referred must have an impact on the outcome of the case. Accordingly, the Court may refuse to give a ruling where "the interpretation of European Union law that is sought bears no relation to the actual facts of the main action or its purpose, [or] where the problem is hypothetical."[15]

But who decides whether the reference question is relevant to the outcome of the case? The wording of Article 267(2) suggests that it is up to the referring court to decide the relevance of the question. However, a rule of strict deference to the referring court would open the door to potential

---

[11] Case C-99/00, Criminal proceedings against Kenny Roland Lyckeskog, 2002 E.C.R. I-4839.

[12] *But see* PAUL CRAIG & GRAINNE DE BURCA, EU LAW 469 (6th ed. 2015) (viewing the Lyckeskog decision as an affirmation of the concrete theory).

[13] Case C-99/00, Criminal proceedings against Kenny Roland Lyckeskog, 2002 E.C.R. I-4839 ¶ 16.

[14] *Id.*

[15] Case C-310/10, Ministerul Justiiei i Libertilor Ceteneti v. Stefan Agafiei, 2011 E.C.R. I-5989 ¶ 27.

abuse, since any Member State court, high or low, could refer any question to the ECJ regardless of the question's actual relevance. Against this background, the Court of Justice has opted for a compromise position. Consider the following excerpt from a 2010 case:

> Where questions submitted by national courts concern the interpretation of a provision of EU law, the Court of Justice is bound, in principle, to give a ruling *unless it is obvious* that the request for a preliminary ruling is in reality designed to induce the Court to give a ruling by means of a fictitious dispute, or to deliver advisory opinions on general or hypothetical questions, or that the interpretation of EU law requested bears no relation to the actual facts of the main action or its purpose, or that the Court does not have before it the factual or legal material necessary to give a useful answer to the questions submitted to it.[16] [emphasis added]

The principle that the European Court of Justice will exercise some scrutiny over whether the preliminary ruling is actually necessary to decide a real dispute was largely developed in the so-called *Foglia* cases.[17]

PASQUALE FOGLIA V. MARIELLA NOVELLO ["FOGLIA I"]
E.C.J., Case 104/79, June 29, 1979, 1981 E.C.R. 745 (citations omitted)

[Mr. Foglia was an Italian wine dealer. He had sold wine to Mariella Novello. The wine was to be delivered to France, and to that end, Foglia entered into a contract with Danzas, a transport company. The contract between Foglia and Novello explicitly stipulated that Foglia would not be liable for any duties that the Italian or French authorities might impose in violation of EU law. In addition, Foglia inserted a similar clause into his contract with Danzas, the transport company.

When the wine was delivered to France, the French authorities promptly imposed a consumption tax. Danzas paid that tax without complaining, but then billed Foglia for it—despite the fact that the contract between Danzas and Foglia explicitly stated that Foglia did not have to bear any illegal duties. Foglia reimbursed Danzas. Subsequently, Foglia contacted Novello and demanded to be reimbursed. Novello refused, and Foglia brought suit against her in an Italian court.

The Italian court asked the Court of Justice for a preliminary ruling to establish whether the relevant French consumption tax violated EU law. However, in what is known as the *Foglia I* decision, the Court of Justice

---

[16] Case C-439/08, Vlaamse federatie van verenigingen van Brood en Banketbakkers, Ijsbereiders en Chocoladebewerkers (VEBIC) VZW, 2010 E.C.R. I-12471¶ 42.

[17] Case 244/80, Pasquale Foglia v. Mariella Novello, 1981 E.C.R. 3045; Case 104/79, Pasquale Foglia v. Mariella Novello, 1981 E.C.R. 745.

refused to answer this question.[18] Consider the following excerpt from the Court's opinion.]

10. It thus appears that the parties to the main action are concerned [with obtaining] a ruling that the French tax system is invalid for liqueur wines by the expedient of proccedings before an Italian Court between two private individuals who are in agreement as to the result to be attained and who have inserted a clause in their contract [regarding the question of who bears the relevant French taxes] in order to induce the Italian Court to give a ruling on the point. The artificial nature of this expedient is underlined by the fact that Danzas [the transportation company] did not exercise its rights under French law to institute proceedings over the consumption tax although it undoubtedly had an interest in doing so in view of the clause of the contract by which it was also bound and moreover of the fact that Foglia paid without protest that undertaking's bill which included a sum paid in respect of that tax.

11. The duty of the Court of Justice under Article 177 [now Article 267] of the EEC Treaty [now the TFEU] is to supply all courts in the Community [now the Union] with the information on the interpretation of Community law which is necessary to enable them to settle genuine disputes which are brought before them. A situation in which the Court was obliged by the expedient of arrangements like those described above to give rulings would jeopardize the whole system of legal remedies available to private individuals to enable them to protect themselves against tax provisions which are contrary to the Treaty.

12. This means that the questions asked by the national court, having regard to the circumstances of this case, do not fall within the framework of the duties of the Court of Justice under Article 177 [now Article 267 TFEU] of the Treaty.[19] ∎

QUESTIONS

1. Why would "the whole system of legal remedies available to private individuals to enable them to protect themselves against tax provisions which are contrary to the Treaty" be jeopardized if the Court were obliged to give rulings in cases like *Foglia I*?

2. What arguments can be adduced in support of the Court's conclusion that the dispute in *Foglia I* is not a genuine dispute?

3. In your view, should the referring court determine whether a particular question is relevant to the outcome of a case, or should that question be determined by the Court of Justice?

---

[18] *Id.* ¶ 13.
[19] *Id.* ¶¶ 10–12.

PASQUALE FOGLIA V. MARIELLA NOVELLO ["FOGLIA II"]
Case 244/80, Dec. 16, 1981, 1981 E.C.R. 3045 (citations omitted)

[In *Foglia I*, the Court of Justice refused to answer the questions submitted by the referring court on the ground that the dispute was not a genuine one. This answer apparently did not satisfy the Italian court, which promptly reacted with a new request for a preliminary ruling, this one aimed at clarifying the division of powers between national courts and the European Court of Justice in the preliminary rulings procedure.[20] This new request led to the famous *Foglia II* decision, which is of interest not least because it illuminates how the Court of Justice understands the function of the preliminary rulings procedure.]

14. With regard to the first question it should be recalled, as the Court has had occasion to emphasize in very varied contexts, that Article 177 [now Article 267 TFEU] is based on cooperation which entails a division of duties between the national courts and the Court of Justice in the Interest of the proper application and uniform interpretation of Community [now Union] law throughout all the Member States.

15. With this in view it is for the national court—by reason of the fact that it is seized of the substance of the dispute and that it must bear the responsibility for the decision to be taken—to assess, having regard to the facts of the case, the need to obtain a preliminary judgment to enable it to give judgment.

16. In exercising that power of appraisal the national court, in collaboration with the Court of Justice, fulfills a duty entrusted to them both of ensuring that in the interpretation and application of the Treaty the law is observed. Accordingly, the problems which may be entailed in the exercise of its power of appraisal by the national court and the relations which it maintains within the framework of [Article 267 TFEU] with the Court of Justice are governed exclusively by the provisions of Community law.

17. In order that the Court of Justice may perform its task in accordance with the Treaty it is essential for national courts to explain, when the reasons do not emerge beyond any doubt from the file, why they consider that a reply to their questions is necessary to enable them to give judgment.

18. It must in fact be emphasized that the duty assigned to the Court by [Article 267 TFEU] is not that of delivering advisory opinions on general or hypothetical questions but of assisting in the administration of justice in the member states. It accordingly does not have jurisdiction to reply to questions of interpretation which are submitted to it within the framework of procedural devices arranged by the parties in order to induce the court

---

[20] Case 244/80, Pasquale Foglia v. Mariella Novello, 1981 E.C.R. 3045 ¶ 11.

to give its view on certain problems of Community law which do not correspond to an objective requirement inherent in the resolution of a dispute. A declaration by the Court that it does not have jurisdiction in such circumstances does not in any way trespass upon the prerogatives of the national court but makes it possible to prevent the application of the procedure under [Article 267] for purposes other than those appropriate for it.

19. Furthermore, it should be pointed out that, whilst the Court of Justice must be able to place as much reliance as possible upon the assessment by the national court of the extent to which the questions submitted are essential, it must be in a position to make any assessment inherent in the performance of its own duties in particular order to check, as all courts must, whether it has jurisdiction. Thus, the Court, taking into account the repercussions of its decisions in this matter, must have regard, in exercising the jurisdiction conferred upon it by [Article 267], not only to the interests of the parties to the proceedings but also to those of the Community of the Member States. Accordingly it cannot without disregarding the duties assigned to it, remain indifferent to the assessments made by the courts of the Member States in the exceptional cases in which such assessments may affect the proper working of the procedure laid down by Article [Article 267].

20. [While] the spirit of cooperation which must govern the performance of the duties assigned by [Article 267] to the national courts on the one hand and the Court of Justice on the other requires the latter to have regard to the national court's proper responsibilities, it implies at the same time that the national court, in the use which it makes of the facilities provided by [Article 267], should have regard to the proper function of the Court of Justice in this field.

21. The reply to the first question must accordingly be that [while], according to the intended role of [Article 267 TFEU], an assessment of the need to obtain an answer to the questions of interpretation raised, regard being had to the circumstances of fact and of law involved in the main action, is a matter for the national court it is nevertheless for the Court of Justice, in order to confirm its own jurisdiction, to examine, where necessary, the conditions in which the case has been referred to it by the national court. ∎

QUESTIONS

1. What, according to the Court, are the goals of the preliminary rulings procedure? Do you think that the allocation of responsibilities between the national courts and the Court of Justice, as defined in *Foglia II*, serves these goals?

2. How does the Court envision the general relationship between the Court of Justice and the national courts?

3. How does the Court of Justice justify its refusal to defer to the national court with respect to the question of whether the referred question is necessary to decide the case? Do you find the Court's arguments to be persuasive?

D. LIMITATIONS ON THE DUTY TO REFER

Over time, two limitations on the duty to refer cases to the Court of Justice have developed. First and most importantly, the issue involved may already have been decided by the Court of Justice in a previous case. Second, a reference to the European Court of Justice may not be necessary because the meaning of the relevant provision in EU law is so clear as to require no interpretation.

1. ISSUES THAT HAVE ALREADY BEEN DECIDED

In many cases, litigation before Member State courts raises questions of EU law that the Court of Justice has already addressed. In this case, the Member State court does not have to refer the question to the Court of Justice again. Consider the following excerpt from the 1963 *Costa* decision:

> Although the third paragraph of Article 177 [now Article 267 TFEU] unreservedly requires courts or tribunals of member states against whose decisions there is no judicial remedy under national law . . . to refer to the Court every question of interpretation before them, the authority of an interpretation under [Article 267 TFEU] already given by the Court may deprive the obligation of its purpose and thus empty it of its substance. Such is the case especially when the question raised is materially identical with a question which has already been the subject of a preliminary rulings procedure in a similar case.[21]

This said, the Court also made it clear that while a Member State court is under no duty to refer to the Court of Justice a question that was already decided in the past, the Member State court can refer such questions voluntarily:

> It is no less true that Article [Article 267 TFEU] allows a national court, if it considers it desirable, to refer questions of interpretation to the court again. This follows from Article 20 of the Statute of the Court of Justice under which the Procedure laid down for the settlement of preliminary questions is automatically

---

[21] Joined Cases 28 to 30–62, Da Costa en Schaake NV v. Netherlands Inland Revenue Admin., 1963 E.C.R. 31.

set in motion as soon as such a question is referred by a national court.[22]

QUESTIONS

1. Can you think of legal policy reasons for why Member State courts should be free to request preliminary rulings on legal issues that have already been decided?

2. Is there reason to believe that national courts will try to avoid their duty to refer questions to the Court of Justice by arguing that the same issue has already been decided in the past? Or do you think that that risk is fairly small?

3. The Court seems to rely on the Statute of the Court of Justice in interpreting Article 267 of the Treaty on the Functioning of the European Union? Is that appropriate?

2. THE *ACTE CLAIR* DOCTRINE

Under the so-called *acte clair* doctrine, which has its origin in the French legal tradition, Member State courts do not have to make a request for a preliminary ruling if the meaning of the relevant provision of EU law is so clear that it does not raise any questions of interpretation.

The doctrinal argument underlying the *acte clair* doctrine is the following: if the meaning of a provision is so clear that no interpretation is necessary, then there exists no question of interpretation within the meaning of Article 267 TFEU. Of course, this line of reasoning is subject to an obvious objection: a determination that the meaning of a provision is clear is itself an act of interpretation.

The more interesting justification for the *acte clair* doctrine, therefore, rests on a legal policy argument: if the meaning of a provision is obvious, then there is no reason to believe that a failure to refer the matter to the Court of Justice will threaten the uniform interpretation and application of EU law. Accordingly, there is no need to involve the ECJ and force the parties to incur the inevitable delay connected with a preliminary ruling procedure. This said, the doctrine's potential for abuse is substantial. The obvious danger is that Member States could simply declare their preferred interpretation of EU law to be obviously correct in order to avoid having to involve the Court of Justice. Indeed, this is precisely what happened in the early years of the *acte clair* doctrine. For example, courts would declare the meaning of a particular provision to be clear even though courts in other Member States had interpreted the relevant provision quite differently.

In its famous CILFIT decision of 1982, the Court of Justice largely put an end to such abuses. On the one hand, the Court of Justice explicitly

---

[22] *Id.*

recognized the *acte clair* doctrine. On the other hand, it defined its requirements quite strictly.

SRL CILFIT AND LANIFICIO DI GAVARDO SPA v. MINISTRY OF HEALTH

Case 283/81, Judgment of Oct. 6, 1982 (citations omitted)

[Under Article 267 TFEU, national courts against whose decision there is no judicial remedy under national law are under an obligation to refer questions pertaining to the interpretation of EU law to the Court of Justice. The highest Italian court in non-constitutional matters—the Corte Suprema di Cassazione—wanted to know if that obligation applies even in those cases where the meaning of EU law is clear.

In answering this question, the Court of Justice first emphasized that the third paragraph of what is now Article 267 TFEU seeks to ensure that national courts across the EU apply EU law in a uniform manner. The Court then noted that the duty to make a preliminary ruling request only arises when there is a "question of interpretation. Thus, according to the Court of Justice, the crucial issue is what the Treaty means by a "question of interpretation."]

9. In this regard, it must in the first place be pointed out that [Article 267 TFEU] does not constitute a means of redress available to the parties to a case pending before a national court or tribunal. Therefore the mere fact that a party contends that the dispute gives rise to a question concerning the interpretation of Community law does not mean that the court or tribunal concerned is compelled to consider that a question has been raised within the meaning of [Article 267 TFEU]. [. . .]

16. [T]he correct application of community law may be so obvious as to leave no scope for any reasonable doubt as to the manner in which the question raised is to be resolved. Before it comes to the conclusion that such is the case, the national court or tribunal must be convinced that the matter is equally obvious to the courts of the other member states and to the court of justice. Only if those conditions are satisfied, may the national court or tribunal refrain from submitting the question to the court of justice and take upon itself the responsibility for resolving it.

17. However, the existence of such a possibility must be assessed on the basis of the characteristic features of community law and the particular difficulties to which its interpretation gives rise.

18. To begin with, it must be borne in mind that community legislation is drafted in several languages and that the different language versions are all equally authentic. An interpretation of a provision of Community law thus involves a comparison of the different language versions.

19. It must also be borne in mind, even where the different language versions are entirely in accord with one another, that community law uses terminology which is peculiar to it. Furthermore, it must be emphasized that legal concepts do not necessarily have the same meaning in Community law and in the law of the various Member States.

20. Finally, every provision of community law must be placed in its context and interpreted in the light of the provisions of community law as a whole, regard being had to the objectives thereof and to its state of evolution at the date on which the provision in question is to be applied.

21. In the light of all those considerations, the answer to the question submitted by the Corte Suprema di Cassazione must be that the third paragraph of [Article 267] of the EEC Treaty [now the TFEU] is to be interpreted as meaning that a court or tribunal against whose decisions there is no judicial remedy under national law is required, where a question of community law is raised before it, to comply with its obligation to bring the matter before the court of justice, unless it has established that the question raised is irrelevant or that the community provision in question has already been interpreted by the court or that the correct application of community law is so obvious as to leave no scope for any reasonable doubt. The existence of such a possibility must be assessed in the light of the specific characteristics of community law, the particular difficulties to which its interpretation gives rise and the risk of divergences in judicial decisions within the community. ■

NOTES AND QUESTIONS

1. While Article 267 TFEU imposes a duty on Member State courts, against whose decision no remedy exists under national law, to refer questions of interpretation to the Court of Justice, Member State courts have not always met that requirement. In particular, the German Bundesfinanzhof, Germany's highest court in tax matters, the French Conseil d'État, France's constitutional court, and Greece's constitutional court famously disregarded the duty to refer questions to the Court of Justice in certain cases.[23] Against that background, why would the Court of Justice be so generous as to recognize the *acte clair* doctrine instead of simply rejecting it flat-out?

2. After CILFIT, how often do you think Member State courts invoke the *acte clair* doctrine in practice? Why?

3. Could one argue that the *acte clair* doctrine establishes the primacy of the wording of a provision over other criteria of interpretation?

4. In paragraph 9, the Court notes that the preliminary rulings procedure "does not constitute a means of redress available to the parties to a

---

[23] G. Frederico Mancini & David T. Keeling, *From CILFIT to ERT: the Constitutional Challenge Facing the European Court*, 11 YEARBOOK OF EUROPEAN LAW [YEL] 1, 4 (1992).

case pending before a national court or tribunal." What does the Court of Justice mean and how is this relevant to the issue at hand?

CHAPTER 6

ENFORCEMENT ACTIONS

∎ ∎ ∎

European Union law imposes substantial duties on the Member States. As in any contract, or any treaty between nations, these duties are incurred in the expectation that the other parties will also fulfill their respective duties. But of course, there is the ever-present risk of shirking: individual Member States may try to avoid their legal obligations, even though they and their citizens profit from other Member States complying with EU law. This presents a potentially grave threat to the whole European edifice: if some Member States start violating EU law, others may follow, and in the end, a general state of non-compliance may result. Accordingly, in order for the European Union to survive, it is essential to have mechanisms that force individual Member States to comply.

The most obvious of such mechanisms lies in so-called enforcement actions under Articles 257–260 TFEU: if a Member State violates EU law, the Commission or another Member State can bring a so-called enforcement proceeding before the European Court of Justice, Articles 257, 258. If the Court finds that a violation of EU law has indeed occurred, the Member State in question is under a duty to take the necessary steps to comply with the judgment, Article 260(1). If the Member State fails to comply with the judgment, the Commission can initiate a proceeding before the Court of Justice that will result in the imposition of a monetary lump sum or penalty payments, Article 260(2).

In practice, enforcement proceedings are one of the most common types of procedure before the Court of Justice; in terms of the number of ECJ judgments, they come second only to the preliminary rulings procedure.

A. OVERVIEW OF THE PROCEDURE

Typically, enforcement actions are brought by the Commission. In this case, the procedure comprises six main phases.

1. First, as a preliminary matter, the Commission will contact the Member State and voice its concerns regarding the alleged violation of EU law. In many cases, this will prompt the Member State to cease the violation of EU law or allow the Member State to convince the Commission that the relevant conduct does not, in fact, violate EU law. Either way, an enforcement action is avoided.

2. Should these informal contacts fail to resolve the conflict, the procedure enters into its second, more formal stage. At this stage, the Member State receives a formal letter from the Commission notifying the Member State of the alleged violation of EU law. The Member State then has the opportunity to reply to this letter. In response to the Member State's reply, the Commission can either drop the case or proceed to the next stage.

3. At the third stage, the Commission provides the Member State with a reasoned opinion. This opinion not only specifies the alleged violation of EU law, but also explains the reasons why the Commission believes that EU law has been violated. Moreover, the reasoned opinion sets a deadline for ceasing the violation of EU law.

4. If the Member State fails to comply with the reasoned opinion, the conflict enters into its fourth phase, in which the Commission brings suit before the European Court of Justice and the Court of Justice ascertains whether EU law has, in fact, been violated.

5. If the Court of Justice finds a violation of EU law, the conflict enters into its fifth stage: the Member State now has to take the necessary steps to comply with the judgment, Article 260(1).

6. Should the Member State still fail to comply, there is a potential sixth stage: the Commission, "after giving that State the opportunity to submit its observations" may bring the case yet again before the Court, and the Court, if it finds that the Member State has indeed failed to comply with the ECJ's judgment, "may impose a lump sum or penalty payment," Article 260(2). In practice, the imposition of lump sum or penalty payments still constitutes a rare exception, but has become somewhat more common in recent years.

As noted above, enforcement proceedings can be brought not only by the Commission, but also by the other Member States. In this case, the procedure is a little more complicated. If a Member State believes that another Member State has violated EU law, the former Member State first has to bring the matter before the Commission, Article 259. Both Member States can then submit their observations. If this does not resolve the matter, the Commission will deliver a reasoned opinion.

B. THE REASONED OPINION

A key role in enforcement proceedings is played by the reasoned opinion that the Commission issues to the Member State accused of violating EU law. The reasoned opinion determines the subject matter of the subsequent proceeding. For that reason, the content of the reasoned opinion has to meet certain requirements. More specifically,

...the reasoned opinion must contain a coherent and detailed statement of the reasons which persuaded the Commission that the State concerned had failed to fulfill one of its obligations under the Treaty. However, the Commission cannot be required to indicate in the reasoned opinion what steps should be taken to eliminate the impugned conduct.[1]

Crucially, the Commission cannot later base its claims of a violation of EU law on grounds that were not part of the reasoned opinion.[2] This requirement serves a dual purpose: it constitutes a central protection for the defendant Member State,[3] and it also ensures that the enforcement proceeding has "a clearly defined dispute as its subject-matter."[4]

This said, the Court is not overly formalistic in applying the principle that the Commission's claim in the enforcement proceeding must be based on the same grounds as the reasoned opinion. Minor deviations that do not change the subject matter are harmless. For example, it does not matter if the Commission's application to the Court of Justice is simply more detailed than the reasoned opinion. Consider the following excerpt from a 2010 case involving an enforcement proceeding against the Portuguese Republic:

> 44. [T]he requirement [that the application must be based on the same grounds as the reasoned opinion] cannot be stretched so far as to mean that in every case the formal statement of objections set out in the reasoned opinion and the form of order sought in the application must be exactly the same, provided that the subject-matter of the proceedings as defined in the reasoned opinion has not been extended or altered.
>
> 47. Therefore, the fact that, in its application [to the Court], the Commission set out in detail the arguments supporting its conclusion as to the alleged failure to fulfill obligations, arguments which had already been put forward in more general terms in the letter of formal notice and the reasoned opinion, and merely explained further why it takes the view that that scheme is incompatible with the freedom to provide services, did not alter the subject of that infringement and has thus had no effect on the scope of the proceedings.[5]

---

[1] Case C-247/89, Comm'n v. Portuguese Republic, 1991 E.C.R. I-3659 ¶ 22 (citations omitted).

[2] Id. ¶ 43 ("It follows that the subject-matter of the proceedings under Article 226 EC [now Article 258] is delimited by the pre-litigation procedure provided for in that provision. Accordingly, the application must be based on the same grounds and pleas as the reasoned opinion...").

[3] Id. ¶ 42.

[4] Id.

[5] Case C-458/08, Comm'n v. Portuguese Republic, 2010 E.C.R. I-11599 ¶¶ 42–44.

There is also another basis on which Member States accused of breaching EU law sometimes attack the Commission's reasoned opinion: they argue that the deadline for remedying the situation is too short. In general, however, the Court of Justice has shown little sympathy for this type of argument.

COMMISSION V. GRAND DUCHY OF LUXEMBOURG
Case C-473/93, July 2, 1996, E.C.R. 1996, I-3207

[By statute, Luxembourg reserved employment in various state-run sectors to its own citizens. These sectors included research, inland transport, teaching, health, and telecommunication as well as water, gas, and electricity distribution services. The Commission took the view that the relevant rules violated the Treaty's provisions on the free movement of workers and brought enforcement proceedings against Luxemburg.]

17. First of all, the Grand Duchy of Luxembourg challenges the admissibility of the Commission's action on the ground that the Commission gave it a period of only four months in which to comply with the reasoned opinions. That period was manifestly insufficient to allow it to carry out the major reform demanded, which required it to overhaul its administrative system starting at its very roots.

18. In response, the Commission maintains first of all that the period of four months given in the reasoned opinions was exceptionally long since the usual period allowed is only one or two months. The Commission goes on to point out that the entire pre-litigation procedure lasted more than 33 months, not to mention the fact that at the time when that procedure commenced the Grand Duchy of Luxembourg had long been aware of the Commission's intentions because of the strategy it had announced. Finally, the Grand Duchy never asked for the period to be extended but always insisted that it would not amend its legislation.

19. In view of those arguments, the Court must reiterate that the purpose of the pre-litigation procedure is to give the Member State concerned an opportunity, on the one hand, to comply with its obligations under Community law and, on the other, to avail itself of its right to defend itself against the objections raised by the Commission.

20. In view of that dual purpose the Commission must allow Member States a reasonable period to reply to the letter of formal notice and to comply with a reasoned opinion, or, where appropriate, to prepare their defence. In order to determine whether the period allowed is reasonable, account must be taken of all the circumstances of the case.

21. In the present case, the period of four months laid down in the reasoned opinions was twice as long as the period normally allowed by the Commission.

22. Furthermore, the Grand Duchy of Luxembourg had been aware of the Commission's position since 18 March 1988 when it published Communication 88/C 72/02, mentioned above, which was therefore nearly three years before it received the letters, dated 12 March 1991, giving it formal notice, which in turn allowed it a period of six months.

23. In the replies which it gave to the Commission the Grand Duchy of Luxembourg made it clear that it was not going to carry out any legislative reforms.

24. In those circumstances the four-month period imposed by the reasoned opinions cannot be regarded as unreasonable. The action is therefore admissible. . . . ■

QUESTIONS

1. Is it always reasonable to expect Member States to change their law before the Commission has issued a reasoned opinion?

2. Do you think it might have been possible for Luxembourg to adopt a statute ending discrimination based on citizenship within four months?

C. INFRINGEMENT

In an enforcement proceeding, the Court of Justice will ascertain whether the "Member State has failed to fulfill an obligation under the Treaties," Article 260(1) TFEU. This wording is broader than it may seem at first glance. Since the Treaties require the Member States to comply not just with primary but also with secondary EU law, violations of both primary and secondary EU law can form the object of an enforcement proceeding.

As a general rule, the burden of proof is borne by the Commission. In the words of the Court, "it is incumbent upon the Commission to prove the allegation that the obligation has not been fulfilled."[6]

For the most part, whether EU law has been violated is a question of substantive EU law. For example, the Court may find that a certain Member State law violates the fundamental freedoms guaranteed by the TFEU. Such questions will be discussed in later chapters. There exist, however, two issues that arise specifically in the context of enforcement proceedings. One concerns the extent to which an administrative practice that defies EU law can form the object of an enforcement proceeding. The other is whether an enforcement proceeding can be based on a violation of EU law by Member State courts.

---

[6] Case C-494/01, Comm'n v. Ireland, 2005 E.C.R. I-3331 ¶ 41.

1. ADMINISTRATIVE PRACTICE

Obviously, EU law is binding not only on the legislature and courts of a Member State, but also on the Member State's administration. A separate question is, however, to what extent enforcement proceedings can target not just specific, individual instances of EU law violations by a Member State's administration, but also more broadly defined, systematic practices that violate EU law. The distinction between an individual administrative act that violates EU law and an administrative practice in violation of EU law may seem subtle but it has important procedural implications.

COMMISSION V. IRELAND
E.C.J., Case 494/01, April 26, 2005, 2005 E.C.R. I-3331

[Council Directive 75/442/EEC governs the disposal of waste and, in this context, imposes various duties on the Member States. Inter alia, the Member States are required to ensure that waste is disposed of without endangering human health or the environment. Furthermore, the directive imposed various more detailed duties to ensure the proper disposal of waste. The Commission received numerous complaints about instances in which Irish authorities were accused of violating their duties under the directive. After sending Ireland formal letters of notification regarding various instances of alleged violations of the directive, the Commission finally issued a reasoned opinion in which it accused Ireland of having repeatedly violated the directive. In the reasoned opinion, the Commission made it clear that it viewed the various breaches of the directive described in the opinion as mere illustrations of Ireland's more general failure to adhere to the directive. The Commission also stressed that it reserved the right to cite further examples later on. When Ireland failed to comply with the reasoned opinion, the Commission brought an enforcement action. In its application to the Court of Justice, the Commission not only invoked violations of the directive that it had mentioned in the reasoned opinion. but also cited, as part of its case, the illegal disposal of waste in County Wicklow. At the time of the reasoned opinion, the Commission had not yet been aware of the events in County Wicklow.]

28. It is accepted that an administrative practice can be the subject-matter of an action for failure to fulfill obligations when it is, to some degree, of a consistent and general nature.

29. [. . .] [T]he question whether a Member State has failed to fulfill its obligations must be determined by reference to the situation prevailing in the Member State at the end of the period laid down in the reasoned opinion. . . .

33. [. . .] [T]he purpose of the pre-litigation phase is to give the Member State concerned an opportunity, on the one hand, to comply with its obligations under Community law and, on the other, to avail itself of its right to defend itself against the charges formulated by the Commission.

34. The proper conduct of that procedure constitutes an essential guarantee required by the EC Treaty not only in order to protect the rights of the Member State concerned, but also so as to ensure that any contentious procedure will have a clearly defined dispute as its subject-matter.

35. The subject-matter of proceedings under Article 226 EC [now Article 258] is accordingly delimited by the pre-litigation procedure governed by that provision. The Commission's reasoned opinion and the application must be based on the same grounds and pleas, with the result that the Court cannot examine a ground of complaint which was not formulated in the reasoned opinion, which for its part must contain a cogent and detailed exposition of the reasons which led the Commission to the conclusion that the Member State concerned had failed to fulfil one of its obligations under the Treaty.

36. It indeed follows that the Commission cannot seek a declaration of a specific failure by Ireland to fulfill its obligations under the Directive regarding a particular factual situation that was not referred to in the course of the pre-litigation procedure. A specific ground of complaint of that kind must necessarily have been relied on at the pre-litigation stage, in order that the Member State concerned has the opportunity to remedy the particular situation complained of or to avail itself of its right to defend itself in that regard; such defence may in particular prompt the Commission to withdraw the ground of complaint and/or help to delimit the subject-matter of the dispute that the Court will subsequently have before it.

37. On the other hand, in so far as the action seeks to raise a failure of a general nature to comply with the Directive's provisions, concerning in particular the Irish authorities' systemic and consistent tolerance of situations not in accordance with the Directive, the production of additional evidence intended, at the stage of proceedings before the Court, to support the proposition that the failure thus alleged is general and consistent cannot be ruled out in principle.

38. It should be noted that in its application the Commission may clarify its initial grounds of complaint provided, however, that it does not alter the subject-matter of the dispute. In producing fresh evidence intended to illustrate the grounds of complaint set out in its reasoned opinion, which allege a failure of a general nature to comply with the provisions of a directive, the Commission does not alter the subject-matter of the dispute.

39. In the present case, contrary to the Irish Government's submissions, although they were not referred to during the pre-litigation procedure the facts relating to massive illegal dumping of, on occasions hazardous, waste in County Wicklow, of which the Commission became aware after issue of the reasoned opinion, could therefore properly be mentioned by the latter in support of its application for the purpose of illustrating the failures of a general nature to fulfil obligations raised by it. . . . ∎

QUESTIONS

1. According to the Court, when exactly can an administrative practice—rather than individual administrative acts—form the subject-matter of an enforcement proceeding? Can you think of an example where the line between an administrative practice and individual administrative acts might be blurred?

2. Assuming that the Commission accuses a Member State of having developed an administrative practice that violates EU law, how does the nature of this complaint affect the ability of the Commission to invoke state conduct that was not mentioned in the reasoned opinion?

3. As the Court notes, under settled case law, "the question whether a Member State has failed to fulfill its obligations must be determined by reference to the situation prevailing in the Member State at the end of the period laid down in the reasoned opinion."[7] This means that the Court will find a violation of EU law even if the Member State has in fact ceased to violate EU law before the Court's judgment, but after the deadline set in the reasoned opinion. Do you believe that this rule is desirable as a matter of legal policy? Can you name any arguments one way or the other?

4. How does the Court allocate the burden of proof between the Commission and the Member States? Is the Court's position compatible with the general principle that, in enforcement proceedings, it is incumbent on the Commission to prove that a Member State has breached EU law?

2. ENFORCEMENT PROCEEDINGS AND MEMBER STATE COURTS

As a practical matter, the Commission until recently abstained from initiating enforcement proceedings based on violations of EU law by Member State courts.[8] However, the Court of Justice has made it very clear that such enforcement proceedings are entirely possible.[9] After all, Member

---

[7] Case 494/01, Comm'n v. Ireland, 2005 E.C.R. I-3331 ¶ 29.

[8] However, this changed in 2004, when the Commission delivered a reasoned opinion to Sweden based on the failure of the Swedish Supreme Court to make adequate use of the preliminary rulings procedure. See Doc. C (2004), 3899, Oct. 7, 2004. The case never made it to the Court of Justice, though, because Sweden credibly assured the Commission that its courts would comply in the future.

[9] Case C-129/00, Commission v. Italy, 2003 E.C.R. I-8003 ¶ 29 ("A Member State's failure to fulfill obligations may, in principle, be established under Article 226 EC [insert TFEU equivalent]

State courts are bound by EU law and can breach EU law just like any other Member State institution can. In the words of the Court:

> 32. In international law a State which incurs liability for breach of an international commitment is viewed as a single entity, irrespective of whether the breach which gave rise to the damage is attributable to the legislature, the judiciary or the executive. That principle must apply a fortiori in the Community legal order since all State authorities . . . are bound in performing their tasks to comply with the rules laid down by Community law which directly govern the situation of individuals.[10]

That said, the truly difficult question involving enforcement proceedings and Member State courts is a different one. Quite often, the Member State laws that form the object of enforcement proceedings have to be interpreted in order to ascertain whether they are incompatible with EU law. In this context, the question arises what weight should be given to individual decisions by Member State courts.

COMMISSION V. ITALY

E.C.J., Case C-129/00, December 9, 2003, 2003 E.C.R. I-8003 (citations omitted)

[Italian law explicitly provided that duties and taxes levied in breach of EU law had to be repaid to the taxpayer. However, the relevant Italian statute included an important exception from that duty to repay illegally raised taxes: no such repayment was required if the relevant duties and taxes had already been passed on to other persons such as consumers. The Commission took the view that this exception, as interpreted and applied by the Italian courts and the Italian administration, violated EU law. More specifically, the Commission took umbrage at the fact that the law, as it was interpreted and applied, allowed the use of evidentiary rules that made it exceedingly difficult or even impossible for the taxpayer to show that the duties and taxes had *not* been passed on. When Italy failed to remedy the situation in response to the Commission's reasoned opinion, the Commission brought an enforcement action.]

28. The Commission's complaint in support of its action has three aspects. First, many Italian courts, especially and repeatedly the Corte suprema di cassazione [*the highest Italian court in civil matters*], consider that the passing on of charges to third parties is established from the sole fact that the claimant is a commercial undertaking. . . . Secondly, the authorities systematically seek the production of claimants' accounting documents. The courts before which claimants bring objections accede to such

---

whatever the agency of that State whose action or inaction is the cause of the failure to fulfill its obligations, even in the case of a constitutionally independent institution.").

[10] Case C-224/01, Gerhard Kobler v. Republik Osterreich, 2003 E.C.R. I-10239 ¶ 32 (citations omitted).

applications by adopting the same sort of reasoning as that set out above and they regard with disfavor claimants' failure to produce the documents even though the statutory period for their preservation has expired. Thirdly, the authorities regard failure to account for the amount of the taxes in question, from the year of their payment, as payments to the public purse for undue tax and credited as an asset in the balance-sheet of the undertaking which is claiming their repayment, as proof that those charges have been passed on to third parties.

29. A Member State's failure to fulfill obligations may, in principle, be established under Article 226 EC [Article 258 TFEU] whatever the agency of that State whose action or inaction is the cause of the failure to fulfill its obligations, even in the case of a constitutionally independent institution.

30. The scope of national laws, regulations or administrative provisions must be assessed in the light of the interpretation given to them by national courts.

31. In this case what is at issue is Article 29(2) of Law No 428/1990 which provides that duties and charges levied under national provisions incompatible with Community legislation are to be repaid, unless the amount thereof has been passed on to others. Such a provision is in itself neutral in respect of Community law in relation both to the burden of proof that the charge has been passed on to other persons and to the evidence which is admissible to prove it. Its effect must be determined in the light of the construction which the national courts give it.

32. In that regard, isolated or numerically insignificant judicial decisions in the context of case-law taking a different direction, or still more a construction disowned by the national supreme court, cannot be taken into account. That is not true of a widely-held judicial construction which has not been disowned by the Supreme Court, but rather confirmed by it.

33. Where national legislation has been the subject of different relevant judicial constructions, some leading to the application of that legislation in compliance with Community law, others leading to the opposite application, it must be held that, at the very least, such legislation is not sufficiently clear to ensure its application in compliance with Community law.

34. In the present case, the Italian Government does not dispute that a certain number of judgments of the Corte suprema di cassazione lead, by deductive reasoning, to the conclusion that, in the absence of evidence to the contrary, commercial undertakings trading normally pass on an indirect tax by subsequent sales, in particular if it is levied throughout the national territory for an appreciable period without objection. The Italian Government confines itself to explaining that numerous trial courts do not accept such reasoning as proof of such passing on and to providing examples of taxpayers who secured repayment of charges contrary to

Community law, since the authorities did not succeed in those cases in proving to the relevant court that the taxpayers had passed on those charges. [. . .]

41. In the light of the foregoing considerations, it must be declared that, by failing to amend Article 29(2) of Law No 428/1990, which is construed and applied by the administrative authorities and a substantial [portion] of the courts, including the Corte suprema di cassazione, in such a way that the exercise of the right to repayment of charges levied in breach of Community rules is made excessively difficult for the taxpayer, the Italian Republic has failed to fulfil its obligations under the EC Treaty.[11] ∎

NOTES AND QUESTIONS

1. According to the Court of Justice, wherein exactly lies the Italian Republic's failure to fulfill its obligations under European law?

2. According to the Court, to what extent can judgments by Member State courts be taken into account in ascertaining whether national statutory law violates EU law?

3. In paragraph 33 of the opinion, the Court notes that "[w]here national legislation has been the subject of different relevant judicial constructions, some leading to the application of that legislation in compliance with Community law, others leading to the opposite application, it must be held that, at the very least, such legislation is not sufficiently clear to ensure its application in compliance with Community law." What might be the logic behind this argument?

4. In the context of the implementation of directives, the Court of Justice has also taken a hard line vis-à-vis Member State legislation that is not sufficiently clear to allow citizens to exercise their rights. For example, in case C-131/88, *Commission v. Germany*,[12] Germany had sought to avoid the enactment of a statute to implement a particular directive on the protection of groundwater on the ground that the German practice already corresponded to the requirements imposed by the directive. The Court was not persuaded by this reasoning. Instead, it pointed out that "the fact that a practice is consistent with the protection afforded under a directive does not justify failure to implement that directive in the national legal order by means of provisions which are capable of creating a situation which is sufficiently precise, clear and open to permit individuals to be aware of and enforce their rights."[13] Should the Member States be subject to a general requirement that their legislation must be sufficiently transparent such as not to burden the exercise of rights granted by EU law?

---

[11] Case C-129/00, Comm'n v. Italy, 2003 E.C.R. I-8003 (citations omitted).
[12] Case C-131/88, Comm'n v. Germany, 1991 E.C.R. I-825.
[13] *Id.* ¶ 8.

D. DEFENSES

As one would expect, Member States have been quite creative in coming up with various arguments designed to protect them from being held accountable in enforcement proceedings. However, the Court of Justice has rejected the vast majority of these defenses.

1. FORCE MAJEURE

One defense that the Member States may sometimes successfully invoke is *force majeure:* at least in some situations, a Member State will not be found in violation of EU law if compliance was absolutely impossible.[14] However, the concept of force majeure is defined quite narrowly, and it remains unclear in which cases this excuse applies.

COMMISSION V. HELLENIC REPUBLIC
Case 70/86, Sept. 17, 1987, 1987 E.C.R. I-3545 (citations omitted)

[Greece failed to pay its annual financial contributions to the European Community on time. Under the applicable EU law, states that fail to pay their contributions in a timely manner have to pay interest, and the interest rate increases by one quarter of a percentage point for each month of delay. The Greek authorities blamed the delay on a general strike by bank employees. This, they argued, must be considered "force majeure."]

8. As the Court has consistently held, apart from special features of specific areas in which it is used, the concept of force majeure essentially covers extraneous circumstances which make it impossible for the relevant action to be carried out, even though it does not presuppose absolute impossibility it nevertheless requires abnormal difficulties which are independent of the will of the person concerned and appear inevitable even if all due care is taken.

9. Those conditions are not met in this case. It appears from the documents before the court that at least since 25 May the press had warned of strikes affecting several occupations, including bank employees, for 26 and 27 May. On 29 May, the press warned of further industrial action and stated that the unions had called a strike for 1 and 2 June. The strike which in fact took place on those dates was therefore foreseeable and the delay in the entry of the financial contributions in question could have been avoided.

---

[14] Case C-349/93, Comm'n v. Italy, 1995 E.C.R. I-343 ¶ 12 ("The only defence available to a Member State in opposing an application by the Commission under Article 93(2) of the Treaty for a declaration that it has failed to fulfil its Treaty obligations is to plead that it was absolutely impossible for it to implement the decision properly.") (citations omitted). *Cf.* Case 101/84, Comm'n v. Italy, 1985 E.C.R. 2629 ¶ 16 (recognizing that a bomb attack could potentially constitute force majeure, but rejecting this defense in the case at hand on the grounds that enough time had elapsed since the bombing for Italy to fulfill its duties anyway).

10. It is not necessary to consider the question whether or not, in the event of force majeure, the Member States are obliged to pay interest pursuant to article 11 of regulation no 2891/77. The strike relied on as an excuse by the Greek government cannot be regarded as a case of force majeure.

11. Consequently, by failing to enter the financial contributions for the month of June 1983 in the Commission's account in due time and by refusing to pay interest pursuant to article 11 of regulation no 2891/77 in respect of the late entry, the Hellenic republic has failed to fulfill its obligations under the treaty. ∎

QUESTIONS

1. From a legal policy perspective, does it make sense to recognize force majeure as a defense in enforcement proceedings?

2. What might be circumstances that *could* qualify as force majeure?

3. Should an obstacle's foreseeability always preclude a finding of force majeure?

2. INTERNAL DIFFICULTIES

The paradigmatic excuse advanced by Member States involves some kind of internal difficulties such as an overburdened legislature or the difficulty of reaching the political consensus necessary to enact legislation that complies with EU law. The Court of Justice has consistently rejected this type of excuse. In the Court's words, "a Member State may not plead provisions, practices or circumstances existing in its internal legal system in order to justify a failure to comply with its obligations under Community law."[15]

3. RECIPROCITY

A more interesting defense involves the argument by a Member State that other Member States or the Commission are also violating the relevant EU rules. In the famous *van Gend en Loos* decision, the Court of Justice rejected this defense with the following arguments:

> The defendants ... complain that the Community [now the European Union] failed to comply with the obligations falling on it ... and was thus responsible for the continuance of the alleged infringement of the Treaty, which should have ceased before the issue of the reasoned opinion under Article 169 [now Article 259 TFEU]. In their view, since international law allows a party, injured by the failure of another party to perform its obligations, to withhold performance of its own, the Commission has lost the right to plead infringement of the Treaty. However this

---

[15] Case C-349/93, Comm'n v. Italy, 1995 E.C.R. I-343 ¶ 11 (citations omitted).

relationship between the obligations of parties cannot be recognized under Community law.

In fact the Treaty is not limited to creating reciprocal obligations between the different natural and legal persons to whom it is applicable, but establishes a new legal order which governs the powers, rights and obligations of the said persons, as well as the necessary procedures for taking cognizance of and penalizing any breach of it. Therefore, except where otherwise expressly provided, the basic concept of the treaty requires that the Member States shall not take the law into their own hands. Therefore the fact that the council failed to carry out its obligations cannot relieve the defendants from carrying out theirs.[16]

4. OTHER EXCUSES

The Member States have also tried to invoke a number of other excuses that proved unsuccessful. The Court of Justice has made it clear that it does not matter whether the Member State *intentionally* breached EU law:

> 81. It should be stated in that regard that the procedure provided for in Article 258 TFEU presupposes an objective finding that a Member State has failed to fulfill its obligations under the Treaty or secondary legislation.
>
> 82. Where such a finding has been made, as in the present case, it is irrelevant whether the failure to fulfill obligations is the result of intention or negligence on the part of the Member State responsible, or of technical difficulties encountered by it.[17]

Similarly, a Member State cannot invoke opposition from its populace to justify noncompliance with EU law:

> With regard to the local inhabitants' opposition to the establishment of certain disposal installations, it is settled case-law that a Member State may not plead internal situations, such as difficulties of implementation which emerge at the stage of putting a Community [now Union] measure into effect, including difficulties relating to opposition on the part of certain individuals, in order to justify a failure to comply with obligations and time-limits laid down by Community law.[18]

Furthermore, a Member State cannot escape a finding that it has violated EU law by arguing that the infringement was remedied after the

---

[16] Joined Cases 90/63 and 91/63, Comm'n v. Grand Duchy of Luxembourg and Kingdom of Belgium, 1964 E.C.R. 94.

[17] Case C-297/08, Comm'n v. Italian Republic, 2010 E.C.R. I-1749 ¶¶ 81–82 (citations omitted).

[18] *Id.* ¶ 83 (citations omitted).

deadline set in the reasoned opinion had expired but before the Court handed down its decision:

> [T]he Court has held on numerous occasions that the question whether a Member State has failed to fulfill its obligations must be determined by reference to the situation [existing] in that Member State at the time of the deadline set in the reasoned opinion and that the Court cannot take account of any subsequent changes.[19]

---

[19] *Id.* ¶ 79 (citations omitted).

PART 3

CHARACTERISTICS OF EU LAW

■ ■ ■

In this Part, we will take a closer look at the characteristics of EU law as well as at the legislative process.

As has already been noted, EU law comes in two main flavors—primary EU law and secondary EU law. The term "primary EU law" refers to the Treaty on European Union and the Treaty on the Functioning of the European Union. The protocols and annexes of the Treaty are also part of EU primary law because they constitute an "integral part" of the Treaties.[1] Similarly, the general principles of EU law that the Court of Justice has derived from the provisions of the Treaties are deemed part of primary EU law.[2]

By contrast, the term "secondary EU law" refers to the legal acts (regulations, directives, decisions, etc.) of the institutions of the European Union. For example, whereas the Statute of the Court of Justice of the European Union is part of primary EU law because it was enacted as Protocol No. 3 annexed to the Treaties, the Rules of Procedure of the Court of Justice constitute secondary law because they were adopted by the Court of Justice.[3]

---

[1] TEU, art. 51.
[2] RUDOLF STREINZ, EUROPARECHT § 5.1.2. (10th ed. 2016).
[3] *See* JENS DAMMANN, MATERIELLES RECHT UND BEWEISRECHT IM SYSTEM DER GRUNDFREIHEITEN 17 (2007).

CHAPTER 7

THE DIRECT EFFECT PRINCIPLE

■ ■ ■

One central question for EU law concerns its effects on individuals. To what extent are EU norms addressed only to the Member States, and to what extent do they create rights and duties for individuals? This question is generally discussed under the notion of "direct effect." According to the conventional terminology, a provision has "direct effect" if it "confers ... rights [on individuals] upon which they are entitled to rely directly before the national courts."[1] By contrast, a provision that is merely addressed to the Member States and does not confer rights upon individuals lacks direct effect.

A. BACKGROUND: MONISM V. DUALISM

To understand the importance of the direct effect issue, it is helpful to begin with a time-honored debate in international law regarding the impact of international treaties on national legal systems: According to one view, international treaties only create rights and duties for the nations that conclude them. On that view, private individuals cannot directly invoke international treaties in domestic courts; instead, they have to wait for their country to transform international law into national law, e.g. by way of legislation. This view is traditionally known as "dualism" because it posits that international law and national law are two separate legal systems, and international treaties that are concluded in the former cannot have any impact on the latter unless a nation decides to change its national law in compliance with the treaty. By contrast, according to a view known as "monism," international treaties can directly create individual rights.[2]

This dualism v. monism debate has important practical implications. What happens if a country concludes an international treaty but then fails to enact legislation that incorporates the treaty into its domestic legal

---

[1] E.C.J., Case C-429/09, Günter Fuß v. Stadt Halle, 2010 E.C.R. I-12167para. 35. *See* E.C.J., Case C-203/10, Direktsia "Obzhalvane i upravlenie na izpalnenieto" Varna v. Auto Nikolovi OOD, E.C.R. 2011 Page 1083 para. 65 (referring to "direct effect which authorises an individual to rely on [provisions of EU law] before a national court"); Case C-372/06, Asda Stores Ltd v. Commissioners of Her Majesty's Revenue and Custom, E.C.R. 2007 Page I-11223, para. 90 ("direct effect . . . implies that the individuals to whom they apply have the right to rely on them before the courts of the Member States").

[2] For a more general analysis of dualist and monist approaches to international law see Rett R. Ludwikowski, *Supreme Law or Basic Law? The Decline of the Concept of Constitutional Supremacy*, 9 CARDOZO J. INT'L & COMP. L. 253 (2001).

system? Under a theory of pure dualism, the relevant country may be in breach of the treaty by failing to implement it. However, that does not change the fact that the treaty has not become part of the country's legal system. Hence, if a private party tried to invoke the treaty before a national court, that court would refuse to apply the treaty's provision.

For example, assume that countries Alpha and Beta conclude an international treaty whereby each country has to allow the other country's citizens to visit for up to three months for touristic purposes without a visa. Further assume that Alpha never enacts legislation that incorporates the treaty's provision into Alphanian law. If a citizen of Beta now tried to enter Alphanian territory without a visa, he would be denied, and if he took his case to an Alphanian court, his suit would be dismissed. For even though Alpha would be in breach of the treaty it has concluded, that does not change the fact that the treaty's provision have not become part of Alphanian law.

Moreover, even if a country that is bound by a treaty has in fact enacted legislation incorporating that treaty into its domestic legal system, that country may later reverse course and change its domestic law. To stick to the above hypothetical, assume that Alpha originally enacted legislation according to which Betanian tourists can visit Alpha for up to three months without a visa. However, two years later, Alpha changes its mind and repeals the relevant statute. In that case, Alpha is in breach of its international obligations, but that does not change the fact that Alpha's domestic law no longer incorporates the content of the treaty.

Different countries have traditionally taken different positions in the monism v. dualism debate, and many nations have taken approaches that can best be described as a mixture of dualism and monism.[3]

COMMITMENT AND DIFFUSION, HOW AND WHY NATIONAL CONSTITUTIONS INCORPORATE INTERNATIONAL LAW

Tom Ginsburg, Svitlana Chernykh, & Zachary Elkins
2008 Ill. L. Rev. 201, 204–6

National constitutional provisions vary widely in terms of their relationship with international law. International lawyers and scholars have traditionally used the concept of monism and dualism to describe the relationship between international legal order and the domestic legal order. Monism sees international law and the domestic legal system as part of the same legal order. International law has a primary place in this unitary legal system, such that domestic legal systems must always conform to the requirements of international law or find themselves in violation. This would be true whether or not domestic legal actors had

---

[3] Note, *Constitutional Courts and International Law: Revisiting the Transatlantic Divide*, 129 HARV. L. REV. 1362, 1367 (2016).

taken any formal steps to introduce international legal norms into the domestic legal order in accordance with domestic constitutional rules.

In contrast, dualism views the international legal order as distinct, only penetrating the domestic legal order by explicit consent of the state involved. When the two systems conflict, national courts would apply their own national law. From a dualist perspective, the international legal order could purport to bind actors within states, but consent is required to do so as a matter of domestic law. International legal obligations would require transposition into the domestic order to take effect. Absent such transposition, there is the distinct possibility of an action being legal in national law but illegal in international law; in which case, a dualist would presume that courts should apply the rules of national law.

A further complexity is that monism and dualism can vary with the type of obligation, so that some states are monist with regard to treaty law but dualist with regard to customary international law. For example, the Netherlands Constitution of 1983 places international treaties above the Constitution, and explicitly states that statutes that conflict with international law are void. But the Dutch Constitution does not give the same status to customary international law. In Germany, Italy and Austria, by contrast, customary international law is superior to domestic statutes, but treaties are equal to domestic statues, with the last-in-time rule determining which is valid. This is the opposite configuration of the Dutch Constitution. To take another example, the Constitution of Russia states that the "[u]niversally recognized principles and norms of international law as well as international agreements of the Russian Federation should be an integral part of its legal system. If an international agreement of the Russian Federation establishes rules, which differ from those stipulated by law, then the rules of international agreement shall be applied." France has yet another configuration, in which treaties have higher status than subsequent legislation, but the French constitution is silent on customary international law. In Switzerland, preemptory norms of jus cogens, but not other rules of customary international law, are superior to the Constitution. Finally, constitutions can require that courts interpret the document in conformity with international human rights law.

The United Kingdom, with its long tradition of parliamentary supremacy, would seem to be dualist. Parliamentary sovereignty was famously defined by Albert Dicey as "the right to make or unmake any law whatever; and further, that no person or body is recognized by the law of England as having a right to override or set aside the legislation of Parliament." This means that parliament is unconstrained by national courts and also by international bodies; parliament is also free to pass statutes that conflict with prior treaties. This stance came under some pressure from the European Union and the European Court of Human

Rights, because the British treaty commitments accept European law to be superior. Nevertheless, the doctrine of parliamentary sovereignty survives.

At the same time, customary international law (CIL) was traditionally viewed as part of the common law, and directly applicable so long as it was not overruled by subsequent statute or judicial decision. This is called the doctrine of incorporation, whereby changes in CIL are automatically "incorporated" into the common law. For many decades, scholars have asserted that the UK has followed the competing doctrine of transformation, so that courts require some evidence of governmental intent to incorporate the international rule into domestic law before it will be applied; but the conventional view is that the doctrine of incorporation remains intact.

The United States Constitution establishes a scheme somewhat similar to that of the UK. Customary international law, or the "law of nations," was traditionally viewed as part of federal common law. Article I Section 8 of the Constitution also gives Congress the power to "define . . . offences against the law of nations." This provision would seem to give the legislative branch primary control over the treatment of custom, but legislation is seldom based on this provision. Treaties are the "Supreme Law of the Land" according to the supremacy clause, although later-in-time statutes can supersede them. Thus Congress and the President can together supersede a treaty adopted by the President and Senate alone.

These examples illustrate the great variety of ways in which states treat international law vis-à-vis domestic obligations. There is no necessary relationship between the treatment of customary international law and treaty law, nor any general convergence among states in terms of the manner in which they treat international obligations. ∎

QUESTIONS

1. From a policy perspective, wherein lie the advantages of a monist approach to international law? Wherein lie the disadvantages?

2. Why might some countries be more open to a monist approach than others?

B. TREATY PROVISIONS

In the case of the European Union, the direct effect question had its own special flavor and combined a number of issues: Should European law be treated as just another type of international law, such that the traditional national approaches to the monism/dualism debate should apply to EU law as well? Or should EU law be treated as a different type of supranational law, so that the traditional approaches to international law would not apply? And who would get to decide this question? Would the Court of Justice define a mandatory and uniform approach for all Member States, or would each Member State be entitled to define their own position regarding the effect of European Union law?

In the case law of the Court of Justice, these questions first arose with respect to the Treaty Establishing the European Economic Community, today's European Union. Many treaty provisions were—and still are—written in such a way that their wording does not expressly address the issue of whether they create rights for individuals. For example, Article 34 of the Treaty on the Functioning of the European Union prohibits quantitative restrictions on imports as well as measures having equivalent effect. But does this mean that an individual can invoke Article 34 before a national court? Or does a violation simply imply that a Member State that imposes quantitative restrictions on imports can be sued by the Commission or by another Member State? The Court of Justice has long opted for a generous position. According to the Court, treaty provisions have direct effects as long as they are "clear and unconditional."

NV ALGEMENE TRANSPORTEN EXPEDITIE ONDERNEMING VAN GEND & LOOS V. NETHERLANDS INLAND REVENUE ADMINISTRATION

E.C.J., Case 26/62, Feb. 15, 1963, 1963 E.C.R. 1 (citations omitted)

[Article 12 of the EEC Treaty—now superseded by Article 30 TFEU—provided that "[c]ustoms duties on imports and exports and charges having equivalent effect shall be prohibited between Member States." The Netherlands changed the tariff classification for a certain chemical. This change in classification meant that a higher tariff applied. In the ensuing litigation, the question arose whether private parties could invoke the prohibition in Article 12 EEC [30 TFEU] in Member State courts.]

[. . .] The first question . . . is whether [the general prohibition against increasing existing customs duties in] Article 12 of the Treaty [30 TFEU] has direct application in national law in the sense that nationals of member states may on the basis of this article lay claim to rights which the national court must protect.

To ascertain whether the provisions of an international treaty extend so far in their effects it is necessary to consider the spirit, the general scheme and the wording of those provisions.

The objective of the EEC Treaty, which is to establish a Common Market, the functioning of which is of direct concern to interested parties in the Community, implies that this Treaty is more than an agreement which merely creates mutual obligations between the contracting states. This view is confirmed by the Preamble to the Treaty which refers not only to governments but to peoples. It is also confirmed more specifically by the establishment of institutions endowed with sovereign rights, the exercise of which affects member states and also their citizens. Furthermore, it must be noted that the nationals of the states brought together in the Community are called upon to cooperate in the functioning of this Community through the intermediary of the European Parliament and the Economic and Social Committee.

In addition the task assigned to the Court of Justice under Article 177 [267 TFEU], the object of which is to secure uniform interpretation of the treaty by national courts and tribunals, confirms that the states have acknowledged that community law has an authority which can be invoked by their nationals before those courts and tribunals. The conclusion to be drawn from this is that the community constitutes a new legal order of international law for the benefit of which the states have limited their sovereign rights, albeit within limited fields, and the subjects of which comprise not only member states but also their nationals. Independently of the legislation of Member States, Community law therefore not only imposes obligations on individuals but is also intended to confer upon them rights which become part of their legal heritage. These rights arise not only where they are expressly granted by the treaty, but also by reason of obligations which the Treaty imposes in a clearly defined way upon individuals as well as upon the Member States and upon the institutions of the Community.

With regard to the general scheme of the Treaty as it relates to customs duties and charges having equivalent effect, it must be emphasized that Article 9 28 TFEU], which bases the community upon a customs union, includes as an essential provision the prohibition of these customs duties and charges. This provision is found at the beginning of the part of the Treaty which defines the "foundations of the community". It is applied and explained by Article 12 [now Article 30 TFEU].

The wording of Article [30 TFEU] contains a clear and unconditional prohibition which is not a positive but a negative obligation. This obligation, moreover, is not qualified by any reservation on the part of states which would make its implementation conditional upon a positive legislative measure enacted under national law. The very nature of this prohibition makes it ideally adapted to produce direct effects in the legal relationship between member states and their subjects.

The implementation of Article [30 TFEU] does not require any legislative intervention on the part of the states. The fact that under this Article it is the Member States who are made the subject of the negative obligation does not imply that their nationals cannot benefit from this obligation.

In addition the argument based on Articles 169 and 170 of the treaty [259, 260 TFEU], which the three governments submitted to the court in their statements of case, is misconceived. The mere fact that these articles enable the Commission and the Member States to bring states that have not fulfilled their obligations before the court does not mean that individuals cannot plead these obligations before a national court. By that same logic the commission's power to ensure that obligations imposed upon the Treaty's subjects are observed could preclude the possibility of pleading infringements of these obligations in actions between individuals before a national court.

A restriction of the guarantees against an infringement of Article 12 [30 TFEU] by Member States to the procedures under [259 TFEU] and [260 TFEU] would remove all direct legal protection of the individual rights of their nationals. There is the risk that recourse to the procedure under these articles would be [ineffective] if it were to occur after the implementation of a national decision taken contrary to the provisions of the Treaty.

The vigilance of individuals concerned to protect their rights amounts to an effective supervision in addition to the supervision entrusted by [Article 259 TFEU] and [Article 260 TFEU] to the diligence of the commission and of the Member States.

It follows from the foregoing considerations that, according to the spirit, the general scheme and the wording of the Treaty, Article 12 [30 TFEU] must be interpreted as producing direct effects and creating individual rights which national courts must protect. . . . ■

NOTES AND QUESTIONS

1. The Court maintains that the EEC Treaty's objective of creating a common market implies that the Treaty is "more than an agreement which merely creates mutual obligations between the contracting states." Do you agree?

2. The Court also invokes the preliminary rulings procedure as evidence in support of its argument. Do you agree that Article 267 TFEU implies that EU law has direct effect? Can you imagine a situation in which EU law is not directly applicable, but the national Court still refers a question of interpretation to the Court of Justice?

3. One of the arguments advanced by the Court of Justice is that recognizing the direct effect of EU law will allow individuals to protect their rights—thereby complementing the enforcement proceeding as a mechanism to ensure that the Member States adhere to EU law. Is this reasoning circular?

4. As a practical matter, which mechanism do you believe is more important in securing adherence to EU law—the direct effect of EU law or enforcement proceedings?

5. Following *van Gend & Loos*, many of the central provisions of the Treaties were found to be directly applicable. This is true, for example, for most of the basic provisions that constitute the fundamental freedoms.

THE TRANSFORMATION OF EUROPE
J.H.H. Weiler
100 YALE L.J. 2403, 2413–2414 (1991)

The implications of [the doctrine of direct effect] were and are far reaching. The European Court reversed the normal presumption of public international law whereby international legal obligations are . . . addressed to states. Public international law typically allows the internal constitutional order of a state to determine the method and extent to which international obligations may, if at all, produce effects for individuals within the legal order of the state. Under the normal canons of international law, even when the international obligation itself, such as a trade agreement or a human rights convention, is intended to bestow rights (or duties) on individuals within a state, if the state fails to bestow the rights, the individual cannot invoke the international obligation before national courts, unless internal constitutional or statutory law, to which public international law is indifferent, provides for such a remedy. The typical remedy under public international law in such a case would be an inter-state claim. The main import of the Community doctrine of direct effect was not simply the conceptual change it ushered forth. In practice direct effect meant that Member States violating their Community obligations could not shift the locus of dispute to the interstate or Community plane. They would be faced with legal actions before their own courts at the suit of individuals within their own legal order.

Individuals (and their lawyers) noticed this practical implication, and the number of cases brought on the basis of this doctrine grew exponentially. Effectively, individuals in real cases and controversies (usually against state public authorities) became the principal "guardians" of the legal integrity of Community law within Europe similar to the way that individuals in the United States have been the principal actors in ensuring the vindication of the Bill of Rights and other federal law. ∎

QUESTIONS

1. According to Joseph Weiler, why is the direct effect doctrine of great practical importance?

2. Do you think that EU law might have developed very differently if the Court of Justice had not developed the direct effect doctrine? Explain!

C. REGULATIONS

Regulations are the EU equivalent of federal statutes. As Article 288(2) TFEU makes clear, regulations are "binding in [their] entirety and directly applicable in all Member States."[4] In conjunction with the direct

---

[4] TFEU, art. 288(2).

effect doctrine, this implies that no action on the part of the Member States is necessary in order for regulations to have direct effect for the European Union's citizens.

Incidentally, could the Court of Justice have argued that the Treaty's provisions on regulations provide a direct answer to the monism v. dualism debate? The answer is no. By their wording, traditional international treaties also seem to create direct rights and duties for individuals. Dualists, however, maintain that even if a Treaty purports to create direct rights and duties for individuals, it cannot have any effect within national legal systems unless the nations that are parties to the treaty transpose it into their national law. In other words, Article 288(2) TFEU decrees that regulations are directly applicable. But Article 288(2) can only have that effect because the Court of Justice has opted for a monist approach regarding the relationship between European Union law and Member State law.

D. DIRECTIVES

According to Article 288(3) TFEU, "[a] directive shall be binding, as to the result to be achieved, upon each Member State to which it is addressed, but shall leave to the national authorities the choice of form and methods."[5] In other words, the basic idea is that directives specify the outcome to be achieved and that Member States should then adopt national legislation that secures the relevant outcome. This seems to imply that directives should only impose obligations on Member States and that only the national legislation transposing the directive into Member State law should have direct effect for individuals.

Note that this approach does not contradict the Court of Justice's position that EU law can have direct effect. Even monism does not posit that all Treaties must create rights and/or duties for individuals. It only maintains that international treaties *can* create such duties. In other words, the fact that the Court of Justice has taken the position that EU law *can* have direct effect does not imply that all of EU law *must* have direct effect.

Even though Article 288(3) TFEU does not at all contradict the direct effect principle embraced in *van Gend & Loos*, the European Court of Justice has gradually chipped away at the principle that directives lack direct effect. It still remains true that in litigation between two private parties, the general rule is that neither party can directly invoke a directive that has not yet been implemented. In other words, directives lack *horizontal* direct effect: they do not have any direct impact on the relationship between two private parties. Nevertheless, even directives that have not been transposed into national law are quite relevant to

---

[5] *Id.*

individuals. There are three main ways in which such directives acquire importance.

The first and most important one is known as *vertical direct* effect, and it constitutes an explicit exception from the principle that directives lack direct effect: if a directive is unconditional and sufficiently precise and the prescribed time for transposing the directive has expired, then individuals *can* invoke the directive in proceedings against the Member State that has failed to transpose it.[6] For example, if a directive gives the EU citizens the unconditional right to reside in another Member State for a certain period of time, that directive is directly applicable once the deadline for transposing it has expired.

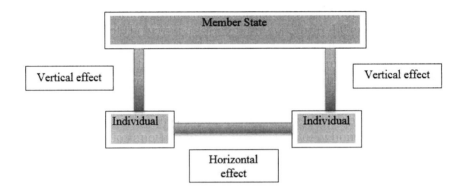

Second, there are some cases where the dividing line between horizontal cases and vertical cases is not all that clear. In such situations, the Court has shown a certain tendency to frame cases as vertical, thereby allowing the Court to directly apply the directive. In such cases, one may speak of a *quasi-horizontal* direct effect, since the relevant cases do in fact involve litigation between private parties. The most important examples are cases in which construction or other permits are issued to a private party in violation of a directive and another private party, e.g. the neighbor, objects. Such cases have a horizontal dimension, because they essentially involve a conflict between two private parties, but they also have a vertical dimension in that the government has exercised its public power by issuing a permit.

The third area in which directives are relevant to private parties concerns the interpretation of Member State law. While the rule remains that directives are not *directly* applicable between private individuals, such directives can gain indirect relevance in that they may determine the meaning of Member State law: In the words of the Court of Justice, "when national courts apply domestic law, they are bound to interpret it, to the

---

[6] Case C-194/08, Susanne Gassmayr v. Bundesminister für Wissenschaft und Forschung, 2010 E.C.R. I-6281 paras. 44–45.

fullest extent possible, in the light of the wording and the purpose of the directive concerned in order to achieve the result sought by the directive and consequently comply with the third paragraph of Article 288 TFEU."[7]

The principle that Member State law has to be interpreted in conformity with EU law—including directives—does not constitute an explicit exception from the principle that directives lack direct effect between private individuals. However, in many cases, the result is the same: it matters little whether a plaintiff or defendant can directly invoke a directive, or whether he invokes some vague provision of national law—such as a good faith requirement—that is then interpreted to require exactly the same as the directive.

In the following sections, all three of the above-described phenomena—the vertical direct effect of directives, their quasi-horizontal direct effect, and the requirement to interpret national law in conformity with EU law—will be discussed in more detail.

1. VERTICAL DIRECT EFFECT

According to the well established case law of the Court of Justice, once the time for transposing a directive has expired, the directive has *direct vertical effect* as long as it is unconditional and sufficiently precise.[8] In the Court's own words:

> According to settled case-law, whenever the provisions of a directive appear, so far as their subject-matter is concerned, to be unconditional and sufficiently precise, they may be relied on before the national courts by individuals against the State where the latter has failed to implement the directive in domestic law by the end of the period prescribed or where it has failed to implement the directive correctly.[9]

To justify the direct effect of directives, the Court of Justice has invoked two main arguments. First, a Member State should not profit from the fact that it has failed to transpose the directive within the prescribed time.[10] Second, the recognition of a vertical direct effect increases the effectiveness of directives.[11] How persuasive do you find these arguments? Can they also be invoked in favor of recognizing a direct horizontal effect?

---

[7] Case C-109/09, Deutsche Lufthansa AG v. Gertraud Kumpan, 2011 E.C.R. I-1309 para. 52.

[8] ECJ, Case C-194/08, Susanne Gassmayr v. Bundesminister für Wissenschaft und Forschung, 2010 E.C.R. I-6281 para. 44.

[9] *Id.*

[10] *Cf.* ECJ, Case 148/78, Criminal proceedings against Tullio Ratti, E.C.R. 1979, 1629 para. 22 ("[A] Member State which has not adopted the implementing measures required by the directive in the prescribed periods may not rely, as against individuals, on its own failure to perform the obligations which the directive entails.").

[11] *Id.* 21.

The precondition that the time has expired for transposing the directive is quite clear. The other two, namely that the directive be *unconditional* and *sufficiently precise*, are somewhat less determinate.

a) Unconditional

The requirement that the directive be unconditional has been clarified as follows:

> 45. A provision of European Union law is unconditional where it sets forth an obligation which is not qualified by any condition, or subject, in its implementation or effects, to the taking of any measure either by the institutions of the European Union or by the Member States.[12]

This definition nicely illustrates the purpose of the *unconditional*-prong: if a directive makes it clear that its provisions shall not be applicable until some EU institution or a Member State takes further action, then it would be contrary to the intention of the legislature to give that directive direct effect.

However, it is important to note that some provisions of a directive can be unconditional while others are not. Moreover, in those cases where the directive allows the Member States to choose between different options, the directive can still be unconditional as long as it imposes a minimum obligation on the Member State that can be clearly identified.[13]

For example, assume that a directive limits the fees that the Member States can impose, but gives Member States the choice between different levels of fees. In that case, the directive can be said to impose an unconditional obligation to the extent that it imposes some upper limit on the fees that can legally be levied by the Member States.[14]

b) Sufficiently Precise

The Court of Justice has also clarified the requirement that the directive be sufficiently precise. According to the Court, a directive "is sufficiently precise to be relied on by an individual and applied by a court where it sets out an obligation in unequivocal terms."[15] While this definition is still a bit vague, the idea simply seems to be that the directive must be clear enough so that a vertical application is possible even in the absence of any measure transposing the directive into Member State law.

---

[12] ECJ, Case C-194/08, Susanne Gassmayr v. Bundesminister für Wissenschaft und Forschung, 2010 E.C.R. I-6281 para. 45.

[13] Case C-374/97, Anton Feyrer v. Landkreis Rottal-Inn, 1999 E.C.R. I-5153 ¶ 27.

[14] *Id.*

[15] Case C-194/08, Susanne Gassmayr v. Bundesminister für Wissenschaft und Forschung, 2010 E.C.R. I-6281 ¶ 45.

ANDREA FRANCOVICH & DANILA BONIFACI ET AL. V. ITALIAN REPUBLIC

E.C.J., Joined cases C-6/90 and C-9/90, November 19, 1991, 1991 E.C.R. I-5357
(citations omitted)

[Community Directive 80/987 required the Member States to provide a certain minimum level of protection to employees in the case of their employer's insolvency. More specifically, under the directive, the Member States were to take measures to ensure that employees could collect their wages even if the employer fell into insolvency.

Italy failed to transpose the directive in a timely fashion. Andrea Francovich and the other plaintiffs were employees of an insolvent company. They sued Italy for damages in an Italian Court. Among other things, the plaintiffs argued that the directive had vertical direct effect. The Italian court asked the European Court of Justice for a preliminary ruling.]

11. As the Court has consistently held, a Member State which has not adopted the implementing measures required by a directive within the prescribed period may not, against individuals, plead its own failure to perform the obligations which the directive entails. Thus wherever the provisions of a directive appear, as far as their subject-matter is concerned, to be unconditional and sufficiently precise, those provisions may, in the absence of implementing measures adopted within the prescribed period, be relied upon as against any national provision which is incompatible with the directive or in so far as the provisions of the directive define rights which individuals are able to assert against the State.

12. It is therefore necessary to see whether the provisions of Directive 80/987 which determine the rights of employees are unconditional and sufficiently precise. There are three points to be considered: the identity of the persons entitled to the guarantee provided, the content of that guarantee and the identity of the person liable to provide the guarantee. [. . .]

13. With regard first of all to the identity of the persons entitled to the guarantee, it is to be noted that, according to Article 1(1), the directive applies to employees' claims arising from contracts of employment or employment relationships and existing against employers who are in a state of insolvency . . . .

14. Those provisions are sufficiently precise and unconditional to enable the national court to determine whether or not a person should be regarded as a person intended to benefit under the directive. . . .

15. With regard to the content of the guarantee, Article 3 of the directive provides that measures must be taken to ensure the payment of outstanding claims resulting from contracts of employment or employment

relationships and relating to pay for the period prior to a date determined by the Member State, which may choose one of three possibilities: (a) the date of the onset of the employer's insolvency; (b) that of the notice of dismissal issued to the employee concerned on account of the employer's insolvency; (c) that of the onset of the employer's insolvency or that on which the contract of employment or the employment relationship with the employee concerned was discontinued on account of the employer's insolvency.

16. Depending on the choice it makes, the Member State has the option, under Article 4(1) and (2), to restrict liability to periods of three months or eight weeks respectively, calculated in accordance with detailed rules laid down in that article. Finally, Article 4(3) provides that the Member States may set a ceiling on liability, in order to avoid the payment of sums going beyond the social objective of the directive. . . .

17. Article 3 of the directive thus leaves the Member State a discretion in determining the date from which payment of claims must be ensured. However, as is already implicit in the Court's case-law, the right of a State to choose among several possible means of achieving the result required by a directive does not preclude the possibility for individuals of enforcing before the national courts rights whose content can be determined sufficiently precisely on the basis of the provisions of the directive alone.

18. In this case, the result required by the directive in question is a guarantee that the outstanding claims of employees will be paid in the event of the insolvency of their employer. The fact that Articles 3 and 4(1) and (2) give the Member States some discretion as regards the means of establishing that guarantee and the restriction of its amount do not affect the precise and unconditional nature of the result required.

19. As the Commission and the plaintiffs have pointed out, it is possible to determine the minimum guarantee provided for by the directive by taking the date whose choice entails the least liability for the guarantee institution. That date is that of the onset of the employer's insolvency, since the two other dates, that of the notice of dismissal issued to the employee and that on which the contract of employment or the employment relationship was discontinued, are, according to the conditions laid down in Article 3, necessarily subsequent to the onset of the insolvency and thus define a longer period in respect of which the payment of claims must be ensured.

20. The possibility under Article 4(2) of limiting the guarantee does not make it impossible to determine the minimum guarantee. It follows from the wording of that article that the Member States have the option of limiting the guarantees granted to employees to certain periods prior to the date referred to in Article 3. Those periods are fixed in relation to each of the three dates provided for in Article 3, so that it is always possible to

determine to what extent the Member State could have reduced the guarantee provided for by the directive depending on the date which it would have chosen if it had transposed the directive.

21. As regards Article 4(3), according to which the Member States may set a ceiling on liability in order to avoid the payment of sums going beyond the social objective of the directive, and Article 10, which states that the directive does not affect the option of Member States to take the measures necessary to avoid abuses, it should be observed that a Member State which has failed to fulfil its obligations to transpose a directive cannot defeat the rights which the directive creates for the benefit of individuals by relying on the option of limiting the amount of the guarantee which it could have exercised if it had taken the measures necessary to implement the directive.

22. It must therefore be held that the provisions in question are unconditional and sufficiently precise as regards the content of the guarantee.

23. Finally, as regards the identity of the person liable to provide the guarantee, Article 5 of the directive provides that:

"Member States shall lay down detailed rules for the organization, financing and operation of the guarantee institutions, complying with the following principles in particular: (a) the assets of the institutions shall be independent of the employers' operating capital and be inaccessible to proceedings for insolvency; (b) employers shall contribute to financing, unless it is fully covered by the public authorities; (c) the institutions' liabilities shall not depend on whether or not obligations to contribute to financing have been fulfilled."

24. It has been submitted that since the directive provides for the possibility that the guarantee institutions may be financed entirely by the public authorities, it is unacceptable that a Member State may thwart the effects of the directive by asserting that it could have required other persons to bear part or all of the financial burden resting upon it.

25. That argument cannot be upheld. It follows from the terms of the directive that the Member State is required to organize an appropriate institutional guarantee system. Under Article 5, the Member State has a broad discretion with regard to the organization, operation and financing of the guarantee institutions. The fact, referred to by the Commission, that the directive envisages as one possibility among others that such a system may be financed entirely by the public authorities cannot mean that the State can be identified as the person liable for unpaid claims. The payment obligation lies with the guarantee institutions, and it is only in exercising its power to organize the guarantee system that the State may provide that the guarantee institutions are to be financed entirely by the public

authorities. In those circumstances the State takes on an obligation which in principle is not its own.

26. Accordingly, even though the provisions of the directive in question are sufficiently precise and unconditional as regards the determination of the persons entitled to the guarantee and as regards the content of that guarantee, those elements are not sufficient to enable individuals to rely on those provisions before the national courts. Those provisions do not identify the person liable to provide the guarantee, and the State cannot be considered liable on the sole ground that it has failed to take transposition measures within the prescribed period.

27. The answer to the first part of the first question must therefore be that the provisions of Directive 80/987 which determine the rights of employees must be interpreted as meaning that the persons concerned cannot enforce those rights against the State before the national courts where no implementing measures are adopted within the prescribed period. . . . ■

NOTES AND QUESTIONS

1. According to the Court, Directive 80/987 is sufficiently precise and unconditional regarding the content of the guarantee as well as regarding the persons entitled to the guarantee, but not with respect to the person liable. How does the Court justify this conclusion? Why does the Court feel able to identify a "minimum" duty regarding the content of the guarantee, but not regarding the person liable?

2. Do you think the Commission could have succeeded in bringing an enforcement proceeding against Italy for failure to implement the directive despite the directive's lack of clarity? If yes, should we be surprised that the Commission did not initiate such a proceeding?

3. As we shall see later on in this casebook, the fact that the directive was not directly applicable did not leave the plaintiffs unprotected. Rather, *Francovich* was the case in which the Court developed the doctrine that Member States can be held liable for damages if they fail to transpose directives in a timely manner.

2. QUASI-HORIZONTAL EFFECT

According to the well-established case law of the Court of Justice, directives cannot be invoked *horizontally*. That is, they do not create rights or duties directly between private individuals. However, in some cases, the dividing line between vertical direct effect and horizontal direct effect becomes fuzzy. Essentially, these cases fall into one of two categories.

First, there are so-called triangular cases involving both a Member State and two private parties. Typically, one private party objects to a permit granted to another private party on the ground that the granting of the permit violates EU law. In these cases, too, the Court has recognized a direct effect of directives on the ground that the effect really is a vertical one: the party fighting the permit is asserting a right vis-à-vis the Member State, not a right against a third party.[16]

Second, there are situations where a directive imposes certain procedural requirements that the Member States have to respect in order to enact valid legislation and where a Member State's legislation violates those procedural requirements. In that case, the Court has allowed private parties to invoke the nullity of the relevant Member State legislation vis-à-vis other private parties.[17] The Court's main argument was that this is not a matter of direct effect, since the directive itself does not create rights or duties—it only invalidates national legislation.[18]

UNILEVER ITALIA SpA V. CENTRAL FOOD SpA
E.C.J., Case C-443/98, Sept. 26, 2000, 2000 E.C.R. I-7535 (citations omitted)

[Diverging technical standards for goods in the various Member States make it difficult to market goods throughout the European Union. Against that background, Council Directive 83/189/EEC imposes certain duties on Member States when they promulgate technical standards. In particular, Article 8(1) of that Directive requires the Member States to provide the Commission immediately with any draft of any technical regulation. Moreover, Article 9 of the same directive requires the Member States to postpone the adoption of any such draft for a period of three months after the Commission has received the draft.

In 1998, Italy adopted a law that governed the labeling of olive oil. However, Italy failed to postpone the adoption of the draft as prescribed by Article 9(1).

In the litigation underlying the case at hand, Unilever Italia SpA ("Unilever") had entered into a contract for the sale of olive oil to Central Food SpA ("Central Food"). The question was whether Unilever had breached that contract by delivering improperly labeled olive oil. This, in turn, depended on whether the Italian statute governing the labeling of olive oil was applicable. Unilever argued that the Italian law on labeling could not be applied because its enactment violated Directive 83/189/EEC. However, the question was whether this directive could be invoked in litigation between two private parties.

The Italian court requested a preliminary ruling from the Court of Justice.]

---

[16] E.C.J., Case C-431/92, Commission of the European Communities v. Federal Republic of Germany, 1995 E.C.R. I-2189 para. 26 (failure to assess the environmental impact of a project before granting development consent).

[17] E.C.J., Case C-443/98, Unilever Italia Spa v. Central Food Spa, 2000 E.C.R. I-7535 para. 52.

[18] *Cf. id.* para. 51.

45. It is therefore necessary to consider . . . whether the inapplicability of technical regulations adopted in breach of Article 9 of Directive 83/189 can be invoked in civil proceedings between private individuals concerning contractual rights and obligations.

46. First, in civil proceedings of that nature, application of technical regulations adopted in breach of Article 9 of Directive 83/189 may have the effect of hindering the use or marketing of a product which does not conform to those regulations.

47. That is the case in the main proceedings, since application of the Italian rules is liable to hinder Unilever in marketing the extra virgin olive oil which it offers for sale. [. . .]

50. Whilst it is true . . . that a directive cannot of itself impose obligations on an individual and cannot therefore be relied on as such against an individual, that case-law does not apply where non-compliance with Article 8 or Article 9 of Directive 83/189, which constitutes a substantial procedural defect, renders a technical regulation adopted in breach of either of those articles inapplicable.

51. In such circumstances, and unlike the case of non-transposition of directives with which the case-law cited by those two Governments is concerned, Directive 83/189 does not in any way define the substantive scope of the legal rule on the basis of which the national court must decide the case before it. It creates neither rights nor obligations for individuals.

52. In view of all the foregoing considerations, the answer to the question submitted must be that a national court is required, in civil proceedings between individuals concerning contractual rights and obligations, to refuse to apply a national technical regulation which was adopted during a period of postponement of adoption prescribed in Article 9 of Directive 83/189. ■

NOTES AND QUESTIONS

1. The Court maintains that Directive 83/189 "creates neither rights nor obligations for individuals." But is this correct? Does the directive create the right for Unilever to market olive oil that does not conform to the labeling provisions of the relevant Italian statute?

2. Perhaps the most plausible interpretation of the decision is that national rules are inapplicable between private parties if their enactment violated important procedural requirements imposed by EU directives. Can you think of a good policy argument why the horizontal effect of directives is or is not more acceptable in this scenario than in other cases? Can private parties be expected to know of such procedural violations?

3. States most often violate directives by not implementing them in a timely fashion. What do you think are the reasons for such delay? Now consider

directives imposing procedural requirements for national legislation like Council Directive 83/189/EEC. Why do you think states might violate such procedural requirements?

3. THE REQUIREMENT TO INTERPRET MEMBER STATE LAW IN CONFORMITY WITH EU LAW

Even if directives cannot be applied directly, this does not at all mean that they are without relevance for the relationship between private parties. This is because courts applying national law "are bound to interpret it to the fullest extent possible" in conformity with EU law.[19] In other words, to the extent that Member State law leaves room for interpretation, Member State courts have to look to EU law to determine which interpretation to choose. This requirement is of immense practical importance because the national legal rules governing contractual and other relationships between private parties tend to be full of vague standards.

MARLEASING SA v. LA COMERCIAL INTERNACIONAL DE ALIMENTACION SA

Case C-106/89, Nov. 13, 1990, 1990 E.C.R. 1990, I-4135 (citations omitted)

[La Comercial Internacional de Alimentacion SA—hereinafter: "Comercial"—was a public limited company formed under Spanish law.[20] Public limited companies are the Spanish equivalent of public corporations. According to the Spanish Civil Code, contracts concluded for an unlawful purpose are void. At some point, Comercial sued another company, Marleasing. Marleasing argued that the suit should be dismissed because Comercial had been formed for fraudulent purposes such that its formation was void. Comercial countered that the nullity of public limited companies was governed by European Community law. In fact, Directive 68/151/EEC contained an exhaustive enumeration of circumstances that could lead to the nullity of a company, but that list did not include formation for an illegal purpose. The problem, in this case, was that Spain had not yet transposed the directive into national law. Against this backdrop, the Spanish Court asked the Court of Justice for a preliminary ruling to clarify the role of the directive.]

4. ... [T]he national court referred the following question to the Court: "Is Article 11 of Council Directive 68/151/EEC ..., which has not been implemented in national law, directly applicable so as to preclude a declaration of nullity of a public limited company on a ground other than those set out in the said article?"

---

[19] ECJ, Case C-109/09, Deutsche Lufthansa AG v. Gertraud Kumpan, 2011 E.C.R. I-1309 para. 52.

[20] Para. 2.

6. ... [A]s the Court has consistently held, a directive may not of itself impose obligations on an individual and, consequently, a provision of a directive may not be relied upon as such against such a person.

7. However, it is apparent from the documents before the Court that the national court seeks in substance to ascertain whether a national court hearing a case which falls within the scope of Directive 68/151 is required to interpret its national law in the light of the wording and the purpose of that directive in order to preclude a declaration of nullity of a public limited company on a ground other than those listed in Article 11 of the directive.

8. In order to reply to that question, it should be observed that ... the Member States' obligation arising from a directive to achieve the result envisaged by the directive and their duty under Article 5 of the Treaty [now Article 4 TEU] to take all appropriate measures, whether general or particular, to ensure the fulfilment of that obligation, is binding on all the authorities of Member States including, for matters within their jurisdiction, the courts. It follows that, in applying national law, whether the provisions in question were adopted before or after the directive, the national court called upon to interpret it is required to do so, as far as possible, in the light of the wording and the purpose of the directive in order to achieve the result pursued by the latter and thereby comply with the third paragraph of Article 189 of the Treaty [now Article 288 TFEU].

9. It follows that the requirement that national law must be interpreted in conformity with Article 11 of Directive 68/151 precludes the interpretation of provisions of national law relating to public limited companies in such a manner that the nullity of a public limited company may be ordered on grounds other than those exhaustively listed in Article 11 of the directive in question. ■

NOTES AND QUESTIONS

1. According to the Court of Justice, what is the doctrinal basis for the duty of Member State courts to interpret national law in conformity with EU law?

2. From a legal policy perspective, can you think of any arguments in favor of or against the principle that Member State law should be interpreted in conformity with EU law? How does such a rule affect the citizens of the European Union? Will they be more likely to reap the benefits of EU legislation? Will they be more likely to misunderstand the meaning of their own Member State's law because they fail to take into account the fact that that law has to be interpreted in conformity with EU law? How does the rule that national law must be interpreted in conformity with EU law affect the incentives of states that are wondering whether or not to implement EU directives in a timely fashion?

3. The principle that national law has to be interpreted in accordance with EU law raises an interesting question in those cases where EU law employs vague, indeterminate standards rather than precise rules. One example is Council Directive 93/13/EEC of 5 April 1993 on unfair terms in consumer contracts.[21] According to Article 6(1) of the directive, the Member States shall ensure that unfair terms in a consumer contract are not binding on the consumer. Furthermore, Article 3(1) makes it clear that a "contractual term which has not been individually negotiated shall be regarded as unfair if, contrary to the requirement of good faith, it causes a significant imbalance in the parties' rights and obligations arising under the contract, to the detriment of the consumer."

Consider the following hypothetical: Alpha is a Member State of the European Union. It has transposed Council Directive 93/13/EEC by adopting a general prohibition against unfair terms in consumer contracts. In litigation between two Alphanian parties, one of them a merchant and the other a consumer, the question arises whether a forum selection clause in a consumer contract is valid. The relevant clause designates a court in the city where the merchant is headquartered as the exclusive forum for all litigation between the parties. The consumer maintains that this clause is unfair and therefore invalid under Alphanian law; the merchant argues that it is not. The case eventually reaches the Alphanian Supreme Court which wonders whether it must refer the question to the Court of Justice. Could you argue that any question pertaining to the interpretation of the term "unfair" in national consumer contract legislation has to be referred to the Court of Justice because the question of what is unfair depends on how the term "unfair" in Council Directive 93/13/EEC has to be interpreted? Would this be a desirable outcome?

KONSTANTINOS ADENELER ET AL. V. ELLINIKOS ORGANISMOS GALAKTOS (ELOG)

E.C.J., Case C-212/04, July 4, 2006, 2006 E.C.R. I-6057 (citations omitted)

[In the United States, firms can hire and fire employees whenever they wish—a principle known as employment at will. By contrast, in many European countries, the basic rule is that employees can only be fired for cause. Against that background, employment contracts with a fixed duration are typically something that European workers consider to be undesirable. That is because with a fixed duration contract, the employment relationship ends once the term specified in the contract has been completed unless the employer decides to offer the employee a new contract. By contrast, in case of an employment contract of unspecified duration, the employee keeps his job and the employer cannot fire him unless he has cause to do so.

Left to their own devices, some employers might try to circumvent the for-cause rule by hiring employees for a fixed term and then offering them

---

[21] O.J. L 95, April 21, 1993, 29–34.

new fixed-term contracts when the need arises. For that reason, Member State law typically limits the ability of employers to resort to fixed-term contracts, and so does EU law. A so-called Framework Agreement annexed to Directive 1999/70 requires Member States to "prevent abuse arising from the use of successive fixed-term employment contracts." There are various ways for Member States to meet this requirement. For example, they can limit the maximum *number* of permissible renewals, impose an upper limit for the total aggregate *duration* of repeated fixed term employment contracts, or require employers to show objective reasons for relying on successive fixed-term contracts. In the case at hand, the plaintiffs were employed on the basis of a series of fixed-term employment contracts. They believed that the contract clauses that limited the duration of their employment contracts violated E.U. rules on fixed-term employment contracts and were therefore void. They brought suit and sought a judicial declaration that the relevant contracts had to be viewed as employment contracts of unlimited duration.

The relevant E.U. legislation had not yet been transposed into Greek law. Therefore, the Greek court considered the possibility that existing Greek law had to be interpreted in conformity with European law. However, one of the key issues in the case was timing. At the time that the fixed-term employment contracts at issue had been signed, the deadline for transposing the directive into Member State law had not yet expired.

Against this background, the Greek court asked the Court of Justice for a preliminary ruling. Inter alia, the Greek court wanted to know at what point in time the duty to interpret national law in conformity with EU law would arise.]

107. [T]his question is essentially designed to determine—where a directive is transposed belatedly into a Member State's domestic law and the relevant provisions of the directive do not have direct effect—the time from which the national courts are required to interpret rules of domestic law in conformity with those provisions. Specifically, the referring court is unsure whether the relevant point in time is the date on which the directive in question was published in the Official Journal of the European Communities and which corresponds to the date on which it entered into force for the Member States to which it was addressed, the date on which the period for transposing the directive expired or the date on which the national provisions implementing it entered into force.

108. When national courts apply domestic law, they are bound to interpret it, so far as possible, in the light of the wording and the purpose of the directive concerned in order to achieve the result sought by the directive and consequently comply with the third paragraph of Article 249 EC [now Article 288 TFEU]. This obligation to interpret national law in conformity

with Community law concerns all provisions of national law, whether adopted before or after the directive in question.

109. The requirement for national law to be interpreted in conformity with Community law is inherent in the system of the Treaty, since it permits national courts, for the matters within their jurisdiction, to ensure the full effectiveness of Community law when they determine the disputes before them. . . .

114. . . . [B]efore the period for transposition of a directive has expired, Member States cannot be reproached for not having yet adopted measures implementing it in national law.

115. Accordingly, where a directive is transposed belatedly, the general obligation owed by national courts to interpret domestic law in conformity with the directive exists only once the period for its transposition has expired.

116. It necessarily follows from the foregoing that, where a directive is transposed belatedly, the date . . . on which the national implementing measures actually enter into force in the Member State concerned does not constitute the relevant point in time. Such a solution would be liable seriously to jeopardise the full effectiveness of Community law and its uniform application by means, in particular, of directives.

117. In addition, . . . it should be pointed out that it is already clear from the Court's case-law that the obligation on Member States, under the second paragraph of Article 10 EC [now Article 4 TEU], the third paragraph of Article 249 EC [now Article 288(3) TFEU] and the directive in question itself, to take all the measures necessary to achieve the result prescribed by the directive is binding on all national authorities, including, for matters within their jurisdiction, the courts.

118. Also, directives are either (i) published in the Official Journal of the European Communities in accordance with Article 254(1) EC [now Article 297(1) TFEU] and, in that case, enter into force on the date specified in them or, in the absence thereof, on the 20th day following that of their publication, or (ii) notified to those to whom they are addressed, in which case they take effect upon such notification, in accordance with Article 254(3) EC [now Article 297(3) TFEU].

119. It follows that a directive produces legal effects for a Member State to which it is addressed—and, therefore, for all the national authorities—following its publication or from the date of its notification, as the case may be.

121. In accordance with the Court's settled case-law, it follows from the second paragraph of Article 10 EC [now Article 4(3)(2) TEU] in conjunction with the third paragraph of Article 249 EC [Article 288(3) TFEU] and the directive in question itself that, during the period prescribed for

transposition of a directive, the Member States to which it is addressed must refrain from taking any measures liable seriously to compromise the attainment of the result prescribed by it. In this connection it is immaterial whether or not the provision of national law at issue which has been adopted after the directive in question entered into force is concerned with the transposition of the directive.

122. Given that all the authorities of the Member States are subject to the obligation to ensure that provisions of Community law take full effect, the obligation to refrain from taking measures, as set out in the previous paragraph, applies just as much to national courts.

123. It follows that, from the date upon which a directive has entered into force, the courts of the Member States must refrain as far as possible from interpreting domestic law in a manner which might seriously compromise, after the period for transposition has expired, attainment of the objective pursued by that directive. ∎

NOTES AND QUESTIONS

1. According to the Court of Justice, the general duty to interpret national law in conformity with a directive "exists only once the period for its transposition has expired." On what argument does the Court base this view? Do you agree with the Court's position?

2. The Court also points out that "from the date upon which a directive has entered into force, the courts of the Member States must refrain as far as possible from interpreting domestic law in a manner which might seriously compromise, after the period for transposition has expired, attainment of the objective pursued by that directive." How can this statement be reconciled with the previously cited statement that the general duty to interpret national law in conformity with the directive "exists only once the period for its transition has expired"?

3. How real is the danger that an interpretation of a national statute by a Member State court which was adopted before the deadline for implementing a directive had expired will compromise the attainment of the directive's goals?

4. Does your answer to the previous question depend on whether the relevant Member State adheres to the common law tradition in which legal precedents are binding or to the civil law tradition in which precedents are not deemed to be formally binding? Note that even in civil law countries, courts typically attach substantial importance to prior decisions.

5. In many respects, the legal protections enjoyed by workers vary strongly across Member States. In particular, there are no uniform rules on when employers can fire workers.[22] While Member State laws generally

---

[22] Cf. Carol D. Rasnic, *Balancing Respective Rights in the Employment Contract: Contrasting the U.S. "Employment-at-Will" Rule with the Worker Statutory Protections Against Dismissal in European Community Countries*, 4 J. INT'L L. & PRAC. 441, 478–93 (1995) (summarizing the law

require cause for dismissal, they diverge greatly on what constitutes such cause as well as on when exactly the for-cause rule applies. Is the dismissal of employees an area where harmonization, that is, the introduction of uniform rules, seems desirable? Or are there good reasons why Member State laws should be allowed to differ in this area?

6. Whereas the general rules on firing employees have not, so far, been harmonized, there is one area of employment law where EU law plays a particularly important role: EU law contains wide-ranging protections against employment discrimination. The relevant directives include Directive 2006/54/EC (gender discrimination in employment); Directive 2000/43/EC (discrimination based on racial or ethnic origin); and Directive 2000/78/EC (discrimination based on disability, sexual orientation, religion or belief and age). Importantly, these directives allow Member States to offer additional protections beyond what is required by EU law.

7. Why do you think the Member States have managed to agree on EU-wide protections against discrimination in the workplace, despite the fact that no such agreement has been possible on the general question of when employers should be allowed to fire employees?

8. Does the rule that employees can only be fired for cause render employment discrimination law more important or less important?

---

governing the termination of employees in Austria, Denmark, Finland, Luxembourg, the Netherlands, Portugal, Spain, Sweden, and the United Kingdom); Carol Daugherty Rasnic, *Die Kündigung, Licenciement, Recesso dal Contrato, Firing, or Sacking: Comparing European and American Laws on Management Prerogatives and Discretion in Termination Decisions*, 18 IND. INT'L & COMP. L. REV. 19, 24–66 (2008) (describing the law governing termination decisions in various European countries); Michael Kittner & Thomas C. Kohler, *Conditioning Expectations: The Protection of the Employment Bond in German and American Law*, 21 COMP. LAB. L. & POL'Y J. 263, 314 (2000) (summarizing the German rules on the termination of employees).

CHAPTER 8

THE SUPREMACY OF EU LAW

∎ ∎ ∎

One of the central principles of European Union law is the so-called supremacy principle: in case of a conflict between EU law and Member State law, EU law prevails. This principle is also referred to as the primacy of EU law or as the precedence of EU law.

Note that the direct effect doctrine and the supremacy doctrine are closely related. If the Court of Justice had opted for a dualist model in which EU law and national law exist in different spheres, it would be impossible for EU law and national law to clash. However, because of the direct effect principle, both national law and EU law claim to govern the legal relationships between citizens and Member States as well as between citizens. As a result, it becomes necessary to determine which legal system prevails in case of a conflict. The supremacy principle answers that question by giving priority to EU law.

It should be noted, however, that national law violating EU law is not void. Rather, the consequence of such a violation is that, in the specific case, the relevant Member State law cannot be applied. Accordingly, the supremacy of EU law is often referred to as a primacy in application rather than primacy in validity.

A. FLAMINIO COSTA V. E.N.E.L.

The landmark case that established the supremacy of EU law is *Flaminio Costa v. E.N.E.L.*[1]

FLAMINIO COSTA V. E.N.E.L.
E.C.J., Case 6/64, July 15, 1964, E.C.R. 1964, 585

[In a proceeding before an Italian court, one party claimed that several of the relevant Italian statutory provisions and presidential decrees violated the Treaty Establishing the European Economic Community. The Italian court thereupon requested a preliminary ruling from the Court of Justice. In this context, the Court of Justice addressed the question to what extent Community law enjoyed priority over the law of the Member States.]

---

[1] E.C.J., Case 6/64, July 15, 1964, E.C.R. 1964, 585.

By contrast with ordinary international treaties, the EEC Treaty has created its own legal system which, on the entry into force of the treaty, became an integral part of the legal systems of the Member States and which their courts are bound to apply.

By creating a Community of unlimited duration, having its own institutions, its own personality, its own legal capacity and capacity of representation on the international plane and, more particularly, real powers stemming from a limitation of sovereignty or a transfer of powers from the states to the community, the member states have limited their sovereign rights, albeit within limited fields, and have thus created a body of law which binds both their nationals and themselves.

The integration into the laws of each member state of provisions which derive from the Community, and more generally the terms and the spirit of the Treaty, make it impossible for the states, as a corollary, to accord precedence to a unilateral and subsequent measure over a legal system accepted by them on a basis of reciprocity. Such a measure cannot therefore be inconsistent with that legal system. [T]he executive force of Community law cannot vary from one state to another in deference to subsequent domestic laws, without jeopardizing the attainment of the objectives of the Treaty set out in Article 5(2) [now Article 3 TEU] and giving rise to the discrimination prohibited by [A]rticle 7 [now Article 18 TFEU].

The obligations undertaken under the Treaty establishing the Community would not be unconditional, but merely contingent, if they could be called in question by subsequent legislative acts of the signatories. Wherever the [T]reaty grants the states the right to act unilaterally, it does this by clear and precise provisions. . . . Applications, by member states for authority to derogate from the treaty are subject to a special authorization procedure . . . which would lose their purpose if the member states could renounce their obligations by means of an ordinary law.

The precedence of Community law is confirmed by Article 189 [now Article 288 TFEU], whereby a regulation "shall be binding" and "directly applicable in all member states". This provision, which is subject to no reservation, would be quite meaningless if a state could unilaterally nullify its effects by means of a legislative measure which could prevail over community law.

It follows from all these observations that the law stemming from the Treaty, an independent source of law, could not, because of its special and original nature, be overridden by domestic legal provisions, however framed, without being deprived of its character as Community law and without the legal basis of the Community itself being called into question.

The transfer by the states from their domestic legal system to the Community legal system of the rights and obligations arising under the treaty carries with it a permanent limitation of their sovereign rights, against which a subsequent unilateral act incompatible with the concept of the Community cannot prevail. . . . ∎

NOTES AND QUESTIONS

1. The Court argues, inter alia, that "the terms and the spirit of the Treaty make it impossible for the states . . . to accord precedence to a unilateral and subsequent measure over a legal system accepted by them on a basis of reciprocity." How persuasive is that argument?

2. The Court also argues that Article 189 [now Article 288] "would be quite meaningless if a state could unilaterally nullify its effects by means of a legislative measure which could prevail." Is this true?

3. Is it correct to assert, as the Court does, that "[t]he obligations undertaken under the Treaty establishing the Community would . . . be . . . merely contingent, if they could be called in question by subsequent legislative acts of the signatories"? Does the Court's argument imply that, as a general rule, international treaties only impose contingent duties?

4. As a legal policy matter, can you think of arguments supporting the supremacy of EU law? What would be the likely consequences if EU law did not prevail over conflicting Member State law?

5. The Court goes to great length to stress that EU law has a "special and original nature." In the Court's opinion, what exactly are the features that give EU law its special and original nature? Do you agree with the Court?

6. Assuming that the supremacy of EU law is in fact desirable from a policy perspective, does it follow that other international treaties should also enjoy supremacy over national law?

B. SUBSEQUENT CASES

The *Costa* decision laid the foundation for the supremacy doctrine. However, it took several more cases to establish this doctrine in its present form.

1. MEMBER STATE LAW PREDATING THE ESTABLISHMENT OF THE EUROPEAN ECONOMIC COMMUNITY

In *Costa*, the Court only noted that "subsequent" Member State legislation could not prevail against Community law. It did not address the question of whether the same was true for Member State law predating the Treaty Establishing the European Economic Community. In a later case, *Simmenthal*, the Court filled that gap and made it clear that the supremacy of EU law did not depend on whether national law predated or postdated the Treaty:

[E]very national court must, in a case within its jurisdiction, apply Community law in its entirety and protect rights which the latter confers on individuals and must accordingly set aside any provision of national law which may conflict with it, whether prior or subsequent to the Community rule.[2]

Do you think that the case for EU law's supremacy is stronger vis-à-vis national law predating the Treaty or vis-à-vis law postdating the Treaty?

2. MEMBER STATE CONSTITUTIONAL LAW

Another question left open by *Costa* was whether the supremacy principle also applied in case of a conflict between EU law and the constitutional—as opposed to statutory—law of the Member States. In *Internationale Handelsgesellschaft,* the Court answered this question in the affirmative:

> Recourse to the legal rules or concepts of national law in order to judge the validity of measures adopted by the institutions of the Community would have an adverse effect on the uniformity and efficacy of Community law. The validity of such measures can only be judged in the light of Community law. In fact, the law stemming from the Treaty, which is an independent source of law, by its very nature cannot be overridden by rules of national law, however framed, without depriving it of its character as Community law and calling into question the legal basis of the community itself. Therefore the validity of a Community measure or its effect within a member state cannot be affected by allegations that it runs counter to either fundamental rights as formulated by the constitution of that state or the principles of a national constitutional structure.[3]

3. MEMBER STATE ADMINISTRATIVE ACTS

The Court also extended the supremacy doctrine beyond Member State law in the strict sense (statutes and cases), to administrative acts of the Member States:

> 31. ... [P]rovisions of national law which conflict with ... a provision of Community law may be legislative or administrative. ...
>
> 33. There is no reason why the legal protection which individuals derive from the direct effect of provisions of Community law and

---

[2] E.C.J., Case 106/77, Amministrazione delle Finanze dello Stato v. Simmenthal SpA, 1978 page 629 para. 21.

[3] Case 11-70, Internationale Handelsgesellschaft mbH v. Einfuhr und Vorratsstelle für Getreide und Futtermittel, E.C.R. 1970, 1125, para. 3.

which the national courts must ensure should be refused to those individuals in cases where the dispute concerns the validity of an administrative measure. The existence of such protection cannot depend on the nature of the conflicting provision of national law.

4. MEMBER STATE JUDICIAL DECISIONS

The most difficult question arises in regard to decisions by Member State courts. If a judicial decision violates EU law, does this mean that the judicial decision has to be ignored? On the one hand, one could argue that ignoring court decisions that violate EU law would increase the effectiveness of EU law. On the other hand, the impact of such a rule on legal certainty would be highly troublesome. In *Kapferer*, the Court opted for a compromise.[4]

ROSMARIE KAPFERER V. SCHLANK & SCHICK GMBH
Case C-234/04, 16 March 2006, 2006 E.C.R. I-2585 (citations omitted)

[As part of an advertising campaign, Schlank & Schick GmbH, a German mail order company, sent Ms. Kapferer a letter, personally addressed to her, which conveyed the impression that Ms. Kapferer had won a prize. Ms. Kapferer lived in Austria, and under Austrian consumer protection law, such letters allow the consumer to actually claim the prize.

EU law provides that in consumer contract cases, the courts in the consumer's state of domicile have jurisdiction to hear cases brought by the consumer. Accordingly, Ms. Kapferer filed suit against Schlank & Schick in an Austrian district court. Schlank & Schick, however, asserted that the court lacked jurisdiction because a mere letter could not suffice to form a contract and that therefore, the consumer contract necessary to establish the jurisdiction of Austrian courts was lacking.

The Austrian district court affirmed its jurisdiction, but rejected Ms. Kapferer's claim on the merits. Schlank & Schick did not appeal this decision because of the favorable outcome on the merits. Ms. Kapferer, however, brought an appeal.

The Austrian court of appeals once more addressed the jurisdictional question. More specifically, the court considered the possibility that the district court's decision to affirm its own jurisdiction might have violated EU law. At this point, the court of appeal faced the following problem:

On the one hand, Schlank & Schick had not appealed the lower court's decision to affirm its own jurisdiction. Under Austrian law, this meant that the jurisdictional issue could no longer be raised.

---

[4] Case C-234/04, Rosmarie Kapferer v. Schlank & Schick GmbH, 2006 E.C.R. I-2585.

On the other hand, the court of appeals thought that the lower court's decision might have violated EU law, and so the question was whether, as a matter of European law, the lower court's decision had to be set aside anyway to secure the supremacy of EU law. To clarify this issue, the Austrian court of appeals requested a preliminary ruling from the Court of Justice.]

19. ... [T]he referring court asks essentially whether, and, where relevant, in what conditions, the principle of cooperation arising from Article 10 EC [now Article 3 TEU] imposes on a national court an obligation to review and set aside a final judicial decision if that decision should infringe Community law.

20. In that regard, attention should be drawn to the importance, both for the Community legal order and national legal systems, of the principle of res judicata. In order to ensure both stability of the law and legal relations and the sound administration of justice, it is important that judicial decisions which have become definitive after all rights of appeal have been exhausted or after expiry of the time-limits provided for in that connection can no longer be called into question.

21. Therefore, Community law does not require a national court to disapply domestic rules of procedure conferring finality on a decision, even if to do so would enable it to remedy an infringement of Community law by the decision at issue.

22. By laying down the procedural rules for proceedings designed to ensure protection of the rights which individuals acquire through the direct effect of Community law, Member States must ensure that such rules are not less favourable than those governing similar domestic actions (principle of equivalence) and are not framed in such a way as to render impossible in practice the exercise of rights conferred by Community law (principle of effectiveness). However, compliance with the limits of the power of the Member States in procedural matters has not been called into question in the dispute in the main proceedings as regards appeal proceedings. . . .

24. Having regard to the foregoing considerations, the answer to [the question referred by the Austrian court of appeal] must be that the principle of cooperation under Article 10 EC [3 TEU] does not require a national court to disapply its internal rules of procedure in order to review and set aside a final judicial decision if that decision should be contrary to Community law. ∎

QUESTIONS

1. According to the Court of Justice, do Member State courts enjoy a special status with respect to the primacy of EU law?

2. Given that the Court of Justice does not require that national courts suspend their internal rules of procedure to set aside final judicial decisions, how does the Court ensure that the Member States do not use their procedural rules as a way of circumventing the supremacy of EU law?

3. Does the Court of Justice's approach to the supremacy principle create an incentive for Member States to let courts rather than lawmakers create new legal principles?

C. SUPREMACY: PRIORITY IN APPLICATION

As noted in the introduction, a conflict between EU law and Member State law does not imply that Member State law is void. Rather, the conflict simply means that, in the particular case, the pertinent provision of Member State law cannot be applied. Consider the following passage from the Court's decision in *IN.CO.GE.'90*:

> 20. ... [I]n Simmenthal, the Court held that every national court must, in a case within its jurisdiction, apply Community law in its entirety and protect rights which the latter confers on individuals, setting aside any provision of national law which may conflict with it, whether prior or subsequent to the Community rule.
>
> 21. It cannot ... be inferred from the judgment in Simmenthal that the incompatibility with Community law of a subsequently adopted rule of national law has the effect of rendering that rule of national law non-existent. Faced with such a situation, the national court is, however, obliged to disapply that rule, provided always that this obligation does not restrict the power of the competent national courts to apply, from among the various procedures available under national law, those which are appropriate for protecting the individual rights conferred by Community law.[5]

NOTES AND QUESTIONS

1. That a violation of EU law does not render the relevant Member State rules void is of great practical importance. In many cases, the scope of application of EU rules is limited to certain areas. For example, the so-called *fundamental freedoms* such as the free movement of goods apply to cross-border activities, but do not apply to purely domestic situations. If a violation of EU law rendered national rules void, then courts would have to abstain from applying these rules regardless of whether the situation before them is covered by EU law. However, since a breach of EU law merely bars the application of Member State law in the specific case, the relevant Member State rules can still be applied to those situations that do not fall within the ambit of EU law.

---

[5] E.C.J., Joined cases C-10/97 to C-22/97, Ministero delle Finanze v. IN.CO.GE.'90 Srl et al., 1998 E.C.R. I-6307.

2. One result of the Court's position is a phenomenon sometimes referred to as "reverse discrimination."[6] Some norms in EU law, most notably the fundamental freedoms that we will discuss in later chapters, apply only in those cases that have some cross-border element. For example, the so-called free movement of goods applies when goods produced in one state are sold in another state, whereas it does not apply to purely domestic situations: A baker in Germany selling bread to consumers in the Netherlands is protected by the free movement of goods, but a baker in the Netherlands selling bread to Dutch customers is not. This means that some burdensome Member State laws may be perfectly legal when applied to purely domestic situations, but illegal when applied to cross-border situations.

For example, assume, hypothetically, that the Netherlands enacts a statute according to which bread must not contain salt. Such a statute violates the free movement of goods of foreign producers selling their bread in the Netherlands because it limits, without sufficient justification, their ability to sell their products in the Netherlands. Yet at the same time, the no-salt rule does not fall afoul of EU law when applied to Dutch bakers selling their bread in the Netherlands because that case is purely domestic in nature and thus does not fall within the scope of application of the free movement of goods. As a result, foreign bakers exporting their bread to the Netherlands are better off than Dutch bakers selling their bread in the Netherlands.

The Court of Justice has consistently held that such "reverse discrimination" does not violate European law since it simply follows from the fact that the scope of application of the fundamental freedoms is limited.[7] Crucially, this problem arises only because a Member State law violating EU law is rendered inapplicable rather than void. If the no-salt statute were *void*, then it would no longer apply to anyone, including Dutch bakers selling their bread in the Netherlands. However, since Member State law is only *inapplicable* in those cases where it violates EU law, said Member State law remains in force and can therefore still be applied in those situations that are purely domestic in nature.

3. Can you think of any policy argument for why "reverse discrimination" in this sense is not a major concern? Consider again the example of the no-salt rule. Is the relevant regulation likely to endure? Assuming that Member States understand that they will not be able to apply the no-salt rule to foreign producers, are they likely to adopt such a rule in the first place?

---

[6] *See, e.g.*, Case C-127/08, Blaise Baheten Metock et al. v. Minister for Justice, Equality and Law Reform, 2008 E.C.R. I-6241 para. 76 (noting that several governments had argued that a particular interpretation of EU law would lead "to unjustified reverse discrimination, in so far as nationals of the host Member State who have never exercised their right of freedom of movement would not derive" the rights at issue from Community law).

[7] *Id.* para. 77–78.

D. THE SUPREMACY OF EU LAW AND THE MEMBER STATE COURTS

While the European Court of Justice has always been consistent in insisting on the supremacy of EU law, this does not mean that the Member State courts have always been willing to accept this position. The most famous opposition came from the German Constitutional Court.

"SOLANGE I"
Case BvL 52/71, May 29, 1974, German Constitutional Court, Second Chamber
(citations omitted, translation by author)

... In accordance with the case law of the Court of Justice, the Senate [i.e. one of the two chambers of the Constitutional Court] adheres to its case law according to which Community law is neither part of the national legal system nor part of international law. Instead, it constitutes an independent legal system flowing from an autonomous source of law; for the Community is no nation, particularly no federal system, but a Community *sui generis* in the process of progressive integration ...

It follows that the two legal systems [the German legal system and the legal system of the European Economic Community] are binding concurrently and independently of each other. Accordingly ... the Community institutions including the Court of Justice have to decide over the binding character, the interpretation, and the observance of Community law, whereas the competent national institutions have to decide over the binding character, the interpretation, and the observance of the Constitutional law of the Federal Republic of Germany. The European Court of Justice cannot make a binding decision as to whether a norm of Community law is compatible with the [German Constitution], and neither can the German Constitutional Court decide whether—and with what content—a norm or secondary Community law is compatible with primary Community law.

This [division of responsibilities] does not cause any difficulties as long as the two legal systems do not come into conflict with each other. Therefore, the special relationship that the establishment of the Community has created between the Community and the Member States, creates a special duty for the competent institutions, especially for the ... European Court of Justice and the German Constitutional Court: their first objective must be to strive for the mutual compatibility of the two legal systems involved.

It is not enough, in this context, to simply speak of the supremacy of EU law vis-à-vis the national Constitutions in order to justify the [desired] result that Community law can always claim priority over national law on the ground that otherwise the Community would be put into question.

Article 25 of the German Constitution provides that the general rules of international law enjoy priority over German statutory law, but not over German constitutional law. This provision does not put into question international law. Neither is a foreign legal system put into question when [under the rules governing the conflict of laws], that legal system has to give way to the German *ordre public*. Accordingly, Community law is not put into question either, if, in exceptional cases, Community law cannot claim priority over mandatory Constitutional law.

The duties of the Federal Republic of Germany (and of all other Member States) under the Treaty are not unidirectional. Rather, under the spirit of the Treaties, the Community, too, is required to do its part in solving the conflict at issue. That means searching for a resolution which is compatible with the mandatory Constitutional law of the Federal Republic of Germany. Therefore, invoking this principle does not constitute a violation of the Treaty. Rather, it simply initiates the process under the Treaty, by which, within the European institutions, the conflict can be resolved by political means.

Article 24 of the German constitution allows the transfer of sovereign rights to international organizations. This [provision, however,] cannot be taken literally. Like every other provision in the Constitution, Article 24 has to be understood and interpreted within the context of the Constitution as a whole. Article 24 of the German Constitution does not create a mechanism for changing the fundamental structure of the Constitution . . . through rules adopted by an international organization without [formally amending the Constitution]. Admittedly, the competent Community institutions can enact laws that the competent German institutions could not enact under the German Constitution—laws that are nonetheless directly binding and applicable in the Federal Republic of Germany. However, Article 24 limits what is possible in this respect. Article 24 does not allow a change to the Treaty that would eliminate the identity of the current Constitution of the Federal Republic of Germany by interfering with the very structures that constitute this Constitution. The same limit is imposed on rules of secondary Community legislation based on a particular interpretation of the Treaty inasmuch as such secondary legislation interferes with the essential structures of the [German Constitution]. Article 24 of the German Constitution does not, properly speaking, authorize the transfer of sovereign rights. Rather, this provision opens up the national legal system (within the limits described above) such that the Federal Republic of Germany's exclusive claim to sovereign power . . . leaves room . . . for the direct validity and application of a law from another source within the national sovereign sphere.

One essential part of the current [German Constitution] which cannot be ceded is that part of the German Constitution that contains the [constitutionally guaranteed civil rights]. Article 24 of the German

Constitution does not authorize unlimited changes to this Part of the Constitution. In this context, the present state of integration of the European Community is of decisive importance. The Community still lacks a Parliament, that has direct democratic legitimacy, is elected via a general election, has the power to legislate and can hold the [other] institutions involved in the legislative process fully accountable... [In addition,] the Community ... lacks a codified catalogue of civil rights the content of which is guaranteed as clearly and unambiguously for the future as that of the German Constitution—a catalogue of civil rights that would allow a ... determination, whether the level of protection ... accorded to fundamental rights under the law of the European Community is sufficient to permanently secure the level of protection for fundamental rights prescribed by the German Constitution in such a way that the limit imposed by Article 24 is not violated.

The case law of the European Court of Justice, which is admittedly favorable to the protection of civil rights, is not sufficient to [guarantee such a permanent level of protection for fundamental rights under European Community law]. And as long as the progressive integration of the European Community fails to secure [such a permanent level of protection for civil rights], the limit imposed by Article 24 of the German Constitution remains applicable. Thus, we are dealing with a legal problem that is owed solely to the still ongoing progressive process of integration of the Community and that will be solved as the present phase of transition comes to an end.

Thus, for the present time, any ... conflict between Community law with certain norms of national Constitutional law, namely with the civil rights guaranteed by the Constitution, raises the question which law prevails and thereby leads to the inapplicability of the other law. In this conflict of norms, the civil rights guaranteed by the German Constitution prevail as long as the competent institutions of the Community have not eliminated the conflict of norms...

The protection of the civil rights guaranteed by the German Constitution falls ... solely within the responsibility of the German Constitutional Court.... No other court can take over that task from the German Constitutional Court. Accordingly, to the extent that German citizens have a right to judicial protection of their civil rights by the German Constitution, their status must not suffer any deterioration, simply because the courts or administrative institutions that have interfered with their German rights were enforcing Community law. Otherwise, the judicial protection accorded to a citizen's most elementary rights would become substantially incomplete.

In any case, what is true for a free and democratic federal state also remains true for the free and democratic Constitution of a Community of

States: It cannot harm the Community and its free (and democratic) Constitution if the Members [of the Community], in their Constitution, provide stronger guarantees of their citizens basic rights than the Community itself does. . . .

The result can be summarized as follows: As long as the process of integration of the Community has not advanced so far that Community law contains a catalogue of civil rights that is in force and that has been adopted by a Parliament, a catalogue of civil rights that adequately secures the fundamental rights guaranteed by the catalogue of civil rights of the German Constitution, [German courts]—once they have obtained a preliminary ruling from the European Court of Justice under Article 177 of the Treaty [now Article 267 TFEU]—are both authorized and required to [request a decision by the German Constitutional Court] if these German courts believe that the relevant provision of European Community law, as interpreted by the European Court of Justice, is inapplicable because and to the extent that it violates one of the civil rights guaranteed by the German Constitution. ∎

NOTES AND QUESTIONS

1. The decision above is aptly named "Solange I" ("As-long-as I") after the decisive sentence in its concluding paragraph; the "I" being a Roman numeral indicating that this is the first of two decisions on this issue. Many scholars credit *Solange I* with motivating the European Court of Justice to develop strong protections for civil rights.[8] However, this view is by no means uncontroversial. Manfred Zuleeg, a former judge at the European Court of Justice, called this narrative a "myth" and insisted that the Court of Justice's push towards greater protections for civil rights at the Community level began long before the German Constitutional Court's decision.[9]

2. The German Constitutional Court is rather dismissive of some of the arguments that the Court of Justice had previously invoked to defend the supremacy of Community law. Does the Constitutional Court's reasoning do justice to the arguments of the Court of Justice?

3. The German Constitutional Court finds itself in the uncomfortable position of having to justify why it wants to second-guess legislation adopted by an institution based on an international Treaty that Germany has signed and ratified. In other words, the German Constitutional Court has to defend its approach against the anticipated criticism that Germany is breaching its duties under the Treaty Establishing the European Economic Community. How does the German Constitutional Court forestall that criticism? In other

---

[8] *E.g.*, Cathryn Costello, *The Bosphorus Ruling of the European Court of Human Rights: Fundamental Rights and Blurred Boundaries in Europe*, 6 HUM. RTS. L. REV. 87 (2006); Ward Ferdinandusse, *Out of the Black-Box? The International Obligation of State Organs*, 29 BROOK. J. INT'L L. 45, 138–39 (2003).

[9] Manfred Zuleeg, *A Community of Law: Legal Cohesion in the European Union*, 20 FORDHAM INT'L L.J. 623, 627 (1997).

words, what arguments does the Court advance that suggest that Germany is not breaching the Treaty Establishing the European Economic Community by scrutinizing European law under the civil rights guaranteed by the German Constitution?

4. If Member State courts were to refuse to apply EU law in more than a handful of cases, what would the consequences be for the European Union?

5. Part of the reason why Germany's Constitutional Court refused to recognize the supremacy of European law lies in a peculiar feature of German Constitutional law, the so-called eternity clause (*Ewigkeitsgarantie*). Most national constitutions are entirely subject to later amendments. However, that is not true for the German Constitution. According to its Article 79(3), certain core principles of German constitutional law, including the commitment to democracy, the rule of law, and the inviolability of human dignity, are beyond the reach of constitutional amendments, and so is the eternity clause itself. It is not difficult to see a certain tension between the eternity clause on the one hand and an unconditional transfer of sovereignty to the European Union on the other hand. Why do you think the Framers of the German Constitution included the eternity clause?

The *Solange I* decision was not the last word on the matter. When, in 1986, the German Constitutional Court was confronted with the supremacy issue once more, it opted for a more generous position.

"SOLANGE II"
German Constitutional Court, Case 2 BvR 197/83, Oct. 22, 1986, BVerfGE 73, 399
(citations omitted, translation by author)

In its decision of May 29, 1974, . . . the Constitutional Court made it clear that in light of the state of integration at the time, the level of protection generally accorded to civil rights in the European Communities was insufficient to guarantee with the necessary certainty, that this level of protection would permanently . . . be adequate to ensure that the limits, which Article 24 imposes on the application of secondary Community law . . . within the sovereign sphere of the Federal Republic of Germany, are not exceeded. . . .

It is the view of this Court that the level of protection afforded to civil rights within the . . . European Community has now reached the point where . . . it has to be considered essentially equal to that . . . of the German Constitution. All of the main institutions of the Community have, by now, made legally meaningful commitments to respect, as legally binding, . . . the civil rights, as they are guaranteed by the Constitutions of the Member States and by the European Convention of Human Rights. There is no persuasive evidence that the present state of the protection afforded to civil rights in the Community is insufficiently secured or merely of a temporary nature. . . .

Compared to the level of protection for civil rights guaranteed by the German Constitution, the level of protection afforded to such rights by way of the case law of the Court of Justice of the European Community, which has naturally been developed on a case by case basis, may still contain certain gaps. . . . However, what matters is the general attitude that the European Court of Justice now shows vis-à-vis the Community's obligation to respect civil rights . . . as well as the actual importance that civil rights have now gained in the case law of the European Court of Justice. While the relevant declarations of the Community's institutions . . . may not be part of primary Community law and while the Community is not, as such, a Member of the European Convention of Human Rights, these declarations are legally relevant both within the Community and in the relationship between the Community and the Member States. They attest, in a formal manner, to the unanimous legal position of the Member States and the Community institutions that the Community is bound by the civil rights as they flow from the Member State Constitutions and, as general [ ] legal principles, are part of primary Community law. Moreover, as a unanimous declaration of an intent to apply the Community Treaties in a certain way, these declarations, under international law, are relevant to the interpretation of the Treaties. These declarations also reinforce the competence and the duty of the Court of Justice, to secure the protection of civil rights . . . according to its rules of procedure. These rules of procedure are . . . designed in a way, that generally secure[s] an effective protection of civil rights which has to be considered essentially equal to that which is inalienably guaranteed by the German Constitution. . . .

In its decision from May 29, 1974, this Court pointed out that the Community lacked a parliament with direct democratic legitimacy and with members elected in general elections, a parliament that had the power to legislate and could hold the institutions involved in the legislative process fully politically accountable. However, this [critique] was [merely] an element of the state of integration as it presented itself at the time. The reason for this statement was . . . the idea that the protection of civil rights must begin at the level of legislation and that parliamentary accountability provides an effective mechanism of protection in this context. By contrast, this Court was not trying to postulate a Constitutional requirement that had to be met before this Court could decline to exercise its jurisdiction over secondary Community law. . . .

In light of this development, we hold: As long as the European Communities, particularly by way of the decisions of the European Court of Justice, generally guarantee an effective protection of civil rights against the governmental powers of the Communities, and as long as this protection is essentially equal to that which the German Constitution views as inalienable, the German Constitutional Court will no longer exercise its jurisdiction over the applicability of secondary Community law on which German courts and administrative bodies . . . base their actions. Accordingly, under these conditions, the Court will no longer scrutinize such law under the standards imposed by the civil rights of the German Constitution. It follows that applications of such a nature . . . are inadmissible. ∎

NOTES AND QUESTIONS

1. The *Solange II* decision represents a substantial step towards the recognition of the supremacy of EU law by the German Constitutional Court. Apart from the improved protection of civil rights in the European Community, what other factors, do you think, might have prompted the German Constitutional Court to be more generous this time around?

2. In *Solange II*, the German Constitutional Court faced an obvious dilemma. In its earlier *Solange I* decision, the Court had held that it would continue to scrutinize European Community law under the civil rights guaranteed by the German Constitution as long as the Community did not have "a binding catalogue of civil rights that has been adopted by a Parliament," and, in addition, the German Constitutional Court had based its decision in part on the lack of a directly elected European Parliament. In *Solange II*, the German Constitutional Court announced that it would no longer subject Community law to scrutiny under the German Constitution's civil rights. However, technically speaking, its earlier demands had not been met. While the members of the European Parliament had been directly elected since 1979—and hence since before *Solange II*—the European Parliament took a clear backseat to the Council in matters of legislation. Moreover, when the German Constitutional Court handed down the *Solange II* decision in 1986, the Community still lacked a binding catalogue of civil rights (as opposed to mere case law recognizing civil rights). How does the German Constitutional Court finesse these issues without expressly overruling its earlier opinion?

3. Interestingly, current EU law meets both of the German Constitutional Court's original demands. The European Parliament now has direct democratic legitimacy because its members are elected "by direct universal suffrage in a free and secret ballot."[10] Moreover, it is the main legislative body, albeit together with the Council.[11] Furthermore, EU law now contains a binding catalogue of civil rights. In fact, this latter requirement is now met for two reasons. First, the European Union is now itself a party to the European Convention of Human Rights, which means that the catalogue of civil rights contained in that convention is now formally binding on the European Union.[12] Second, Article 6(3) of the Treaty on European Union now

---

[10] TEU, art. 14(3).

[11] TEU, art. 14(1).

[12] The Treaty on European Union itself calls upon the European Union to accede to the European Convention of Human Rights. TEU, art. 6(2).

explicitly incorporates the civil rights guaranteed by the European Convention on Human Rights into European Union law by providing that "[f]undamental rights, as guaranteed by the European Convention for the Protection of Human Rights and Fundamental Freedoms and as they result from the constitutional traditions common to the Member States, shall constitute general principles of the Union's law."[13]

4. Germany was not the only country where the supremacy principle was only gradually and reluctantly accepted. Other Member States witnessed similar controversies.[14] Over the years, however, the courts in the Member States accepted the position that, as a practical matter and notwithstanding theoretical reservations, Member State law (whether statutory or constitutional) conflicting with EU law must be set aside.[15]

5. Finally, a short note on the terminology employed in this chapter seems in order. The rights known to American constitutionalists as civil rights, such as the right to free speech, bear different names elsewhere. In the European Convention of Human Rights, they are referred to as human rights. In the German Constitution, the so-called Basic Law (Grundgesetz), they are named basic rights, and in EU law, they are often termed fundamental rights to distinguish them from the fundamental freedoms such as the free movement of goods. To avoid confusion, this chapter has generally used the term civil rights.

---

[13] TEU, art. 6(3).

[14] Rett R. Ludwikowski, *Supreme Law or Basic Law? The Decline of the Concept of Constitutional Supremacy*, 9 CARDOZO J. INT'L & COMP. L. 253, 281–87 (2001); Craig T. Smith & Thomas Fetzer, *The Uncertain Limits of the European Court of Justice's Authority: Economic Freedom versus Human Dignity*, 10 COLUM. J. EUR. L. 445, 470 (2004).

[15] Ludwikowski, at 281–87.

CHAPTER 9

STATE LIABILITY FOR VIOLATIONS OF EU LAW

■ ■ ■

We have already discussed various mechanisms designed to ensure that the Member States adhere to EU law. On the procedural side, the enforcement proceeding allows the Commission as well as other Member States to react to violations of EU law. On the side of substantive law, the rules governing the direct effect of EU law play an important role: to the extent that Member State courts are called upon to give direct effect to EU law, Member State governments cannot escape EU law by refusing to transpose it into national legislation. For the same reason, the duty to interpret national law in conformity with EU law contributes to the enforcement of EU law.

In this chapter, we will discuss yet another way of securing the Member States' adherence to EU law, namely the principles governing state liability for breaching EU law: under certain conditions, individual plaintiffs can demand damages from Member States that have violated their obligations under EU law. According to the case law of the Court of Justice, "the principle of State liability for loss and damage caused to individuals as a result of breaches of EU law for which the State can be held responsible" is "inherent in the legal order of the Union."[1] In its recent *Infrabouw* decision, the Court summarized the preconditions for state liability as follows:

> The Court has held that individuals harmed have a right to reparation where three conditions are met: the rule of EU law infringed must be intended to confer rights on them; the breach of that rule must be sufficiently serious; and there must be a direct causal link between the breach and the loss or damage sustained by the individuals.[2]

---
[1] Case C-568/08, Spijker Infrabouw-De Jonge Konstruktie v. Provincie Drenthe. 2010 E.C.R. 2010 para. 87.
[2] *Id.*

A. THE ORIGIN OF THE STATE LIABILITY DOCTRINE

Neither the Treaty on European Union nor the Treaty on the Functioning of the European Union explicitly mentions the principle that states can be held liable for violations of EU law. Rather, the doctrine of state liability was developed by the Court of Justice. The leading case is the 1991 *Francovich* decision which remains one of the most well-known and important cases in EU law. To this day, it defines many of the principles governing state liability.

ANDREA FRANCOVICH & DANILA BONIFACI ET AL. V. ITALIAN REPUBLIC

Joined cases C-6/90 and C-9/90, November 19, 1991, 1991 E.C.R. I-5357
(citations omitted)

[Community Directive 80/987 required the Member States to provide a certain minimum level of protection to employees in the case of their employer's insolvency. Italy failed to transpose this directive by the deadline that the directive specified. Andrea Francovich and the other plaintiffs were employees whose employer had become insolvent. They sued Italy for damages in an Italian Court. The Italian court asked the European Court of Justice for a preliminary ruling.

In the first part of the decision, the Court holds that the directive cannot be applied directly because the it is not sufficiently clear and precise. That part of the decision was discussed in Chapter 7 of this casebook.

In the second part of the decision, the Court focuses on whether the States can at least be held liable for damages.]

28. ... [T]he national court seeks to determine whether a Member State is obliged to make good loss and damage suffered by individuals as a result of the failure to transpose Directive 80/987.

29. The national court thus raises the issue of the existence and scope of a State's liability for loss and damage resulting from breach of its obligations under Community law.

30. That issue must be considered in the light of the general system of the Treaty and its fundamental principles.

(a) The existence of State liability as a matter of principle

31. It should be borne in mind at the outset that the EEC Treaty has created its own legal system, which is integrated into the legal systems of the Member States and which their courts are bound to apply. The subjects of that legal system are not only the Member States but also their nationals. Just as it imposes burdens on individuals, Community law is

also intended to give rise to rights which become part of their legal patrimony. Those rights arise not only where they are expressly granted by the Treaty but also by virtue of obligations which the Treaty imposes in a clearly defined manner both on individuals and on the Member States and the Community institutions

32. Furthermore, it has been consistently held that the national courts whose task it is to apply the provisions of Community law in areas within their jurisdiction must ensure that those rules take full effect and must protect the rights which they confer on individuals.

33. The full effectiveness of Community rules would be impaired and the protection of the rights which they grant would be weakened if individuals were unable to obtain redress when their rights are infringed by a breach of Community law for which a Member State can be held responsible.

34. The possibility of obtaining redress from the Member State is particularly indispensable where, as in this case, the full effectiveness of Community rules is subject to prior action on the part of the State and where, consequently, in the absence of such action, individuals cannot enforce before the national courts the rights conferred upon them by Community law.

35. It follows that the principle whereby a State must be liable for loss and damage caused to individuals as a result of breaches of Community law for which the State can be held responsible is inherent in the system of the Treaty.

36. A further basis for the obligation of Member States to make good such loss and damage is to be found in Article 5 of the Treaty (Article 4 TEU), under which the Member States are required to take all appropriate measures, whether general or particular, to ensure fulfilment of their obligations under Community law. Among these is the obligation to nullify the unlawful consequences of a breach of Community law.

37. It follows from all the foregoing that it is a principle of Community law that the Member States are obliged to make good loss and damage caused to individuals by breaches of Community law for which they can be held responsible.

(b) The conditions for State liability

38. Although State liability is thus required by Community law, the conditions under which that liability gives rise to a right to reparation depend on the nature of the breach of Community law giving rise to the loss and damage.

39. Where, as in this case, a Member State fails to fulfil its obligation under the third paragraph of Article 189 [now Article 288 TFEU] of the Treaty to take all the measures necessary to achieve the result prescribed

by a directive, the full effectiveness of that rule of Community law requires that there should be a right to reparation provided that three conditions are fulfilled.

40. The first of those conditions is that the result prescribed by the directive should entail the grant of rights to individuals. The second condition is that it should be possible to identify the content of those rights on the basis of the provisions of the directive. Finally, the third condition is the existence of a causal link between the breach of the State's obligation and the loss and damage suffered by the injured parties.

41. Those conditions are sufficient to give rise to a right on the part of individuals to obtain reparation, a right founded directly on Community law.

42. Subject to that reservation, it is on the basis of the rules of national law on liability that the State must make reparation for the consequences of the loss and damage caused. In the absence of Community legislation, it is for the internal legal order of each Member State to designate the competent courts and lay down the detailed procedural rules for legal proceedings intended fully to safeguard the rights which individuals derive from Community law.

43. Further, the substantive and procedural conditions for reparation of loss and damage laid down by the national law of the Member States must not be less favourable than those relating to similar domestic claims and must not be so framed as to make it virtually impossible or excessively difficult to obtain reparation.

44. In this case, the breach of Community law by a Member State by virtue of its failure to transpose Directive 80/987 within the prescribed period has been confirmed by a judgment of the Court. The result required by that directive entails the grant to employees of a right to a guarantee of payment of their unpaid wage claims. As is clear from the examination of the first part of the first question, the content of that right can be identified on the basis of the provisions of the directive.

45. Consequently, the national court must, in accordance with the national rules on liability, uphold the right of employees to obtain reparation of loss and damage caused to them as a result of failure to transpose the directive.

46. The answer to be given to the national court must therefore be that a Member State is required to make good loss and damage caused to individuals by failure to transpose Directive 80/987. ■

NOTES AND QUESTIONS

1. In a later case, *Factortame*, the Court summarized the preconditions of state liability as follows: "Community law confers a right to reparation

where three conditions are met: the rule of law infringed must be intended to confer rights on individuals; the breach must be sufficiently serious; and there must be a direct causal link between the breach of the obligation resting on the State and the damage sustained by the injured parties."[3] How does this test differ from the one used in the *Francovich* decision? What might have prompted the change?

2. What arguments does the Court advance to support the recognition of the principle that states shall be liable for violations of EU law? Are these arguments convincing? Do they fit into the Court's general view of the EU legal system?

3. To what extent is the decision about the state liability system left to the Member States? Can the Member States hope to undermine the state liability doctrine via procedural means? Might it be desirable, from a legal policy perspective, for the EU to adopt a directive or regulation on state liability for violations of EU law?

4. Instead of recognizing state liability for violations of EU law, might it have been preferable to allow the direct application of Directive 80/987?

B. THE PRECONDITIONS OF STATE LIABILITY

According to the Court of Justice, the liability of Member States for violations of EU law has three basic preconditions: the EU rule that is violated must be intended to confer rights on individuals; the breach must be sufficiently serious; and there must be a direct causal link between the breach of the obligation resting on the State and the damage sustained by the injured parties."[4] In a number of judgments over the last decades, the Court has clarified the state liability doctrine further.

1. A SUFFICIENTLY SERIOUS VIOLATION OF EU LAW

In its 1996 *Factortame* decision, the Court provided detailed information on what it means for a violation of EU law to be "sufficiently serious."

BRASSERIE DU PECHEUR SA V. BUNDESREPUBLIK DEUTSCHLAND AND THE QUEEN V. SECRETARY OF STATE FOR TRANSPORT, EX PARTE: FACTORTAME LTD AND OTHERS

Joined Cases C-46/93 & C-48/93, E.C.R. 1996, I-1029 para. 51

[German law prohibited marketing beer containing additives. More generally, it also prohibited marketing beer that that did not comply with

---

[3] Joined Cases C-46/93 & C-48/93, Brasserie du Pecheur SA v. Bundesrepublik Deutschland and The Queen v. Secretary of State for Transport, ex parte: Factortame Ltd and others, E.C.R. 1996 Page I-01029 para. 51.

[4] *Id.*

the so-called German beer purity requirement (Reinheitsgebot).[5] The beer purity requirement limits the ingredients that can be used in brewing beer. Both the prohibition against additives and the beer purity requirement were found to violate the free movement of goods,[6] since they prevented foreign brewers from marketing their non-compliant beers in Germany and since there was no sufficient justification for this restriction.

A French brewery had incurred losses as a result of the relevant German rules.[7] It therefore sought damages for violation of EU law. However, for the purpose of holding Germany liable, the question was whether the relevant Germany statutory provisions, namely the prohibition against additives and the more general beer purity requirement, constituted "sufficiently serious" violations of EU law.]

55. [T]he decisive test for finding that a breach of Community law is sufficiently serious is whether the Member State or the Community institution concerned manifestly and gravely disregarded the limits on its discretion.

56. The factors which the competent court may take into consideration include the clarity and precision of the rule breached, the measure of discretion left by that rule to the national or Community authorities, whether the infringement and the damage caused was intentional or involuntary, whether any error of law was excusable or inexcusable, the fact that the position taken by a Community institution may have contributed towards the omission, and the adoption or retention of national measures or practices contrary to Community law.

57. On any view, a breach of Community law will clearly be sufficiently serious if it has persisted despite a judgment finding the infringement in question to be established, or a preliminary ruling or settled case-law of the Court on the matter from which it is clear that the conduct in question constituted an infringement.

58. While . . . the Court cannot substitute its assessment for that of the national courts, which have sole jurisdiction to find the facts in the main proceedings and decide how to characterize the breaches of Community law at issue, it will be helpful to indicate a number of circumstances which the national courts might take into account.

59. In Case C-46/93 a distinction should be drawn between the question of the German legislature's having maintained in force provisions of the Biersteuergesetz [Beer Tax Act] concerning the purity of beer prohibiting the marketing under the designation "Bier" of beers imported from other Member States which were lawfully produced in conformity

---
[5] Para. 4.
[6] Para. 4.
[7] Para. 5.

with different rules, and the question of the retention of the provisions of that same law prohibiting the import of beers containing additives. As regards the provisions of the German legislation relating to the designation of the product marketed, it would be difficult to regard the breach of Article 30 [now Article 34 TFEU] by that legislation as an excusable error, since the incompatibility of such rules with Article 30 was manifest in the light of earlier decisions of the Court, in particular Case 120/78 Rewe-Zentral 1979 ECR 649 ("Cassis de Dijon") and Case 193/80 Commission v. Italy 1981 ECR 3019 ("vinegar"). In contrast, having regard to the relevant case-law, the criteria available to the national legislature to determine whether the prohibition of the use of additives was contrary to Community law were significantly less conclusive until the Court's judgment of 12 March 1987 in Commission v. Germany, cited above, in which the Court held that prohibition to be incompatible with Article 30. ■

QUESTIONS ON FACTORTAME

1. What criteria does the Court apply in determining whether a breach of EU law is sufficiently serious to hold the Member State liable?

2. Do these criteria make sense from a legal policy perspective?

3. Can you think of any other criteria that the Court should use?

2. STATE LIABILITY FOR COURT DECISIONS?

One of the more delicate questions raised in the wake of *Francovich* was whether Member States could be held liable for decisions by state courts. The obvious argument against such an extension of state liability is that courts are independent. Accordingly, one could argue that there is little that Member States can do to prevent violations of EU law by their courts. Moreover, allowing state liability actions against judgments by a Member State's highest court creates the risk that every major decision by such courts will be relitigated in the guise of a damages action.

GERHARD KÖBLER V. REPUBLIK ÖSTERREICH
Case C-224/01, Sept. 30, 2003, 2003 E.C.R. I-10239

[Mr. Köbler was employed by the Austrian state as a university professor. After ten years, he applied for an increase in salary usually due after fifteen years. His argument was that while he had not been employed as a university professor in Austria for fifteen years, he had previously been employed by universities in other Member States, and he demanded that this previous service be taken into account, the idea being that under the free movement of workers, Member States cannot discriminate against those of their citizens who have chosen to work in another Member State.

In the litigation that ensued, Mr. Köbler was unsuccessful. In particular, the highest Austrian court in matters of administrative law, the Verwaltungsgerichtshof, decided against Mr. Köbler. Thereupon, Mr. Köbler filed an action for damages against the Republic of Austria in an Austrian Court, the Landesgericht fur Zivilrechtssachen Wien. He claimed that the Verwaltungsgerichtshof's decision violated EU law. The Landesgericht requested a preliminary ruling from the Court of Justice. Among other things, it wanted to know whether Member States could be held liable for violations of EU law committed by their highest courts and, if so, whether the Member States were free to determine which court should adjudicate such disputes.]

Principle of State liability

30. First, as the Court has repeatedly held, the principle of liability on the part of a Member State for damage caused to individuals as a result of breaches of Community law for which the State is responsible is inherent in the system of the Treaty.

31. The Court has also held that that principle applies to any case in which a Member State breaches Community law, whichever is the authority of the Member State whose act or omission was responsible for the breach.

32. In international law a State which incurs liability for breach of an international commitment is viewed as a single entity, irrespective of whether the breach which gave rise to the damage is attributable to the legislature, the judiciary or the executive. That principle must apply a fortiori in the Community legal order since all State authorities, including the legislature, are bound in performing their tasks to comply with the rules laid down by Community law which directly govern the situation of individuals.

33. In the light of the essential role played by the judiciary in the protection of the rights derived by individuals from Community rules, the full effectiveness of those rules would be called in question and the protection of those rights would be weakened if individuals were precluded from being able, under certain conditions, to obtain reparation when their rights are affected by an infringement of Community law attributable to a decision of a court of a Member State adjudicating at last instance.

34. It must be stressed, in that context, that a court adjudicating at last instance is by definition the last judicial body before which individuals may assert the rights conferred on them by Community law. Since an infringement of those rights by a final decision of such a court cannot thereafter normally be corrected, individuals cannot be deprived of the possibility of rendering the State liable in order in that way to obtain legal protection of their rights.

35. Moreover, it is, in particular, in order to prevent rights conferred on individuals by Community law from being infringed that under the third paragraph of Article 234 EC [now Article 267 TFEU] a court against whose decisions there is no judicial remedy under national law is required to make a reference to the Court of Justice.

36. Consequently, it follows from the requirements inherent in the protection of the rights of individuals relying on Community law that they must have the possibility of obtaining redress in the national courts for the damage caused by the infringement of those rights owing to a decision of a court adjudicating at last instance.

37. Certain of the governments which submitted observations in these proceedings claimed that the principle of State liability for damage caused to individuals by infringements of Community law could not be applied to decisions of a national court adjudicating at last instance. In that connection arguments were put forward based, in particular, on the principle of legal certainty and, more specifically, the principle of res judicata, the independence and authority of the judiciary and the absence of a court competent to determine disputes relating to State liability for such decisions.

38. In that regard the importance of the principle of res judicata cannot be disputed. In order to ensure both stability of the law and legal relations and the sound administration of justice, it is important that judicial decisions which have become definitive after all rights of appeal have been exhausted or after expiry of the time-limits provided for in that connection can no longer be called in question.

39. However, it should be borne in mind that recognition of the principle of State liability for a decision of a court adjudicating at last instance does not in itself have the consequence of calling in question that decision as res judicata. Proceedings seeking to render the State liable do not have the same purpose and do not necessarily involve the same parties as the proceedings resulting in the decision which has acquired the status of res judicata. The applicant in an action to establish the liability of the State will, if successful, secure an order against it for reparation of the damage incurred but not necessarily a declaration invalidating the status of res judicata of the judicial decision which was responsible for the damage. In any event, the principle of State liability inherent in the Community legal order requires such reparation, but not revision of the judicial decision which was responsible for the damage.

40. It follows that the principle of res judicata does not preclude recognition of the principle of State liability for the decision of a court adjudicating at last instance.

41. Nor can the arguments based on the independence and authority of the judiciary be upheld.

42. As to the independence of the judiciary, the principle of liability in question concerns not the personal liability of the judge but that of the State. The possibility that under certain conditions the State may be rendered liable for judicial decisions contrary to Community law does not appear to entail any particular risk that the independence of a court adjudicating at last instance will be called in question.

43. As to the argument based on the risk of a diminution of the authority of a court adjudicating at last instance owing to the fact that its final decisions could by implication be called in question in proceedings in which the State may be rendered liable for such decisions, the existence of a right of action that affords, under certain conditions, reparation of the injurious effects of an erroneous judicial decision could also be regarded as enhancing the quality of a legal system and thus in the long run the authority of the judiciary.

44. Several governments also argued that application of the principle of State liability to decisions of a national court adjudicating at last instance was precluded by the difficulty of designating a court competent to determine disputes concerning the reparation of damage resulting from such decisions.

45. In that connection, given that, for reasons essentially connected with the need to secure for individuals protection of the rights conferred on them by Community rules, the principle of State liability inherent in the Community legal order must apply in regard to decisions of a national court adjudicating at last instance, it is for the Member States to enable those affected to rely on that principle by affording them an appropriate right of action. Application of that principle cannot be compromised by the absence of a competent court.

46. According to settled case-law, in the absence of Community legislation, it is for the internal legal order of each Member State to designate the competent courts and lay down the detailed procedural rules for legal proceedings intended fully to safeguard the rights which individuals derive from Community law.

47. Subject to the reservation that it is for the Member States to ensure in each case that those rights are effectively protected, it is not for the Court to become involved in resolving questions of jurisdiction to which the classification of certain legal situations based on Community law may give rise in the national judicial system.

48. It should be added that, although considerations to do with observance of the principle of res judicata or the independence of the judiciary have caused national legal systems to impose restrictions, which may sometimes be stringent, on the possibility of rendering the State liable for damage caused by mistaken judicial decisions, such considerations have not been such as absolutely to exclude that possibility. Indeed, application of the

principle of State liability to judicial decisions has been accepted in one form or another by most of the Member States, as the Advocate General pointed out at paragraphs 77 to 82 of his Opinion, even if subject only to restrictive and varying conditions.

49. It may also be noted that, in the same connection, the ECHR and, more particularly, Article 41 thereof enables the European Court of Human Rights to order a State which has infringed a fundamental right to provide reparation of the damage resulting from that conduct for the injured party. The case-law of that court shows that such reparation may also be granted when the infringement stems from a decision of a national court adjudicating at last instance (see ECt.HR, Dulaurans v. France, 21 March 2000, not yet published).

50. It follows from the foregoing that the principle according to which the Member States are liable to afford reparation of damage caused to individuals as a result of infringements of Community law for which they are responsible is also applicable where the alleged infringement stems from a decision of a court adjudicating at last instance. It is for the legal system of each Member State to designate the court competent to adjudicate on disputes relating to such reparation.

Conditions governing State liability

51. As to the conditions to be satisfied for a Member State to be required to make reparation for loss and damage caused to individuals as a result of breaches of Community law for which the State is responsible, the Court has held that these are threefold: the rule of law infringed must be intended to confer rights on individuals; the breach must be sufficiently serious; and there must be a direct causal link between the breach of the obligation incumbent on the State and the loss or damage sustained by the injured parties.

52. State liability for loss or damage caused by a decision of a national court adjudicating at last instance which infringes a rule of Community law is governed by the same conditions.

53. With regard more particularly to the second of those conditions and its application with a view to establishing possible State liability owing to a decision of a national court adjudicating at last instance, regard must be had to the specific nature of the judicial function and to the legitimate requirements of legal certainty, as the Member States which submitted observations in this case have also contended. State liability for an infringement of Community law by a decision of a national court adjudicating at last instance can be incurred only in the exceptional case where the court has manifestly infringed the applicable law.

54. In order to determine whether that condition is satisfied, the national court hearing a claim for reparation must take account of all the factors which characterise the situation put before it.

55. Those factors include, in particular, the degree of clarity and precision of the rule infringed, whether the infringement was intentional, whether the error of law was excusable or inexcusable, the position taken, where applicable, by a Community institution and non-compliance by the court in question with its obligation to make a reference for a preliminary ruling under the third paragraph of Article 234 EC [now Article 267 TFEU].

56. In any event, an infringement of Community law will be sufficiently serious where the decision concerned was made in manifest breach of the case-law of the Court in the matter (see to that effect Brasserie du Pecheur and Factortame, cited above, paragraph 57).

57. The three conditions mentioned at paragraph 51 hereof are necessary and sufficient to found a right in favour of individuals to obtain redress, although this does not mean that the State cannot incur liability under less strict conditions on the basis of national law (see Brasserie du Pecheur and Factortame, cited above, paragraph 66).

58. Subject to the existence of a right to obtain reparation which is founded directly on Community law where the conditions mentioned above are met, it is on the basis of rules of national law on liability that the State must make reparation for the consequences of the loss and damage caused, with the proviso that the conditions for reparation of loss and damage laid down by the national legislation must not be less favourable than those relating to similar domestic claims and must not be so framed as to make it in practice impossible or excessively difficult to obtain reparation.

59. In the light of all the foregoing, the reply to the first and second questions must be that the principle that Member States are obliged to make good damage caused to individuals by infringements of Community law for which they are responsible is also applicable where the alleged infringement stems from a decision of a court adjudicating at last instance where the rule of Community law infringed is intended to confer rights on individuals, the breach is sufficiently serious and there is a direct causal link between that breach and the loss or damage sustained by the injured parties. In order to determine whether the infringement is sufficiently serious when the infringement at issue stems from such a decision, the competent national court, taking into account the specific nature of the judicial function, must determine whether that infringement is manifest. It is for the legal system of each Member State to designate the court competent to determine disputes relating to that reparation. ∎

NOTES AND QUESTIONS

1. In paragraph 32, the Court of Justice takes the view that for purposes of finding a breach of European law, a Member State must be viewed as a single entity. In other words, it does not matter which branch of the government breaches EU law. For legal purposes, it is still the Member State that is considered to be in breach. Can you find any argument in the Treaties supporting this claim. Read, for example, Articles 258, 259, 260 TFEU.

2. One of the chief arguments against applying the doctrine of state liability to decisions by Member State courts lies in the principle of res judicata. However, the Court of Justice flatly denies that the principle of res judicata is put at risk. Indeed, critics of the *Köbler* decision have accused the Court of essentially ignoring the principle of res judicata.[8] Can you summarize the Court's arguments?

3. The Court of Justice also denies that allowing state liability claims based on Member State court decisions will put the independence of the judiciary at risk. How does the Court support this conclusion?

4. According to the Court of Justice, does every decision by a Member State court that violates EU law give rise to state liability?

5. Does the *Köbler* decision increase the likelihood that Member State courts will make a good faith effort to apply EU law correctly in the first place?

6. Does the *Köbler* decision increase the likelihood that Member State courts will refer genuine questions of interpretation to the Court of Justice under Article 267 TFEU? It has been suggested that the *Köbler* decision increases the likelihood of preliminary ruling requests by national courts eager to avoid subsequent damages lawsuits.[9]

7. In practice, it is not just the Member States that may violate EU law, but also the institutions of the European Union itself. Who is liable then? Read Article 340 TFEU.

---

[8] *See, e.g.*, Peter J. Wattel, *Köbler, CILFIT, & Welthgrove, We Can't Go on Meeting Like This*, 41 COMM. MKT. L. REV. 177, 177 (2004).

[9] Oreste Pollicino, *The New Relationship between National and the European Courts after the Enlargement of Europe: Towards a Unitary Theory of Jurisprudential Supranational Law?*, 29 YEARBOOK EUR. L. 65, 98 (2010); James Pfander, *Köbler v. Austria: Expositional Supremacy and Member State Liability*, 17 EUR. BUS. L. REV. 275 (2006).

CHAPTER 10

THE LEGISLATIVE PROCESS

■ ■ ■

The rules governing the legislative process in the European Union are notoriously complex and technical.

In part, this reflects the dynamic character of EU law: over time, power has shifted from the Council to the European Parliament as well as from the Member States to the European Union. Accordingly, the current rules are the result of a complex web of political compromises that has evolved over decades. In addition, the European Union has traditionally sought to allay concerns over being too distant from EU citizens by institutionalizing pluralistic input into the democratic process even outside of the Parliament. Thus, auxiliary institutions such as the Committee of the Regions are also involved in the legislative process, which further adds to its complexity.

This chapter provides an overview over the relevant rules and principles.

A. COMPETENCE

In order for the European Union to enact legislation, it first needs a so-called competence to legislate in the relevant area. Unless the Treaties bestow on the Union the power to adopt legislation in a given area, the relevant field is reserved to the Member States. This principle—which is akin to the approach of the U.S. Constitution—is expressed very clearly in Article 5(2) of the Treaty on European Union:

> Under the principle of conferral, the Union shall act only within the limits of the competences conferred upon it by the Member States in the Treaties to attain the objectives set out therein. Competences not conferred upon the Union in the Treaties remain with the Member States.

The obvious question, then, is which competences the Treaties assign to the European Union as opposed to the Member States. In this context, one has to distinguish between different types of competences.

1. EXCLUSIVE COMPETENCES

In some areas, the European Union enjoys an exclusive competence—meaning that whereas the European Union can legislate in these areas, the Member States are barred from legislating even if the EU has failed to exercise its powers. The areas in which the European Union enjoys an exclusive competence are enumerated in Article 3 TFEU. They include, inter alia, the customs union, the competition rules necessary for the functioning of the internal market, the monetary policy for the Member States whose currency is the euro, and the common commercial policy.

2. SHARED COMPETENCES

In other areas, the European Union has a shared competence to legislate. This means that both the European Union and the Member States can enact legislation.

A list of shared competences can be found in Article 4(2) TFEU. The list includes numerous matters of great practical importance. Examples are the internal market, social policy, economic, social and territorial cohesion, the environment, consumer protection, transport, energy, and common safety concerns in public health matters.

The list in Article 4(2) is complemented by various provisions throughout the Treaty on the Functioning of the European Union. Perhaps most important is Article 114(1) TFEU. Under this provision, the Parliament and the Council can adopt measures for the approximation of Member State laws seeking to contribute to the functioning of the internal market. Approximation of laws means that law is made more uniform across Member States. The term "internal market" is defined in Article 26(2) TFEU: an "area without internal frontiers in which the free movement of goods, persons, services and capital is ensured in accordance with the provisions of the Treaties."[1]

The basic idea underlying Article 114(a) is that differences between legal systems can make it difficult for citizens and firms from one Member State to gain access to the markets of another Member State. For example, if two Member States impose very different safety regulations for consumer products, then manufacturers may struggle to develop products that can be sold in both states.

Article 114(1) TFEU therefore authorizes the Parliament and the Council to adopt legislation that makes the law more uniform across Member States to facilitate the internal market's functioning. Because most legal disparities have some adverse impact on the internal market's functioning, Article 114(1) TFEU offers a broad basis for measures to harmonize laws throughout the European Union.

Note that harmonization is a technical term in EU law. It means that legislation at the EU level is used to eliminate or at least reduce differences between the legal systems of the Member States. To the extent that

---

[1] TFEU, art. 26(2).

harmonization occurs by EU regulation, the result is a uniform "federal" rule. However, in many cases, harmonization occurs by directive. Because directives typically leave the Member States at least some discretion, harmonization via directives does not usually eliminate the differences between the various systems, but at least reduces them.

As a general rule, once the European Union has enacted legislation in the area of shared competences, that legislation preempts Member State legislation dealing with the same issue. However, under Article 4(3) TFEU and 4(4) TFEU, there are a few limited exceptions from this principle. For example, under Article 4(4), the Union has competence to carry out activities in the areas of development cooperation and humanitarian aid, but the exercise of that competence does not prevent the Member States from exercising their competence in the same area.

3. SUPPLEMENTARY COMPETENCES

In a few areas, the Union can adopt legislation only to "support, coordinate, or supplement" action by the Member States, and that legislation does not supersede the legislation that the Member States have adopted in these areas, Article 2(5) TFEU.

4. IMPLIED POWERS AND ARTICLE 352(1) TFEU

Finally, Article 352(1) TFEU provides a catch-all provision that seeks to ensure that the European Union has the necessary competences to achieve the goals specified by the Treaty. According to that provision, "[i]f action by the Union should prove necessary . . . to attain one of the objectives set out in the Treaties, and the Treaties have not provided the necessary powers, the Council, acting unanimously on a proposal from the Commission and after obtaining the consent of the European Parliament, shall adopt the appropriate measures." Obviously, this type of indeterminate empowerment poses a substantial risk to the sovereignty of the Member States. However, Article 352(1) TFEU anticipates that risk by requiring that the Council act unanimously. Thus, any single Member State—even tiny Member States like Malta or Luxembourg—can thwart legislation based on Article 352 through its representative in the Council.

B. SUBSIDIARITY

An additional hurdle for EU legislation lies in the so-called subsidiary principle. This principle is expressed in Article 5(3) of the Treaty on European Union:

> Under the principle of subsidiarity, in areas which do not fall within its exclusive competence, the Union shall act only if and in so far as the objectives of the proposed action cannot be sufficiently achieved by the Member States, either at central level

or at regional and local level, but can rather, by reason of the scale or effects of the proposed action, be better achieved at Union level.

The principle of subsidiarity was introduced to limit centralist tendencies within the European Union: to the extent that the Member States can deal with a problem better or at least as well as the European Union, the latter shall not have the power to intervene. Note, however, that the subsidiarity principle applies only outside the areas that fall into the Union's exclusive competence. That makes sense: because the Member States are barred from enacting legislation in areas that fall into the Union's exclusive competence, there is no alternative to EU action in these areas.

As a practical matter, the legal relevance of the subsidiarity principle seems quite limited. The Court of Justice appears determined to grant EU institutions substantial discretion when it comes to observing the principle of subsidiarity. To date, not a single EU measure has been declared void for violating the subsidiarity principle. However, that does not necessarily mean that the subsidiarity principle is without importance. Its true significance may lie in its impact on the political discourse.

C. NECESSITY TO ACHIEVE OBJECTIVES OF THE TREATY

One of the most important general principles of EU law is the principle of proportionality.

This principle is generally thought to impose three requirements. First, there is the principle of suitability: Measures must at least make a contribution to the aim that they purport to achieve. Second, there is the principle of *necessity*. Under that principle, a measure is illegal if its aim can be achieved by an alternative measure that is equally effective but less burdensome. And finally, there is the principle of proportionality in the strict sense. A measure is illegal if it imposes a burden out of proportion to the benefits brought by the measure.

While the principle of proportionality is a general principle of EU law, Article 5(4) TEU highlights its importance in one specific context, namely the exercise of legislative powers. Under that provision, "the content and form of Union action shall not exceed what is necessary to achieve the objectives of the Treaties."

D. PROCEDURE

Assuming the European Union has acted within its competences in adopting legislation, the next question is whether the legislative procedure has been satisfied. The Treaty on the Functioning of the European Union contains no less than three different procedures for enacting legislation. In the following, we will mainly focus on the so-called ordinary legislative procedure, which is governed by Article 289(1) TFEU and is by far the most common.

1. COMMISSION PROPOSAL

The first step in the legislative process is for the Commission to submit a proposal to the European Parliament and the Council. This rule is much more striking than it may appear at first glance. After all, the Commission is the executive arm of the European Union, and its democratic accountability is less direct than that of either the Council or the European Parliament. Yet, as a general rule,[2] the Commission nonetheless retains a monopoly on legislative proposals.[3]

To compensate for the Parliament's inability to make proposals, Article 225 TFEU explicitly empowers the Parliament to "request the Commission to submit any appropriate proposal on matters on which it considers that a Union act is required for the purpose of implementing the Treaties." However, whether the Commission follows that request lies within its discretion. If the Commission fails to submit the requested proposal, it simply has to "inform the European Parliament of the reasons," Article 225 TFEU.

2. FIRST READING IN THE EUROPEAN PARLIAMENT

Once the European Parliament has received the Commission's proposal, it undertakes the first reading and adopts its own position regarding the proposal. That position is then communicated to the Council.

3. THE COUNCIL'S RESPONSE

When the Council receives the Parliament's position, it has two options. First, it can approve the Parliament's position without changes. In that case, the European Parliament's position is deemed adopted with its original wording, Article 294(4) TFEU.

Alternatively, the Council may disagree with the European Parliament's position. In that case, the Council will adopt its own position at first reading and communicate that position to the European Parliament, Article 294(5) TFEU. The Council also has to inform the Parliament of the reasons behind the Council's position. Furthermore, once the Council has adopted its own position, the Commission has to weigh in

---

[2] *But see* Article 289(4) TFEU: "In the specific cases provided for by the Treaties, legislative acts may be adopted on the initiative of a group of Member States or of the European Parliament, on a recommendation from the European Central Bank or at the request of the Court of Justice or the European Investment Bank."

[3] This principle is further strengthened in Article 17(2)(1) of the Treaty on European Union, which reads: "Union legislative acts may only be adopted on the basis of a Commission proposal, except where the Treaties provide otherwise."

and inform the Parliament of its own views regarding the Council's position.

The Council takes its decisions with a qualified majority, Article 16(3) TEU. The rules governing what constitutes a qualified majority can be found in Article 16(3) TEU as well as in the Protocol on Transitional Provisions. They have been described in Chapter 3 of this casebook.

4. SECOND READING IN THE EUROPEAN PARLIAMENT

When the European Parliament receives the Council's position, it has several choices.

To begin, it can approve the Council's position at first reading. In that case, the Council's version of the legislation is deemed to be adopted. The same result occurs if the Parliament fails to make a decision within three months after receiving the Council's position.

Alternatively, the Parliament can reject the Council's position at first reading by a majority of its members. In that case, the legislative process comes to an end.

The Parliament also has the option of proposing, by a majority of its members, to amend the Council's position at first reading. In that case, the ball is back in the Council's court.

5. THE COUNCIL'S RESPONSE TO AMENDMENTS SUGGESTED BY THE PARLIAMENT

Once the Council receives the Parliament's suggested amendments to the Council's position, the Council again has to decide how to react. It can approve the amendments suggested by the Parliament within three months of receiving them, in which case the legislation is deemed to be adopted as amended by the Parliament. By contrast, if the Parliament fails to approve all of the amendments, the President of the Council will call a meeting of the so-called Conciliation Committee.

6. THE CONCILIATION COMMITTEE

The Conciliation Committee is composed of the members of the Council or their representatives and an equal number of members representing the Parliament, Article 294(10) TFEU. Its mission is to reach an agreement regarding a joint text; this joint text has to be approved by a qualified majority of the Committee members representing the Council as well as by a simple majority of the Committee members representing the Parliament.

The Conciliation Committee has only six weeks to complete this task. If the Conciliation Committee cannot reach an agreement within six weeks, then the legislative process comes to an end and the legislation is not adopted. By contrast, if the Committee manages to agree on a joint text, then the Council and the European Parliament get a last chance to lead the legislative process to a successful outcome.

7. APPROVAL BY PARLIAMENT AND COUNCIL

The joint text arrived at by the Conciliation Committee is communicated to the Council and the European Parliament. If, within six weeks after the Conciliation Committee has approved the joint text, that joint text is approved by the Parliament by a majority of the votes cast as well as by the Council by a qualified majority, the legislation is deemed to have been adopted in accordance with the joint text, Article 294(13) TFEU. Otherwise, the legislation has not been adopted.

8. PRESIDENT'S SIGNATURE AND PUBLICATION

Once the legislation has been successfully adopted in the ordinary procedure, it still has to be signed by the President of the European Parliament as well as by the President of the Council, Article 297(1) TFEU. After that, the legislation will be published in the Official Journal of the European Union. It enters into force either on the specified date or on the twentieth day following the day of its publication, Art. 297(1) TFEU.

GERMANY V. EUROPEAN PARLIAMENT AND COMMISSION
Case C-380/03, December 12, 2006, 2006 E.C.R. I-11573

[One of the central goals of the European Union is the creation of an "internal market," Article 3(1); 26(1) TFEU. The internal market is defined as "an area without internal frontiers in which the free movement of goods, persons, services and capital is ensured in accordance with the provisions of the Treaties," Article 26(2) TFEU.

As a practical matter, one of the main obstacles to the creation of an internal market is differences between the legal systems of the Member States. For example, imagine that you are a car manufacturer trying to sell cars in different Member States. If the various Member States have different and perhaps mutually incompatible rules on safety and emissions, that makes selling cars across the EU much more difficult. Moreover, different rules in different Member States may distort competition between producers in different Member States. To stick with our example, local manufacturers are already used to their Member State's safety and emissions standards, whereas those same standards impose an additional cost on foreign manufacturers.

Against that background, Article 114 TFEU authorizes EU measures aimed at reducing differences between the legal systems of the Member State in order to facilitate the functioning of the internal market. Such a reduction of differences between different legal systems is known as the "approximation" of Member State laws. Thus Article 114 TFEU, formerly known as Article 95 TEC, provides:

"The European Parliament and the Council shall, acting in accordance with the ordinary legislative procedure and after consulting the Economic and Social Committee, adopt the measures for the approximation of the provisions laid down by law, regulation or administrative action in Member States which have as their object the establishment and functioning of the internal market."

Based on that provision, the EU adopted Directive 2003/33/EC governing advertisement for tobacco products. However, to critics, the main purpose of that directive seemed to lie less in the advancement of the internal market than in the protection of human health against the danger of tobacco products. More specifically, the directive's central provisions imposed sharp limitations on the ability of tobacco manufacturers to advertise their products.

Thus, Article 3 of the directive imposed a general prohibition against advertisements in printed publications for tobacco products. Exceptions from this prohibition were provided for publications aimed solely at professionals in the tobacco trade and for publications printed in countries outside the EU and not primarily intended for the EU market.

Article 4 of the directive prohibited all forms of radio advertisement for tobacco products and also banned tobacco companies from sponsoring radio programs.

To justify these prohibitions, the Directive, in its preamble, pointed out that uniform rules on tobacco advertising were necessary to facilitate the functioning of the internal market with respect to press products (such as newspapers) as well as with respect to radio programs. The idea was that publishers of press products and providers of radio services would find it difficult to supply different Member States if they were subject to different rules on tobacco advertising in these different states. In other words, even though the directive governed advertisements for tobacco products, it was not the creation of an internal market with respect to tobacco products that the directive was supposed to facilitate, but the creation of an internal market with respect to press products, radio programs, and advertising space.

Not all Member States welcomed the new restrictions. Germany initiated an action for annulment under what is now Article 263 TFEU, seeking the annulment of both Article 3 and Article 4 of the directive.]

Arguments of the parties

17. The applicant [Germany] submits that the conditions justifying recourse to Article 95 EC [now Article 114(1) TFEU] for the adoption of

Articles 3 and 4 of the Directive are not met. None of the prohibitions laid down in those articles actually contributes to eliminating obstacles to the free movement of goods or to removing appreciable distortions of competition.

18. As regards, first, "the press and other printed publications", referred to in Article 3(1) of the Directive, more than 99.9% of products are marketed not in a number of Member States but only regionally or locally, so that the general prohibition on the advertising of tobacco products which is laid down in that provision responds only very marginally to the supposed need to eliminate barriers to trade.

19. "Press" products are traded between Member States only rarely, on account of not only linguistic and cultural reasons, but also policy reasons of publishers. There is no actual obstacle to their movement within the Community even though certain Member States prohibit tobacco advertising in the press since in those States the foreign press is not subject to such a prohibition. . . .

21. Nor does Article 3(1) of the Directive meet the objective of removing appreciable distortions of competition. There is no competitive relationship between local publications in one Member State and those in other Member States or between newspapers, periodicals and magazines with a wider circulation and comparable foreign newspapers, periodicals and magazines.

23. Likewise, in the applicant's submission, the choice of Article 95 EC [now Article 114 TFEU] as legal basis for the Directive is incorrect with regard to the prohibition, laid down in Article 4 of the Directive, on radio advertising and the sponsorship of radio programmes since the vast majority of radio programmes are addressed to the public in a locality or region and cannot be picked up outside a given area because of the limited range of the transmitters. . . .

24. Finally, [Germany submits that] Article 95 EC [now Article 114 TFEU] cannot constitute an appropriate legal basis for the prohibitions on the advertising of tobacco products set out in Articles 3 and 4 of the Directive since the true purpose of those prohibitions is not to improve the conditions for the establishment and functioning of the internal market, but solely to protect public health. The applicant submits that recourse to Article 95 EC as legal basis for the Directive is also contrary to Article 152(4)(c) EC [now superseded by Article 168(4)(c) TFEU], which expressly excludes any harmonisation of the laws and regulations of the Member States in the field of public health.

Findings of the Court

36. Article 95(1) EC [now Article 114(1) TFEU] establishes that the Council is to adopt measures for the approximation of provisions laid down

by law, regulation or administrative action in the Member States which have as their object the establishment and functioning of the internal market.

37. While a mere finding of disparities between national rules is not sufficient to justify having recourse to Article [114 TFEU], it is otherwise where there are differences between the laws, regulations or administrative provisions of the Member States which are such as to obstruct the fundamental freedoms and thus have a direct effect on the functioning of the internal market.

38. It is also settled case-law that, although recourse to Article [114 TFEU] as a legal basis is possible if the aim is to prevent the emergence of future obstacles to trade resulting from multifarious development of national laws, the emergence of such obstacles must be likely and the measure in question must be designed to prevent them.

39. The Court has also held that, provided that the conditions for recourse to Article [114 TFEU] as a legal basis are fulfilled, the Community legislature cannot be prevented from relying on that legal basis on the ground that public health protection is a decisive factor in the choices to be made.

40. It should be noted that the first subparagraph of Article 152(1) EC [now Article 168(1) TFEU] provides that a high level of human health protection is to be ensured in the definition and implementation of all Community policies and activities, and that Article 95(3) EC [now Article 114(3) TFEU] explicitly requires that, in achieving harmonisation, a high level of protection of human health should be guaranteed.

41. It follows from the foregoing that when there are obstacles to trade, or it is likely that such obstacles will emerge in the future, because the Member States have taken, or are about to take, divergent measures with respect to a product or a class of products, which bring about different levels of protection and thereby prevent the product or products concerned from moving freely within the Community, [Article 114 TFEU] authorises the Community legislature to intervene by adopting appropriate measures, in compliance with Article 95(3) EC [now Article 114(3) TFEU] and with the legal principles mentioned in the EC Treaty or identified in the case-law, in particular the principle of proportionality.

42. It is also to be observed that, by using the words 'measures for the approximation' in Article [114 TFEU], the authors of the Treaty intended to confer on the Community legislature a discretion, depending on the general context and the specific circumstances of the matter to be harmonised, as regards the method of approximation most appropriate for achieving the desired result, in particular in fields with complex technical features.

43. Depending on the circumstances, those measures may consist in requiring all the Member States to authorise the marketing of the product or products concerned, subjecting such an obligation of authorisation to certain conditions, or even provisionally or definitively prohibiting the marketing of a product or products.

44. It is in the light of those principles that it must be ascertained whether the conditions for recourse to Article [114 TFEU] as a legal basis for Articles 3 and 4 of the Directive were met.

45. First of all, it is to be recalled that the Court has already found that, at the time of adoption of Directive 98/43, disparities existed between national laws on the advertising of tobacco products and that there was a trend in national legislation towards ever greater restrictions (the tobacco advertising judgment, paragraphs 96 and 97).

46. [. . .] According to the information given by the Commission in its written observations, when the draft directive was submitted advertising and/or sponsorship in respect of such products were partially prohibited in six Member States, totally prohibited in four, and the subject of legislative proposals seeking a total prohibition in the remaining five.

47. Having regard, in addition, to the enlargement of the European Union through the accession of 10 new Member States, there was an appreciable risk that those disparities would increase. According to the Commission, some of the new Member States envisaged a total prohibition on advertising and sponsorship in respect of tobacco products while others accepted such acts subject to compliance with certain conditions. [. . .]

51. It follows that, at the time of the Directive's adoption, disparities existed between national rules on advertising and sponsorship in respect of tobacco products which justified intervention by the Community legislature.

52. It is in that context that it is necessary to examine the effects of such disparities, in the fields covered by Articles 3 and 4 of the Directive, on the establishment and functioning of the internal market, in order to determine whether the Community legislature was able to use Article [114 TFEU] as a basis for adoption of the contested provisions.

53. The market in press products, like the radio market, is a market in which trade between Member States is relatively sizeable and is set to grow further as a result, in particular, of the link between the media in question and the internet, which is the cross-border medium par excellence.

54. Having regard, first of all, to press products, the movement of newspapers, periodicals and magazines is a reality common to all the Member States and is not limited only to States sharing the same language. The proportion of publications from other Member States may even in certain cases come to more than half of the publications on the

market, according to information provided at the hearing by the Parliament, the Council and the parties intervening in support of them which was not challenged. It is necessary to include, in that intra-Community trade in press products on paper, trade made possible by information society services, especially the internet which enables direct access in real time to publications distributed in other Member States.

55. Also, on the date when the Directive was adopted, several Member States already prohibited advertising of tobacco products, as indicated in paragraph 46 of the present judgment, while others were about to do so. Consequently, disparities existed between the Member States' national laws and, contrary to the applicant's submissions, those disparities were such as to impede the free movement of goods and the freedom to provide services.

56. First, measures prohibiting or restricting the advertising of tobacco products are liable to impede access to the market by products from other Member States more than they impede access by domestic products.

57. Second, such measures restrict the ability of undertakings established in the Member States where they are in force to offer advertising space in their publications to advertisers established in other Member States, thereby affecting the cross-border supply of services.

58. Moreover, even if, in reality, certain publications are not sold in other Member States, the fact remains that the adoption of divergent laws on the advertising of tobacco products creates, or is likely to create, incontestably, legal obstacles to trade in respect of press products and other printed publications (see, to this effect, the tobacco advertising judgment, paragraph 97). Such obstacles therefore also exist for publications placed essentially on a local, regional or national market that are sold in other Member States, even if only by way of exception or in small quantities.

59. Furthermore, it is common ground that certain Member States which have prohibited the advertising of tobacco products exclude the foreign press from that prohibition. The fact that those Member States have chosen to accompany the prohibition with such an exception confirms that, in their eyes at least, there is significant intra-Community trade in press products.

60. Finally, the risk that new barriers to trade or to the freedom to provide services would emerge as a result of the accession of new Member States was real.

61. The same finding must be made with regard to the advertising of tobacco products in radio broadcasts and information society services. Many Member States had already legislated in those areas or were preparing to do so. Given the increasing public awareness of the harm caused to health by the consumption of tobacco products, it was likely that new barriers to trade or to the freedom to provide services were going to

emerge as a result of the adoption of new rules reflecting that development and intended to discourage more effectively the consumption of tobacco products.... [...]

66. As pointed out in the first and fifth recitals in the preamble to the Directive, those differences also meant that there was an appreciable risk of distortions of competition.

67. In any event, as the Court has already held, when the existence of obstacles to trade has been established, it is not necessary also to prove distortions of competition in order to justify recourse to Article 95 EC [now Article 114 TFEU].

68. It follows from the foregoing that the barriers and the risks of distortions of competition warranted intervention by the Community legislature on the basis of Article [114 TFEU].

69. It remains to determine whether, in the fields covered by Articles 3 and 4 of the Directive, those articles are in fact designed to eliminate or prevent obstacles to the free movement of goods or the freedom to provide services or to remove distortions of competition.

70. As regards, first of all, Article 3 of the Directive, the Court has already held that a prohibition on the advertising of tobacco products in periodicals, magazines and newspapers with a view to ensuring the free movement of those goods may be adopted on the basis of Article 95 EC [now Article 114 TFEU]....

71. The adoption of such a prohibition, which is designed to apply uniformly throughout the Community, is intended to prevent intra-Community trade in press products from being impeded by the national rules of one or other Member State. [...]

73. Furthermore, unlike Directive 98/43, Article 8 of the Directive provides that the Member States are not to prohibit or restrict the free movement of products which comply with the Directive. This article consequently precludes Member States from impeding the movement within the Community of publications intended exclusively for professionals in the tobacco trade, inter alia by means of more restrictive provisions which they consider necessary in order to protect human health with regard to advertising or sponsorship for tobacco products.

74. In preventing the Member States in this way from opposing the provision of advertising space in publications intended exclusively for professionals in the tobacco trade, Article 8 of the Directive gives expression to the objective laid down in Article 1(2) of improving the conditions for the functioning of the internal market.

75. The same finding must be made with regard to the freedom to provide services, which is also covered by Article 8 of the Directive. Under this

article, the Member States cannot prohibit or restrict that freedom where services comply with the Directive. . . .

77. Likewise, in prohibiting the sponsorship of radio programmes by undertakings whose principal activity is the manufacture or sale of tobacco products, Article 4(2) of the Directive seeks to prevent the freedom to provide services from being impeded by the national rules of one or other Member State.

78. It follows from the foregoing that Articles 3 and 4 of the Directive do in fact have as their object the improvement of the conditions for the functioning of the internal market and, therefore, that they were able to be adopted on the basis of Article 95 EC.

79. This conclusion is not called into question by the applicant's line of argument that the prohibition laid down in Articles 3 and 4 of the Directive concerns only advertising media which are of a local or national nature and lack cross-border effects.

80. Recourse to Article 95 EC [now Article 114 TFEU] as a legal basis does not presuppose the existence of an actual link with free movement between the Member States in every situation covered by the measure founded on that basis. As the Court has previously pointed out, to justify recourse to Article 95 EC [now Article 114 TFEU] as the legal basis what matters is that the measure adopted on that basis must actually be intended to improve the conditions for the establishment and functioning of the internal market.

81. Accordingly, it must be held that, as has been stated in paragraph 78 of the present judgment, Articles 3 and 4 of the Directive are intended to improve the conditions for the functioning of the internal market. . . .

88. It follows from the foregoing that Article [114 TFEU] constitutes an appropriate legal basis for Articles 3 and 4 of the Directive.

89. The first plea is accordingly not well founded and must be dismissed. [. . .]

The second plea: circumvention of Article 152(4)(c) EC [superseded by Article 168(4)(c) TFEU]

Arguments of the parties

90. The applicant maintains that, since the true purpose of the prohibition laid down in Articles 3 and 4 of the Directive is not to improve the conditions for the establishment and functioning of the internal market, the Community legislature, in adopting the provisions at issue, infringed the prohibition laid down in Article 152(4)(c) EC] [now Article 168(4)(c) TFEU] on any harmonisation of the laws and regulations of the Member States in the field of public health.

Findings of the Court

92. ... [I]t is settled case-law that, provided that the conditions for recourse to Article [114 TFEU] as a legal basis are fulfilled, the Community legislature cannot be prevented from relying on that legal basis on the ground that public health protection is a decisive factor in the choices to be made.

93. Article [114(3) TFEU] explicitly requires that, in achieving harmonisation, a high level of protection of human health should be guaranteed.

94. The first subparagraph of Article [168(1) TFEU] provides that a high level of human health protection is to be ensured in the definition and implementation of all Community policies and activities.

[. . .]

96. With regard to the applicant's argument that public health protection largely prompted the choices made by the Community legislature when adopting the Directive, in particular so far as concerns Articles 3 and 4, suffice it to state that the conditions for recourse to Article [114 TFEU] were met in this instance.

97. The Community legislature therefore did not infringe Article 152(4)(c) EC [now Article 168(4)(c) TFEU] by adopting Articles 3 and 4 of the Directive on the basis of Article [114 TFEU].

98. Accordingly, the second plea is unfounded and must also be dismissed.

[The following part of the Court's decision concerns the codecision procedure for enacting Community legislation. The so-called codecision procedure was the equivalent of today's ordinary legislative procedure. The codecision procedure was so called because it gave a central role to both the Council and the European Parliament. This represented a break with the previous legal tradition in the European Community in which the Council had been the central legislative body and in which the European Parliament played only a strictly secondary role.]

The fourth plea: infringement of the codecision procedure

Arguments of the parties

118. The applicant contends that the Directive was adopted in breach of the codecision procedure set out in Article 251 EC [now Article 294 TFEU]. It submits that substantive amendments were made by the Council after the vote of the Parliament in plenary sitting on the proposal for a directive.

119. According to the applicant, those amendments go beyond mere linguistic or editorial adjustment of the various language versions or the mere correction of manifest factual errors. Article 10(2) of the Directive was added to the text of the Directive after its approval, and Article 11 was

substantially amended compared with the version approved by the Parliament since the date of the Directive's entry into force was brought forward. Furthermore, Article 3 was amended and, in the German version at least, permits a broader interpretation of "printed media" which enlarges the Directive's field of application.

120. The Parliament, the Council and the parties intervening in support of them submit that, under the codecision procedure, measures are not adopted solely by the Council but, pursuant to Article 254 EC [now Article 297 TFEU], are jointly signed by the President of the Parliament and by the President of the Council who, by their signatures, take formal notice that the Directive corresponds to the Commission's proposal coupled with the amendments approved by the Parliament. . . .

Findings of the Court

124. By the present action, the applicant seeks to call into question the validity of Articles 3 and 4 of the Directive alone.

125. Accordingly, the plea alleging infringement of the codecision procedure laid down in Article [294 TFEU] with regard to the adoption of Articles 10 and 11 of the Directive in their final form is immaterial to the assessment of the validity of Articles 3 and 4 of the Directive.

126. In any event, the amendments to Articles 10 and 11 of the Directive were the subject of a corrigendum, a fact which is indeed not disputed, and this corrigendum was signed pursuant to Article [297 TFEU] by the President of the Parliament and by the President of the Council, and then published in the Official Journal of the European Union.

127. The amendments made to Article 3 of the Directive, as the Advocate General has rightly stated in point 197 of his Opinion, do not appear to have exceeded the limits applicable when the various language versions of a Community measure are harmonised.

128. The fourth plea must therefore necessarily be dismissed. ■

NOTES AND QUESTIONS

1. Article 114(1) TFEU seeks to allow harmonizing measures "which have as their object the establishment and functioning of the internal market." One concern regarding this provision is that it may be unduly broad. Can you think of any business-related rule or regulation where harmonization would not benefit the establishment and functioning of the internal market? How about non-business-related rules and regulations?

2. In parts of the legal literature, the Court's decision drew sharp criticism for allowing the use of Article 95 TEC [now Article 114 TFEU] as a basis for EU legislation that mainly seems to serve public health

considerations.[4] Are there any good reasons to preclude reliance on Article 114 TFEU when the legislation's main purpose is the protection of public health? For example, can one argue that using Article 114 TFEU as a basis for legislation in such cases would render Article 152 TFEU redundant? Can one argue that the prohibition in 168(4)(c) TFEU ("excluding any harmonisation of the laws and regulations of the Member States") is undermined if Article 114 TFEU can be used as a basis for legislation in cases like the one at issue?

3. One of Germany's arguments was that there is really no need to harmonize the law on press products because these are, for the most part, sold locally. However, the Court of Justice is unimpressed with this argument and claims that "the movement of newspapers, periodicals and magazines is a reality common to all the Member States." Can you think of any manufactured product where there is unlikely to be interstate trade? Or can you think of any services that are unlikely to be provided across Member State borders?

4. In the part of the decision dealing with the codecision procedure—now the ordinary legislative procedure—the Court accepts the argument that minor changes to the language are harmless even when they are undertaken after the Parliament has approved the legislation. Are there any safeguards to ensure that this does not undermine the power of the European Parliament?

5. Part of the Court's argument for allowing minor changes to the text is that these changes merely served to harmonize the various language versions of the directive. How does the Court's position fit in with the CILFIT principle that the various different language versions of EU law are all equally authentic and must all be considered in interpreting EU law?

6. In 2014, the European Union enacted yet another directive on tobacco products, namely Directive 2014/40/EU on the manufacture, sale, and presentation of tobacco products. This directive contains, among other things, detailed rules on ingredients, emissions, packaging, labeling, and health warnings. It also contains rules pertaining to e-cigarettes. This new directive was once again based on Article 114 TFEU, and, when challenged, met with the Court of Justice's approval.[5]

---

[4] H-W. Liu, *Harmonizing the Internal Market, or Public Health?—Revisiting the Case C-491/01 and C-380/03*, 15 COLUM. J. EUROP. L. ONL. 41 (2009).

[5] Case C-547/14, *Philip Morris*, OJ ECLI:EU:C:2016:325.

PART 4

THE INTERNAL MARKET

■ ■ ■

At the core of the European Union lies the so-called internal market. A definition of the internal market can be found in Article 26(2) TFEU:

> The internal market shall comprise an area without internal frontiers in which the free movement of goods, persons, services and capital is ensured in accordance with the provisions of the Treaties.[1]

The creation of an internal market has historically been—and still is—one of the main rationales for the existence of the European Union. Accordingly, Article 3 of the Treaty on European Union lists the creation of the internal market as one of the European Union's aims.

In order to achieve an internal market, the Treaties provide two main mechanisms.

The first is legal harmonization. The underlying idea is that an internal market cannot function if firms are faced with incoherent and contradictory legal rules in the various national markets. Accordingly, Article 114 of the TFEU, in order to facilitate the creation of an internal market, allows the European Union to adopt legislation aimed at legal harmonization. Legal harmonization is often said to constitute *positive* integration, since, by creating a uniform set of rules, it makes a positive contribution to European integration.

The second main mechanism is the guarantee of fundamental freedoms which guarantee, within certain limits, the free movement of goods, workers, services, and capital, as well as the freedom of establishment within the European Union. Like the Dormant Commerce Clause doctrine in U.S. law, the fundamental freedoms eliminate obstacles resulting from, inter alia, the existing legal framework. For that reason, their contribution is often referred to as *negative integration*.

The fundamental freedoms are at the very heart of EU law, and their importance to the development of the European Union cannot be overstated. In the following chapters, therefore, we will take a close look at the different freedoms.

---

[1] TFEU art. 26(2).

Chapter 11

Free Movement of Goods: The Customs Union

■ ■ ■

One reason for creating an internal market is to ensure the free movement of goods within the European Union, Article 26(2) TFEU. The free movement of goods requires that Member States do not disrupt the flow of goods within the Union via customs duties and equivalent charges. For that reason, Article 28 TFEU provides that "[t]he Union shall comprise a customs union which shall cover all trade in goods and which shall involve the prohibition between Member States of customs duties on imports and exports and of all charges having equivalent effect. . . ."

Abolishing customs duties and equivalent charges *within* the European Union makes it necessary that all Member States use uniform tariffs vis-à-vis non-EU countries. Otherwise, exporters in third countries could simply export their goods to the Member State with the lowest external tariffs and then exploit the absence of intra-Union customs duties to sell their goods to customers in other Member States without incurring additional customs duties. For this reason, Article 29 TFEU provides for "the adoption of a common customs tariff in [the Member States'] relations with third countries." The duties imposed by the common customs tariff are set by the Council based on a proposal from the Commission, Article 31 TFEU.

A. CUSTOMS DUTIES AND CHARGES HAVING EQUIVALENT EFFECT

Regarding the goal of eliminating intra-Union customs duties and other charges having equivalent effect, the central Treaty provision can be found in sentence one of Article 30 TFEU:

Customs duties on imports and exports and charges having equivalent effect shall be prohibited between Member States.

Crucially, this provision imposes an unconditional prohibition: If a burden qualifies as a customs duty or as a measure having equivalent effect, it is per se illegal. No attempt at justification will be permitted. Accordingly, it is essential that the provision's scope of application is stated precisely. However, while formal customs duties are easily identified, applying the prohibition against charges having equivalent effect has proven more complex. In its 1977 *Bauhuis* decision, the Court of Justice opted for a broad definition:

> 9. The justification for the prohibition of charges having an effect equivalent to customs duties lies in the fact that any pecuniary charge, however small, imposed on goods by reason of the fact that they cross a frontier constitutes an obstacle to the movement of goods, which is aggravated by the resulting administrative formalities.
>
> 10. Consequently, any pecuniary charge, whatever its designation and mode of application, which is imposed unilaterally on goods by reason of the fact that they cross a frontier and which is not a customs duty in the strict sense, constitutes a charge having equivalent effect . . ., even if it is not imposed for the benefit of the state.

In other words, Article 30 in its entirety contains an absolute prohibition against (a) any pecuniary charge, (b) which is unilaterally imposed (c) on goods (d) by reason of the fact that the goods cross a frontier. While this definition may seem straightforward, its application can nonetheless be difficult.

1. BY REASON OF THE FACT THAT A FRONTIER IS CROSSED

In order to fall under the prohibition of Article 30 TFEU, the pecuniary charge has to be imposed by reason of the fact that a border is crossed. By contrast, Article 30 is not applicable if the charge "relates to a general system of internal dues applied systematically to categories of products in accordance with objective criteria irrespective of the origin or destination of the products."[1] This makes sense: if the charge is imposed "irrespective of origin or destination," then it is not imposed by reason of the fact that a frontier is crossed. However, as the following case demonstrates, this principle can be quite difficult to apply.

CARBONATI APUANI SRL V. COMUNE DI CARRARA
Case C-72/03, Sept. 9 2004, E.C.R. 2004, I-8027

[The Italian municipality of Carrara is famous for its marble. The municipality imposed a "tax" on marble "excavated within its territory on its being transported across the boundaries of municipal territory."[2] Thus, the question arose whether the relevant charge could fall under Article 30 TFEU even though it applied regardless of whether the marble was

---

[1] ECJ, Case C-72/03, Carbonati Apuani Srl v. Comune di Carrara, 2004 E.C.R. I-8027 para. 17.

[2] *Id.* para. 2.

destined for another Member State or simply for another municipality within Italy.]

19. The next question to be considered is whether a tax such as the marble tax constitutes a charge having effect equivalent to a customs duty . . . .

20. As the Court has held before on many occasions, any pecuniary charge, however small, and whatever its designation and mode of application, which is imposed unilaterally on domestic or foreign goods by reason of the fact that they cross a frontier, and which is not a customs duty in the strict sense, constitutes a charge having equivalent effect . . . .

21. The Italian Government and the Comune di Carrara argue, nevertheless, that the prohibition . . . [in what is now Article 30 TFEU] must refer only to customs duties and charges having equivalent effect in trade "between Member States."

22. On this point it ought to be recalled that the justification for the prohibition of customs duties and charges having equivalent effect is that any pecuniary charges imposed on goods by reason of the fact that they cross a frontier constitutes an obstacle to the movement of such goods. The very principle of a customs union . . . requires the free movement of goods to be ensured within the union generally, not in trade between Member States alone, but more broadly throughout the territory of the customs union. If [the prohibition against customs duties and charges having equivalent effect] . . . make[s] express reference only to trade between Member States, that is because the framers of the Treaty took it for granted that there were no charges exhibiting the features of a customs duty in existence within the Member States.

23. . . . Article 14(2) EC [now Article 26 TFEU] defines the internal market as "an area without internal frontiers in which the free movement of goods, persons, services and capital is ensured", without drawing any distinction between inter-State frontiers and frontiers within a State.

24. Since [the prohibition against customs duties and charges having equivalent effect] must be read in conjunction with Article 14(2) EC [now Article 26 TFEU], the absence of charges—whether between States or within a State—exhibiting the features of a customs duty is a precondition essential to the realisation of a customs union in which the free movement of goods is ensured. . . .

26. It must moreover be emphasised that the issue raised in the case in the main proceedings does not appear to be a situation in which all the components are wholly confined to one Member State. Indeed, it has been established that the marble tax is imposed on all marble from Carrara that crosses that municipality's territorial boundaries, no distinction being made between marble the final destination of which is in Italy and marble

destined for other Member States. By its nature and terms, the marble tax therefore impinges on trade between Member States.

27. Nevertheless, the Comune di Carrara argues that various facts militate against the classifying of the marble tax as a charge having an effect equivalent to a customs duty. On this point it observes that the tax at issue in the main proceedings . . . is levied by a territorial administrative authority of no great size, and that it is imposed on one class of goods, viz., Carrara marble, and not on all goods crossing the municipality's territorial boundaries.

28. Those arguments cannot be accepted. Indeed, it must be borne in mind that . . . [the prohibition against customs duties and charges having equivalent effect] prohibits any pecuniary charge, albeit minimal, that might create an impediment to trade in the form of customs duty, unilaterally imposed by a competent public authority of a Member State. For the purposes of classifying a tax as a charge having effect equivalent to a customs duty, the size of the territorial administrative authority which levied the tax is therefore immaterial, in so far as that tax constitutes an obstacle to trade in the internal market.

29. In addition, given that [the prohibitions against customs duties and charges having equivalent effect] seek to abolish all obstacles to trade created by customs duties, it is irrelevant that the tax in question is imposed on one specific category of goods.

30. In addition, the defendant in the main proceedings stresses the particular purpose of the tax at issue in the main proceedings. The revenue from the tax is intended to cover the expenses borne by the Comune di Carrara as a consequence of the marble industry's activities in its territory. The tax responds to an interest of all operators in that industry, including those that market the goods concerned abroad.

31. The Court has held before that customs duties and charges having equivalent effect are prohibited regardless of the purpose for which they were introduced and the destination of the revenue from them. None the less, the Court has accepted that a charge which represents payment for a service actually rendered to an economic operator, of an amount in proportion to that service, does not constitute a charge having an effect equivalent to a customs duty.

32. That is not, however, the case in the present circumstances. As a matter of fact there is at best an indirect link between the tax at issue and the services provided for the operators on which the tax is imposed. The Comune di Carrara's observations make it clear that that charge is intended, in particular, to cover the costs incurred by the municipal authority in repairing and maintaining the road network, installing infrastructure for the harbour, the upkeep of a museum, research into safety in quarries, training activities in the field of mining engineering, or

social benefits for workers. Some of those services do not specifically benefit the operators that transport marble out of the territory of the Comune di Carrara.

33. With regard to the argument that "local" operators paying municipal taxes are already contributing to the expenses which the marble industry causes the municipal authority to bear, it has to be recalled that the chargeable event in respect of this tax occurs when marble crosses the municipality's territorial boundaries, irrespective of whether the operator concerned is subject to municipal taxes.

34. In any case, the fact that a tax imposed on the crossing of a frontier between States or within a State was introduced in order to compensate for a local charge applying to similar domestic products is not sufficient to exempt that tax from being classified as a charge having equivalent effect. If it were, it would make the prohibition on charges having an effect equivalent to customs duties empty and meaningless.

35. It follows therefore from all the foregoing that a tax proportionate to the weight of goods, levied in one municipality of a Member State only and imposed on one class of goods when those goods are transported across the territorial boundaries of that municipality, constitutes a charge having effect equivalent to a customs duty on exports . . ., despite the fact that the tax is imposed also on goods the final destination of which is within the Member State concerned. ■

NOTES AND QUESTIONS

1. Recall our earlier analysis of the Court of Justice's interpretive methodology. Which criteria of interpretation does the Court use in this case?

2. The Court rejects the argument that Carrara's residents should not have to pay the tax because they already contribute to the costs of extraction through other taxes. What argument does the Court invoke? Does this argument convince you?

3. Suppose the government of Carrara could not in fact afford to provide the services necessary (maintenance of public roads and harbor infrastructure) to keep its marble industry in good working order. Does it have an alternative means of raising the necessary revenue, and does that means restrict the free movement of goods less than the tax at issue here?

4. The fundamental freedoms, including the free movement of goods, do not apply to purely domestic situations without a cross-border element. The Court therefore has to come up with some argument as to why the case is not of a purely domestic nature. In paragraph 26, the Court simply notes that "the issue raised in the case in the main proceedings does not appear to be a situation in which all the components are wholly confined to one Member State."

5. Now consider the following hypothetical: Let us assume that Georgio buys Carrara marble in Italy, which he wants to use it to decorate his apartment in Rome. Can the Community of Carrara impose the tax in this case without violating EU law? Does it help Georgio's chances that other buyers buy marble in Carrara in order to decorate houses in France and Germany?

6. Let us take our hypothetical a step further. Assume, once more, that some buyers of Carrara marble are from France, whereas others are Italians who buy the marble in order to use it in Italy. The Commission learns of the tax that the Community of Carrara imposes and, after going through the required procedural steps, commences enforcement proceedings against Italy. Will the Commission win the case? Can Italy defend itself on the ground that it was the Community of Carrara, rather than the Italian government, that imposed the tax.

2. INSPECTION FEES

Another area that can cause some difficulties involves so-called inspection fees. Member state or EU laws frequently require inspections for imported goods. The Member States may then try to impose a fee to cover the costs of the relevant inspection. This then prompts the question of whether the fee has to be viewed as a charge having an equivalent effect to a customs duty because the fee is levied in response to the movement of goods from one Member State to another. As a general rule, the Court of Justice has answered that question in the affirmative. In other words, inspection fees levied on imported goods, but not on domestically produced goods, are charges having an effect equivalent to customs duties.[3]

That domestically produced goods are "through other charges subjected to a similar burden" does not matter in this context unless the charges imposed on domestic goods are applied "according to the same criteria and at the same stage of production, thus making it possible for them to be regarded as falling within a general system of internal taxation applying systematically and in the same way to domestic and imported products."[4]

But, even though it is usually the case that charging inspection fees imposed solely on imported goods violates Article 30 TFEU, the following case demonstrates that this rule has exceptions.

COMMISSION V. GERMANY
Case C-18/87, Sept. 27, 1988, E.C.R. 1988, 5427 (citations omitted)

[Council Directive 81/389/EEC provides that when live animals are imported, the importing Member State as well as those Member States

---

[3] ECJ, Case 87/75, Conceria Daniele Bresciani v. Amministrazione Italiana delle Finanze, E.C.R. 1976, 129 paras. 9–11.

[4] Id. para. 11.

through which the animals are transported on the way to their final destination ("transit states") are required to carry out certain veterinary inspections.[5] To cover the costs of these veterinary inspections, some of the German states ("Länder") imposed a fee on the importation or transit of live animals from other Member States.[6] The Commission believed that these fees constituted charges having an equivalent effect to customs duties and therefore initiated an enforcement proceeding against Germany.]

5. It should be observed in the first place that, as the Court has held on a number of occasions, the justification for the prohibition of customs duties and any charges having an equivalent effect lies in the fact that any pecuniary charge, however small, imposed on goods by reason of the fact that they cross a frontier, constitutes an obstacle to the movement of goods which is aggravated by the resulting administrative formalities. It follows that any pecuniary charge, whatever its designation and mode of application, which is imposed unilaterally on goods by reason of the fact that they cross a frontier and is not a customs duty in the strict sense constitutes a charge having an equivalent effect to a customs duty . . . .

6. However, the Court has held that such a charge escapes that classification if it relates to a general system of internal dues applied systematically and in accordance with the same criteria to domestic products and imported products alike, if it constitutes payment for a service in fact rendered to the economic operator of a sum in proportion to the service, or again, subject to certain conditions, if it attaches to inspections carried out to fulfill obligations imposed by Community law.

7. The contested fee, which is payable on importation and transit, cannot be regarded as relating to a general system of internal dues. Nor does it constitute payment for a service rendered to the operator, because this condition is satisfied only if the operator in question obtains a definite specific benefit, which is not the case if the inspection serves to guarantee, in the public interest, the health and life of animals in international transport.

8. Since the contested fee was charged in connection with inspections carried out pursuant to a Community provision, it should be noted that according to the case-law of the Court such fees may not be classified as charges having an effect equivalent to a customs duty if the following conditions are satisfied:

   (a) they do not exceed the actual costs of the inspections in connection with which they are charged;

---

[5] *Id.* para. 10.
[6] *Id.* para 1.

(b) the inspections in question are obligatory and uniform for all the products concerned in the Community;

(c) they are prescribed by Community law in the general interest of the Community;

(d) they promote the free movement of goods, in particular by neutralizing obstacles which could arise from unilateral measures of inspection adopted in accordance with Article 36 of the Treaty [now Article 36 TFEU].

9. In this instance these conditions are satisfied by the contested fee. In the first place it has not been contested that it does not exceed the real cost of the inspections in connection with which it is charged.

10. Moreover, all the Member States of transit and destination are required, under, inter alia, Article 2(1) of Directive 81/389/EEC, cited above, to carry out the veterinary inspections in question when the animals are brought into their territories, and therefore the inspections are obligatory and uniform for all the animals concerned in the Community.

11. Those inspections are prescribed by Directive 81/389/EEC, which establishes the measures necessary for the implementation of Council Directive 77/489/EEC of 18 July 1977 on the protection of animals during international transport, with a view to the protection of live animals, an objective which is pursued in the general interest of the Community and not a specific interest of individual States.

12. Finally, it appears from the preambles to the two abovementioned directives that they are intended to harmonize the laws of the Member States regarding the protection of animals in international transport in order to eliminate technical barriers resulting from disparities in the national laws (see third, fourth and fifth recitals in the preamble to Directive 77/489/EEC and third recital in the preamble to Directive 81/389/EEC). In addition, failing such harmonization, each Member State was entitled to maintain or introduce, under the conditions laid down in Article 36 of the Treaty, measures restricting trade which were justified on grounds of the protection of the health and life of animals. It follows that the standardization of the inspections in question is such as to promote the free movement of goods.

13. The Commission has claimed, however, that the contested fee is to be regarded as a charge having equivalent effect to a customs duty because, in so far as fees of this type have not been harmonized, such harmonization, moreover, being unattainable in practice—their negative effect on the free movement of goods could not be compensated or, consequently, justified by the positive effects of the Community standardization of inspections.

14. In this respect, it should be noted that since the fee in question is intended solely as the financially and economically justified compensation

for an obligation imposed in equal measure on all the Member States by Community law, it cannot be regarded as equivalent to a customs duty. . . .

15. The negative effects which such a fee may have on the free movement of goods in the Community can be eliminated only by virtue of Community provisions providing for the harmonization of fees, or imposing the obligation on the Member States to bear the costs entailed in the inspections or, finally, establishing that the costs in question are to be paid out of the Community budget.

16. It follows from the foregoing that the Commission's application must be dismissed. ■

NOTES AND QUESTIONS

1. In paragraph 6, the Court mentions that fees imposed on imported goods do not constitute charges having an effect equivalent to a customs duty if they constitute "payment for a service in fact rendered to the economic operator of a sum in proportion to the service." In other words, (1) the firm or citizen made to pay the fine must have received a service, and (2) the fee must have been commensurate with that service. This fee-in-exchange-for-services exception goes back to a 1983 decision.[7] There, the Danish government had sought to justify an inspection fee on the ground that it constituted payment for a laboratory analysis rather than a charge imposed on the importer.[8] However, the argument did not persuade the Court, which argued that the inspection (including the laboratory analysis) was undertaken in the public interest and therefore did not constitute a service to the importer. Because mandatory inspections almost always serve the public interest—why else would they be mandatory?—the fee-in-exchange-for-services exception has little practical relevance when it comes to mandatory inspections.

2. According to the Court, fees imposed for inspections prescribed by Community law may pass judicial scrutiny as long as certain other requirements are met. Why would the Court make such an exception for inspections prescribed by Community law (now: EU law)? Think about what would happen if EU law required the Member States to undertake certain inspections without being able to charge for them. Also note that, in the past, Member States often used extensive mandatory inspections as a way of making imports more burdensome and thereby shield local producers from foreign competition. When it comes to inspections prescribed by Community law, do we have to be concerned that they serve such anticompetitive purposes?

3. How does it benefit the internal market if the European Union standardizes border inspections by means of regulations or directives?

---

[7] Case 158/82, Commission v. Denmark, E.C.R. 1983, page 3573.
[8] Para. 12.

B. ARTICLE 110 TFEU

While Article 30 TFEU seeks to eliminate customs duties and charges having equivalent effect, the goal of Article 110 TFEU is to eradicate the obstacles to the free movement of goods that result from discriminatory tax regimes.

> No Member State shall impose, directly or indirectly, on the products of other Member States any internal taxation of any kind in excess of that imposed directly or indirectly on similar domestic products.
>
> Furthermore, no Member State shall impose on the products of other Member States any internal taxation of such a nature as to afford indirect protection to other products.

Article 110 TFEU contains two separate but closely related prohibitions: Article 110(1) prohibits Member States from imposing higher taxes on foreign products than on *similar* domestic products. For example, Article 110(1) would be violated if Germany imposed a higher sales tax on Spanish apples than on German apples. This would be true even if both types of apples are not exactly the same because they differ in color. After all, in order for the prohibition in Article 110(1) to apply, the relevant foreign products only have to be similar, not identical, to the domestic products in question.

Article 110(2) TFEU does not even require that the foreign products be similar to domestic ones. Instead, Article 110(2) applies in those cases where taxes on foreign products indirectly protect domestic products. For example, assume France imposes a higher sales tax on beer than on wine, and that beer is mostly produced in other Member States whereas wine is mostly produced in France. Assuming that wine and beer are not deemed to be similar products—a distinction to which we will return later on—the relevant tax regime does not violate Article 110(1). However, the Court may still find a violation of Article 110(2), because, to some extent, beer and wine compete for buyers such that a higher tax on beer affords indirect protection to wine.

1. ARTICLE 110(1) TFEU

Under Article 110(1) TFEU, the Member States cannot impose higher taxes on foreign products than on similar domestic ones. The notion of taxes is interpreted generously in this context and includes, for example, inspection fees or mandatory contributions to funds.

a) Similar Products

Unfortunately, the notion of similarity remains somewhat vague. The Court has provided the following definition:

5. The first paragraph of Article 95 [now Article 110 TFEU], which is based on a comparison of the tax burdens imposed on domestic products and on imported products which may be classified as "similar," is the basic rule in this respect. This provision . . . must be interpreted widely so as to cover all taxation procedures which conflict with the principle of the equality of treatment of domestic products and imported products; it is therefore necessary to interpret the concept of "similar products" with sufficient flexibility. The court specified . . . that it is necessary to consider as similar products which "have similar characteristics and meet the same needs from the point of view of consumers". It is therefore necessary to determine the scope of the first paragraph of Article 95 [now 110] on the basis not of the criterion of the strictly identical nature of the products but on that of their similar and comparable use.[9]

Of course, this definition raises more questions than it answers. For example, how does one determine what similar characteristics are?

COMMISSION V. GERMANY
Case C-184/85, May 7, 1987, 1987 E.C.R. 2013 (citations omitted)

9. It must . . . be considered . . . whether bananas and other table fruit . . . have similar characteristics and meet the same consumer needs. Consequently, in order to assess similarity, account must be taken . . . of a set of objective characteristics of the two categories of product in question, such as their organoleptic[10] characteristics and their water content, and, on the other hand, whether or not the two categories of fruit can satisfy the same consumer needs.

10. It must be observed in this case that the two categories of fruit in question, that is to say, on the one hand, bananas, and, on the other, table fruit typically produced in Italy mentioned above have different characteristics. As the Commission has conceded, the organoleptic characteristics and the water content of the two categories of product differ. By way of example, the higher water content of pears and other fruit typically grown in Italy [apples, pears, peaches, plums, apricots, cherries, oranges, and mandarins] give them thirst-quenching properties which bananas do not possess. Moreover, the observation of the Italian government, which has not been challenged by the Commission, that the banana is regarded, at least on the Italian market, as a foodstuff which is particularly nutritious, of a high energy content and well-suited for infants must be accepted. It must therefore be held that those two categories of

---

[9] Case 171/78, Commission v. Denmark, E.C.R. 1980, p. 447 para. 5.
[10] ["Organoleptic" refers to the sensory properties of a food (taste, color, feel, smell).]

fruit are not similar within the meaning of the first paragraph of Article 95 [now Article 110 TFEU]. ∎

JOHN WALKER & SONS LTD. V. MINISTERIET FOR SKATTER OG AFGIFTER
Case C-243/84, March 4, 1986, 1988 E.C.R. 875 (citations omitted)

9. The Danish government, supported by the Italian government, observes that scotch whisky and fruit wine of the liqueur type differ in terms of both the raw materials used and the method of manufacture (distillation in the case of whisky and natural fermentation in the case of fruit wine) and in terms of their characteristics and organoleptic properties. For that reason, in its view, the products are classified under different headings of the common customs tariff. The addition of neutral alcohol cannot transform fruit wine into spirits.

10. The commission shares the view that the products in question do not have similar and comparable uses and cannot be regarded as similar products within the meaning of the first paragraph of Article 95 [now 110 TFEU].

11. In order to determine whether products are similar within the terms of the prohibition laid down in the first paragraph of Article 95 [110 TFEU] it is necessary to consider, whether they have similar characteristics and meet the same needs from the point of view of consumers. The court endorsed a broad interpretation of the concept of similarity in its judgments . . . and assessed the similarity of the products not according to whether they were strictly identical, but according to whether their use was similar and comparable. Consequently, in order to determine whether products are similar it is necessary first to consider certain objective characteristics of both categories of beverages, such as their origin, the method of manufacture and their organoleptic properties, in particular taste and alcohol content, and secondly to consider whether or not both categories of beverages are capable of meeting the same needs from the point of view of consumers.

12. It should be noted that the two categories of beverages exhibit manifestly different characteristics. Fruit wine of the liqueur type is a fruit-based product obtained by natural fermentation, whereas Scotch whisky is a cereal-based product obtained by distillation. The organoleptic properties of the two products are also different. As the court held in Rewe . . ., the fact that the same raw material, for example alcohol, is to be found in the two products is not sufficient reason to apply the prohibition contained in the first paragraph of Article 95 [110 TFEU]. For the products to be regarded as similar that raw material must also be present in more or less equal proportions in both products. In that regard, it must be pointed out that the alcoholic strength of Scotch whisky is 40% by volume,

whereas the alcoholic strength of fruit wine of the liqueur type, to which the Danish tax legislation applies, does not exceed 20% by volume.

13. The contention that Scotch whisky may be consumed in the same way as fruit wine of the liqueur type, as an aperitif diluted with water or with fruit juice, even if it were established, would not be sufficient to render scotch whisky similar to fruit wine of the liqueur type, whose intrinsic characteristics are fundamentally different.

14. The answer to the first question must therefore be that the first paragraph of Article 95 [110 TFEU] must be interpreted as meaning that products such as Scotch whisky and fruit wine of the liqueur type may not be regarded as similar products. ■

NOTES AND QUESTIONS

1. In the two excerpts above, the Court arguably opts for a fairly narrow definition of the term "similar." For example, it does not seem farfetched to argue that bananas and other table fruit are similar in the sense that they are conventionally regarded as fruit. Does the Court's approach threaten to undermine the importance of Article 110 TFEU?

2. Should "light" tobacco cigarettes be regarded as similar to "dark" tobacco cigarettes? What about "mountain bikes" versus "road bikes," skim milk versus whole milk, soy milk versus almond milk, or almonds versus walnuts?

3. Note that the Court is willing to accord some importance to the "point of view of consumers." Does this make sense from a policy perspective?

b) Direct and Indirect Discrimination

Once it has been determined that foreign products and domestic products are similar, the question remains whether the Member State has imposed on the foreign products "any internal taxation . . . in excess of that imposed directly or indirectly" on the domestic ones. Crucially, the prohibition covers indirect as well as direct discrimination.

The distinction between direct and indirect discrimination plays a substantial role in various areas of EU law. Direct discrimination—also referred to as formal discrimination—occurs where the discriminatory rule explicitly references the prohibited distinction. For example, a tax that explicitly imposes higher taxes on "imported goods" than on "domestic goods" discriminates directly. By contrast, indirect discrimination occurs where a rule, on its face, seems to treat foreign and domestic goods alike, but de facto imposes a higher burden on foreign goods. For example, imagine that a country's domestic car manufacturers produce mostly small, environmentally friendly automobiles, whereas most larger cars are imported from other Member States. In that case, a tax rule that imposes additional taxes on larger cars de facto imposes a higher burden on foreign cars than on domestic ones.

In other words, the fact that a national tax regime does not explicitly target foreign goods may not prevent a violation of Article 110(1). Rather, even a facially neutral tax regime discriminates if, de facto, it imposes a higher burden on foreign than on domestic goods. Indeed, according to the Court of Justice, "a system of taxation may be considered compatible with Article 95 [110 TFEU] only if it is so arranged as to exclude any possibility of imported products being taxed more heavily than similar domestic products."[11]

There exists, however, an important distinction between those cases involving direct discrimination and those involving only indirect discrimination: direct discrimination is per se illegal. By contrast, in the absence of direct discrimination, the situation is more complicated. Even if the less favorable regime de facto applies more frequently—or even exclusively—to foreign goods, the Court will conclude that the relevant regime does not constitute discrimination as long as the differential treatment is justified by objective reasons. In other words, the Court nominally insists on an absolute prohibition against discriminatory tax regimes, but it seems willing to exclude from the notion of indirect discrimination cases where (a) Member State law distinguishes between different types of products based on objective criteria and (b) the objectives of that differentiation are themselves compatible with EU law. The leading case is *Chemical Farmaceutici SpA v. DAF SpA*.[12]

CHEMICAL FARMACEUTICI SPA V. DAF SPA
Case 140/79, January 14, 1981, 1981 E.C.R. 1 (citations omitted)

[Italy imposed higher taxes on synthetic alcohol than on alcohol produced by fermentation.[13] De facto, this differentiation came at the expense of foreign products since synthetic alcohol was produced exclusively outside of Italy.[14] Nonetheless, the Court refused to find that the Italian tax regime was discriminatory within the meaning of Article 95 EEC [now Article 110 TFEU].]

12. The Italian government recalls that in a number of judgments the court has recognized that the member states may lay down differing tax arrangements, even for identical products, on the basis of objective criteria such as the conditions of production and the raw materials used. According to the court, such arrangements are compatible with the Treaty if they are

---

[11] Case 228/98, Charalampos Dounias v. Ypourgio Oikonomikon, E.C.R. 2000, I-577 para. 41.
[12] Case 140/79, Chemical Farmaceutici SpA v. DAF SpA, E.C.R. 1981, 1.
[13] *Id.* para 10.
[14] *Id.*

laid down on the basis of objective factors and are not discriminatory or protective in their nature.

13. The arrangements challenged before the national court meet these requirements. In fact the different taxation of synthetic alcohol and of alcohol produced by fermentation in Italy is the result of an economic policy decision to favour the manufacture of alcohol from agricultural products and, correspondingly, to restrain the processing into alcohol of ethylene, a derivative of petroleum, in order to reserve that raw material for other more important economic uses. It accordingly constitutes a legitimate choice of economic policy to which effect is given by fiscal means. The implementation of that policy does not lead to any discrimination since although it results in discouraging imports of synthetic alcohol into Italy, it also has the consequence of hampering the development in Italy itself of production of alcohol from ethylene, that production being technically perfectly possible.

14. As the court has stated on many occasions, particularly in the judgments cited by the Italian government, in its present stage of development community law does not restrict the freedom of each member state to lay down tax arrangements which differentiate between certain products on the basis of objective criteria, such as the nature of the raw materials used or the production processes employed. Such differentiation is compatible with community law if it pursues economic policy objectives which are themselves compatible with the requirements of the treaty and its secondary law and if the detailed rules are such as to avoid any form of discrimination, direct or indirect, in regard to imports from other member states or any form of protection of competing domestic products.

15. Differential taxation such as that which exists in Italy for denatured synthetic alcohol on the one hand and denatured alcohol obtained by fermentation on the other satisfies these requirements. It appears in fact that that system of taxation pursues an objective of legitimate industrial policy in that it is such as to promote the distillation of agricultural products as against the manufacture of alcohol from petroleum derivatives. That choice does not conflict with the rules of community law or the requirements of a policy decided within the framework of the community.

16. The detailed provisions of the legislation at issue before the national court cannot be considered as discriminatory since, on the one hand, it is not disputed that imports from other member states of alcohol obtained by fermentation qualify for the same tax treatment as Italian alcohol produced by fermentation and, on the other hand, although the rate of tax prescribed for synthetic alcohol results in restraining the importation of synthetic alcohol originating in other member states, it has an equivalent economic effect in the national territory in that it also hampers the

establishment of profitable production of the same product by Italian industry. ■

QUESTIONS

1. Why might Italy have been keen to ensure that alcohol is produced from agricultural products rather than petroleum derivatives? In answering this question, note the date of the decision.

2. Assume that instead of imposing a tax on synthetic alcohol, Italy had enacted legislation according to which importers of synthetic alcohol have to pay a fee in the amount of one euro for every gallon of synthetic alcohol imported from other countries. Would this fee violate EU law?

3. Also consider the following hypothetical: What if Germany imposed a tax on synthetic alcohol as well as on alcohol produced from olives (which do not grow in Germany), but not on alcohol produced from potatoes (which do grow in Germany)? Would such a rule violate EU law?

2. ARTICLE 110(2) TFEU

Under Article 110(2) TFEU, the Member States cannot impose taxes on foreign goods that afford indirect protection to domestic goods.

a) Protective Effect

In determining whether the tax regime of a Member State offers indirect protection to domestic goods, the Court places central importance on the competitive relationship between the different goods involved. The state of the case law is nicely summarized in the following excerpt:

> 38. ... [T]he Court has already observed that the second paragraph of Article 95 [now Article 110 TFEU] of the Treaty is intended to prevent any form of indirect fiscal protectionism affecting imported products which, although not similar, within the meaning of the first paragraph . . ., to domestic products, are nevertheless in a competitive relationship with some of them, even if only partially, indirectly or potentially.
>
> 39. The Court has also consistently held that the assessment of the compatibility of a fiscal charge with the second paragraph of Article [110 TFEU] must take account of the impact of that charge on the competitive relationships between the products concerned. The essential question is therefore whether or not the charge is of such a kind as to have the effect, on the market in question, of reducing potential consumption of the imported products to the advantage of competing domestic products. In that connection, the national court must have regard to the difference between the selling prices of the products in question and the impact of that

difference on the consumer's choice, as well as to changes in the consumption of those products.[15]

b) Discriminatory Nature

On its face, the prohibition in Article 110(2) TFEU seems to require only that a Member State's taxes afford indirect protection to domestic goods. However, such a literal interpretation would be problematic because the prohibition would also apply to measures that pursue legitimate public policy goals and merely de facto apply more frequently to foreign than to domestic goods.

For example, assume that a Member State imposes higher sales taxes on fuel to protect the environment. Furthermore, assume that the relevant Member State has a car industry that produces only small, fuel-efficient cars. Now, it is easy to argue that sellers of small cars compete for customers with sellers of larger cars, and high fuel prices clearly give the producers of small cars an advantage in that competition. However, as a matter of public policy, there are good reasons to allow a tax of the type at issue.

It is unsurprising, therefore, that the Court of Justice has made it clear that Article 110(2) TFEU only applies to discriminatory taxes and that adverse tax regimes, which pursue legitimate policy goals and are based on objective criteria, are not discriminatory simply because they apply more frequently to foreign goods than to domestic ones.

JOHN WALKER & SONS LTD. v. MINISTERIET FOR SKATTER OG AFGIFTER

Case 243/84, March 4, 1986, 1986 E.C.R. 875 (citations omitted)

[Under Danish law, fruit wine of the liqueur type with an alcohol content not exceeding 20% was subject to lower taxes than Scotch whisky, fruit wine of the liqueur type with more than 20% alcohol, and grape wine with more than 23% alcohol. In the context of a preliminary ruling procedure, the Court of Justice was faced with the question of whether this tax regime was compatible with the prohibitions now contained in Article 110 TFEU. The Court first held that the products at issue were not "similar" within the meaning of what is now Article 110(1) TFEU. The Court then addressed the question of whether the Danish tax regime violated the prohibition which is now contained in Article 110(2) TFEU.]

15. In its second question the national court seeks to ascertain whether, if they are not similar products, Scotch whisky and fruit wine of the liqueur type are to be regarded as competing products and, if so, whether taxation that differentiates between the two products, of the kind imposed by the

---

[15] ECJ, Joined Cases C-367/93 to C-377/93, E.C.R. 1995 Page I-2229 paras. 38–39.

aforesaid Danish legislation, is to be regarded as incompatible with the second paragraph of Article 95 of the EEC Treaty [now Article 110 TFEU]. . . .

19. The second paragraph of Article 95 of the EEC Treaty [now Article 110 TFEU] provides that no member state may impose on the products of other member states any internal taxation of such a nature as to afford indirect protection to other domestic products.

20. That provision therefore pursues the general aim of guaranteeing fiscal neutrality and seeks to ensure that member states do not discriminate against products originating in other member states by favouring domestic products under their national tax legislation, thereby creating barriers to the free movement of goods between the Member States.

21. It is clear from the documents forwarded by the national court and from the observations submitted to the court of justice that the product which bears the lightest tax burden is manufactured almost exclusively in Denmark and that whisky, which is exclusively an imported product, is taxed not as such but as an alcoholic beverage included in the tax category of spirits—that is to say beverages with a high alcohol content—which comprises other products, the vast majority of which are Danish.

22. In order to enable the national court to determine whether, in those circumstances, the differential taxation imposed by the Danish tax system constitutes an infringement of the second paragraph of Article 95 [now Article 110 TFEU], it is necessary to recall that the Court has consistently held that Community law at its present stage of development does not restrict the freedom of each member state to lay down tax arrangements which differentiate between certain products on the basis of objective criteria, such as the nature of the raw materials used or the production processes employed. Such differentiation is compatible with community law if it pursues objectives of economic policy which are themselves compatible with the requirements of the treaty and its secondary legislation, and if the detailed rules are such as to avoid any form of discrimination, direct or indirect, in regard to imports from other member states or any form of protection of competing domestic products.

23. Accordingly, without there being any need to ascertain whether there exists a competitive relationship between Scotch whisky and fruit wine of the liqueur type, the answer to the second question must be that at the present stage of its development community law, and in particular the second paragraph of Article 95 of the EEC Treaty [now Article 110 TFEU], does not preclude the application of a system of taxation which differentiates between certain beverages on the basis of objective criteria. Such a system does not favour domestic producers if a significant

proportion of domestic production of alcoholic beverages falls within each of the relevant tax categories. ■

QUESTIONS

1. Why does the Court believe that it is not necessary to ascertain whether whisky competes with fruit wine of the liqueur type?

2. Why might Denmark tax products with a higher percentage of alcohol more highly? Do you think the case would have been decided differently if Denmark had taxed drinks with lower alcohol content more highly than drinks with higher alcohol content?

Article 110 TFEU

A] Art. 110(1) TFEU: Higher taxes on foreign products than on similar domestic products

   I. Taxes

   II. On foreign products and similar domestic products

   - Similar means: "hav[ing] similar characteristics and meet[ing] the same needs from the point of view of consumers"

   III. Higher

   - The pertinent taxes must discriminate against foreign products ("higher")

   - Article 110(1) TFEU covers both direct discrimination (which explicitly treats foreign products differently from domestic ones) and indirect discrimination (where foreign products are only de facto burdened more than domestic ones)

   - But note that direct discrimination is always prohibited, whereas indirect discrimination can be justified by objective reasons

B] Article 110(2) TFEU: indirect protection for domestic goods

   I. Taxes

   II. On foreign goods

   - Note that Article 110(2) TFEU does not require that only foreign goods be taxed. For example, high taxes on wine may be prohibited by Article 110(2) TFEU if they serve to protect competing domestic alcoholic beverages such as fruit liquor despite the fact that some of the wine consumed in the pertinent country is of domestic origin

III. Indirect protection for domestic goods
1. Competitive relationship
   a. In order for taxes to afford indirect protection to domestic goods, there must be a competitive relationship between the goods involved
   b. The relevant products need only compete partially, indirectly, or potentially
   c. But note that if the competing products are similar, Art. 110(1) TFEU rather than Article 110(2) TFEU should be applied
2. Discrimination
   a. Furthermore, in order for the taxes to protect domestic products, they must discriminate against foreign products. As in the case of Article 110(1) TFEU, one can distinguish between direct discrimination (where foreign products are explicitly treated differently from domestic products) and indirect discrimination (where the burden on domestic products is only de facto higher than on foreign ones)
   b. Taxes that directly discriminate against foreign products are always illegal
   c. Indirect discrimination can be justified by objective reasons

CHAPTER 12

FREE MOVEMENT OF GOODS: QUANTITATIVE RESTRICTIONS

■ ■ ■

One obvious way of thwarting the free movement of goods within the European Union is for Member States to impose limits on the amount of goods that can be imported or exported. Accordingly, the Treaty on the Functioning of the European Union bans both quantitative restrictions on imports and exports and measures having equivalent effect. The relevant prohibitions can be found in articles 34 and 35 TFEU.

> Article 34
>
> Quantitative restrictions on imports and all measures having equivalent effect shall be prohibited between Member States.
>
> Article 35
>
> Quantitative restrictions on exports, and all measures having equivalent effect, shall be prohibited between Member States.

A. QUANTITATIVE RESTRICTIONS

According to the Court of Justice, quantitative restrictions are "measures which amount to a total or partial restraint of, according to the circumstances, imports, exports or goods in transit."[1] Restrictions meeting this definition have become rare. The main importance of articles 34 and 35, therefore, lies in the prohibition against measures having equivalent effect. These prohibitions are used to police a wide array of Member State rules that do not constitute quantitative restrictions in the formal sense, but nonetheless have an adverse effect on the flow of goods within the European Union.

B. MEASURES HAVING EQUIVALENT EFFECT

Whereas the Court of Justice had little trouble defining quantitative restrictions on imports and exports, the concept of measures having equivalent effect to such quantitative restrictions proved more complex. In particular, the Court distinguishes between measures having equivalent

---

[1] Case 2-73, Riseria Luigi Geddo v. Ente Nazionale Risi, 1973 E.C.R. 865 ¶ 7.

effect to quantitative restrictions on *imports* and measures having equivalent effect to quantitative restrictions on *exports*.

1. IMPORTS

Measures having equivalent effect to quantitative restrictions on imports play a much greater role since Member States seem perennially tempted to protect their domestic industries by shielding them from foreign competitors. Against this background, it is not surprising that the Court of Justice, in its famous judgment in *Dassonville*, opted for a very broad definition of what constitutes a measure having equivalent effect to a quantitative restriction.

PROCUREUR DU ROI V. BENOÎT AND GUSTAVE DASSONVILLE

Cases 8/74, July 11, 1974, E.C.R. 1974, 837 (citations omitted)

[Belgian law prohibited the import of products bearing a designation of origin unless these products were accompanied by a certificate of origin issued by the country of origin. In defiance of this rule, certain merchants acquired Scotch whiskey in France and imported it into Belgium without a certificate of origin from the British authorities. The relevant merchants were criminally prosecuted. The Court of First Instance of Brussels, where the criminal proceedings took place, requested a preliminary ruling from the Court of Justice regarding, inter alia, the question of whether the Belgian prohibition at issue violated Article 34 of the EEC Treaty (now Article 34 TFEU).]

2. By the first question it is asked whether a national provision prohibiting the import of goods bearing a designation of origin where such goods are not accompanied by an official document issued by the government of the exporting country certifying their right to such designation constitutes a measure having an effect equivalent to a quantitative restriction within the meaning of Article 30 of the Treaty.

3. This question was raised within the context of criminal proceedings instituted in Belgium against traders who duly acquired a consignment of Scotch whisky in free circulation in France and imported it into Belgium without being in possession of a certificate of origin from the British customs authorities, thereby infringing Belgian rules.

4. It emerges from the file and from the oral proceedings that a trader, wishing to import into Belgium Scotch whisky which is already in free circulation in France, can obtain such a certificate only with great difficulty, unlike the importer who imports directly from the producer country.

5. All trading rules enacted by Member States which are capable of hindering, directly or indirectly, actually or potentially, intra-community trade are to be considered as measures having an effect equivalent to quantitative restrictions.

6. In the absence of a Community system guaranteeing for consumers the authenticity of a product's designation of origin, if a member state takes measures to prevent unfair practices in this connection, it is however subject to the condition that these measures should be reasonable and that the means of proof required should not act as a hindrance to trade between member states and should, in consequence, be accessible to all community nationals. . . .

9. Consequently, the requirement by a Member State of a certificate of authenticity which is less easily obtainable by importers of an authentic product which has been put into free circulation in a regular manner in another Member State than by importers of the same product coming directly from the country of origin constitutes a measure having an effect equivalent to a quantitative restriction as prohibited by the Treaty. ■

NOTES AND QUESTIONS

1. What standard did the court apply to determine whether regulations have an "equivalent effect" to quantitative restrictions on imports?

2. Do consumers have a legitimate interest in knowing the place of origin of the goods they purchase?

3. Assume, hypothetically, that a Member State were to enact a statute requiring all goods sold in that Member State to have a label showing their country of origin. Would this statute constitute a measure having equivalent effect to a quantitative restriction on imports?

In the decades after the Court decided *Dassonville*, it became increasingly apparent that the Court's definition of measures having equivalent effect was overly broad. Parties grew increasingly inventive at challenging Member State legislation, and the *Dassonville* formula was worded so generously that any Member State rule that could plausibly be argued to have some direct or indirect effect on interstate trade seemed subject to scrutiny under the free movement of goods. Therefore, in the landmark 1993 *Keck* decision, the Court imposed an important limitation on the *Dassonville* test.

CRIMINAL PROCEEDINGS AGAINST BERNARD KECK AND DANIEL MITHOUARD

Joined cases C-267/91 and C-268/91, November 24, 1993, E.C.R. 1993, I-431
(citations omitted)

[French law prohibited reselling unaltered products for less than their actual purchase price ("resale at a loss"). Mr. Keck and Mr. Mithouard violated this law and were therefore criminally prosecuted. They defended themselves by arguing, inter alia, that a general ban on resale at a loss violated the prohibition against measures having equivalent effect to quantitative restrictions on imports. Thereupon, the Tribunal de Grande Instance de Strasbourg requested a preliminary ruling from the Court of Justice. Among other things, the Tribunal de Grande Instance asked whether a general prohibition against resale at a loss was compatible with the free movement of goods.]

11. By virtue of Article 30 [now Article 34 TFEU], quantitative restrictions on imports and all measures having equivalent effect are prohibited between Member States. The Court has consistently held that any measure which is capable of directly or indirectly, actually or potentially, hindering intra-Community trade constitutes a measure having equivalent effect to a quantitative restriction.

12. National legislation imposing a general prohibition on resale at a loss is not designed to regulate trade in goods between Member States.

13. Such legislation may, admittedly, restrict the volume of sales, and hence the volume of sales of products from other Member States, in so far as it deprives traders of a method of sales promotion. But the question remains whether such a possibility is sufficient to characterize the legislation in question as a measure having equivalent effect to a quantitative restriction on imports.

14. In view of the increasing tendency of traders to invoke Article 30 of the Treaty [Art. 34 TFEU] as a means of challenging any rules whose effect is to limit their commercial freedom even where such rules are not aimed at products from other Member States, the Court considers it necessary to re-examine and clarify its case-law on this matter.

15. It is established by the case-law beginning with "Cassis de Dijon" that, in the absence of harmonization of legislation, obstacles to free movement of goods which are the consequence of applying, to goods coming from other Member States where they are lawfully manufactured and marketed, rules that lay down requirements to be met by such goods (such as those relating to designation, form, size, weight, composition, presentation, labelling, packaging) constitute measures of equivalent effect prohibited by Article 30 [34 TFEU]. This is so even if those rules apply without distinction to all products unless their application can be justified

by a public-interest objective taking precedence over the free movement of goods.

16. By contrast, contrary to what has previously been decided, the application to products from other Member States of national provisions restricting or prohibiting certain selling arrangements is not such as to hinder directly or indirectly, actually or potentially, trade between Member States within the meaning of the Dassonville judgment, so long as those provisions apply to all relevant traders operating within the national territory and so long as they affect in the same manner, in law and in fact, the marketing of domestic products and of those from other Member States.

17. Provided that those conditions are fulfilled, the application of such rules to the sale of products from another Member State meeting the requirements laid down by that State is not by nature such as to prevent their access to the market or to impede access any more than it impedes the access of domestic products. Such rules therefore fall outside the scope of Article 30 of the Treaty [now Article 34 of the TFEU].

18. Accordingly, the reply to be given to the national court is that Article 30 of the EEC Treaty [now Article 34 of the TFEU] is to be interpreted as not applying to legislation of a Member State imposing a general prohibition on resale at a loss. ∎

NOTES AND QUESTIONS

1. Why might French law have prohibited "resale at a loss"? And why would anyone want to sell products in an unaltered state at a price lower than their actual purchase price?

2. The Court of Justice concludes that a prohibition against resale at a loss does not constitute a measure having equivalent effect. But how exactly does the Court distinguish between those national rules that continue to fall under the *Dassonville* test and those rules that do not?

3. The Court's position that certain selling arrangements do not constitute measures having equivalent effect is known as the *Keck* exemption. Do you believe the *Keck* exemption is justified? What arguments might be advanced in favor or against of the Court's position?

4. As we shall see later in this book, the same basic challenge that the Court faces in defining the scope of the free movement of goods also presents itself within the context of the other fundamental freedoms, such as the freedom to provide services or the freedom of establishment. It should be unsurprising, therefore, that there have been repeated calls to extend the *Keck* exemption to other fundamental freedoms.[2] So far, however, the Court has not

---

[2] *See, e.g.*, Case C-543/08, Commission v. Portugal, 2010 E.C.R. I-11241, ¶ 32 (noting that the defendant invited the Court to make use of the Keck doctrine in the context of the free movement of capital and the freedom of establishment).

indicated that it is willing to apply the Keck doctrine beyond the free movement of goods.[3]

5. In light of *Keck* exemption, which of the following hypothetical statutes can be qualified as a measure having equivalent effect to a quantitative restriction on imports: a statute imposing a general speed limit of 65 mph on highways, a statute prohibiting supermarkets from handing out free single-use plastic bags to their customers, a statute requiring all processed foods to have a label displaying the amount of sodium they contain, a statute requiring graphic warnings to be displayed on cigarette packages, a statute prohibiting the use of chlorine-bleached paper as a packaging material for groceries?

2. EXPORTS

Member States are generally less likely to try to impede exports than they are to impede imports. After all, most European countries are very much interested in increasing their exports, for the benefit of local manufacturers. This does not mean that export restrictions are unheard of. For example, a country may make it difficult for works of art to leave the country in order to protect its cultural heritage, or it may seek to give domestic manufacturers an edge by making it difficult to export the raw materials needed in the manufacture of the relevant goods.

In light of the relatively limited practical importance of export restrictions, the Court of Justice long applied a fairly narrow definition of measures having equivalent effect to quantitative export restrictions. Consider, for example, the following excerpt from its 2008 *Gysbrechts* decision:

> [T]he Court has classified as measures having equivalent effect to quantitative restrictions on exports national measures which have as their specific object or effect the restriction of patterns of exports and thereby the establishment of a difference in treatment between the domestic trade of a Member State and its export trade in such a way as to provide a particular advantage for national production or for the domestic market of the State in question, at the expense of the production or of the trade of other Member States (Case 15/79 *Groenveld* [1979] E.C.R. 3409, paragraph 7).[4]

However, in its 2016 *New Valmar* decision, the Court seems to embrace a broader understanding of measures having equivalent effect to export restrictions.

---

[3] *E.g., id.*, ¶ 67.
[4] Case 2-205/07, Lodewijk Gysbrechts & Santurel Inter BVBA, 2008 E.C.R. I-9947 para. 40.

NEW VALMAR BVBA V. GLOBAL PHARMACIES PARTNER HEALTH SRL.

Case C-15/15, June 21, 2016, ECLI:EU:C:2016:464 (citations omitted)

[Under Belgian law, private undertakings are required to use the language of the region in which their establishment is located for any documents required by law or regulation. Furthermore, documents that do not meet this language requirement are deemed null and void.

New Valmar was a Belgian Company established in the Dutch-speaking region of Belgium. GPPH was an Italian company established in Italy. In 2010, New Valmar entered into a contract with GPPH, granting the latter a concession for the distribution of children's articles. In the course of the contractual relationship, New Valmar sent GPPH invoices written in Italian. The two companies subsequently argued over whether these invoices were to be regarded as null and void for failure to satisfy the Dutch language requirement imposed Belgian law. New Valmar argued inter alia that the Dutch language requirement violated Article 35 of the Treaty on the Functioning of the European Union and was therefore inapplicable. In the litigation that ensued, the Ghent Commercial Court asked the Court of Justice for a preliminary ruling.]

36. The Court has held that a national measure applicable to all traders active in the national territory whose actual effect is greater on goods leaving the market of the exporting Member State than on the marketing of goods in the domestic market of that Member State is covered by the prohibition laid down by Article 35 TFEU (see, to that effect, judgment of 16 December 2008 in Gysbrechts and Santurel Inter, C-205/07, EU:C:2008:730, paragraphs 40 to 43).

37. Moreover, it should be borne in mind that any restriction, even minor, of one of the fundamental freedoms enshrined by the FEU Treaty is prohibited by it [. . .].

38. In this case, it is stated in the order for reference that, under the legislation at issue in the main proceedings, it is mandatory that invoices, including those relating to cross-border transactions, issued by undertakings which have their place of establishment within the Dutch-speaking region of the Kingdom of Belgium, must be drawn up in Dutch, that language alone being authentic, failing which those invoices will be declared by the national courts of their own motion to be null and void.

39. According to the Belgian Government, such legislation cannot be considered a restriction on the free movement of goods, since invoices, which are the sole subject matter of that legislation, merely confirm liability arising out of a contract concluded by the parties concerned. Such legislation . . . does not affect the freedom of the parties to draw up such a contract in the language of their choice and, therefore, does not impinge on

the establishment of *consensus ad idem*. Consequently, the view cannot be taken that the legislation at issue in the main proceedings has an impact on trade between Member States.

40. Nevertheless, in depriving the traders concerned of the possibility of choosing freely a language which they are both able to understand for the drawing-up of their invoices and in imposing on them to that end a language which does not necessarily correspond to the one they agreed to use in their contractual relations, legislation such as that at issue in the main proceedings is likely to increase the risk of disputes and non-payment of invoices, since the recipients of those invoices could be encouraged to rely on their actual or alleged inability to understand the invoices' content in order to refuse to pay them.

41. Conversely, the recipient of an invoice drawn up in a language other than Dutch could, given that such an invoice is null and void, be encouraged to dispute its validity for that reason alone, even if it were drawn up in a language he understands. Such nullity could, moreover, be the source of significant disadvantages for the issuer of the invoice, including the loss of default interest, since it is apparent from the file submitted to the Court that, in the absence of a contractual term to the contrary, interest will begin to run, in principle, only from the issue of a new invoice drawn up in Dutch.

42. It follows that legislation, such as that at issue in the main proceedings, even if it concerns the language version in which the details on an invoice—not the content of the underlying contractual relationship—must be drawn up, produces, because of the legal uncertainty it creates, restrictive effects on trade which are likely to deter the initiation or continuation of contractual relationships with an undertaking established in the Dutch-speaking region of the Kingdom of Belgium.

43. While it is true that such legislation, since it applies indiscriminately to all invoices issued by an undertaking which has its place of establishment within that region, can affect both domestic trade within the Member State concerned and cross-border trade, the fact remains that it is more likely to affect the latter, as the Advocate General observed in points 61 to 68 of his Opinion, given that a purchaser established in a Member State other than the Kingdom of Belgium is less likely to be able to understand Dutch than a purchaser established in the latter Member State, where that language is one of the official languages. [. . .]

45. Furthermore, the restrictive effects of that legislation cannot be considered to be too indirect or too uncertain for it to be possible to regard that legislation . . . as not constituting a restriction within the meaning of Article 35 TFEU.

46. As is apparent from paragraphs 40 to 43 of this judgment, such legislation is likely to have an impact, however minor, on contractual relations, particularly since, as was indicated at the hearing, it is not unusual for the drawing-up of an invoice to be the only concrete manifestation of those relations. Moreover, as the Advocate General observed in point 69 of his Opinion, that impact depends not on a future and hypothetical event, but on the exercise of the right to free movement of goods . . . .

47. It follows that legislation such as that at issue in the main proceedings constitutes a restriction falling within the scope of Article 35 TFEU. ∎

NOTES AND QUESTIONS

1. Why do you think Belgian law required firms to use the language of their region?

2. How would the case have been decided if the *Dassonville* and *Keck* judgments were applicable to export restrictions?

3. More generally, after *New Valmar*, how much of a difference remains between the standards governing import restrictions and export restrictions?

C. JUSTIFICATIONS

The fact that a Member State regulation qualifies as a quantitative restriction on imports or exports or as a measure having equivalent effect does not necessarily mean that the relevant measure violates the free movement of goods. Rather, there is still the possibility that the measure may be justified. According to the case law of the European Court of Justice, there are two ways of justifying measures that interfere with the free movement of goods.

In some cases, the Member State may be able to invoke Article 36 TFEU, which expressly permits quantitative restrictions and measures having equivalent effect in order to pursue legitimate policy goals like public security, the protection of health, or the protection of human life.

Yet even in those cases where Article 36 TFEU does not apply, a Member State measure interfering with the free movement of goods is not necessarily illegal. Rather, the Court of Justice has developed an unwritten justification, which is typically referred to as the *mandatory requirements doctrine* or the *rule of reason*. Under this doctrine, certain types of restrictions on the free movement of goods can be "justified as being necessary in order to satisfy mandatory requirements relating, inter alia, to consumer protection or fair trading."[5] As a doctrinal matter, the

---

[5] Case C-126/91, Schutzverband gegen Unwesen in der Wirtschaft e.V. v. Yves Rocher GmbH, 1993 E.C.R. I-2361 ¶ 12.

mandatory requirements doctrine serves as an unwritten element of Articles 34 and 35. Hence, in keeping with the approach embraced by the Court of Justice, we discuss the mandatory requirements doctrine before addressing Article 36.

1. THE MANDATORY REQUIREMENTS DOCTRINE

Given the broad scope of the free movement of goods, Article 36 TFEU soon proved insufficient: many legitimate forms of regulation could not be based on Article 36 because the public goods at issue were not listed in Article 36. One solution to this dilemma would have been to opt for a broad interpretation of the concepts of public morality, public policy, and public security, all of which are mentioned in Article 36. However, the Court of Justice went a different way. It developed an unwritten justification for measures interfering with the free movement of goods, often referred to as the *mandatory requirements doctrine*, the *imperative requirements doctrine*, or *the rule of reason*. The Court of Justice has summarized this doctrine as follows:

> [I]n the absence of common rules applying to the products concerned, the obstacles to free movement within the Community resulting from disparities between national provisions must be accepted in so far as those national provisions, which are applicable without distinction to national products and to imported products, can be justified as being necessary in order to satisfy imperative requirements of Community law. . . .[6]

In its case law, the Court of Justice has elaborated upon these requirements.

a) Serving an Imperative Requirement of Community Law

A state regulation must serve an imperative requirement of EU law. This requirement is interpreted broadly. The Court of Justice has given numerous examples of goals that represent mandatory requirements. They include, for example, the protection of consumers,[7] the fairness of commercial transactions,[8] the protection of public health,[9] and the effectiveness of fiscal supervision.[10] Moreover, the Court of Justice has

---

[6] Joined cases C-388/00 and C-429/00, Radiosistemi Srl v. Prefetto di Genova, 2002 E.C.R. I-05845 ¶ 41.

[7] Case 120/78, Rewe-Zentral AG v. Bundesmonopolverwaltung für Branntwein 1979 E.C.R. 649 ¶ 8.

[8] *Id.*

[9] *Id.*

[10] *Id.*

made it clear that the list is not exhaustive. In principle, any legitimate regulatory goal can constitute an imperative requirement.[11]

b) Proportionality

In addition, the regulation must satisfy the principle of proportionality,[12] which constitutes a general principle of European Union law:[13] The measure has to contribute to the aim it purports to pursue (suitability),[14] there must be no less burdensome but equally effective measure (necessity),[15] and the burden imposed by the measure must not be out of proportion in light of the benefits that the measure yields (proportionality in the strict sense).[16] In practice, the Court of Justice often discusses only the first two prongs of the proportionality requirement and omits the principle of proportionality in the strict sense.

c) Applicability Without Distinction

Furthermore, the relevant state measures must apply "without distinction to national products and to imported products."[17] The exact meaning of this requirement is somewhat controversial, and the pertinent case law of the European Court of Justice is not entirely free from contradictions.

As the reader may recall, discriminatory state measures come in two flavors. First, there are so-called "formally" or "directly" discriminating measures, which have in common that they explicitly use the prohibited criterion. Within the context of the free movement of goods, these are measures that explicitly distinguish between goods from other Member States and goods of domestic origin. Second, there are measures that discriminate only "de facto" or "indirectly." These measures do not explicitly use the banned criterion, but in fact impose a greater burden on foreign than on domestic goods.

In principle, the mandatory requirements doctrine cannot be applied to state measures that engage in formal (direct) discrimination. However,

---

[11] JENS DAMMANN, MATERIELLES RECHT UND BEWEISRECHT IM SYSTEM DER GRUNDFREIHEITEN (2008).

[12] *E.g.*, Case C-126/9, Schutzverband gegen Unwesen in der Wirtschaft e.V. v. Yves Rocher GmbH, 1993 E.C.J. I-2361 ¶ 12.

[13] *E.g.*, joined cases C-27/00 and C-122/00, The Queen v. Secretary of State for the Environment, 2002 E.C.R. I-02569 ¶ 62.

[14] *See, e.g., id.* ¶ 15 ("[T]he Court must examine, in accordance with the settled case-law, whether the national provisions are suitable for attaining the aim pursued and do not go beyond what is necessary for that purpose.").

[15] *Id.*

[16] *E.g.*, joined cases C-27/00 and C-122/00, The Queen v. Secretary of State for the Environment, 2002 E.C.R. I-02569 ¶ 62 (noting that the "the disadvantages caused must not be disproportionate to the aims pursued").

[17] Joined cases C-388/00 & C-429/00, Radiosistemi Srl v. Prefetto di Genova, 2002 E.C.R. I-5845 ¶ 41.

even on this point, the Court of Justice has not always been entirely consistent: in its famous *Belgian Waste* decision, the Court of Justice applied the mandatory requirements doctrine to a measure that clearly distinguished based on the good's origin.[18] However, that case constitutes the exception to the rule. In general, it is safe to say that formally discriminating state measures cannot be justified by invoking mandatory requirements. Herein lies a crucial difference between the mandatory requirements doctrine and Article 36 TFEU: the latter can be applied even to formally discriminating state measures.

Whether the mandatory requirements doctrine can be applied to those state measures that only discriminate de facto is more difficult to say. In the case law of the European Court of Justice, one can find examples where the mandatory requirements doctrine was successfully invoked despite indirect discrimination.[19] In other cases, however, indirect discrimination was held to bar the application of the mandatory requirements doctrine.[20]

REWE-ZENTRAL AG V. BUNDESMONOPOLVERWALTUNG FÜR BRANNTWEIN

Case 120/78, February 20, 1979, 1979 E.C.R. 649 (citations omitted)

[The plaintiff, a German corporation, wanted to import "Cassis de Dijon"—a specific type of fruit liquor—from France to sell it in Germany. So, the plaintiff requested an import authorization from the German Federal Monopoly Administration for Spirits. However, the German Federal Monopoly Administration for Spirit rejected the plaintiff's request on the ground that the alcohol content of Cassis de Dijon was too low. Under German law, fruit liquor could only be marketed if its alcohol content was at least 25%, whereas Cassis de Dijon only contained between 15% and 20% alcohol.

The case ended up before the German Finanzgericht (tax court), and the German Finanzgericht requested a preliminary ruling from the Court of Justice. In particular, the German court wanted to know whether the prescription of a minimum alcohol content for fruit liquor constituted a measure having equivalent effect to a restriction on imports.]

6. The national court is thereby asking for assistance in the matter of interpretation in order to enable it to assess whether the requirement of a minimum alcohol content may be covered . . . by the prohibition on all measures having an effect equivalent to quantitative restrictions in trade between Member States contained in Article 30 of the Treaty . . . .

---

[18] Case C-2/90, Commission v. Belgium, 1992 E.C.R. I-4431 paras. 32–34.
[19] *E.g.,* Case C-204/90, Hanns-Martin Bachmann v. Belgium, 1990 E.C.R. I-249 paras. 9, 28.
[20] *E.g.,* Case C-224/97, Erich Ciola v. Land Vorarlberg, 1999 E.C.R. I-2517 paras. 14–17.

8. In the absence of common rules relating to the production and marketing of alcohol—a proposal for a regulation submitted to the Council by the Commission on 7 December 1976 . . . not yet having received the Council's approval—it is for the Member States to regulate all matters relating to the production and marketing of alcohol and alcoholic beverages on their own territory.

Obstacles to movement within the community resulting from disparities between the national laws relating to the marketing of the products in question must be accepted in so far as those provisions may be recognized as being necessary in order to satisfy mandatory requirements relating in particular to the effectiveness of fiscal supervision, the protection of public health, the fairness of commercial transactions and the defence of the consumer.

9. The government of the Federal Republic of Germany, intervening in the proceedings, put forward various arguments which, in its view, justify the application of provisions relating to the minimum alcohol content of alcoholic beverages, adducing considerations relating on the one hand to the protection of public health and on the other to the protection of the consumer against unfair commercial practices.

10. As regards the protection of public health the German government states that the purpose of the fixing of minimum alcohol contents by national legislation is to avoid the proliferation of alcoholic beverages on the national market, in particular alcoholic beverages with a low alcohol content, since, in its view, such products may more easily induce a tolerance towards alcohol than more highly alcoholic beverages.

11. Such considerations are not decisive since the consumer can obtain on the market an extremely wide range of weakly or moderately alcoholic products and furthermore a large proportion of alcoholic beverages with a high alcohol content freely sold on the German market is generally consumed in a diluted form.

12. The German government also claims that the fixing of a lower limit for the alcohol content of certain liqueurs is designed to protect the consumer against unfair practices on the part of producers and distributors of alcoholic beverages.

This argument is based on the consideration that the lowering of the alcohol content secures a competitive advantage in relation to beverages with a higher alcohol content, since alcohol constitutes by far the most expensive constituent of beverages by reason of the high rate of tax to which it is subject.

Furthermore, according to the German government, to allow alcoholic products into free circulation wherever, as regards their alcohol content, they comply with the rules laid down in the country of production would have the effect of imposing as a common standard within the community the lowest alcohol content permitted in any of the member states, and even of rendering any requirements in this field inoperative since a lower limit of this nature is foreign to the rules of several Member States.

13. As the Commission rightly observed, the fixing of limits in relation to the alcohol content of beverages may lead to the standardization of products placed on the market and of their designations, in the interests of a greater transparency of commercial transactions and offers for sale to the public.

However, this line of argument cannot be taken so far as to regard the mandatory fixing of minimum alcohol contents as being an essential guarantee of the fairness of commercial transactions, since it is a simple matter to ensure that suitable information is conveyed to the purchaser by requiring the display of an indication of origin and of the alcohol content on the packaging of products.

14. It is clear from the foregoing that the requirements relating to the minimum alcohol content of alcoholic beverages do not serve a purpose which is in the general interest and such as to take precedence over the requirements of the free movement of goods, which constitutes one of the fundamental rules of the Community.

In practice, the principle effect of requirements of this nature is to promote alcoholic beverages having a high alcohol content by excluding from the national market products of other member states which do not answer that description.

It therefore appears that the unilateral requirement imposed by the rules of a Member State of a minimum alcohol content for the purposes of the sale of alcoholic beverages constitutes an obstacle to trade which is incompatible with the provisions of Article 30 of the Treaty [now Article 34 TFEU].

There is therefore no valid reason why, provided that they have been lawfully produced and marketed in one of the member states, alcoholic beverages should not be introduced into any other member state; the sale of such products may not be subject to a legal prohibition on the marketing of beverages with an alcohol content lower than the limit set by the national rules.

15. Consequently, the first question should be answered to the effect that the concept of "measures having an effect equivalent to quantitative restrictions on imports" contained in Article 30 of the Treaty [now Article 34 TFEU] is to be understood to mean that the fixing of a minimum alcohol content for alcoholic beverages intended for human consumption by the legislation of a member state also falls within the prohibition laid down in

that provision where the importation of alcoholic beverages lawfully produced and marketed in another member state is concerned. ∎

NOTES AND QUESTIONS

1. How does the German government defend setting a minimum alcohol content?

2. Why does the Court of Justice fail to accept the German government's arguments regarding the protection of consumers?

3. In their 2014 book *More than You Wanted to Know*, Omri Ben-Shahar and Carl E. Schneider argue that mandated disclosure is generally ineffective.[21] Reviewing numerous empirical studies, they conclude that consumers generally fail to notice disclosures, that they fail to read them even if they notice them, and that they fail to understand them even if they read them.[22] Do you believe that disclosure is sufficient to protect consumers?

3. We will see, in the context of the protection of public morality, that the Court of Justice expects Member States to be consistent in their pursuit of public policy goals. To what extent does this line of reasoning seem to have influenced the Court of Justice in the case at hand?

4. Assume, hypothetically, that Germany enacts a statute requiring iodine to be added to salt sold to consumers. Would such a statute violate the free movement of goods? Assume, for the purpose of this question, that iodine can also be purchased separately.

COMMISSION V. GERMANY
Cases 178/84, March 12, 1987, E.C.R. 1987, 37 (citations omitted)

[Under German law, commercial use of the term "Bier" ["beer"] was limited to beverages that complied with the requirements of the Biersteuergesetz (Beer Tax Act): So-called bottom-fermented beers could only be manufactured from "malted barley, hops, yeast and water."[23] The same was true for so-called top-fermented beers except that for the latter, the law allowed the use of "other malts, technically pure cane sugar, beet sugar or invert sugar and glucose and colourants obtained from those sugars."[24] These requirements were known as the "Reinheitsgebot" [purity requirement] for beer.[25] In addition, German law also imposed an absolute ban on the marketing of beer containing so-called additives.]

The European Commission was of the opinion that these rules—both the beer purity requirement and the general prohibition against marketing

---
[21] OMRI BEN-SHAHAR & CARL E. SCHNEIDER, MORE THAN YOU WANTED TO KNOW 12 (2014).
[22] *Id.* at 55.
[23] Para. 5.
[24] Para. 5.
[25] Para. 15.

beer with additives—violated EU law inasmuch as they created a bar for the importation of beers from other Member States that did not satisfy the requirements imposed by German law but had been brewed in accordance with the laws of their Member States of origin. Ultimately, the Commission initiated an enforcement proceeding, and so the matter came before the Court of Justice.]

27. According to a consistent line of decisions of the Court the prohibition of measures having an effect equivalent to quantitative restrictions under Article 30 of the EEC Treaty covers "all trading rules enacted by member states which are capable of hindering, directly or indirectly, actually or potentially, intra-community trade."

28. The court has also consistently held . . . that "in the absence of common rules relating to the marketing of the products concerned, obstacles to free movement within the community resulting from disparities between the national laws must be accepted in so far as such rules, applicable to domestic and to imported products without distinction, may be recognized as being necessary in order to satisfy mandatory requirements relating inter alia to consumer protection. It is also necessary for such rules to be proportionate to the aim in view. If a member state has a choice between various measures to attain the same objective it should choose the means which least restricts the free movement of goods".

29. It is not contested that the application of . . . the Biersteuergesetz [Beer Tax Act] to beers from other Member States in whose manufacture raw materials other than malted barley have been lawfully used, in particular rice and maize, is liable to constitute an obstacle to their importation into the Federal Republic of Germany.

30. Accordingly, it must be established whether the application of that provision may be justified by imperative requirements relating to consumer protection.

31. The German government's argument that [the relevant provision of the Beer Tax Act] is essential in order to protect German consumers because, in their minds, the designation "bier" is inseparably linked to the beverage manufactured solely from the ingredients laid down in . . . [the relevant provision] of the Biersteuergesetz must be rejected.

32. Firstly, consumers' conceptions which vary from one member state to the other are also likely to evolve in the course of time within a Member State. The establishment of the common market is, it should be added, one of the factors that may play a major contributory role in that development. Whereas rules protecting consumers against misleading practices enable such a development to be taken into account, legislation of the kind contained . . . Biersteuergesetz prevents it from taking place. As the court has already held in another context . . ., the legislation of a member state must not "crystallize given consumer habits so as to

consolidate an advantage acquired by national industries concerned to comply with them".

33. Secondly, in the other member states of the community the designations corresponding to the German designation "bier" are generic designations for a fermented beverage manufactured from malted barley, whether malted barley on its own or with the addition of rice or maize. The same approach is taken in Community law as can be seen from heading no 22.03 of the Common Customs Tariff. The German legislature itself utilizes the designation "bier" in that way in article 9(7) and (8) of the Biersteuergesetz in order to refer to beverages not complying with the manufacturing rules laid down in article 9(1) and (2).

34. The German designation "bier" and its equivalents in the languages of the other Member States of the Community may therefore not be restricted to beers manufactured in accordance with the rules in force in the Federal Republic of Germany.

35. It is admittedly legitimate to seek to enable consumers who attribute specific qualities to beers manufactured from particular raw materials to make their choice in the light of that consideration. However, as the court has already emphasized . . ., that possibility may be ensured by means which do not prevent the importation of products which have been lawfully manufactured and marketed in other member states and, in particular, "by the compulsory affixing of suitable labels giving the nature of the product sold". [. . .]

37. It follows from the foregoing that by applying the rules on designation in article 10 of the Biersteuergesetz to beers imported from other member states which were manufactured and marketed lawfully in those states the federal republic of Germany has failed to fulfil its obligations under article 30 of the EEC Treaty [now Article 34 TFEU].

The absolute ban on the marketing of beers containing additives

38. In the Commission's opinion the absolute ban on the marketing of beers containing additives cannot be justified on public-health grounds. It maintains that the other member states control very strictly the utilization of additives in foodstuffs and do not authorize the use of any given additive until thorough tests have established that it is harmless. In the Commission's view, there should be a presumption that beers manufactured in other member states which contain additives authorized there represent no danger to public health. The Commission argues that if the Federal Republic of Germany wishes to oppose the importation of such beers then it bears the onus of proving that such beers are a danger to public health. The commission considers that in this case that burden of proof has not been discharged. In any event, the rules on additives applying to beer in the federal republic of Germany are disproportionate in so far as

they completely preclude the use of additives whereas the rules for other beverages, such as soft drinks, are much more flexible.

39. For its part, the German government considers that in view of the dangers resulting from the utilization of additives whose long-term effects are not yet known and in particular of the risks resulting from the accumulation of additives in the organism and their interaction with other substances, such as alcohol, it is necessary to minimize the quantity of additives ingested. Since beer is a foodstuff of which large quantities are consumed in Germany, the German government considers that it is particularly desirable to prohibit the use of any additive in its manufacture, especially in so far as the use of additives is not technologically necessary and can be avoided if only the ingredients laid down in the Biersteuergesetz are used. In those circumstances, the German rules on additives in beer are fully justified by the need to safeguard public health and do not infringe the principle of proportionality.

40. It is not contested that the prohibition on the marketing of beers containing additives constitutes a barrier to the importation from other member states of beers containing additives authorized in those states, and is to that extent covered by article 30 of the EEC Treaty [now Article 34 TFEU]. However, it must be ascertained whether it is possible to justify that prohibition under article 36 of the treaty on grounds of the protection of human health.

41. The court has consistently held that "in so far as there are uncertainties at the present state of scientific research it is for the member states, in the absence of harmonization, to decide what degree of protection of the health and life of humans they intend to assure, having regard however to the requirements of the free movement of goods within the community".

42. As may also be seen from the decisions of the court, in such circumstances community law does not preclude the adoption by the member states of legislation whereby the use of additives is subjected to prior authorization granted by a measure of general application for specific additives, in respect of all products, for certain products only or for certain uses. Such legislation meets a genuine need of health policy, namely that of restricting the uncontrolled consumption of food additives.

43. However, the application to imported products of prohibitions on marketing products containing additives which are authorized in the member state of production but prohibited in the member state of importation is permissible only in so far as it complies with the requirements of Article 36 of the treaty as it has been interpreted by the Court.

44. It must be borne in mind, in the first place, that in its judgments in the Sandoz, Motte and Muller cases, cited above, the court inferred from

the principle of proportionality underlying the last sentence of Article 36 of the treaty that prohibitions on the marketing of products containing additives authorized in the member state of production but prohibited in the member state of importation must be restricted to what is actually necessary to secure the protection of public health. The court also concluded that the use of a specific additive which is authorized in another member state must be authorized in the case of a product imported from that member state where, in view, on the one hand, of the findings of international scientific research, and in particular of the work of the Community's Scientific Committee for food, the Codex Alimentarius Committee of the Food and Agriculture Organization of the United Nations (FAO) and the World Health Organization, and, on the other hand, of the eating habits prevailing in the importing member state, the additive in question does not present a risk to public health and meets a real need, especially a technical one.

45. Secondly, it should be remembered that ... by virtue of the principle of proportionality, traders must also be able to apply, under a procedure which is easily accessible to them and can be concluded within a reasonable time, for the use of specific additives to be authorized by a measure of general application.

46. It should be pointed out that it must be open to traders to challenge before the courts an unjustified failure to grant Authorization. Without prejudice to the right of the competent national authorities of the importing member state to ask traders to produce the information in their possession which may be useful for the purpose of assessing the facts, it is for those authorities to demonstrate ... that the prohibition is justified on grounds relating to the protection of the health of its population.

47. It must be observed that the German rules on additives applicable to beer result in the exclusion of all the additives authorized in the other member states and not the exclusion of just some of them for which there is concrete justification by reason of the risks which they involve in view of the eating habits of the German population; moreover those rules do not lay down any procedure whereby traders can obtain authorization for the use of a specific additive in the manufacture of beer by means of a measure of general application.

48. As regards more specifically the harmfulness of additives, the German government, citing experts' reports, has referred to the risks inherent in the ingestion of additives in general. It maintains that it is important, for reasons of general preventive health protection, to minimize the quantity of additives ingested, and that it is particularly advisable to prohibit altogether their use in the manufacture of beer, a foodstuff consumed in considerable quantities by the German population.

49. However, it appears from the tables of additives authorized for use in the various foodstuffs submitted by the German government itself that some of the additives authorized in other member states for use in the manufacture of beer are also authorized under the German rules, in particular the regulation on additives, for use in the manufacture of all, or virtually all, beverages. Mere reference to the potential risks of the ingestion of additives in general and to the fact that beer is a foodstuff consumed in large quantities does not suffice to justify the imposition of stricter rules in the case of beer. [. . .]

53. Consequently, in so far as the German rules on additives in beer entail a general ban on additives, their application to beers imported from other member states is contrary to the requirements of Community law as laid down in the case-law of the Court, since that prohibition is contrary to the principle of proportionality and is therefore not covered by the exception provided for in Article 36 of the EEC Treaty [now Article 36 TFEU]. ■

Notes and Questions

1. The German beer purity requirement has a long tradition. A well-known version was enacted by the German state of Bavaria in 1516, though earlier versions in other states date back to at least the 14th century.

2. While the German Beer Tax Act was amended following the Court of Justice's decision, the German beer purity requirement, which is now part of a different statute,[26] remains in force and continues to be applied to purely domestic situations where the free movement of goods does not apply. However, as a matter of legal policy, the merits of the beer purity requirement are quite controversial. Critics believe that the beer purity requirement stifles innovation and limits variety.[27] Why do you think the German beer purity law has endured even though it effectively appears to put German brewers at a competitive disadvantage?

3. Consider the following hypothetical. Assume that in one Member State, a manufacturer starts selling a fruit juice made from blackberries under the name "beer," and, after a few years, it becomes customary in that Member State to call blackberry juice "beer." Now the producer in question wants to sell his blackberry juice in Germany and the U.K. under the name "beer." Does he have a right to do so under the free movement of goods?

4. What is Germany's argument for why additives that are legal in other foods should be illegal in beer.

5. Which party bears the burden of proof that the requirements of Article 36 TFEU are satisfied? In particular, what happens if the health risks posed by certain goods are not yet known?

---

[26] Vorläufiges Biergesetz (Provisional Beer Act), July 29, 1993, BGBl. I, 1422.
[27] *German Beer Laws: Pure Swill*, THE ECONOMIST, Apr. 16, 2016.

6. In what sense does the ban on additives raise problems distinct from those raised by the beer purity requirement? In particular, why does the court not simply declare that a ban on additives fails the proportionality test because mandatory disclosure is a less burdensome means of protecting consumers?

7. Can the Court's decision be read to imply that if a product can legally be sold in one Member State, then it is also legal to sell it in other Member States?

COMMISSION V. HELLENIC REPUBLIC
Cases C-391/92, June 29, 1995, E.C.R. 1995, I-1621 (citations omitted)

[Under Greek law, processed milk for infants (formula) could be sold only by pharmacies. Other establishments could sell formula only if the relevant municipality did not have a pharmacy. The Commission took the view that this rule violated Article 30 EC (now Article 34 TFEU) and brought enforcement proceedings against Greece. There were no Greek manufacturers of formula, so all formula sold in Greece was imported.]

9. Under Article 30 [now Article 34 TFEU] of the Treaty, quantitative restrictions on imports and all measures having equivalent effect are prohibited between Member States.

10. The Court has consistently held that any measure which is capable of, directly or indirectly, actually or potentially, hindering intra-Community trade constitutes a measure having an effect equivalent to a quantitative restriction . . . .

11. National legislation which reserves the sale of processed milk for infants solely to pharmacies is not designed to regulate trade in goods between Member States.

12. Such legislation may, admittedly, restrict the volume of sales and hence the volume of sales of processed milk for infants originating in other Member States inasmuch as it deprives traders other than pharmacists of the possibility of marketing that product. But the question remains whether such a possibility is sufficient to characterize the legislation in question as a measure having equivalent effect to a quantitative restriction on imports, within the meaning of Article 30 of the Treaty [now Article 34 TFEU].

13. In that respect it should be observed that the application to products from other Member States of national provisions restricting or prohibiting certain selling arrangements is not such as to hinder directly or indirectly, actually or potentially, trade between Member States within the meaning of the Dassonville judgment, cited above, so long as those provisions apply to all relevant traders operating within the national territory and so long as they affect in the same manner, in law and in fact, the marketing of domestic products and of those from other Member States.

Provided that those conditions are fulfilled, the application of such rules to the sale of products from another Member State meeting the requirements laid down by that State is not by nature such as to prevent their access to the market or to impede access any more than it impedes the access of domestic products. Such rules therefore fall outside the scope of Article 30 of the Treaty [now Article 34 TFEU].

14. So far as concerns the Greek legislation called in question in this case by the Commission, those conditions are fulfilled.

15. Thus, that legislation, the effect of which is to limit the commercial freedom of traders irrespective of the actual characteristics of the product referred to, concerns the selling arrangements of certain goods, inasmuch as it prohibits the sale, other than exclusively by pharmacies, of processed milk for infants and thus generally determines the points of sale where they may be distributed.

16. Moreover, the legislation objected to by the Commission, which applies, without distinction according to the origin of the products in question, to all of the traders operating within the national territory, does not affect the sale of products originating in other Member States any differently from that of domestic products.

17. The fact, invoked by the Commission, that the Hellenic Republic does not itself produce processed milk for infants does not undermine those findings. The applicability of Article 30 of the Treaty [now Article 34 TFEU] to a national measure for the general regulation of commerce, which concerns all the products concerned without distinction according to their origin, cannot depend on such a purely fortuitous factual circumstance, which may, moreover, change with the passage of time. If it did, this would have the illogical consequence that the same legislation would fall under Article 30 [now Article 34 TFEU] in certain Member States but fall outside the scope of that provision in other Member States.

18. The situation would be different only if it was apparent that the legislation at issue protected domestic products which were similar to processed milk for infants from other Member States or which were in competition with milk of that type.

19. In this instance, the Commission has not shown that that was the case.

20. It follows from the foregoing considerations that the Greek legislation called in question by the Commission is confined to limiting the places where the product concerned may be distributed by regulating the marketing of that product, without thereby preventing access to the market of products from other Member States or specifically placing them at a disadvantage.

21. That being so, the Greek legislation reserving the sale of processed milk for infants in principle exclusively to pharmacies falls outside the scope of Article 30 of the Treaty [now Article 34 TFEU]. The Commission's application must therefore be dismissed. ■

NOTES AND QUESTIONS

1. Do you believe there are good policy reasons for limiting the sale of infant formula to pharmacies? What are the potential downsides of such a rule?

2. How is this case different from the beer purity law case? In other words, why did the Court not simply hold that buyers of infant formula can be sufficiently protected by appropriate disclosure.

3. The Court argues that the legislation applies without distinction to domestic and foreign goods despite the fact that no formula is produced in Greece. Can you think of any policy reasons that support the Court's conclusion? For example, why do you think the Court has limited the mandatory requirements doctrine to measures that apply without distinction in the first place?

4. Consider the following hypothetical: Alphaland, a Member State of the European Union, has two main modes of transportation: cars and bicycles. The bicycles sold in Alphaland are mostly produced in Alphaland, whereas there are no car manufacturers in Alphaland. One fine day, Alphaland enacts legislation under which cars can be sold only by licensed car dealers with at least 50 employees. Does this statute violate the free movement of goods?

KONSUMENTOMBUDSMANNEN V. GOURMET INTERNATIONAL PRODUCTS AB

Cases C-405/98., March 8, 2001, E.C.R. 2001, I-1795 (citations omitted)

[Swedish law imposed sweeping prohibitions against advertising for alcoholic beverages.[28] In particular, such beverages could not be advertised on television or radio.[29] Further, they could not be advertised in periodicals.[30] An exception was allowed for "publications distributed solely at the point of sale of such beverages."[31] In litigation before the Stockholm District Court, the question arose whether these prohibitions were compatible with the fundamental freedoms. The Stockholm District Court requested a preliminary ruling from the Court of Justice.[32]]

14. The Consumer Ombudsman and the intervening Governments accept that the prohibition on advertising in Sweden affects sales of alcoholic beverages there, including those imported from other Member

---
[28] Para. 4.
[29] Para. 4.
[30] Para. 4.
[31] Para. 4.
[32] Para. 1.

States, since the specific purpose of the Swedish legislation is to reduce the consumption of alcohol.

15. However, observing that the Court held in [its *Keck* decision] [. . .] that national provisions restricting or prohibiting certain selling arrangements are not liable to hinder intra-Community trade, so long as they apply to all relevant traders operating within the national territory and so long as they affect in the same manner, in law and in fact, the marketing of domestic products and of those from other Member States, the Consumer Ombudsman and the intervening Governments contend that the prohibition on advertising in issue in the main proceedings does not constitute an obstacle to trade between Member States, since it satisfies the criteria laid down by the Court in that judgment. [. . .]

18. It should be pointed out that, according to paragraph 17 of its judgment in Keck and Mithouard, if national provisions restricting or prohibiting certain selling arrangements are to avoid being caught by Article 30 of the Treaty [now Article 34 TFEU], they must not be of such a kind as to prevent access to the market by products from another Member State or to impede access any more than they impede the access of domestic products.

19. The Court has also held . . . that it cannot be excluded that an outright prohibition, applying in one Member State, of a type of promotion for a product which is lawfully sold there might have a greater impact on products from other Member States.

20. It is apparent that a prohibition on advertising such as that at issue in the main proceedings not only prohibits a form of marketing a product but in reality prohibits producers and importers from directing any advertising messages at consumers, with a few insignificant exceptions.

21. Even without its being necessary to carry out a precise analysis of the facts characteristic of the Swedish situation, which it is for the national court to do, the Court is able to conclude that, in the case of products like alcoholic beverages, the consumption of which is linked to traditional social practices and to local habits and customs, a prohibition of all advertising directed at consumers in the form of advertisements in the press, on the radio and on television, the direct mailing of unsolicited material or the placing of posters on the public highway is liable to impede access to the market by products from other Member States more than it impedes access by domestic products, with which consumers are instantly more familiar. [. . .]

25. A prohibition on advertising such as that at issue in the main proceedings must therefore be regarded as affecting the marketing of products from other Member States more heavily than the marketing of domestic products and as therefore constituting an obstacle to trade between Member States caught by Article 30 [now Article 34] of the Treaty.

26. However, such an obstacle may be justified by the protection of public health, a general interest ground recognised by Article 36 of the Treaty.

27. In that regard, it is accepted that rules restricting the advertising of alcoholic beverages in order to combat alcohol abuse reflects public health concerns. . . .

28. In order for public health concerns to be capable of justifying an obstacle to trade such as that inherent in the prohibition on advertising at issue in the main proceedings, the measure concerned must also be proportionate to the objective to be achieved and must not constitute either a means of arbitrary discrimination or a disguised restriction on trade between Member States.

29. The Consumer Ombudsman and the intervening Governments claim that the derogation provided for in Article 36 of the Treaty [Article 36 TFEU] can cover the prohibition on advertising at issue in the main proceedings. The Consumer Ombudsman and the Swedish Government emphasise in particular that the prohibition is not absolute and does not prevent members of the public from obtaining information, if they wish, in particular in restaurants, on the Internet, in an editorial context or by asking the producer or importer to send advertising material. Furthermore, the Swedish Government observes that the Court of Justice has acknowledged that, in the present state of Community law, Member States are at liberty, within the limits set by the Treaty, to decide on the degree of protection which they wish to afford to public health and on the way in which that protection is to be achieved . . . . The Swedish Government maintains that the legislation at issue in the main proceedings constitutes an essential component of its alcohol policy.

30. GIP claims that the outright prohibition on advertising laid down by the legislation at issue in the main proceedings is disproportionate, since the protection sought could be obtained by prohibitions of a more limited nature, concerning, for example, certain public places or the press aimed at children and adolescents. It must be borne in mind that the Swedish policy on alcoholism is already catered for by the existence of the monopoly on retail sales, by the prohibition on sales to persons under the age of 20 years and by information campaigns. [. . .]

32. It should be pointed out, first, that there is no evidence before the Court to suggest that the public health grounds on which the Swedish authorities rely have been diverted from their purpose and used in such a way as to discriminate against goods originating in other Member States or to protect certain national products indirectly . . .

33. Second, the decision as to whether the prohibition on advertising at issue in the main proceedings is proportionate, and in particular as to whether the objective sought might be achieved by less extensive

prohibitions or restrictions or by prohibitions or restrictions having less effect on intra-Community trade, calls for an analysis of the circumstances of law and of fact which characterise the situation in the Member State concerned, which the national court is in a better position than the Court of Justice to carry out.

34. The answer to the question must therefore be that, as regards the free movement of goods, Articles 30 and 36 of the Treaty [now Articles 34 and 36 TFEU] do not preclude a prohibition on the advertising of alcoholic beverages such as that laid down in [the relevant Swedish statute], unless it is apparent that, in the circumstances of law and of fact which characterise the situation in the Member State concerned, the protection of public health against the harmful effects of alcohol can be ensured by measures having less effect on intra-Community trade. ■

NOTES AND QUESTIONS

1. According to the Court of Justice, the *Keck* exemption does not apply in this case. Why?

2. Note that the Court does not decide whether the near-total ban on advertising satisfies the proportionality principle. Rather, it limits itself to outlining the general legal principles that govern this question and then lets the national court decide. As a technical matter, this approach is perfectly legal given that Article 267 TFEU does not specify in how much detail the Court of Justice has to answer the national court's questions. Nonetheless, the fact that the Court of Justice sometimes leaves the details of the proportionality test to the national court raises interesting questions. As a normative matter, do you think that the Court of Justice should have provided the national court with a more detailed answer?

3. Why do you think the Court of Justice did not go into detail regarding the proportionality test? And, more generally, in which cases do you think the Court of Justice is likely to leave the details of the proportionality test to the national court?

4. Do you think that the near-total ban on advertising satisfies the proportionality principle?

5. Assume, hypothetically, that a Member State imposes a complete ban on cars and motorcycles in order to reduce the number of traffic accidents, while still allowing the use of buses. Would such a statute violate EU law?

6. Assume, hypothetically, that a Member State enacts a statute according to which all cars and motorcycles must be powered by electricity rather than gas. Would such a statute violate EU law?

7. As a policy matter, should each Member State be able to determine the level of protection afforded against alcohol and/or substance abuse, or would it be desirable for the European Union to harmonize the pertinent rules?

2. ARTICLE 36 TFEU

In order for a measure to be justified under Article 36 TFEU, several conditions must be met.

To begin, the measure must be aimed at one of the goals listed in Article 36. The list is long and includes "public morality, public policy [and] public security; the protection of health and human life, animals [and] plants; the protection of national treasures possessing artistic, historic or archaeological value; [and] the protection of industrial and commercial property."[33]

Moreover, the relevant regulation must satisfy the principle of proportionality, which means that the measure must satisfy three prongs: suitability, necessity, and proportionality in the strict sense. In other words, the state measure must be suitable to advance the goals that it purports to protect (suitability). There must not be another way of achieving the same goal that is less burdensome for those who are adversely affected by the measure (necessity). And the burden imposed by the measure must not be out of proportion to the benefits that the measure yields (proportionality in the strict sense).

Finally, in order to be justified under Article 36 TFEU, the measure must not "constitute a means of arbitrary discrimination or a disguised restriction on trade between Member States." In other words, the Member States must not abuse Article 36 by adopting measures that purport to protect the goals listed in that provision but in fact aim at restricting trade or discriminating against foreign goods. Crucially, though, Article 36 prohibits only "arbitrary" discrimination. The mere fact that a measure discriminates, even if the discrimination is "formal" in the sense that the measure explicitly distinguishes between foreign and domestic goods, does not preclude the measure from being justified under Article 36 TFEU. Rather, as long as such discrimination is necessary to achieve the goals listed in Article 36—and hence is not arbitrary—the discriminatory nature of the measure does not stand in the way of justifying the measure under Article 36.

While some of the goals listed in Article 36 TFEU are fairly self-explanatory, such as the protection of health, others have proven more difficult to define. This is particularly true for the notions of public morality, public policy and public security. By and large, the Court of Justice has opted for a relatively narrow understanding of public morality, public policy and public security.

The public policy exception in Article 36 can only be invoked if there is a "genuine and sufficiently serious threat to a fundamental interest of

---

[33] TFEU, art. 36.

society."[34] The same is true for the public security exception, which also requires "a genuine and sufficiently serious threat to a fundamental interest of society."[35]

As regards public morality, the Member States are given somewhat more leeway in that each Member State can determine its own moral values.[36] However, to prevent abuse of the public morality clause, the Court of Justice has made it clear that the Member States have to be consistent in protecting the values that they claim to uphold. For example, in *Conegate Limited*, the Court was faced with the question of whether a Member State could prohibit the importation of pornographic materials on public morality grounds despite the fact that the same Member State did not prohibit the marketing of such products within its territory.[37] Consider the following excerpt.

> 14. ... [I]n principle it is for each member state to determine in accordance with its own scale of values and in the form selected by it the requirements of public morality in its territory.
>
> 15. However, although Community law leaves the Member States free to make their own assessments of the indecent or obscene character of certain articles, it must be pointed out that the fact that goods cause offence cannot be regarded as sufficiently serious to justify restrictions on the free movement of goods where the Member State concerned does not adopt, with respect to the same goods manufactured or marketed within its territory, penal measures or other serious and effective measures intended to prevent the distribution of such goods in its territory.
>
> 16. It follows that a Member State may not rely on grounds of public morality in order to prohibit the importation of goods from other Member States when its legislation contains no prohibition on the manufacture or marketing of the same goods on its territory.[38]

All of the public goods listed in Article 36 have in common that they relate to what the Court of Justice has called "matters of a non-economic nature."[39] By that, the Court means that Article 36 cannot be invoked to defend measures that seek to prevent the economic consequences, such as

---

[34] *E.g.*, Case C-137/09, Marc Michel Josemans v. Burgemeester van Maastricht, 2010 E.C.R. I-3019 ¶ 62 (regarding the freedom to provide services).

[35] *E.g.*, Case C-543/08, Commission v. Portugal, 2010 E.C.R. I-11241 ¶ 85.

[36] Case 121/85, Conegate Limited v. HM Customs & Excise, 1986 E.C.R. 1007 ¶ 14.

[37] *Id.* ¶ 13.

[38] *Id.* ¶¶ 14–16.

[39] Case 72/83, Campus Oil Limited et al. v. Minister for Industry and Energy, 1984 E.C.R. 2727 ¶ 35.

unemployment, that result from the very increase in competition that the fundamental freedoms are designed to create.[40]

CAMPUS OIL LIMITED ET AL. V. MINISTER FOR INDUSTRY AND ENERGY ET AL.
Case 72/83, July 10, 1984, E.C.R. 1984, 2727 (citations omitted)

[The Irish State owned an oil refining company. Under Irish law, firms importing oil into Ireland were under an obligation to buy a certain percentage, which could be as much as 35%, of their oil from that state-owned company. Furthermore, the Irish government was authorized to set the purchase price based on its costs. The Irish government defended these rules on the ground that they were necessary to ensure that Ireland could maintain a certain capacity to refine oil within its territory. However, in litigation before Irish courts the plaintiffs argued that the relevant Irish rules violated the free movement of goods. In response, the High Court of Ireland requested a preliminary ruling from the Court of Justice.

In its opinion, the Court of Justice first notes that the statute at issue constitutes a measure having equivalent effect to a quantitative restriction on imports. Then, it addresses the question of whether the statute can nonetheless be justified.]

21. The second question asks whether Article 36 of the Treaty [now Article 36 TFEU] and, in particular, the concepts of "public policy" and of "public security" contained therein are to be interpreted as meaning that a system such as the one at issue in this case, established by a Member State which is totally dependent on imports for its supplies of petroleum products, can be exempt from the prohibition laid down in Article 30 [now Article 34] of the Treaty. [...]

34. It should be stated in this connection that petroleum products, because of their exceptional importance as an energy source in the modern economy, are of fundamental importance for a country's existence since not only its economy but above all its institutions, its essential public services and even the survival of its inhabitants depend upon them. An interruption of supplies of petroleum products, with the resultant dangers for the country's existence, could therefore seriously affect the public security that Article 36 allows states to protect.

35. It is true that ... Article 36 refers to matters of a non-economic nature. A Member State cannot be allowed to avoid the effects of measures provided for in the treaty by pleading the economic difficulties caused by the elimination of barriers to intra-Community trade. However, in the light of the seriousness of the consequences that an interruption in supplies of

---

[40] *Cf. id.* ("A member state cannot be allowed to avoid the effects of measures provided for in the treaty by pleading the economic difficulties caused by the elimination of barriers to intra-Community trade.").

petroleum products may have for a country's existence, the aim of ensuring a minimum supply of petroleum products at all times is to be regarded as transcending purely economic considerations and thus as capable of constituting an objective covered by the concept of public security.

36. It should be added that to come within the ambit of Article 36, the rules in question must be justified by objective circumstances corresponding to the needs of public security. Once that justification has been established, the fact that the rules are of such a nature as to make it possible to achieve, in addition to the objectives covered by the concept of public security, other objectives of an economic nature which the member state may also seek to achieve, does not exclude the application of Article 36 . . . .

37. As the court has previously stated . . ., Article 36, as an exception to a fundamental principle of the Treaty, must be interpreted in such a way that its scope is not extended any further than is necessary for the protection of the interests which it is intended to secure and the measures taken pursuant to that article must not create obstacles to imports which are disproportionate to those objectives. Measures adopted on the basis of Article 36 can therefore be justified only if they are such as to serve the interest which that article protects and if they do not restrict intra-Community trade more than is absolutely necessary.

38. In that connection, the plaintiffs in the main action and the commission cast doubt, in the first place, on whether the installation of a refinery can ensure supplies of petroleum products in the event of a crisis, since a crisis gives rise above all to a shortage of crude oil, so that the refinery would be unable to operate in such circumstances.

39. It is true that as the world oil market now stands, the immediate effect of a crisis would probably be an interruption or a severe reduction in deliveries of crude oil. It should, however, be pointed out that the fact of having refining capacity on its territory enables the state concerned to enter into long-term contracts with the oil-producing countries for the supply of crude oil to its refinery which offer a better guarantee of supplies in the event of a crisis. It is thus less at risk than a state which has no refining capacity of its own and which has no means of covering its needs other than by purchases on the free market.

40. Furthermore, the existence of a national refinery constitutes a guarantee against the additional risk of an interruption in deliveries of refined products to which a state with no refining capacity of its own is exposed. Such a state would be dependent on the major oil companies which control refineries in other countries and on those companies' commercial policy.

41. It may, therefore, be concluded that the presence of a refinery on the national territory, by reducing both of those types of risks, can

effectively contribute to improving the security of supply of petroleum products to a state which does not have crude oil resources of its own.

42. The plaintiffs in the main action and the commission consider, however, that even if the operation of a refinery is justified in the interest of public security, it is not necessary in order to achieve that objective, and, in any event, it is disproportionate in relation to that objective, to oblige importers to satisfy a certain proportion of their requirements by purchase from the national refinery at a price fixed by the competent minister.

44. It must be pointed out in this connection that a Member State may have recourse to Article 36 to justify a measure having equivalent effect to a quantitative restriction on imports only if no other measure, less restrictive from the point of view of the free movement of goods, is capable of achieving the same objective.

45. In the present case, therefore, it is necessary to consider whether the obligation placed on importers of petroleum products to purchase at prices determined on the basis of the costs incurred by the refinery in question is necessary, albeit only temporarily, for the purpose of ensuring that enough of the refinery's production can be marketed so as to guarantee, in the interest of public security, a minimum supply of petroleum products to the state concerned in the event of a supply crisis.

46. That obligation could be necessary if the distributors that hold the major share of the market concerned refuse, as the Irish government contends, to purchase supplies from the refinery in question. It is on the assumption that the refinery charges prices which are competitive on the market concerned that it must be determined whether the refinery's products could be freely marketed. If it is not possible by means of industrial and commercial measures to avoid any financial losses resulting from such prices, those losses must be borne by the Member State concerned, subject to the application of Articles 92 and 93 of the Treaty [now Articles 87, 88 TFEU].

47. As regards, in the next place, the quantities of petroleum products which may, as the case may be, be covered by such a system of purchasing obligations, it should be stressed that they must in no case exceed the minimum supply requirements of the state concerned without which its public security, as defined above, and in particular the operation of its essential public services and the survival of its inhabitants, would be affected.

48. Furthermore, the quantities of petroleum products whose marketing can be ensured under such a system must not exceed the quantities which are necessary, so far as production is concerned, on the one hand, for technical reasons in order that the refinery may operate currently at a sufficient level of its production capacity to ensure that its plant will be available in the event of a crisis and, on the other hand, in

order that it may continue to refine at all times the crude oil covered by the long-term contracts which the state concerned has entered into so that it may be assured of regular supplies.

49. The proportion of the total needs of importers of petroleum products that may be made subject to a purchasing obligation must not, therefore, exceed the proportion which the quantities set out above represent of the current total consumption of petroleum products in the Member State concerned.

50. It is for the national court to decide whether the system established by the 1982 order complies with those limits.

51. The answer to the second question should therefore be that a member state which is totally or almost totally dependent on imports for its supplies of petroleum products may rely on grounds of public security within the meaning of Article 36 of the treaty for the purpose of requiring importers to cover a certain proportion of their needs by purchases from a refinery situated in its territory at prices fixed by the competent minister on the basis of the costs incurred in the operation of that refinery, if the production of the refinery cannot be freely disposed of at competitive prices on the market concerned. The quantities of petroleum products covered by such a system must not exceed the minimum supply requirement without which the public security of the state concerned would be affected or the level of production necessary to keep the refinery's production capacity available in the event of a crisis and to enable it to continue to refine at all times the crude oil for the supply of which the state concerned has entered into long-term contracts. ■

NOTES AND QUESTIONS

1. The Campus Oil decision has to be read in its historical context. The year 1979 saw the Iranian revolution; Iran became an Islamic Republic under the leadership of the Ayatollah Khomeini. The following year, Iraq, headed by Saddam Hussein, invaded Iran. As a result of these events, Iranian oil production decreased dramatically, and Iraq's oil production sank as well. This prompted the so-called second oil crisis. As a result, the prospect of oil shortages was widely thought to constitute a potentially serious threat to national security. For example, a 1980 article in *The New York Times* cites a panel report suggesting that a sudden loss of access to foreign oil might lead to another Great Depression and could possibly result in a confrontation with the Soviet Union.[41]

2. Can you identify the "genuine and sufficiently serious threat to a fundamental interest of society" that the Court of Justice found compelling in *Campus Oil?*

---

[41] Robert D. Hershey, Jr., *Warning By Energy Group: Security Peril in Oil Cutoff Cited*, NY Times, July 4, 1980, at D2.

3. Why did the Court conclude that the statute served a non-economic goal?

4. According to the Court, can Article 36 TFEU justify a national measure that serves both one of the goods listed in Article 36 and economic interests of the Member States?

5. Does the statute contribute to protecting Ireland against a shortage of petroleum products? Or is the statute useless for this purpose since substantial refining capacity does not help against a shortage of crude oil? What does the Court say? Do you agree?

6. According to the Court, Ireland's refinery must charge competitive prices (para. 46) in order to avoid a violation of EU law. Assume, hypothetically, that Ireland needs additional funds to keep its refinery running. Could Ireland legally impose a petrol tax on fuel sold in Ireland in order to generate additional funds? Or would such a tax violate EU law? Assume that Ireland is not an oil producing country.

D. PRACTICE QUESTIONS

For the purpose of the following hypotheticals, assume that Alpha and Beta are Member States of the European Union.

1. In January 2019, several major Alphanian newspapers publish credible reports that *Alphanian Blues*, a type of parrot native to Alpha, have begun to show signs of an unknown disease. Highly respected scientists voice concerns that this disease may well be dangerous to humans, although no studies had been conducted on this issue. Beta thereupon enacts a statute strictly prohibiting the import of all Alphanian animals. Does the Betanian statute violate the free movement of goods? Discuss!

2. In February 2019, the Alphanian government enacts a new statute, the so-called "Beer Fairness Act (BFA)." According to the BFA, it is illegal to sell beer with more than 6% alcohol in Alpha under the name "beer." As it happens, 90 % of all beer produced in Alpha as of January 2019 contain 6% or less alcohol. By contrast, 80% of the beer produced in the rest of the European Union contain more than 6% alcohol.

Francois is a Betanian brewer whose brewery is located in Beta. He wants to export his beer to Alpha. His beer contains 9% alcohol. He believes, however, that the BFA violates EU law. The Alphanian government truthfully points out that, according to surveys, 95% of Alphanian consumers believe that alcoholic beverages sold as beer contain at most 6% alcohol. The Alphanian government also argues that if beer were to contain more than six percent alcohol, then consumers might be more likely to later transition from beer to beverages with higher alcohol content, thus contributing to the problem of alcoholism. Assume that there is no secondary EU legislation on the issue. Does the Alphanian statute violate the free movement of goods?

3. Assume that an Alphanian law subjects the sale of fruit liquor with an alcohol content of up to 20% to an excise tax of 20%. By contrast, whiskey is subject to an excise tax of 30%. Whiskey has an alcohol content between 30 and 40%. Assume, for the sake of this question, that Alpha produces copious amounts of fruit liquor but no whiskey. Rather, whiskey is imported mainly from Beta. The Alphanian government defends the higher excise tax for whiskey on the ground that whiskey has a higher alcohol content and that the excise tax is designed to deter the consumption of whiskey because alcoholism is already a significant problem in Alpha. Other alcoholic beverages that are typically produced in Alpha and have an alcohol content equal to or higher than that of whiskey such as Alpha's famous "apple schnapps" are also subject to an excise tax of 30%. Linda is a Betanian citizen who wants to export whiskey from Beta to Alpha. She believes that the relevant Alphanian tax regime violates EU law. Discuss!

4. The Alphanian town of Victoria is famous for its locally produced pottery, including the so-called "beard man," a beer mug decorated with the shape of bearded human face. Unfortunately, the various potteries use heavy trucks to transport their wares to other cities located both in Alpha and in other EU Member States, and these heavy trucks impose a heavy burden on the local roads in and around Victoria. Therefore, the town of Victoria decides to impose a special "pottery sales tax" of 5% on pottery sold in Victoria. This "pottery sales tax" is added to the regular sales tax imposed by Alphanian law. Does the "pottery sales tax" violate EU law? Assume, for the purpose of this question, that EU law does not contain any special rules on sales taxes.[42] Discuss!

5. In April 2018, there are several cases in which Europeans suffer from food poisoning as a result of consuming fish imported from Alpha that was not properly stored in its country of origin. Therefore, in May 2018, Beta adopts a statute according to which all imported fish has to undergo an inspection to ensure that it does not pose health risks. The inspection does not necessarily take place at the border. Rather, the statute only provides that it has to take place before the imported fish is sold to consumers. The importer has to pay the costs of the relevant inspection—roughly $1 per kilo of fish. Assume, for the purpose of this question, that there exists no secondary EU law dealing with the import of fish. Does the Betanian statute violate EU law?

---

[42] As an aside, note that in the European Union, Member States actually use added-value taxes rather than sales taxes. Whereas a sales tax taxes the sale of goods, an added-value tax is aimed at taxing consumption. The European Union has adopted a directive aimed at ensuring that added-value taxes are harmonized at least to some extent. *See* Council Directive 2006/112/EC of 28 Nov. 2006 on the common system of value-added tax, O.J. 347, Dec. 11, 2006, pp. 1–118, art. 97 (setting a minimum standard rate of 15%).

6. In 2018, Alpha adopts a statute according to which all book importers are required to contribute 0.01% of a book's price to a so-called "social benefits fund," which is used to finance health and retirement benefits for workers in the publishing industry. The purpose of the law is to "level the playing field" for foreign and Alphanian publishers since the workers employed by Alphanian publishers are typically older than those employed by publishers in other Member States. The contribution is not levied on books produced in Alpha itself. Does the statute violate EU law?

Article 34 TFEU

I. Goods

II. Quantitative restriction on imports or measure having equivalent effect (MHEE)

   a. A quantitative restriction is given both in cases where a specific Member State imposes a limit on the quantity of goods that can be imported and in cases where the import of a specific type of goods is prohibited entirely

   b. Measure having equivalent effect

   i. *Dassonville*: any rules that are "capable of hindering, directly or indirectly, actually or potentially, intra-community trade are to be considered as measures having an effect equivalent to quantitative restrictions"

   ii. *Keck*: "national provisions restricting or prohibiting certain selling arrangements" do not constitute MHEE if "those provisions apply to all relevant traders operating within the national territory and so long as they affect in the same manner, in law and in fact, the marketing of domestic products and of those from other Member States"

   1. Rules governing selling arrangements

   - Examples: rules on when stores can be open, prohibition against resale at a loss

   - Counterexamples: no mere selling arrangements in case of rules "relating to designation, form, size, weight, composition, presentation, labelling, packaging"

   2. No direct discrimination ("affect in the same manner . . . in law")

   3. No indirect discrimination ("affect in the same manner . . . in fact")

c. Mandatory requirements doctrine ("rule of reason")
   i. Any legitimate goal that does not contradict the purpose of the free movement of goods can serve as a mandatory requirement, e.g. consumer protection
   ii. Proportionality
      1. Suitability: measure must make some contribution to the goal it pursues
      2. Necessity: there must be no less burdensome and equally effective means of furthering the goal in question
      3. Proportionality in the strict sense: the costs imposed by the measure must not be grossly out of proportion to the benefits obtained
   iii. The mandatory requirements doctrine cannot be used to justify discriminatory measures. However, it is not entirely clear what types of discrimination are precluded from being justified
      1. Directly discriminating measures cannot be justified
      2. But the case law of the Court of Justice is not entirely consistent on whether indirectly discriminating measures are capable of being justified
d. Justification under Art. 36 TFEU
   i. Quantitative restriction or MHEE must serve one of the goods listed in Article 36 TFEU
   ii. Measure must satisfy the principle of proportionality (see above)
   iii. Note that Article 36 TFEU can even justify (directly or indirectly) discriminating measures as long as the measures are not a means of arbitrary discrimination or hidden restrictions of trade

Chapter 13

Free Movement of Workers: Personal Scope of Application

■ ■ ■

Article 45 TFEU guarantees the free movement of workers within the European Union. That freedom entails, first, a prohibition against any discrimination based on nationality regarding employment, wages, and other working conditions.[1] Moreover, the free movement of workers includes "the right . . . to accept offers of employment actually made; to move freely within the territory of Member States for this purpose . . . to stay in a Member State for the purpose of employment"[2] and "to remain in the territory of a Member State after having been employed in that State."[3]

A. WORKER

The free movement of workers applies only to workers. That, of course, raises the question of how the notion of worker should be defined. The Court of Justice has answered that question as follows:

> "The Court has consistently held that the concept of worker, within the meaning of the abovementioned provisions, has a specific Community meaning and must not be interpreted narrowly. Any person who pursues activities which are effective and genuine, to the exclusion of activities on such a small scale as to be regarded as purely marginal and ancillary, must be regarded as a worker. The essential feature of an employment relationship is, according to that case-law, that for a certain period of time a person performs services for and under the direction of another person in return for which he receives remuneration."[4]

While this definition has proved quite robust, determining whether a person qualifies as a worker can nonetheless be difficult. In practice, there are mainly two legal issues that can arise in this context. First, at what point is the volume and/or duration of a person's work so marginal that he cannot be considered a worker? Second, how do policy-driven work

---

[1] TFEU, art. 45(1).
[2] TFEU, art. 45(2).
[3] Id.
[4] Case C-337/97, C.P.M. Meeusen v. Hoofdirectie van de Informatie Beheer Groep, 1999 E.C.R. I-3289 ¶ 13 (citations omitted).

programs, such as programs designed to reintegrate drug users into society, affect a person's status as a worker?

D.M. LEVIN V. STAATSSECRETARIS VAN JUSTITIE

Case 53/81, March 23, 1982, E.C.R. 1982, 1035 (citations omitted)

[Mrs. Levin, a citizen of the United Kingdom, sought a permit to reside in the Netherlands. The Dutch authorities denied her request, arguing that she was not engaged in gainful employment in the Netherlands and was therefore not entitled to a residence permit. Thereupon, Mrs. Levin brought suit. With respect to EU law, the issue was whether a person can qualify as a worker despite the fact that the income derived from the relevant occupation is less than the amount generally considered to be the minimum necessary to support oneself.]

6. [T]he national court is essentially asking whether the provisions of community law relating to freedom of movement for workers also cover a national of a member state whose activity as an employed person . . . provides him with an income less than the minimum required for subsistence within the meaning of the legislation of the second member state. [. . .]

7. Under article 48 of the Treaty [now article 45 TFEU] freedom of movement for workers is to be secured within the Community. That freedom is to entail the abolition of any discrimination based on nationality between workers of the member states as regards employment, remuneration and other conditions of work and is to include the right, subject to limitations justified on grounds of public policy, public security or public health, to accept offers of employment actually made, to move freely within the territory of member states for this purpose, to stay in a member state for the purpose of employment and to remain there after the termination of that employment. [. . .]

10. The Netherlands and Danish governments have maintained that the [free movement of workers] may only be relied upon by persons who receive a wage at least commensurate with the means of subsistence considered as necessary by the legislation of the member state in which they work, or who work at least for the number of hours considered as usual in respect of full-time employment in the sector in question. In the absence of any provisions to that effect in community legislation, it is suggested that it is necessary to have recourse to national criteria for the purpose of defining both the minimum wage and the minimum number of hours.

11. That argument cannot, however, be accepted. As the court has already stated . . . the terms "worker" and "activity as an employed person" may not be defined by reference to the national laws of the member states but have a Community meaning. If that were not the case, the Community rules on freedom of movement for workers would be frustrated, as the

meaning of those terms could be fixed and modified unilaterally, without any control by the Community institutions, by national laws which would thus be able to exclude at will certain categories of persons from the benefit of the treaty.

12. Such would, in particular, be the case if the enjoyment of the rights conferred by the principle of freedom of movement for workers could be made subject to the criterion of what the legislation of the host state declares to be a minimum wage, so that the field of application ratione personae of the Community rules on this subject might vary from one member state to another. The meaning and the scope of the terms "worker" and "activity as an employed person" should thus be clarified in the light of the principles of the legal order of the community.

13. In this respect it must be stressed that these concepts define the field of application of one of the fundamental freedoms guaranteed by the treaty and, as such, may not be interpreted restrictively. [. . .]

15. An interpretation which reflects the full scope of these concepts is also in conformity with the objectives of the Treaty which include, according to Articles 2 and 3, the abolition, as between Member States, of obstacles to freedom of movement for persons, with the purpose inter alia of promoting throughout the community a harmonious development of economic activities and a raising of the standard of living. Since part-time employment, although it may provide an income lower than what is considered to be the minimum required for subsistence, constitutes for a large number of persons an effective means of improving their living conditions, the effectiveness of community law would be impaired and the achievement of the objectives of the treaty would be jeopardized if the enjoyment of rights conferred by the principle of Freedom of Movement for Workers were reserved solely to persons engaged in full-time employment and earning, as a result, a wage at least equivalent to the guaranteed minimum wage in the sector under consideration.

16. It follows that the concepts of "worker" and "activity as an employed person" must be interpreted as meaning that the rules relating to freedom of movement for workers also concern persons who pursue or wish to pursue an activity as an employed person on a part-time basis only and who, by virtue of that fact obtain or would obtain only remuneration lower than the minimum guaranteed remuneration in the sector under consideration. In this regard no distinction may be made between those who wish to make do with their income from such an activity and those who supplement that income with other income, whether the latter is derived from property or from the employment of a member of their family who accompanies them.

17. It should however be stated that whilst part-time employment is not excluded from the field of application of the rules on freedom of

movement for workers, those rules cover only the pursuit of effective and genuine activities, to the exclusion of activities on such a small scale as to be regarded as purely marginal and ancillary. It follows both from the statement of the principle of freedom of movement for workers and from the place occupied by the rules relating to that principle in the system of the treaty as a whole that those rules guarantee only the free movement of persons who pursue or are desirous of pursuing an economic activity.

18. The answer to be given to the first and second questions must therefore be that the provisions of community law relating to freedom of movement for workers also cover a national of a member state who pursues, within the territory of another member state, an activity as an employed person which yields an income lower than that which, in the latter state, is considered as the minimum required for subsistence, whether that person supplements the income from his activity as an employed person with other income so as to arrive at that minimum or is satisfied with means of support lower than the said minimum, provided that he pursues an activity as an employed person which is effective and genuine. ∎

NOTES AND QUESTIONS

1. What principle of interpretation does the Court invoke when it asserts, in paragraph 11, that the words "worker" and "activity as an employed person" "may not be defined by reference to the national laws of the member states but have a Community meaning"?

2. How does the Court justify the conclusion that a person can be a worker within the meaning of the free movement of workers despite the fact that his or her activity "yields an income lower than that which, in the latter state, is considered as the minimum required for subsistence"?

3. Consider the situation from a legal policy perspective. Are there good reasons to include or exclude low-income workers? For example, can one argue that such workers are particularly likely to suffer from discrimination based on nationality or from other obstacles to the free movement of workers? Also consider in this context whether the Member States have legitimate reasons to object to the influx of foreign workers whose activity yields an income below the minimum required for subsistence.

4. In paragraph 17 of the opinion, the Court stresses that the free movement of workers "cover[s] only the pursuit of effective and genuine activities, to the exclusion of activities on such a small scale as to be regarded as purely marginal and ancillary." How does the Court justify this limitation and what might be the legal policy rationale underlying it? Why has the Court not established a similar restriction for the free movement of goods, e.g., in the sense that imports, in order to be protected by the free movement of goods, have to reach a certain volume?

5. The principles established in *Levin* were reaffirmed in the 1986 decision *Kempf*.[5] There, the free movement of workers was invoked by a German citizen who lived in the Netherlands and worked there as a music teacher.[6] Crucially, Mr. Kempf gave only about 12 lessons per week and received supplemental income from public funds under the Dutch law on employment benefits.[7] The Dutch government took the view that "work providing an income below the minimum means of subsistence as defined by the host member state cannot be regarded as effective and genuine work if the person who does it is claiming social assistance drawn from public funds."[8] The Court, however, was not persuaded. It held that "a person in effective and genuine part-time employment cannot be excluded . . . merely because the remuneration he derives from it is below the level of the minimum means of subsistence and he seeks to supplement it by other lawful means of subsistence."[9] Moreover, the court stressed that "in that regard it is irrelevant whether those supplementary means of subsistence are derived from property or from the employment of a member of his family, as was the case in Levin, or whether, as in this instance, they are obtained from financial assistance drawn from the public funds of the member state in which he resides, provided that the effective and genuine nature of his work is established."[10]

FRANCA NINNI-ORASCHE V. BUNDESMINISTER FÜR WISSENSCHAFT, VERKEHR UND KUNST

Case C-413/01, November 6, 2003, 2003 E.C.R. I-13187 (citations omitted)

[Mrs. Ninni-Orasche was an Italian citizen living in Austria and married to an Austrian. From July 1995 to September 1995, she worked as a waitress on the basis of a fixed-term contract. Subsequently, she sought work, but was unsuccessful. In March 1996, she therefore enrolled as a student at an Austrian university and studied romance languages and literature. In this context, Mrs. Ninni-Orasche also requested financial aid ("study finance") from the Austrian state. Under Austrian law, financial aid was to be paid not only to Austrians but also to foreign nationals, to the extent that Community law gave such foreign nationals the right to be treated like Austrian nationals. Mrs. Ninni-Orasche argued that she qualified as a worker within the meaning of the free movement of workers and therefore had to be treated like a national. However, her request for financial aid was denied. Litigation ensued, and the case eventually reached the Austrian Verwaltungsgerichtshof. The Verwaltungsgerichtshof requested a preliminary ruling from the Court of Justice in order to clarify the notion of worker.]

---

[5] Case 139/85, R. H. Kempf v. Staatssecretaris van Justitie, 1986 E.C.R. 1741.
[6] *Id.* ¶ 2.
[7] *Id.*
[8] *Id.* ¶ 7.
[9] *Id.* ¶ 14.
[10] *Id.*

18. By its first question, the national court is essentially asking, first, whether the fact that a national of a Member State has worked for a temporary period of two and a half months in the territory of another Member State . . . can confer on him the status of a worker within the meaning of Article 48 of the Treaty [now article 45 TFEU] and, second, whether circumstances preceding and subsequent to that period of employment, such as the fact that the person concerned:

— took up the job only some years after his entry into the host Member State,

— shortly after the end of his short, fixed-term employment relationship, became eligible for entry to university in the host Member State by virtue of having completed his schooling in his country of origin, or

— attempted to find a new job in the period between the end of the short, fixed-term employment relationship and the time when he took up his studies, are relevant in that regard.

[. . .]

23. First of all, it is settled case-law that the concept of "worker", within the meaning of Article 48 of the Treaty [45 TFEU], has a specific Community meaning and must not be interpreted narrowly.

24. Moreover, that concept must be defined in accordance with objective criteria characterising the employment relationship in view of the rights and duties of the persons concerned. The essential feature of an employment relationship is that, for a certain period of time, a person performs services for and under the direction of another person in return for which he receives remuneration.

25. In the light of that case-law, it must be held that the fact that employment is of short duration cannot, in itself, exclude that employment from the scope of Article 48 [45 TFEU] of the Treaty.

26. In order to be treated as a worker, a person must nevertheless pursue an activity which is effective and genuine, to the exclusion of activities on such a small scale as to be regarded as purely marginal and accessory.

27. When establishing whether that condition is satisfied, the national court must base its examination on objective criteria and assess as a whole all the circumstances of the case relating to the nature of both the activities concerned and the employment relationship at issue.

28. It should be stated that, with respect to the assessment whether employment is capable of conferring the status of worker within the meaning of Article 48 [45 TFEU] of the Treaty, factors relating to the conduct of the person concerned before and after the period of employment

are not relevant in establishing the status of worker within the meaning of that article. Such factors are not in any way related to the objective criteria referred to in the case-law cited in paragraphs 23 and 24 of this judgment.

29. In particular, the three factors referred to by the national court, namely the fact that the person concerned took up employment as a waitress only several years after her entry into the host Member State, that, shortly after the end of her short term of employment, she obtained a diploma entitling her to enroll at university in that State and that, after that employment had come to an end, she attempted to find a new job, are not linked either to the possibility that the activity pursued by the appellant in the main proceedings was ancillary or to the nature of that activity or of the employment relationship.

30. For the same reasons, nor can the Court accept the argument put forward by the Danish Government that, in order to assess whether activities pursued as an employed person are effective and genuine, it is necessary to take account of the short term of the employment in relation to the total duration of residence by the person concerned in the host Member State, which, in the main proceedings, was two and a half years.

31. Finally, as regards the argument that the national court is under an obligation to examine, on the basis of the circumstances of the case, whether the appellant in the main proceedings has sought abusively to create a situation enabling her to claim the status of a worker within the meaning of Article 48 of the Treaty with the aim of acquiring advantages linked to that status, it is sufficient to state that any abusive use of the rights granted by the Community legal order under the provisions relating to freedom of movement for workers presupposes that the person concerned falls within the scope ratione personae of that Treaty because he satisfies the conditions for classification as a "worker" within the meaning of that article. It follows that the issue of abuse of rights can have no bearing on the answer to the first question.

32. Having regard to the preceding considerations, the answer to the first question must be that the fact that a national of a Member State has worked for a temporary period of two and a half months in the territory of another Member State, of which he is not a national, can confer on him the status of a worker within the meaning of Article 48 of the Treaty [45 TFEU] provided that the activity performed as an employed person is not purely marginal and ancillary. It is for the national court to carry out the examinations of fact necessary in order to determine whether that is so in the case before it. . . . ∎

NOTES AND QUESTIONS

1. Member States differ substantially in the extent to which they provide students with financial support for their studies. Moreover, Member

States have very different positions on tuition. Most European universities are public institutions rather than private ones. However, in some Member States, such as the United Kingdom, public universities are allowed to charge substantial tuition, whereas in other Member States there is little or no charge for attending university. Does the Court's decision in *Ninni-Orasche* threaten to invite free riding and thereby undermine the position of those Member States that offer substantial financial aid to students and/or fail to charge tuition?

2. In defense of the Court's decision, could you argue that encouraging young workers and students to work or study in other Member States is crucial to the future of European integration?

3. Under EU law, would it be legal for a public university to charge different amounts of tuition based on a student's nationality? How about a tuition regime that provides for different amounts of tuition based on whether a student has lived in the relevant Member State for at least two years before beginning his studies? Would your answers to these questions change if the university were private rather than public?

I. BETTRAY V. STAATSSECRETARIS VAN JUSTITIE
Case C-344/87, May 31, 1989, 1989 E.C.R. 1621

[Mr. Bettray was a German national living in the Netherlands. Suffering from drug addiction, he was employed in accordance with the provisions of the Dutch Social Employment Law.]

5. ... [T]he Social Employment Law constitutes a body of rules intended to provide work for the purpose of maintaining, restoring or improving the capacity for work of persons who, for an indefinite period, are unable, by reason of circumstances related to their situation, to work under normal conditions. For that purpose, Netherlands local authorities are to set up, with financial support from the State, undertakings or work associations the sole purpose of which is to provide the persons involved with an opportunity to engage in paid work under conditions which correspond as far as possible to the legal rules and practices applicable to paid employment under normal conditions in so far as the physical and mental capacities of the workers do not justify a derogation in that regard. . . .

9. The question raised by the national court seeks essentially to ascertain whether Article 48(1) of the EEC Treaty [now Article 45 TFEU] must be interpreted as meaning that a national of a Member State employed in another Member State in the framework of a scheme such as that provided for in the Social Employment Law may be regarded on that ground alone as a worker for the purposes of Community law. . . .

11. It should be pointed out first of all that according to now established case-law the term "worker" in Article 48 [now Article 45 TFEU]

of the Treaty has a Community meaning and, inasmuch as it defines the scope of one of the fundamental freedoms of the Community, must be interpreted broadly.

12. According to the same judgment, that concept must be defined in accordance with objective criteria which distinguish the employment relationship by reference to the rights and duties of the persons concerned, and the essential feature of an employment relationship is that for a certain period of time a person performs services for and under the direction of another person in return for which he receives remuneration.

13. It is clear both from the terms in which the principle of freedom of movement for workers is expressed and the place occupied by the provisions concerning that principle in the structure of the Treaty that those provisions guarantee freedom of movement only for persons pursuing or wishing to pursue an economic activity and that, consequently, they cover only the pursuit of an effective and genuine activity.

14. It appears from the order for reference that persons employed under the scheme set up by the Social Employment Law perform services under the direction of another person in return for which they receive remuneration. The essential feature of an employment relationship is therefore present.

15. That conclusion is not altered by the fact that the productivity of persons employed in the scheme is low and that, consequently, their remuneration is largely provided by subsidies from public funds. Neither the level of productivity nor the origin of the funds from which the remuneration is paid can have any consequence in regard to whether or not the person is to be regarded as a worker.

16. Nor can the person cease to be regarded as a worker merely by virtue of the fact that the employment relationship under the Social Employment Law is of a sui generis nature in national law. As the Court has held, the nature of the legal relationship between the employee and the employer is of no consequence in regard to the application of Article 48 of the Treaty [now Article 45 TFEU].

17. However, work under the Social Employment Law cannot be regarded as an effective and genuine economic activity if it constitutes merely a means of rehabilitation or reintegration for the persons concerned and the purpose of the paid employment, which is adapted to the physical and mental possibilities of each person, is to enable those persons sooner or later to recover their capacity to take up ordinary employment or to lead as normal as possible a life.

18. It appears from the order for reference that the jobs in question are reserved for persons who, by reason of circumstances relating to their situation, are unable to take up employment under normal conditions and

that the social employment ends once the local authority is informed by the employment office that the person concerned will be able within a short period to take up employment under normal conditions.

19. It also appears from the order for reference that persons employed under the Social Employment Law are not selected on the basis of their capacity to perform a certain activity; on the contrary, it is the activities which are chosen in the light of the capabilities of the persons who are going to perform them in order to maintain, re-establish or develop their capacity for work. Finally, the activities involved are pursued in the framework of undertakings or work associations created solely for that purpose by local authorities.

20. The reply to the national court's question must therefore be that Article 48(1) of the EEC Treaty [now Article 45(1) TFEU] is to be interpreted as meaning that a national of a Member State employed in another Member State under a scheme such as that established under the Social Employment Law, in which the activities carried out are merely a means of rehabilitation or reintegration, cannot on that basis alone be regarded as a worker for the purposes of Community law. ■

MICHEL TROJANI V. CENTRE PUBLIC D'AIDE SOCIALE DE BRUXELLES (CPAS)

Case C-456/02, Sept. 7, 2004, 2004 E.C.R. I-7573

[Mr. Trojani was a French citizen who had been living in a Salvation Army hostel in Belgium since January 8, 2002. In exchange for "board and lodging and some pocket money" he did "various jobs for about 30 hours a week as part of a personal socio-occupational reintegration [program]."]

13. By its first question, the national court essentially asks whether a person in a situation such as that of the claimant in the main proceedings can claim a right of residence as a worker, a self-employed person or a provider or recipient of services, within the meaning of Articles 39 EC, 43 EC and 49 EC [now Articles 45, 49, 56 TFEU] respectively.

14. In the context of freedom of movement for workers, it should be recalled that Article 39(3)(c) EC [now Article 45(3) (c) TFEU] grants nationals of the Member States the right of residence in the territory of a Member State for the purpose of employment.

15. As the Court has held, the concept of 'worker' within the meaning of Article [45 TFEU] has a specific Community meaning and must not be interpreted narrowly. Any person who pursues activities which are real and genuine, to the exclusion of activities on such a small scale as to be regarded as purely marginal and ancillary, must be regarded as a 'worker'. The essential feature of an employment relationship is, according to that case-law, that for a certain period of time a person performs services for

and under the direction of another person in return for which he receives remuneration.

16. Moreover, neither the sui generis nature of the employment relationship under national law, nor the level of productivity of the person concerned, the origin of the funds from which the remuneration is paid or the limited amount of the remuneration can have any consequence in regard to whether or not the person is a worker for the purposes of Community law.

17. With respect more particularly to establishing whether the condition of the pursuit of real and genuine activity for remuneration is satisfied, the national court must base its examination on objective criteria and make an overall assessment of all the circumstances of the case relating to the nature both of the activities concerned and of the employment relationship at issue.

18. In this respect, the Court has held that activities cannot be regarded as a real and genuine economic activity if they constitute merely a means of rehabilitation or reintegration for the persons concerned.

19. However, that conclusion can be explained only by the particular characteristics of the case in question, which concerned the situation of a person who, by reason of his addiction to drugs, had been recruited on the basis of a national law intended to provide work for persons who, for an indefinite period, are unable, by reason of circumstances related to their situation, to work under normal conditions.

20. In the present case, as is apparent from the decision making the reference, Mr Trojani performs, for the Salvation Army and under its direction, various jobs for approximately 30 hours a week, as part of a personal reintegration programme, in return for which he receives benefits in kind and some pocket money.

21. Under the relevant provisions of the decree of the Commission communautaire francaise of 27 May 1999 on the grant of authorisation and subsidies to hostels . . ., the Salvation Army has the task of receiving, accommodating and providing psycho-social assistance appropriate to the recipients in order to promote their autonomy, physical well-being and reintegration in society. For that purpose it must agree with each person concerned a personal reintegration programme setting out the objectives to be attained and the means to be employed to attain them.

22. Having established that the benefits in kind and money provided by the Salvation Army to Mr Trojani constitute the consideration for the services performed by him for and under the direction of the hostel, the national court has thereby established the existence of the constituent elements of any paid employment relationship, namely subordination and the payment of remuneration.

23. For the claimant in the main proceedings to have the status of worker, however, the national court, in the assessment of the facts which is within its exclusive jurisdiction, would have to establish that the paid activity in question is real and genuine.

24. The national court must in particular ascertain whether the services actually performed by Mr Trojani are capable of being regarded as forming part of the normal labour market. For that purpose, account may be taken of the status and practices of the hostel, the content of the social reintegration programme, and the nature and details of performance of the services.

25. On the question of the applicability of Articles [49 TFEU] and [56 TFEU], it must be stated that, in the case at issue in the main proceedings, neither of those provisions of the EC Treaty may be relied on as a legal basis for a right of residence.

26. As may be seen from paragraph 20 above, Mr Trojani performs services on a continuing basis for and under the direction of the Salvation Army, in return for which he receives a remuneration.

27. Now, first, the freedom of establishment provided for in Articles [49 TFEU] to [55 TFEU] includes only the right to take up and pursue all types of self-employed activity, to set up and manage undertakings, and to set up agencies, branches or subsidiaries. Paid activities are therefore excluded.

28. Second, according to the settled case-law of the Court, an activity carried out on a permanent basis, or at least without a foreseeable limit to its duration, does not fall within the Community provisions concerning the provision of services.

29. In those circumstances, the answer to the first question must be that a person in a situation such as that of the claimant in the main proceedings, first, does not come under Articles [49 TFEU] and [Article 56 TFEU] and, second, can claim a right of residence as a worker within the meaning of Article [45 TFEU] only if the paid activity he carries out is real and genuine. It is for the national court to carry out the examinations of fact necessary to determine whether that is so in the case pending before it. ∎

NOTES AND QUESTIONS

1. What led the Court to categorize Mr. Trojani, but not Mr. Bettray, as a worker?

2. From a legal policy perspective, can you think of justifications for the distinct outcomes? Consider, in particular, the incentives for Member States to create reintegration programs of the type seen in *Bettray*.

3. In *Trojani*, the Court does not spend any time explaining when a paid activity is "real and genuine." Instead, the Court simply notes that it "is for the national court to carry out the examinations of fact necessary to determine whether that is so in the case pending before it." Could the Court have gone into more detail without violating the principle that it is for the national court to apply the law to the case at hand? Should the Court of Justice have gone into more detail?

4. On what basis did the Court of Justice come to the conclusion that Mr. Trojani was not protected by the freedom to provide services or the freedom of establishment?

B. THE PUBLIC SERVICE EXCEPTION

According to Article 45(4) TFEU, the free movement of workers does "not apply to employment in the public service." Over time, two interpretations of this provision have been suggested. One of these interpretations relies on an institutional perspective: according to this approach, the decisive question is whether, institutionally, a worker is part of a Member State's civil service.[11] The second approach is a functional one and accordingly focuses on the functions exercised by the employee at issue.[12]

The Court of Justice has embraced this second approach, holding that "the criterion for determining whether [the public service exemption] is applicable must be functional and must take account of the nature of the tasks and responsibilities inherent in the post. . . ."[13]

So what requirements does a function have to meet in order to be deemed part of a Member State's civil service? The Court has given the following answer:

> "That provision removes from the ambit of Article 48(1) to (3) [now Article 45(1) to (3) TFEU] a series of posts which involve direct or indirect participation in the exercise of powers conferred by public law and duties designed to safeguard the general interests of the state or of other public authorities. Such posts in fact presume on the part of those occupying them the existence of a special relationship of allegiance to the state and reciprocity of rights and duties which form the foundation of the bond of nationality."[14]

---

[11] This approach was taken, for example, by the Luxembourg government in Case C-473/93, Commission v. Grand Duchy of Luxemburg, 1996 E.C.R. I-3207 ¶ 25.

[12] This approach was adopted, in particular, by Court of Justice. *E.g., id.* ¶ 27 (noting that "the criterion for determining whether Article 48(4) of the Treaty [now Article 45(4) TFEU] is applicable must be functional and must take account of the nature of the tasks and responsibilities inherent in the post").

[13] *Id.*

[14] Case 149/79, Commission v. Belgium, 1980 E.C.R. 3881 ¶ 10.

In a later case, the Court added a quantitative requirement:

"[R]ecourse to the derogation from the freedom of movement for workers provided for by Article 39(4) EC [now Article 45(5) TFEU] cannot be justified solely on the ground that rights under powers conferred by public law are granted by national law to holders of the posts in question. It is still necessary that such rights are in fact exercised on a regular basis by those holders and do not represent a very minor part of their activities."[15]

In other words, it is not only necessary to adopt a functional perspective and focus on the nature of the tasks assigned to the worker. Rather, in order for a function to be qualified as falling under Article 45(5) TFEU, the relevant work has to meet high standards. It has to involve (1) direct or indirect participation (2) in the exercise of powers conferred public law and (3) duties to safeguard the general interests of public authorities. Furthermore, (4) the rights conferred by public law must be exercised regularly rather than representing a minor part of the worker's activities, and the work has to be such as to (5) require a special relationship of allegiance between the state on the one hand and the civil service on the other hand.

In applying this definition, the Court has also made it clear that Article 45(4) TFEU must be interpreted narrowly.[16] In the words of the Court, this provision "must be construed in such a way as to limit its scope to what is strictly necessary for safeguarding the interests which that provision allows the Member States to protect."[17]

Indeed, the case law of the Court of Justice clearly reflects this approach. For example, university lecturers are not part of the civil service in this sense,[18] and neither are teachers.[19] Similarly, managerial employees in the administration of hospitals also are not necessarily civil servants.[20] The posts of master and chief mate of a merchant ship are also all outside of the civil service exemption, unless the powers to represent the relevant Member State are regularly exercised and make up more than a minor part of the relevant activities.[21]

---

[15] Case C-405/01, Colegio de Oficiales de la Marina Mercante Española v. Administración del Estado, 2003 E.C.R. I-10391 ¶ 44.

[16] *Id.* ¶ 41.

[17] *Id.*

[18] Joined Cases C-259/91, C-331/91 and C-332/91, Allué, 1989 E.C.R. 1591 ¶ 21.

[19] Case C-195/98, Österreichischer Gewerkschaftsbund, 2000 E.C.R. I-10497 ¶ 36.

[20] Case C-285/01, Burbaud, 2003 E.C.R. I-8219 ¶ 40.

[21] Case C-405/01, Colegio de Oficiales de la Marina Mercante Española v. Administración del Estado, 2003 E.C.R. I-10391 ¶ 50.

COMMISSION V. GRAND DUCHY OF LUXEMBURG
Case C-473/93, July 2, 1996, E.C.R. 1996, I-3207 (citations omitted)

[By statute, Luxembourg reserved employment in various state-run sectors to its own employees. These sectors included research, inland transport, teaching, health, telecommunication as well as water, gas, and electricity distribution services. The Commission took the view that the relevant rules violated the free movement of workers and so brought enforcement proceedings against Luxemburg.]

25. On the substance, the Grand Duchy of Luxembourg submits first of all that Article 48(4) of the Treaty [now Article 45(4) TFEU] must be interpreted in an "institutional" sense so that the exception which it lays down should cover all posts which under national law constitute public service posts, including those involving purely executory, technical or manual duties if they are performed for the State or for public authorities. Only nationals can be depended on to show the special degree of integrity and trustworthiness which must be capable of being required of civil servants and public employees.

26. With regard to that argument, it suffices to refer to the Court's settled case-law according to which the concept of public service within the meaning of Article [45(4) TFEU] of the Treaty requires uniform interpretation and application throughout the Community and cannot therefore be left entirely to the discretion of the Member States....

27. So, in order to determine whether posts fall within the scope of Article [45(4) TFEU] of the Treaty, it is necessary to consider whether or not the posts in question typify the specific activities of the public service in so far as it exercises powers conferred by public law and has responsibility for safeguarding the general interests of the State or of other public bodies. For that reason, the criterion for determining whether Article 48(4) of the Treaty is applicable must be functional and must take account of the nature of the tasks and responsibilities inherent in the post, in order to ensure that the effectiveness and scope of the provisions of the Treaty on freedom of movement of workers and equal treatment of nationals of all Member States is not restricted by interpretations of the concept of public service which are based on domestic law alone and which would obstruct application of Community rules. [...]

31. The Court observes in this regard that, as the Luxembourg Government itself admits, the generality of posts in the areas of research, health, inland transport, posts and telecommunications and in the water, gas and electricity supply services are remote from the specific activities of the public service because they do not involve direct or indirect participation in the exercise of powers conferred by public law or duties designed to safeguard the general interests of the State or of other public authorities.

32. As regards the area of education, the Luxembourg Government submits in particular that teachers must be Luxembourg nationals in order to transmit traditional values and that, in view of the size of the country and its specific demographic situation, the nationality requirement is therefore an essential condition for preserving Luxembourg's national identity. Its identity could not be preserved if the majority of teachers came from other States of the Community. In the case of primary and secondary school teachers, the Luxembourg Government points out that these teachers perform non-commercial functions which do actually entail safeguarding the general interests of the State.

33. As to that argument, the Court has already stated that the very strict conditions which posts must satisfy in order to come within the exception laid down in Article [45(4) TFEU] of the Treaty are not fulfilled in the case of trainee teachers, in the case of foreign-language assistants or in the case of secondary school teachers.

34. For the same reasons, the same applies to primary school teachers.

35. This conclusion cannot be shaken by considerations relating to the preservation of national identity in a demographic situation as specific as that prevailing in the Grand Duchy of Luxembourg. Whilst the preservation of the Member States' national identities is a legitimate aim respected by the Community legal order (as is indeed acknowledged in Article F(1) of the Treaty on European Union), the interest pleaded by the Grand Duchy can, even in such particularly sensitive areas as education, still be effectively safeguarded otherwise than by a general exclusion of nationals from other Member States. As the Advocate General points out in ... his Opinion, nationals of other Member States must, like Luxembourg nationals, still fulfil all the conditions required for recruitment, in particular those relating to training, experience and language knowledge.

36. Consequently, the protection of national identity cannot justify exclusion of nationals of other Member States from all the posts in an area such as education, with the exception of those involving direct or indirect participation in the exercise of powers conferred by public law and duties designed to safeguard the general interests of the State or of other public authorities.

37. Thirdly, the Grand Duchy of Luxembourg refers to the second paragraph of Article 11 of its Constitution, according to which only Luxembourg nationals may occupy civil and military posts, save where a Law makes an exception in an individual case. Being a supreme rule of domestic law, that provision precludes the breach of obligations alleged by the Commission from being found.

38. In reply to that argument it is sufficient to refer to the Court's settled case-law according to which recourse to provisions of the domestic legal systems to restrict the scope of the provisions of Community law would have the effect of impairing the unity and efficacy of that law and consequently cannot be accepted.

39. Fourthly, the Grand Duchy of Luxembourg relies on Article 13 of the European Convention on Establishment of 13 December 1955, which provides: "Any Contracting Party may reserve for its own nationals the exercise of public functions or of occupations connected with national security or defence, or make the exercise of these occupations by aliens subject to special conditions." The Grand Duchy points out that this Convention has been signed by most of the Member States, including the Grand Duchy.

40. In that regard, the Court observes that it is settled case-law that, whilst the first paragraph of Article 234 of the Treaty [now Article 267 TFEU] allows Member States to honour obligations owed to non-Member States under international agreements preceding the Treaty, it does not authorize them to exercise rights under such agreements in intra-Community relations. Even if Article 13 of the European Convention on Establishment must be given a broader interpretation than Article [45(4) TFEU] of the Treaty, the Grand Duchy of Luxembourg cannot therefore rely on the former provision in order to escape its Community obligations. [. . .]

44. Finally, the Grand Duchy of Luxembourg draws attention to its special demographic situation. It states that its tiny population, the attraction which civil servants' and public employees' posts continue to have in this country, as well as the economic crisis may cause a massive influx of workers from other Member States who would monopolize the vacant posts so that the very future of the country could be put in question. That is why the States which signed the EEC Treaty on 25 March 1957 adopted the Protocol on the Grand Duchy of Luxembourg which, in Article 2, provides that: "When framing the regulations on freedom of movement for workers provided for in Article 48(3) of this Treaty, the Commission shall take account, as regards the Grand Duchy of Luxembourg, of the special demographic situation in that country." The Grand Duchy argues that this provision should also apply in this case.

45. In this regard, it is sufficient to state that Article 2 of that Protocol allowed the Grand Duchy of Luxembourg to request specific changes, required by its special demographic situation, to be made upon enactment of the regulations for implementing freedom of movement for workers. However, the existence of that right cannot authorize it unilaterally to exclude workers from other Member States from entire areas of occupational activity.

46. It follows from the foregoing considerations that the Grand Duchy of Luxembourg may not generally make all posts in the areas concerned subject to a nationality condition without exceeding the limits of the exception provided for by Article [45(4) TFEU].

47. The fact that some posts in those areas may, in certain circumstances, be covered by Article [45(4) TFEU] cannot justify such a general prohibition.

48. In those circumstances, in order to give full effect to the principles of freedom of movement for workers and equal treatment in access to employment, the Grand Duchy of Luxembourg was obliged to open the areas in question to nationals of other Member States by restricting application of the nationality condition to only those posts which actually involve direct or indirect participation in the exercise of powers conferred by public law and duties designed to safeguard the general interest of the State or of other public authorities. [. . .]

50. It must accordingly be declared that, in not restricting the requirement of Luxembourg nationality to access to civil servants' and public employees' posts involving direct or indirect participation in the exercise of powers conferred by public law and duties designed to safeguard the general interests of the State or of other public authorities in the public sectors of research, education, health, inland transport, posts and telecommunications, and in the water, gas and electricity distribution services, the Grand Duchy of Luxembourg has failed to fulfil its obligations under Article [45 TFEU] y and Article 1 of Regulation No 1612/68. ∎

NOTES AND QUESTIONS

1. Does the Court define the public service exemption in a functional or in an institutional sense? What is the difference between the approaches? How does the Court of Justice justify its choice of approach?

2. Luxembourg argues that a broad interpretation of the public service exemption is necessary to allow Luxembourg to protect its national identity. Why might Luxembourg think that its national identity is at stake? What does Luxembourg's size have to do with this? What would be the broader consequence to the EU legal system if the Court allowed Luxembourg to invoke its small size?

3. The Court argues that Luxembourg's national identity can "be effectively safeguarded otherwise than by a general exclusion of nationals from other Member States." How so?

4. What type of proceeding gave rise to the decision? What are the possible consequences if Luxembourg fails to bring its national laws in conformity with EU law?

C. DISCRIMINATORY AND NON-DISCRIMINATORY OBSTACLES

All fundamental freedoms—including the free movement of workers[22]—include a prohibition against discriminatory Member State measures. This includes both measures that discriminate formally by explicitly relying on the prohibited criterion and measures that discriminate solely de facto.

The more difficult question has traditionally been to what extent the fundamental freedoms also apply to non-discriminatory measures. In the context of the free movement of goods, the Court early on opted for an extensive approach: by adopting the *Dassonville* formula, it secured the general application of the free movement of goods to non-discriminatory obstacles, exempting only those state measures that meet the restrictive *Keck* conditions.

With respect to the free movement of workers, the Court's approach has been more gradual and subtle. One landmark decision was the 1995 *Bosman* decision. *Bosman* involved the rules governing the transfer of soccer players between different clubs. Under those rules, the new club had to make a transfer payment to the old club, and the plaintiff, Pierre Bosman, complained that this rule prevented him from transferring from his Belgian club to a new club in France. In this context, the Court of Justice made it clear that at least some non-discriminatory rules were subject to the free movement of workers:

> "Provisions which preclude or deter a national of a Member State from leaving his country of origin in order to exercise his right to freedom of movement therefore constitute an obstacle to that freedom even if they apply without regard to the nationality of the workers concerned."[23]

Of course, this raises the question of when a national rule deters workers from moving to other Member States. How much of an obstacle must it be? In *Bosman*, the Court seemed to suggest a distinction between those rules that bar a worker's access to employment markets and those that do not:

> It is sufficient to note that, although the rules in issue in the main proceedings apply also to transfers between clubs belonging to different national associations within the same Member State and are similar to those governing transfers between clubs belonging

---

[22] Case C-155/09, Commission v. Hellenic Republic, 2011 E.C.R. I-65 ¶ 45 (affirming that the free movement of goods prohibits "not only overt discrimination by reason of nationality but also all covert forms of discrimination which, by the application of other criteria of differentiation, lead in fact to the same result").

[23] Case C-415/93, Union royale belge des societes de football association ASBL v. Jean-Marc Bosman, 1995 E.C.R. I-4921 ¶ 96.

to the same national association, they still directly affect players' access to the employment market in other Member States and are thus capable of impeding freedom of movement for workers.[24]

However, in subsequent cases the Court of Justice has put less emphasis on the *access* criterion and more on the question of deterrence.[25] Moreover, the Court has made it clear that the threshold for deterrence is not to be understood too strictly. Rather, a deterrence effect will be found in those cases where the relevant national rule makes the exercise of the free movement of workers "less attractive"[26] and is therefore "likely to discourage"[27] the worker from working in another Member State.

VOLKER GRAF V. FILZMOSER MASCHINENBAU GMBH
Case C-190/98, January 27, 2000, 2000 E.C.R. I-493

[Mr. Graf was a German national living and working in Austria. His employer was Filzmoser Maschinenbau GmbH ("Filzmoser"), an Austrian company.

Under Austrian law, an employee whose employment relationship has lasted for at least three years is entitled to a compensation payment if the employment relationship is terminated. However, no such claim arises if it is the employee who terminates the employment relationship or if the employee is responsible for his own dismissal.

At some point, Mr. Graf terminated his employment contract because he wanted to move to Germany and work there. He demanded a compensation payment, but Filzmoser refused, pointing out that it was Mr. Graf himself who had terminated the employment contract. Litigation ensued. Mr. Graf argued that the rule under which no compensation payment was due in cases where the employee terminated the employment contract violated the free movement of workers. The case ended up before the Austrian Court of Appeals of Linz which requested a preliminary ruling from the Court of Justice.]

13. By its question, the national court essentially asks whether Article 48 of the Treaty [now Article 45 TFEU] precludes national provisions which deny a worker entitlement to compensation on termination of employment if he terminates his contract of employment himself in order to take up employment in another Member State, when those provisions grant him entitlement to such compensation if the

---

[24] *Id.* ¶ 103.
[25] *E.g.*, Case C-325/08, Olympique Lyonnais SASP v. Olivier Bernard and Newcastle UFC, 2010 E.C.R. I-2177 ¶¶ 33–37 (discussing the scope of the free movement of workers).
[26] *Id.* ¶ 36.
[27] *Id.* ¶ 35.

contract ends without the termination being at his own initiative or attributable to him.

14. First, it must be borne in mind that Article 48(2) of the Treaty [now Article 45(2)] expressly provides that freedom of movement for workers is to entail the abolition of any discrimination based on nationality between workers of the Member States as regards employment, remuneration and other conditions of work and employment. In addition, according to the Court's case-law, the rule of equal treatment, laid down in Article [45 TFEU], prohibits not only overt discrimination based on nationality but also all covert forms of discrimination which, by applying other distinguishing criteria, achieve in practice the same result.

15. Legislation such as that at issue in the main proceedings applies irrespective of the nationality of the worker concerned.

16. Moreover, legislation of that kind denies compensation on termination of employment to all workers who end their contract of employment themselves in order to take up employment with a new employer, regardless of whether the latter is established in the same Member State as the previous employer or in another Member State. In those circumstances, it cannot be maintained that such legislation affects migrant workers to a greater extent than national workers and that it might therefore place at a disadvantage the former in particular.

17. Furthermore, as the national court expressly stated in its order for reference, there is nothing on the file to indicate that such legislation operates to the disadvantage of a particular group of workers wishing to take up new employment in another Member State.

18. Second, it is clear from the Court's case-law, in particular from the judgment in Bosman, cited above, that Article 48 of the Treaty [now Article 45 TFEU] prohibits not only all discrimination, direct or indirect, based on nationality but also national rules which are applicable irrespective of the nationality of the workers concerned but impede their freedom of movement.

19. According to Mr. Graf, the loss of compensation on termination of employment where the worker himself terminates the contract constitutes such an obstacle to freedom of movement for workers, comparable to the obstacle which was at issue in Bosman. In his submission, it is largely immaterial in this connection whether the worker suffers a financial loss because he changes employer or the new employer is required to make a payment in order to take him on.

20. By contrast, the other parties who have submitted observations to the Court maintain that national legislation applicable irrespective of the nationality of the workers concerned which is liable to dissuade the latter

from deciding to exercise their right to freedom of movement does not necessarily constitute an obstacle to freedom of movement for workers.

21. In that regard, the Court has held on numerous occasions that the Treaty provisions relating to freedom of movement for persons are intended to facilitate the pursuit by Community nationals of occupational activities of all kinds throughout the Community, and preclude measures which might place Community nationals at a disadvantage when they wish to pursue an economic activity in the territory of another Member State.

22. Nationals of Member States have in particular the right, which they derive directly from the Treaty, to leave their country of origin to enter the territory of another Member State and reside there in order to pursue an economic activity.

23. Provisions which, even if they are applicable without distinction, preclude or deter a national of a Member State from leaving his country of origin in order to exercise his right to freedom of movement therefore constitute an obstacle to that freedom. However, in order to be capable of constituting such an obstacle, they must affect access of workers to the labour market.

24. Legislation of the kind at issue in the main proceedings is not such as to preclude or deter a worker from ending his contract of employment in order to take a job with another employer, because the entitlement to compensation on termination of employment is not dependent on the worker's choosing whether or not to stay with his current employer but on a future and hypothetical event, namely the subsequent termination of his contract without such termination being at his own initiative or attributable to him.

25. Such an event is too uncertain and indirect a possibility for legislation to be capable of being regarded as liable to hinder freedom of movement for workers where it does not attach to termination of a contract of employment by the worker himself the same consequence as it attaches to termination which was not at his initiative or is not attributable to him.

26. In view of all the foregoing considerations, the answer to the question submitted must be that Article 48 of the Treaty [now Article 45 TFEU] does not preclude national provisions which deny a worker entitlement to compensation on termination of employment if he terminates his contract of employment himself in order to take up employment in another Member State, when those provisions grant him entitlement to such compensation if the contract ends without the termination being at his own initiative or attributable to him. ∎

NOTES AND QUESTIONS

1. The Court argues that the Austrian law at issue does not interfere with the free movement of workers because its adverse impact is "too uncertain and indirect" to deter workers from exercising their right to free movement. As a practical matter, what incentives for workers would result if the Court of Justice had resolved the question in favor of Mr. Graf?

2. As we will see in the next section, one of the possible grounds of justification for measures interfering with the free movement of workers is the mandatory requirements doctrine, which applies not only to the free movement of goods, but also to all other fundamental freedoms. Assume, hypothetically, that the Court of Justice had categorized the Austrian statute as a measure interfering with the free movement of workers. In that case, the next question would have been whether the measure could be justified. Do you believe that the statute at issue could be justified on the basis of the mandatory requirements doctrine?

D. JUSTIFICATIONS

Even if a measure interferes with the free movement of workers, this does not necessarily mean that the measure is illegal. Rather—just as in the case of the free movement of goods—measures interfering with the free movement of workers can be justified.

The structure of available justifications is quite similar to that which we have observed in the context of the free movement of goods. The Treaty itself contains an explicit justification for restrictions that Member States impose on the free movement of workers: Article 45(3) TFEU makes it clear that the free movement of workers is subject to "limitations justified on grounds of public policy, public security or public health."[28] In addition to these explicit limitations, the Court of Justice has made it clear that the unwritten mandatory-requirements doctrine also applies to the free movement of workers.

Because we have already discussed these justifications in the context of the free movement of goods, the relevant principles need not be repeated here.

E. EMPLOYERS

In most cases involving the free movement of workers, it is the worker himself who invokes this fundamental freedom. However, the Court of Justice has held that employers, too, can invoke the free movement of workers.

---

[28] TFEU, art. 45(3).

CLEAN CAR AUTOSERVICE GESMBH V LANDESHAUPTMANN VON WIEN

Case C-350/96, May 7, 1998, 1998 E.C.R. I-2521 (citations omitted)

[Clear Car Autoservice GesmbH [hereinafter Clean Car] was an Austrian Company established in Vienna. It sought to register for trade, which was necessary for doing business. However, Clean Car's application was rejected on the ground that under Austrian law, a company seeking to register for trade in Austria had to have a manager residing in Austria. But Clean Car's manager was a German national residing in Berlin. Clean Car sued against this decision, and the Austrian Court asked the Court of Justice for a preliminary ruling.]

18. Next, it must be noted that Article 48(1) [now Article 45(1) TFEU] states, in general terms, that freedom of movement for workers is to be secured within the Community. Under Article 48(2) and (3) [now Article 45(2) & (3) TFEU], such freedom of movement is to entail the abolition of any discrimination based on nationality between workers of the Member States as regards employment, remuneration and other conditions of work and employment, and to entail the right, subject to limitations justified on grounds of public policy, public security or public health, to accept offers of employment actually made, to move freely within the territory of Member States for that purpose, to stay in a Member State in order to be employed there under the same conditions as nationals of that State and to remain there after such employment.

19. Whilst those rights are undoubtedly enjoyed by those directly referred to—namely, workers—there is nothing in the wording of Article [45 TFEU] to indicate that they may not be relied upon by others, in particular employers.

20. It must further be noted that, in order to be truly effective, the right of workers to be engaged and employed without discrimination necessarily entails as a corollary the employer's entitlement to engage them in accordance with the rules governing freedom of movement for workers.

21. Those rules could easily be rendered nugatory if Member States could circumvent the prohibitions which they contain merely by imposing on employers requirements to be met by any worker whom they wish to employ which, if imposed directly on the worker, would constitute restrictions on the exercise of the right to freedom of movement to which that worker is entitled under Article 48 of the Treaty [now Article 45 TFEU].

22. Finally, the above interpretation is corroborated both by Article 2 of Regulation No 1612/68 and by the Court's case-law.

23. It is made explicitly clear in Article 2 of Regulation No 1612/68 that any employer pursuing an activity in the territory of a Member State and any national of a Member State must be able to conclude and perform contracts of employment in accordance with the provisions in force laid down by law, regulation or administrative action, without any discrimination resulting therefrom.

24. It is, furthermore, clear from, in particular, [the Court's case law] that justifications on grounds of public policy, public security or public health, as envisaged in Article [45(3)] of the Treaty, may be relied upon not only by Member States in order to justify limitations on freedom of movement for workers under their laws, regulations or administrative provisions but also by individuals in order to justify such limitations under agreements or other measures adopted by persons governed by private law. Thus, if an employer may rely on a derogation under Article [45(3) TFEU], he must also be able to rely on the same principles under, in particular, Article [45(1) and (2) TFEU].

25. In the light of those considerations, the answer to the first question must be that the rule of equal treatment in the context of freedom of movement for workers, enshrined in Article 48 of the Treaty, may also be relied upon by an employer in order to employ, in the Member State in which he is established, workers who are nationals of another Member State.

The second question

26. By its second question, the national court wishes to ascertain, in substance, whether Article [45 TFEU] precludes a Member State from providing that the owner of an undertaking exercising a trade on the territory of that State may not appoint as manager a person not resident there.

27. The Court has consistently held that the rules of equal treatment prohibit not only overt discrimination based on nationality but also all covert forms of discrimination which, by applying other distinguishing criteria, achieve in practice the same result.

28. It is true that a provision such as [the Austrian statute at issue] applies without regard to the nationality of the person to be appointed as manager.

29. However, as the Court has already held . . ., national rules under which a distinction is drawn on the basis of residence are liable to operate mainly to the detriment of nationals of other Member States, as non-residents are in the majority of cases foreigners.

30. A requirement that nationals of the other Member States must reside in the State concerned in order to be appointed managers of

undertakings exercising a trade is therefore such as to constitute indirect discrimination based on nationality, contrary to Article 48(2) of the Treaty.

31. It would be otherwise only if the imposition of such a residence requirement were based on objective considerations independent of the nationality of the employees concerned and proportionate to a legitimate aim pursued by the national law . . .

32. In that context, as stated at paragraph 15 above, the national court has expressly referred in its order for reference to the fact that, under [the Austrian state in question], the person appointed as manager is responsible for compliance with the applicable statutory provisions in the exercise of the trade concerned and fines may be imposed upon him.

33. In their written observations, the Landeshauptmann von Wien and the Austrian Government have explained that the residence requirement is intended to ensure that the manager can be served with notice of the fines which may be imposed upon him and that they can be enforced against him. The intention is also to ensure that the manager satisfies the other requirement imposed on him by [the Austrian statute] namely that he must be in a position to act effectively as such in the business.

34. In that regard, the residence requirement must be held either to be inappropriate for ensuring that the aim pursued is achieved or to go beyond what is necessary for that purpose.

35. In the first place, the fact that the manager resides in the Member State in which the undertaking is established and exercises its trade does not itself necessarily ensure that he will be in a position to act effectively as manager in the business. A manager residing in the State but at a considerable distance from the place at which the undertaking exercises its trade should normally find it more difficult to act effectively in the business than a person whose place of residence, even if in another Member State, is at no great distance from that at which the undertaking exercises its trade.

36. Secondly, other less restrictive measures, such as serving notice of fines at the registered office of the undertaking employing the manager and ensuring that they will be paid by requiring a guarantee to be provided beforehand, would make it possible to ensure that the manager can be served with notice of any such fines imposed upon him and that they can be enforced against him.

37. Finally, it must be added, even such measures as those just indicated are not justified by the aims in question if the service of notice of fines imposed on a manager resident in another Member State and their enforcement against him are guaranteed by an international convention

concluded between the Member State in which the undertaking exercises its trade and that in which the manager resides.

38. It must be concluded, therefore, that the residence requirement in question constitutes indirect discrimination.

39. As regards the justifications based on Article 45(3) TFEU to which the national court has also referred, it must be observed that a general rule of the kind in issue in the main proceedings cannot be justified on any grounds of public security or public health.

40. As regards the justification on grounds of public policy, also envisaged in Article 48(3) of the Treaty, the Court has already held . . . that in so far as it may justify certain restrictions on the free movement of persons subject to Community law, recourse to the concept of public policy as used in that provision presupposes, in any event, the existence, in addition to the perturbation of the social order which any infringement of the law involves, of a genuine and sufficiently serious threat affecting one of the fundamental interests of society.

41. Here, however, it does not appear from the documents in the case that any such interest is liable to be affected if the owner of an undertaking is free to appoint, for the purpose of exercising that undertaking's trade, a manager who does not reside in the Member State concerned.

42. It is thus also impossible for a national provision such as that in issue in the main proceedings, which requires any worker appointed as manager for the exercise of a trade to reside in the State concerned, to be justified on grounds of public policy within the meaning of Article [45(3) TFEU].

43. In view of the foregoing considerations, the answer to the second question must be that Article [45(3) TFEU] of the Treaty precludes a Member State from providing that the owner of an undertaking exercising a trade on the territory of that State may not appoint as manager a person not resident there. ∎

NOTES AND QUESTIONS

1. In earlier cases, the Court of Justice had held that, in certain situations, the free movement of workers may bind not only the Member States but also private employers. In particular, when confronted with rules issued by sports associations, the Court had held that the free movement of workers "not only applies to the action of public authorities but extends also to rules of any other nature aimed at regulating gainful employment in a collective manner."[29] Consequently, the Court had also allowed private employers to

---

[29] Case C-415/93, Union royale belge des societes de football association ASBL v. Jean-Marc Bosman, 1995 E.C.R. I-4921 ¶ 82. *See* Case 36/74, Walrave v. Union Cycliste Internationale, 1974 E.C.R. 1405, para. 17 (holding that the general prohibition against discrimination on the basis of nationality, the prohibition against discrimination inherent in the free movement of workers, as

invoke the various grounds for justifying measures interfering with the free movement of workers.[30] In paragraph 24 of the *Clean Car* judgment, the Court of Justice relies on this case law to justify why employers must be able to invoke the free movement of workers. More specifically, the Court argues that if an employer is entitled to invoke the provisions justifying measures restricting the free movement of workers, then the employer must also be able to invoke the free movement of workers itself. Is this reasoning persuasive?

2. Why might it make sense from a legal policy perspective to allow employers to invoke the free movement of workers? In particular, is there any reason to think that this will substantially improve the protection of workers against measures violating the free movement of workers?

3. In Article 22, the Court invokes Regulation 1612/68 in support of its interpretation of the Treaty. Is it persuasive to justify a particular interpretation of primary EU law based in part on the content of secondary EU law? What concerns might such an approach raise?

F. PRACTICE QUESTIONS

For the purpose of the following hypotheticals, assume that Alpha and Beta are Member States of the European Union.

1. Alpha enacts a statute whereby every employee automatically receives a one-time bonus at the end of his fifth year of employment, to be paid by the employer, in the amount of 20% of the worker's annual wage. The declared goal of the statute is to reward the loyalty of employees who stay with a single employer for five years or more. Carl has worked for his employer in Alpha for four years, at which point he receives a more attractive employment offer from a firm located in Beta. He now argues that the Alphanian statute violates the free movement of workers because it deters him from accepting the Betanian firm's offer. Is he right?

2. Alpha enacts a statute whereby every employee who has worked in Alpha for ten years without any period of unemployment is entitled to a one-time bonus in the amount of 30% of his current annual wage. The bonus must be paid by the employer at the time that the ten-year mark is reached. The official goal of the statute is to reward employees who have, over a long time, provided financial benefits in terms of taxes and social security contributions. Maria is an Alphanian citizen who has worked without interruption for ten years. However, only the first four years and the last four years were spent working in Alpha, whereas the two years in the middle were spent working for an investment bank in Beta. Maria

---

well as the prohibition against discrimination inherent in the freedom to provide services do "not only apply to the action of public authorities, but [extend] likewise to rules of any other nature aimed at regulating in a collective manner gainful employment and the provision of services."

[30] Case C-415/93, Union royale belge des societes de football association ASBL v. Jean-Marc Bosman, 1995 E.C.R. I-4921 ¶¶ 84–86.

believes that the Alphanian statute violates the free movement of workers. Is she right?

3. Lisa is an Alphanian citizen living in Beta. One fine day, she applies for a job as a bus driver in Beta. Only one day later, Lisa receives a rejection letter pointing out that under Betanian law, only Betanian citizens can become bus drivers. When she asks why, she is told that under Betanian law bus drivers have various public powers in emergency situations: If no police are present or available, bus drivers can arrest persons who pose a threat to the safety of their passengers. Moreover, where the death of a passenger is imminent, but the passenger wants to marry another passenger before he dies, the bus driver can perform an emergency marriage. Lisa believes that the statute requiring Betanian citizenship for bus drivers violates EU law. Is she right?

Free Movement of Workers

I. Scope of Application

    A. Worker

        1. "[P]erson [who] performs services for and under the direction of another person in return for which he receives remuneration"

        2. Quantitative thresholds

            a. No requirement that workers earn enough to make a living

            b. "[A]ctivities which are effective and genuine, to the exclusion of activities on such a small scale as to be regarded as purely marginal and ancillary"

    B. Public service exemption

        1. Working for the government is not enough

        2. Public service exemption only applies to "posts which involve direct or indirect participation in the exercise of powers conferred by public law and duties designed to safeguard the general interests of the state or of other public authorities"

        3. Moreover, it is "necessary that such rights are in fact exercised on a regular basis by those holders and do not represent a very minor part of their activities"

II. Restriction

    A. Measures that discriminate directly or indirectly against workers from other Member States restrict the free movement of workers

    B. Even non-discriminating measures can restrict the free movement of workers if they "preclude or deter a national of a Member State from leaving his country of origin in order to exercise his right to freedom of movement"

III. Mandatory requirements doctrine

    A. Legitimate goal

    B. Proportionality

    C. Absence of discrimination

        1. Mandatory requirements doctrine does not apply in the case of formal discrimination

        2. Court of Justice not consistent on whether mere indirect discrimination can be justified

IV. Justification under Article 45(3) TFEU

    A. Measure must protect public policy, public security or public health

    B. Even discriminatory measures can be justified

    C. Proportionality

CHAPTER 14

DIRECTIVE 2004/38/EC AND REGULATION 1612/68/EEC

■ ■ ■

All fundamental freedoms have to be seen in conjunction with the numerous pieces of secondary legislation that the European Union has enacted. In many cases, the relevant legislation is relatively specialized and technical and does not, therefore, form a central part of the analysis offered in this casebook. However, within the context of the free movement of workers, the importance of secondary legislation is paramount not least because the relevant directives and regulations offer far-ranging protections that in some cases go well beyond the guarantees afforded by the Treaties themselves.

Two pieces of secondary legislation are particularly crucial in this context. One is Regulation 1612/68/EEC on freedom of movement for workers within the Community.[1] The other is Directive 2004/38/EC, which governs the rights of EU citizens and their family members to move and reside freely within the territory of the EU.[2] Directive 2004/38/EC amends Regulation 1612/68/EEC and largely renders many of the latter's provisions redundant. In the following, therefore, we will begin by focusing on Directive 2004/38/EC before proceeding to analyze Regulation 1612/68/EEC.

A. DIRECTIVE 2004/38/EC

As already noted, directive 2004/38/EC governs the rights of EU citizens and their family members to move and reside freely within the territory of the EU.

---

[1] Regulation (EEC) No 1612/68 of the Council of 15 October 1968 on freedom of movement for workers within the Community, OJ L 257, 19.10.1968, pp. 2–12.

[2] Directive 2004/38/EC of the European Parliament and of the Council of 29 April 2004 on the right of citizens of the Union and their family members to move and reside freely within the territory of the Member States amending Regulation (EEC) No 1612/68 and repealing Directives 64/221/EEC, 68/360/EEC, 72/194/EEC, 73/148/EEC, 75/34/EEC, 75/35/EEC, 90/364/EEC, 90/365/EEC and 93/96/EEC (Text with EEA relevance), OJ L 158, 30.4.2004, pp. 77–123.

1. BENEFICIARIES

Who benefits from directive 2004/38/EC? To differing degrees, the Directive protects both EU citizens and their family members. EU citizens are persons who are citizens of at least one Member State.[3]

The term "family members" includes, first and foremost, spouses.[4] The same is true for children, but only if they qualify as dependents or are under the age of 21.

As regards registered partnerships, which often constitute the sole form of a legally protected union for same-sex partners, the Directive defers to the law of the host state: Partners in registered partnerships are protected as family members, but only to the extent that the host Member State recognizes registered partnerships as "equivalent to marriage."[5] In other words, if the host state generally recognizes registered partnerships as equivalent to marriage, it cannot deny recognition as family members to the foreign partners of EU citizens. If, by contrast, the host state generally refuses to recognize registered partnerships as marriage-equivalent, then it can also do so within the context of Directive 2004/38/EC. Note that this compromise reflects the general importance of the consistency principle in EU law: while the European Union generally tends to be deferential to different values prevailing in different Member States, it at least requires Member States to be consistent in their actions.

Crucially, Directive 2004/38/EC protects only those EU citizens "who move to or reside in a Member State other than that of which they are a national" as well as family members of these citizens.[6] In other words, Directive 2004/38/EC cannot be invoked in cases that do not involve other Member States. This reflects the principle that the freedom of movement—just like the other fundamental freedoms—does not apply to purely internal situations.[7]

SHIRLEY MCCARTHY V. SECRETARY OF STATE FOR THE HOME DEPARTMENT

Case C-434/09, 5 May 2011, 2011 E.C.R. I-3375 (citations omitted)

[Mrs. McCarthy was a citizen of both the United Kingdom and Ireland. However, she was born in the United Kingdom and had always lived there. She was never a worker or self-employed person. Rather, she received state benefits.

---

[3] Directive 2004/38/EC, art. 2(1).
[4] *Id.* art. 2(2).
[5] *Id.* art. 2(3).
[6] *Id.* art. 3(1).
[7] Case C-127/08, Blaise Baheten Metock v. Minister of Justice, Equality and Law Reform, 2008 E.C.R. I-6241 ¶ 77.

In 2002, Mrs. McCarthy married a citizen of Jamaica. In 2004, Mrs. McCarthy and her husband applied to the British authorities for a residence permit and residence document under EU law for Mr. McCarthy, arguing that they were entitled to such permit and document in their quality as an EU citizen and a spouse of an EU citizen, respectively. British authorities denied the application, and litigation ensued.

One of the main legal issues in the case involved Mrs. McCarthy's citizenship. More specifically, the question was whether she and her husband could invoke Directive 2004/38/EC in their quarrel with the U.K. authorities despite the fact that Mrs. McCarthy was herself a U.K. citizen and had always lived in the United Kingdom. Eventually, the case reached the highest court of the United Kingdom, which requested a preliminary ruling from the Court of Justice.]

30. The first part of the first question . . . concerns whether Article 3(1) of Directive 2004/38 is to be interpreted as meaning that that directive applies to a citizen in a situation such as that of Mrs. McCarthy, who has never exercised his right of free movement, who has always resided in a Member State of which he is a national and who is also a national of another Member State.

31. A literal, teleological and contextual interpretation of that provision leads to a negative reply to that question.

32. First, according to Article 3(1) of Directive 2004/38, all Union citizens who 'move to' or reside in a Member State 'other' than that of which they are a national are beneficiaries of that directive.

33. Secondly, whilst it is true that . . . Directive 2004/38 aims to facilitate and strengthen the exercise of the primary and individual right to move and reside freely within the territory of the Member States that is conferred directly on each citizen of the Union, the fact remains that the subject of the directive concerns, as is apparent from Article 1(a), the conditions governing the exercise of that right.

34. Since . . . the residence of a person residing in the Member State of which he is a national cannot be made subject to conditions, Directive 2004/38, concerning the conditions governing the exercise of the right to move and reside freely within the territory of the Member States, cannot apply to a Union citizen who enjoys an unconditional right of residence due to the fact that he resides in the Member State of which he is a national.

35. Thirdly, it is apparent from Directive 2004/38, taken as a whole, that the residence to which it refers is linked to the exercise of the freedom of movement for persons. . . .

39. Hence, in circumstances such as those of the main proceedings, in so far as the Union citizen concerned has never exercised his right of free movement and has always resided in a Member State of which he is a

national, that citizen is not covered by the concept of 'beneficiary' for the purposes of Article 3(1) of Directive 2004/38, so that that directive is not applicable to him.

40. That finding cannot be influenced by the fact that the citizen concerned is also a national of a Member State other than that where he resides.

41. Indeed, the fact that a Union citizen is a national of more than one Member State does not mean that he has made use of his right of freedom of movement.

42. Lastly, it should also be noted that, since a Union citizen such as Mrs McCarthy is not covered by the concept of 'beneficiary' for the purposes of Article 3(1) of Directive 2004/38, her spouse is not covered by that concept either, given that the rights conferred by that directive on the family members of a beneficiary of that directive are not autonomous rights of those family members, but derived rights, acquired through their status as members of the beneficiary's family.

43. It follows that Article 3(1) of Directive 2004/38 is to be interpreted as meaning that that directive is not applicable to a Union citizen who has never exercised his right of free movement, who has always resided in a Member State of which he is a national and who is also a national of another Member State. ∎

NOTES AND QUESTIONS

1. At the core of this case lies the fact that Mrs. McCarthy was a dual citizen. Note that Member States' laws on acquiring citizenship vary. Being a child of a citizen is generally sufficient. Whether being born in a Member State leads to citizenship or at least opens up a path to citizenship depends on the Member State. Do you think that dual citizenship is a common phenomenon in the European Union? Do you think that having persons with citizenship from multiple EU Member States benefits EU integration? Why or why not?

2. Would the outcome of the case have been different if both Mr. and Mrs. McCarthy were living and working in Germany, and if they had applied for permission to stay in Germany?

3. If the EU has an interest in ensuring that a citizen who moves from one Member State to another may bring along his or her spouse, why might it not have a similar interest in ensuring that citizens can bring foreign spouses into the EU? Is there some countervailing interest?

2. RIGHT OF RESIDENCE

Regarding the right to reside in another Member State, Directive 2004/38/EC distinguishes between stays lasting up to three months and those lasting longer.

a) Stays of up to Three Months

Any EU citizen has the right to reside up to three months in another Member State, the only requirement being that he holds a valid identity card or passport.[8] Moreover, family members of EU citizens who are not EU citizens themselves have that same right as long as they accompany or join the EU citizen.[9]

b) Stays of More than Three Months

If a Union citizen wants to reside in another Member State for more than three months, he has to meet at least one of several substantive requirements set forth in Article 7 of Directive 2004/38/EC.

The first and most obvious possibility is that the Union citizen is a worker or self-employed in the chosen state of residence.[10] It is worth noting that temporary unemployment, a temporary inability to work or even the interruption of work to take up vocational training does not necessarily terminate a person's status as a worker or self-employed person.[11]

The second possibility is that the Union citizen has "sufficient resources for [himself] and [his] family members not to become a burden on the social assistance system of the host Member State during their period of residence and [that he and his family members] have comprehensive sickness insurance cover[age] in the host Member State."[12] In this scenario, the fundamental freedoms do not protect the worker; rather, Directive 2004/38/EC goes well beyond what is required by the Treaty on the Functioning of the European Union. However, the purpose behind this provision is obvious: if a Union citizen has sufficient funds and insurance coverage not to be a burden on his chosen state of residence, then why not let him stay in the host state?

The third category involves persons who are engaged in studies or vocational training in the host state.[13] These persons also have to meet additional requirements in order to ensure that they do not burden the host state: they need comprehensive health insurance, and they also have to declare that they have sufficient funds for themselves and their family such that they do not have to draw on social assistance in the state of residence.[14]

---

[8] Directive 2004/38/EC, art. 6(1).
[9] *Id.* art. 6(2).
[10] *Id.* art. 7(1)(a).
[11] *Id.* art. 7(4).
[12] *Id.* art. 7(1) (b).
[13] *Id.* art. 7(1)(c).
[14] *Id.* art. 7(1)(c).

The fourth category includes family members who either accompany or join an EU citizen, provided that the latter has a right of residence under one of the three scenarios described above.[15] It is not necessary that the family members be EU citizens themselves, as long as the EU citizen whom they accompany or join has a right of residence.[16]

One question of considerable practical importance is whether family members of EU citizens can invoke the protection of Directive 2004/38/EC if they originally stayed in the host country illegally. For example, assume that a non-EU national enters an EU Member State illegally and then marries an EU national? Can the relevant individual invoke the rights granted by Directive 2003/38/EC? The ECJ's 2003 *Akrich* decision,[17] which concerned Regulation 1612/68/EEC rather than Directive 2003/38/EC and in fact predated the enactment of the latter, suggested that the answer might be no.[18] In 2008, the Court of Justice addressed the issue again:

BLAISE BAHETEN METOCK V. MINISTER OF JUSTICE, EQUALITY AND LAW REFORM
Case C-127/08, July 25, 2008, 2008 E.C.R. I-6241

[In Ireland, the statutory provisions implementing Directive 2004/38/EC added a requirement not contained in the text of that directive: under Irish statutory law, family members of EU citizens could not invoke the rights granted by Directive 2000/38/EC unless these family members were "lawfully resident" in the host state.

This requirement of lawful residency proved contentious, eventually leading to a request for a preliminary ruling. One of the cases underlying this request involved Mr. Metock, a citizen of Cameroon. Since 1994, Mr. Metock had been in a relationship with Ms. Ikeng, a U.K. citizen working and living in Ireland. In June 2006, Mr. Metock came to Ireland and applied for asylum. In October 2006, he married Ms. Ikeng, while the asylum proceedings were still ongoing. Following the marriage, Mr. Metock also applied for a residence card in Ireland as a spouse of a European citizen. However, both his application for asylum and his application for a residence card were rejected, the latter on the ground that he had never been a lawful resident in Ireland within the meaning of Irish law.]

---

[15] *Id.* art. 7(1)(d).

[16] *Id.* art. 7(2).

[17] Case C-109/01, Secretary of State for the Home Department v. Hacene Akrich, 2003 E.C.R. I-9607.

[18] *Cf. id.* ¶ 50 ("In order to benefit in a situation such as that at issue in the main proceedings from the rights provided for in Article 10 of Regulation No 1612/68, the national of a non-Member State, who is the spouse of a citizen of the Union, must be lawfully resident in a Member State when he moves to another Member State to which the citizen of the Union is migrating or has migrated.").

The first question

48. By its first question the referring court asks whether Directive 2004/38 precludes legislation of a Member State which requires a national of a non-member country who is the spouse of a Union citizen residing in that Member State but not possessing its nationality to have previously been lawfully resident in another Member State before arriving in the host Member State, in order to benefit from the provisions of that directive.

49. In the first place, it must be stated that, as regards family members of a Union citizen, no provision of Directive 2004/38 makes the application of the directive conditional on their having previously resided in a Member State.

50. As Article 3(1) of Directive 2004/38 states, the directive applies to all Union citizens who move to or reside in a Member State other than that of which they are a national, and to their family members as defined in point 2 of Article 2 of the directive who accompany them or join them in that Member State. The definition of family members in point 2 of Article 2 of Directive 2004/38 does not distinguish according to whether or not they have already resided lawfully in another Member State.

51. It must also be pointed out that Articles 5, 6(2) and 7(2) of Directive 2004/38 confer the rights of entry, of residence for up to three months, and of residence for more than three months in the host Member State on nationals of non-member countries who are family members of a Union citizen whom they accompany or join in that Member State, without any reference to the place or conditions of residence they had before arriving in that Member State.

52. In particular, the first subparagraph of Article 5(2) of Directive 2004/38 provides that nationals of non-member countries who are family members of a Union citizen are required to have an entry visa, unless they are in possession of the valid residence card referred to in Article 10 of that directive. In that, as follows from Articles 9(1) and 10(1) of Directive 2004/38, the residence card is the document that evidences the right of residence for more than three months in a Member State of the family members of a Union citizen who are not nationals of a Member State, the fact that Article 5(2) provides for the entry into the host Member State of family members of a Union citizen who do not have a residence card shows that Directive 2004/38 is capable of applying also to family members who were not already lawfully resident in another Member State.

53. Similarly, Article 10(2) of Directive 2004/38, which lists exhaustively the documents which nationals of non-member countries who are family members of a Union citizen may have to present to the host Member State in order to have a residence card issued, does not provide for the possibility of the host Member State asking for documents to demonstrate any prior lawful residence in another Member State.

54. In those circumstances, Directive 2004/38 must be interpreted as applying to all nationals of non-member countries who are family members of a Union citizen within the meaning of point 2 of Article 2 of that directive and accompany or join the Union citizen in a Member State other than that of which he is a national, and as conferring on them rights of entry and residence in that Member State, without distinguishing according to whether or not the national of a non-member country has already resided lawfully in another Member State. . . .

80. The answer to the first question must therefore be that Directive 2004/38 precludes legislation of a Member State which requires a national of a non-member country who is the spouse of a Union citizen residing in that Member State but not possessing its nationality to have previously been lawfully resident in another Member State before arriving in the host Member State, in order to benefit from the provisions of that directive. ∎

QUESTIONS

1. Assume the following hypothetical facts: Ms. Ikeng and Mr. Metock met and eventually married in Cameroon during a time when Ms. Ikeng still lived and worked in the United Kingdom. At some point, Ms. Ikeng moves to Ireland to live and work there. Now Mr. Metock, still living in Cameroon, seeks permission to enter Ireland and live there with his wife. Would he be successful?

2. Can you think of any reason(s) why the Court of Justice's decision might be desirable as a matter of legal policy? Are there any counterarguments?

3. Would the original case have been decided differently if Mr. Metock and Ms. Ikeng had been engaged, but not married? What if Mr. Metock and Ms. Ikeng had been married, but had already divorced before requesting a residence card for Mr. Metock?

4. What if Ms. Ikeng had married Mr. Metock in exchange for 5000 euros from him for the sole purpose of securing a residence card?

3. RIGHT OF PERMANENT RESIDENCE

As noted above, the right to reside in the host Member State for more than three months generally depends on meeting certain substantive requirements such as having the status of worker or having sufficient funds and insurance coverage not to burden the host Member State. However, once the person has resided long enough in the host state, he acquires a right of permanent residence and no longer has to meet any of these substantive conditions. More specifically, Union citizens acquire a right of permanent residence after having legally resided in the host

Member State for five years.[19] The same is true for family members who are not EU citizens but who have resided in the host state for five years.[20]

4. RESTRICTIONS ON THE RIGHT OF ENTRY AND RESIDENCE

The rights of entry and residence granted by Directive 2004/38/EC are not absolute. Rather, these rights can be restricted "on grounds of public policy, public security or public health."[21] Crucially, however, the Directive defines these justifications quite narrowly.

Thus, while public health constitutes one potential reason for restricting the right of residence and entry, the Directive sharply limits the spectrum of public health threats that qualify: in order for a disease to justify restrictions it (1) has to have "epidemic potential" as defined by the World Health Organization, or (2) it has to be an "infectious diseas[e] or contagious parasitic diseas[e]" that, if transmitted to one of the State's own nationals, would also give rise to protective measures.[22] Moreover, any disease occurring later than three months after an EU citizen has arrived in the host state does not justify the citizen's expulsion.[23]

Restrictions based on public policy and public security also have to meet very demanding requirements. The typical case involves the expulsion of foreign citizens who have committed some sort of criminal offense. However, any restriction based on grounds of public policy or public security not only has to comply with the general principle of proportionality, but also has to be based "exclusively on the personal conduct of the individual concerned."[24] Moreover, to justify restrictions on the right of residence or entry, the relevant personal conduct has to "represent a genuine, present and sufficiently serious threat affecting one of the fundamental interests of society."[25] Thus, minor offenses such as shoplifting do not qualify. The Directive also requires that justifications for restrictions have to take into account the individual circumstances of the case and that they must not be on "considerations of general prevention"—meaning that measures restricting the right of residence cannot be justified on grounds of public deterrence.

There are a number of additional restrictions on Member States' power to expel non-citizens based on public policy or public health. Specifically, the chosen state of residence has to "take account of considerations such as

---

[19] Art. 16(1).
[20] Art. 16(2).
[21] Art. 27(1).
[22] Art. 29(1).
[23] Art. 29(2).
[24] Art. 27(2).
[25] Art. 27(2).

how long the individual concerned has resided on its territory, his/her age, state of health, family and economic situation, social and cultural integration into the host Member State and the extent of his/her links with the country of origin."[26] In other words, the chosen state of residence cannot simply rubber stamp expulsions.

Moreover, the threshold for expulsion is even higher if the non-citizen has the right of permanent residence. In that case, the expulsion can only be based on "serious" grounds of public policy or public security.[27] If the EU citizen has resided in the host state for ten years (rather than for the five years required for a right of permanent residence) or if the EU citizen is a minor, the relevant grounds must meet an even stricter "imperative" grounds standard.[28]

Together with various procedural requirements imposed by the Directive, these substantive hurdles mean that expulsions of EU citizens and their family members are quite difficult to undertake.

5. EQUAL TREATMENT

Directive 2004/38/EC does not only govern the right to enter and reside in other Member States. It also contains important guarantees regarding the rights that EU citizens and their family members enjoy in the host state. Thus, citizens from other Member States and their family members are entitled to take up employment or self-employment in the host state.[29] Just as importantly, the directive seeks to ensure that citizens from other EU Member States as well as certain non-EU family members enjoy a general right to equal treatment in the host state. See Article 24 of Directive 2004/38/EC:

Equal treatment

1. Subject to such specific provisions as are expressly provided for in the Treaty and secondary law, all Union citizens residing on the basis of this Directive in the territory of the host Member State shall enjoy equal treatment with the nationals of that Member State within the scope of the Treaty. The benefit of this right shall be extended to family members who are not nationals of a Member State and who have the right of residence or permanent residence.

2. By way of derogation from paragraph 1, the host Member State shall not be obliged to confer entitlement to social assistance during the first three months of residence or, where appropriate, the longer period provided for in Article 14(4)(b), nor shall it be

---

[26] Art. 28(1).
[27] Art. 28(2).
[28] Art. 28(3).
[29] Art. 24.

obliged, prior to acquisition of the right of permanent residence, to grant maintenance aid for studies, including vocational training, consisting in student grants or student loans to persons other than workers, self-employed persons, persons who retain such status and members of their families.

B. REGULATION 1612/68/EEC

Regulation 1612/68/EEC complements—and sometimes overlaps with—Directive 2004/38/EC. Of particular relevance are the provisions contained in Part I of the Regulation. These provisions govern eligibility for employment (Title 1), equal treatment in employment (Title 2), and workers' families (Title 3). In large part, these provisions have been made redundant by Directive 2004/38/EC. Nonetheless, they continue to be invoked, and it is helpful to be familiar with them.

1. ELIGIBILITY FOR EMPLOYMENT

Title 1, which governs eligibility for employment, essentially clarifies rights that can easily be derived from Article 45 TFEU. For example, under Article 1 of Regulation 1612/68/EEC, an EU citizen has "the right to take up an activity as an employed person, and to pursue such activity, within the territory of another Member State in accordance with the provisions laid down by law, regulation or administrative action governing the employment of nationals of that State." This, of course, is nothing but the core guarantee contained in Article 45 TFEU, and equivalent guarantees can be found in Articles 23 and 24 of Directive 2004/38/EC.

2. EQUAL TREATMENT IN EMPLOYMENT

Title 2 of Regulation 1612/68/EEC prohibits discrimination in employment and, in particular, makes it clear that that prohibition not only applies to Member States but also to private employers. The core guarantee can be found in Article 7(1) under which an EU citizen from another Member State must not be treated differently from the citizens of the host state with respect to "any conditions of employment and work, in particular as regards remuneration, dismissal, and should he become unemployed, reinstatement or re-employment." Crucially, the general right to equal treatment in Article 24 of Directive 2004/38/EC does not make Article 7(1) of Regulation 1612/68/EEC redundant, since Article 24 of Directive 204/38/EC does not apply to private employers. However, as we shall see in more detail later on, Article 7(1) is not the only norm preventing private employers from discriminating against citizens from other Member States. Rather, Article 45 TFEU also fulfills that function since Article 45 binds not only Member States but also private employers.

Under Article 7(2), the foreign worker shall also "enjoy the same social and tax advantages as national workers." Of course, the guarantee contained in Article 7(2) can also be derived from Article 24 of Directive 2004/38/EC as well as from Article 45 TFEU.

3. WORKERS' FAMILIES

Like Directive 2004/38/EC, Regulation 1612/68/EEC not only concerns the rights of workers but also accords rights to their family members. Of crucial importance in this context is Article 12 of the Regulation. Under that provision, the children of an EU citizen who is or has been employed in another Member State "shall be admitted to that State's general educational, apprenticeship and vocational training courses under the same conditions as the nationals of that State, if such children are residing in its territory."

Article 12 has been interpreted expansively. Contrary to what a literal reading of this provision might suggest, it not only grants migrant workers' children access to education but also implies a right of residence for those children:[30]

> The Court has previously held that the children of a citizen of the Union who have installed themselves in a Member State during the exercise by their parent of rights of residence as a migrant worker in that Member State are entitled to reside there in order to attend general educational courses there, pursuant to Article 12 of Regulation No 1612/68. The fact that the parents of the children concerned have meanwhile divorced, the fact that only one parent is a citizen of the Union, and the fact that that parent has ceased to be a migrant worker in the host Member State are irrelevant in this regard.[31]

Moreover, the right of residence is not only granted to the children of EU citizens themselves, but also to their parents because "a refusal to allow those parents to remain in the host Member State during the period of their children's education might deprive those children of a right which has been granted to them by the legislature of the European Union."[32]

C. PRACTICE QUESTIONS

For the purpose of the following practice questions, assume that Alpha and Beta are Member States of the European Union.

---

[30] *E.g.*, Case C-310/08, London Borough of Harrow v. Nimco Hassan Ibrahim and Secretary of State for the Home Department, 2010 E.C.R. I-01065 ¶ 29.
[31] *Id.*
[32] *Id.* at ¶ 30.

1. As a matter of EU law, how long can an EU citizen stay in another Member State based solely on the fact that he has his identity card or passport?

2. Klaus is an Alphanian citizen, whereas his wife Maria is a U.S. citizen. Both live in Alpha. One fine day, Maria—who holds an Alphanian residence card—decides to move to Beta for 80 days. Under EU law, does she have the right to enter Beta and stay in Beta for that long?

3. Louis is a Betanian citizen. On January 1, 2019, he moves to Alpha and takes on a job as a waiter. Alphanian law requires every foreign citizen who intends to stay for more than 3 months to register with the local authorities no longer than 6 weeks after arrival. However, Louis does not register until 7 weeks after he first arrives in Alpha. Therefore, the Alphanian authorities fine Louis in the amount of €50,000. Does the fine violate EU law?

4. Can the host Member State deny the protection of directive 2004/38/EC to those spouses of EU citizens who have entered into a "pretend" marriage?

5. Can the Member States be even more generous to the citizens of other EU Member States than directive 2004/38/EC calls for?

6. George is a Betanian citizen working and living in Alpha. In January 2019, George's brother James, who works for the Betanian government, plays a central role in capturing various members of a terrorist network. In February 2019, the Alphanian government receives various threats from other members of the same terrorist network, threatening that they will commit serious terrorist acts unless Alpha deports George. Would the Alphanian government violate directive 2004/38/EC if it deported George on grounds of public policy or public security?

7. Paul is an Alphanian national living and working in Beta. Paul's Alphanian passport expired in 2018, and Paul never bothered to renew it. In 2019, Paul is convicted in a Betanian court of committing 20 counts of arson directed at public buildings as well as 23 murders. Beta wants to deport Paul to Alpha so that Paul can serve his sentence there. However, Alpha refuses to let Paul enter Alphanian territory. It argues that (a) Beta has no sufficient reason to deport Paul and that (b) Alpha is under no duty to let Paul enter Alphanian territory given that the free movement of workers does not protect EU citizens against their own Member States. Is Alpha correct?

8. Gustav is an Alphanian living in Beta. In January 2019, Gustav is convicted of dealing in illegal narcotics. Two months later, Gustav is ordered to leave Beta. The reasons accompanying the administration's decision make it clear that Gustav is ordered to leave the country because

the Betanian administration wants to "set an example to other foreigners living in Beta that dealing in narcotics will not be tolerated." Does this decision violate directive 2004/38/EC?

9. Assume that Alpha enacts a law requiring all aliens who wish to work or live in Alpha for more than three months to undergo a medical exam to show that they are free of diseases of epidemic potential. Does this rule violate directive 2004/38/EC?

10. George is an Alphanian citizen. He wants to live in Beta for two years, but he neither wants to study nor work there. He has a very sizable fortune and just wants to enjoy Beta. Does George have the right to live in Beta under directive 2004/38/EC?

11. Hans and George have entered into a same-sex "civil union" under Alphanian law. Hans is an Alphanian citizen. George is an American citizen. After having lived in the United States for several years, Hans and George want to move to Beta. Assume that Beta also recognizes civil unions between same sex partners and generally treats them as equivalent to married couples. Further assume that Hans has a job in Beta. Do Hans and George have the right to live in Beta under the provisions of directive 2004/38/EC?

12. George is a Betanian citizen who has lived in Alpha since 2001. In 2007, he wonders whether he should apply for a permanent resident card and wants to know whether there are any benefits to being a permanent resident that he does not already enjoy.

13. Martin is a U.S. national married to Lucy, an Alphanian national. They were married in 2001. In 2005, Martin and Lucy moved to Beta where Lucy worked as a teacher. In 2019, they divorced. Assuming that Martin, who works as a cook in Beta, can support himself, does directive 2004/38/EC give him the right to stay in Beta?

14. John is an Alphanian national working in the United States. His wife, Mary, is a U.S. citizen. Both live in the United States, but want to move to Alpha. Does EU law give Mary the right to live in Alpha?

15. John is an Alphanian citizen. His wife, Mary, is a U.S. citizen. Both live in Beta, but want to move to Alpha. Does EU law give Mary the right to move to Alpha?

16. In Alpha, possession of small amounts of marijuana is a criminal offense, but one which is not prosecuted. Luigi is an Betanian citizen living in Alpha. The Alphanian police discover that he possesses a small amount of marijuana. The Alphanian administration invokes the public security exemption to expel Luigi. Can they do so without violating directive 2004/38/EC?

17. Susan is a private employer in Alpha. Francois is a Betanian citizen living in Alpha who works for Susan. One day, Francois finds out that Susan is paying her Alphanian employees higher wages than her foreign employees for the same work. When Francois confronts Susan, she freely admits that she is paying her Alphanian employees more because they are Alphanians. Does Susan's conduct violate EU law?

18. Under Alphanian law, every firm with at least five regular employees has to allow its workers to elect, from among their midst, a number of special representatives who form the so-called "works council." The intuition underlying the works council is that employees need a firm-level institution that represents their interests vis-à-vis employers. In particular, the works council engages in monitoring to ensure that the firm complies with its legal duties regarding working conditions and worker safety. Assume, for the purpose of this question, that Alphanian law limits membership in the works council to workers of Alphanian nationality. Would such a provision violate Directive 2004/38/EC or Regulation 1612/68/EEC?

Chapter 15

Freedom of Establishment

■ ■ ■

The freedom of establishment, guaranteed by Article 49 TFEU, gives EU citizens the right to "take up and pursue activities as self-employed persons and to set up and manage undertakings . . ." in another Member State under the same conditions that apply to that state's citizens.[1]

A. DISCRIMINATORY AND NON-DISCRIMINATORY OBSTACLES

Like the other fundamental freedoms, the freedom of establishment includes a prohibition against discrimination.[2] But—also like the other fundamental freedoms—the freedom of establishment is not limited to a prohibition against discrimination: any state measure that is "liable to hinder or render less attractive the exercise by Union nationals of the freedom of establishment"[3] interferes with the freedom of establishment.

B. JUSTIFICATIONS

The justifications that Member States can invoke for interfering with the freedom of establishment are also similar to what we have seen for the other fundamental freedoms.

First, there are written justifications: under Article 52(1) TFEU, the freedom of establishment does not prohibit national restrictions based on grounds of public policy, public security, or public health. In order to be justified, of course, these measures have to comply with the principle of proportionality.

Second, measures interfering with the freedom of establishment can be justified based on the unwritten mandatory requirements doctrine,

---

[1] TFEU, art. 49(2).

[2] *E.g.*, Case C-51/08, European Commission v. Grand Duchy of Luxemburg, 2011 E.C.R. I-4231 ¶ 80 ("Article 43 EC [now Article 49 TFEU] is thus intended to ensure that all nationals of all Member States who establish themselves in another Member State for the purpose of pursuing activities there as self-employed persons receive the same treatment as nationals of that State, and it prohibits, as a restriction on freedom of establishment, any discrimination on grounds of nationality resulting from national legislation. . .").

[3] *E.g.* Case C-148/10, DHL International NV, formerly Express Line NV v. Belgisch Instituut voor Postdiensten en Telecommunicatie, 2011 E.C.R. I-9543 ¶ 60.

which we have already discussed in the context of the free movement of goods.

C. COMPANIES

The freedom of establishment applies not only to natural persons, but also to companies: under Article 54(1) TFEU, companies that have been "formed in accordance with the law of a Member State and having their registered office, central administration or principal place of business within the Union shall, for the purposes of [the freedom of establishment], be treated in the same way as natural persons who are nationals of Member States."

The central question in this context is to what extent Article 54(1) TFEU contains a guarantee of "corporate mobility." Next, we will focus on a number of cases that address this issue. On a doctrinal level, these cases are closely related. On a policy level, however, it is noteworthy that these cases raise questions on two very different planes: tax policy and corporate law policy.

1. TAXATION

It should first be noted that, as a matter of tax policy, under the relevant treaties on double taxation, a corporation that has ties to various countries will, for tax purposes, be considered a resident of the country where its place of effective management—usually its central administration—is located.[4] Hence, each Member State has a fiscal interest in keeping corporations from moving their central administrations elsewhere.

As a matter of legal policy, states should not be able to indulge that interest by way of legal prohibitions: according to standard economic theory it is, by and large, desirable that different Member States compete for corporations. In the absence of externalities, corporations should be able to establish their headquarters in the state that offers the most attractive mix of low taxes and high quality public services such as good courts, well-maintained roads, etc.

However, beyond the general interest that states have in keeping a corporation's central administration in their territories, there is also a more particular interest that relates to "hidden reserves:" discrepancies between the book value of a corporation's assets and its market value. For example, a corporation may have acquired a piece of real estate for $1,000,000. Five years later, that same piece of real estate could be worth $5,000,000. However, under the relevant tax accounting rules, the

---

[4] *Cf.* art. 4(3) of the OECD Model Tax Convention on Income and Capital, *available* at http://www.oecd.org/tax/treaties/47213736.pdf.

corporation may still be able to accord a book value of $1,000,000 to the relevant asset. The $4,000,000 difference between the book value and the market value constitutes a hidden reserve.

Normally, the existence of such hidden reserves does not impose an undue burden on the state. This is because once the corporation sells the relevant piece of real estate, the difference between the book value and the market value is "realized" and thus becomes taxable income. In other words, the state only has to be patient. However, the balance of this system is upset if corporations are allowed to move their places of residence from one country to another before selling their assets. In that situation, the former country of residence may never be able to tax the increase in value. After all, by the time that the asset is sold—and hence by the time that the relevant income is realized for tax purposes—the corporation would no longer be subject to taxation in its original country of residence. This outcome is problematic inasmuch as it leaves the former country of residence unable to tax an increase in value that took place while the corporation was a tax resident in that country. Moreover, it creates an obvious potential for abuse: corporations with substantial hidden reserves could systematically exploit such a system by moving their tax residence from countries with high corporate tax rates to countries with low corporate tax rates.

It is therefore unsurprising that some of the obstacles that countries have placed in the way of corporate mobility have precisely the purpose of preventing corporations from leaving their old states of residence without paying taxes on their hidden reserves.

2. CORPORATE LAW

In the arena of corporate law, the question is a very different one—namely, to what extent should corporations be able to choose freely between the corporate law systems of different Member States? Consider the following excerpt.

FREEDOM OF CHOICE IN EUROPEAN CORPORATE LAW
Jens Dammann
29 YALE J. INT'L L. 477 (2004)

U.S. corporations are free to choose the state law governing their internal affairs, a concept that this Article will refer to as free choice. The legal mechanism by which U.S. law ensures free choice is the state of incorporation doctrine. Under that doctrine, the internal affairs of a corporation are governed by the law of the state of incorporation, regardless of where the corporation's headquarters is located. At any time, therefore, corporations can change the state law which applies to them by choosing to reincorporate elsewhere.

The concept of free choice has long been the topic of intensive legal research. In particular, scholars have focused on the question of whether the freedom of corporations to choose between the law of different states will lead to more efficient rules. Amid the variety of positions that have been developed on this issue, the two most prominent ones are commonly known as the race-to-the-bottom and the race-to-the-top views. While both assume that states compete for corporate charters in order to maximize the revenues derived from incorporation fees, they differ as to the direction that such competition takes. Under the race-to-the-bottom view, states will compete for corporate charters not by making their corporate law more efficient, but by making their law more management-friendly. Proponents of the race-to-the-top view reject that reasoning, claiming that it neglects the influence exerted by capital markets. Managers, they argue, have a strong incentive to make the corporation's shares attractive to shareholders, lest capital markets punish the corporation and—by extension—its managers.

In the European Community, the debate over free choice has, at least until recently, rarely inspired close scrutiny. This is unsurprising, given that the ability of corporations to choose the applicable corporate law regime has long faced a formidable obstacle in the so-called real seat doctrine. Under this doctrine, which prevailed until recently in many Member States of the European Community, the internal affairs of a corporation are governed not by the law of the state of incorporation but by the law of the state where the corporation's headquarters are located. As a result, corporations cannot choose the law of another Member State unless they are willing to move their headquarters as well. Since the costs of such a move will usually outweigh the advantages connected with a more efficient corporate law regime, the real seat doctrine effectively prevents free choice. ∎

NOTES AND QUESTIONS

1. One of the questions underlying the ECJ decisions on the freedom of establishment for corporations relates precisely to the freedom of corporations to choose the applicable law. That is, to what extent should the Member State where the corporation's central administration is located be able to force the corporation to make use of that state's corporate law—as required by the real seat doctrine?

2. As pointed out in the excerpt above, the so-called race-to-the-top theory assumes that corporations that incorporate in states with low quality corporate law are punished by capital markets? How exactly might this work?

3. A simple answer to the tax policy issue underlying Daily Mail would be to shift corporate taxation from the Member State level to the level of the European Union: if corporations were taxed by the European Union rather than by the Member States, then they could no longer avoid corporate income

taxes by moving their headquarters from one Member State to another. In addition, such an approach would make life much simpler for corporations that operate across Member States. At present, such firms have to deal with up to 28 different corporate income tax regimes. So what might be the reasons that the Treaties do not give the European Union the power to tax corporations?

THE QUEEN V. H. M. TREASURY AND COMMISSIONERS OF INLAND REVENUE, EX PARTE DAILY MAIL AND GENERAL TRUST PLC.

Case 81/87, September 27, 1988, 1988 E.C.R. 5483

[The United Kingdom allows a company to be formed under U.K. law as long as its registered office is located in the United Kingdom, even if its headquarters (central management and control) is located elsewhere. Daily Mail and General Trust PLC ("Daily Mail") was a company that had been formed under U.K. law and also had its central management and control in the United Kingdom.

At some point, Daily Mail decided to move its central management and control to the Netherlands. However, U.K. law prohibits companies residing in the United Kingdom from ceasing their resident status without the consent of the British Treasury.

In part, this has to do with the taxation of hidden reserves—that is, assets whose book values are below their market value. Under U.K. law, a company is deemed a resident of the country where its central management and control is located, and only companies that are residents of the United Kingdom are subject to the United Kingdom's corporation tax. If a company accumulates hidden reserves in the United Kingdom and then moves to another Member State where it eventually realizes taxable income by selling the undervalued assets, then the United Kingdom does not participate in the relevant tax revenues even though the hidden reserves were originally created in the United Kingdom.

Daily Mail, however, took the position that the consent requirement violated the Freedom of Establishment. The ensuing litigation eventually led to a request for a preliminary ruling.]

18. [. . .] [The provision of United Kingdom law at issue does not] stand in the way of a partial or total transfer of the activities of a company incorporated in the United Kingdom to a company newly incorporated in another Member State, if necessary after winding-up and, consequently, the settlement of the tax position of the United Kingdom company. It requires Treasury consent only where such a company seeks to transfer its central management and control out of the United Kingdom while maintaining its legal personality and its status as a United Kingdom company.

19. In that regard it should be borne in mind that, unlike natural persons, companies are creatures of the law and, in the present state of Community law, creatures of national law. They exist only by virtue of the varying national legislation which determines their incorporation and functioning.

20. As the Commission has emphasized, the legislation of the Member States varies widely in regard to both the factor providing a connection to the national territory required for the incorporation of a company and the question whether a company incorporated under the legislation of a Member State may subsequently modify that connecting factor. Certain States require that not merely the registered office but also the real head office, that is to say the central administration of the company, should be situated on their territory, and the removal of the central administration from that territory thus presupposes the winding-up of the company with all the consequences that winding-up entails in company law and tax law. The legislation of other States permits companies to transfer their central administration to a foreign country but certain of them, such as the United Kingdom, make that right subject to certain restrictions, and the legal consequences of a transfer, particularly in regard to taxation, vary from one Member State to another.

21. The Treaty has taken account of that variety in national legislation. In defining, in Article 58 [now Article 53], the companies which enjoy the right of establishment, the Treaty places on the same footing, as connecting factors, the registered office, central administration and principal place of business of a company. Moreover, Article 220 of the Treaty provides for the conclusion, so far as is necessary, of agreements between the Member States with a view to securing inter alia the retention of legal personality in the event of transfer of the registered office of companies from one country to another. No convention in this area has yet come into force. [The former Article 220 EC has no equivalent in the TFEU or the TEU.]

22. It should be added that none of the directives on the coordination of company law adopted under Article 54(3)(g) [now Article 50(2)(g)] of the Treaty deal with the differences at issue here.

23. It must therefore be held that the Treaty regards the differences in national legislation concerning the required connecting factor and the question whether—and if so how—the registered office or real head office of a company incorporated under national law may be transferred from one Member State to another as problems which are not resolved by the rules concerning the right of establishment but must be dealt with by future legislation or conventions.

24. Under those circumstances, Articles 52 and 58 [now Articles 49 and 54] of the Treaty cannot be interpreted as conferring on companies

incorporated under the law of a Member State a right to transfer their central management and control and their central administration to another Member State while retaining their status as companies incorporated under the legislation of the first Member State.

25. The answer to the first part of the first question must therefore be that in the present state of Community law Articles 52 [now Article 49] and 58 [now Article 54] of the Treaty, properly construed, confer no right on a company incorporated under the legislation of a Member State and having its registered office there to transfer its central management and control to another Member State. ∎

NOTES AND QUESTIONS

1. As the Court of Justice points out in paragraph 18 of the decision, the consent requirement does not apply when—after winding-up the old corporation—a company is newly formed in another Member State. Given what you know about the problem of hidden reserves, why might U.K. law treat this case differently?

2. As the Court of Justice notes in paragraph 20, the corporation laws of the various Member States differ greatly when it comes to the question of what connection a company has to have to a Member State in order to be formed under that Member State's law. In some Member States—such as Germany—a corporation can only be formed under local law if the corporation's headquarters is located in that state. Other Member States are more generous: they allow corporations to be formed under their laws as long as the corporation's registered office is located there—a crucial difference because the registered office does not require any real economic presence. But why is it relevant to the dispute in *Daily Mail* that Member States differ with respect to the connection that a company has to have to a Member State in order to be formed under that Member State's law?

3. What consequences might have resulted if the Court of Justice had decided in favor of Daily Mail?

Doctrinally, the *Daily Mail* decision relies heavily on the assumption that "unlike natural persons, companies are creatures of the law and, in the present state of Community law, creatures of national law."[5] In adopting this view, the Court of Justice positions itself, without explicitly saying so, in an age old doctrinal debate regarding the nature of the firm. In the European tradition, this debate is generally associated with the legal fiction theory favored by German lawyers Friedrich Carl von Savigny and the real entity theory advanced by Otto von Gierke. This debate is of

---

[5] The Queen v. H. M. Treasury and Commissioners of Inland Revenue, ex parte Daily Mail and General Trust plc., Case 81/87, September 27, 1988, 1988 E.C.R. 5483 para. 17.

interest in part because of its international character. Consider the following excerpt.

RECONCEPTUALIZING THE THEORY OF THE FIRM—FROM NATURE TO FUNCTION

Martin Petrin
118 PENN STATE L. REV. 1, 5 (2013)

1. Fiction Theory

[. . .] [T]he fiction theory is strongly connected to German jurist Friedrich Carl von Savigny, whose work on the subject greatly influenced common law scholars.

Savigny contended that because legal persons could only have recognized rights and duties as a consequence of an act of the State, they were nothing but artificial beings or fictions. He and other fiction theorists insisted that due to its artificial personality, a firm could only have a very limited set of rights and duties, namely those pertaining to property. The nature of legal persons, which represented but a small fraction of a human's personality, did not allow for recognition of non-monetary rights and duties. Because of these limitations, the fiction theory also held that legal entities—apart from instances of strict liability—could not themselves be liable, either civilly or criminally.

The reason for this, in addition to the fact that a tort or crime was not necessary for exercising property rights, is that liability was conditioned upon a finding of culpability or mens rea. Mens rea, however, was something that a legal person, if thought of as only an artificial being, could not possess. According to Savigny, a legal person could never be liable, but a legal person's representatives or agents who actually committed a tort or a crime could be.

2. Real Entity Theory

In response to the fiction theory, particularly as promulgated by Savigny, another group of German scholars—under the leadership of historian and legal academic Otto von Gierke—developed the late nineteenth century "real entity theory" or "organic theory." According to this premise, legal entities were not fictions. Rather, they were real and capable of possessing their own mind and will. In addition, legal entities enjoyed any rights and duties that they could exercise. While the real entity theory recognized that legal entities gained their personality through the law and an act of the State, its proponents still contended that the legal person was not something created by the law, but rather a pre-existing reality that was solely "found" and recognized by the law.

In contrast to the fiction theory, the real entity view held that the firm is a distinct, autonomous being that is separate from, and more than just the sum of, its individual (human) parts. In a manner of speaking, the legal entity, under this approach, leads its own "life," in the sense of a psychological or sociological existence, and was thought to have attributes not found among its human components. The only difference between firms and human beings was that legal entities did not represent corporal organisms, but instead composite, social organisms.

Nevertheless, real entity theorists were confronted with the obvious problem that a legal entity, although thought to be "real" and likened to a living organism, was not capable of acting by itself. However, they solved this problem by providing the entity with "organs," its metaphorical "hands and mouth." Acts undertaken by these organs—generally higher-ranking officials within the legal entity—were fully and directly binding upon the legal entity. Yet, these organs were not viewed as agents. Instead, real entity theorists argued that the organs were part of, and reflected, the legal entity itself.

The real entity theory further acknowledged that legal entities, as "living creatures," could be liable both under tort and criminal law. However, because they were only able to act through their organs, legal entities could solely incur liability as a consequence of a tort or criminal offense if committed by one or more organs acting within their official capacities. These individuals, moreover, remained personally liable to third parties. Contrariwise, misconduct by lower-level employees, who were not considered to be organs, was insufficient to incur liability for the legal entity. Importantly, therefore, corporate liability depended on the seniority of the person or employee committing the offense.

B. The Debate's "Export" to Anglo-American Law

Around the turn of the early twentieth century, the debate over the nature of the firm was exported from German to Anglo-American law and began to exhibit a strong influence on the practice and theory of the latter. As one commentator writing in 1911 observed, it became "difficult indeed for any American lawyer writing upon the subject of corporations to avoid declaring himself" in the controversy. Thus, as evidenced by a flurry of contributions to the philosophic struggle surrounding the legal entity on this side of the Atlantic, common law authors too grew extensively entangled in this discourse.

1. Fiction Theory and Aggregate Theory

Previously, during the first half of the nineteenth century, the fiction theory predominated in England and the United States. Here, this theory was also known as the "concession theory" or "grant theory," owing to the fact that at the time corporations could only be incorporated based on a state legislature's award of a special concession, grant, or charter. In the landmark case Trustees of Dartmouth College v. Woodward, for instance, Chief Justice Marshall characterized the corporation as an "artificial being, invisible, intangible, and existing only in contemplation of law," which, as a mere creature of law, "possesses only those properties which the charter of its creation confers upon it."

However, during this period, the fiction theory also competed with the "aggregate" or "contractualist" theory, which was particularly popular in nineteenth century England and emerged more clearly in the United States during the latter half of the same century. The "aggregate" or "contractualist" theory asserted that corporations and other legal entities constituted aggregations of natural persons whose relationships were structured by way of mutual agreements. As such, both a legal entity's legal rights and duties were often seen, in an indirect or derivative manner, as simply those of its shareholders or other individuals that made up the entity. In other words, under the aggregate theory, rights and obligations held by individuals can be construed to reflect upon the legal entity itself.

[. . .]

The Ascendance of Real Entity Theory

With the emergence of the twentieth century, the increasing importance and prevalence of corporations led to growing dissatisfaction with the fiction theory's effects, including its hostility toward liability of legal entities. In addition, the fiction theory was difficult to reconcile with the shift from special chartering to general incorporation. At the same time, the aggregate theory failed to provide a plausible explanation for the adoption of limited liability for corporations and the decoupling of corporate and individual rights and duties in general. As a consequence, Gierke's real entity theory, together with previous discourse over its clash with the fiction theory, was "transplanted" from Germany to England and the United States, where it gained traction, challenging both the fiction and aggregate theories.

In England, Cambridge Professor Frederic William Maitland translated some of Gierke's major works and introduced his real entity theory to English and American judges and academics. In the United States, Ernst Freund, a U.S. born academic with German roots, published The Legal Nature of Corporations, which also contributed to the wider recognition of Gierke's theory in the U.S. legal community.

While the real entity theory was not as successful in the common law as in the civil law, where it clearly defeated the fiction theory, it did gain considerable prominence and both U.K. and U.S. courts began to rely increasingly on the ideas it incorporated. In the iconic 1897 case Salomon v. A. Salomon & Co., the House of Lords upheld a company's separate legal personality and limited liability, finding that a company's existence was "real" and rejecting the notion that it was nothing more than a myth or fiction. Similarly, the influence of the real entity theory reinforced the tendency by Anglo-American courts to recognize the tortious liability of companies, followed by a partial recognition of criminal liability as well. Moreover, the real entity theory's ascendance led to the decline of the ultra vires doctrine, helped strengthen limited liability and the business judgment rule, and may have been partially responsible for the introduction of a corporate income tax regime, which treated corporations as separate taxable entities.

The tension between the real entity theory and its counterparts, the fiction and aggregate theories, also made its mark on constitutional law, particularly in the United States. Over the course of the nineteenth and twentieth centuries, a number of Supreme Court cases found that a corporation was akin to a real person and therefore entitled to constitutional rights such as freedom of the press, commercial speech, and protections against unreasonable searches and seizures, among others. Conversely, in other cases decided during that time, the fictional nature of the firm prevailed. For example, the Supreme Court refused to grant legal entities certain Fourth and Fifth Amendment guarantees and limited their right to privacy because they were only "artificial" in nature. Moreover, as discussed in more detail below, all three traditional theories of the firm have had, and continue to have, an impact on corporate political speech rights. ∎

In the legal literature, the *Daily Mail* decision was widely interpreted as giving wide discretion to Member States in choosing rules governing the conflict of laws for corporations. Specifically, it was thought that it was up to each Member State to decide whether to apply the state of incorporation doctrine, under which a corporation's internal affairs are governed by the law of the state of incorporation, or the real seat rule, under which the applicable corporate law is determined by the location of the corporation's real seat.

As a practical matter, this meant that Member States could prevent locally headquartered firms from selecting another Member State's corporate law. For example, assume that a German-based entrepreneur preferred U.K. company law to German corporate law and therefore incorporated his firm in the United Kingdom. As long as the firm's real seat was located in Germany, German courts would apply German corporate law to the firm because Germany traditionally followed the real seat rule. Hence, if the relevant firm was incorporated under U.K. law rather than under German corporate law, German courts would treat the firm as not being incorporated at all. This meant that the firm would be treated as a sole proprietorship (in the case of a single owner) or as a partnership (in the case of two or more owners). Either way, the owners would face unlimited personal liability for the debts of the firm. However, in 1999, the

Court of Justice abruptly put an end to this practice with its landmark *Centros* decision.

CENTROS LTD V. ERHVERVS-OG SELSKABSSTYRELSEN
Case C-212/97, March 9, 1999, 1999 E.C.R. I-1459

[In Denmark, forming a limited liability company required the founders to pay up a minimum capital fixed at (i.e. fund the company with at least) 200,000 Danish Crowns. This rule was designed to protect the creditors of limited liability companies: because the members of a limited liability company are not personally liable to the company's creditors, Danish law sought to ensure at least that entrepreneurs cannot set up a limited liability company without providing it with the requisite minimum capital.

By contrast, forming a private limited company in the United Kingdom required much less capital. This is because U.K. law does not impose any duty on founders to pay up a certain minimum capital when forming a private limited company.

Mr. and Mrs. Bryde, both of whom were Danish citizens, made use of the liberal U.K. provisions in forming a private limited company in the U.K. named *Centros Ltd*. Centros' share capital amounted only to 100 British Pounds, and even this amount had not been paid up. The home of a friend of Mr. Bryde's in the U.K. served as Centros' registered office.

Subsequently, the company sought to have a branch office registered in Denmark. The Danish authorities refused. They pointed out that Centros did not trade in the U.K., so the branch office would not, in fact, be a branch office but the company's principal establishment, and that the whole scheme was aimed at circumventing the Danish minimum capital rules.

Centros argued that the Danish authorities' refusal to let Centros set up a branch office in Denmark violated the freedom of establishment. The ensuring litigation resulted in a request for a preliminary ruling.]

14. By its question, the national court is in substance asking whether it is contrary to Articles 52 [now Article 49 TFEU] and 58 [now Article 54 TFEU] of the Treaty for a Member State to refuse to register a branch of a company formed in accordance with the legislation of another Member State in which it has its registered office but where it does not carry on any business when the purpose of the branch is to enable the company concerned to carry on its entire business in the State in which that branch is to be set up, while avoiding the formation of a company in that State, thus evading application of the rules governing the formation of companies which are, in that State, more restrictive so far as minimum paid-up share capital is concerned. . . .

16. According to the Danish Government, Article [49 TFEU] is not applicable in the case in the main proceedings, since the situation is purely internal to Denmark. Mr and Mrs Bryde, Danish nationals, have formed a company in the United Kingdom which does not carry on any actual business there with the sole purpose of carrying on business in Denmark through a branch and thus of avoiding application of Danish legislation on the formation of private limited companies. . . .

17. In this respect, it should be noted that a situation in which a company formed in accordance with the law of a Member State in which it has its registered office desires to set up a branch in another Member State falls within the scope of Community law. In that regard, it is immaterial that the company was formed in the first Member State only for the purpose of establishing itself in the second, where its main, or indeed entire, business is to be conducted.

18. That M[r] and Mrs Bryde formed the company Centros in the United Kingdom for the purpose of avoiding Danish legislation requiring that a minimum amount of share capital be paid up has not been denied either in the written observations or at the hearing. That does not, however, mean that the formation by that British company of a branch in Denmark is not covered by freedom of establishment for the purposes of Article [49] and [54 TFEU]. The question of the application of those articles of the Treaty is different from the question whether or not a Member State may adopt measures in order to prevent attempts by certain of its nationals to evade domestic legislation by having recourse to the possibilities offered by the Treaty.

19. As to the question whether, as Mr and Mrs Bryde claim, the refusal to register in Denmark a branch of their company formed in accordance with the law of another Member State in which it has its registered office constitutes an obstacle to freedom of establishment, it must be borne in mind that that freedom, conferred by Article [49 TFEU] on Community nationals, includes the right for them to take up and pursue activities as self-employed persons and to set up and manage undertakings under the same conditions as are laid down by the law of the Member State of establishment for its own nationals. Furthermore, under Article [54] of the Treaty companies or firms formed in accordance with the law of a Member State and having their registered office, central administration or principal place of business within the Community are to be treated in the same way as natural persons who are nationals of Member States.

20. The immediate consequence of this is that those companies are entitled to carry on their business in another Member State through an agency, branch or subsidiary. The location of their registered office, central administration or principal place of business serves as the connecting

factor with the legal system of a particular State in the same way as does nationality in the case of a natural person.

21. Where it is the practice of a Member State, in certain circumstances, to refuse to register a branch of a company having its registered office in another Member State, the result is that companies formed in accordance with the law of that other Member State are prevented from exercising the freedom of establishment conferred on them by Articles [49] and [54] of the Treaty.

22. Consequently, that practice constitutes an obstacle to the exercise of the freedoms guaranteed by those provisions.

23. According to the Danish authorities, however, Mr and Mrs Bryde cannot rely on those provisions, since the sole purpose of the company formation which they have in mind is to circumvent the application of the national law governing formation of private limited companies and therefore constitutes abuse of the freedom of establishment. In their submission, the Kingdom of Denmark is therefore entitled to take steps to prevent such abuse by refusing to register the branch.

24. It is true that according to the case-law of the Court a Member State is entitled to take measures designed to prevent certain of its nationals from attempting, under cover of the rights created by the Treaty, improperly to circumvent their national legislation or to prevent individuals from improperly or fraudulently taking advantage of provisions of Community law.

25. However, although, in such circumstances, the national courts may, case by case, take account—on the basis of objective evidence—of abuse or fraudulent conduct on the part of the persons concerned in order, where appropriate, to deny them the benefit of the provisions of Community law on which they seek to rely, they must nevertheless assess such conduct in the light of the objectives pursued by those provisions (Paletta II, paragraph 25).

26. In the present case, the provisions of national law, application of which the parties concerned have sought to avoid, are rules governing the formation of companies and not rules concerning the carrying on of certain trades, professions or businesses. The provisions of the Treaty on freedom of establishment are intended specifically to enable companies formed in accordance with the law of a Member State and having their registered office, central administration or principal place of business within the Community to pursue activities in other Member States through an agency, branch or subsidiary.

27. That being so, the fact that a national of a Member State who wishes to set up a company chooses to form it in the Member State whose rules of company law seem to him the least restrictive and to set up branches in

other Member States cannot, in itself, constitute an abuse of the right of establishment. The right to form a company in accordance with the law of a Member State and to set up branches in other Member States is inherent in the exercise, in a single market, of the freedom of establishment guaranteed by the Treaty. . . .

31. The final question to be considered is whether the national practice in question might not be justified for the reasons put forward by the Danish authorities.

32. Referring both to Article 56 of the Treaty [now Article 52 TFEU] and to the case-law of the Court on imperative requirements in the general interest, the Board argues that the requirement that private limited companies provide for and pay up a minimum share capital pursues a dual objective: first, to reinforce the financial soundness of those companies in order to protect public creditors against the risk of seeing the public debts owing to them become irrecoverable since, unlike private creditors, they cannot secure those debts by means of guarantees and, second, and more generally, to protect all creditors, whether public or private, by anticipating the risk of fraudulent bankruptcy due to the insolvency of companies whose initial capitalisation was inadequate.

33. The Board adds that there is no less restrictive means of attaining this dual objective. The other way of protecting creditors, namely by introducing rules making it possible for shareholders to incur personal liability, under certain conditions, would be more restrictive than the requirement to provide for and pay up a minimum share capital.

34. It should be observed, first, that the reasons put forward do not fall within the ambit of Article [52 TFEU] of the Treaty. Next, it should be borne in mind that, according to the Court's case-law, national measures liable to hinder or make less attractive the exercise of fundamental freedoms guaranteed by the Treaty must fulfil four conditions: they must be applied in a non-discriminatory manner; they must be justified by imperative requirements in the general interest; they must be suitable for securing the attainment of the objective which they pursue; and they must not go beyond what is necessary in order to attain it.

35. Those conditions are not fulfilled in the case in the main proceedings. First, the practice in question is not such as to attain the objective of protecting creditors which it purports to pursue since, if the company concerned had conducted business in the United Kingdom, its branch would have been registered in Denmark, even though Danish creditors might have been equally exposed to risk.

36. Since the company concerned in the main proceedings holds itself out as a company governed by the law of England and Wales and not as a company governed by Danish law, its creditors are on notice that it is covered by laws different from those which govern the formation of private

limited companies in Denmark and they can refer to certain rules of Community law which protect them, such as the Fourth Council Directive 78/660/EEC of 25 July 1978 based on Article 54(3)(g) [now Article 50(2)(g)] of the Treaty on the annual accounts of certain types of companies (OJ 1978 L 222, p. 11), and the Eleventh Council Directive 89/666/EEC of 21 December 1989 concerning disclosure requirements in respect of branches opened in a Member State by certain types of company governed by the law of another State (OJ 1989 L 395, p. 36).

37. Second, contrary to the arguments of the Danish authorities, it is possible to adopt measures which are less restrictive, or which interfere less with fundamental freedoms, by, for example, making it possible in law for public creditors to obtain the necessary guarantees.

38. Lastly, the fact that a Member State may not refuse to register a branch of a company formed in accordance with the law of another Member State in which it has its registered office does not preclude that first State from adopting any appropriate measure for preventing or penalising fraud, either in relation to the company itself, if need be in cooperation with the Member State in which it was formed, or in relation to its members, where it has been established that they are in fact attempting, by means of the formation of the company, to evade their obligations towards private or public creditors established on the territory of a Member State concerned. In any event, combating fraud cannot justify a practice of refusing to register a branch of a company which has its registered office in another Member State.

39. The answer to the question referred must therefore be that it is contrary to Articles [49] and [54 TFEU] of the Treaty for a Member State to refuse to register a branch of a company formed in accordance with the law of another Member State in which it has its registered office but in which it conducts no business where the branch is intended to enable the company in question to carry on its entire business in the State in which that branch is to be created, while avoiding the need to form a company there, thus evading application of the rules governing the formation of companies which, in that State, are more restrictive as regards the paying up of a minimum share capital. That interpretation does not, however, prevent the authorities of the Member State concerned from adopting any appropriate measure for preventing or penalising fraud, either in relation to the company itself, if need be in cooperation with the Member State in which it was formed, or in relation to its members, where it has been established that they are in fact attempting, by means of the formation of a company, to evade their obligations towards private or public creditors established in the territory of the Member State concerned. ∎

NOTES AND QUESTIONS

1. How can the present case be distinguished from the *Daily Mail* decision?

2. Why can't the Danish authorities' decision to deny the registration of the branch office be justified on the ground that Mr. and Mrs. Bryde were circumventing Danish law?

3. Why can't the Danish authorities' decision be justified on the ground that it protects creditors?

4. How might this case be analyzed in terms of the race-to-the-top vs. race-to-the-bottom framework?

When the *Centros* decision was handed down, many scholars saw it as the end of the real seat doctrine. Others, however, were skeptical. Their argument could be summarized as follows: *Daily Mail* implied that each Member State could decide freely whether to follow the state of incorporation doctrine, under which a corporation's internal affairs are governed by the corporation's state of incorporation, or the real seat doctrine, under which a corporation's internal affairs are governed by the state where the corporation is headquartered. The peculiarity of the facts underlying *Centros* was that Denmark generally adhered to the state of incorporation doctrine. But if Denmark adhered to the state of incorporation doctrine, then it recognized Centros Ltd. as a legal person and therefore could not then impose unjustified limits on Centros Ltd.'s freedom of establishment. By contrast, these scholars suggested, if Denmark had embraced the real seat doctrine, then Denmark would have been well within its rights to refrain from treating Centros Ltd. as a legal person and thus to deny Centros any rights under the freedom of establishment. Under this reading of *Centros* decision, the only real problem lay in the inconsistency of Denmark's approach: recognizing Centros Ltd as a person, but denying its right to open up a branch office in Denmark.

The dispute over the proper reading of *Centros* was put to rest, however, in the 2002 *Überseering* decision.[6]

ÜBERSEERING BV v. NORDIC CONSTRUCTION COMPANY BAUMANAGEMENT GMBH (NCC)

Case C-208/00, November 5, 2002, 2002 E.C.R. I-9919

[Überseering BV was a company that had been formed under Dutch law and originally had its central administration in the Netherlands.

---

[6] Case C-208/00, Überseering BV v. Nordic Construction Company Baumanagement GmbH (NCC), 2002 E.C.R. I-9919.

Subsequently, two Germans became the owners of Überseering BV and moved its central administration to Germany. They did not, however, reincorporate the company under German law.

Once Überseering BV was headquartered in Germany, it tried to sue another corporation before a German court. However, under Germany's real seat doctrine, Überseering was governed by German corporate law because its central administration was located in Germany. Given that Überseering was subject to German corporate law, the German rules on the formation of corporations applied as well. And from the perspective of German law, any firm that had its central administration in Germany had to be formed under German corporate law in order to be considered a validly formed corporation. But, of course, Überseering BV had only been formed under Dutch law. Hence, from the point of view of German law, Überseering had not been validly formed and therefore was not actually a corporation. Therefore, under German law, Überseering did not have the capacity to bring suit.

Überseering, however, argued that the application of the real seat doctrine violated the freedom of establishment, and the matter was referred to the Court of Justice for a preliminary ruling.]

40. Daily Mail and General Trust applies only to the relationship between the Member State of incorporation and the company which wishes to leave that State whilst retaining the legal personality conferred on it by the legislation thereof. Since companies are creatures of national law, they must continue to observe the requirements laid down by the legislation of their State of incorporation. Daily Mail and General Trust therefore formally acknowledges the right of the Member State of incorporation to set rules on the incorporation and legal existence of companies in accordance with its rules of private international law. It does not, in contrast, decide the question whether a company formed under the law of one Member State must be recognised by another Member State. [. . .]

78. The Court must next consider whether the refusal by the German courts to recognise the legal capacity and capacity to be a party to legal proceedings of a company validly incorporated under the law of another Member State constitutes a restriction on freedom of establishment.

79. In that regard, in a situation such as that in point in the main proceedings, a company validly incorporated under the law of, and having its registered office in, a Member State other than the Federal Republic of Germany has under German law no alternative to reincorporation in Germany if it wishes to enforce before a German court its rights under a contract entered into with a company incorporated under German law.

80. Überseering, which is validly incorporated in the Netherlands and has its registered office there, is entitled under Articles 43 EC [now Article 49] and 48 EC [now Article 54] to exercise its freedom of establishment in

Germany as a company incorporated under Netherlands law. It is of little significance in that regard that, after the company was formed, all its shares were acquired by German nationals residing in Germany, since that has not caused Überseering to cease to be a legal person under Netherlands law.

81. Indeed, its very existence is inseparable from its status as a company incorporated under Netherlands law since, as the Court has observed, a company exists only by virtue of the national legislation which determines its incorporation and functioning. The requirement of reincorporation of the same company in Germany is therefore tantamount to outright negation of freedom of establishment. [. . .]

92. It is not inconceivable that overriding requirements relating to the general interest, such as the protection of the interests of creditors, minority shareholders, employees and even the taxation authorities, may, in certain circumstances and subject to certain conditions, justify restrictions on freedom of establishment.

93. Such objectives cannot, however, justify denying the legal capacity and, consequently, the capacity to be a party to legal proceedings of a company properly incorporated in another Member State in which it has its registered office. Such a measure is tantamount to an outright negation of the freedom of establishment conferred on companies by Articles 43 EC [now Article 49 TFEU] and 48 EC [now Article 54 TFEU]. ■

NOTES AND QUESTIONS

1. Following *Überseering*, can Member States still apply the real seat doctrine to firms that have been formed in other Member States in accordance with the laws of those other Member States?

2. Can Member States still apply the real seat doctrine to corporations that are incorporated under their own laws? For example, assume that an enterprise is headquartered in Hungary, but its owners want to incorporate the relevant enterprise in Germany. Can German law make the formation of a German corporation contingent on the firm's headquarters being located in Germany?

3. What, if any, are the implications of the *Überseering* decision for firms incorporated in jurisdictions outside the European Union? For example, assume that a firm is headquartered in Germany, but incorporated in Delaware. Does *Überseering* imply that Germany must apply Delaware law to the question of whether the relevant corporation has been validly formed?

In *Überseering*, the Court suggested that "the protection of the interests of creditors, minority shareholders, [and] employees" might "in certain circumstances and subject to certain conditions, justify restrictions on freedom of establishment." This seemed to imply that Member States might be able to impose at least some of their corporate law norms on corporations formed in another Member State. The Court of Justice soon had the opportunity to address this question, in the 2003 case *Inspire Art*.

KAMER VAN KOOPHANDEL EN FABRIEKEN VOOR AMSTERDAM V. INSPIRE ART
Case C-167/01, September 30, 2003, 2003 E.C.R. I-10155

[The Netherlands had adopted a statute on so-called "formally foreign companies." Such companies were defined as foreign companies that carried on all or almost all of their activities in the Netherlands and did not have any real connection with the country under the law of which they had been formed. Under the Dutch statute, these companies were subject to, inter alia, the Dutch requirements on minimum share capital and certain rules regarding the liability of directors.

Inspire Art was a U.K. company that did all of its business in the Netherlands and was therefore subject to the relevant Dutch statute. It argued, however, that the statute violated the freedom of establishment. The ensuing legal proceedings prompted a request for a preliminary ruling.

Given the burden that the Dutch law imposed on formally foreign companies operating in the Netherlands, the Court of Justice had no trouble finding that the relevant provisions of the Dutch statute constituted restrictions of the free movement of establishment. The question, however, was whether that restriction could be justified.]

133. ... [A]ccording to the Court's case-law, national measures liable to hinder or make less attractive the exercise of fundamental freedoms guaranteed by the Treaty must, if they are to be justified [under the mandatory requirements doctrine], fulfil four conditions: they must be applied in a non-discriminatory manner; they must be justified by imperative requirements in the public interest; they must be suitable for securing the attainment of the objective which they pursue, and they must not go beyond what is necessary in order to attain it.

134. In consequence, it is necessary to consider whether those conditions are fulfilled by provisions relating to minimum capital such as those at issue in the main proceedings.

135. First, with regard to protection of creditors, and there being no need for the Court to consider whether the rules on minimum share capital constitute in themselves an appropriate protection measure, it is clear that Inspire Art holds itself out as a company governed by the law of England and Wales and not as a Netherlands company. Its potential creditors are put on sufficient notice that it is covered by legislation other than that regulating the formation in the Netherlands of limited liability companies

and, in particular, laying down rules in respect of minimum capital and directors' liability. They can also refer . . . to certain rules of Community law which protect them, such as the Fourth and Eleventh Directives.

136. Second, with regard to combating improper recourse to freedom of establishment, it must be borne in mind that a Member State is entitled to take measures designed to prevent certain of its nationals from attempting, under cover of the rights created by the Treaty, improperly to circumvent their national legislation or to prevent individuals from improperly or fraudulently taking advantage of provisions of Community law.

137. However, while in this case Inspire Art was formed under the company law of a Member State, in the case in point the United Kingdom, for the purpose in particular of evading the application of Netherlands company law, which was considered to be more severe, the fact remains that the provisions of the Treaty on freedom of establishment are intended specifically to enable companies formed in accordance with the law of a Member State and having their registered office, central administration or principal place of business within the Community to pursue activities in other Member States through an agency, branch or subsidiary.

138. That being so, as the Court confirmed in paragraph 27 of Centros, the fact that a national of a Member State who wishes to set up a company can choose to do so in the Member State the company-law rules of which seem to him the least restrictive and then set up branches in other Member States is inherent in the exercise, in a single market, of the freedom of establishment guaranteed by the Treaty.

139. In addition, it is clear from settled case-law that the fact that a company does not conduct any business in the Member State in which it has its registered office and pursues its activities only or principally in the Member State where its branch is established is not sufficient to prove the existence of abuse or fraudulent conduct which would entitle the latter Member State to deny that company the benefit of the provisions of Community law relating to the right of establishment.

140. Last, as regards possible justification of the [Dutch statute] on grounds of protection of fairness in business dealings and the efficiency of tax inspections, it is clear that neither the Chamber of Commerce nor the Netherlands Government has adduced any evidence to prove that the measure in question satisfies the criteria of efficacy, proportionality and non-discrimination mentioned in paragraph 132 above.

141. To the extent that the provisions concerning minimum capital are incompatible with freedom of establishment, as guaranteed by the Treaty, the same must necessarily be true of the penalties attached to non-compliance with those obligations, that is to say, the personal joint and several liability of directors where the amount of capital does not reach the

minimum provided for by the national legislation or where during the company's activities it falls below that amount. ∎

NOTES AND QUESTIONS

1. In *Inspire Art*, the Court argues that it is unnecessary to apply minimum capital requirements to foreign corporations headquartered in the Netherlands since "creditors are put on sufficient notice." The intuition here is that creditors who deal with a foreign company know who they are dealing with and can therefore protect themselves, e.g. by refusing to extend credit to firms incorporated under foreign law. However, does this logic apply to all types of creditors? Or are there some creditors who are essentially unable to protect themselves?

2. How does the Court arrive at the conclusion that the Dutch statute cannot be justified as an attempt to prevent entrepreneurs from circumventing Dutch law?

3. Various Member States have adopted some type of employee codetermination regime for public corporations.[7] In these Member States, the employees of public firms have the right to elect some of the members of the firm's board. For example, under German corporate law, public corporations have two boards: a managing board that runs the corporation and a supervisory board that appoints and supervises the members of the managing board.[8] In public corporations with more than 2000 employees, the firm's employees have the right to elect half the members of the supervisory board.[9] At present, this codetermination regime only applies to firms incorporated under German law. Would it be legal for Germany to subject firms that are headquartered in Germany, but incorporated in some other Member State, to the same rules on codetermination that apply to German firms?

In the 1988 *Daily Mail* decision, the company had invoked the freedom of establishment against the Member State in which it had been formed. By contrast, in *Centros*, *Überseering*, and *Inspire Art*, the companies involved invoked the freedom of establishment not against the state in which they had been formed, but against the state in which they conducted their business. In the 2008 *Cartesio* decision, the Court of Justice was once again confronted with a case in which a company invoked the freedom of

---

[7] *E.g.*, Jens Dammann, *The Mandatory Law Puzzle: Redefining American Exceptionalism in Corporate Law*, 65 HASTINGS L.J. 441, 454 (2014); Henry Hansmann & Reinier Kraakman, *The End of History for Corporate Law*, 89 GEO. L.J. 439, 445 (2001); Klaus J. Hopt, *Comparative Corporate Governance: The State of the Art and International Regulation*, 59 AM. J. COMP. L. 1, 52 (2011). For a very useful survey of the various codetermination regimes see MADS ANDENAS & FRANK WOOLDRIDGE, EUROPEAN COMPARATIVE COMPANY LAW 417–47 (2009).

[8] *E.g.*, Jens C. Dammann, *The Future of Codetermination After Centros: Will German Corporate Law Move Closer to the U.S. Model?*, 8 FORDHAM J. CORP. & FIN. L. 607, 619 (2003).

[9] *Id.* at 619–20.

establishment against its state of formation. Thus, the Court had the opportunity to revisit its opinion in *Daily Mail*.

CARTESIO OKTATÓ ÉS SZOLGÁLTATÓ BT
Case C-210/06, December 16, 2008, 2008 E.C.R. I-9641

[Cartesio was a limited partnership formed under Hungarian law. Under Hungarian law, a company's "seat" is the place of the company's central administration. Originally, Cartesio's central administration was located in Hungary. At some point, however, Cartesio moved its central administration to Italy. Subsequently, it sought to have its new seat entered into the Hungarian commercial register. The Hungarian authorities denied its request on the ground that Hungarian law did not allow a company to move its seat abroad while retaining its status as a company formed under Hungarian law. Cartesio appealed this decision, arguing that the relevant Hungarian rules violated the freedom of establishment. The Hungarian court, in turn, requested a preliminary ruling from the Court of Justice.]

99. . . . [T]he referring court essentially asks whether Articles [49 TFEU] and 48 EC [now Article 54 TFEU] are to be interpreted as precluding legislation of a Member State under which a company incorporated under the law of that Member State may not transfer its seat to another Member State whilst retaining its status as a company governed by the law of the Member State of incorporation.

109. [I]n accordance with Article [54 TFEU], in the absence of a uniform Community law definition of the companies which may enjoy the right of establishment on the basis of a single connecting factor determining the national law applicable to a company, the question whether Article [49 TFEU] applies to a company which seeks to rely on the fundamental freedom enshrined in that article—like the question whether a natural person is a national of a Member State, hence entitled to enjoy that freedom—is a preliminary matter which, as Community law now stands, can only be resolved by the applicable national law. In consequence, the question whether the company is faced with a restriction on the freedom of establishment, within the meaning of Article [49 TFEU], can arise only if it has been established, in the light of the conditions laid down in Article [54 TFEU], that the company actually has a right to that freedom.

110. Thus a Member State has the power to define both the connecting factor required of a company if it is to be regarded as incorporated under the law of that Member State and, as such, capable of enjoying the right of establishment, and that required if the company is to be able subsequently to maintain that status. That power includes the possibility for that Member State not to permit a company governed by its law to retain that status if the company intends to reorganise itself in another Member State

by moving its seat to the territory of the latter, thereby breaking the connecting factor required under the national law of the Member State of incorporation. . . .

124. In the light of all the foregoing, the answer to the . . . question [referred by the national court] must be that, as Community law now stands, Articles [49] and [54 TFEU] are to be interpreted as not precluding legislation of a Member State under which a company incorporated under the law of that Member State may not transfer its seat to another Member State whilst retaining its status as a company governed by the law of the Member State of incorporation. ■

QUESTIONS

1. How does the Court distinguish the situation in *Cartesio* from that in *Centros* or *Überseering*? How much do you think the varying policies surrounding taxation and corporate law, respectively, have to do with this distinction?

2. Does this distinction make sense from a legal policy perspective? If so, on what grounds?

Centros and subsequent cases on the freedom of establishment make it clear that entrepreneurs from one Member State can choose the corporate law of another Member State at the time that they form a new corporation, provided that the chosen Member State follows the state of incorporation doctrine. As a practical matter, the United Kingdom—with its very low incorporation fees—has proven especially popular among entrepreneurs. However, that popularity has mostly been limited to fairly small firms. Consider the following excerpt:

INDETERMINACY IN CORPORATE LAW: A THEORETICAL AND COMPARATIVE ANALYSIS
Jens Dammann
49 STAN. J. INTL. L. 54, 70 (2013)

[C]orporate mobility in the European Union has thus-far remained a phenomenon whose importance is strictly limited to very small privately held firms. At least some of these firms make use of the changes brought by Centros to avoid the often high costs of forming a corporation in their home state. Their destination of choice is the United Kingdom, where the costs of incorporating are relatively low. According to one study, over 67,000 new companies were formed in the United Kingdom from 2003 to 2006 by entrepreneurs located in other Member States. However, even among small privately-held firms, the trend to incorporate in the United Kingdom seems to be losing steam in recent years. Even more importantly, corporate mobility has not yet obtained any relevance for publicly traded firms. ∎

In the years immediately following the *Centros* decision, one reason that large public corporations did not make use of *Centros* to select another Member State's law was that *Centros* seemed to apply only to newly formed firms. At the time a corporation is formed, *Centros* gives entrepreneurs the ability to incorporate their firm under their preferred state of incorporation, even if their firm's real seat is located in some other Member State.

However, what if an existing public corporation wants to reincorporate, say from Germany to the United Kingdom, without moving its real seat? At the time of the Centros decision, neither European Union law nor German law allowed existing corporations to reincorporate in another Member State. Thus, the German corporation would have had to dissolve, and then a new corporation would have to be created in the United Kingdom. As a result, the hidden reserves of the German corporation would have been subject to taxation. Moreover, every single asset previously held by the German corporation would have had to be transferred piecemeal to the new U.K. corporation, possibly leading to substantial transaction costs.

In the following years, EU law addressed this problem. Consider the following excerpt:

INDETERMINACY IN CORPORATE LAW: A THEORETICAL AND COMPARATIVE ANALYSIS

Jens Dammann
49 STAN. J. INTL. L. 54, 69–70 (2013)

[. . .] Centros and its progeny only allowed corporations to choose the applicable corporate law at the time of their initial formation. By contrast, the relevant cases did not allow existing corporations to change the applicable corporate law by way of reincorporation, at least not without suffering adverse tax consequences. As a result, corporate "mobility" was limited to newly formed firms, whereas it remained off limits to the vast majority of corporations, namely those that already existed.

The problem of reincorporating an existing company was only addressed much later. In 2005, the European Union adopted the so-called Cross-Border Merger Directive, which the Member States had to implement by the end of 2007. In combination with an earlier directive, the Cross-Border Merger Directive ensures that European corporations can merge with companies from other Member States without suffering adverse tax consequences. This, in turn, allows corporations to reincorporate freely since a reincorporation can be undertaken by merging the old corporation into a newly formed corporation in the chosen state of destination.

The Cross-Border Merger Directive is not the only step that was undertaken in the direction of allowing existing corporations to reincorporate. Rather, the European Court of Justice also seemed to be sympathetic toward recognizing a constitutional right to corporate mobility in its case law. In *Sevic Systems*, the Court was faced with a German statute that allowed mergers between domestic corporations, but did not allow for the possibility of cross-border mergers. The Court made it clear that this rule violated the Treaty Establishing the European Community—suggesting that as a matter of European Constitutional law, states cannot allow domestic mergers while prohibiting cross-border mergers. ■

NOTES AND QUESTIONS

1. Even though both the merger directive and the *Sevic* decision provided existing corporations with a relatively easy way to reincorporate in another Member State—namely forming a new corporation in the chosen state of destination and then merging the old corporation into the newly formed corporation—large public firms have generally abstained from making use of this possibility. What might be some of the reasons for this?

2. European entrepreneurs now also have a new option for incorporating, namely the European Company or Societas Europaea (SE).[10] The SE, which was created by a 2001 regulation, is effectively designed as a hybrid between EU law and national law. The SE must have its registered office in one of the Member States. SEs are primarily governed by the norms contained in the SE regulation. However, to the extent that SE regulation has gaps, these gaps are filled by applying the corporate law of the state where the SE regulation has its registered office. Moreover, the state in which the registered office is located cannot be chosen freely. Rather, the registered office must be located in the same Member State as the firm's head office.

D. PRACTICE QUESTIONS

For the purpose of the following hypotheticals, assume that Alpha and Beta are Member States of the European Union.

1. Under an Alphanian statute enacted in 2017, a corporation must have a pro-forma statutory seat in Alpha in order to be validly formed. The corporation's effective place of management, by contrast, can be located elsewhere. In other words, it would be perfectly legal, under the relevant Alphanian law, to form a corporation under Alphanian law that has its statutory seat in Alpha, and its effective place of management in Beta. However, in 2018, Alpha enacts a new statute to complement the 2017

---

[10] Council Regulation 2157/2001 on the Statute of the European Company, 2001 O.J. (L294) 1 (EC).

statute. The 2018 statute provides that if an existing corporation that has been formed under Alphanian law and has its effective place of management in Alpha moves its effective place of management to another Member State without the prior permission of the Alphanian government, that corporation is automatically dissolved. Does the 2018 statute violate EU law?

2. Profit Corp. is a corporation that was formed under Alphanian law, but is headquartered in Beta. In 2018, Alpha enacts a statute which provides that an Alphanian corporation will be automatically dissolved on January 1, 2019, unless, by that date, it is either headquartered in Alpha or has a board of directors the majority of whom are Alphanian citizens. Does the 2018 statute violate EU law?

3. Loss Corp. is a corporation that was formed under Alphanian law, but is headquartered in Beta. In 2019, Beta adopts a statute according to which employees that are working for foreign corporations headquartered in Beta are entitled to a yearly bonus of 1000 euros. The statute only applies to jobs located in Beta and it explicitly states that its applicability does not depend on the employee's citizenship. The statute does not entitle employees working for Betanian corporations headquartered in Beta to any bonus. Does the statute violate the free movement of workers? Does it violate the freedom of establishment?

Freedom of Establishment

I. Scope of application

    A. Personal scope

        1. Individuals

        2. Companies under Article 54 TFEU

    B. Activities involving the exercise of official authority are not covered, Article 51 TFEU

    C. Distinguish the freedom of establishment from the free movement of workers

    D. Setting up firms or creating branch offices or subsidiaries is also covered, Article 49 TFEU

II. Restriction

    A. The freedom of establishment prohibits both directly and indirectly discriminating measures

    B. In addition, it covers measures that apply without distinction to the extent they are "liable to hinder or render less attractive the exercise by Union nationals of the freedom of establishment"

C. But recall that corporations cannot invoke the freedom of establishment against the corporate law rules governing their formation and continued existence that were adopted by the state of incorporation (Daily Mail, Cartesio). By contrast, they can invoke the freedom of establishment against corporate law rules imposed by the states other than the state of incorporation (Centros, Überseering)

III. Mandatory requirements doctrine

A. Legitimate goal

B. Proportionality

C. Absence of discrimination

1. Mandatory requirements doctrine does not apply in the case of formal discrimination

2. The Court of Justice is not consistent on whether mere indirect discrimination can be justified

IV. Justification under Articles 62, 52 TFEU

A. Measure must protect public policy, public security or public health

B. Proportionality

C. Even discriminatory measures can be justified

CHAPTER 16

FREEDOM TO PROVIDE SERVICES

■ ■ ■

The freedom to provide services protects the cross-border provision of services. What matters, under Article 56 TFEU, is that the provider of the services is established in a Member State other than that of the recipient of the services.

A. SERVICES

According to Article 57 TFEU, "[s]ervices shall be considered to be 'services' within the meaning of the Treaties where they are normally provided for remuneration, in so far as they are not governed by the provisions relating to freedom of movement for goods, capital and persons." Activities involving the exercise of official authority are not covered, Articles 62, 51 TFEU.

In defining the scope of application of the freedom of services, one has to determine the dividing line between that freedom and other freedoms. In practice, this need arises with respect to the free movement of workers and, more importantly, the freedom of establishment.

The difference between the free movement of workers and the freedom to provide services is that the former applies to employees, whereas the latter governs the activities of self-employed persons.[1] The more difficult distinction is that between the freedom to provide services and the freedom of establishment. The decisive question, in this context, is whether the provider of services has an establishment in the state where the recipient of the services is located. If the answer is yes, the freedom of establishment applies. If the answer is no, then we can apply the freedom to provide services. However, the question of whether an establishment exists can be tricky.

---

[1] *E.g.*, Case C-152/03, Hans-Jürgen Ritter-Coulais and Monique Ritter-Coulais v. Finanzamt Germersheim, 2006 E.C.R. I-1711 ¶ 19 ("With regard to freedom of establishment, it should be noted that, according to settled case-law, this includes the right to take up and practice activities as a self-employed person . . . .").

REINHARD GEBHARD V. CONSIGLIO DELL'ORDINE DEGLI AVVOCATI E PROCURATORI DI MILANO

Case C-55/94, November 30, 1995, 1995 E.C.R. I-4165 (citations omitted)

[Mr. Gebhard was a German national. Having obtained a German law degree, he was a member of the bar in Stuttgart (Germany). Since 1978, Mr. Gerhard resided in Italy with his family. In 1989, he opened a law office in Milan (Italy). Soon thereafter, the Milan Bar Council initiated proceedings against Mr. Gebhard on the ground that he had "pursued a professional activity in Italy on a permanent basis in chambers set up by himself whilst using the title avvocato [lawyer]." Mr. Gerhard believed that the relevant Italian rules that restricted his activities in Italy violated the fundamental freedoms, and, via the preliminary rulings procedure, the matter found its way to the Court of Justice. In this context, the Court had to decide whether Mr. Gebhard's activities fell under the freedom of establishment or under the freedom to provide services.]

22. The provisions of the chapter on services are subordinate to those of the chapter on the right of establishment in so far, first, as the wording of the first paragraph of Article 59 [now Article 56 TFEU] assumes that the provider and the recipient of the service concerned are "established" in two different Member States and, second, as the first paragraph of Article 60 [now Article 57 TFEU] specifies that the provisions relating to services apply only if those relating to the right of establishment do not apply. It is therefore necessary to consider the scope of the concept of "establishment."

23. The right of establishment, provided for in Articles 52 to 58 [now Articles 49 to 55 TFEU] of the Treaty, is granted both to legal persons within the meaning of Article 58 [now Article 54 TFEU] and to natural persons who are nationals of a Member State of the Community. Subject to the exceptions and conditions laid down, it allows all types of self-employed activity to be taken up and pursued on the territory of any other Member State, undertakings to be formed and operated, and agencies, branches or subsidiaries to be set up.

24. It follows that a person may be established, within the meaning of the Treaty, in more than one Member State. In particular, in the case of companies, through the setting-up of agencies, branches or subsidiaries (Article 52 [now Article 49 TFEU]) and, as the Court has held, in the case of members of the professions, by establishing a second professional base.

25. The concept of establishment within the meaning of the Treaty is therefore a very broad one, allowing a Community national to participate, on a stable and continuous basis, in the economic life of a Member State other than his State of origin and to profit therefrom, so contributing to economic and social interpenetration within the Community in the sphere of activities as self-employed persons.

26. In contrast, where the provider of services moves to another Member State, the provisions of the chapter on services, in particular the third paragraph of Article 60 [now Article 57 TFEU], envisage that he is to pursue his activity there on a temporary basis.

27. As the Advocate General has pointed out, the temporary nature of the activities in question has to be determined in the light, not only of the duration of the provision of the service, but also of its regularity, periodicity or continuity. The fact that the provision of services is temporary does not mean that the provider of services within the meaning of the Treaty may not equip himself with some form of infrastructure in the host Member State (including an office, chambers or consulting rooms) in so far as such infrastructure is necessary for the purposes of performing the services in question.

28. However, that situation is to be distinguished from that of Mr Gebhard who, as a national of a Member State, pursues a professional activity on a stable and continuous basis in another Member State where he holds himself out from an established professional base to, amongst others, nationals of that State. Such a national comes under the provisions of the chapter relating to the right of establishment and not those of the chapter relating to services.

29. The Milan Bar Council has argued that a person such as Mr Gebhard cannot be regarded for the purposes of the Treaty as being "established" in a Member State, in his case, Italy, unless he belongs to the professional body of that State or, at least, pursues his activity in collaboration or in association with persons belonging to that body.

30. That argument cannot be accepted.

31. The provisions relating to the right of establishment cover the taking-up and pursuit of activities. Membership of a professional body may be a condition of taking up and pursuit of particular activities. It cannot itself be constitutive of establishment. ■

NOTES AND QUESTIONS

1. Does the outcome of the case depend on whether one applies the freedom of establishment or the freedom to provide services?

2. From a policy perspective, who, if anyone, should be afforded greater protection: EU citizens established in another Member State or EU citizens providing cross-border services?

3. According to the Court, what is required in order for a person to be established in another Member State?

B. PERSONAL SCOPE OF PROTECTION

Contrary to what the wording of Article 56 TFEU might suggest, the freedom to provide services protects not only the service-provider, but also the person receiving the services. Moreover, according to Articles 62, 54, it is not just individuals who can invoke the freedom to provide services; rather, companies can as well.

IAN WILLIAM COWAN V. TRESOR PUBLIC
Case 186/87, February 2, 1989, 1989 E.C.R. 195 (citations omitted)

[Ian William Cowan was a British citizen. While visiting Paris as a tourist, he was assaulted at the exit of a metro station. Under French law, victims of certain violent crimes were entitled to compensation from the French state when they were otherwise unable to obtain compensation. However, under the relevant statute, non-French victims could only obtain compensation from the French state if they either held a residence permit or if their Member State had entered into a reciprocity agreement with France. Mr. Cowan, who did not satisfy either of these conditions, was denied compensation. He brought suit, arguing that the relevant French rules violated European law. The French court requested a preliminary ruling from the Court of Justice.]

15. ... [T]he Court [has previously] held that the freedom to provide services includes the freedom for the recipients of services to go to another Member State in order to receive a service there, without being obstructed by restrictions, and that tourists, among others, must be regarded as recipients of services.

16. At the hearing the French Government submitted that as Community law now stands a recipient of services may not rely on the prohibition of discrimination to the extent that the national law at issue does not create any barrier to freedom of movement. A provision such as that at issue in the main proceedings, it says, imposes no restrictions in that respect. ...

17. That reasoning cannot be accepted. When Community law guarantees a natural person the freedom to go to another Member State the protection of that person from harm in the Member State in question, on the same basis as that of nationals and persons residing there, is a corollary of that freedom of movement. It follows that the prohibition of discrimination is applicable to recipients of services within the meaning of the Treaty as regards protection against the risk of assault and the right to obtain financial compensation provided for by national law when that risk materializes. The fact that the compensation at issue is financed by the Public Treasury cannot alter the rules regarding the protection of the rights guaranteed by the Treaty. ∎

QUESTIONS

1. In a passage of this case that is not reprinted above, the French government also argued that the rules of compensation could not violate the freedom to provide services because they were part of the law on criminal procedure, which is outside the scope of the Treaty. What should we think of this argument?

2. As a matter of legal policy, does it make sense to extend the protection of the freedom to provide services to the recipient of the services? Can you think of any arguments one way or the other?

3. If the relevant French rules on compensation were adopted today, would they violate Directive 38/2004/EC?

C. THE INTERSTATE ELEMENT

The fundamental freedoms do not apply to purely internal situations—i.e. situations lacking a cross-border element—and the freedom to provide services is no exception.

However, it should be noted that the free movement of services does not require the service provider to cross a border. Rather, what matters under Article 56 TFEU is that the provider of the services is established in a Member State other than that of the recipient of the services. Thus, the freedom to provide services applies when the service-provider crosses a border, but it also applies when the recipient of the services crosses a border. Finally, it also applies in those cases where both parties stay in their respective states—as in the case of services rendered online or by phone.

D. DISCRIMINATORY AND NON-DISCRIMINATORY OBSTACLES

Like the other fundamental freedoms, the freedom to provide services contains not only a prohibition against discrimination, but also applies to non-discriminatory obstacles. In the words of the Court of Justice, "national measures which prohibit, impede or render less attractive the exercise of the freedom to provide services are restrictions on that freedom."[2]

ALPINE INVESTMENTS BV v. MINISTER VAN FINANCIEN
Case C-384/93, May 10, 1995, 1995 E.C.R. I-1141 (citations omitted)

[Under Dutch law, it was illegal for firms offering certain types of financial services to engage in so-called "cold calling"—i.e. trying to gain

---

[2] Case C-9/11, Waypoint Aviation SA v. Belgian State—SPF Finances, 2011 E.C.R. I-9697.

customers by calling individuals who had not previously consented to be contacted.

Alpine Investments BV ("Alpine Investments") was a company formed under Dutch law and established in the Netherlands. It offered an array of financial services—including those triggering the prohibition against cold calling—and had customers in the Netherlands, Belgium, France, and the United Kingdom. In a lawsuit brought in a Dutch court, Alpine Investments challenged the prohibition against cold calling, arguing that it violated the freedom to provide services. The Dutch Court, in turn, requested a preliminary ruling from the Court of Justice.

The Court's opinion begins by addressing whether the prohibition against cold-calling can constitute a restriction on the freedom to provide services, even though the prohibition does not distinguish between customers located in the Netherlands and customers located in other Member States.]

26. First, it must be determined whether the prohibition against telephoning potential clients in another Member State without their prior consent can constitute a restriction on freedom to provide services.

27. A prohibition such as that at issue in the main proceedings does not constitute a restriction on freedom to provide services within the meaning of Article 59 [now Article 56] solely by virtue of the fact that other Member States apply less strict rules to providers of similar services established in their territory.

28. However, such a prohibition deprives the operators concerned of a rapid and direct technique for marketing and for contacting potential clients in other Member States. It can therefore constitute a restriction on the freedom to provide cross-border services.

29. Secondly, it must be considered whether that conclusion may be affected by the fact that the prohibition at issue is imposed by the Member State in which the provider is established and not by the Member State in which the potential recipient is established.

30. The first paragraph of Article 59 of the Treaty [now Article 56 TFEU] prohibits restrictions on freedom to provide services within the Community in general. Consequently, that provision covers not only restrictions laid down by the State of destination but also those laid down by the State of origin. As the Court has frequently held, the right freely to provide services may be relied on by an undertaking as against the State in which it is established if the services are provided for persons established in another Member State.

31. It follows that the prohibition of cold calling does not fall outside the scope of Article 59 of the Treaty [now Article 56 TFEU] simply because it is imposed by the State in which the provider of services is established.

32. Finally, certain arguments adduced by the Netherlands Government and the United Kingdom must be considered.

33. They submit that the prohibition at issue falls outside the scope of Article 59 of the Treaty [now Article 56 TFEU] because it is a generally applicable measure, it is not discriminatory and neither its object nor its effect is to put the national market at an advantage over providers of services from other Member States. Since it affects only the way in which the services are offered, it is analogous to the non-discriminatory measures governing selling arrangements which, according to the decision in Joined Cases C-267 and 268/91 Keck and Mithouard 1993 ECR I-6097, paragraph 16, do not fall within the scope of Article 30 of the Treaty.

34. Those arguments cannot be accepted.

35. Although a prohibition such as the one at issue in the main proceedings is general and non-discriminatory and neither its object nor its effect is to put the national market at an advantage over providers of services from other Member States, it can none the less, as has been held above (see paragraph 28), constitute a restriction on the freedom to provide cross-border services.

36. Such a prohibition is not analogous to the legislation concerning selling arrangements held in Keck and Mithouard to fall outside the scope of Article 30 of the Treaty.

37. According to that judgment, the application to products from other Member States of national provisions restricting or prohibiting, within the Member State of importation, certain selling arrangements is not such as to hinder trade between Member States so long as, first, those provisions apply to all relevant traders operating within the national territory and, secondly, they affect in the same manner, in law and in fact, the marketing of domestic products and of those from other Member States. The reason is that the application of such provisions is not such as to prevent access by the latter to the market of the Member State of importation or to impede such access more than it impedes access by domestic products.

38. A prohibition such as that at issue is imposed by the Member State in which the provider of services is established and affects not only offers made by him to addressees who are established in that State or move there in order to receive services but also offers made to potential recipients in another Member State. It therefore directly affects access to the market in services in the other Member States and is thus capable of hindering intra-Community trade in services.

39. The answer to the second question is therefore that rules of a Member State which prohibit providers of services established in its territory from making unsolicited telephone calls to potential clients established in other Member States in order to offer their services

constitute a restriction on freedom to provide services within the meaning of Article 59 [now Article 56] of the Treaty.

[Despite this finding, the Court ultimately concluded that the relevant rules were justified on the basis of the mandatory requirements doctrine because they were necessary to protect the good reputation of the Dutch financial sector.] ■

QUESTIONS

1. Does the Court, in principle, accept the applicability of the Keck doctrine to the freedom to provide services?

2. Why does the Court believe that the rules at issue are not comparable to selling arrangements within the meaning of the Keck doctrine?

E. JUSTIFICATIONS

Even if a measure restricts the freedom to provide services, it may nonetheless be justified. As was the case with other fundamental freedoms, justifications come in two flavors. First are the written justifications. Article 62 TFEU, referring to Article 52 TFEU, allows national measures that restrict the free movement of services on grounds of public policy, public security or public health. Second, the mandatory requirements doctrine also applies to the freedom to provide services.

OMEGA SPIELHALLEN- UND AUTOMATENAUFSTELLUNGS-GMBH v. OBERBÜRGERMEISTERIN DER STADT BONN
Case C-36/02, October 14, 2004, E.C.R. 2004, I 9609 (citations omitted)

[Omega Spielhallen- und Automatenaufstellungs-GmbH ("Omega") was a German corporation established in Bonn, Germany. It owned and operated a facility—the "laserdrome"—that was used for "laser sport." The equipment used for these games was delivered and installed by Pulsar, a British Company. Pulsar also provided specifically designed games. Subsequently, Pulsar and Omega entered into a franchising relationship.

In one of the activities offered in the laserdrome, players would wear sensory tags on their jackets, which other players would then have to hit with laser guns.

The state police were concerned about this type of game, on the grounds that it amounted to allowing players to "play at killing." Under the applicable state law, the police were authorized to "take measures necessary to avert a risk to public order or safety in an individual case." At some point, the police issued a prohibition against games that involved firing at human targets with a laser beam. The prohibition was based on the argument that the relevant games represented a danger to public order because they trivialized violence against humans. Litigation ensued, and the case ended up before the Federal Administrative Court.

Omega argued, inter alia, that because of Pulsar's involvement, the prohibition violated the free movement of goods. Against that background, the Federal Administrative Court requested a preliminary ruling from the European Court of Justice.]

11. According to the Bundesverwaltungsgericht [the highest German court in administrative law matters], the Oberverwaltungsgericht [court of appeals] was right to hold that the commercial exploitation of a 'killing game' in Omega's "laserdrome' constituted an affront to human dignity, a concept established in the first sentence of Paragraph 1(1) of the German Basic (Constitutional) Law.

12. The referring court states that human dignity is a constitutional principle which may be infringed either by the degrading treatment of an adversary, which is not the case here, or by the awakening or strengthening in the player of an attitude denying the fundamental right of each person to be acknowledged and respected, such as the representation, as in this case, of fictitious acts of violence for the purposes of a game. It states that a cardinal constitutional principle such as human dignity cannot be waived in the context of an entertainment, and that, in national law, the fundamental rights invoked by Omega cannot alter that assessment.

23. By its question, the referring court asks, first, whether the prohibition of an economic activity for reasons arising from the protection of fundamental values laid down by the national constitution, such as, in this case, human dignity, is compatible with Community law, and, second, whether the ability which Member States have, for such reasons, to restrict fundamental freedoms guaranteed by the Treaty, namely the freedom to provide services and the free movement of goods, is subject, as the judgment in Schindler might suggest, to the condition that that restriction be based on a legal conception that is common to all Member States.

24. As a preliminary issue, it needs to be determined to what extent the restriction which the referring court has found to exist is capable of affecting the freedom to provide services and the free movement of goods, which are governed by different Treaty provisions.

25. In that respect, this Court finds that the contested order, by prohibiting Omega from operating its 'laserdrome' in accordance with the form of the game developed by Pulsar and lawfully marketed by it in the United Kingdom, particularly under the franchising system, affects the freedom to provide services which Article 49 EC [now Article 56 TFEU] guarantees both to providers and to the persons receiving those services established in another Member State. Moreover, in so far as use of the form of the game developed by Pulsar involves the use of specific equipment, which is also lawfully marketed in the United Kingdom, the prohibition

imposed on Omega is likely to deter it from acquiring the equipment in question, thereby infringing the free movement of goods ensured by Article 28 EC [now Article 34 TFEU].

26. However, where a national measure affects both the freedom to provide services and the free movement of goods, the Court will, in principle, examine it in relation to just one of those two fundamental freedoms if it is clear that, in the circumstances of the case, one of those freedoms is entirely secondary in relation to the other and may be attached to it.

27. In the circumstances of this case, the aspect of the freedom to provide services prevails over that of the free movement of goods. The Bonn police authority and the Commission of the European Communities have rightly pointed out that the contested order restricts the importation of goods only as regards equipment specifically designed for the prohibited variant of the laser game and that that is an unavoidable consequence of the restriction imposed with regard to supplies of services by Pulsar. Therefore, as the Advocate General has concluded in paragraph 32 of her Opinion, there is no need to make an independent examination of the compatibility of that order with the Treaty provisions governing the free movement of goods.

28. Concerning justification for the restriction of the freedom to provide services imposed by the order of 14 September 1994, Article 46 EC [52 TFEU], which applies here by virtue of Article 55 EC [62 TFEU], allows restrictions justified for reasons of public policy, public security or public health. In this case, the documents before the Court show that the grounds relied on by the Bonn police authority in adopting the prohibition order expressly mention the fact that the activity concerned constitutes a danger to public policy. . . .

29. In these proceedings, it is undisputed that the contested order was adopted independently of any consideration linked to the nationality of the providers or recipients of the services placed under a restriction. In any event, since measures for safeguarding public policy fall within a derogation from the freedom to provide services set out in Article 46 EC [Article 52 TFEU], it is not necessary to verify whether those measures are applied without distinction both to national providers of services and those established in other Member States.

30. However, the possibility of a Member State relying on a derogation laid down by the Treaty does not prevent judicial review of measures applying that derogation. In addition, the concept of 'public policy' in the Community context, particularly as justification for a derogation from the fundamental principle of the freedom to provide services, must be interpreted strictly, so that its scope cannot be

determined unilaterally by each Member State without any control by the Community institutions.

31. The fact remains, however, that the specific circumstances which may justify recourse to the concept of public policy may vary from one country to another and from one era to another. The competent national authorities must therefore be allowed a margin of discretion within the limits imposed by the Treaty.

32. In this case, the competent authorities took the view that the activity concerned by the prohibition order was a threat to public policy by reason of the fact that, in accordance with the conception prevailing in public opinion, the commercial exploitation of games involving the simulated killing of human beings infringed a fundamental value enshrined in the national constitution, namely human dignity. According to the Bundesverwaltungsgericht, the national courts which heard the case shared and confirmed the conception of the requirements for protecting human dignity on which the contested order is based, that conception therefore having to be regarded as in accordance with the stipulations of the German Basic Law.

33. It should be recalled in that context that, according to settled case-law, fundamental rights form an integral part of the general principles of law the observance of which the Court ensures, and that, for that purpose, the Court draws inspiration from the constitutional traditions common to the Member States and from the guidelines supplied by international treaties for the protection of human rights on which the Member States have collaborated or to which they are signatories. The European Convention on Human Rights and Fundamental Freedoms has special significance in that respect.

34. As the Advocate General argues in ... her Opinion, the Community legal order undeniably strives to ensure respect for human dignity as a general principle of law. There can therefore be no doubt that the objective of protecting human dignity is compatible with Community law, it being immaterial in that respect that, in Germany, the principle of respect for human dignity has a particular status as an independent fundamental right.

35. Since both the Community and its Member States are required to respect fundamental rights, the protection of those rights is a legitimate interest which, in principle, justifies a restriction of the obligations imposed by Community law, even under a fundamental freedom guaranteed by the Treaty such as the freedom to provide services.

36. However, measures which restrict the freedom to provide services may be justified on public policy grounds only if they are necessary for the protection of the interests which they are intended to guarantee and only in so far as those objectives cannot be attained by less restrictive measures.

37. It is not indispensable in that respect for the restrictive measure issued by the authorities of a Member State to correspond to a conception shared by all Member States as regards the precise way in which the fundamental right or legitimate interest in question is to be protected. Although, in paragraph 60 of Schindler, the Court referred to moral, religious or cultural considerations which lead all Member States to make the organisation of lotteries and other games with money subject to restrictions, it was not its intention, by mentioning that common conception, to formulate a general criterion for assessing the proportionality of any national measure which restricts the exercise of an economic activity.

38. On the contrary, as is apparent from well-established case-law subsequent to Schindler, the need for, and proportionality of, the provisions adopted are not excluded merely because one Member State has chosen a system of protection different from that adopted by another State.

39. In this case, it should be noted, first, that, according to the referring court, the prohibition on the commercial exploitation of games involving the simulation of acts of violence against persons, in particular the representation of acts of homicide, corresponds to the level of protection of human dignity which the national constitution seeks to guarantee in the territory of the Federal Republic of Germany. It should also be noted that, by prohibiting only the variant of the laser game the object of which is to fire on human targets and thus 'play at killing' people, the contested order did not go beyond what is necessary in order to attain the objective pursued by the competent national authorities.

40. In those circumstances, the order [prohibiting games in which laser beams were aimed at other players] cannot be regarded as a measure unjustifiably undermining the freedom to provide services.

41. In the light of the above considerations, the answer to the question must be that Community law does not preclude an economic activity consisting of the commercial exploitation of games simulating acts of homicide from being made subject to a national prohibition measure adopted on grounds of protecting public policy by reason of the fact that that activity is an affront to human dignity. ∎

NOTES AND QUESTIONS

1. The Treaty on European Union now contains an explicit commitment to the protection of human dignity. Consider Article 2 TEU:

> The Union is founded on the values of respect for human dignity, freedom, democracy, equality, the rule of law and respect for human rights, including the rights of persons belonging to minorities.

These values are common to the Member States in a society in which pluralism, non-discrimination, tolerance, justice, solidarity and equality between women and men prevail.

2. More generally, the Treaty on European Union now also contains various mechanisms to commit the European Union to the protection of human rights. Read Article 6 TEU. How does that provision seek to ensure that the European Union is committed to the protection of human rights?

3. As you may recall, the Court of Justice has made it very clear that in case of a conflict between EU law and Member State constitutional law, the former prevails. Why, then, does the Court come to the conclusion that Germany can restrict the freedom to provide services in order to protect human dignity as enshrined in the German Constitution?

4. Assume, for the sake of the argument, that in most other Member States, laser games of the type at issue are not seen as a threat to human dignity. Would this change the outcome of the case? Should it?

F. PRACTICE QUESTIONS

For the purpose of the following hypothetical, assume that Alpha, Beta, and Gamma are Member States of the European Union.

1. Tom is an Alphanian citizen. In the summer of 2019, he travels to Beta for three months to stay at local hotels, enjoy local restaurants, and visit theatres and parks. Unfortunately, that same year, a volcano in Gamma erupts, showering all of Europe in a mist of black ash. Air traffic breaks down completely, and Beta is soon swamped with travelers who cannot leave. Beta reacts by enacting a statute according to which Betanian citizens are to be given priority when it comes to hotel rooms. Does this statute violate EU law?

2. Luke is a Alphanian citizen who owns his own business, located in Alpha. Specifically, he owns a bus and organizes guided tours of the Betanian city of Victoria, which is located close to the Alphanian border. These tours include a visit to Victoria's famous cathedral. In 2018, Beta adopts a statute according to which guided tours of certain nationally recognized monuments—including Victoria's cathedral—can only be offered by "authorized tour guides." In order to obtain such an authorization, tour guides have to take part in a three-month intensive course on Beta's cultural heritage and pass a four-hour written exam at the end. Beta defends this statute on the grounds that it is necessary to preserve the reputation and fame of its national cultural heritage. Does the statute violate EU law?

3. Georg is an Alphanian citizen. He is the sole proprietor of a transportation company and makes most of his money transporting goods by truck on the European continent. In 2017, Beta adopts a statute requiring all trucking companies operating in Beta, regardless of where

they are headquartered and incorporated, to pay a yearly "road maintenance fee" in the amount of 1000 Euros per truck. The Betanian government points out, correctly, that trucks cause a disproportionate fraction of the wear and tear suffered by Betanian highways. Furthermore, for those transportation companies that are headquartered or operate a branch office in Beta and therefore pay income taxes in Beta, the road maintenance fee can be deducted from the firm's income tax. Georg, whose transportation company is located in Alpha and who only pays income taxes in Alpha, believes that this new Betanian statute violates EU law. He also believes that Alpha violates EU law by not allowing him to deduct from his Alphanian income tax the maintenance fees that he has to pay in Beta. Discuss!

4. Assume that Alpha allows assisted suicide for terminally ill patients in so-called "assisted dying clinics." Frank owns and operates such a clinic. However, given the relatively small population of Alpha, he decides to advertise his clinic's services in neighboring Beta via radio commercials and flyers. Beta promptly adopts a statute imposing criminal sanctions against anyone advertising assisted suicide programs in Beta, no matter where they are located. Does the new Betanian statute violate the freedom to provide services?

5. Assume the same facts as in the previous hypo, except that this time, the statute enacted by the Betanian legislature does not mention suicide programs and instead provides that anyone advertising health-related services that "violate human dignity" faces imprisonment. Moreover, assume that Betanian courts are split on whether assisted suicide programs violate human dignity. The Betanian Supreme Court has not yet weighed in on the matter. Does Beta violate EU law, and if so, how?

6. Alpha and Beta were both involved in World War II, but on opposite sides. Alpha is a popular tourist destination. Its world famous National Art Gallery, which is owned and operated by the Alphanian city of Victoria, charges 50 euros for adults and 10 euros for children. However, the Museum charges only 30 euros for veterans who fought on Alpha's side in World War II. Thomas is a Betanian citizen who fought in World War II as a soldier in Beta's army. He believes that excluding him from the reduced admission price for veterans violates EU law. Is he right?

Freedom to Provide Services

I. Scope of Application

A. "Services shall be considered to be 'services' within the meaning of the Treaties where they are normally provided for remuneration, in so far as they are not governed by the provisions relating to freedom of movement for goods, capital and persons." To distinguish the freedom of services from the freedom of establishment, focus not only on the duration of the provision of the service, but also on its regularity, periodicity or continuity

 B. Personal scope: not only the service provider, but also the recipient can invoke the freedom to provide services. Moreover, companies can invoke the freedom to provide services under Articles 62, 54 TFEU

 C. Interstate element: while an interstate element is required, it is sufficient that the recipient or the provider or merely the service itself crosses a border

 D. Activities involving the exercise of official authority are not covered, Articles 62, 51 TFEU

II. Restriction

 A. The freedom to provide services prohibits both directly and indirectly discriminating measures

 B. In addition, the freedom to provide services prohibits measures that apply without distinction, at least where they "directly affects access to the market in services in the other Member States"

III. Mandatory requirements doctrine

 A. Legitimate goal

 B. Proportionality

 C. Absence of discrimination

  1. Mandatory requirements doctrine does not apply in the case of formal discrimination

  2. Court of Justice not consistent on whether mere indirect discrimination can be justified

IV. Justification under Articles 62, 52 TFEU

 A. Measure must protect public policy, public security or public health

 B. Even directly discriminating measures can be justified

 C. Proportionality

CHAPTER 17

FREE MOVEMENT OF CAPITAL

■ ■ ■

The right to free movement of capital seeks to secure the free flow of capital and payments within the European Union: Article 56(1) TFEU prohibits "all restrictions on the movement of capital between Member States and between Member States and third countries." Article 56(2) TFEU then extends that prohibition to "all restrictions on payments between Member States and between Member States and third countries."

A. MOVEMENT OF CAPITAL AND PAYMENTS

The Treaty on the Functioning of the European Union does not define "movement of capital." The Court of Justice, however, has made it clear that it will look to the non-exhaustive listing in the Annex of Directive 88/361/EEC,[1] which enumerates various financial transactions, including direct investments in companies, investments in real estate, operations in publicly-traded securities, etc.[2]

In practice, it is often necessary to distinguish the scope of application of Article 56 from that of the other fundamental freedoms. The Court of Justice has made it clear early on that payments which constitute consideration for goods and services protected by the other fundamental freedoms are protected by those other fundamental freedoms rather than by the free movement of capital.[3] For example, the payment for a good imported from another Member State is protected by the free movement of goods rather than by the free movement of capital.[4] In that sense, the other

---

[1] Council Directive 88/361/EEC of 24 June 1988 for the implementation of Article 67 of the Treaty, O.J. L 178, 08/07/1988, pp. 5–18.

[2] Case C-222/97, Manfred Trummer & Peter Mayer, 1999 E.C.R. I-1661 ¶ 21 ("20 It should be noted in that connection that the EC Treaty does not define the terms movements of capital' and payments'. 21 However, inasmuch as Article 73b of the EC Treaty substantially reproduces the contents of Article 1 of Directive 88/361, and even though that directive was adopted on the basis of Articles 69 and 70(1) of the EEC Treaty, which have since been replaced by Article 73b et seq. of the EC Treaty, the nomenclature in respect of movements of capital annexed to Directive 88/361 still has the same indicative value, for the purposes of defining the notion of capital movements, as it did before the entry into force of Article 73b et seq., subject to the qualification, contained in the introduction to the nomenclature, that the list set out therein is not exhaustive.").

[3] Joint cases 286/82 & 26/83, Graziana Luisi v. Ministero del Tesoro & Guiseppe Carbone v. Ministero del Tesoro, 1984 E.C.R. 377 ¶ 22.

[4] *Id.*

fundamental freedoms are *leges speciales* vis-à-vis the free movement of capital.

A different question is whether coins made from precious metals can sometimes be categorized as goods or whether their import falls under the free movement of capital.

REGINA V. ERNEST GEORGE THOMPSON, BRIAN ALBERT JOHNSON AND COLIN ALEX NORMAN WOODIWISS

Case 7/78, November 23, 1978, 1978 E.C.R. 2247 (citations omitted)

[U.K. law imposed certain restrictions on the import and export of gold and silver coins: gold coins could not be *imported* into the United Kingdom without a license granted by the board of trade. At the same time, silver alloy coins minted before 1947, and not more than 100 years old, could not be *exported* from the United Kingdom in a quantity of more than ten coins, without a license.

Mr. Thompson et al. imported gold coins—namely South African Krugerrands—from Germany into the United Kingdom and exported silver alloy coins from the United Kingdom to Germany, thus breaching the relevant U.K. regulations. The ensuing criminal proceedings resulted in a request for a preliminary ruling to the Court of Justice, and the Court had to decide, inter alia, whether the import and export of coins fell under the free movement of goods or the free movement of capital.]

19. . . . [The purpose of questions referred by the national court] is to find out whether these coins are goods falling within the provisions [of the Treaty regarding the free movement of goods] or constitute a means of payment falling within the scope of other provisions. . . .

25. . . . [U]nder the system of the treaty means of payment are not to be regarded as goods . . . .

26. Silver alloy coins which are legal tender in a member state are, by their very nature, to be regarded as means of payment and it follows that their transfer does not fall within the provisions of Articles 30 to 37 of the Treaty [now Articles 28 to 37].

27. Although doubts may be entertained on the question whether Krugerrands are to be regarded as means of legal payment it can nevertheless be noted that on the money markets of those member states which permit dealings in these coins they are treated as being equivalent to currency.

28. Their transfer must consequently be designated as a monetary transfer which does not fall within the provisions of the said articles 30 to 37. ∎

The scope of application of the free movement of capital also has to be distinguished from that of the free movement of establishment. In particular, this issue arises where an investor holds shares in a company from another Member State. Is that investor making use of the freedom of establishment—because he owns part of a company established in another Member State, or is he making use of the free movement of capital—because he has undertaken a cross-border investment?

C. BAARS V. INSPECTEUR DER BELASTINGEN PARTICULIEREN/ONDERNEMINGEN GORINCHEM
Case C-251/98, April 13, 2000, 2000 E.C.R. I-02787 (citations omitted)

[Mr. Baars was a Dutch citizen residing in the Netherlands. He held 100% of the shares of an Irish company established in Dublin, Ireland. One of the questions facing the Court of Justice was whether his investment was protected by the freedom of establishment or by the free movement of capital.]

21. [T]he situation from which the main proceedings have arisen concerns a national of a Member State who resides in that Member State and who holds all the shares in a company established in another Member State. A 100% holding in the capital of a company having its seat in another Member State undoubtedly brings such a taxpayer within the scope of application of the Treaty provisions on the right of establishment.

22. It is clear from the second paragraph of Article 52 [Article 49(2)] of the Treaty that Freedom of Establishment includes the right to set up and manage undertakings, in particular companies or firms, in a Member State by a national of another Member State. So, a national of a Member State who has a holding in the capital of a company established in another Member State which gives him definite influence over the company's decisions and allows him to determine its activities is exercising his right of establishment. ∎

EUROPEAN COMMISSION V. PORTUGUESE REPUBLIC
Case C-212/09, November 10, 2011, 2011 E.C.R. I-10889 (citations omitted)

[The Portuguese Republic sought to privatize its energy sector. For this purpose, it set up various stock corporations to own and operate former state enterprises. One of these stock corporations was GALP Energia SGPS SA ("GALP"). Its shares were offered to the public. However, the Portuguese state retained so-called "golden shares" that granted their holder—i.e. the Portuguese state—special powers. In particular, the state could veto amendments to the articles of incorporation, and it could appoint the chairman of the board of directors.

The Commission believed that the creation of such golden shares violated the freedom of establishment as well as the free movement of capital and eventually initiated an infringement proceeding.

The Court of Justice first addresses whether the relevant national legislation falls within the scope of the freedom of establishment or the free movement of capital.]

The applicability of Articles 43 EC [now Article 49 TFEU] and 56 EC [now Article 63 TFEU]

41. As regards the question whether national legislation falls within the scope of one or other of the fundamental freedoms, it is clear from well-established case-law that the purpose of the legislation concerned must be taken into consideration.

42. Provisions of national law which apply to the possession by nationals of one Member State of holdings in the capital of a company established in another Member State, allowing them to exert a definite influence on that company's decisions and to determine its activities, fall within the scope ratione materiae of Article 43 EC [now Article 49 TFEU] on freedom of establishment.

43. Direct investments, that is to say, investments of any kind made by natural or legal persons which serve to establish or maintain lasting and direct links between the persons providing the capital and the company to which that capital is made available in order to carry out an economic activity, fall within the scope of Article 56 EC [now Article 63 TFEU] on the free movement of capital. That object presupposes that the shares held by the shareholder enable the latter to participate effectively in the management or control of that company.

44. National legislation not intended to apply only to those shareholdings which enable the holder to exert a definite influence on a company's decisions and to determine its activities but which applies irrespective of the size of the holding which the shareholder has in a company may fall within the scope of both Article 43 EC [now Article 49 TFEU] and Article 56 EC [now Article 63 TFEU].

45. It must be stated that, in the present action for failure to fulfil obligations, it is not inconceivable that the national provisions at issue might affect all shareholders and potential investors and not solely those shareholders capable of exerting a definite influence on the management and control of GALP. Consequently, the contested provisions must be examined in the light of both Article 43 EC [now Article 49 TFEU] and Article 56 EC [now Article 63 TFEU].

Failure to fulfil obligations under Article 56 EC [now Article 63 TFEU]

46. It should be noted at the outset that, according to consistent case-law, Article 56(1) EC [now Article 63(1) TFEU] generally prohibits restrictions on movements of capital between Member States.

47. In the absence of an EC-Treaty definition of 'movements of capital' within the meaning of Article 56(1) EC [now Article 63(1) TFEU], the Court has acknowledged the indicative value of the nomenclature of movements of capital set out in Annex I to Council Directive 88/361/EEC of 24 June 1988 for the implementation of Article [67] of the Treaty (article repealed by the Treaty of Amsterdam) (OJ 1988 L 178, p. 5). Thus, the Court has held that movements of capital within the meaning of Article 56(1) EC include, in particular, 'direct' investments, that is to say, investments in the form of participation in an undertaking through the holding of shares which confers the possibility of effectively participating in its management and control, and 'portfolio' investments, that is to say, investments in the form of the acquisition of shares on the capital market solely with the intention of making a financial investment without any intention to influence the management and control of the undertaking.

48. Concerning those two forms of investment, the Court has stated that national measures must be regarded as 'restrictions' within the meaning of Article 56(1) EC [now Article 63(1) TFEU] if they are liable to prevent or limit the acquisition of shares in the undertakings concerned or to deter investors from other Member States from investing in their capital. . . .

55. As regards the restrictive nature of the Portuguese State's holding of golden shares in the share capital of GALP to which special rights attach, as provided for by the national legislation—in part, in conjunction with GALP's articles of association—, it must be held that such shares are liable to deter traders from other Member States from investing in the capital of that company. . . .

63. . . . [T]he national measures here at issue are not comparable to the rules concerning selling arrangements which, as the Court found in Keck and Mithouard, did not come within the scope of Article 28 EC [now Article 30 TFEU].

64. According to that judgment, the application to products from other Member States of national provisions restricting or prohibiting certain selling arrangements, within the Member State of importation, is not such as to hinder trade between Member States so long as, first, those provisions apply to all relevant traders operating within the national territory and, secondly, they affect in the same manner, in law and in fact, the marketing of domestic products and of those from other Member States. The reason is that the application of such provisions is not such as to prevent access by

the latter products to the market of the Member State of importation or to impede such access more than it impedes access by domestic products.

65. In the present case, while it is true that the national provisions at issue apply without distinction to both residents and non-residents, it must none the less be held that they affect the position of a person acquiring a shareholding as such and are thus liable to deter investors from other Member States from making such investments and, consequently, affect access to the market.

66. Furthermore, the finding that those national provisions constitute restrictions on the free movement of capital cannot be called into question by the Portuguese Republic's argument that the special rights at issue have no effect on either direct investments or portfolio investments in GALP's share capital given that a large number of that company's shares are in the hands of investors from other Member States.

67. It is clear, as has been stated in paragraphs 58 and 61 of the present judgment, that the national provisions at issue, to the extent to which they create instruments liable to limit the ability of investors to participate in the share capital of GALP with a view to establishing or maintaining lasting and direct economic links with it which would make possible effective participation in the management or control of that company, reduce the interest in acquiring a stake in that capital.

68. That finding is not affected by the fact that GALP's shareholders include direct investors. That circumstance is not such as to cast doubt, in the present case, on the fact that, because of the provisions of national law at issue, direct investors from other Member States, whether actual or potential, may have been deterred from acquiring a stake in the capital of that company in order to participate in it with a view to establishing or maintaining lasting and direct economic links with it which would make possible effective participation in the management or control of that company, even though they were entitled to benefit from the principle of the free movement of capital and from the protection which that principle affords them.

69. In the light of the foregoing, it must be held that the Portuguese State's holding of golden shares, in conjunction with the special rights which such shares confer on their holder, constitutes a restriction on the free movement of capital within he terms of Article 56(1) EC [now Article 63(1) TFEU].

Whether the restrictions are justified...

77. The Portuguese Republic contends that, even if it is accepted that the national measures at issue do constitute restrictions on freedom of establishment and on the free movement of capital, they are none the less justified with regard to Articles 46 EC [now Article 52 TFEU] and 58 EC

[now Article 62 TFEU] in that they are necessary in order to guarantee the country's security of supply for oil and natural gas and to enable this to be done in an appropriate way, given, inter alia, the absence of suitable instruments at European Union level. . . .

Findings of the Court

81. According to well-established case-law, national measures which restrict the free movement of capital may be justified on the grounds set out in Article [62 TFEU] or by overriding reasons in the public interest, provided that they are appropriate to secure the attainment of the objective which they pursue and do not go beyond what is necessary in order to attain it.

82. As regards the derogations permitted under Article [62 TFEU], it cannot be denied that the objective invoked by the Portuguese Republic of safeguarding a secure energy supply in that Member State in case of crisis, war or terrorism may constitute a ground of public security and may possibly justify an obstacle to the free movement of capital. The importance attached by Member States and the European Union to the protection of a secure energy supply can, moreover, be seen, for example, with regard to oil, in Directive 2006/67 and, with regard to the natural gas sector, in Directive 2003/55.

83. However, it is common ground that requirements of public security must, in particular as a derogation from the fundamental principle of the free movement of capital, be interpreted strictly, with the result that their scope cannot be determined unilaterally by each Member State without any control by the institutions of the European Union. Thus, public security may be relied on only if there is a genuine and sufficiently serious threat to a fundamental interest of society.

84. In this regard, the Portuguese Republic points out, inter alia, that at the present time concerns exist about certain investments made particularly by sovereign wealth funds, or investments that might be linked to terrorist organisations, in undertakings in strategic sectors, which constitute a threat of that nature in relation to energy supply. Given that a Member State is under an obligation to guarantee the security of a regular and uninterrupted supply of oil and natural gas, that State can legitimately equip itself with the means required to guarantee the fundamental interest of security of supply in the event of a crisis and it is the duty of the State concerned to ensure that adequate mechanisms are put in place which will enable it to react rapidly and effectively to guarantee that the security of that supply is not interrupted.

85. However, as the Portuguese Republic has done no more than put forward the ground relating to the security of the energy supply, without stating clearly the exact reasons why it considers that the special rights at issue, considered either individually or as a whole, would make it possible

to prevent such interference with a fundamental interest such as energy supply, a justification based on public security cannot be upheld in the present case....

88. For the sake of completeness, as regards the proportionality of the provisions of national law at issue, it should be noted that, as has correctly been pointed out by the Commission, the exercise of the special rights which the holding of golden shares in GALP's share capital confers on the Portuguese State is not subject to any specific and objective condition or circumstance, contrary to what is claimed by the Portuguese Republic.

89. ... [N]either that law nor GALP's articles of association lay down any criteria for determining the specific circumstances in which ... [the] special rights [associated with the golden shares] may be exercised....

90. Thus, such uncertainty constitutes serious interference with the free movement of capital in that it confers on the national authorities, as regards the use of such rights, a latitude so discretionary in nature that it cannot be regarded as proportionate to the objectives pursued....

97. It must consequently be declared that, by maintaining in favour of the Portuguese State and other public bodies special rights in GALP, such as those provided for in the present case by the LQP, Decree-Law No 261-A/99 and the company's articles of association, granted in connection with the Portuguese State's golden shares in the share capital of GALP, the Portuguese Republic has failed to fulfil its obligations under Article 56 EC.

Failure to fulfil obligations under Article 43 EC

98. With regard to the Commission's application for a declaration that the Portuguese Republic has failed to fulfil its obligations under Article 43 EC [now Article 49 TFEU], suffice it to note that, in accordance with settled case-law, since the national measures at issue involve restrictions on freedom of establishment, such restrictions are a direct consequence of the obstacles to the free movement of capital considered above, to which they are inextricably linked. Consequently, since a breach of Article 56(1) EC [now Article 63(1) TFEU] has been established, there is no need for a separate examination of the measures at issue in the light of the Treaty rules concerning freedom of establishment. ∎

NOTES AND QUESTIONS

1. According to the Court of Justice, when does the freedom of establishment apply to direct investments? When does the free movement of capital apply? When do both freedoms apply?

2. Does it make a practical difference whether an investment is protected by the freedom of establishment or by the free movement of capital?

3. Why might the "golden shares" be likely to deter private investors from acquiring shares?

4. The Court argues that the "golden shares" cannot be compared to a selling arrangement within the meaning of *Keck*. Is the Court's reasoning persuasive?

5. The Court rejects Portugal's argument that the "golden shares" are necessary to protect the security of Portugal's energy supply. Do you find the Court's position persuasive? How does the case compare to the *Campus Oil* decision discussed earlier in this casebook?

6. The Court also argues that the "golden shares" violate the proportionality principle. How does the Court of Justice arrive at this conclusion?

7. Could you argue that the Court's decision is likely to deter Member States from privatizing state-owned companies? If so, is that a desirable outcome with a view to the creation of an internal market?

B. DISCRIMINATORY AND NON-DISCRIMINATORY OBSTACLES

Like the other fundamental freedoms, the free movement of capital contains not only a prohibition against discrimination, but also a prohibition against non-discriminatory obstacles.[5]

C. JUSTIFICATIONS

Measures that restrict the free movement of capital may nonetheless be justified. Article 62 TFEU refers to Article 52 TFEU on the freedom of establishment and thus incorporates the justification of restrictions on grounds related to public policy, public security and public health. In addition, though, Article 65 TFEU allows far-reaching restrictions in the area of taxation."

D. PRACTICE QUESTIONS

For the purpose of the following hypotheticals, assume that Alpha and Beta are Member States of the European Union.

1. In Alpha, the state has traditionally owned a chain of banks. The Alphanian government decides to privatize the relevant chain of banks. Alpha therefore adopts a law that provides for the relevant banks to be privatized and to be auctioned off to the highest bidder. Article 17 of the relevant law also provides that a government authorization shall be required before foreign ownership can exceed 49% of the capital of the

---

[5] Case C-212/09, European Commission v. Portuguese Republic, November 10, 2011, 2011 E.C.R. I-10889 ¶ 48.

privatized banks. Following an inquiry by the European commission, the Alphanian government declares that it will likely grant that authorization if control is acquired by a citizen or corporation in another Member State. Does the new Alphanian law violate EU law?

2. In 2018, the Betanian government adopts a statute according to which wire transfers between domestic bank accounts and bank accounts in third countries are prohibited, unless the transferor first files a form providing information regarding the money's origin and the transfer's purpose. According to the Betanian government, this filing requirement helps to prevent money laundering and potential financing of terrorist activities. Does this statute violate EU law?

Free Movement of Capital

I. Scope of application

   A. The free movement of capital covers, inter alia, both portfolio and direct investments, whereas only the latter are also covered by the freedom of establishment

   B. The free movement of capital covers not just the movement of capital between Member States, but also the movement of capital between a Member State and third country

II. Restriction

   A. The freedom to provide services prohibits both directly and indirectly discriminating measures

   B. In addition, it covers measures that apply without distinction

III. Mandatory requirements doctrine

   A. Legitimate goal

   B. Proportionality

   C. Absence of discrimination

      1. Mandatory requirements doctrine does not apply in the case of formal discrimination

      2. Court of Justice not consistent on whether mere indirect discrimination can be justified

IV. Justification under Articles 65, 66 TFEU

CHAPTER 18

FUNDAMENTAL FREEDOMS: COMMON PROBLEMS

■ ■ ■

While each of the fundamental freedoms has its own peculiarities, the various freedoms are in many ways structurally similar, and they have some problems in common. In this chapter, we will focus on two such problems: the extent to which Member States can violate fundamental freedoms through inaction and the extent to which the fundamental freedoms bind private parties.

A. FAILURE TO ACT

The Member States can restrict the fundamental freedoms in many ways. For example, a Member State that enacts a statute prohibiting the import of certain goods restricts the free movement of goods. Similarly, a Member State whose administration denies construction permits to construction companies headquartered in other Member States restricts the freedom to provide services.

It does not make any difference, in this context, whether or not the origin of the relevant state action precedes the creation of the European Economic Community or the European Union. For example, a statute that restricts the free movement of goods may date back to the 19th century, but this does not prevent us from classifying the statute as a state action that violates the fundamental freedoms.

But can the Member States also restrict—and possibly violate—the fundamental freedoms by having done nothing at all? The issue arises in those cases where private parties are prevented from exercising their fundamental freedoms by other private parties. For example, what if farmers, angry at being underpriced by foreign agricultural products, erect physical barriers on highways to prevent the import of foreign produce?

Under such circumstances, can we argue that a Member State violates the fundamental freedoms by failing to protect the party trying to exercise its fundamental freedoms? The Court of Justice has, in principle, answered that question in the affirmative: in some cases, Member States are under a duty to protect the exercise of the fundamental freedoms against interference by nongovernmental third parties. Of course, the difficulty lies in defining when exactly such a duty arises.

COMMISSION OF THE EUROPEAN COMMUNITIES
v FRENCH REPUBLIC

Case C-265/95, December 9, 1997, 1997 E.C.R. I-6959

[Beginning in 1993, certain groups of French farmers made systematic efforts to hinder the sale of foreign produce in France, in particular by threatening wholesalers and retailers to ensure that they only sell French products and by imposing minimum prices for the relevant products.

In this context, various acts of vandalism occurred, including the destruction of foreign produce and means of transport. In one case, such violent acts took place twice within a two-week period at the same location, and although the police were present, they did not interfere. The Commission repeatedly intervened with the French authorities, but these interventions proved fruitless. The Commission eventually initiated enforcement proceedings against France. The Commission argued that France had violated the free movement of goods by failing to take appropriate measures to ensure that the free movement of goods was not obstructed by the criminal actions of private parties.]

28. [. . .] Article 30 [now Article 34 TFEU] provides that quantitative restrictions on imports and all measures having equivalent effect are prohibited between Member States.

29. That provision, taken in its context, must be understood as being intended to eliminate all barriers, whether direct or indirect, actual or potential, to flows of imports in intra-Community trade.

30. As an indispensable instrument for the realization of a market without internal frontiers, Article 30 [34 TFEU] therefore does not prohibit solely measures emanating from the State which, in themselves, create restrictions on trade between Member States. It also applies where a Member State abstains from adopting the measures required in order to deal with obstacles to the free movement of goods which are not caused by the State.

31. The fact that a Member State abstains from taking action or, as the case may be, fails to adopt adequate measures to prevent obstacles to the free movement of goods that are created, in particular, by actions by private individuals on its territory aimed at products originating in other Member States is just as likely to obstruct intra-Community trade as is a positive act.

32. Article 30 [now Article 34] therefore requires the Member States not merely themselves to abstain from adopting measures or engaging in conduct liable to constitute an obstacle to trade but also, when read with Article 5 of the Treaty [now Article 4 TEU], to take all necessary and appropriate measures to ensure that that fundamental freedom is respected on their territory.

33. In the latter context, the Member States, which retain exclusive competence as regards the maintenance of public order and the safeguarding of internal security, unquestionably enjoy a margin of discretion in determining what measures are most appropriate to eliminate barriers to the importation of products in a given situation.

34. It is therefore not for the Community institutions to act in place of the Member States and to prescribe for them the measures which they must adopt and effectively apply in order to safeguard the free movement of goods on their territories.

35. However, it falls to the Court, taking due account of the discretion referred to above, to verify, in cases brought before it, whether the Member State concerned has adopted appropriate measures for ensuring the free movement of goods.

36. It should be added that . . . the foregoing considerations apply also to Council regulations on the common organization of the markets for the various agricultural products.

37. As regards more specifically the present case, the facts which gave rise to the action brought by the Commission against the French Republic for failure to fulfil obligations are not in dispute.

38. The acts of violence committed in France and directed against agricultural products originating in other Member States, such as the interception of lorries transporting those products, the destruction of their loads and violence towards drivers, as well as threats to wholesalers and retailers and the damaging of goods on display, unquestionably create obstacles to intra-Community trade in those products.

39. It is therefore necessary to consider whether in the present case the French Government complied with its obligations under Article 30 [now Article 34], in conjunction with Article 5 [now Article 4 TEU], of the Treaty, by adopting adequate and appropriate measures to deal with actions by private individuals which create obstacles to the free movement of certain agricultural products.

40. It should be stressed that the Commission's written pleadings show that the incidents to which it objects in the present proceedings have taken place regularly for more than 10 years.

41. It was as long ago as 8 May 1985 that the Commission first sent a formal letter to the French Republic calling on it to adopt the preventive and penal measures necessary to put an end to acts of that kind.

42. Moreover, in the present case the Commission reminded the French Government on numerous occasions that Community law imposes an obligation to ensure de facto compliance with the principle of the free

movement of goods by eliminating all restrictions on the freedom to trade in agricultural products from other Member States.

43. In the present case the French authorities therefore had ample time to adopt the measures necessary to ensure compliance with their obligations under Community law.

44. Moreover, notwithstanding the explanations given by the French Government, which claims that all possible measures were adopted in order to prevent the continuation of the violence and to prosecute and punish those responsible, it is a fact that, year after year, serious incidents have gravely jeopardized trade in agricultural products in France.

45. According to the summary of the facts submitted by the Commission, which is not contested by the French Government, there are particular periods of the year which are primarily concerned and there are places which are particularly vulnerable where incidents have occurred on several occasions during one and the same year.

46. Since 1993 acts of violence and vandalism have not been directed solely at the means of transport of agricultural products but have extended to the wholesale and retail sector for those products.

47. Further serious incidents of the same type also occurred in 1996 and 1997.

48. Moreover, it is not denied that when such incidents occurred the French police were either not present on the spot, despite the fact that in certain cases the competent authorities had been warned of the imminence of demonstrations by farmers, or did not intervene, even where they far outnumbered the perpetrators of the disturbances. Furthermore, the actions in question were not always rapid, surprise actions by demonstrators who then immediately took flight, since in certain cases the disruption continued for several hours.

49. Furthermore, it is undisputed that a number of acts of vandalism were filmed by television cameras, that the demonstrators' faces were often not covered and that the groups of farmers responsible for the violent demonstrations are known to the police.

50. Notwithstanding this, it is common ground that only a very small number of the persons who participated in those serious breaches of public order has been identified and prosecuted.

51. Thus, as regards the numerous acts of vandalism committed between April and August 1993, the French authorities have been able to cite only a single case of criminal prosecution.

52. In the light of all the foregoing factors, the Court, while not discounting the difficulties faced by the competent authorities in dealing with situations of the type in question in this case, cannot but find that,

having regard to the frequency and seriousness of the incidents cited by the Commission, the measures adopted by the French Government were manifestly inadequate to ensure freedom of intra-Community trade in agricultural products on its territory by preventing and effectively dissuading the perpetrators of the offences in question from committing and repeating them.

53. That finding is all the more compelling since the damage and threats to which the Commission refers not only affect the importation into or transit in France of the products directly affected by the violent acts, but are also such as to create a climate of insecurity which has a deterrent effect on trade flows as a whole.

54. The above finding is in no way affected by the French Government's argument that the situation of French farmers was so difficult that there were reasonable grounds for fearing that more determined action by the competent authorities might provoke violent reactions by those concerned, which would lead to still more serious breaches of public order or even to social conflict.

55. Apprehension of internal difficulties cannot justify a failure by a Member State to apply Community law correctly.

56. It is for the Member State concerned, unless it can show that action on its part would have consequences for public order with which it could not cope by using the means at its disposal, to adopt all appropriate measures to guarantee the full scope and effect of Community law so as to ensure its proper implementation in the interests of all economic operators.

57. In the present case the French Government has adduced no concrete evidence proving the existence of a danger to public order with which it could not cope.

58. Moreover, although it is not impossible that the threat of serious disruption to public order may, in appropriate cases, justify non intervention by the police, that argument can, on any view, be put forward only with respect to a specific incident and not, as in this case, in a general way covering all the incidents cited by the Commission.

59. As regards the fact that the French Republic has assumed responsibility for the losses caused to the victims, this cannot be put forward as an argument by the French Government in order to escape its obligations under Community law.

60. Even though compensation can provide reparation for at least part of the loss or damage sustained by the economic operators concerned, the provision of such compensation does not mean that the Member State has fulfilled its obligations.

61. Nor is it possible to accept the arguments based on the very difficult socio-economic context of the French market in fruit and vegetables after the accession of the Kingdom of Spain.

62. It is settled case-law that economic grounds can never serve as justification for barriers prohibited by Article 30 [now Article 34] of the Treaty.

63. As regards the suggestion by the French Government, in support of those arguments, that the destabilization of the French market for fruit and vegetables was brought about by unfair practices, and even infringements of Community law, by Spanish producers, it must be remembered that a Member State may not unilaterally adopt protective measures or conduct itself in such a way as to obviate any breach by another Member State of rules of Community law.

64. This must be so a fortiori in the sphere of the common agricultural policy, where it is for the Community alone to adopt, if necessary, the measures required in order to deal with difficulties which some economic operators may be experiencing, in particular following a new accession.

65. Having regard to all the foregoing considerations, it must be concluded that in the present case the French Government has manifestly and persistently abstained from adopting appropriate and adequate measures to put an end to the acts of vandalism which jeopardize the free movement on its territory of certain agricultural products originating in other Member States and to prevent the recurrence of such acts.

66. Consequently, it must be held that, by failing to adopt all necessary and proportionate measures in order to prevent the free movement of fruit and vegetables from being obstructed by actions by private individuals, the French Government has failed to fulfil its obligations under Article 30 [now Article 34], in conjunction with Article 5, of the Treaty [now Article 4 TFEU] and under the common organizations of the markets in agricultural products. ∎

NOTES AND QUESTIONS

1. How does the Court arrive at the conclusion that Member States have to "take all necessary and appropriate measures to ensure" that private parties do not undermine the free movement of goods?

2. Does the Member States' duty to protect the free movement of goods against private parties imply that private parties are bound by the free movement of goods?

3. The Court explicitly recognizes that the Member States enjoy a "margin of discretion" in determining how to safeguard the free movement of goods. Why does the Court nonetheless come to the conclusion that France violated the free movement of goods?

EUGEN SCHMIDBERGER, INTERNATIONALE TRANSPORTE UND PLANZÜGE V. REPUBLIK ÖSTERREICH

Case C-112/00, 12 June 12, 2003, 2003 E.C.R. I-5659 (citations omitted)

[Under Austrian law, a person planning a public assembly has to notify the authorities 24 hours in advance. If the assembly's purpose violates criminal law or if the assembly is likely to pose a threat to public order, it must be banned by the authorities.

On May 15, 1988, the Transitforum Austria, an environmental group, gave notice to the authorities that it would hold a demonstration on the Brenner motorway, thereby preventing that motorway from being used for traffic. The Austrian authorities decided not to ban the demonstration, and the demonstration took place as planned. As a result, the motorway was closed to traffic from Friday 9 am to Saturday 3.30 pm and the vehicles that had planned to use the motorway were immobilized.

Schmidberger was a transportation business owning and operating six trucks. Its main business lay in transporting steel and timber between Italy and Germany, and its trucks usually use the Brenner motorway. Schmidberger brought an action for damages against Austria on the ground that the Austrian authorities had violated the free movement of goods by not banning the assembly on the Brenner. The Austrian court requested a preliminary ruling from the Court of Justice.]

57. ... Article 30 does not prohibit only measures emanating from the State which, in themselves, create restrictions on trade between Member States. It also applies where a Member State abstains from adopting the measures required in order to deal with obstacles to the free movement of goods which are not caused by the State.

58. The fact that a Member State abstains from taking action or, as the case may be, fails to adopt adequate measures to prevent obstacles to the free movement of goods that are created, in particular, by actions by private individuals on its territory aimed at products originating in other Member States is just as likely to obstruct intra-Community trade as is a positive act.

59. Consequently, Articles 30 and 34 [now Articles 34 and 35] of the Treaty require the Member States not merely themselves to refrain from adopting measures or engaging in conduct liable to constitute an obstacle to trade but also, when read with Article 5 of the Treaty [now Article 4 TEU], to take all necessary and appropriate measures to ensure that that fundamental freedom is respected on their territory. Article 5 of the Treaty [now Article 4 TEU] requires the Member States to take all appropriate measures, whether general or particular, to ensure fulfilment of the obligations arising out of the Treaty and to refrain from any measures which could jeopardise the attainment of the objectives of that Treaty.

60. Having regard to the fundamental role assigned to the free movement of goods in the Community system, in particular for the proper functioning of the internal market, that obligation upon each Member State to ensure the free movement of products in its territory by taking the measures necessary and appropriate for the purposes of preventing any restriction due to the acts of individuals applies without the need to distinguish between cases where such acts affect the flow of imports or exports and those affecting merely the transit of goods. . . .

62. It follows that, in a situation such as that at issue in the main proceedings, where the competent national authorities are faced with restrictions on the effective exercise of a fundamental freedom enshrined in the Treaty, such as the free movement of goods, which result from actions taken by individuals, they are required to take adequate steps to ensure that freedom in the Member State concerned even if, as in the main proceedings, those goods merely pass through Austria en route for Italy or Germany.

63. It should be added that that obligation of the Member States is all the more important where the case concerns a major transit route such as the Brenner motorway, which is one of the main land links for trade between northern Europe and the north of Italy.

64. In the light of the foregoing, the fact that the competent authorities of a Member State did not ban a demonstration which resulted in the complete closure of a major transit route such as the Brenner motorway for almost 30 hours on end is capable of restricting intra-Community trade in goods and must, therefore, be regarded as constituting a measure of equivalent effect to a quantitative restriction which is, in principle, incompatible with the Community law obligations arising from Articles 30 and 34 [now Articles 34 and 35] of the Treaty, read together with Article 5 thereof [now Article 4 TEU], unless that failure to ban can be objectively justified.

Whether the restriction may be justified

65. In the context of its fourth question, the referring court asks essentially whether the purpose of the demonstration on 12 and 13 June 1998 during which the demonstrators sought to draw attention to the threat to the environment and public health posed by the constant increase in the movement of heavy goods vehicles on the Brenner motorway and to persuade the competent authorities to reinforce measures to reduce that traffic and the pollution resulting therefrom in the highly sensitive region of the Alps is such as to frustrate Community law obligations relating to the free movement of goods.

66. However, even if the protection of the environment and public health, especially in that region, may, under certain conditions, constitute a legitimate objective in the public interest capable of justifying a restriction

of the fundamental freedoms guaranteed by the Treaty, including the free movement of goods, it should be noted, as the Advocate General pointed out at paragraph 54 of his Opinion, that the specific aims of the demonstration are not in themselves material in legal proceedings such as those instituted by Schmidberger, which seek to establish the liability of a Member State in respect of an alleged breach of Community law, since that liability is to be inferred from the fact that the national authorities did not prevent an obstacle to traffic from being placed on the Brenner motorway.

67. Indeed, for the purposes of determining the conditions in which a Member State may be liable and, in particular, with regard to the question whether it infringed Community law, account must be taken only of the action or omission imputable to that Member State.

68. In the present case, account should thus be taken solely of the objective pursued by the national authorities in their implicit decision to authorise or not to ban the demonstration in question.

69. It is apparent from the file in the main case that the Austrian authorities were inspired by considerations linked to respect of the fundamental rights of the demonstrators to freedom of expression and freedom of assembly, which are enshrined in and guaranteed by the ECHR and the Austrian Constitution.

70. In its order for reference, the national court also raises the question whether the principle of the free movement of goods guaranteed by the Treaty prevails over those fundamental rights.

71. According to settled case-law, fundamental rights form an integral part of the general principles of law the observance of which the Court ensures. For that purpose, the Court draws inspiration from the constitutional traditions common to the Member States and from the guidelines supplied by international treaties for the protection of human rights on which the Member States have collaborated or to which they are signatories. The ECHR [European Court of Human Rights] has special significance in that respect.

72. The principles established by that case-law were reaffirmed in the preamble to the Single European Act and subsequently in Article F.2 of the Treaty on European Union. That provision states that "the Union shall respect fundamental rights, as guaranteed by the European Convention for the Protection of Human Rights and Fundamental Freedoms signed in Rome on 4 November 1950 and as they result from the constitutional traditions common to the Member States, as general principles of Community law."

73. It follows that measures which are incompatible with observance of the human rights thus recognised are not acceptable in the Community.

74. Thus, since both the Community and its Member States are required to respect fundamental rights, the protection of those rights is a legitimate interest which, in principle, justifies a restriction of the obligations imposed by Community law, even under a fundamental freedom guaranteed by the Treaty such as the free movement of goods.

75. It is settled case-law that where, as in the main proceedings, a national situation falls within the scope of Community law and a reference for a preliminary ruling is made to the Court, it must provide the national courts with all the criteria of interpretation needed to determine whether that situation is compatible with the fundamental rights the observance of which the Court ensures and which derive in particular from the ECHR.

76. In the present case, the national authorities relied on the need to respect fundamental rights guaranteed by both the ECHR and the Constitution of the Member State concerned in deciding to allow a restriction to be imposed on one of the fundamental freedoms enshrined in the Treaty.

77. The case thus raises the question of the need to reconcile the requirements of the protection of fundamental rights in the Community with those arising from a fundamental freedom enshrined in the Treaty and, more particularly, the question of the respective scope of freedom of expression and freedom of assembly, guaranteed by Articles 10 and 11 of the ECHR, and of the free movement of goods, where the former are relied upon as justification for a restriction of the latter.

78. First, whilst the free movement of goods constitutes one of the fundamental principles in the scheme of the Treaty, it may, in certain circumstances, be subject to restrictions for the reasons laid down in Article 36 of that Treaty [now Article 36 TFEU] or for overriding requirements relating to the public interest, in accordance with the Court's consistent case-law since the judgment in Case 120/78 Rewe-Zentral ("Cassis de Dijon") 1979 ECR 649.

79. Second, whilst the fundamental rights at issue in the main proceedings are expressly recognised by the ECHR and constitute the fundamental pillars of a democratic society, it nevertheless follows from the express wording of paragraph 2 of Articles 10 and 11 of the Convention that freedom of expression and freedom of assembly are also subject to certain limitations justified by objectives in the public interest, in so far as those derogations are in accordance with the law, motivated by one or more of the legitimate aims under those provisions and necessary in a democratic society, that is to say justified by a pressing social need and, in particular, proportionate to the legitimate aim pursued.

80. Thus, unlike other fundamental rights enshrined in that Convention, such as the right to life or the prohibition of torture and inhuman or degrading treatment or punishment, which admit of no restriction, neither

the freedom of expression nor the freedom of assembly guaranteed by the ECHR appears to be absolute but must be viewed in relation to its social purpose. Consequently, the exercise of those rights may be restricted, provided that the restrictions in fact correspond to objectives of general interest and do not, taking account of the aim of the restrictions, constitute disproportionate and unacceptable interference, impairing the very substance of the rights guarantee.

81. In those circumstances, the interests involved must be weighed having regard to all the circumstances of the case in order to determine whether a fair balance was struck between those interests.

82. The competent authorities enjoy a wide margin of discretion in that regard. Nevertheless, it is necessary to determine whether the restrictions placed upon intra-Community trade are proportionate in the light of the legitimate objective pursued, namely, in the present case, the protection of fundamental rights.

83. As regards the main case, it should be emphasised at the outset that the circumstances characterising it are clearly distinguishable from the situation in the case giving rise to the judgment in Commission v. France, cited above, referred to by Schmidberger as a relevant precedent in the course of its legal action against Austria.

84. By comparison with the points of fact referred to by the Court at paragraphs 38 to 53 of the judgment in Commission v. France, cited above, it should be noted, first, that the demonstration at issue in the main proceedings took place following a request for authorization presented on the basis of national law and after the competent authorities had decided not to ban it.

85. Second, because of the presence of demonstrators on the Brenner motorway, traffic by road was obstructed on a single route, on a single occasion and during a period of almost 30 hours. Furthermore, the obstacle to the free movement of goods resulting from that demonstration was limited by comparison with both the geographic scale and the intrinsic seriousness of the disruption caused in the case giving rise to the judgment in Commission v. France, cited above.

86. Third, it is not in dispute that by that demonstration, citizens were exercising their fundamental rights by manifesting in public an opinion which they considered to be of importance to society; it is also not in dispute that the purpose of that public demonstration was not to restrict trade in goods of a particular type or from a particular source. By contrast, in Commission v. France, cited above, the objective pursued by the demonstrators was clearly to prevent the movement of particular products originating in Member States other than the French Republic, by not only obstructing the transport of the goods in question, but also destroying those

goods in transit to or through France, and even when they had already been put on display in shops in the Member State concerned.

87. Fourth, in the present case various administrative and supporting measures were taken by the competent authorities in order to limit as far as possible the disruption to road traffic. Thus, in particular, those authorities, including the police, the organisers of the demonstration and various motoring organisations cooperated in order to ensure that the demonstration passed off smoothly. Well before the date on which it was due to take place, an extensive publicity campaign had been launched by the media and the motoring organisations, both in Austria and in neighbouring countries, and various alternative routes had been designated, with the result that the economic operators concerned were duly informed of the traffic restrictions applying on the date and at the site of the proposed demonstration and were in a position timeously to take all steps necessary to obviate those restrictions. Furthermore, security arrangements had been made for the site of the demonstration.

88. Moreover, it is not in dispute that the isolated incident in question did not give rise to a general climate of insecurity such as to have a dissuasive effect on intra-Community trade flows as a whole, in contrast to the serious and repeated disruptions to public order at issue in the case giving rise to the judgment in Commission v. France, cited above.

89. Finally, concerning the other possibilities envisaged by Schmidberger with regard to the demonstration in question, taking account of the Member States' wide margin of discretion, in circumstances such as those of the present case the competent national authorities were entitled to consider that an outright ban on the demonstration would have constituted unacceptable interference with the fundamental rights of the demonstrators to gather and express peacefully their opinion in public.

90. The imposition of stricter conditions concerning both the site for example by the side of the Brenner motorway and the duration limited to a few hours only of the demonstration in question could have been perceived as an excessive restriction, depriving the action of a substantial part of its scope. Whilst the competent national authorities must endeavour to limit as far as possible the inevitable effects upon free movement of a demonstration on the public highway, they must balance that interest with that of the demonstrators, who seek to draw the aims of their action to the attention of the public.

91. An action of that type usually entails inconvenience for non-participants, in particular as regards free movement, but the inconvenience may in principle be tolerated provided that the objective pursued is essentially the public and lawful demonstration of an opinion.

92. In that regard, the Republic of Austria submits, without being contradicted on that point, that in any event, all the alternative solutions

which could be countenanced would have risked reactions which would have been difficult to control and would have been liable to cause much more serious disruption to intra-Community trade and public order, such as unauthorised demonstrations, confrontation between supporters and opponents of the group organising the demonstration or acts of violence on the part of the demonstrators who considered that the exercise of their fundamental rights had been infringed.

93. Consequently, the national authorities were reasonably entitled, having regard to the wide discretion which must be accorded to them in the matter, to consider that the legitimate aim of that demonstration could not be achieved in the present case by measures less restrictive of intra-Community trade.

94. In the light of those considerations, the answer . . . must be that the fact that the authorities of a Member State did not ban a demonstration in circumstances such as those of the main case is not incompatible with Articles 30 and 34 of the Treaty [now Articles 34 and 35], read together with Article 5 thereof [now Article 4 TEU]. ∎

QUESTIONS

1. In *Commission v. France*, the Court found that the free movement of goods had been violated by the French authorities' passivity. By contrast, in *Schmidberger*, the Court of Justice came to the opposite conclusion. What distinguishes the two cases?

2. How would you summarize the case law on when Member States have to take action to protect fundamental freedoms?

3. Why does the Court invoke the common traditions of the Member States when it comes to fundamental rights? Does this not violate the principle of autonomous interpretation of EU law?

4. The principle that Member States are required to protect the fundamental freedoms against private parties has so far been applied only in cases dealing with the free movement of goods. Can you think of any reasons not to apply this principle to the other fundamental freedoms?

B. PRIVATE PARTIES

As noted above, the Member States are required, in principle to protect the fundamental freedoms against obstacles created by private parties. An entirely different question is, however, whether private parties are also bound directly by the fundamental freedoms.

ROMAN ANGONESE V. CASSA DI RISPARMIO DI BOLZANO SPA

Case C-281/98, June 6, 2000, 2000 E.C.R. I-4139

[Mr. Angonese was an Italian citizen from Bolzano whose native language was German. Bolzano is part of an Italian region in Northern Italy where many citizens' native language is German. From 1993 to 1997, Mr. Angonese undertook studies in Austria. In 1997, he applied to participate in a competition for a job at a private bank in Bolzano, Italy.

In order to be allowed to participate in the relevant competition, the candidates were required to present a so-called "type B certificate of bilingualism" signifying that they were bilingual in German and Italian. The public administration of the province of Bolzano issues that certificate after an examination of the candidate's language skills. The relevant examination takes place only at certain times during the year and only in Bolzano.

Residents of Bolzano usually undertake the relevant examination as a matter of course. Mr. Angonese had not obtained the relevant certificate. However, he was in fact perfectly bilingual and had presented evidence of that fact. According to him, the requirement to obtain a type B certificate of bilingualism ("Certificate") in order to prove bilingualism was discriminatory in nature, since that certificate was much easier to obtain for those candidates who lived in Bolzano, where the examination took place, than for those candidates who lived in other Member States.

Accordingly, Mr. Angonese sued the bank holding the competition—the Cassa di Risparmio di Bolzano. The Italian court requested a preliminary ruling from the European Court of Justice.]

29. [F]reedom of movement for workers within the Community entails the abolition of any discrimination based on nationality between workers of the Member States as regards employment, remuneration and other conditions of work and employment.

30. It should be noted at the outset that the principle of non-discrimination set out in Article 48 [now Article 45 TFEU] is drafted in general terms and is not specifically addressed to the Member States.

31. Thus, the Court has held that the prohibition of discrimination based on nationality applies not only to the actions of public authorities but also to rules of any other nature aimed at regulating in a collective manner gainful employment and the provision of services.

32. The Court has held that the abolition, as between Member States, of obstacles to freedom of movement for persons would be compromised if the abolition of State barriers could be neutralised by obstacles resulting from the exercise of their legal autonomy by associations or organisations not governed by public law.

33. Since working conditions in the different Member States are governed sometimes by provisions laid down by law or regulation and sometimes by agreements and other acts concluded or adopted by private persons, limiting application of the prohibition of discrimination based on nationality to acts of a public authority risks creating inequality in its application.

34. The Court has also ruled that the fact that certain provisions of the Treaty are formally addressed to the Member States does not prevent rights from being conferred at the same time on any individual who has an interest in compliance with the obligations thus laid down (see Case 43/75 Defrenne v. Sabena 1976 ECR 455, paragraph 31). [The *Defrenne* judgment concerned the prohibition against gender discrimination in what is now Article 157 TFEU.] The Court accordingly held, in relation to a provision of the Treaty which was mandatory in nature, that the prohibition of discrimination applied equally to all agreements intended to regulate paid labour collectively, as well as to contracts between individuals (see Defrenne, paragraph 39).

35. Such considerations must, a fortiori, be applicable to Article 48 [now Article 45] of the Treaty, which lays down a fundamental freedom and which constitutes a specific application of the general prohibition of discrimination contained in Article 6 of the EC Treaty . . . [now Article 18 TFEU]. . . .

36. Consequently, the prohibition of discrimination on grounds of nationality laid down in Article 48 of the Treaty [now Article 45 TFEU] must be regarded as applying to private persons as well.

37. The next matter to be considered is whether a requirement imposed by an employer, such as the Cassa di Risparmio, which makes admission to a recruitment competition conditional on possession of one particular diploma, such as the Certificate, constitutes discrimination contrary to Article 48 of the Treaty.

38. According to the order for reference, the Cassa di Risparmio accepts only the Certificate as evidence of the requisite linguistic knowledge and the Certificate can be obtained only in one province of the Member State concerned.

39. Persons not resident in that province therefore have little chance of acquiring the Certificate and it will be difficult, or even impossible, for them to gain access to the employment in question.

40. Since the majority of residents of the province of Bolzano are Italian nationals, the obligation to obtain the requisite Certificate puts nationals of other Member States at a disadvantage by comparison with residents of the province.

41. That is so notwithstanding that the requirement in question affects Italian nationals resident in other parts of Italy as well as nationals of other Member States. In order for a measure to be treated as being discriminatory on grounds of nationality under the rules relating to the free movement of workers, it is not necessary for the measure to have the effect of putting at an advantage all the workers of one nationality or of putting at a disadvantage only workers who are nationals of other Member States, but not workers of the nationality in question.

42. A requirement, such as the one at issue in the main proceedings, making the right to take part in a recruitment competition conditional upon possession of a language diploma that may be obtained in only one province of a Member State and not allowing any other equivalent evidence could be justified only if it were based on objective factors unrelated to the nationality of the persons concerned and if it were in proportion to the aim legitimately pursued.

43. The Court has ruled that the principle of non-discrimination precludes any requirement that the linguistic knowledge in question must have been acquired within the national territory.

44. So, even though requiring an applicant for a post to have a certain level of linguistic knowledge may be legitimate and possession of a diploma such as the Certificate may constitute a criterion for assessing that knowledge, the fact that it is impossible to submit proof of the required linguistic knowledge by any other means, in particular by equivalent qualifications obtained in other Member States, must be considered disproportionate in relation to the aim in view.

45. It follows that, where an employer makes a person's admission to a recruitment competition subject to a requirement to provide evidence of his linguistic knowledge exclusively by means of one particular diploma, such as the Certificate, issued only in one particular province of a Member State, that requirement constitutes discrimination on grounds of nationality contrary to Article 48 [now Article 45] of the EC Treaty.

46. The reply to be given to the question submitted must therefore be that Article 48 of the Treaty [now Article 45 TFEU] precludes an employer from requiring persons applying to take part in a recruitment competition to provide evidence of their linguistic knowledge exclusively by means of one particular diploma issued only in one particular province of a Member State. ∎

QUESTIONS

1. Even if the requirement of a type B certificate violated the free movement of workers, why was Mr. Angonese able to invoke that violation, given that he was himself an Italian citizen?

2. Why was the requirement of a type B certificate not justified?

3. Can the arguments that the Court adduces in favor of a direct application of Article 45 TFEU to private parties be extended to the other fundamental freedoms? Is the free movement of workers somehow unique?

C. PRACTICE QUESTIONS

1. Alpha unexpectedly loses the final of the World Soccer Championship to Beta. Frustrated by this outcome, Alphanian consumers start boycotting Betanian products in supermarkets. In television interviews, Alphanian shoppers frankly state that they refuse to buy Betanian products unless the captain of Beta's national soccer squad apologizes for scoring seventeen goals in the final. The Betanian government believes that Alphanian consumers are violating the free movement of goods by refusing to buy Betanian products. Moreover, it argues that the Alphanian government violates the free movement of goods by failing to intervene against the boycott. Discuss!

2. In 2016, the European Union adopts a new directive according to which the Member States must not authorize the building of new waste disposal sites without undertaking a prior formal inquiry into the likely impact that the waste disposal site would have on the health and quality of life of persons residing within a ten mile radius of the site. This hypothetical directive also provides that residents within a ten-mile radius have an unconditional right that no permit be granted without such prior inquiry and that permits granted in violation of this rule be revoked without delay. The directive further provides, inter alia, that the Member States are required to implement the directive by December 31, 2017. However, Alpha never implements the directive. In June 2018, the Alphanian city of Victoria grants George a permit for the construction of a new waste disposal site in Victoria. Tanusha lives directly next to the planned site. She submits a formal objection to the permit, citing the city's obligations under the 2018 directive. Assume that, if one does not consider the directive, Alphanian law imposes a duty on the city of Victoria to grant the permit for the site. Does the city of Victoria have to revoke the permit granted to George?

3. Hans, an Alphanian citizen, who lives in Beta and works for the Betanian police, has been a federal employee since 1973. In 2017, the European Union adopts a "general bonus" directive. This directive has several articles. Article 1 provides: "Every employer employing more than five employees has to pay each of his employees an annual New Year's bonus on December 31 of each year. The bonus amounts to 10% of the monthly salary during the month of December." Article 5 provides: "This directive shall be implemented by June 1, 2018." Beta never implements the directive. At the end of 2018, Hans expects to be paid a New Year's

bonus, but none is forthcoming. More specifically, his employer announces that every worker will receive a 10% bonus, but also notes that this bonus will only be paid to Betanian citizens. Does Hans have a right to be paid the bonus?

4. Assume the same facts as in the previous hypothetical except that this time, Hans works for a private employer. Can Hans demand to be paid the bonus?

Part 5

Current Challenges

∎ ∎ ∎

CHAPTER 19

THE MONETARY UNION

■ ■ ■

Most countries in the European Union now famously share a common currency, the Euro, and a common monetary policy set by the European Central Bank. Those countries that have adopted the euro constitute the Eurozone.

The creation of the Eurozone is among the most important and visible elements of European integration. However, the common currency remains controversial, and some of the European Union's most salient legal questions revolve around the Eurozone.

A. HISTORICAL BACKGROUND

Regarding the historical background of the Eurozone, consider the following excerpt:

PARADISE LOST: CAN THE EUROPEAN UNION EXPEL COUNTRIES FROM THE EUROZONE
Jens Dammann
49 VAND. J. TRANSNAT'L L. 693 (2016) (citations omitted)

The history of European monetary unification did not start with the introduction of a common currency. Long before the euro was introduced on January 1, 1999, most member states of the European Union sought to stabilize their currency exchange rates by means of the so-called European Monetary System (EMS). At the core of EMS, which was created in 1979, was the so-called Exchange Rate Mechanism (ERM). Currency exchange rates were permitted to fluctuate within certain narrow boundaries—usually 2.25 percent up or down—but were otherwise fixed.

In practice, this system was not without limitations. Because the economies of the member states developed differently over time, the relevant exchange rates had to be adjusted—or "realigned"—regularly. In addition, both the United Kingdom and Italy had to withdraw from the Exchange Rate Mechanism because their currencies came under too much pressure; and whereas Italy eventually returned to the Exchange Rate Mechanism, the United Kingdom did not.

In any case, supporters of European integration had much loftier goals than the mere stabilization of currency exchange rates; they strove for a

European currency. However, this project faced both political and economic obstacles, and an understanding of these obstacles is crucial to comprehending the Eurozone's current crisis.

Political opposition to a common currency arose from the fact that citizens in states with stable currencies were reluctant to exchange it for a common European currency and a common European monetary policy, which they feared might bring the high inflation rates common in Southern Europe. This fear was particularly pronounced in Germany, a country that had experienced hyperinflation after both World War I and World War II and whose citizens were therefore particularly afraid of exchanging a hard currency for a soft one.

To allay German fears of inflation, the member states went out of their way to design a European monetary system that would address this concern, and as a result, European constitutional law imposes much more rigid strictures on monetary policy than U.S. federal law, let alone U.S. constitutional law, does.

To begin with, the Treaty on the Functioning of the European Union explicitly provides that the European Central Bank must focus primarily on price stability in fashioning its monetary policy, a principle often referred to as the "primacy of price stability." This principle stands in obvious contrast to other areas of European law, where institutions can choose between a broad range of policy goals and weigh them according to political expediency. It also contrasts quite vividly with U.S. law, since the Federal Reserve is authorized to balance the goal of stable prices with other competing policy goals, including "maximum employment" and "moderate long-term interest rates."

Moreover, in order to become part of the Eurozone, a member state first has to meet the so-called convergence criteria. These criteria include, inter alia, a high degree of price stability, stable currency exchange rates, the sustainability of the government's financial position, as well as stable long-term interest-rate levels. Of particular practical importance is the second one of these requirements. Under this criterion, a country's total government debt must not exceed 60 percent of GDP, and the budget deficit must not be more than 3 percent of GDP.

To enforce even greater fiscal discipline, the member states entered into the so-called Stability and Growth Pact. The Stability and Growth Pact effectively perpetuates the convergence criteria by requiring each member state to stay within the limits on government debt and budget deficits described above even after joining the Eurozone. Moreover, the requirements of the Stability and Growth Pact are accompanied by a regime of escalating interventions, culminating in the imposition of fines of up to 0.5 percent of a member state's GDP.

In addition to these various legal mechanisms designed to safeguard monetary stability, the European Union took the symbolically important step of locating the European Central Bank in Frankfurt, the same city that is home to the Bundesbank, Germany's equivalent of the Federal Reserve. In the end, Germany was ready to part with the Deutsche Mark, thereby creating the political consensus necessary for a common European currency.

Of course, there were also challenges of an economic nature. The European Union simply did not satisfy the economic requirements for a successful common currency that the literature on optimal currency areas had developed. In particular, the member states remained in charge of fiscal policy, the general level of political integration remained low, and the same was true for interstate labor mobility. Not surprisingly, therefore, many economists were pessimistic regarding the Eurozone's future.

In the end, these economic reservations were set aside; on January 1, 1999, eleven member states of the European Union, including France, Germany, Italy, and Spain, switched from their national currencies to the euro. Only two years later, Greece followed. Since then, seven other member states have joined the Eurozone, which is now comprised of nineteen of the European Union's twenty-eight member states.

In the first years after the introduction of the euro, the new currency seemed to refute its skeptics. Predictions that the euro might become a soft currency failed to come to pass. Rather, inflation remained low, and the euro held its own vis-à-vis other currencies. Moreover, those member states that had had soft currencies before introducing the euro were now able to borrow at the low rates previously reserved for more stable economies. For some of these member states, the result was rapid growth. This was particularly true for Greece, whose economy expanded dramatically after it joined the Eurozone: In 2000, the year before Greece was admitted to the Eurozone, its per capita GDP was $11,961.67 By 2008, the year that the financial crisis began, Greek per capita GDP had risen to $31,700.68 During that same time, Greek government debt stayed fairly stable as a percentage of GDP. Thus, in 2000, Greek national debt was 108.9 percent of GDP and rose to only 110.6 percent by 2008.

Not surprisingly, therefore, the euro was widely hailed as a stunning success. Indeed, in 2008, shortly before the financial crisis broke, the Chief European Economist at Goldman Sachs, Erik Nielsen, declared that "the Euro and the Euro-zone economy have all the hallmarks of a success, including ... contributing to an unprecedented degree of financial stability."

However, the financial crisis of 2008 proved that such initial enthusiasm had been too sanguine. In Europe, the financial crisis of 2008 quickly turned into a sovereign debt crisis as investors grew fearful that some of the more economically fragile member states—particularly Greece, Ireland, Italy, Portugal, and Spain—might no longer be able to shoulder their debts. By 2010, Greece was on the verge of insolvency. European institutions, in cooperation with member state governments and the IMF, managed to prevent that outcome via a 110 billion euro rescue package adopted in May 2010. However, the financial crisis escalated further, resulting in bailouts for Ireland (2010), Portugal (2011), Greece (2012), Spain (2012), and Cyprus (2012). ∎

B. JOINING AND LEAVING THE EUROZONE

The legal framework of the monetary union is quite complex, but some key elements stand out.

1. BECOMING PART OF THE EUROZONE

While the Treaty on the Functioning of the European Union seeks to establish a common currency, there was some concern that not all Member States were immediately ready for such a step. Against that background, the Treaty imposes a peculiar transition system. Only those Member States that satisfy the so-called convergence criteria defined in the treaty—price stability, stable exchange rates, stable long-term interest rates, and a sustainable financial position on the part of the government—can join the Eurozone.[1]

Member States that have not yet joined the Eurozone for failure to satisfy the convergence criteria are called "Member States with a derogation."[2] At least every two years, the European Central Bank and the Commission are required to report to the Council on the progress made by Member States with a derogation towards fulfilling the convergence criteria. Moreover, any Member State with a derogation can demand that such a report be made even sooner.[3] It is up to the Council to decide, after consulting with the European Parliament, which Member States satisfy the convergence criteria. Crucially, the Treaty imposes a special decision rule for this purpose: the Council "acts having received a recommendation by a qualified majority of those among its Members representing Member States whose currency is the Euro."[4] In other words, it is up to those Members of the European Union, which have already adopted the euro as their currency, to decide who else gets to join the club.

---

[1] Consolidated Version of the Treaty on the Functioning of the European Union, May 9, 2008, 2008 O.J. (C 115) 47 (as in effect after the Treaty of Lisbon) [hereinafter TFEU], art. 140 (listing the convergence criteria); Protocol (No. 13) on the Convergence Criteria, 2010 O.J. (C83) 281 [hereinafter Convergence Protocol] (providing more detailed rules on the meaning and application of the convergence criteria).

[2] TFEU, art. 139.

[3] TFEU, art. 140.

[4] Id.

Note that this framework does not leave it up to the Member States with a derogation to decide whether or not they want to join the Eurozone. Rather, a Member State that satisfies the convergence criteria has a duty to join. However, this duty does not apply to all Member States alike. Two Member States, Denmark and the United Kingdom, negotiated for the right to abstain from adopting the Euro.[5]

QUESTIONS

1. Why might Denmark and the United Kingdom have been reluctant to join the Eurozone?

2. Read Article 140 of the Treaty on European Union. Does this provision impose an explicit duty to join the Eurozone? If not, what arguments can be adduced in support of the claim that Member States with a derogation have to join the Eurozone once they satisfy the convergence criteria.

2. LEAVING THE EUROZONE

Whether and how Member States can leave the Eurozone is controversial.

PARADISE LOST: CAN THE EUROPEAN UNION EXPEL COUNTRIES FROM THE EUROZONE

Jens Dammann
49 VAND. J. TRANSNAT'L L. 693 (2016)

[There are several options for leaving the Eurozone.] These include an amendment to the Treaty on the Functioning of the European Union, a unilateral withdrawal from the European Union, or, more controversially, a unilateral withdrawal from the Eurozone. [. . .]

A. *Exit by Treaty Amendment*

One option that would allow Greece—or any other member state—to leave the Eurozone while staying in the European Union would be to amend the Treaty on the Functioning of the European Union. By universal agreement, the member states remain the "masters of the treaties" and are therefore free to amend the treaties. Hence, one could complement the relevant rules with an explicit right to leave the Eurozone or with an explicit expulsion right. For example, one could provide that, once a member state's total government debt exceeds a certain level relative to the member state's GDP, the other member states can expel that member state by unanimous resolution.

---

[5] Protocol (No. 16) on Certain Provisions Relating to Denmark, 2008 O.J. (C 83) 287; Protocol (No. 15) on Certain Provisions Relating to the United Kingdom of Great Britain and Northern Ireland, 2008 O.J. (C 83) 284.

Alternatively, one could amend the Treaty on the Functioning of the European Union on a case-by-case basis and simply include special rules for individual member states such as Greece. After all, there are already two member states, the United Kingdom and Denmark, that are subject to special treatment vis-à-vis the introduction of the euro: unlike other member states, which are under an obligation to join the Eurozone once they fulfill the relevant preconditions, both the United Kingdom and Denmark have reserved the right to stay outside the Eurozone, and, so far, both countries have made full use of that right.

However, amending the Treaties is a rather challenging task. Every single member state would have to sign and ratify such an amendment. Given that the European Union now has twenty-eight different member states, a unanimous consensus is rather difficult to achieve. In any case, given that the current Greek government is firmly opposed to leaving the Eurozone, a treaty amendment aimed at facilitating such an exit seems out of the question for the time being.

B. Withdrawal from the European Union

Another way for a member state to leave the Eurozone is to leave the European Union entirely. This option has the advantage that it is legally uncontroversial. Article 50 of the Treaty on European Union (TEU) explicitly provides that each member state has the right to withdraw from the European Union. Such a withdrawal would automatically terminate the member state's membership in the Eurozone as well.

Of course, even if a member state were willing to withdraw from the Eurozone, it would hardly be ready to withdraw from the European Union to achieve this aim. Membership in the European Union is the key to accessing Europe's markets. Under the so-called Fundamental Freedoms, firms from one member state can sell their goods and services in other member states without having to worry about customs duties or equivalent measures, workers are free to take up employment in other states, citizens of one state are free to establish companies in another state, and capital can be moved freely from member state to member state. If a member state were to leave the European Union, its firms and citizens would lose these rights. Of course, some access to European markets may still be granted via bilateral agreements. However, the outcome of bilateral negotiations is difficult to predict. All this suggests that leaving the European Union would be a recipe for economic disaster.

C. Withdrawal from the Eurozone

The question remains whether EU law allows a member state to withdraw unilaterally from the Eurozone, while remaining in the European Union. Neither the Treaty on European Union nor the Treaty on the Functioning of the European Union explicitly mentions a right to withdraw from the Eurozone. However, scholars disagree about how to interpret this silence.

The traditional view has been that EU law does not permit such a unilateral withdrawal. However, in related work, I have argued that this traditional view is mistaken. A more persuasive interpretation of the Treaty on the Functioning of the European Union is that any member state can withdraw from the Eurozone if it no longer fulfills the preconditions for joining the Eurozone in the first place. ■

QUESTIONS

1. What arguments, if any, might support a right to leave the Eurozone?

2. What arguments, if any, could be adduced against the existence of a right to leave the Eurozone without, at the same time, leaving the European Union?

3. The Treaty does not mention any right to expel the Member States from the Eurozone. Can you think of any arguments in favor or against such a right?

4. Would Member States be more or less likely to join the Eurozone if they knew they had the right to withdraw from the Eurozone later on? Would they be more likely or less likely to join the Eurozone if there existed a right to expel Member States from the Eurozone?

5. In the above excerpt, I argue that no Member State would want to leave the Eurozone if doing so would mean leaving the European Union as well. Shortly after the article was published, the United Kingdom formally notified the European Council of its intention to withdraw from the EU under Article 50 TEU. Does this suggest that a Member State in economic difficulties will simply choose to leave the European Union in order to get rid of the euro?

C. THE MONETARY UNION: AN ECONOMIC PERSPECTIVE

Before examining the rules that govern economic and monetary policy in the European Union, it is helpful to address some of the economic objections against the monetary union.

Long before the creation of the monetary union, economists contemplated the problem of the so-called optimal currency area (OCA). In 1961, the Canadian economist Robert Mundell published a landmark paper in which he posited four main criteria for an optimal currency area.[6] These include labor mobility, capital mobility, similar business cycles across the currency area, and currency risk-sharing in the sense that economically

---

[6] Robert A. Mundell, *A Theory of Optimal Currency Areas*, 51 AM. ECON. REV. 657 (1961).

prosperous regions within the currency union make transfers to economically troubled areas.[7]

More recently, economists have particularly stressed the importance of two of these factors, namely labor mobility and risk-sharing.[8] They also note that the latter—risk sharing—will require "fiscal integration." The term "fiscal integration" is used with different meanings. In the narrow sense, it means implies the adoption of a common budget and common fiscal rules. In the context of the European Union, this would mean aggressively expanding the European Union's budget at the expense of Member State budgets, thereby enabling the European Union to effect transfers to Member States that are hit by economic crises. However, in a broader sense, fiscal integration is also used to refer to other mechanisms that allow for risk-sharing. These would include, for example, an EU-wide unemployment insurance. Because unemployment insurance benefits are more likely to be received by households situated in countries whose economies perform poorly, an EU-wide unemployment insurance would essentially transfer funds from countries whose economies do well to countries in economic difficulties.

To illustrate these concepts, consider the following stylized example. Assume that two European countries, Alpha and Beta, have quite different economies. Alpha produces cars, whereas Beta produces bicycles. Owing to language barriers, workers cannot usually relocate from one country to the other. Moreover, assume that firms cannot shift production from one Member State to another. Furthermore, for the sake of simplicity, assume that all bicycles and cars are exported to a foreign country, say the United States. All exported goods are paid in the currency of the exporting country.[9]

Now assume an exogenous change in circumstances, a so-called "shock," that impacts both economies differently ("asymmetrically"). For example, let us say that oil prices—and hence the cost of fuel—suddenly drop due to technological advances in oil exploration. As a result, driving a car suddenly becomes cheaper, and some consumers will switch from riding a bicycle to driving a car. How will this impact the economies of Alpha and Beta?

Consider, first, a scenario in which Alpha and Beta have different currencies. Let's say that Alpha has alphadollars and Beta has betadollars. And let's say that before the shock occurred, the value of the U.S. dollar

---

[7] *Id.*

[8] *Cf.* Paul Krugman, *Revenge of the Optimal Currency* Area, 27 NBER MACROECONOMICS ANNUAL 439 (2013).

[9] This assumption helps to make the following discussion easier to understand. However, nothing would change if one assumed that foreign customers paid in US dollar and the sellers then converted their revenues into their home country's currency in order to pay their workers, suppliers, etc.

was the same as that of the alphadollar and also identical to that of the betadollar. As the price of fuel drops, more U.S. customers will want to buy cars and fewer of them will want to buy bicycles. It follows that fewer customers will want to exchange their U.S. dollars for Beta's currency to pay for Beta's bicycles, whereas more U.S. customers will want to exchange their U.S. dollars for Alpha's currency to pay for cars produced in Alpha. As a result, the value of Beta's currency will fall relative to the U.S. dollar, whereas the value of Alpha's currency will rise relative to the U.S. dollar. So let's say that one alphadollar now trades at two US dollars, whereas one betadollar now trades 0.5 US dollars.

These changes in currency exchange rates have important implications. To begin, as Beta's currency loses value relative to the US Dollar, Beta's exports become cheaper for U.S. customers. Therefore, the declining value of Beta's currency counterbalances, to some extent, the reduced demand for bicycles. This is quite intuitive. If a bicycle cost 100 betadollars before the shock and 100 betadollars after the shock, this means that the price in U.S. dollars declined by half. 100 US dollars would buy 1 bicycle from Beta before the shock occurred, but the same 100 US dollars will buy 2 bicycles from Beta after the shock and the accompanying devaluation of the betadollar. Beta's bicycle producers may still have to lower their prices as the demand for bicycles declines, but because Beta's currency is now cheaper for foreigners to buy, they don't have to lower the price of their bicycles as much as they would if Beta's currency had not declined in value. On the other hand, the rising value of Alpha's currency means that Alpha's cars will become more expensive for foreigners to buy. Because of this currency effect, Alpha's exporters cannot raise the prices of their cars as much as they otherwise would.

But the changes in exchange rates also impact consumers in countries Alpha and Beta. As the currency of Alpha rises, it becomes cheaper for Alpha's workers to buy foreign goods. Thus, for Alpha's workers and retirees, the fact that Alpha's currency becomes more valuable functions like a pay increase. By contrast, Beta's workers effectively suffer a pay cut: they may still receive the same amount of betadollars each month, but their salary will now buy them fewer U.S. goods.

Note that this de-facto paycut is rather important for employers in Beta. Without the devaluation of the betadollar, Beta's firms would be caught between a rock and a hard place. They would have to slash their prices in order to be able to sell their bicycles in the face of weakened demand for bicycles. At the same time, they would still have to pay the same wages as before. Of course, they could try to reduce wages. But, in practice, this is hard to do, especially in Europe, where wages are frequently set by collective bargaining agreements. Thus, Beta's firms might find it very difficult to manufacture bicycles as a profit. As a result, they might be tempted to decrease production, leading to higher unemployment. The devaluation of the betadollar attenuates this problem by lowering the real wages of workers in Beta and making Beta's goods more competitive in international markets.

Alpha's firms and workers experience the opposite effects. As a result of the alphadollar's rise against the U.S. dollar, Alpha's workers experience a de-facto pay-increase: their salary now allows them to buy more goods produced in the United States. At the same time, the alphadollar's rise against the U.S. dollar also means that Alpha's goods become more expensive for U.S. buyers. Thus, Alpha's firms will not expand their production as much as they otherwise would.

Now let us assume that Alpha and Beta have the same currency in the form of the euro, and let us further assume that they are the only two countries sharing that currency. What happens then?

As before, lower fuel prices means that U.S. consumers will want to buy fewer bicycles and more cars. But since both bicycles and cars are produced in countries that have the euro as their currency, the value of the euro relative to the dollar may not change as much as in the previous hypothetical: after the fuel prices fall, fewer U.S. consumers will exchange their U.S. dollars into euros to buy bicycles, but more of them will exchange their U.S. dollars into euros to buy cars, so these shifts counterbalance each other to some extent.

Because the bicycle-producing firms in Beta can no longer count as much on a devalued currency to make their exports to the U.S. cheaper for U.S. consumers, they need to slash their prices. But for the reasons explained above, they will often find it difficult to also lower the wages they pay to their workers. As a result, they will decrease production, and high unemployment follows. For Alpha's car manufacturers, things look much brighter. They can increase the prices for their cars without having to worry as much as without the existence of the euro that their own currency's rise against the dollar makes their exports more expense to U.S. consumers. Thus Alpha's car manufacturers will expand production. This will work well as long as additional job applicants are available. But at some point, Alpha's firms have to contend with labor shortages.

The resulting situation with unemployment in Beta and potential labor shortages in Alpha not only threatens to lead to substantial human misery, but also creates obvious inefficiencies. From an economic perspective, a good should be produced in the way that creates the lowest costs. But in the situation at hand, highly productive workers in Beta remain unemployed, whereas employers in Alpha have to resort to hiring much less productive workers to respond to labor shortages.

This is where labor mobility enters the picture. The human and economic costs of asymmetric shocks in a common currency area could be greatly reduced if workers were completely mobile. Differently put, if

Beta's workers could easily migrate from Beta to Alpha and work in Alpha's automobile industry, Beta would avoid high unemployment and Alpha would avoid labor shortages.

Of course, other problems would remain. For example, what about Beta's retirees and welfare recipients? If production moves from Beta to Alpha, so will tax revenues. This is where fiscal integration comes in. As long as transfers are made between from Alpha to Beta, the hardships that the citizens of Beta suffer can be attenuated.

In countries like the United States, both of these requirements for an optimal currency union—labor mobility and transfer payments—are met to a substantial degree. It is fairly common for Americans to move from one state to another for employment related reasons. And mechanisms like social security or federal income taxes help to facilitate substantial wealth transfers between states.[10] For example, assume that one state—say Florida—undergoes a severe recession. In that case, Florida taxpayers will have less income and thus pay lower federal income and Medicare taxes as well as lower Social Security contributions. At the same time, they receive at least the same amount of federal spending. Typically, federal spending will even increase given that Medicaid payments and other forms of support tend to increase during recessions.

By contrast, in the European Union the economic case for a common currency area is much more difficult to make. The fact that the Treaty on the Functioning of the European Union guarantees the free movement of workers helps to increase labor mobility. But workers still face language, cultural, and numerous other barriers. Imagine if you had to emigrate to Finland, France or Germany after having grown up and attended college in some other country with a different language. Moreover, the European Union still lacks an EU-level income tax or an EU-level social safety net. The Member States make financial contributions to the EU budget, but in terms of sheer size these contributions remain far below what would be necessary for EU spending to rival federal spending in the United States. For example, the 2018 EU budget is set at 160.1 billion Euros (or about 182 billion US dollars). Compare this to the federal budget in the United States, which is set at 4.1 trillion US dollars).

NOTES AND QUESTIONS

1. Do you think that worker mobility in the United States and/or Europe has increased or decreased over time? What role does home ownership play in this context?

---

[10] *Cf.* Paul Krugman, *Revenge of the Optimal Currency* Area, 27 NBER MACROECONOMICS ANNUAL 439 (2013).

2. Can you think of any reforms that might bring the European Union closer to satisfying the preconditions for an optimal currency area? Why might these reforms face political obstacles?

3. Some argue that even if fiscal integration within the European Union has been insufficient to justify the introduction of a common currency, the creation of the Eurozone was nonetheless a savvy move since it forces Europe to finally embark on a course towards more fiscal integration? Do you agree with this logic? Can you think of any counterarguments?

4. Can one argue that in practice, firms' ability to shift production to other Member States essentially eliminates the need for worker mobility?

D. THE STATE OF ECONOMIC AND FISCAL INTEGRATION

The Treaty on the Functioning of the European Union contains various provisions to ensure not only a European monetary policy, but also a certain amount of coordination regarding economic policies. Nonetheless, it is quite striking that the European Union has gone much further in the former field than in the latter.

1. MONETARY POLICY

Within the Eurozone, European monetary policy is now within the hands of the European Central Bank (ECB).

a) The European Central Bank's Organization

The European Central Bank has two governing bodies: the governing council and the executive board.[11] The executive board consists of the president, the vice president, and four other members. All of the executive board's members, including the president and vice president, are appointed by the European Council.[12] The appointment is for an eight-year term and none of the members can be reappointed.[13] The governing council includes both the members of the executive board and the governors of the central banks of the Eurozone countries.[14] Each member of the governing council has one vote.[15] In order to vote, a two-thirds quorum of the voting members is necessary.[16] As a general rule, the governing council acts by simple majority.[17]

---

[11] TFEU, art. 129(1).
[12] TFEU, art. 283(2).
[13] *Id.*
[14] TFEU, art. 283(1).
[15] Protocol on the Statute of the European System of Central Banks and of the European Central Bank, art. 10(2).
[16] *Id.*
[17] *Id.*

b) Responsibility for Monetary Policy

Under Art. 282(1) TFEU, the European Central Bank, together with the national central banks of those member states whose currency is the Euro, conducts the European Union's monetary policy. Together, the European Central Bank and the central banks of the Eurozone countries form the European System of Central Banks (ECBS).[18]

Within the European System of Central Banks, however, it is the European Central Bank—rather than the national central banks—that holds the reins. Thus, the European Central Bank has "the exclusive right to authorize the issue of euro banknotes."[19] The national banks, meanwhile, are under an obligation to follow guidelines and instructions issued by the European Central Bank.[20]

Crucially, though, the Treaty on the Function of the European Union seeks to impose strong substantive constraints on the European Union's monetary policy. The "primary objective" of the European System of Central Banks (ECBS) is to "maintain price stability."[21] Admittedly, the ECBS is also tasked with supporting "the general economic policies in the Union," but that responsibility must not come at the expense of the primary goal of maintaining price stability.[22] In other words, the ECBS can pursue goals such as low unemployment or economic growth, but only to the extent that doing so does not come at the expense of price stability. This is quite different from the rules governing the U.S. Federal Reserve's policy, which authorizes the Federal Reserve to balance the goal of stable prices with other goals such as "maximum employment" and "moderate long-term interest rates."[23]

In recent years, much controversy has surrounded the question to what extent the European Central Bank has stayed faithful to the goal of maintaining price stability. One particularly thorny question involved the European Central Bank's so-called Outright Monetary Transactions (OMTs): in the course of the euro crisis, several of the economically weaker Member States, most notably Greece, had trouble borrowing money from private lenders. Private investors feared that these Member States might eventually become insolvent and fail to repay their debts. In part to alleviate this problem, the European Central Bank resorted to buying large quantities of bonds issued by Member State governments, thereby providing these Member State governments with liquidity. This policy met with severe criticism from some of the wealthier Member States that

---

[18] TFEU, art. 282(1).
[19] TFEU, art. 128.
[20] Protocol on the Statute of the European System of Central Banks and of the European Central Bank, art. 14(3).
[21] *Id.* art. 282(2).
[22] *Id.*
[23] 12 U.S.C. § 225a (2018).

viewed it as a transfer of wealth from richer to poorer states and argued that the European Central Bank had overstepped its authority under the Treaty.

In fact, the European Central Bank's OMT program could be argued to have two main goals. First, it provided the economically weaker Member States with much needed liquidity and thereby protected their economies against collapse. Second, though, the OMT program could potentially be viewed as a tool for restoring the European Central Bank's control over the European monetary system.

This second point is a bit less obvious, and hence an explanation is in order. Central banks play an important role in the economy by exercising a certain amount of control over the amount of money in the economy as well as the inflation rate. To do so, central banks have various instruments at their disposal. These instruments include reserve requirements, discount rates, and open market transactions.

For example, assume that a central bank is concerned that the economy is suffering from a shortage of credit, meaning that firms and perhaps consumers find it too hard to borrow. In that case, the central bank can lower reserve requirements—the amount of funds that ordinary banks are obligated to hold in reserve when they extend loans. As a result, ordinary banks can more easily extend credit, which in turn makes it easier for households or firms to borrow. The central bank can also lower the so-called discount rate, which is the interest rate paid by ordinary banks on short term loans that they receive from the central bank. If ordinary banks have to pay a lower interest rate to the central bank, they can afford to extend credit more cheaply to firms and households. Finally, the central bank can engage in so-called open market transactions. For example, assume that the central bank buys large quantities of bonds issued by ordinary banks or firms. In that case, the central bank creates additional demand for such bonds. Under the law of supply and demand, this will mean that firms and banks issuing the relevant bonds find it easier to sell them and can therefore lower the interest rate that they are offering to the investors who buy the pertinent bonds. In other words, buying bonds on the open market is one more way for the central bank of making it cheaper for private banks or firms to borrow money.

At the time of the euro crisis, one could reasonably argue that traditional instruments of monetary policy such as the discount rate or reserve requirements were no longer functioning properly: if investors feared that one or more of the economically weaker Member States might become insolvent and that the euro area might break up as a result, then investors might be reluctant to extend credit regardless of the reserve rates or the discount rate.

Against that background, providing liquidity to Member States in trouble via open market transactions (OMTs) could be viewed as a way of restoring the effectiveness of the European Central Bank's control over monetary policy.

PETER GAUWEILER ET AL. V. DEUTSCHER BUNDESTAG
ECJ, Case C-62/14, June 16, 2015

1. This request for a preliminary ruling concerns the validity of the decisions of the Governing Council of the European Central Bank (ECB) of 6 September 2012 [. . .] regarding the Eurosystem's outright monetary transactions in secondary sovereign bond markets ("the OMT decisions") . . . .

33. The referring court raises the question of whether a programme for the purchase of government bonds on secondary markets, such as the programme announced in the press release [by which the ECB's governing council announced the OMT program], can be covered by the powers of the ESCB, as defined by primary law. [. . .]

The delimitation of monetary policy

46. The Court has held that in order to determine whether a measure falls within the area of monetary policy it is appropriate to refer principally to the objectives of that measure. The instruments which the measure employs in order to attain those objectives are also relevant [. . .].

50. The ability of the ESCB to influence price developments by means of its monetary policy decisions in fact depends, to a great extent, on the transmission of the "impulses" which the ESCB sends out across the money market to the various sectors of the economy. Consequently, if the monetary policy transmission mechanism is disrupted, that is likely to render the ESCB's decisions ineffective in a part of the euro area and, accordingly, to undermine the singleness of monetary policy. Moreover, since disruption of the transmission mechanism undermines the effectiveness of the measures adopted by the ESCB, that necessarily affects the ESCB's ability to guarantee price stability. Accordingly, measures that are intended to preserve that transmission mechanism may be regarded as pertaining to the primary objective laid down in Article 127(1) TFEU.

51. The fact that a programme such as that announced in the press release might also be capable of contributing to the stability of the euro area, which is a matter of economic policy . . ., does not call that assessment into question.

52. Indeed, a monetary policy measure cannot be treated as equivalent to an economic policy measure merely because it may have indirect effects on the stability of the euro area. . . .

55. As regards the selective nature of the programme announced in the press release, it should be borne in mind that the programme is intended to rectify the disruption to the monetary policy transmission mechanism caused by the specific situation of government bonds issued by certain Member States. In those circumstances, the mere fact that the programme is specifically limited to those government bonds is thus not of a nature to imply, of itself, that the instruments used by the ESCB fall outside the realm of monetary policy. Moreover, no provision of the TFEU Treaty requires the ESCB to operate in the financial markets by means of general measures that would necessarily be applicable to all the States of the euro area.

56. In the light of those considerations, it is apparent that a programme such as that announced in the press release, in view of its objectives and the instruments provided for achieving them, falls within the area of monetary policy. [. . .]

Proportionality

66. It follows from Articles 119(2) TFEU and 127(1) TFEU, read in conjunction with Article 5(4) TEU, that a bond-buying programme forming part of monetary policy may be validly adopted and implemented only in so far as the measures that it entails are proportionate to the objectives of that policy.

67. In that regard, it should be borne in mind that, according to the settled case-law of the Court, the principle of proportionality requires that acts of the EU institutions be appropriate for attaining the legitimate objectives pursued by the legislation at issue and do not go beyond what is necessary in order to achieve those objectives . . . .

68. As regards judicial review of compliance with those conditions, since the ESCB is required, when it prepares and implements an open market operations programme of the kind announced in the press release, to make choices of a technical nature and to undertake forecasts and complex assessments, it must be allowed, in that context, a broad discretion . . . .

72. As regards, in the first place, the appropriateness of a programme such as that announced in the press release for achieving the ESCB's objectives, it is apparent from the press release and from the explanations provided by the ECB that the programme is based on an analysis of the economic situation of the euro area, according to which, at the date of the programme's announcement, interest rates on the government bonds of various States of the euro area were characterised by high volatility and extreme spreads. According to the ECB, those spreads were not accounted for solely by macroeconomic differences between the States concerned but were caused, in part, by the demand for excessive risk premia for the bonds

issued by certain Member States, such premia being intended to guard against the risk of a break-up of the euro area.

73. According to the ECB, that special situation severely undermined the ESCB's monetary policy transmission mechanism in that it gave rise to fragmentation as regards bank refinancing conditions and credit costs, which greatly limited the effects of the impulses transmitted by the ESCB to the economy in a significant part of the euro area.

74. Having regard to the information placed before the Court in the present proceedings, it does not appear that that analysis of the economic situation of the euro area as at the date of the announcement of the programme in question is vitiated by a manifest error of assessment. [. . .]

77. In those circumstances, the ESCB was entitled to take the view that such a development in interest rates is likely to facilitate the ESCB's monetary policy transmission and to safeguard the singleness of monetary policy. . . .

80. It follows from the foregoing that, in economic conditions such as those described by the ECB at the date of the press release, the ESCB could legitimately take the view that a programme such as that announced in the press release is appropriate for the purpose of contributing to the ESCB's objectives and, therefore, to maintaining price stability.

81. Accordingly, it should, in the second place, be established whether such a programme does not go manifestly beyond what is necessary to achieve those objectives.

82. It must be noted in that regard that the wording of the press release makes quite clear that, under the programme at issue in the main proceedings, the purchase of government bonds on secondary markets is permitted only in so far as it is necessary to achieve the objectives of that programme and that such purchases will cease as soon as those objectives have been achieved. [. . .]

91. In the third place, the ESCB weighed up the various interests in play so as to actually prevent disadvantages from arising, when the programme in question is implemented, which are manifestly disproportionate to the programme's objectives.

92. It follows from the foregoing considerations that a programme such as that announced in the press release does not infringe the principle of proportionality.

Article 123(1) TFEU

93. The referring court raises the issue of the compatibility with Article 123(1) TFEU of a programme for the purchase of government bonds on secondary markets, such as the programme announced in the press release.

94. It is clear from its wording that Article 123(1) TFEU prohibits the ECB and the central banks of the Member States from granting overdraft facilities or any other type of credit facility to public authorities and bodies of the Union and of Member States and from purchasing directly from them their debt instruments [. . .].

95. It follows that that provision prohibits all financial assistance from the ESCB to a Member State [. . .], but does not preclude, generally, the possibility of the ESCB purchasing from the creditors of such a State, bonds previously issued by that State. [. . .]

97. Nevertheless, the ESCB does not have authority to purchase government bonds on secondary markets under conditions which would, in practice, mean that its action has an effect equivalent to that of a direct purchase of government bonds from the public authorities and bodies of the Member States, thereby undermining the effectiveness of the prohibition in Article 123(1) TFEU.

98. In addition, in order to determine which forms of purchases of government bonds are compatible with Article 123(1) TFEU, it is necessary to take account of the objective pursued by that provision [. . .].

99. To that end, it must be recalled that the origin of the prohibition laid down in Article 123 TFEU is to be found in Article 104 of the EC Treaty (which became Article 101 EC), which was inserted in the EC Treaty by the Treaty of Maastricht.

100. It is apparent from the preparatory work relating to the Treaty of Maastricht that the aim of Article 123 TFEU is to encourage the Member States to follow a sound budgetary policy, not allowing monetary financing of public deficits or privileged access by public authorities to the financial markets to lead to excessively high levels of debt or excessive Member State deficits [. . .].

102. It follows that, as the Advocate General has observed in point 227 of his Opinion, when the ECB purchases government bonds on secondary markets, sufficient safeguards must be built into its intervention to ensure that the latter does not fall foul of the prohibition of monetary financing in Article 123(1) TFEU.

103. As regards a programme such as that announced in the press release, it must in the first place be stated that, in the framework of such a programme, the ESCB is entitled to purchase government bonds—not directly, from public authorities or bodies of the Member States—but only indirectly, on secondary markets. Intervention by the ESCB of the kind provided for by a programme such as that at issue in the main proceedings thus cannot be treated as equivalent to a measure granting financial assistance to a Member State. [. . .]

109. In the third place, a programme such as that announced in the press release would circumvent the objective of Article 123(1) TFEU, recalled in paragraph 100 of this judgment, if that programme were such as to lessen the impetus of the Member States concerned to follow a sound budgetary policy. In fact, since it follows from Articles 119(2) TFEU, 127(1) TFEU and 282(2) TFEU that, without prejudice to the objective of price stability, the ESCB is to support the general economic policies in the Union, the action taken by the ESCB on the basis of Article 123 TFEU cannot be such as to contravene the effectiveness of those polices by lessening the impetus of the Member States concerned to follow a sound budgetary policy.

110. Moreover, the conduct of monetary policy will always entail an impact on interest rates and bank refinancing conditions, which necessarily has consequences for the financing conditions of the public deficit of the Member States.

111. In any event, the Court finds that the features of a programme such as that announced in the press release exclude the possibility of that programme being considered of such a kind as to lessen the impetus of the Member States to follow a sound budgetary policy.

112. In that regard, it must be borne in mind, first, that the programme provides for the purchase of government bonds only in so far as is necessary for safeguarding the monetary policy transmission mechanism and the singleness of monetary policy and that those purchases will cease as soon as those objectives are achieved.

113. That limitation on the ESCB's intervention means (i) that the Member States cannot, in determining their budgetary policy, rely on the certainty that the ESCB will at a future point purchase their government bonds on secondary markets and (ii) that the programme in question cannot be implemented in a way which would bring about a harmonisation of the interest rates applied to the government bonds of the Member States of the euro area regardless of the differences arising from their macroeconomic or budgetary situation.

114. The adoption and implementation of such a programme thus do not permit the Member States to adopt a budgetary policy which fails to take account of the fact that they will be compelled, in the event of a deficit, to seek financing on the markets, or result in them being protected against the consequences which a change in their macroeconomic or budgetary situation may have in that regard.

127. In view of all the foregoing considerations, the answer to the questions referred is that Articles 119 TFEU, 123(1) TFEU and 127(1) and (2) TFEU and Articles 17 to 24 of the Protocol on the ESCB and the ECB must be interpreted as permitting the ESCB to adopt a programme for the purchase of government bonds on secondary markets, such as the

programme announced in the press release [announcing the OMT program]. ∎

NOTES AND QUESTIONS

1. How does the level of scrutiny that the Court applies to the ECB's measures compare to that which the Court applies to measures taken by the Member States?

2. What might be the purpose of Article 123(1) TFEU? How does the Court deal with that provision? Do you find the Court's reasoning convincing?

3. Critics of outright monetary transactions are concerned that they amount to a redistribution of wealth between richer and poorer Member States. Setting aside the question of whether such redistribution is desirable as a matter of fairness or policy, are outright monetary transactions likely to have a redistributive effect?

4. Assume that the primacy of price stability provided for in the Treaty on the Functioning of European Union or the prohibition in Article 123 TFEU prove to be highly undesirable as a matter of economic policy. In this case, one possibility would be for the Member States to change the Treaty, though the unanimity requirement makes such a change quite difficult. Another possibility is for the Court of Justice to interpret the relevant norms restrictively. What might be the advantages of the latter approach, and what might be the downsides?

5. Read Article 125 TFEU. In what sense does that provision complement Article 123 TFEU? Could you argue that one of the two provisions is superfluous?

6. The Court of Justice considers the possibility that OTMs might weaken the Member States' resolve to "follow a sound budgetary policy." How does the Court address this concern? Is the Court's position convincing?

7. The Member States whose government bonds are bought in open market transactions are immediate beneficiaries of such transactions. Can you argue that the remaining Member States benefit as well? Or are they simply bearing the burden of such transactions?

CHAPTER 20

LEAVING THE EUROPEAN UNION

■ ■ ■

Art. 50 of the Treaty on European Union explicitly grants Member States the right to leave the European Union.

Until recently, this so-called withdrawal right was largely considered to be of mere theoretical interest. However, that drastically changed when, following a referendum in 2016, the United Kingdom formally notified the European Council of its intention to withdraw from the European Union effective March 29, 2018.[1]

Now the withdrawal right in Article 50 TFEU has moved to the forefront of the scholarly debate. However, European scholarship is only beginning to tackle the numerous legal issues associated with a State's withdrawal from the European Union.

A. HISTORICAL BACKGROUND

The withdrawal right in Article 50 of the Treaty on European Union is of relative recent origin.

REVOKING BREXIT: CAN MEMBER STATES RESCIND THEIR DECLARATION OF WITHDRAWAL FROM THE EUROPEAN UNION?

Jens Dammann
23 COLUM. J. EUR. L. 265, 271 (2017) (citations omitted)

Article 50 of the Treaty on European Union explicitly gives the Member States a right to withdraw. Yet this provision is of fairly recent origin. It was introduced into European law only with the Treaty of Lisbon of 2007, which entered into force in 2009. Before the Treaty of Lisbon, the question of whether countries could leave the European Union without the consent of the other Member States had long been the subject of heated debate.

A. From 1957 to the European Convention

When the European Economic Community (EEC), the precursor of today's European Union, was created in 1957, the relevant Treaty provided

---

[1] Stephen Castle, *U.K. Initiates 'Brexit' and Wades Into a Thorny Thicket*, N.Y. TIMES (Mar. 29, 2017), https://www.nytimes.com/2017/03/29/world/europe/brexit-uk-eu-article-50.html.

that it was concluded "for an unlimited period." However, whether this wording could be read to exclude a withdrawal right was rather unclear, in part because the Treaty's history is ambiguous. On the one hand, when the Treaty was drafted, the inclusion of an explicit withdrawal right had been proposed and rejected. On the other hand, the parties had abandoned an earlier wording according to which the Treaty could not be dissolved. Against this background, the question of whether Member States could withdraw from the European Economic Community, which was later renamed the European Community before it eventually became the European Union, remained controversial.

In the following years, various countries left or came close to leaving the European Union; yet the existence of a withdrawal right remained unresolved. As early as 1962, Algeria gained independence from France. It thus became, strictly speaking, the first country to leave the European Union. However, because Algeria had never been a party to the Treaty Establishing the European Economic Community (EEC Treaty), its departure did not raise the question of a formal withdrawal.

In the seventies, the withdrawal issue almost gained practical relevance. Even though the United Kingdom had only joined the European Economic Community in 1973, Britons soon developed second thoughts. As early as 1974, polls indicated that more British voters disapproved than approved of Britain's membership in the European Economic Community. That same year, Harold Wilson, the Labour Party's candidate for Prime Minister, promised that if elected, he would not only renegotiate the terms of Britain's membership in the European Economic Community, but also hold a referendum on the continuation of that membership. Upon his election, Wilson kept these promises. However, because he managed to portray the fairly modest results of his negotiations as a substantial success, the referendum, which took place in 1975, ended with a landslide victory for the pro-European camp.

In 1981, the Greek government also seemed to be reconsidering its membership in the European Economic Community. Greece had ratified its accession to the Community only two years earlier, in 1979. Yet in 1981, the year that Greece's entry into the European Economic Community took effect, the left-wing party PASOK, which had been opposed to Greece's accession to the EEC and supported a referendum, gained a solid majority in Greece's parliament. However, once in power, PASOK grew more moderate and the referendum never took place.

Soon thereafter, Greenland, which had long been part of Denmark, left the European Economic Community. In 1979, Denmark adopted the so-called Home Rule Act, which granted Greenland far-reaching autonomy. After a referendum in which a clear majority of voters cast their votes in favor of leaving the European Union, Greenland in 1985 submitted a formal request for withdrawal from the EEC. The matter was solved via negotiations, and so Greenland ended up leaving the EEC via multilateral Treaty rather than by unilateral withdrawal. Accordingly, the question of whether a right to unilateral withdrawal existed remained unresolved.

B. From the European Convention to the Treaty of Lisbon

The issue of a formal withdrawal right resurfaced in the context of the so-called European Convention. Chaired by former French President Giscard d'Estaing, the European Convention was established in December 2001 in order to draft a European Constitution, began its work in 2002, and lasted until July 2003. The European Convention consisted of a total of 105 members (conventionnels) as well as numerous other invitees. Aside from the Convention's president and vice-presidents, the voting members represented either the European Union's institutions or the Member State governments or parliaments. Various so-called "candidate countries"—countries formally recognized as prospective Member States—had been allowed to send nonvoting members.

Crucially, of the 105 members of the Convention, only twelve (and one invitee) formed the so-called Praesidium, where many of the most important decisions were made or at least prepared. These twelve members consisted of the chairman Giscard d'Estaing, his various vice-chairmen, and a few other select members.

When the Praesidium presented its preliminary draft for a European Constitution on October 28, 2002, this draft proposed, for the first time, the inclusion of an explicit right to withdraw from the European Union, without, however, going into detail. The Praesidium's next draft, presented on February 4, 2003, contained a fully fleshed out withdrawal right. This version already made it clear that the withdrawal right was to be unconditional and unilateral. The next version, which the Praesidium presented on May 26, 2003, remained largely unchanged but, for the first time, included comments by the Praesidium aimed at justifying the withdrawal right:

The Praesidium considers that the Constitution must contain a provision on voluntary withdrawal from the Union. Although many consider that it is possible to withdraw even in the absence of a specific provision to that effect, the Praesidium feels that inserting a specific provision in the Constitution on voluntary withdrawal from the Union clarifies the situation and allows the introduction of a procedure for negotiating and concluding an agreement between the Union and the Member State concerned setting the arrangements for withdrawal and the framework for future relations. Moreover, the existence of a provision to that effect is an important political signal to anyone inclined to argue that the Union is a rigid entity which it is impossible to leave.

This draft drew numerous comments, and various members of the Convention suggested amendments. Some members of the Convention feared that the provision might be abused as a blunt bargaining tool and that it might even endanger the stability of the European Union. Others voiced the concern that the withdrawal right was contrary to the spirit of European integration as well as to the idea of solidarity between the Member States. Accordingly, many members suggested that the withdrawal right be stricken entirely, made contingent on the conclusion of a Treaty between the European Union and the withdrawing state, or at least limited to certain narrowly defined circumstances. One member even suggested that any withdrawing state should be liable for any damages that such withdrawal caused. Others, however, supported the proposal, and some argued that the withdrawal right was an important affirmation of state sovereignty.

By and large, there was a certain division between old Western European Member States and Central European Member States, which had only recently escaped the Soviet Union. The former sought to have the withdrawal right severely limited or even abolished. But the latter, who had only recently reacquired full national sovereignty with the collapse of the Soviet Union, welcomed the withdrawal right. Moreover, many believed that this was a crucial issue for the newer Member States. In the end, the supporters of the explicit withdrawal right won the day, and the provision was included in the final draft.

Of course, the European Constitution as such never went into force. Signed with great fanfare, it went out with a whimper. Having been ratified by eighteen out of twenty-five Member States, it lost any chance of entering into force when it was rejected by popular referenda in both France and the Netherlands in 2005. However, much of its substance was incorporated into the Treaty of Lisbon that was adopted in 2007 and took effect in 2009. Hence, the withdrawal right survived the inglorious death of the European Constitution with minor changes and can now be found in Article 50 of the Treaty on European Union. ∎

NOTES AND QUESTIONS

1. The question of whether or not Member States can leave the European Union is a matter of fundamental importance. So what might be the reason that the original Treaty Establishing the European Economic Community did not include an explicit and unambiguous rule on the matter?

2. Can you make an argument for why an explicit right of withdrawal might be more important now than in 1957 when the Treaty Establishing the European Economic Community was concluded? Can you come up with counterarguments?

3. In the United States, the attempt of states to secede prompted the American Civil War (1861–1865). Why would the European Union be more willing than the United States to grant states a withdrawal right?

4. The existence of an explicit withdrawal right creates the risk that Member States will use the threat of withdrawal in negotiations with other Member States. Arguably, the United Kingdom tried to do exactly that, albeit with limited success. Consider the following excerpt: "After winning the 2015 election by a substantial margin, [British Prime Minister David Cameron] confronted the other Member States with a list of demands. In particular, he sought four main concessions: (1) he wanted the United Kingdom to be exempt from the European Union's declared goal of an ever-closer union; (2) he wanted national parliaments to be able to block EU legislation; (3) he sought protections for non-Eurozone countries; and most importantly, (4) he demanded the ability to deny welfare benefits to immigrants from other Member States. After some back and forth, a compromise was finally achieved at an EU summit in February 2016. That compromise granted Cameron some of the changes he had sought, but the concessions were heavy on symbolism and light on substance. The other Member States agreed on exempting the United Kingdom from the goal of an ever closer union. However, as many observers were quick to point out, the commitment to an ever closer union is more of a symbolic commitment anyway and derives its legal importance mainly from its relevance to the interpretation of other Treaty provisions. The compromise also banned discrimination against non-Eurozone countries, but the practical relevance of this commitment, too, was dubious. By contrast, when it came to the more significant changes sought by Cameron, the other Member States proved far less generous. Rather than allowing national parliaments to block EU legislation, the compromise only included a rule under which the Council had to reassess any legislative drafts that sufficiently many national Parliaments viewed to be in violation of the so-called principle of subsidiarity. Most importantly, though, the Central European Member States forcefully resisted Cameron's demands on welfare benefits for immigrants, and so the Brussels compromise only made a relatively weak concession to Cameron in this regard: the compromise called for the creation of a mechanism to allow Member States to deny welfare benefits to immigrants, but that mechanism could only be applied in exceptional circumstances, could only remain in place for a maximum of seven years, and could not be renewed."[2] Given British concerns over immigration and the impending referendum, why might the rest of Europe and, in particular, the Central European Member States, have been strongly opposed to any concessions on this issue? Are other Member States likely to be more successful than the United Kingdom in using the threat of withdrawal to obtain concessions in negotiations?

5. Past U.K. governments repeatedly bargained for special treatment and enjoyed some success in doing so. The most famous examples are the so-called "British rebate" and the right not to join the Eurozone. Consider the

---

[2] Jens Dammann, *Revoking Brexit: Can Member States Rescind Their Declaration of Withdrawal from the European Union?*, 23 COLUM. J. EUR. L. 265, 281–82 (2017).

following excerpt: "One of the earlier sources of conflict [between the United Kingdom and the European Economic Community] concerned agricultural subsidies, which made up a large portion of the European Community's budget. Given its relatively small agricultural sector, Britain received a relatively meager share of these subsidies but still had to pay hefty financial contributions to the EEC budget. Moreover, the financial contributions that Member States had to pay to the European Union depended in part on the revenues a Member State derived from its Value Added Tax (VAT); and the United Kingdom had disproportionately high VAT revenues relative to its GDP. In fact, though relatively less prosperous than various other Member States, it was the second largest net contributor to the Community Budget, surpassed only by the then much more prosperous Germany. This enraged British voters and politicians who saw the United Kingdom at a disadvantage vis-à-vis other large Member States, such as France and Italy. The conflict culminated at the Dublin summit in 1979 with Margaret Thatcher's famous demand: "I want my money back." Years of negotiations followed, and at the 1984 European Council meeting at Fontainebleau, the Member States agreed on a mechanism—the so-called "British rebate"—that reduced the United Kingdom's contributions to the Community's budget by about two-thirds. Of course, this compromise came at a cost. Aside from sowing discord among European governments, it has traditionally been exploited as a political argument by euro-skeptics in other countries who complain gleefully about the United Kingdom's special deal. Over the following years, Britain managed to obtain obtained various other exemptions from EU law. Perhaps the most obvious one concerned the European Union's common currency, the euro. Together with Denmark, the United Kingdom negotiated the right to remain outside of the Eurozone, a right that both countries have exercised to this day."[3] Why might Margaret Thatcher have been more successful in demanding concessions from the rest of Europe than David Cameron?

---

[3] Jens Dammann, *Revoking Brexit: Can Member States Rescind Their Declaration of Withdrawal from the European Union?*, 23 COLUM. J. EUR. L. 265, 278–79 (2017).

> ### Margaret Thatcher (1925–2013)
>
>
>
> Margaret Thatcher was a British stateswoman, who served as the first female Prime Minister of the United Kingdom from 1979–90. She was first elected to Parliament in 1959, and twenty years later led the Conservative Party to win the general election of 1979.
>
> Once in office, Thatcher implemented a series of conservative and pro-market reforms that are often referred to as Thatcherism. She privatized public services, abandoned the Keynesian economic policy of prior governments in favor of a more supply-side oriented approach, and closed numerous unprofitable coal mines against the fierce resistance of labor unions. Believing that labor unions had a harmful impact on the economy, she successfully championed legislation that greatly reduced the rights of unions, dealing a harsh blow to organized labor in the United Kingdom. Her policies met with substantial criticism, not just outside, but also from within her own party. However, Thatcher, dubbed the "Iron Lady," pursued her political approach with great determination. When confronted with calls for a change of course at the Conservative Party Conference of 1980, she gave a speech that included her now famous phrase: "The lady's not for turning."
>
> In foreign affairs, Thatcher became a close ally of U.S. President Ronald Reagan. When in 1982, the military regime governing Argentina invaded the Falkland Islands and South Georgia, she had the Islands retaken by British Forces in what is known as the Falkland War.
>
> Thatcher was in favor of the United Kingdom's membership in the European Economic Community, but also took the view that the EEC should mainly focus on free trade.

B. CAN WITHDRAWING MEMBER STATES CHANGE THEIR MINDS?

Article 50 TEU explicitly recognizes that each Member State has the right to withdraw from the European Union. To exercise that right, the Member State has to formally notify the European Council of its intention to withdraw.[4] Following that notification, the European Union and the

---
[4] TFEU, art. 50(1).

withdrawing Member State have two years to negotiate a withdrawal agreement,[5] though that deadline can be extended by a unanimous decision of the Council in agreement with the withdrawing Member State.[6] If no agreement is reached by the original two-year deadline or the extended deadline, if applicable, the withdrawing Member State's membership in the European Union ceases automatically.[7]

Despite these seemingly clear rules, crucial questions remain open. In particular, the Treaty does not explicitly address the issue of whether the withdrawing Member State can change its mind after having notified the European Council of its intention to withdraw.

ANDY WRIGHTMAN ET AL. V. SECRETARY OF STATE FOR EXITING THE EUROPEAN UNION
ECJ, Case C-621/18, December 10, 2018

[The petitioners had lodged a petition in the Court of Session (Scotland, United Kingdom). They sought a declaratory judgment ("declarator") specifying "when and how" the United Kingdom could withdraw its notification of intent to withdraw from the European Union. The first instance judge of the Court of Session, the Lord Ordinary, refused the request for a preliminary reference to the Court of Justice, asserting, inter alia, that the issue was a merely hypothetical one. However, on appeal, the Court of Session, Inner House, First Division (Scotland, United Kingdom), decided to ask the Court of Justice for a preliminary ruling.]

Admissibility

20. The United Kingdom Government argues that the question referred is inadmissible because it is hypothetical. In particular, the United Kingdom Government submits that no draft act of revocation of the notification of the United Kingdom's intention to withdraw from the European Union has been adopted or even contemplated, that there is no dispute in the main proceedings and that the question referred is actually intended to obtain an advisory opinion on a constitutional issue, namely the correct interpretation of Article 50 TEU and of acts adopted pursuant to that article.

21. According to the United Kingdom Government, there is no concrete dispute, since the question referred addresses events that have not occurred and may not occur. The United Kingdom Government submits that it has consistently reiterated its intention to honour the result of the referendum by giving notice under Article 50 TEU and thereby

---

[5] TEU, art. 50(3).
[6] *Id.*
[7] *Id.*

withdrawing from the European Union, whether on the basis of an agreement or without any agreement.

22. The question, according to the United Kingdom Government, actually concerns the legal implications of a situation that does not currently exist. It is based on the assumption, first, that there will be an attempt by the United Kingdom, whether at the instigation of its Parliament or otherwise, to revoke the notification and, secondly, that the European Commission or the other 27 Member States will oppose that revocation. Only in the event of such opposition would a dispute arise. [. . .]

26. In that regard, it should be borne in mind that it is solely for the national court before which the dispute has been brought, and which must assume responsibility for the subsequent judicial decision, to determine in the light of the particular circumstances of the case, both the need for a preliminary ruling in order to enable it to deliver judgment and the relevance of the questions which it submits to the Court. Consequently, where the questions submitted concern the interpretation of a rule of EU law, the Court is in principle bound to give a ruling [. . .].

27. It follows that questions relating to EU law enjoy a presumption of relevance. The Court may refuse to rule on a question referred for a preliminary ruling by a national court only where it is quite obvious that the interpretation of EU law that is sought bears no relation to the actual facts of the main action or its purpose, where the problem is hypothetical, or where the Court does not have before it the factual or legal material necessary to give a useful answer to the questions submitted to it [. . .].

28. It should also be borne in mind that, in accordance with settled case-law, the justification for a reference for a preliminary ruling is not that it enables advisory opinions on general or hypothetical questions to be delivered but rather that it is necessary for the effective resolution of a dispute [. . .].

29. In the present case, it must be noted that an appeal has been brought before the referring court against a decision of the first instance court delivered in the context of an action seeking a declarator specifying whether the notification of the United Kingdom's intention to withdraw from the European Union, given under Article 50 TEU, may be unilaterally revoked before the expiry of the two-year period laid down in that article, with the effect that, if the notification made by the United Kingdom were revoked, that Member State would remain in the European Union. The referring court states, in that respect, that it is required to rule on that question of law, which represents a genuine and live issue, of considerable practical importance, and which has given rise to a dispute. That court emphasises that one of the petitioners and the two interveners, who are Members of the United Kingdom Parliament, must vote on the withdrawal of the United Kingdom from the European Union and, in particular [. . .]

on the ratification of the agreement negotiated between the United Kingdom Government and the European Union pursuant to Article 50 TEU. The referring court states that those Members of the United Kingdom Parliament have an interest in the answer to that question of law, since that answer will clarify the options open to them in exercising their parliamentary mandates.

30. It is not for the Court to call into question the referring court's assessment of the admissibility of the action in the main proceedings, which falls, in the context of the preliminary ruling proceedings, within the jurisdiction of the national court; nor is it for the Court to determine whether the order for reference was made in accordance with the rules of national law governing the organisation of the courts and legal proceedings [. . .].

36. It follows that the question referred is admissible.

Substance

37. The petitioners and the interveners in the main proceedings, while acknowledging that Article 50 TEU does not contain any express rule on the revocation of a notification of the intention to withdraw from the European Union, submit that a right of revocation exists and is unilateral in nature. However, that right may only be exercised in accordance with the constitutional requirements of the Member State concerned, by analogy with the right of withdrawal itself, laid down in Article 50(1) TEU. According to those parties to the main proceedings, the withdrawal procedure therefore continues for as long as the Member State concerned intends to withdraw from the European Union, but comes to an end if, before the end of the period laid down in Article 50(3) TEU, that Member State changes its mind and decides not to withdraw from the European Union.

38. The Council and the Commission, while agreeing that a Member State is entitled to revoke the notification of its intention to withdraw before the Treaties have ceased to apply to that Member State, dispute the unilateral nature of that right.

39. According to those institutions, the recognition of a right of unilateral revocation would allow a Member State that has notified its intention to withdraw to circumvent the rules set out in Article 50(2) and (3) TEU, which are intended to ensure an orderly withdrawal from the European Union, and would open the way for abuse by the Member State concerned to the detriment of the European Union and its institutions.

40. The Council and the Commission argue that the Member State concerned could thus use its right of revocation shortly before the end of the period laid down in Article 50(3) TEU and notify a new intention to withdraw immediately after that period expired, thereby triggering a new

two-year negotiation period. By doing so, the Member State would enjoy, de facto, a right to negotiate its withdrawal without any time limit, rendering the period laid down in Article 50(3) TEU ineffective.

41. In addition, according to those institutions, a Member State could at any time use its right of revocation as leverage in negotiations. If the terms of the withdrawal agreement did not suit that Member State, it could threaten to revoke its notification and thus put pressure on the EU institutions in order to alter the terms of the agreement to its own advantage.

42. In order to guard against such risks, the Council and the Commission propose that Article 50 TEU should be interpreted as allowing revocation, but only with the unanimous consent of the European Council.

43. The United Kingdom Government has not taken a position on the right, for a Member State that has notified its intention to withdraw from the European Union under Article 50 TEU, to revoke that notification.

44. In that respect, it must be borne in mind that the founding Treaties, which constitute the basic constitutional charter of the European Union [. . .], established, unlike ordinary international treaties, a new legal order, possessing its own institutions, for the benefit of which the Member States thereof have limited their sovereign rights, in ever wider fields, and the subjects of which comprise not only those States but also their nationals [. . .].

45. According to settled case-law of the Court, that autonomy of EU law with respect both to the law of the Member States and to international law is justified by the essential characteristics of the European Union and its law, relating in particular to the constitutional structure of the European Union and the very nature of that law. EU law is characterised by the fact that it stems from an independent source of law, namely the Treaties, by its primacy over the laws of the Member States, and by the direct effect of a whole series of provisions which are applicable to their nationals and to the Member States themselves. Those characteristics have given rise to a structured network of principles, rules and mutually interdependent legal relations binding the European Union and its Member States reciprocally as well as binding its Member States to each other (judgment of 6 March 2018, *Achmea*, C-284/16, EU:C:2018:158, paragraph 33 and the case-law cited).

46. The question referred must therefore be examined in the light of the Treaties taken as a whole.

47. In that respect, it should be borne in mind that, according to settled case-law of the Court, the interpretation of a provision of EU law requires that account be taken not only of its wording and the objectives it pursues, but also of its context and the provisions of EU law as a whole.

The origins of a provision of EU law may also provide information relevant to its interpretation [. . .].

48. As regards the wording of Article 50 TEU, it should be noted that that article does not explicitly address the subject of revocation. It neither expressly prohibits nor expressly authorises revocation.

49. That being said, as the Advocate General pointed out in points 99 to 102 of his Opinion, it follows from the wording of Article 50(2) TEU that a Member State which decides to withdraw is to notify the European Council of its 'intention'. An intention is, by its nature, neither definitive nor irrevocable.

50. In addition, Article 50(1) TEU provides that any Member State may decide to withdraw from the European Union in accordance with its own constitutional requirements. It follows that the Member State is not required to take its decision in concert with the other Member States or with the EU institutions. The decision to withdraw is for that Member State alone to take, in accordance with its constitutional requirements, and therefore depends solely on its sovereign choice.

51. Article 50(2) and (3) TEU then set out the procedure to be followed if a Member State decides to withdraw. As the Court held in the judgment of 19 September 2018, *RO* (C-327/18 PPU, EU:C:2018:733, paragraph 46), that procedure consists of, first, notification to the European Council of the intention to withdraw, secondly, negotiation and conclusion of an agreement setting out the arrangements for withdrawal, taking into account the future relationship between the State concerned and the European Union and, thirdly, the actual withdrawal from the Union on the date of entry into force of that agreement or, failing that, two years after the notification given to the European Council, unless the latter, in agreement with the Member State concerned, unanimously decides to extend that period.

52. Article 50(2) TEU refers to Article 218(3) TFEU, according to which the Commission is to submit recommendations to the Council, which is to adopt a decision authorising the opening of negotiations and nominating the European Union negotiator or the head of the European Union's negotiating team.

53. Article 50(2) TEU thus defines the role of the various institutions in the procedure to be followed in order to negotiate and conclude the withdrawal agreement, the conclusion of which requires a decision of the Council, acting by a qualified majority, after obtaining the consent of the European Parliament.

54. In addition, Article 50(3) TEU determines when the withdrawal of the Member State concerned from the European Union will take effect, in providing that the Treaties are to cease to apply to that Member State

from the date of entry into force of the withdrawal agreement or, failing that, two years after the notification by that Member State of its intention to withdraw. That maximum period of two years applies unless the European Council decides, unanimously and in agreement with the Member State concerned, to extend it.

55. After its withdrawal from the European Union, the Member State concerned may ask to rejoin, under the procedure set out in Article 49 TEU.

56. It follows that Article 50 TEU pursues two objectives, namely, first, enshrining the sovereign right of a Member State to withdraw from the European Union and, secondly, establishing a procedure to enable such a withdrawal to take place in an orderly fashion.

57. As the Advocate General stated in points 94 and 95 of his Opinion, the sovereign nature of the right of withdrawal enshrined in Article 50(1) TEU supports the conclusion that the Member State concerned has a right to revoke the notification of its intention to withdraw from the European Union, for as long as a withdrawal agreement concluded between the European Union and that Member State has not entered into force or, if no such agreement has been concluded, for as long as the two-year period laid down in Article 50(3) TEU, possibly extended in accordance with that provision, has not expired.

58. In the absence of an express provision governing revocation of the notification of the intention to withdraw, that revocation is subject to the rules laid down in Article 50(1) TEU for the withdrawal itself, with the result that it may be decided upon unilaterally, in accordance with the constitutional requirements of the Member State concerned.

59. The revocation by a Member State of the notification of its intention to withdraw, before the occurrence of one of the events referred to in paragraph 57 of the present judgment, reflects a sovereign decision by that State to retain its status as a Member State of the European Union, a status which is not suspended or altered by that notification [. . .], subject only to the provisions of Article 50(4) TEU.

60. That revocation is fundamentally different in that respect from any request by which the Member State concerned might ask the European Council to extend the two-year period referred to in Article 50(3) TEU; the analogy that the Commission and the Council seek to make between that revocation and such an extension request cannot therefore be accepted.

61. As regards the context of Article 50 TEU, reference must be made to the 13th recital in the preamble to the TEU, the first recital in the preamble to the TFEU and Article 1 TEU, which indicate that those treaties have as their purpose the creation of an ever closer union among the peoples of Europe, and to the second recital in the preamble to the

TFEU, from which it follows that the European Union aims to eliminate the barriers which divide Europe.

62. It is also appropriate to underline the importance of the values of liberty and democracy, referred to in the second and fourth recitals of the preamble to the TEU, which are among the common values referred to in Article 2 of that Treaty and in the preamble to the Charter of Fundamental Rights of the European Union, and which thus form part of the very foundations of the European Union legal order [. . .].

63. As is apparent from Article 49 TEU, which provides the possibility for any European State to apply to become a member of the European Union and to which Article 50 TEU, on the right of withdrawal, is the counterpart, the European Union is composed of States which have freely and voluntarily committed themselves to those values, and EU law is thus based on the fundamental premises that each Member State shares with all the other Member States, and recognises that those Member States share with it, those same values [. . .].

64. It must also be noted that, since citizenship of the Union is intended to be the fundamental status of nationals of the Member States [. . .], any withdrawal of a Member State from the European Union is liable to have a considerable impact on the rights of all Union citizens, including, inter alia, their right to free movement, as regards both nationals of the Member State concerned and nationals of other Member States.

65. In those circumstances, given that a State cannot be forced to accede to the European Union against its will, neither can it be forced to withdraw from the European Union against its will.

66. However, if the notification of the intention to withdraw were to lead inevitably to the withdrawal of the Member State concerned from the European Union at the end of the period laid down in Article 50(3) TEU, that Member State could be forced to leave the European Union despite its wish—as expressed through its democratic process in accordance with its constitutional requirements—to reverse its decision to withdraw and, accordingly, to remain a Member of the European Union.

67. Such a result would be inconsistent with the aims and values referred to in paragraphs 61 and 62 of the present judgment. In particular, it would be inconsistent with the Treaties' purpose of creating an ever closer union among the peoples of Europe to force the withdrawal of a Member State which, having notified its intention to withdraw from the European Union in accordance with its constitutional requirements and following a democratic process, decides to revoke the notification of that intention through a democratic process.

68. The origins of Article 50 TEU also support an interpretation of that provision as meaning that a Member State is entitled to revoke

unilaterally the notification of its intention to withdraw from the European Union. That article largely adopts the wording of a withdrawal clause first set out in the draft Treaty establishing a Constitution for Europe. Although, during the drafting of that clause, amendments had been proposed to allow the expulsion of a Member State, to avoid the risk of abuse during the withdrawal procedure or to make the withdrawal decision more difficult, those amendments were all rejected on the ground, expressly set out in the comments on the draft, that the voluntary and unilateral nature of the withdrawal decision should be ensured.

69. It follows from the foregoing that the notification by a Member State of its intention to withdraw does not lead inevitably to the withdrawal of that Member State from the European Union. On the contrary, a Member State that has reversed its decision to withdraw from the European Union is entitled to revoke that notification for as long as a withdrawal agreement concluded between that Member State and the European Union has not entered into force or, if no such agreement has been concluded, for as long as the two-year period laid down in Article 50(3) TEU, possibly extended in accordance with that provision, has not expired.

70. That conclusion is corroborated by the provisions of the Vienna Convention on the Law of Treaties, which was taken into account in the preparatory work for the Treaty establishing a Constitution for Europe.

71. In the event that a treaty authorises withdrawal under its provisions, Article 68 of that convention specifies inter alia, in clear and unconditional terms, that a notification of withdrawal, as provided for in Article 65 or 67 thereof, may be revoked at any time before it takes effect.

72. As regards the proposal of the Council and the Commission that the right of the Member State concerned to revoke the notification of its intention to withdraw should be subject to the unanimous approval of the European Council, that requirement would transform a unilateral sovereign right into a conditional right subject to an approval procedure. Such an approval procedure would be incompatible with the principle, referred to in paragraphs 65, 67 and 69 of the present judgment, that a Member State cannot be forced to leave the European Union against its will.

73. It follows, in the first place, that, for as long as a withdrawal agreement concluded between the European Union and that Member State has not entered into force or, if no such agreement has been concluded, for as long as the two-year period laid down in Article 50(3) TEU, possibly extended in accordance with that provision, has not expired, that Member State—which enjoys, subject to Article 50(4) TEU, all of the rights and remains bound by all of the obligations laid down in the Treaties—retains the ability to revoke unilaterally the notification of its intention to

withdraw from the European Union, in accordance with its constitutional requirements.

74. In the second place, the revocation of the notification of the intention to withdraw must, first, be submitted in writing to the European Council and, secondly, be unequivocal and unconditional, that is to say that the purpose of that revocation is to confirm the EU membership of the Member State concerned under terms that are unchanged as regards its status as a Member State, and that revocation brings the withdrawal procedure to an end.

75. In view of all the foregoing, the answer to the question referred is that Article 50 TEU must be interpreted as meaning that, where a Member State has notified the European Council, in accordance with that article, of its intention to withdraw from the European Union, that article allows that Member State—for as long as a withdrawal agreement concluded between that Member State and the European Union has not entered into force or, if no such agreement has been concluded, for as long as the two-year period laid down in Article 50(3) TEU, possibly extended in accordance with that paragraph, has not expired—to revoke that notification unilaterally, in an unequivocal and unconditional manner, by a notice addressed to the European Council in writing, after the Member State concerned has taken the revocation decision in accordance with its constitutional requirements. The purpose of that revocation is to confirm the EU membership of the Member State concerned under terms that are unchanged as regards its status as a Member State, and that revocation brings the withdrawal procedure to an end. ∎

NOTES AND QUESTIONS

1. The Court's ruling in *Wightman* is remarkable for many reasons. One of them relates to the timing of the decision. The Court's ruling was announced after the EU and the United Kingdom had concluded their negotiations regarding the withdrawal agreement, but before the U.K. Parliament had voted on the withdrawal agreement. Moreover, at the time of the Court's decision, it was entirely unclear whether the House of Commons would give its blessing to the withdrawal agreement. Assume, hypothetically, that the Court chose the timing of its decision strategically. Would the timing of the decision be likely to increase or decrease the chances that the United Kingdom would reverse its decision to withdraw from the European Union?

2. The Court goes to great length to explain why the request for a preliminary ruling is admissible. In light of what you have learned about the preliminary rulings procedure, does the Court's reasoning seem persuasive?

3. The Court invokes the fact that the withdrawal right was modeled in part on the Vienna Convention on the Law of Treaties. This author had

previously made the same argument[8] and therefore, unsurprisingly, finds it quite convincing. However, can you think of arguments why EU law should be less generous in this respect than the Vienna Convention?

4. Perhaps the Court's most important argument is that no country should be forced to leave the European Union against its will. But is it plausible to assert that the United Kingdom would be forced to leave the European Union against its will if it could not revoke its notification of intent to withdraw?

5. The Council and the Commission had argued against the unilateral right to revoke the notification under Art. 50 TEU. In particular, they had reasoned that such a right could be abused to prolong the two-year negotiation period. Is that argument plausible?

6. Assume, hypothetically, that after the United Kingdom leaves the European Union, a majority of Scots want Scotland to secede from the United Kingdom and join the European Union as an independent nation. Would the European Union likely welcome such a step?

7. In substantial part, the outcome of the 2016 Brexit referendum appears to have been driven by concerns over immigration. As an empirical matter, there is little evidence that immigration to United Kingdom has led to more unemployment or strained public finances. For example, a much-cited study by Christian Dustmann and Tommaso Frattini finds that the immigrants who have entered the United Kingdom since the year 2000 have made positive financial contributions via tax payments that far outweigh the financial benefits that they have received.[9]

C. THE EUROPEAN UNION'S INTERNATIONAL TREATIES

A Member State's withdrawal from the European Union does not suddenly end existing economic, political, and personal ties between the former Member State and the European Union. Consequently, a Member State's withdrawal may engender numerous practical problems. For example, what happens to EU citizens living in the former Member State or, for that matter, citizens of the former Member State who continue to live in the EU? How can existing trade and other economic relationships such as supply chains be protected despite the Member State's withdrawal?

As a practical matter, therefore, the EU and the withdrawing Member State will seek to enter into a treaty or even numerous treaties governing the future relationship between the EU and the former Member State. The

---

[8] Jens Dammann, *Revoking Brexit: Can Member States Rescind Their Declaration of Withdrawal from the European Union?*, 23 COLUM. J. EUR. L. 265, 301–02 (2017).

[9] Christian Dustmann & Tommaso Frattini, *The Fiscal Effects of Immigration on the U.K.*, 124 ECON. J. 593, 628 (2014).

law governing treaties between the European Union and third countries is quite complex, but it is helpful to understand some basic principles.

As a preliminary matter, one might ask whether the European Union, as opposed to the Member States, is at all able to conclude international treaties. The answer to that question is a clear yes. According to Article 47 of the Treaty on European Union, "[t]he Union shall have legal personality."[10] Moreover, the Treaty on the Functioning of the European Union contains detailed rules on how the European Union can conclude international treaties. Of course, even if the European Union is capable of concluding international treaties in principle, one still needs to ask whether the EU has the competence to conclude a particular treaty and how that treaty can be concluded.

1. THE COMPETENCE TO CONCLUDE INTERNATIONAL TREATIES

In concluding international treaties, the European Union must still obey by the division of competences between the Member States and the European Union. From the chapter on legislation, you may recall that there are different types of competences: In case of an exclusive EU competence, only the European Union can legislate, whereas the Member States must abstain from legislation. In case of a shared competence, the Member States are free to legislate, but only as long as the European Union does not enact exhaustive legislation. Finally, where the Member States retain an exclusive competence to act, there is no room for EU legislation.

The same general system applies when it comes to international treaties. In other words, to the extent that the European Union enjoys an exclusive competence over a specific field, only the European Union can enact international treaties in that area. The most important example is trade agreements. According to Article 3 of the Treaty on the Functioning of the European Union, the European Union has exclusive competence for the Union's common commercial policy.[11] Hence, Member States are no longer able to conclude individual trade agreements with third countries that touch upon the areas covered by the common commercial policy, and the common commercial policy in particular includes trade in goods and trade in services. Shared competences include, for example, rules on portfolio investments or rules on investor state dispute settlements.[12] In areas where the European Union lacks the competence to conclude international agreements, only the Member States can conclude such agreements.

---

[10] TEU, art. 47.
[11] TFEU, art. 3(1).
[12] ECJ, May 16, 2017, Case C-2/15, *Free Trade Agreement With Singapore*, para. 305.

Note that the competences of the European Union to conclude international treaties are defined quite generously in the Treaty on the Functioning of the European Union. Under Article 216(1), "[t]he Union may conclude an agreement with one or more third countries or international organisations where the Treaties so provide or where the conclusion of an agreement is necessary in order to achieve, within the framework of the Union's policies, one of the objectives referred to in the Treaties, or is provided for in a legally binding Union act or is likely to affect common rules or alter their scope."[13]

This provision effectively lists several different grounds on which an EU competence for the conclusion of international treaties can be based. To begin, 216(1) mentions that the EU can conclude international agreements, "where the Treaties so provide." This alludes to the fact that there are numerous treaty provisions that accord the EU competence for the conclusion of international treaties. Among them are, in particular, Article 37 of the Treaty on European Union (common foreign and security policy) as well as Articles 79 (immigration policy), 191 (environmental policy), 207 (common commercial policy), and 219 (monetary policy) of the Treaty on the Functioning of the European Union.

No less important is the fact that Article 216(1) TFEU authorizes the European Union to conclude international treaties "where the conclusion of an agreement is necessary in order to achieve [. . .] one of the objectives referred to in the Treaties." This provision implies that if the European Union has legislated in a certain area, it also has the competence to conclude international agreements in that area.[14] In the words of the European Court of Justice,

> The competence of the EU to conclude international agreements may arise not only from an express conferment by the Treaties but may equally flow implicitly from other provisions of the Treaties and from measures adopted, within the framework of those provisions, by the EU institutions. In particular, whenever EU law creates for those institutions powers within its internal system for the purpose of attaining a specific objective, the EU has authority to undertake international commitments necessary for the attainment of that objective even in the absence of an express provision to that effect (Opinion 1/03, EU:C:2006:81, paragraph 114 and the case-law cited). The last-mentioned possibility is also referred to in Article 216(1) TFEU.[15]

---

[13] TFEU, art. 216(1).

[14] *E.g.*, Astrid Epiney, *Außenbeziehungen von EU und Mitgliedstaaten: Kompetenzverteilung, Zusammenwirken, und wechselseitige Pflichten am Beispiel des Datenschutzes*, 74 ZEITSCHRIFT FÜR AUSLÄNDISCHES ÖFFENTLICHES RECHT UND VÖLKERRECHT [ZAÖRV] 465, 482 (2014).

[15] ECJ, Case C-1/13, Oct. 14, 2014, *Hague Convention*, para. 67.

2. DIFFERENT TYPES OF TREATIES

Even if the European Union has the competence to conclude a particular international agreement, the question remains what procedural requirements have to be met. Most importantly, which institutions within the European Union have the right to be involved in the decision-making process. The answer to that question, it turns out, depends on the type of treaty. Consider the following excerpt.

A LITTLE BIT BREXIT? AN ANALYSIS OF THE RULES GOVERNING POST-WITHDRAWAL TREATIES
Jens Dammann
53 TEXAS INT'L L.J. 153, 162–67 (2018)

I. THE GENERAL RULES ON TREATIES

[. . .] There are four [main] types of agreements with third countries: association agreements, trade agreements, neighborhood treaties, and mixed agreements. These types of agreements could be relied on to create a special relationship between the United Kingdom and the European Union after the UK's withdrawal. The crucial question, in each case, is whether the available rules under each Treaty make it possible to conclude a comprehensive treaty (or set of treaties) between the United Kingdom and the EU (hereinafter EU-UK Treaty) without having to obtain the consent of every single Member State (or its representative in the Council).

A. Association Agreements

Under the general rules of European Union law, the most straightforward basis for a comprehensive EU-UK Treaty would be to enter into an association agreement under Article 217 of the Treaty on the Functioning of the European Union (TFEU). According to this provision "[t]he Union may conclude with one or more third countries or international organizations agreements establishing an association involving reciprocal rights and obligations, common action and special procedure."

Despite a seemingly simple definition, determining whether a treaty satisfies the necessary elements of an association agreement is difficult in practice.

One of the main purposes of Article 217 is to allow for the conclusion of Treaties with countries that ultimately plan to join the European Union but, for some reason or other, are not yet ready or permitted to join. However, the provision is not limited to treaties with aspiring EU members. Rather, it can be, and has been, used to conclude treaties with countries that do not seek to join the European Union.

In order for a treaty to qualify as an association agreement, it must create "common action and special procedure." The meaning of this requirement is not entirely clear. In its landmark *Demirel* decision, the European Court of Justice referred to an association agreement as "creating special, privileged links with a non-member country which must, at least to a certain extent, take part in the Community system." However, the decision is ambiguous as to whether taking part in the Community system was meant to be a necessary requirement for finding an association agreement or simply happened to be an attribute of the association agreement at issue in the case. As a practical matter, the answer to this question may not matter much in the case of the United Kingdom. Even if an association agreement requires taking part in the EU system, the United Kingdom's participation, to a greater or lesser extent, in the internal market, would presumably satisfy this requirement.

Alternatively, some voices in the literature interpret the "common action and special procedure" requirement to mean that the parties to the treaty must be subject to binding decisions by common institutions. However, such a requirement should not present any challenges for the United Kingdom either. Given the volume and depth of the economic relationship between the United Kingdom and the European Union, it is clear that any comprehensive EU-UK Treaty would require the establishment of a court or other governing body to adjudicate legal issues arising under the contract. In fact, another European agreement has already established a court for a similar purpose: the Court of Justice of the European Free Trade Association States was created to adjudicate disputes arising under the EEA Agreement. The EEA agreement includes Norway, Iceland, and Liechtenstein in the so-called internal market. To ensure the proper application of the pertinent rules, the EEA Agreement of 2 May 1992 requires those EFTA states that take part in the EEA agreement—namely Norway, Iceland, and Liechtenstein—to establish a court of Justice. A future EU-UK Treaty could create a similar institution, thereby subjecting the parties to the binding authority of a common institution.

Crucially, though, an association agreement requires not just the consent of the European Parliament, but also the unanimous decision in the Council where the Member States are represented. Hence, while an association agreement within the meaning of Article 217 may well constitute an appropriate way of fashioning the future EU-UK relationship, it does not help to solve the problem that individual Member States may block the agreement.

B. Trade Agreements

A second option for a comprehensive Brexit Treaty is a trade agreement under Article 207 of the Treaty on the Functioning of the

European Union. This is a less ambitious approach because, as a general rule, the Council acts with a so-called qualified majority when negotiating and concluding such trade agreements. However, there are various important exceptions to this principle when unanimity is required.

For example, the Council has to act unanimously if the agreement contains "provisions for [which] unanimity is required for the adoption of internal rules" and the agreement is to cover trade in services, commercial aspects of intellectual property rights, or foreign direct investment. For rules governing the trade in services or commercial aspects of intellectual property rights, unanimity will rarely be required because EU law generally embraces decisions by qualified majority in these areas. However, the issue of direct investments is trickier, and the rules needed to implement trade agreements in this area can much more easily trigger a unanimity requirement. Furthermore, unanimity is required, under certain conditions, for trade agreements in the fields of cultural and audiovisual services as well as in the fields of social, education, and health services. It is likely that some, if not all, of these types of provisions would be included in a post-Brexit agreement. In practice, therefore, it would be difficult to conclude a comprehensive post-Brexit agreement as a trade agreement under Article 207 TFEU without a unanimous decision in the Council.

C. Neighborhood Treaties

Another potential basis for a post-Brexit treaty is a neighborhood treaty based on Article 8 TEU. The provision states that the European Union will "develop a special relationship with neighboring countries" and that the EU "may conclude specific agreements with the countries concerned." The permissible scope of such neighborhood agreements is relatively broad. The Treaty only provides that the agreements "may contain reciprocal rights and obligations as well as the possibility of undertaking activities jointly." In other words, Article 8 creates a very open-ended competence for EU agreements with neighboring countries.

Despite the broad scope of neighborhood agreements, questions remain about how to conclude these agreements in practice. Article 8 is a relatively recent addition to the competence arsenal of the European Union and only found its way into the TEU via the Treaty of Lisbon, which entered into force in 2009. To date, the EU has not made use of Article 8. Tellingly, rather than rely on Article 8, a recent treaty between the European Union and the Ukraine was instead framed as an association agreement under Article 217 TFEU.

One of the reasons for Article 8's lack of popularity may lie in the fact that the procedural aspects of this norm remain unclear. Article 8 does not specify the procedure for concluding a neighborhood agreement, and it remains unclear how this gap should be filled. One possibility would be to invoke the general rule of Article 216 TFEU, according to which treaties require the consent of the European Parliament and a qualified majority in the Council. However, owing to the structural similarities between association agreements and neighborhood agreements, it has also been suggested that neighborhood treaties should be subject to the unanimity requirement imposed by Article 217. In fact, there are persuasive reasons to believe that this view is correct. First, Article 8(2) TEU was modeled on Article 217(4) TFEU, so it makes sense to subject it to the same procedural rules. Second, Article 218(8) TFEU imposes the unanimity agreement not only for association agreements, but also for Treaties with those countries that are candidates for accession to the European Union. This suggests a general policy according to which "integration treaties" are meant to be carried by the unanimous consent of the Member States.

D. Mixed Agreements

A comprehensive post-Brexit treaty might qualify as a so-called mixed agreement that includes both provisions falling into the European Union's competence and provisions falling into the competence of the Member States. If a treaty falls partly within the competence of the EU and partly within the competence of the Member States, it must be concluded as a "mixed agreement" to which both the EU and the Member States accede. In other words both the European Union and the Member States must be parties to a mixed treaty.

Investments provide an example of the practical need for mixed agreements. European law traditionally distinguishes between direct investments and portfolio investments. The TFEU grants the European Union the exclusive competence to conclude treaties governing direct foreign investments. By contrast, a recent decision by the Court of Justice on a trade agreement between the European Union and Singapore holds that a trade agreement governing non-direct investments cannot be approved by the European Union alone. However, trade agreements such as the recently negotiated trade agreement between Canada and the European Union typically govern both types of investments.

The mixed nature of an agreement may not necessarily imply a need for unanimity. Rather, it is conceivable that some Member States either fail to become parties to the agreement or are given the right to opt out of certain parts of the agreement. This phenomenon is generally referred to as an "incomplete" mixed agreement. By contrast, "complete" mixed agreements are those to which all the Member states have acceded. [. . .] ∎

D. INTERNATIONAL AGREEMENTS FOLLOWING WITHDRAWAL FROM THE EU

One of the controversial questions in connection with a Member State's exit from the European Union concerns the scope of the withdrawal agreement. Under Article 50(2) of the Treaty on European Union, the withdrawing Member State and the European Union will negotiate a withdrawal agreement "setting out the arrangements for its withdrawal, taking account of the framework for its future relationship with the Union."[16] Crucially, this withdrawal agreement does not require the unanimous consent of the Member States' representatives in the Council. Rather, Article 50(2) provides that the withdrawal agreement "shall be concluded on behalf of the Union by the Council, acting by a qualified majority, after obtaining the consent of the European Parliament."[17]

That raises an important question: Is the withdrawal agreement limited to the terms of the State's withdrawal, or can it also cover the withdrawing Member State's future relationship with the European Union. In the latter case, the withdrawal agreement could avoid the various unanimity requirements imposed by the general rules on international agreements described in the previous subsection. Consider the following excerpt:

A LITTLE BIT BREXIT? AN ANALYSIS OF THE RULES GOVERNING POST-WITHDRAWAL TREATIES
Jens Dammann
53 TEXAS INT'L L.J. 153, 168–69 (2018)

The question remains whether Article 50 of the Treaty on European Union provides a basis for concluding a comprehensive EU-UK Treaty or set of treaties without making it necessary to obtain the support of all the Member States. Article 50(2) TEU explicitly calls for a withdrawal agreement to be concluded between the European Union and the withdrawing Member State. Under said provision, all that is needed, on the European side, for the withdrawal agreement is a qualified majority in the Council and the consent of the European Parliament. The crucial issue, though, is whether the withdrawal agreement can only cover the withdrawal itself, or whether Article 50(2) also provides the basis for a treaty governing the future relationship between the European Union and the United Kingdom.

The reason that the answer to this question is not immediately obvious lies in the somewhat ambiguous wording of this provision. Article 50(2) describes the withdrawal agreement as "an agreement with [the withdrawing Member State] setting out the arrangements for its withdrawal, taking account of the framework for its future relationship with the Union." Some voices in the literature stress that this wording includes an explicit reference to the future relationship with the European Union, from which they deduce that this relationship is meant to be covered

---

[16] TEU, art. 50(2).
[17] *Id.*

by the withdrawal agreement. Other scholars reject such a broad role for the withdrawal agreement, some of them noting that Article 50(2) merely calls for the withdrawal agreement to "take into account," rather than define, the future relationship between the European Union and the withdrawing Member State. According to this latter view, Article 50(2) only provides a special basis for a treaty covering the withdrawal itself, whereas any comprehensive deal regarding the future relationship between the United Kingdom and the European Union must be based on other provisions of the Treaty. ■

NOTES AND QUESTIONS

1. As a matter of legal policy, can you come up with any arguments for why it would make sense to allow the withdrawal agreement to cover the future relationship between the withdrawing Member State and the European Union? How about any counterarguments?

2. Do the general EU rules on international treaties provide arguments in one or the other direction?

3. At the time that this casebook went to print, the fate of the United Kingdom remained uncertain. The U.K. government and the EU had negotiated a withdrawal agreement, but on January 15, 2019, the House of Commons rejected that withdrawal agreement by a landslide. Subsequently, the House of Commons also voted against a Brexit without withdrawal agreement and tasked the government with renegotiating the deal with the EU.

E. EFTA

In the debate over Brexit, much attention has been lavished on what are called the Swiss and the Norwegian models. Switzerland has concluded a net of bilateral agreements with the European Union. These agreements give Switzerland access to the common market despite the fact that Switzerland is not a Member State. However, the pertinent treaties also impose far-reaching duties on Switzerland, requiring, inter alia, that Switzerland recognize the free movement of persons.

A slightly different approach was taken by Norway. Norway is not a Member State of the European Union, but it has traditionally been part of the European Free Trade Association (EFTA), which also includes Iceland, Liechtenstein, and Switzerland. The EFTA was established by the Stockholm Convention of January 4, 1960. At the time, the signatory states included Norway and Switzerland, but also Austria, Denmark, Portugal, Sweden, and the United Kingdom.

From the beginning, the EFTA states were important trading partners for what is now the EU, and these economic ties became even closer over time. Several of the EFTA states, namely Austria, Denmark, Portugal,

Sweden, and the United Kingdom eventually joined the European Union. Switzerland, as noted above, abstained from joining the EU, but concluded numerous bilateral agreements with the EU, which effectively give Switzerland access to the European Union's common market. The remaining EFTA states, namely Iceland, Norway, and Liechtenstein, chose a different path. The Agreement on a European Economic Area, which was signed on May 2, 1992, and entered into force on January 1, 1994, creates an internal market comprising both the European Union and Norway, Liechtenstein, and Iceland.[18] Consider the following excerpt.

SPLENDID ISOLATION OR CONTINUED COOPERATION? OPTIONS FOR A STATE AFTER WITHDRAWAL FROM THE EUROPEAN UNION

Hannes Hofmeister
21 COLUM. J. EUR. L. 249, 255–270 (2015)

The EEA treaty is primarily an association agreement under Article 217 TFEU between the EC and the EFTA states. [. . .] The main objective of the EEA is "to promote a continuous and balanced strengthening of trade and economic relations between the Contracting Parties with equal conditions of competition, and the respect of the same rules, with a view to creating a homogeneous European Economic Area." [. . .] In order to achieve this objective, the EEA Agreement essentially extends the application of EU law to the EFTA states. Hence the four fundamental freedoms apply in the EEA, as do EU competition law and state aid rules. Moreover, within the framework of the EEA, EU and EFTA states also collaborate closely in fields as diverse as education, consumer protection, culture, social policy, and environmental protection.

Outside the scope of the EEA Agreement is the common agricultural policy and the common fisheries policy. Additionally, the common commercial policy, the common foreign and security policy, justice and home affairs, direct and indirect taxation as well as monetary issues are not covered either by the EEA Agreement. Even the four fundamental freedoms are not fully implemented: indeed, since the EEA is not a customs union but only a free trade area (i.e., without a common external customs regime), the free movements of goods regime could not be fully implemented. [. . .]

A key feature of the EEA Agreement is its dynamic nature. EEA rules are "continuously updated by adding new EU legislation. This aspect is essential given the large output of Union legislation on the internal market. Each month, a number of EEA-relevant pieces of legislation are incorporated into the EEA Agreement by decisions of the EEA Joint Committee." But precisely how does incorporation work? [. . .]

---

[18] Agreement on the European Economic Area, O.J. No. L 1, Jan. 3, 1994, p. 3.

The key objective of the EEA's law making mechanism is to foster homogeneity between EEA law and EU law. In order to achieve this objective a number of mechanisms are employed. First of all, EEA primary law (i.e., the EEA Agreement, its annexes and protocols) provides for the identical adoption of a large part of EU law into the EEA acquis. Moreover, future EU legislative acts which are "EEA relevant" will be incorporated without alterations by a decision of the EEA Joint Committee. [. . .]

EEA organs are not granted any supranational decision making powers. All they can do is pass secondary EEA law of an international law nature. For the latter to become effective, it must then be incorporated into the domestic legal orders of the EEA-EFTA states. Incorporation takes place in accordance with the constitutional requirements of the EFTA states (Article 103 EEA). This might necessitate parliamentary approval and subsequent ratification by the head of state. In summary, "law-making" in the EEA is highly complex. It is even more intergovernmental in nature and opaque than law making in the EU. It basically boils down to a collective and reactive incorporation of EEA-relevant EU law. [. . .]

While EEA membership may at first glance appear attractive, there are nonetheless significant drawbacks: [. . .]

First, as regards the functioning of the EEA it has to be said that the latter does not pass its own rules. In effect, it regularly adopts new EU law norms enacted in said areas: "EEA-relevant" laws are thus incorporated into the EEA Agreement by decisions of the EEA Joint Committee. This also highlights one of the main weaknesses of the EEA, at least from the perspective of the non-EU states: they are bound to comply with most EU law obligations while at the same time being excluded from the decision-making process at EU level. In other words, they run into "the problem of regulation without representation." [. . .]

Financially speaking EEA membership is not cheap either. For instance, the EEA-EFTA states are obliged under the EEA Agreement to contribute to a number of EU funds and programs. For instance, in 2012, they paid more than £ 241 million into these funds. Yet the EEA-EFTA states do not get any direct returns from their payments into said EU funds. [. . .] ∎

NOTES AND QUESTIONS

1. Given what you know about Brexit, does joining the EEA and the EFTA sound like a course of action that would allow the United Kingdom to gain access to the common market while addressing the perceived shortcomings of the European Union?

2. Based on the excerpt above, in what sense, if any, is the EEA Agreement less restricting of national sovereignty than the TEU and TFEU?

F. EXPULSION FROM THE EUROPEAN UNION?

Art. 50 of the Treaty on European Union governs a Member State's voluntary withdrawal from the European Union. An entirely different question is whether Member States can be expelled from the European Union against their will. Neither the Treaty on European Union nor the Treaty on the Function of the European Union mention such a possibility. Not surprisingly, therefore, the traditional view has been that European Union law does not allow for the expulsion of Member States.[19] An obiter dictum in the Court of Justice's 2018 Brexit decision also embraces that view.[20]

The broader issue, in this context, is whether European Union law provides sufficient mechanisms to force states to comply with their legal obligations.

1. ARTICLE 7 TEU

One of these mechanisms is contained in Art. 7 of the Treaty on European Union. Under that provision, if a Member State breaches the values listed in Article 2 TEU, "the Council, acting by a qualified majority, may decide to suspend certain of the rights" that the breaching State has under the Treaties.[21]

However, the substantive and procedural hurdles for such a step are quite high. Substantively, not any breach suffices, rather, the Member State must breach the values enumerated in Article 2 TFEU, which include "human dignity, freedom, democracy, equality, the rule of law and respect for human rights, including the rights of persons belonging to minorities."[22] Moreover, under Article 7(2) TEU, only "the existence of a serious and persistent breach" can lead to sanctions under Article 7.[23]

The procedural requirements are daunting as well. The entire procedure has to be initiated by a reasoned proposal by at least one third of the Member States, by the European Parliament, or by the European Commission.[24] Once that reasoned proposal has been submitted, the Council will hear the Member State. Following that hearing, the Council may make the determination that there exists "a clear risk of a serious breach" of the values listed in Article 2.[25] However, that determination

---

[19] Phoebus Athanassiou, Withdrawal and Expulsion from the EU and EMU: Some Reflections 33 (Eur. Cent. Bank, Legal Working Paper No. 10, 2009) (concluding that an expulsion from the EU would be "legally next to impossible").

[20] ECJ, Case C-621/18, Andy Wrightman et al. v. Secretary of State for Exiting the European Union, December 10, 2018, ECLI:EU:C:2018:999 para. 65.

[21] TFEU, art. 7(3).

[22] TFEU, art. 7(2).

[23] *Id.*

[24] TFEU, art. 7(1).

[25] *Id.*

requires the consent of the European Parliament, and the Council has to act with four-fifths majority in making the determination.[26]

Once the Council has made the pertinent determination, a proposal can be advanced by a third of the Member States or the Commission that the European Council make a determination of a "the serious and persistent breach."[27] Following that proposal, the breaching Member State must again be heard.[28] Then, the European Council, with the consent of the European Parliament, may determine that there exists, in fact, a "serious and persistent breach" of the values listed in Art. 2. However, that determination has to be made unanimously, not counting the breaching state.[29] Only once this determination has been made can the Council, acting with a qualified majority, decide to suspend certain rights that the breaching state has under the Treaties.[30] These suspended rights can include the right to vote in the Council.[31] If the situation improves, the Council can lift the suspension, again acting with a qualified majority.[32] In practice, these various substantive and procedural hurdles have proven so exacting, that sanctions based on Article 7 have never been imposed.[33]

2. LUMP SUM AND PENALTY PAYMENTS

A second type of sanction can be imposed in the context of enforcement proceedings. If the Court has found that a Member State is in breach of EU law, and the Member State fails to comply with this judgment, then the Commission, after hearing the breaching Member State, can ask the Court to impose a lump sum or penalty payment. To make lump sum payments and penalty payments predictable, the Commission issued a communication in 2016, that specifies in advance for each state the amount of lump sum or penalty payments that it will request.[34]

3. STATE LIABILITY

As discussed in Chapter 9, individuals may be able to hold Member States liable for violation of EU law. Interestingly, the Court of Justice justified the development of the rules on Member State liability in part

---

[26] *Id.*

[27] TFEU, art. 7(2).

[28] *Id.*

[29] *Id.*

[30] *Id.*

[31] *Id.*

[32] TFEU, art. 7(4).

[33] Jens Dammann, *Paradise Lost: Can the European Union Expel Countries from the Eurozone?*, 49 VAND. J. TRANSNAT'L. L. 693, 740 (2016).

[34] C/2016/5091, Updating of data used to calculate lump sum and penalty payments to be proposed by the Commission to the Court of Justice in infringement proceedings, O.J. C 290, August 10, 2016, pp. 3–5.

based on the consideration that the existing set of sanctions for EU law violations was insufficient.³⁵

NOTES AND QUESTIONS

1. Can you make an argument that the sanctions described above are insufficient in case of Member States that willfully and persistently breach European Union law?

2. What might be potential downsides of allowing the expulsion of Member States from the European Union?

3. As a practical matter, serious and persistent breaches of EU law are by no means unheard of. For example, from the perspective of EU law, the refusal by the German Constitutional Court to accept the unconditional Supremacy of EU law in its *Solange I* decision—a stance that it still has not entirely abandoned—can be viewed as a rather foundational breach of EU law. Another example lies in the conduct of the French government during the so-called "empty chair crisis" of 1965/1966. At the time, France sought to prevent the development of a supranational dimension to the European Economic Community. To that aim, France started boycotting the meetings of the Council of Ministers, thus bringing the Council's work to a standstill. This crisis was only ended by the so-called Luxembourg compromise, which essentially gave in to France's demands.³⁶ Of course, neither the *Solange I* judgment nor France's empty chair policy led to sanctions against either country. Does that surprise you?

---

[35] ECJ, Joined cases C-6/90 and C-9/90, November 19, 1991, 1991 E.C.R. I-5357, Andrea Francovich & Danila Bonifaci et al. v. Italian Republic, para. 34.

[36] Jens Dammann, *Paradise Lost: Can the European Union Expel Countries from the Eurozone?*, 49 VAND. J. TRANSNAT'L. L. 693, 744 (2016). For a more detailed description of the empty chair crisis, see, *e.g.*, Desmond Dinan, *Fifty Years of European Integration: A Remarkable Achievement*, 31 FORDHAM INT'L L.J. 1118, 1129 (2008); Rafael Leal-Arcas, *Is EC Trade Policy up to Par?: A Legal Analysis over Time—Rome, Marrakesh, Amsterdam, Nice, and the Constitutional Treaty*, 13 COLUM. J. EUR. L. 305, 367 (2007).

ANNEX

■ ■ ■

PART 1: EXCERPTS FROM THE TREATY ON EUROPEAN UNION

Consolidated version of the Treaty on European Union, OJ C 326, 26.10.2012, p. 13–390

TITLE I
COMMON PROVISIONS

Article 1

(ex Article 1 TEU)

By this Treaty, the HIGH CONTRACTING PARTIES establish among themselves a EUROPEAN UNION, hereinafter called "the Union", on which the Member States confer competences to attain objectives they have in common.

This Treaty marks a new stage in the process of creating an ever closer union among the peoples of Europe, in which decisions are taken as openly as possible and as closely as possible to the citizen.

The Union shall be founded on the present Treaty and on the Treaty on the Functioning of the European Union (hereinafter referred to as "the Treaties"). Those two Treaties shall have the same legal value. The Union shall replace and succeed the European Community.

Article 2

The Union is founded on the values of respect for human dignity, freedom, democracy, equality, the rule of law and respect for human rights, including the rights of persons belonging to minorities. These values are common to the Member States in a society in which pluralism, non-discrimination, tolerance, justice, solidarity and equality between women and men prevail.

Article 3

(ex Article 2 TEU)

1. The Union's aim is to promote peace, its values and the well-being of its peoples.

2. The Union shall offer its citizens an area of freedom, security and justice without internal frontiers, in which the free movement of persons is ensured in conjunction with appropriate measures with respect to external

border controls, asylum, immigration and the prevention and combating of crime.

3. The Union shall establish an internal market. It shall work for the sustainable development of Europe based on balanced economic growth and price stability, a highly competitive social market economy, aiming at full employment and social progress, and a high level of protection and improvement of the quality of the environment. It shall promote scientific and technological advance.

It shall combat social exclusion and discrimination, and shall promote social justice and protection, equality between women and men, solidarity between generations and protection of the rights of the child.

It shall promote economic, social and territorial cohesion, and solidarity among Member States.

It shall respect its rich cultural and linguistic diversity, and shall ensure that Europe's cultural heritage is safeguarded and enhanced.

4. The Union shall establish an economic and monetary union whose currency is the euro.

5. In its relations with the wider world, the Union shall uphold and promote its values and interests and contribute to the protection of its citizens. It shall contribute to peace, security, the sustainable development of the Earth, solidarity and mutual respect among peoples, free and fair trade, eradication of poverty and the protection of human rights, in particular the rights of the child, as well as to the strict observance and the development of international law, including respect for the principles of the United Nations Charter.

6. The Union shall pursue its objectives by appropriate means commensurate with the competences which are conferred upon it in the Treaties.

Article 4

1. In accordance with Article 5, competences not conferred upon the Union in the Treaties remain with the Member States.

2. The Union shall respect the equality of Member States before the Treaties as well as their national identities, inherent in their fundamental structures, political and constitutional, inclusive of regional and local self-government. It shall respect their essential State functions, including ensuring the territorial integrity of the State, maintaining law and order and safeguarding national security. In particular, national security remains the sole responsibility of each Member State.

3. Pursuant to the principle of sincere cooperation, the Union and the Member States shall, in full mutual respect, assist each other in carrying out tasks which flow from the Treaties.

The Member States shall take any appropriate measure, general or particular, to ensure fulfilment of the obligations arising out of the Treaties or resulting from the acts of the institutions of the Union.

The Member States shall facilitate the achievement of the Union's tasks and refrain from any measure which could jeopardise the attainment of the Union's objectives.

Article 5

(ex Article 5 TEC)

1. The limits of Union competences are governed by the principle of conferral. The use of Union competences is governed by the principles of subsidiarity and proportionality.

2. Under the principle of conferral, the Union shall act only within the limits of the competences conferred upon it by the Member States in the Treaties to attain the objectives set out therein. Competences not conferred upon the Union in the Treaties remain with the Member States.

3. Under the principle of subsidiarity, in areas which do not fall within its exclusive competence, the Union shall act only if and in so far as the objectives of the proposed action cannot be sufficiently achieved by the Member States, either at central level or at regional and local level, but can rather, by reason of the scale or effects of the proposed action, be better achieved at Union level.

The institutions of the Union shall apply the principle of subsidiarity as laid down in the Protocol on the application of the principles of subsidiarity and proportionality. National Parliaments ensure compliance with the principle of subsidiarity in accordance with the procedure set out in that Protocol.

4. Under the principle of proportionality, the content and form of Union action shall not exceed what is necessary to achieve the objectives of the Treaties.

The institutions of the Union shall apply the principle of proportionality as laid down in the Protocol on the application of the principles of subsidiarity and proportionality.

Article 6

(ex Article 6 TEU)

1. The Union recognises the rights, freedoms and principles set out in the Charter of Fundamental Rights of the European Union of 7 December 2000, as adapted at Strasbourg, on 12 December 2007, which shall have the same legal value as the Treaties.

The provisions of the Charter shall not extend in any way the competences of the Union as defined in the Treaties.

The rights, freedoms and principles in the Charter shall be interpreted in accordance with the general provisions in Title VII of the Charter governing its interpretation and application and with due regard to the explanations referred to in the Charter, that set out the sources of those provisions.

2. The Union shall accede to the European Convention for the Protection of Human Rights and Fundamental Freedoms. Such accession shall not affect the Union's competences as defined in the Treaties.

3. Fundamental rights, as guaranteed by the European Convention for the Protection of Human Rights and Fundamental Freedoms and as they result from the constitutional traditions common to the Member States, shall constitute general principles of the Union's law.

Article 7

(ex Article 7 TEU)

1. On a reasoned proposal by one third of the Member States, by the European Parliament or by the European Commission, the Council, acting by a majority of four fifths of its members after obtaining the consent of the European Parliament, may determine that there is a clear risk of a serious breach by a Member State of the values referred to in Article 2. Before making such a determination, the Council shall hear the Member State in question and may address recommendations to it, acting in accordance with the same procedure.

The Council shall regularly verify that the grounds on which such a determination was made continue to apply.

2. The European Council, acting by unanimity on a proposal by one third of the Member States or by the Commission and after obtaining the consent of the European Parliament, may determine the existence of a serious and persistent breach by a Member State of the values referred to in Article 2, after inviting the Member State in question to submit its observations.

3. Where a determination under paragraph 2 has been made, the Council, acting by a qualified majority, may decide to suspend certain of the rights deriving from the application of the Treaties to the Member State in question, including the voting rights of the representative of the government of that Member State in the Council. In doing so, the Council shall take into account the possible consequences of such a suspension on the rights and obligations of natural and legal persons.

The obligations of the Member State in question under the Treaties shall in any case continue to be binding on that State.

4. The Council, acting by a qualified majority, may decide subsequently to vary or revoke measures taken under paragraph 3 in response to changes in the situation which led to their being imposed.

5. The voting arrangements applying to the European Parliament, the European Council and the Council for the purposes of this Article are laid down in Article 354 of the Treaty on the Functioning of the European Union.

Article 8

1. The Union shall develop a special relationship with neighbouring countries, aiming to establish an area of prosperity and good neighbourliness, founded on the values of the Union and characterised by close and peaceful relations based on cooperation.

2. For the purposes of paragraph 1, the Union may conclude specific agreements with the countries concerned. These agreements may contain reciprocal rights and obligations as well as the possibility of undertaking activities jointly. Their implementation shall be the subject of periodic consultation.

TITLE III
PROVISIONS ON THE INSTITUTIONS

[...]

Article 14

1. The European Parliament shall, jointly with the Council, exercise legislative and budgetary functions. It shall exercise functions of political control and consultation as laid down in the Treaties. It shall elect the President of the Commission.

2. The European Parliament shall be composed of representatives of the Union's citizens. They shall not exceed seven hundred and fifty in number, plus the President. Representation of citizens shall be degressively proportional, with a minimum threshold of six members per Member State. No Member State shall be allocated more than ninety-six seats.

The European Council shall adopt by unanimity, on the initiative of the European Parliament and with its consent, a decision establishing the composition of the European Parliament, respecting the principles referred to in the first subparagraph.

3. The members of the European Parliament shall be elected for a term of five years by direct universal suffrage in a free and secret ballot.

4. The European Parliament shall elect its President and its officers from among its members.

Article 15

1. The European Council shall provide the Union with the necessary impetus for its development and shall define the general political directions and priorities thereof. It shall not exercise legislative functions.

2. The European Council shall consist of the Heads of State or Government of the Member States, together with its President and the President of the Commission. The High Representative of the Union for Foreign Affairs and Security Policy shall take part in its work.

3. The European Council shall meet twice every six months, convened by its President. When the agenda so requires, the members of the European Council may decide each to be assisted by a minister and, in the case of the President of the Commission, by a member of the Commission. When the situation so requires, the President shall convene a special meeting of the European Council.

4. Except where the Treaties provide otherwise, decisions of the European Council shall be taken by consensus.

5. The European Council shall elect its President, by a qualified majority, for a term of two and a half years, renewable once. In the event of an impediment or serious misconduct, the European Council can end the President's term of office in accordance with the same procedure.

6. The President of the European Council:

(a) shall chair it and drive forward its work;

(b) shall ensure the preparation and continuity of the work of the European Council in cooperation with the President of the Commission, and on the basis of the work of the General Affairs Council;

(c) shall endeavour to facilitate cohesion and consensus within the European Council;

(d) shall present a report to the European Parliament after each of the meetings of the European Council.

The President of the European Council shall, at his level and in that capacity, ensure the external representation of the Union on issues concerning its common foreign and security policy, without prejudice to the powers of the High Representative of the Union for Foreign Affairs and Security Policy.

The President of the European Council shall not hold a national office.

Article 16

1. The Council shall, jointly with the European Parliament, exercise legislative and budgetary functions. It shall carry out policy-making and coordinating functions as laid down in the Treaties.

2. The Council shall consist of a representative of each Member State at ministerial level, who may commit the government of the Member State in question and cast its vote.

3. The Council shall act by a qualified majority except where the Treaties provide otherwise.

4. As from 1 November 2014, a qualified majority shall be defined as at least 55 % of the members of the Council, comprising at least fifteen of them and representing Member States comprising at least 65 % of the population of the Union.

A blocking minority must include at least four Council members, failing which the qualified majority shall be deemed attained.

The other arrangements governing the qualified majority are laid down in Article 238(2) of the Treaty on the Functioning of the European Union.

5. The transitional provisions relating to the definition of the qualified majority which shall be applicable until 31 October 2014 and those which shall be applicable from 1 November 2014 to 31 March 2017 are laid down in the Protocol on transitional provisions.

6. The Council shall meet in different configurations, the list of which shall be adopted in accordance with Article 236 of the Treaty on the Functioning of the European Union.

The General Affairs Council shall ensure consistency in the work of the different Council configurations. It shall prepare and ensure the follow-up to meetings of the European Council, in liaison with the President of the European Council and the Commission.

The Foreign Affairs Council shall elaborate the Union's external action on the basis of strategic guidelines laid down by the European Council and ensure that the Union's action is consistent.

7. A Committee of Permanent Representatives of the Governments of the Member States shall be responsible for preparing the work of the Council.

8. The Council shall meet in public when it deliberates and votes on a draft legislative act. To this end, each Council meeting shall be divided into two parts, dealing respectively with deliberations on Union legislative acts and non-legislative activities.

9. The Presidency of Council configurations, other than that of Foreign Affairs, shall be held by Member State representatives in the Council on the basis of equal rotation, in accordance with the conditions established in accordance with Article 236 of the Treaty on the Functioning of the European Union.

Article 17

1. The Commission shall promote the general interest of the Union and take appropriate initiatives to that end. It shall ensure the application of the Treaties, and of measures adopted by the institutions pursuant to them. It shall oversee the application of Union law under the control of the Court of Justice of the European Union. It shall execute the budget and manage programmes. It shall exercise coordinating, executive and management functions, as laid down in the Treaties. With the exception of the common foreign and security policy, and other cases provided for in the Treaties, it shall ensure the Union's external representation. It shall initiate the Union's annual and multiannual programming with a view to achieving interinstitutional agreements.

2. Union legislative acts may only be adopted on the basis of a Commission proposal, except where the Treaties provide otherwise. Other acts shall be adopted on the basis of a Commission proposal where the Treaties so provide.

3. The Commission's term of office shall be five years.

The members of the Commission shall be chosen on the ground of their general competence and European commitment from persons whose independence is beyond doubt.

In carrying out its responsibilities, the Commission shall be completely independent. Without prejudice to Article 18(2), the members of the Commission shall neither seek nor take instructions from any Government or other institution, body, office or entity. They shall refrain from any action incompatible with their duties or the performance of their tasks.

4. The Commission appointed between the date of entry into force of the Treaty of Lisbon and 31 October 2014, shall consist of one national of each Member State, including its President and the High Representative of the Union for Foreign Affairs and Security Policy who shall be one of its Vice-Presidents.

5. As from 1 November 2014, the Commission shall consist of a number of members, including its President and the High Representative of the Union for Foreign Affairs and Security Policy, corresponding to two thirds of the number of Member States, unless the European Council, acting unanimously, decides to alter this number.

The members of the Commission shall be chosen from among the nationals of the Member States on the basis of a system of strictly equal rotation between the Member States, reflecting the demographic and geographical range of all the Member States. This system shall be established unanimously by the European Council in accordance with Article 244 of the Treaty on the Functioning of the European Union.

6. The President of the Commission shall:

(a) lay down guidelines within which the Commission is to work;

(b) decide on the internal organisation of the Commission, ensuring that it acts consistently, efficiently and as a collegiate body;

(c) appoint Vice-Presidents, other than the High Representative of the Union for Foreign Affairs and Security Policy, from among the members of the Commission.

A member of the Commission shall resign if the President so requests. The High Representative of the Union for Foreign Affairs and Security Policy shall resign, in accordance with the procedure set out in Article 18(1), if the President so requests.

7. Taking into account the elections to the European Parliament and after having held the appropriate consultations, the European Council, acting by a qualified majority, shall propose to the European Parliament a candidate for President of the Commission. This candidate shall be elected by the European Parliament by a majority of its component members. If he does not obtain the required majority, the European Council, acting by a qualified majority, shall within one month propose a new candidate who shall be elected by the European Parliament following the same procedure.

The Council, by common accord with the President-elect, shall adopt the list of the other persons whom it proposes for appointment as members of the Commission. They shall be selected, on the basis of the suggestions made by Member States, in accordance with the criteria set out in paragraph 3, second subparagraph, and paragraph 5, second subparagraph.

The President, the High Representative of the Union for Foreign Affairs and Security Policy and the other members of the Commission shall be subject as a body to a vote of consent by the European Parliament. On the basis of this consent the Commission shall be appointed by the European Council, acting by a qualified majority.

8. The Commission, as a body, shall be responsible to the European Parliament. In accordance with Article 234 of the Treaty on the Functioning of the European Union, the European Parliament may vote on a motion of censure of the Commission. If such a motion is carried, the members of the Commission shall resign as a body and the High

Representative of the Union for Foreign Affairs and Security Policy shall resign from the duties that he carries out in the Commission.

Article 18

1. The European Council, acting by a qualified majority, with the agreement of the President of the Commission, shall appoint the High Representative of the Union for Foreign Affairs and Security Policy. The European Council may end his term of office by the same procedure.

2. The High Representative shall conduct the Union's common foreign and security policy. He shall contribute by his proposals to the development of that policy, which he shall carry out as mandated by the Council. The same shall apply to the common security and defence policy.

3. The High Representative shall preside over the Foreign Affairs Council.

4. The High Representative shall be one of the Vice-Presidents of the Commission. He shall ensure the consistency of the Union's external action. He shall be responsible within the Commission for responsibilities incumbent on it in external relations and for coordinating other aspects of the Union's external action. In exercising these responsibilities within the Commission, and only for these responsibilities, the High Representative shall be bound by Commission procedures to the extent that this is consistent with paragraphs 2 and 3.

Article 19

1. The Court of Justice of the European Union shall include the Court of Justice, the General Court and specialised courts. It shall ensure that in the interpretation and application of the Treaties the law is observed.

Member States shall provide remedies sufficient to ensure effective legal protection in the fields covered by Union law.

2. The Court of Justice shall consist of one judge from each Member State. It shall be assisted by Advocates-General.

The General Court shall include at least one judge per Member State.

The Judges and the Advocates-General of the Court of Justice and the Judges of the General Court shall be chosen from persons whose independence is beyond doubt and who satisfy the conditions set out in Articles 253 and 254 of the Treaty on the Functioning of the European Union. They shall be appointed by common accord of the governments of the Member States for six years. Retiring Judges and Advocates-General may be reappointed.

3. The Court of Justice of the European Union shall, in accordance with the Treaties:

(a) rule on actions brought by a Member State, an institution or a natural or legal person;

(b) give preliminary rulings, at the request of courts or tribunals of the Member States, on the interpretation of Union law or the validity of acts adopted by the institutions;

(c) rule in other cases provided for in the Treaties.

[...]

TITLE VI
FINAL PROVISIONS

Article 48

(ex Article 48 TEU)

1. The Treaties may be amended in accordance with an ordinary revision procedure. They may also be amended in accordance with simplified revision procedures.

Ordinary revision procedure

2. The Government of any Member State, the European Parliament or the Commission may submit to the Council proposals for the amendment of the Treaties. These proposals may, inter alia, serve either to increase or to reduce the competences conferred on the Union in the Treaties. These proposals shall be submitted to the European Council by the Council and the national Parliaments shall be notified.

3. If the European Council, after consulting the European Parliament and the Commission, adopts by a simple majority a decision in favour of examining the proposed amendments, the President of the European Council shall convene a Convention composed of representatives of the national Parliaments, of the Heads of State or Government of the Member States, of the European Parliament and of the Commission. The European Central Bank shall also be consulted in the case of institutional changes in the monetary area. The Convention shall examine the proposals for amendments and shall adopt by consensus a recommendation to a conference of representatives of the governments of the Member States as provided for in paragraph 4.

The European Council may decide by a simple majority, after obtaining the consent of the European Parliament, not to convene a Convention should this not be justified by the extent of the proposed amendments. In the latter case, the European Council shall define the terms of reference for a conference of representatives of the governments of the Member States.

4. A conference of representatives of the governments of the Member States shall be convened by the President of the Council for the purpose of

determining by common accord the amendments to be made to the Treaties.

The amendments shall enter into force after being ratified by all the Member States in accordance with their respective constitutional requirements.

5. If, two years after the signature of a treaty amending the Treaties, four fifths of the Member States have ratified it and one or more Member States have encountered difficulties in proceeding with ratification, the matter shall be referred to the European Council.

Simplified revision procedures

6. The Government of any Member State, the European Parliament or the Commission may submit to the European Council proposals for revising all or part of the provisions of Part Three of the Treaty on the Functioning of the European Union relating to the internal policies and action of the Union.

The European Council may adopt a decision amending all or part of the provisions of Part Three of the Treaty on the Functioning of the European Union. The European Council shall act by unanimity after consulting the European Parliament and the Commission, and the European Central Bank in the case of institutional changes in the monetary area. That decision shall not enter into force until it is approved by the Member States in accordance with their respective constitutional requirements.

The decision referred to in the second subparagraph shall not increase the competences conferred on the Union in the Treaties.

7. Where the Treaty on the Functioning of the European Union or Title V of this Treaty provides for the Council to act by unanimity in a given area or case, the European Council may adopt a decision authorising the Council to act by a qualified majority in that area or in that case. This subparagraph shall not apply to decisions with military implications or those in the area of defence.

Where the Treaty on the Functioning of the European Union provides for legislative acts to be adopted by the Council in accordance with a special legislative procedure, the European Council may adopt a decision allowing for the adoption of such acts in accordance with the ordinary legislative procedure.

Any initiative taken by the European Council on the basis of the first or the second subparagraph shall be notified to the national Parliaments. If a national Parliament makes known its opposition within six months of the date of such notification, the decision referred to in the first or the second subparagraph shall not be adopted. In the absence of opposition, the European Council may adopt the decision.

For the adoption of the decisions referred to in the first and second subparagraphs, the European Council shall act by unanimity after obtaining the consent of the European Parliament, which shall be given by a majority of its component members.

Article 49

(ex Article 49 TEU)

Any European State which respects the values referred to in Article 2 and is committed to promoting them may apply to become a member of the Union. The European Parliament and national Parliaments shall be notified of this application. The applicant State shall address its application to the Council, which shall act unanimously after consulting the Commission and after receiving the consent of the European Parliament, which shall act by a majority of its component members. The conditions of eligibility agreed upon by the European Council shall be taken into account.

The conditions of admission and the adjustments to the Treaties on which the Union is founded, which such admission entails, shall be the subject of an agreement between the Member States and the applicant State. This agreement shall be submitted for ratification by all the contracting States in accordance with their respective constitutional requirements.

Article 50

1. Any Member State may decide to withdraw from the Union in accordance with its own constitutional requirements.

2. A Member State which decides to withdraw shall notify the European Council of its intention. In the light of the guidelines provided by the European Council, the Union shall negotiate and conclude an agreement with that State, setting out the arrangements for its withdrawal, taking account of the framework for its future relationship with the Union. That agreement shall be negotiated in accordance with Article 218(3) of the Treaty on the Functioning of the European Union. It shall be concluded on behalf of the Union by the Council, acting by a qualified majority, after obtaining the consent of the European Parliament.

3. The Treaties shall cease to apply to the State in question from the date of entry into force of the withdrawal agreement or, failing that, two years after the notification referred to in paragraph 2, unless the European Council, in agreement with the Member State concerned, unanimously decides to extend this period.

4. For the purposes of paragraphs 2 and 3, the member of the European Council or of the Council representing the withdrawing Member State shall not participate in the discussions of the European Council or Council or in decisions concerning it.

A qualified majority shall be defined in accordance with Article 238(3)(b) of the Treaty on the Functioning of the European Union.

5. If a State which has withdrawn from the Union asks to rejoin, its request shall be subject to the procedure referred to in Article 49.

Article 51

The Protocols and Annexes to the Treaties shall form an integral part thereof.

PART 2: EXCERPTS FROM THE TREATY ON THE FUNCTIONING OF THE EUROPEAN UNION

Consolidated version of the Treaty on the Functioning of the European Union, OJ C 326, 26.10.2012, p. 47–390.

PART ONE
PRINCIPLES

Article 1

1. This Treaty organises the functioning of the Union and determines the areas of, delimitation of, and arrangements for exercising its competences.

2. This Treaty and the Treaty on European Union constitute the Treaties on which the Union is founded. These two Treaties, which have the same legal value, shall be referred to as "the Treaties".

TITLE I
CATEGORIES AND AREAS OF UNION COMPETENCE

Article 2

1. When the Treaties confer on the Union exclusive competence in a specific area, only the Union may legislate and adopt legally binding acts, the Member States being able to do so themselves only if so empowered by the Union or for the implementation of Union acts.

2. When the Treaties confer on the Union a competence shared with the Member States in a specific area, the Union and the Member States may legislate and adopt legally binding acts in that area. The Member States shall exercise their competence to the extent that the Union has not exercised its competence. The Member States shall again exercise their competence to the extent that the Union has decided to cease exercising its competence.

3. The Member States shall coordinate their economic and employment policies within arrangements as determined by this Treaty, which the Union shall have competence to provide.

4. The Union shall have competence, in accordance with the provisions of the Treaty on European Union, to define and implement a common foreign and security policy, including the progressive framing of a common defence policy.

5. In certain areas and under the conditions laid down in the Treaties, the Union shall have competence to carry out actions to support, coordinate or supplement the actions of the Member States, without thereby superseding their competence in these areas.

Legally binding acts of the Union adopted on the basis of the provisions of the Treaties relating to these areas shall not entail harmonisation of Member States' laws or regulations.

6. The scope of and arrangements for exercising the Union's competences shall be determined by the provisions of the Treaties relating to each area.

Article 3

1. The Union shall have exclusive competence in the following areas:

(a) customs union;

(b) the establishing of the competition rules necessary for the functioning of the internal market;

(c) monetary policy for the Member States whose currency is the euro;

(d) the conservation of marine biological resources under the common fisheries policy;

(e) common commercial policy.

2. The Union shall also have exclusive competence for the conclusion of an international agreement when its conclusion is provided for in a legislative act of the Union or is necessary to enable the Union to exercise its internal competence, or in so far as its conclusion may affect common rules or alter their scope.

Article 4

1. The Union shall share competence with the Member States where the Treaties confer on it a competence which does not relate to the areas referred to in Articles 3 and 6.

2. Shared competence between the Union and the Member States applies in the following principal areas:

(a) internal market;

(b) social policy, for the aspects defined in this Treaty;

(c) economic, social and territorial cohesion;

(d) agriculture and fisheries, excluding the conservation of marine biological resources;

(e) environment;

(f) consumer protection;

(g) transport;

(h) trans-European networks;

(i) energy;

(j) area of freedom, security and justice;

(k) common safety concerns in public health matters, for the aspects defined in this Treaty.

3. In the areas of research, technological development and space, the Union shall have competence to carry out activities, in particular to define and implement programmes; however, the exercise of that competence shall not result in Member States being prevented from exercising theirs.

4. In the areas of development cooperation and humanitarian aid, the Union shall have competence to carry out activities and conduct a common policy; however, the exercise of that competence shall not result in Member States being prevented from exercising theirs.

[. . .]

TITLE II
PROVISIONS HAVING GENERAL APPLICATION

Article 7

The Union shall ensure consistency between its policies and activities, taking all of its objectives into account and in accordance with the principle of conferral of powers.

Article 8

(ex Article 3(2) TEC) [2]

In all its activities, the Union shall aim to eliminate inequalities, and to promote equality, between men and women.

Article 9

In defining and implementing its policies and activities, the Union shall take into account requirements linked to the promotion of a high level of employment, the guarantee of adequate social protection, the fight against social exclusion, and a high level of education, training and protection of human health.

Article 10

In defining and implementing its policies and activities, the Union shall aim to combat discrimination based on sex, racial or ethnic origin, religion or belief, disability, age or sexual orientation.

Article 11

(ex Article 6 TEC)

Environmental protection requirements must be integrated into the definition and implementation of the Union's policies and activities, in particular with a view to promoting sustainable development.

Article 12

(ex Article 153(2) TEC)

Consumer protection requirements shall be taken into account in defining and implementing other Union policies and activities.

[...]

PART TWO
NON-DISCRIMINATION AND CITIZENSHIP OF THE UNION

Article 18

(ex Article 12 TEC)

Within the scope of application of the Treaties, and without prejudice to any special provisions contained therein, any discrimination on grounds of nationality shall be prohibited.

The European Parliament and the Council, acting in accordance with the ordinary legislative procedure, may adopt rules designed to prohibit such discrimination.

Article 19

(ex Article 13 TEC)

1. Without prejudice to the other provisions of the Treaties and within the limits of the powers conferred by them upon the Union, the Council, acting unanimously in accordance with a special legislative procedure and after obtaining the consent of the European Parliament, may take appropriate action to combat discrimination based on sex, racial or ethnic origin, religion or belief, disability, age or sexual orientation.

2. By way of derogation from paragraph 1, the European Parliament and the Council, acting in accordance with the ordinary legislative procedure, may adopt the basic principles of Union incentive measures, excluding any harmonisation of the laws and regulations of the Member States, to support action taken by the Member States in order to contribute to the achievement of the objectives referred to in paragraph 1.

Article 20

(ex Article 17 TEC)

1. Citizenship of the Union is hereby established. Every person holding the nationality of a Member State shall be a citizen of the Union. Citizenship of the Union shall be additional to and not replace national citizenship.

2. Citizens of the Union shall enjoy the rights and be subject to the duties provided for in the Treaties. They shall have, inter alia:

   (a) the right to move and reside freely within the territory of the Member States;

   (b) the right to vote and to stand as candidates in elections to the European Parliament and in municipal elections in their Member State of residence, under the same conditions as nationals of that State;

   (c) the right to enjoy, in the territory of a third country in which the Member State of which they are nationals is not represented, the protection of the diplomatic and consular authorities of any Member State on the same conditions as the nationals of that State;

   (d) the right to petition the European Parliament, to apply to the European Ombudsman, and to address the institutions and advisory bodies of the Union in any of the Treaty languages and to obtain a reply in the same language.

These rights shall be exercised in accordance with the conditions and limits defined by the Treaties and by the measures adopted thereunder.

Article 21

(ex Article 18 TEC)

1. Every citizen of the Union shall have the right to move and reside freely within the territory of the Member States, subject to the limitations and conditions laid down in the Treaties and by the measures adopted to give them effect.

2. If action by the Union should prove necessary to attain this objective and the Treaties have not provided the necessary powers, the European Parliament and the Council, acting in accordance with the ordinary legislative procedure, may adopt provisions with a view to facilitating the exercise of the rights referred to in paragraph 1.

3. For the same purposes as those referred to in paragraph 1 and if the Treaties have not provided the necessary powers, the Council, acting in accordance with a special legislative procedure, may adopt measures concerning social security or social protection. The Council shall act unanimously after consulting the European Parliament.

[. . .]

PART THREE
UNION POLICIES AND INTERNAL ACTIONS
TITLE I
THE INTERNAL MARKET

Article 26

(ex Article 14 TEC)

1. The Union shall adopt measures with the aim of establishing or ensuring the functioning of the internal market, in accordance with the relevant provisions of the Treaties.

2. The internal market shall comprise an area without internal frontiers in which the free movement of goods, persons, services and capital is ensured in accordance with the provisions of the Treaties.

3. The Council, on a proposal from the Commission, shall determine the guidelines and conditions necessary to ensure balanced progress in all the sectors concerned.

Article 27

(ex Article 15 TEC)

When drawing up its proposals with a view to achieving the objectives set out in Article 26, the Commission shall take into account the extent of the effort that certain economies showing differences in development will have to sustain for the establishment of the internal market and it may propose appropriate provisions.

If these provisions take the form of derogations, they must be of a temporary nature and must cause the least possible disturbance to the functioning of the internal market.

TITLE II
FREE MOVEMENT OF GOODS

Article 28

(ex Article 23 TEC)

1. The Union shall comprise a customs union which shall cover all trade in goods and which shall involve the prohibition between Member States of customs duties on imports and exports and of all charges having equivalent effect, and the adoption of a common customs tariff in their relations with third countries.

2. The provisions of Article 30 and of Chapter 3 of this Title shall apply to products originating in Member States and to products coming from third countries which are in free circulation in Member States.

Article 29

(ex Article 24 TEC)

Products coming from a third country shall be considered to be in free circulation in a Member State if the import formalities have been complied with and any customs duties or charges having equivalent effect which are payable have been levied in that Member State, and if they have not benefited from a total or partial drawback of such duties or charges.

CHAPTER 1
THE CUSTOMS UNION

Article 30

(ex Article 25 TEC)

Customs duties on imports and exports and charges having equivalent effect shall be prohibited between Member States. This prohibition shall also apply to customs duties of a fiscal nature.

Article 31

(ex Article 26 TEC)

Common Customs Tariff duties shall be fixed by the Council on a proposal from the Commission.

[...]

CHAPTER 3
PROHIBITION OF QUANTITATIVE RESTRICTIONS BETWEEN MEMBER STATES

Article 34

(ex Article 28 TEC)

Quantitative restrictions on imports and all measures having equivalent effect shall be prohibited between Member States.

Article 35

(ex Article 29 TEC)

Quantitative restrictions on exports, and all measures having equivalent effect, shall be prohibited between Member States.

Article 36

(ex Article 30 TEC)

The provisions of Articles 34 and 35 shall not preclude prohibitions or restrictions on imports, exports or goods in transit justified on grounds of public morality, public policy or public security; the protection of health and life of humans, animals or plants; the protection of national treasures possessing artistic, historic or archaeological value; or the protection of industrial and commercial property. Such prohibitions or restrictions shall not, however, constitute a means of arbitrary discrimination or a disguised restriction on trade between Member States.

Article 37

(ex Article 31 TEC)

1. Member States shall adjust any State monopolies of a commercial character so as to ensure that no discrimination regarding the conditions under which goods are procured and marketed exists between nationals of Member States.

The provisions of this Article shall apply to any body through which a Member State, in law or in fact, either directly or indirectly supervises, determines or appreciably influences imports or exports between Member States. These provisions shall likewise apply to monopolies delegated by the State to others.

2. Member States shall refrain from introducing any new measure which is contrary to the principles laid down in paragraph 1 or which restricts the scope of the articles dealing with the prohibition of customs duties and quantitative restrictions between Member States.

3. If a State monopoly of a commercial character has rules which are designed to make it easier to dispose of agricultural products or obtain for them the best return, steps should be taken in applying the rules contained in this Article to ensure equivalent safeguards for the employment and standard of living of the producers concerned.

TITLE IV
FREE MOVEMENT OF PERSONS, SERVICES AND CAPITAL
CHAPTER 1
WORKERS

Article 45

(ex Article 39 TEC)

1. Freedom of movement for workers shall be secured within the Union.

2. Such freedom of movement shall entail the abolition of any discrimination based on nationality between workers of the Member States as regards employment, remuneration and other conditions of work and employment.

3. It shall entail the right, subject to limitations justified on grounds of public policy, public security or public health:

    (a) to accept offers of employment actually made;

(b) to move freely within the territory of Member States for this purpose;

(c) to stay in a Member State for the purpose of employment in accordance with the provisions governing the employment of nationals of that State laid down by law, regulation or administrative action;

(d) to remain in the territory of a Member State after having been employed in that State, subject to conditions which shall be embodied in regulations to be drawn up by the Commission.

4. The provisions of this Article shall not apply to employment in the public service.

[. . .]

Article 47

(ex Article 41 TEC)

Member States shall, within the framework of a joint programme, encourage the exchange of young workers.

Article 48

(ex Article 42 TEC)

The European Parliament and the Council shall, acting in accordance with the ordinary legislative procedure, adopt such measures in the field of social security as are necessary to provide freedom of movement for workers; to this end, they shall make arrangements to secure for employed and self-employed migrant workers and their dependents:

(a) aggregation, for the purpose of acquiring and retaining the right to benefit and of calculating the amount of benefit, of all periods taken into account under the laws of the several countries;

(b) payment of benefits to persons resident in the territories of Member States.

Where a member of the Council declares that a draft legislative act referred to in the first subparagraph would affect important aspects of its social security system, including its scope, cost or financial structure, or would affect the financial balance of that system, it may request that the matter be referred to the European Council. In that case, the ordinary legislative procedure shall be suspended. After discussion, the European Council shall, within four months of this suspension, either:

(a) refer the draft back to the Council, which shall terminate the suspension of the ordinary legislative procedure; or

(b) take no action or request the Commission to submit a new proposal; in that case, the act originally proposed shall be deemed not to have been adopted.

CHAPTER 2
RIGHT OF ESTABLISHMENT

Article 49

(ex Article 43 TEC)

Within the framework of the provisions set out below, restrictions on the freedom of establishment of nationals of a Member State in the territory of another Member State shall be prohibited. Such prohibition shall also apply to restrictions on the setting-up of agencies, branches or subsidiaries by nationals of any Member State established in the territory of any Member State.

Freedom of establishment shall include the right to take up and pursue activities as self-employed persons and to set up and manage undertakings, in particular companies or firms within the meaning of the second paragraph of Article 54, under the conditions laid down for its own nationals by the law of the country where such establishment is effected, subject to the provisions of the Chapter relating to capital.

[. . .]

Article 51

(ex Article 45 TEC)

The provisions of this Chapter shall not apply, so far as any given Member State is concerned, to activities which in that State are connected, even occasionally, with the exercise of official authority.

The European Parliament and the Council, acting in accordance with the ordinary legislative procedure, may rule that the provisions of this Chapter shall not apply to certain activities.

Article 52

(ex Article 46 TEC)

1. The provisions of this Chapter and measures taken in pursuance thereof shall not prejudice the applicability of provisions laid down by law, regulation or administrative action providing for special treatment for foreign nationals on grounds of public policy, public security or public health.

2. The European Parliament and the Council shall, acting in accordance with the ordinary legislative procedure, issue directives for the coordination of the abovementioned provisions.

Article 54

(ex Article 48 TEC)

Companies or firms formed in accordance with the law of a Member State and having their registered office, central administration or principal place of business within the Union shall, for the purposes of this Chapter, be treated in the same way as natural persons who are nationals of Member States.

"Companies or firms" means companies or firms constituted under civil or commercial law, including cooperative societies, and other legal persons governed by public or private law, save for those which are non-profit-making.

Article 55

(ex Article 294 TEC)

Member States shall accord nationals of the other Member States the same treatment as their own nationals as regards participation in the capital of companies or firms within the meaning of Article 54, without prejudice to the application of the other provisions of the Treaties.

CHAPTER 3
SERVICES

Article 56

(ex Article 49 TEC)

Within the framework of the provisions set out below, restrictions on freedom to provide services within the Union shall be prohibited in respect of nationals of Member States who are established in a Member State other than that of the person for whom the services are intended.

The European Parliament and the Council, acting in accordance with the ordinary legislative procedure, may extend the provisions of the Chapter to nationals of a third country who provide services and who are established within the Union.

Article 57

(ex Article 50 TEC)

Services shall be considered to be "services" within the meaning of the Treaties where they are normally provided for remuneration, in so far as they are not governed by the provisions relating to freedom of movement for goods, capital and persons.

"Services" shall in particular include:

(a) activities of an industrial character;

(b) activities of a commercial character;

(c) activities of craftsmen;

(d) activities of the professions.

Without prejudice to the provisions of the Chapter relating to the right of establishment, the person providing a service may, in order to do so, temporarily pursue his activity in the Member State where the service is provided, under the same conditions as are imposed by that State on its own nationals.

Article 59

(ex Article 52 TEC)

1. In order to achieve the liberalisation of a specific service, the European Parliament and the Council, acting in accordance with the ordinary legislative procedure and after consulting the Economic and Social Committee, shall issue directives.

2. As regards the directives referred to in paragraph 1, priority shall as a general rule be given to those services which directly affect production costs or the liberalisation of which helps to promote trade in goods.

Article 61

(ex Article 54 TEC)

As long as restrictions on freedom to provide services have not been abolished, each Member State shall apply such restrictions without distinction on grounds of nationality or residence to all persons providing services within the meaning of the first paragraph of Article 56.

Article 62

(ex Article 55 TEC)

The provisions of Articles 51 to 54 shall apply to the matters covered by this Chapter.

CHAPTER 4
CAPITAL AND PAYMENTS

Article 63

(ex Article 56 TEC)

1. Within the framework of the provisions set out in this Chapter, all restrictions on the movement of capital between Member States and between Member States and third countries shall be prohibited.

2. Within the framework of the provisions set out in this Chapter, all restrictions on payments between Member States and between Member States and third countries shall be prohibited.

[. . .]

Article 65

(ex Article 58 TEC)

1. The provisions of Article 63 shall be without prejudice to the right of Member States:

(a) to apply the relevant provisions of their tax law which distinguish between taxpayers who are not in the same situation with regard to their place of residence or with regard to the place where their capital is invested;

(b) to take all requisite measures to prevent infringements of national law and regulations, in particular in the field of taxation and the prudential supervision of financial institutions, or to lay down procedures for the declaration of capital movements for purposes of administrative or statistical information, or to take measures which are justified on grounds of public policy or public security.

2. The provisions of this Chapter shall be without prejudice to the applicability of restrictions on the right of establishment which are compatible with the Treaties.

3. The measures and procedures referred to in paragraphs 1 and 2 shall not constitute a means of arbitrary discrimination or a disguised restriction on the free movement of capital and payments as defined in Article 63.

4. [...]

[...]

TITLE V
AREA OF FREEDOM, SECURITY AND JUSTICE

CHAPTER 1
GENERAL PROVISIONS

Article 67

(ex Article 61 TEC and ex Article 29 TEU)

1. The Union shall constitute an area of freedom, security and justice with respect for fundamental rights and the different legal systems and traditions of the Member States.

2. It shall ensure the absence of internal border controls for persons and shall frame a common policy on asylum, immigration and external border control, based on solidarity between Member States, which is fair towards third-country nationals. For the purpose of this Title, stateless persons shall be treated as third-country nationals.

3. The Union shall endeavour to ensure a high level of security through measures to prevent and combat crime, racism and xenophobia, and through measures for coordination and cooperation between police and judicial authorities and other competent authorities, as well as through the mutual recognition of judgments in criminal matters and, if necessary, through the approximation of criminal laws.

4. The Union shall facilitate access to justice, in particular through the principle of mutual recognition of judicial and extrajudicial decisions in civil matters.

TITLE VII
COMMON RULES ON COMPETITION, TAXATION AND APPROXIMATION OF LAWS

[...]

CHAPTER 2
TAX PROVISIONS

Article 110

(ex Article 90 TEC)

No Member State shall impose, directly or indirectly, on the products of other Member States any internal taxation of any kind in excess of that imposed directly or indirectly on similar domestic products.

Furthermore, no Member State shall impose on the products of other Member States any internal taxation of such a nature as to afford indirect protection to other products.

[...]

CHAPTER 3
APPROXIMATION OF LAWS

Article 114

(ex Article 95 TEC)

1. Save where otherwise provided in the Treaties, the following provisions shall apply for the achievement of the objectives set out in Article 26. The European Parliament and the Council shall, acting in accordance with the ordinary legislative procedure and after consulting the Economic and Social Committee, adopt the measures for the approximation of the provisions laid down by law, regulation or administrative action in Member States which have as their object the establishment and functioning of the internal market.

2. Paragraph 1 shall not apply to fiscal provisions, to those relating to the free movement of persons nor to those relating to the rights and interests of employed persons.

3. The Commission, in its proposals envisaged in paragraph 1 concerning health, safety, environmental protection and consumer protection, will take as a base a high level of protection, taking account in particular of any new development based on scientific facts. Within their respective powers, the European Parliament and the Council will also seek to achieve this objective.

4. If, after the adoption of a harmonisation measure by the European Parliament and the Council, by the Council or by the Commission, a Member State deems it necessary to maintain national provisions on grounds of major needs referred to in Article 36, or relating to the protection of the environment or the working environment, it shall notify the Commission of these provisions as well as the grounds for maintaining them.

5. Moreover, without prejudice to paragraph 4, if, after the adoption of a harmonisation measure by the European Parliament and the Council, by the Council or by the Commission, a Member State deems it necessary to introduce national provisions based on new scientific evidence relating to the protection of the environment or the working environment on grounds of a problem specific to that Member State arising after the adoption of the harmonisation measure, it shall notify the Commission of the envisaged provisions as well as the grounds for introducing them.

6. The Commission shall, within six months of the notifications as referred to in paragraphs 4 and 5, approve or reject the national provisions involved after having verified whether or not they are a means of arbitrary discrimination or a disguised restriction on trade between Member States and whether or not they shall constitute an obstacle to the functioning of the internal market.

In the absence of a decision by the Commission within this period the national provisions referred to in paragraphs 4 and 5 shall be deemed to have been approved.

When justified by the complexity of the matter and in the absence of danger for human health, the Commission may notify the Member State concerned that the period referred to in this paragraph may be extended for a further period of up to six months.

7. When, pursuant to paragraph 6, a Member State is authorised to maintain or introduce national provisions derogating from a harmonisation measure, the Commission shall immediately examine whether to propose an adaptation to that measure.

8. When a Member State raises a specific problem on public health in a field which has been the subject of prior harmonisation measures, it shall bring it to the attention of the Commission which shall immediately examine whether to propose appropriate measures to the Council.

9. By way of derogation from the procedure laid down in Articles 258 and 259, the Commission and any Member State may bring the matter directly before the Court of Justice of the European Union if it considers that another Member State is making improper use of the powers provided for in this Article.

10. The harmonisation measures referred to above shall, in appropriate cases, include a safeguard clause authorising the Member States to take, for one or more of the non-economic reasons referred to in Article 36, provisional measures subject to a Union control procedure.

TITLE VIII
ECONOMIC AND MONETARY POLICY

Article 119

(ex Article 4 TEC)

1. For the purposes set out in Article 3 of the Treaty on European Union, the activities of the Member States and the Union shall include, as provided in the Treaties, the adoption of an economic policy which is based on the close coordination of Member States' economic policies, on the internal market and on the definition of common objectives, and conducted in accordance with the principle of an open market economy with free competition.

2. Concurrently with the foregoing, and as provided in the Treaties and in accordance with the procedures set out therein, these activities shall include a single currency, the euro, and the definition and conduct of a single monetary policy and exchange-rate policy the primary objective of both of which shall be to maintain price stability and, without prejudice to this objective, to support the general economic policies in the Union, in accordance with the principle of an open market economy with free competition.

3. These activities of the Member States and the Union shall entail compliance with the following guiding principles: stable prices, sound public finances and monetary conditions and a sustainable balance of payments.

CHAPTER 1
ECONOMIC POLICY

[. . .]

Article 123

(ex Article 101 TEC)

1. Overdraft facilities or any other type of credit facility with the European Central Bank or with the central banks of the Member States (hereinafter referred to as "national central banks") in favour of Union institutions, bodies, offices or agencies, central governments, regional, local or other public authorities, other bodies governed by public law, or public undertakings of Member States shall be prohibited, as shall the purchase directly from them by the European Central Bank or national central banks of debt instruments.

2. Paragraph 1 shall not apply to publicly owned credit institutions which, in the context of the supply of reserves by central banks, shall be given the same treatment by national central banks and the European Central Bank as private credit institutions.

[. . .]

Article 125

(ex Article 103 TEC)

1. The Union shall not be liable for or assume the commitments of central governments, regional, local or other public authorities, other bodies governed by public law, or public undertakings of any Member State, without prejudice to mutual financial guarantees for the joint execution of a specific project. A Member State shall not be liable for or assume the commitments of central governments, regional, local or other public authorities, other bodies governed by public law, or public undertakings of another Member State, without prejudice to mutual financial guarantees for the joint execution of a specific project.

2. The Council, on a proposal from the Commission and after consulting the European Parliament, may, as required, specify definitions for the application of the prohibitions referred to in Articles 123 and 124 and in this Article.

Article 126

(ex Article 104 TEC)

1. Member States shall avoid excessive government deficits.

2. The Commission shall monitor the development of the budgetary situation and of the stock of government debt in the Member States with a view to identifying gross errors. In particular it shall examine compliance with budgetary discipline on the basis of the following two criteria:

(a) whether the ratio of the planned or actual government deficit to gross domestic product exceeds a reference value, unless:

— either the ratio has declined substantially and continuously and reached a level that comes close to the reference value,

— or, alternatively, the excess over the reference value is only exceptional and temporary and the ratio remains close to the reference value;

(b) whether the ratio of government debt to gross domestic product exceeds a reference value, unless the ratio is sufficiently diminishing and approaching the reference value at a satisfactory pace.

The reference values are specified in the Protocol on the excessive deficit procedure annexed to the Treaties.

3. If a Member State does not fulfil the requirements under one or both of these criteria, the Commission shall prepare a report. The report of the Commission shall also take into account whether the government deficit exceeds government investment expenditure and take into account all other relevant factors, including the medium-term economic and budgetary position of the Member State.

The Commission may also prepare a report if, notwithstanding the fulfilment of the requirements under the criteria, it is of the opinion that there is a risk of an excessive deficit in a Member State.

4. The Economic and Financial Committee shall formulate an opinion on the report of the Commission.

5. If the Commission considers that an excessive deficit in a Member State exists or may occur, it shall address an opinion to the Member State concerned and shall inform the Council accordingly.

6. The Council shall, on a proposal from the Commission, and having considered any observations which the Member State concerned may wish to make, decide after an overall assessment whether an excessive deficit exists.

7. Where the Council decides, in accordance with paragraph 6, that an excessive deficit exists, it shall adopt, without undue delay, on a recommendation from the Commission, recommendations addressed to the Member State concerned with a view to bringing that situation to an end within a given period. Subject to the provisions of paragraph 8, these recommendations shall not be made public.

8. Where it establishes that there has been no effective action in response to its recommendations within the period laid down, the Council may make its recommendations public.

9. If a Member State persists in failing to put into practice the recommendations of the Council, the Council may decide to give notice to the Member State to take, within a specified time limit, measures for the deficit reduction which is judged necessary by the Council in order to remedy the situation.

In such a case, the Council may request the Member State concerned to submit reports in accordance with a specific timetable in order to examine the adjustment efforts of that Member State.

10. The rights to bring actions provided for in Articles 258 and 259 may not be exercised within the framework of paragraphs 1 to 9 of this Article.

11. As long as a Member State fails to comply with a decision taken in accordance with paragraph 9, the Council may decide to apply or, as the case may be, intensify one or more of the following measures:

— to require the Member State concerned to publish additional information, to be specified by the Council, before issuing bonds and securities,

— to invite the European Investment Bank to reconsider its lending policy towards the Member State concerned,

— to require the Member State concerned to make a non-interest-bearing deposit of an appropriate size with the Union until the excessive deficit has, in the view of the Council, been corrected,

— to impose fines of an appropriate size.

The President of the Council shall inform the European Parliament of the decisions taken.

12. The Council shall abrogate some or all of its decisions or recommendations referred to in paragraphs 6 to 9 and 11 to the extent that the excessive deficit in the Member State concerned has, in the view of the Council, been corrected. If the Council has previously made public recommendations, it shall, as soon as the decision under paragraph 8 has been abrogated, make a public statement that an excessive deficit in the Member State concerned no longer exists.

13. When taking the decisions or recommendations referred to in paragraphs 8, 9, 11 and 12, the Council shall act on a recommendation from the Commission.

When the Council adopts the measures referred to in paragraphs 6 to 9, 11 and 12, it shall act without taking into account the vote of the member of the Council representing the Member State concerned.

A qualified majority of the other members of the Council shall be defined in accordance with Article 238(3)(a).

14. Further provisions relating to the implementation of the procedure described in this Article are set out in the Protocol on the excessive deficit procedure annexed to the Treaties.

The Council shall, acting unanimously in accordance with a special legislative procedure and after consulting the European Parliament and the European Central Bank, adopt the appropriate provisions which shall then replace the said Protocol.

Subject to the other provisions of this paragraph, the Council shall, on a proposal from the Commission and after consulting the European Parliament, lay down detailed rules and definitions for the application of the provisions of the said Protocol.

CHAPTER 2
MONETARY POLICY

Article 127

(ex Article 105 TEC)

1. The primary objective of the European System of Central Banks (hereinafter referred to as "the ESCB") shall be to maintain price stability. Without prejudice to the objective of price stability, the ESCB shall support the general economic policies in the Union with a view to contributing to the achievement of the objectives of the Union as laid down in Article 3 of the Treaty on European Union. The ESCB shall act in accordance with the principle of an open market economy with free competition, favouring an efficient allocation of resources, and in compliance with the principles set out in Article 119.

2. The basic tasks to be carried out through the ESCB shall be:

— to define and implement the monetary policy of the Union,

— to conduct foreign-exchange operations consistent with the provisions of Article 219,

— to hold and manage the official foreign reserves of the Member States,

— to promote the smooth operation of payment systems.

3. The third indent of paragraph 2 shall be without prejudice to the holding and management by the governments of Member States of foreign-exchange working balances.

4. The European Central Bank shall be consulted:

— on any proposed Union act in its fields of competence,

— by national authorities regarding any draft legislative provision in its fields of competence, but within the limits and under the conditions set out by the Council in accordance with the procedure laid down in Article 129(4).

The European Central Bank may submit opinions to the appropriate Union institutions, bodies, offices or agencies or to national authorities on matters in its fields of competence.

5. The ESCB shall contribute to the smooth conduct of policies pursued by the competent authorities relating to the prudential supervision of credit institutions and the stability of the financial system.

6. The Council, acting by means of regulations in accordance with a special legislative procedure, may unanimously, and after consulting the European Parliament and the European Central Bank, confer specific tasks upon the European Central Bank concerning policies relating to the

prudential supervision of credit institutions and other financial institutions with the exception of insurance undertakings.

Article 128

(ex Article 106 TEC)

1. The European Central Bank shall have the exclusive right to authorise the issue of euro banknotes within the Union. The European Central Bank and the national central banks may issue such notes. The banknotes issued by the European Central Bank and the national central banks shall be the only such notes to have the status of legal tender within the Union.

2. Member States may issue euro coins subject to approval by the European Central Bank of the volume of the issue. The Council, on a proposal from the Commission and after consulting the European Parliament and the European Central Bank, may adopt measures to harmonise the denominations and technical specifications of all coins intended for circulation to the extent necessary to permit their smooth circulation within the Union.

Article 129

(ex Article 107 TEC)

1. The ESCB shall be governed by the decision-making bodies of the European Central Bank which shall be the Governing Council and the Executive Board.

2. The Statute of the European System of Central Banks and of the European Central Bank (hereinafter referred to as "the Statute of the ESCB and of the ECB") is laid down in a Protocol annexed to the Treaties.

3. Articles 5.1, 5.2, 5.3, 17, 18, 19.1, 22, 23, 24, 26, 32.2, 32.3, 32.4, 32.6, 33.1(a) and 36 of the Statute of the ESCB and of the ECB may be amended by the European Parliament and the Council, acting in accordance with the ordinary legislative procedure. They shall act either on a recommendation from the European Central Bank and after consulting the Commission or on a proposal from the Commission and after consulting the European Central Bank.

4. The Council, either on a proposal from the Commission and after consulting the European Parliament and the European Central Bank or on a recommendation from the European Central Bank and after consulting the European Parliament and the Commission, shall adopt the provisions referred to in Articles 4, 5.4, 19.2, 20, 28.1, 29.2, 30.4 and 34.3 of the Statute of the ESCB and of the ECB.

CHAPTER 5
TRANSITIONAL PROVISIONS

Article 139

1. Member States in respect of which the Council has not decided that they fulfil the necessary conditions for the adoption of the euro shall hereinafter be referred to as "Member States with a derogation".

2. The following provisions of the Treaties shall not apply to Member States with a derogation:

(a) adoption of the parts of the broad economic policy guidelines which concern the euro area generally (Article 121(2));

(b) coercive means of remedying excessive deficits (Article 126(9) and (11));

(c) the objectives and tasks of the ESCB (Article 127(1) to (3) and (5));

(d) issue of the euro (Article 128);

(e) acts of the European Central Bank (Article 132);

(f) measures governing the use of the euro (Article 133);

(g) monetary agreements and other measures relating to exchange-rate policy (Article 219);

(h) appointment of members of the Executive Board of the European Central Bank (Article 283(2));

(i) decisions establishing common positions on issues of particular relevance for economic and monetary union within the competent international financial institutions and conferences (Article 138(1));

(j) measures to ensure unified representation within the international financial institutions and conferences (Article 138(2)).

In the Articles referred to in points (a) to (j), "Member States" shall therefore mean Member States whose currency is the euro.

3. Under Chapter IX of the Statute of the ESCB and of the ECB, Member States with a derogation and their national central banks are excluded from rights and obligations within the ESCB.

4. The voting rights of members of the Council representing Member States with a derogation shall be suspended for the adoption by the Council of the measures referred to in the Articles listed in paragraph 2, and in the following instances:

(a) recommendations made to those Member States whose currency is the euro in the framework of multilateral surveillance, including on stability programmes and warnings (Article 121(4));

(b) measures relating to excessive deficits concerning those Member States whose currency is the euro (Article 126(6), (7), (8), (12) and (13)).

A qualified majority of the other members of the Council shall be defined in accordance with Article 238(3)(a).

Article 140

(ex Articles 121(1), 122(2), second sentence, and 123(5) TEC)

1. At least once every two years, or at the request of a Member State with a derogation, the Commission and the European Central Bank shall report to the Council on the progress made by the Member States with a derogation in fulfilling their obligations regarding the achievement of economic and monetary union. These reports shall include an examination of the compatibility between the national legislation of each of these Member States, including the statutes of its national central bank, and Articles 130 and 131 and the Statute of the ESCB and of the ECB. The reports shall also examine the achievement of a high degree of sustainable convergence by reference to the fulfilment by each Member State of the following criteria:

— the achievement of a high degree of price stability; this will be apparent from a rate of inflation which is close to that of, at most, the three best performing Member States in terms of price stability,

— the sustainability of the government financial position; this will be apparent from having achieved a government budgetary position without a deficit that is excessive as determined in accordance with Article 126(6),

— the observance of the normal fluctuation margins provided for by the exchange-rate mechanism of the European Monetary System, for at least two years, without devaluing against the euro,

— the durability of convergence achieved by the Member State with a derogation and of its participation in the exchange-rate mechanism being reflected in the long-term interest-rate levels.

The four criteria mentioned in this paragraph and the relevant periods over which they are to be respected are developed further in a Protocol annexed to the Treaties. The reports of the Commission and the European Central Bank shall also take account of the results of the integration of markets, the situation and development of the balances of payments on current account and an examination of the development of unit labour costs and other price indices.

2. After consulting the European Parliament and after discussion in the European Council, the Council shall, on a proposal from the Commission, decide which Member States with a derogation fulfil the necessary conditions on the basis of the criteria set out in paragraph 1, and abrogate the derogations of the Member States concerned.

The Council shall act having received a recommendation of a qualified majority of those among its members representing Member States whose currency is the euro. These members shall act within six months of the Council receiving the Commission's proposal.

The qualified majority of the said members, as referred to in the second subparagraph, shall be defined in accordance with Article 238(3)(a).

3. If it is decided, in accordance with the procedure set out in paragraph 2, to abrogate a derogation, the Council shall, acting with the unanimity of the Member States whose currency is the euro and the Member State concerned, on a proposal from the Commission and after consulting the European Central Bank, irrevocably fix the rate at which the euro shall be substituted for the currency of the Member State concerned, and take the other measures necessary for the introduction of the euro as the single currency in the Member State concerned.

TITLE X
SOCIAL POLICY

[...]

Article 157

(ex Article 141 TEC)

1. Each Member State shall ensure that the principle of equal pay for male and female workers for equal work or work of equal value is applied.

2. For the purpose of this Article, "pay" means the ordinary basic or minimum wage or salary and any other consideration, whether in cash or in kind, which the worker receives directly or indirectly, in respect of his employment, from his employer.

Equal pay without discrimination based on sex means:

(a) that pay for the same work at piece rates shall be calculated on the basis of the same unit of measurement;

(b) that pay for work at time rates shall be the same for the same job.

3. The European Parliament and the Council, acting in accordance with the ordinary legislative procedure, and after consulting the Economic and Social Committee, shall adopt measures to ensure the application of the principle of equal opportunities and equal treatment of men and women

in matters of employment and occupation, including the principle of equal pay for equal work or work of equal value.

4. With a view to ensuring full equality in practice between men and women in working life, the principle of equal treatment shall not prevent any Member State from maintaining or adopting measures providing for specific advantages in order to make it easier for the underrepresented sex to pursue a vocational activity or to prevent or compensate for disadvantages in professional careers.

[. . .]

TITLE XIV
PUBLIC HEALTH

Article 168

(ex Article 152 TEC)

1. A high level of human health protection shall be ensured in the definition and implementation of all Union policies and activities.

Union action, which shall complement national policies, shall be directed towards improving public health, preventing physical and mental illness and diseases, and obviating sources of danger to physical and mental health. Such action shall cover the fight against the major health scourges, by promoting research into their causes, their transmission and their prevention, as well as health information and education, and monitoring, early warning of and combating serious cross-border threats to health.

The Union shall complement the Member States' action in reducing drugs-related health damage, including information and prevention.

2. The Union shall encourage cooperation between the Member States in the areas referred to in this Article and, if necessary, lend support to their action. It shall in particular encourage cooperation between the Member States to improve the complementarity of their health services in cross-border areas.

Member States shall, in liaison with the Commission, coordinate among themselves their policies and programmes in the areas referred to in paragraph 1. The Commission may, in close contact with the Member States, take any useful initiative to promote such coordination, in particular initiatives aiming at the establishment of guidelines and indicators, the organisation of exchange of best practice, and the preparation of the necessary elements for periodic monitoring and evaluation. The European Parliament shall be kept fully informed.

3. The Union and the Member States shall foster cooperation with third countries and the competent international organisations in the sphere of public health.

4. By way of derogation from Article 2(5) and Article 6(a) and in accordance with Article 4(2)(k) the European Parliament and the Council, acting in accordance with the ordinary legislative procedure and after consulting the Economic and Social Committee and the Committee of the Regions, shall contribute to the achievement of the objectives referred to in this Article through adopting in order to meet common safety concerns:

(a) measures setting high standards of quality and safety of organs and substances of human origin, blood and blood derivatives; these measures shall not prevent any Member State from maintaining or introducing more stringent protective measures;

(b) measures in the veterinary and phytosanitary fields which have as their direct objective the protection of public health;

(c) measures setting high standards of quality and safety for medicinal products and devices for medical use.

5. The European Parliament and the Council, acting in accordance with the ordinary legislative procedure and after consulting the Economic and Social Committee and the Committee of the Regions, may also adopt incentive measures designed to protect and improve human health and in particular to combat the major cross-border health scourges, measures concerning monitoring, early warning of and combating serious cross-border threats to health, and measures which have as their direct objective the protection of public health regarding tobacco and the abuse of alcohol, excluding any harmonisation of the laws and regulations of the Member States.

6. The Council, on a proposal from the Commission, may also adopt recommendations for the purposes set out in this Article.

7. Union action shall respect the responsibilities of the Member States for the definition of their health policy and for the organisation and delivery of health services and medical care. The responsibilities of the Member States shall include the management of health services and medical care and the allocation of the resources assigned to them. The measures referred to in paragraph 4(a) shall not affect national provisions on the donation or medical use of organs and blood.

TITLE XX
ENVIRONMENT

Article 191

(ex Article 174 TEC)

1. Union policy on the environment shall contribute to pursuit of the following objectives:

— preserving, protecting and improving the quality of the environment,

— protecting human health,

— prudent and rational utilisation of natural resources,

— promoting measures at international level to deal with regional or worldwide environmental problems, and in particular combating climate change.

2. Union policy on the environment shall aim at a high level of protection taking into account the diversity of situations in the various regions of the Union. It shall be based on the precautionary principle and on the principles that preventive action should be taken, that environmental damage should as a priority be rectified at source and that the polluter should pay.

In this context, harmonisation measures answering environmental protection requirements shall include, where appropriate, a safeguard clause allowing Member States to take provisional measures, for non-economic environmental reasons, subject to a procedure of inspection by the Union.

3. In preparing its policy on the environment, the Union shall take account of:

— available scientific and technical data,

— environmental conditions in the various regions of the Union,

— the potential benefits and costs of action or lack of action,

— the economic and social development of the Union as a whole and the balanced development of its regions.

4. Within their respective spheres of competence, the Union and the Member States shall cooperate with third countries and with the competent international organisations. The arrangements for Union cooperation may be the subject of agreements between the Union and the third parties concerned.

The previous subparagraph shall be without prejudice to Member States' competence to negotiate in international bodies and to conclude international agreements.

PART FIVE
THE UNION'S EXTERNAL ACTION

[...]

TITLE II
COMMON COMMERCIAL POLICY

[...]

Article 207

(ex Article 133 TEC)

1. The common commercial policy shall be based on uniform principles, particularly with regard to changes in tariff rates, the conclusion of tariff and trade agreements relating to trade in goods and services, and the commercial aspects of intellectual property, foreign direct investment, the achievement of uniformity in measures of liberalisation, export policy and measures to protect trade such as those to be taken in the event of dumping or subsidies. The common commercial policy shall be conducted in the context of the principles and objectives of the Union's external action.

2. The European Parliament and the Council, acting by means of regulations in accordance with the ordinary legislative procedure, shall adopt the measures defining the framework for implementing the common commercial policy.

3. Where agreements with one or more third countries or international organisations need to be negotiated and concluded, Article 218 shall apply, subject to the special provisions of this Article.

The Commission shall make recommendations to the Council, which shall authorise it to open the necessary negotiations. The Council and the Commission shall be responsible for ensuring that the agreements negotiated are compatible with internal Union policies and rules.

The Commission shall conduct these negotiations in consultation with a special committee appointed by the Council to assist the Commission in this task and within the framework of such directives as the Council may issue to it. The Commission shall report regularly to the special committee and to the European Parliament on the progress of negotiations.

4. For the negotiation and conclusion of the agreements referred to in paragraph 3, the Council shall act by a qualified majority.

For the negotiation and conclusion of agreements in the fields of trade in services and the commercial aspects of intellectual property, as well as foreign direct investment, the Council shall act unanimously where such agreements include provisions for which unanimity is required for the adoption of internal rules.

The Council shall also act unanimously for the negotiation and conclusion of agreements:

(a) in the field of trade in cultural and audiovisual services, where these agreements risk prejudicing the Union's cultural and linguistic diversity;

(b) in the field of trade in social, education and health services, where these agreements risk seriously disturbing the national organisation of such services and prejudicing the responsibility of Member States to deliver them.

5. The negotiation and conclusion of international agreements in the field of transport shall be subject to Title VI of Part Three and to Article 218.

6. The exercise of the competences conferred by this Article in the field of the common commercial policy shall not affect the delimitation of competences between the Union and the Member States, and shall not lead to harmonisation of legislative or regulatory provisions of the Member States in so far as the Treaties exclude such harmonisation.

TITLE V
INTERNATIONAL AGREEMENTS

Article 216

1. The Union may conclude an agreement with one or more third countries or international organisations where the Treaties so provide or where the conclusion of an agreement is necessary in order to achieve, within the framework of the Union's policies, one of the objectives referred to in the Treaties, or is provided for in a legally binding Union act or is likely to affect common rules or alter their scope.

2. Agreements concluded by the Union are binding upon the institutions of the Union and on its Member States.

Article 217

(ex Article 310 TEC)

The Union may conclude with one or more third countries or international organisations agreements establishing an association involving reciprocal rights and obligations, common action and special procedure.

Article 218

(ex Article 300 TEC)

1. Without prejudice to the specific provisions laid down in Article 207, agreements between the Union and third countries or international

organisations shall be negotiated and concluded in accordance with the following procedure.

2. The Council shall authorise the opening of negotiations, adopt negotiating directives, authorise the signing of agreements and conclude them.

3. The Commission, or the High Representative of the Union for Foreign Affairs and Security Policy where the agreement envisaged relates exclusively or principally to the common foreign and security policy, shall submit recommendations to the Council, which shall adopt a decision authorising the opening of negotiations and, depending on the subject of the agreement envisaged, nominating the Union negotiator or the head of the Union's negotiating team.

4. The Council may address directives to the negotiator and designate a special committee in consultation with which the negotiations must be conducted.

5. The Council, on a proposal by the negotiator, shall adopt a decision authorising the signing of the agreement and, if necessary, its provisional application before entry into force.

6. The Council, on a proposal by the negotiator, shall adopt a decision concluding the agreement.

Except where agreements relate exclusively to the common foreign and security policy, the Council shall adopt the decision concluding the agreement:

(a) after obtaining the consent of the European Parliament in the following cases:

(i) association agreements;

(ii) agreement on Union accession to the European Convention for the Protection of Human Rights and Fundamental Freedoms;

(iii) agreements establishing a specific institutional framework by organising cooperation procedures;

(iv) agreements with important budgetary implications for the Union;

(v) agreements covering fields to which either the ordinary legislative procedure applies, or the special legislative procedure where consent by the European Parliament is required.

The European Parliament and the Council may, in an urgent situation, agree upon a time-limit for consent.

(b) after consulting the European Parliament in other cases. The European Parliament shall deliver its opinion within a time-limit which the Council may set depending on the urgency of the matter. In the absence of an opinion within that time-limit, the Council may act.

7. When concluding an agreement, the Council may, by way of derogation from paragraphs 5, 6 and 9, authorise the negotiator to approve on the Union's behalf modifications to the agreement where it provides for them to be adopted by a simplified procedure or by a body set up by the agreement. The Council may attach specific conditions to such authorisation.

8. The Council shall act by a qualified majority throughout the procedure.

However, it shall act unanimously when the agreement covers a field for which unanimity is required for the adoption of a Union act as well as for association agreements and the agreements referred to in Article 212 with the States which are candidates for accession. The Council shall also act unanimously for the agreement on accession of the Union to the European Convention for the Protection of Human Rights and Fundamental Freedoms; the decision concluding this agreement shall enter into force after it has been approved by the Member States in accordance with their respective constitutional requirements.

9. The Council, on a proposal from the Commission or the High Representative of the Union for Foreign Affairs and Security Policy, shall adopt a decision suspending application of an agreement and establishing the positions to be adopted on the Union's behalf in a body set up by an agreement, when that body is called upon to adopt acts having legal effects, with the exception of acts supplementing or amending the institutional framework of the agreement.

10. The European Parliament shall be immediately and fully informed at all stages of the procedure.

11. A Member State, the European Parliament, the Council or the Commission may obtain the opinion of the Court of Justice as to whether an agreement envisaged is compatible with the Treaties. Where the opinion of the Court is adverse, the agreement envisaged may not enter into force unless it is amended or the Treaties are revised.

Article 219

(ex Article 111(1) to (3) and (5) TEC)

1. By way of derogation from Article 218, the Council, either on a recommendation from the European Central Bank or on a recommendation from the Commission and after consulting the European Central Bank, in an endeavour to reach a consensus consistent with the objective of price

stability, may conclude formal agreements on an exchange-rate system for the euro in relation to the currencies of third States. The Council shall act unanimously after consulting the European Parliament and in accordance with the procedure provided for in paragraph 3.

The Council may, either on a recommendation from the European Central Bank or on a recommendation from the Commission, and after consulting the European Central Bank, in an endeavour to reach a consensus consistent with the objective of price stability, adopt, adjust or abandon the central rates of the euro within the exchange-rate system. The President of the Council shall inform the European Parliament of the adoption, adjustment or abandonment of the euro central rates.

2. In the absence of an exchange-rate system in relation to one or more currencies of third States as referred to in paragraph 1, the Council, either on a recommendation from the Commission and after consulting the European Central Bank or on a recommendation from the European Central Bank, may formulate general orientations for exchange-rate policy in relation to these currencies. These general orientations shall be without prejudice to the primary objective of the ESCB to maintain price stability.

3. By way of derogation from Article 218, where agreements concerning monetary or foreign exchange regime matters need to be negotiated by the Union with one or more third States or international organisations, the Council, on a recommendation from the Commission and after consulting the European Central Bank, shall decide the arrangements for the negotiation and for the conclusion of such agreements. These arrangements shall ensure that the Union expresses a single position. The Commission shall be fully associated with the negotiations.

4. Without prejudice to Union competence and Union agreements as regards economic and monetary union, Member States may negotiate in international bodies and conclude international agreements.

PART SIX
INSTITUTIONAL AND FINANCIAL PROVISIONS

TITLE I
INSTITUTIONAL PROVISIONS

CHAPTER 1
THE INSTITUTIONS

SECTION 1
THE EUROPEAN PARLIAMENT

Article 225

(ex Article 192, second subparagraph, TEC)

The European Parliament may, acting by a majority of its component Members, request the Commission to submit any appropriate proposal on matters on which it considers that a Union act is required for the purpose of implementing the Treaties. If the Commission does not submit a proposal, it shall inform the European Parliament of the reasons.

Article 228

(ex Article 195 TEC)

1. A European Ombudsman, elected by the European Parliament, shall be empowered to receive complaints from any citizen of the Union or any natural or legal person residing or having its registered office in a Member State concerning instances of maladministration in the activities of the Union institutions, bodies, offices or agencies, with the exception of the Court of Justice of the European Union acting in its judicial role. He or she shall examine such complaints and report on them.

In accordance with his duties, the Ombudsman shall conduct inquiries for which he finds grounds, either on his own initiative or on the basis of complaints submitted to him direct or through a Member of the European Parliament, except where the alleged facts are or have been the subject of legal proceedings. Where the Ombudsman establishes an instance of maladministration, he shall refer the matter to the institution, body, office or agency concerned, which shall have a period of three months in which to inform him of its views. The Ombudsman shall then forward a report to the European Parliament and the institution, body, office or agency concerned. The person lodging the complaint shall be informed of the outcome of such inquiries.

The Ombudsman shall submit an annual report to the European Parliament on the outcome of his inquiries.

2. The Ombudsman shall be elected after each election of the European Parliament for the duration of its term of office. The Ombudsman shall be eligible for reappointment.

The Ombudsman may be dismissed by the Court of Justice at the request of the European Parliament if he no longer fulfils the conditions required for the performance of his duties or if he is guilty of serious misconduct.

3. The Ombudsman shall be completely independent in the performance of his duties. In the performance of those duties he shall neither seek nor take instructions from any Government, institution, body, office or entity. The Ombudsman may not, during his term of office, engage in any other occupation, whether gainful or not.

4. The European Parliament acting by means of regulations on its own initiative in accordance with a special legislative procedure shall, after seeking an opinion from the Commission and with the consent of the Council, lay down the regulations and general conditions governing the performance of the Ombudsman's duties.

[...]

SECTION 3
THE COUNCIL

Article 237

(ex Article 204 TEC)

The Council shall meet when convened by its President on his own initiative or at the request of one of its Members or of the Commission.

Article 238

(ex Article 205(1) and (2), TEC)

1. Where it is required to act by a simple majority, the Council shall act by a majority of its component members.

2. By way of derogation from Article 16(4) of the Treaty on European Union, as from 1 November 2014 and subject to the provisions laid down in the Protocol on transitional provisions, where the Council does not act on a proposal from the Commission or from the High Representative of the Union for Foreign Affairs and Security Policy, the qualified majority shall be defined as at least 72 % of the members of the Council, representing Member States comprising at least 65 % of the population of the Union.

3. As from 1 November 2014 and subject to the provisions laid down in the Protocol on transitional provisions, in cases where, under the Treaties, not all the members of the Council participate in voting, a qualified majority shall be defined as follows:

(a) A qualified majority shall be defined as at least 55 % of the members of the Council representing the participating Member States, comprising at least 65 % of the population of these States.

A blocking minority must include at least the minimum number of Council members representing more than 35 % of the population of the participating Member States, plus one member, failing which the qualified majority shall be deemed attained;

(b) By way of derogation from point (a), where the Council does not act on a proposal from the Commission or from the High Representative of the Union for Foreign Affairs and Security Policy, the qualified majority shall be defined as at least 72 % of the members of the Council representing the participating Member States, comprising at least 65 % of the population of these States.

4. Abstentions by Members present in person or represented shall not prevent the adoption by the Council of acts which require unanimity.

Article 239

(ex Article 206 TEC)

Where a vote is taken, any Member of the Council may also act on behalf of not more than one other member.

Article 240

(ex Article 207 TEC)

1. A committee consisting of the Permanent Representatives of the Governments of the Member States shall be responsible for preparing the work of the Council and for carrying out the tasks assigned to it by the latter. The Committee may adopt procedural decisions in cases provided for in the Council's Rules of Procedure.

2. The Council shall be assisted by a General Secretariat, under the responsibility of a Secretary-General appointed by the Council.

The Council shall decide on the organisation of the General Secretariat by a simple majority.

3. The Council shall act by a simple majority regarding procedural matters and for the adoption of its Rules of Procedure.

Article 241

(ex Article 208 TEC)

The Council, acting by a simple majority, may request the Commission to undertake any studies the Council considers desirable for the attainment of the common objectives, and to submit to it any appropriate proposals. If the Commission does not submit a proposal, it shall inform the Council of the reasons.

Article 242

(ex Article 209 TEC)

The Council, acting by a simple majority shall, after consulting the Commission, determine the rules governing the committees provided for in the Treaties.

Article 243

(ex Article 210 TEC)

The Council shall determine the salaries, allowances and pensions of the President of the European Council, the President of the Commission, the High Representative of the Union for Foreign Affairs and Security Policy, the Members of the Commission, the Presidents, Members and Registrars of the Court of Justice of the European Union, and the Secretary-General of the Council. It shall also determine any payment to be made instead of remuneration.

SECTION 4
THE COMMISSION

Article 244

In accordance with Article 17(5) of the Treaty on European Union, the Members of the Commission shall be chosen on the basis of a system of rotation established unanimously by the European Council and on the basis of the following principles:

(a) Member States shall be treated on a strictly equal footing as regards determination of the sequence of, and the time spent by, their nationals as members of the Commission; consequently, the difference between the total number of terms of office held by nationals of any given pair of Member States may never be more than one;

(b) subject to point (a), each successive Commission shall be so composed as to reflect satisfactorily the demographic and geographical range of all the Member States.

Article 245

(ex Article 213 TEC)

The Members of the Commission shall refrain from any action incompatible with their duties. Member States shall respect their independence and shall not seek to influence them in the performance of their tasks.

The Members of the Commission may not, during their term of office, engage in any other occupation, whether gainful or not. When entering upon their duties they shall give a solemn undertaking that, both during and after their term of office, they will respect the obligations arising therefrom and in particular their duty to behave with integrity and discretion as regards the acceptance, after they have ceased to hold office, of certain appointments or benefits. In the event of any breach of these obligations, the Court of Justice may, on application by the Council acting by a simple majority or the Commission, rule that the Member concerned be, according to the circumstances, either compulsorily retired in accordance with Article 247 or deprived of his right to a pension or other benefits in its stead.

Article 246

(ex Article 215 TEC)

Apart from normal replacement, or death, the duties of a Member of the Commission shall end when he resigns or is compulsorily retired.

A vacancy caused by resignation, compulsory retirement or death shall be filled for the remainder of the Member's term of office by a new Member of the same nationality appointed by the Council, by common accord with the President of the Commission, after consulting the European Parliament and in accordance with the criteria set out in the second subparagraph of Article 17(3) of the Treaty on European Union.

The Council may, acting unanimously on a proposal from the President of the Commission, decide that such a vacancy need not be filled, in particular when the remainder of the Member's term of office is short.

In the event of resignation, compulsory retirement or death, the President shall be replaced for the remainder of his term of office. The procedure laid down in the first subparagraph of Article 17(7) of the Treaty on European Union shall be applicable for the replacement of the President.

In the event of resignation, compulsory retirement or death, the High Representative of the Union for Foreign Affairs and Security Policy shall be replaced, for the remainder of his or her term of office, in accordance with Article 18(1) of the Treaty on European Union.

In the case of the resignation of all the Members of the Commission, they shall remain in office and continue to deal with current business until they have been replaced, for the remainder of their term of office, in accordance with Article 17 of the Treaty on European Union.

Article 247

(ex Article 216 TEC)

If any Member of the Commission no longer fulfils the conditions required for the performance of his duties or if he has been guilty of serious misconduct, the Court of Justice may, on application by the Council acting by a simple majority or the Commission, compulsorily retire him.

Article 248

(ex Article 217(2) TEC)

Without prejudice to Article 18(4) of the Treaty on European Union, the responsibilities incumbent upon the Commission shall be structured and allocated among its members by its President, in accordance with Article 17(6) of that Treaty. The President may reshuffle the allocation of those responsibilities during the Commission's term of office. The Members of the Commission shall carry out the duties devolved upon them by the President under his authority.

Article 249

(ex Articles 218(2) and 212 TEC)

1. The Commission shall adopt its Rules of Procedure so as to ensure that both it and its departments operate. It shall ensure that these Rules are published.

2. The Commission shall publish annually, not later than one month before the opening of the session of the European Parliament, a general report on the activities of the Union.

Article 250

(ex Article 219 TEC)

The Commission shall act by a majority of its Members.

Its Rules of Procedure shall determine the quorum.

SECTION 5
THE COURT OF JUSTICE OF THE EUROPEAN UNION

Article 251

(ex Article 221 TEC)

The Court of Justice shall sit in chambers or in a Grand Chamber, in accordance with the rules laid down for that purpose in the Statute of the Court of Justice of the European Union.

When provided for in the Statute, the Court of Justice may also sit as a full Court.

Article 252

(ex Article 222 TEC)

The Court of Justice shall be assisted by eight Advocates-General. Should the Court of Justice so request, the Council, acting unanimously, may increase the number of Advocates-General.

It shall be the duty of the Advocate-General, acting with complete impartiality and independence, to make, in open court, reasoned submissions on cases which, in accordance with the Statute of the Court of Justice of the European Union, require his involvement.

Article 253

(ex Article 223 TEC)

The Judges and Advocates-General of the Court of Justice shall be chosen from persons whose independence is beyond doubt and who possess the qualifications required for appointment to the highest judicial offices in their respective countries or who are jurisconsults of recognised competence; they shall be appointed by common accord of the governments of the Member States for a term of six years, after consultation of the panel provided for in Article 255.

Every three years there shall be a partial replacement of the Judges and Advocates-General, in accordance with the conditions laid down in the Statute of the Court of Justice of the European Union.

The Judges shall elect the President of the Court of Justice from among their number for a term of three years. He may be re-elected.

Retiring Judges and Advocates-General may be reappointed.

The Court of Justice shall appoint its Registrar and lay down the rules governing his service.

The Court of Justice shall establish its Rules of Procedure. Those Rules shall require the approval of the Council.

Article 254

(ex Article 224 TEC)

The number of Judges of the General Court shall be determined by the Statute of the Court of Justice of the European Union. The Statute may provide for the General Court to be assisted by Advocates-General.

The members of the General Court shall be chosen from persons whose independence is beyond doubt and who possess the ability required for appointment to high judicial office. They shall be appointed by common accord of the governments of the Member States for a term of six years, after consultation of the panel provided for in Article 255. The membership shall be partially renewed every three years. Retiring members shall be eligible for reappointment.

The Judges shall elect the President of the General Court from among their number for a term of three years. He may be re-elected.

The General Court shall appoint its Registrar and lay down the rules governing his service.

The General Court shall establish its Rules of Procedure in agreement with the Court of Justice. Those Rules shall require the approval of the Council.

Unless the Statute of the Court of Justice of the European Union provides otherwise, the provisions of the Treaties relating to the Court of Justice shall apply to the General Court.

Article 255

A panel shall be set up in order to give an opinion on candidates' suitability to perform the duties of Judge and Advocate-General of the Court of Justice and the General Court before the governments of the Member States make the appointments referred to in Articles 253 and 254.

The panel shall comprise seven persons chosen from among former members of the Court of Justice and the General Court, members of national supreme courts and lawyers of recognised competence, one of whom shall be proposed by the European Parliament. The Council shall adopt a decision establishing the panel's operating rules and a decision appointing its members. It shall act on the initiative of the President of the Court of Justice.

Article 256

(ex Article 225 TEC)

1. The General Court shall have jurisdiction to hear and determine at first instance actions or proceedings referred to in Articles 263, 265, 268, 270 and 272, with the exception of those assigned to a specialised court set up under Article 257 and those reserved in the Statute for the Court of Justice. The Statute may provide for the General Court to have jurisdiction for other classes of action or proceeding.

Decisions given by the General Court under this paragraph may be subject to a right of appeal to the Court of Justice on points of law only, under the conditions and within the limits laid down by the Statute.

2. The General Court shall have jurisdiction to hear and determine actions or proceedings brought against decisions of the specialised courts.

Decisions given by the General Court under this paragraph may exceptionally be subject to review by the Court of Justice, under the conditions and within the limits laid down by the Statute, where there is a serious risk of the unity or consistency of Union law being affected.

3. The General Court shall have jurisdiction to hear and determine questions referred for a preliminary ruling under Article 267, in specific areas laid down by the Statute.

Where the General Court considers that the case requires a decision of principle likely to affect the unity or consistency of Union law, it may refer the case to the Court of Justice for a ruling.

Decisions given by the General Court on questions referred for a preliminary ruling may exceptionally be subject to review by the Court of Justice, under the conditions and within the limits laid down by the Statute, where there is a serious risk of the unity or consistency of Union law being affected.

Article 257

(ex Article 225a TEC)

The European Parliament and the Council, acting in accordance with the ordinary legislative procedure, may establish specialised courts attached to the General Court to hear and determine at first instance certain classes of action or proceeding brought in specific areas. The European Parliament and the Council shall act by means of regulations either on a proposal from the Commission after consultation of the Court of Justice or at the request of the Court of Justice after consultation of the Commission.

The regulation establishing a specialised court shall lay down the rules on the organisation of the court and the extent of the jurisdiction conferred upon it.

Decisions given by specialised courts may be subject to a right of appeal on points of law only or, when provided for in the regulation establishing the specialised court, a right of appeal also on matters of fact, before the General Court.

The members of the specialised courts shall be chosen from persons whose independence is beyond doubt and who possess the ability required for appointment to judicial office. They shall be appointed by the Council, acting unanimously.

The specialised courts shall establish their Rules of Procedure in agreement with the Court of Justice. Those Rules shall require the approval of the Council.

Unless the regulation establishing the specialised court provides otherwise, the provisions of the Treaties relating to the Court of Justice of the European Union and the provisions of the Statute of the Court of Justice of the European Union shall apply to the specialised courts. Title I of the Statute and Article 64 thereof shall in any case apply to the specialised courts.

Article 258

(ex Article 226 TEC)

If the Commission considers that a Member State has failed to fulfil an obligation under the Treaties, it shall deliver a reasoned opinion on the matter after giving the State concerned the opportunity to submit its observations.

If the State concerned does not comply with the opinion within the period laid down by the Commission, the latter may bring the matter before the Court of Justice of the European Union.

Article 259

(ex Article 227 TEC)

A Member State which considers that another Member State has failed to fulfil an obligation under the Treaties may bring the matter before the Court of Justice of the European Union.

Before a Member State brings an action against another Member State for an alleged infringement of an obligation under the Treaties, it shall bring the matter before the Commission.

The Commission shall deliver a reasoned opinion after each of the States concerned has been given the opportunity to submit its own case and its observations on the other party's case both orally and in writing.

If the Commission has not delivered an opinion within three months of the date on which the matter was brought before it, the absence of such opinion shall not prevent the matter from being brought before the Court.

Article 260

(ex Article 228 TEC)

1. If the Court of Justice of the European Union finds that a Member State has failed to fulfil an obligation under the Treaties, the State shall be required to take the necessary measures to comply with the judgment of the Court.

2. If the Commission considers that the Member State concerned has not taken the necessary measures to comply with the judgment of the Court, it may bring the case before the Court after giving that State the opportunity to submit its observations. It shall specify the amount of the lump sum or penalty payment to be paid by the Member State concerned which it considers appropriate in the circumstances.

If the Court finds that the Member State concerned has not complied with its judgment it may impose a lump sum or penalty payment on it.

This procedure shall be without prejudice to Article 259.

3. When the Commission brings a case before the Court pursuant to Article 258 on the grounds that the Member State concerned has failed to fulfil its obligation to notify measures transposing a directive adopted under a legislative procedure, it may, when it deems appropriate, specify the amount of the lump sum or penalty payment to be paid by the Member State concerned which it considers appropriate in the circumstances.

If the Court finds that there is an infringement it may impose a lump sum or penalty payment on the Member State concerned not exceeding the amount specified by the Commission. The payment obligation shall take effect on the date set by the Court in its judgment.

Article 263

(ex Article 230 TEC)

The Court of Justice of the European Union shall review the legality of legislative acts, of acts of the Council, of the Commission and of the European Central Bank, other than recommendations and opinions, and of acts of the European Parliament and of the European Council intended to produce legal effects vis-à-vis third parties. It shall also review the legality of acts of bodies, offices or agencies of the Union intended to produce legal effects vis-à-vis third parties.

It shall for this purpose have jurisdiction in actions brought by a Member State, the European Parliament, the Council or the Commission on grounds of lack of competence, infringement of an essential procedural requirement, infringement of the Treaties or of any rule of law relating to their application, or misuse of powers.

The Court shall have jurisdiction under the same conditions in actions brought by the Court of Auditors, by the European Central Bank and by the Committee of the Regions for the purpose of protecting their prerogatives.

Any natural or legal person may, under the conditions laid down in the first and second paragraphs, institute proceedings against an act addressed to that person or which is of direct and individual concern to them, and against a regulatory act which is of direct concern to them and does not entail implementing measures.

Acts setting up bodies, offices and agencies of the Union may lay down specific conditions and arrangements concerning actions brought by natural or legal persons against acts of these bodies, offices or agencies intended to produce legal effects in relation to them.

The proceedings provided for in this Article shall be instituted within two months of the publication of the measure, or of its notification to the plaintiff, or, in the absence thereof, of the day on which it came to the knowledge of the latter, as the case may be.

Article 264

(ex Article 231 TEC)

If the action is well founded, the Court of Justice of the European Union shall declare the act concerned to be void.

However, the Court shall, if it considers this necessary, state which of the effects of the act which it has declared void shall be considered as definitive.

Article 265

(ex Article 232 TEC)

Should the European Parliament, the European Council, the Council, the Commission or the European Central Bank, in infringement of the Treaties, fail to act, the Member States and the other institutions of the Union may bring an action before the Court of Justice of the European Union to have the infringement established. This Article shall apply, under the same conditions, to bodies, offices and agencies of the Union which fail to act.

The action shall be admissible only if the institution, body, office or agency concerned has first been called upon to act. If, within two months of being so called upon, the institution, body, office or agency concerned has not defined its position, the action may be brought within a further period of two months.

Any natural or legal person may, under the conditions laid down in the preceding paragraphs, complain to the Court that an institution, body, office or agency of the Union has failed to address to that person any act other than a recommendation or an opinion.

Article 266

(ex Article 233 TEC)

The institution whose act has been declared void or whose failure to act has been declared contrary to the Treaties shall be required to take the necessary measures to comply with the judgment of the Court of Justice of the European Union.

This obligation shall not affect any obligation which may result from the application of the second paragraph of Article 340.

Article 267

(ex Article 234 TEC)

The Court of Justice of the European Union shall have jurisdiction to give preliminary rulings concerning:

(a) the interpretation of the Treaties;

(b) the validity and interpretation of acts of the institutions, bodies, offices or agencies of the Union;

Where such a question is raised before any court or tribunal of a Member State, that court or tribunal may, if it considers that a decision on the question is necessary to enable it to give judgment, request the Court to give a ruling thereon.

Where any such question is raised in a case pending before a court or tribunal of a Member State against whose decisions there is no judicial remedy under national law, that court or tribunal shall bring the matter before the Court.

If such a question is raised in a case pending before a court or tribunal of a Member State with regard to a person in custody, the Court of Justice of the European Union shall act with the minimum of delay.

SECTION 6
THE EUROPEAN CENTRAL BANK

Article 282

1. The European Central Bank, together with the national central banks, shall constitute the European System of Central Banks (ESCB). The European Central Bank, together with the national central banks of the Member States whose currency is the euro, which constitute the Eurosystem, shall conduct the monetary policy of the Union.

2. The ESCB shall be governed by the decision-making bodies of the European Central Bank. The primary objective of the ESCB shall be to maintain price stability. Without prejudice to that objective, it shall support the general economic policies in the Union in order to contribute to the achievement of the latter's objectives.

3. The European Central Bank shall have legal personality. It alone may authorise the issue of the euro. It shall be independent in the exercise of its powers and in the management of its finances. Union institutions, bodies, offices and agencies and the governments of the Member States shall respect that independence.

4. The European Central Bank shall adopt such measures as are necessary to carry out its tasks in accordance with Articles 127 to 133, with Article 138, and with the conditions laid down in the Statute of the ESCB and of the ECB. In accordance with these same Articles, those Member States whose currency is not the euro, and their central banks, shall retain their powers in monetary matters.

5. Within the areas falling within its responsibilities, the European Central Bank shall be consulted on all proposed Union acts, and all proposals for regulation at national level, and may give an opinion.

Article 283

(ex Article 112 TEC)

1. The Governing Council of the European Central Bank shall comprise the members of the Executive Board of the European Central Bank and the Governors of the national central banks of the Member States whose currency is the euro.

2. The Executive Board shall comprise the President, the Vice-President and four other members.

The President, the Vice-President and the other members of the Executive Board shall be appointed by the European Council, acting by a qualified majority, from among persons of recognised standing and professional experience in monetary or banking matters, on a recommendation from the Council, after it has consulted the European Parliament and the Governing Council of the European Central Bank.

Their term of office shall be eight years and shall not be renewable.

Only nationals of Member States may be members of the Executive Board.

[...]

CHAPTER 2
LEGAL ACTS OF THE UNION, ADOPTION PROCEDURES AND OTHER PROVISIONS

SECTION 1
THE LEGAL ACTS OF THE UNION

Article 288

(ex Article 249 TEC)

To exercise the Union's competences, the institutions shall adopt regulations, directives, decisions, recommendations and opinions.

A regulation shall have general application. It shall be binding in its entirety and directly applicable in all Member States.

A directive shall be binding, as to the result to be achieved, upon each Member State to which it is addressed, but shall leave to the national authorities the choice of form and methods.

A decision shall be binding in its entirety. A decision which specifies those to whom it is addressed shall be binding only on them.

Recommendations and opinions shall have no binding force.

Article 289

1. The ordinary legislative procedure shall consist in the joint adoption by the European Parliament and the Council of a regulation,

directive or decision on a proposal from the Commission. This procedure is defined in Article 294.

2. In the specific cases provided for by the Treaties, the adoption of a regulation, directive or decision by the European Parliament with the participation of the Council, or by the latter with the participation of the European Parliament, shall constitute a special legislative procedure.

3. Legal acts adopted by legislative procedure shall constitute legislative acts.

4. In the specific cases provided for by the Treaties, legislative acts may be adopted on the initiative of a group of Member States or of the European Parliament, on a recommendation from the European Central Bank or at the request of the Court of Justice or the European Investment Bank.

Article 294

(ex Article 251 TEC)

1. Where reference is made in the Treaties to the ordinary legislative procedure for the adoption of an act, the following procedure shall apply.

2. The Commission shall submit a proposal to the European Parliament and the Council.

First reading

3. The European Parliament shall adopt its position at first reading and communicate it to the Council.

4. If the Council approves the European Parliament's position, the act concerned shall be adopted in the wording which corresponds to the position of the European Parliament.

5. If the Council does not approve the European Parliament's position, it shall adopt its position at first reading and communicate it to the European Parliament.

6. The Council shall inform the European Parliament fully of the reasons which led it to adopt its position at first reading. The Commission shall inform the European Parliament fully of its position.

Second reading

7. If, within three months of such communication, the European Parliament:

(a) approves the Council's position at first reading or has not taken a decision, the act concerned shall be deemed to have been adopted in the wording which corresponds to the position of the Council;

(b) rejects, by a majority of its component members, the Council's position at first reading, the proposed act shall be deemed not to have been adopted;

(c) proposes, by a majority of its component members, amendments to the Council's position at first reading, the text thus amended shall be forwarded to the Council and to the Commission, which shall deliver an opinion on those amendments.

8. If, within three months of receiving the European Parliament's amendments, the Council, acting by a qualified majority:

(a) approves all those amendments, the act in question shall be deemed to have been adopted;

(b) does not approve all the amendments, the President of the Council, in agreement with the President of the European Parliament, shall within six weeks convene a meeting of the Conciliation Committee.

9. The Council shall act unanimously on the amendments on which the Commission has delivered a negative opinion.

Conciliation

10. The Conciliation Committee, which shall be composed of the members of the Council or their representatives and an equal number of members representing the European Parliament, shall have the task of reaching agreement on a joint text, by a qualified majority of the members of the Council or their representatives and by a majority of the members representing the European Parliament within six weeks of its being convened, on the basis of the positions of the European Parliament and the Council at second reading.

11. The Commission shall take part in the Conciliation Committee's proceedings and shall take all necessary initiatives with a view to reconciling the positions of the European Parliament and the Council.

12. If, within six weeks of its being convened, the Conciliation Committee does not approve the joint text, the proposed act shall be deemed not to have been adopted.

Third reading

13. If, within that period, the Conciliation Committee approves a joint text, the European Parliament, acting by a majority of the votes cast, and the Council, acting by a qualified majority, shall each have a period of six weeks from that approval in which to adopt the act in question in accordance with the joint text. If they fail to do so, the proposed act shall be deemed not to have been adopted.

14. The periods of three months and six weeks referred to in this Article shall be extended by a maximum of one month and two weeks respectively at the initiative of the European Parliament or the Council.

Special provisions

15. Where, in the cases provided for in the Treaties, a legislative act is submitted to the ordinary legislative procedure on the initiative of a group of Member States, on a recommendation by the European Central Bank, or at the request of the Court of Justice, paragraph 2, the second sentence of paragraph 6, and paragraph 9 shall not apply.

In such cases, the European Parliament and the Council shall communicate the proposed act to the Commission with their positions at first and second readings. The European Parliament or the Council may request the opinion of the Commission throughout the procedure, which the Commission may also deliver on its own initiative. It may also, if it deems it necessary, take part in the Conciliation Committee in accordance with paragraph 11.

[...]

SECTION 2
PROCEDURES FOR THE ADOPTION OF ACTS AND OTHER PROVISIONS

[...]

Article 297

(ex Article 254 TEC)

1. Legislative acts adopted under the ordinary legislative procedure shall be signed by the President of the European Parliament and by the President of the Council.

Legislative acts adopted under a special legislative procedure shall be signed by the President of the institution which adopted them.

Legislative acts shall be published in the Official Journal of the European Union. They shall enter into force on the date specified in them or, in the absence thereof, on the twentieth day following that of their publication.

2. Non-legislative acts adopted in the form of regulations, directives or decisions, when the latter do not specify to whom they are addressed, shall be signed by the President of the institution which adopted them.

Regulations and directives which are addressed to all Member States, as well as decisions which do not specify to whom they are addressed, shall be published in the Official Journal of the European Union. They shall enter into force on the date specified in them or, in the absence thereof, on the twentieth day following that of their publication.

Other directives, and decisions which specify to whom they are addressed, shall be notified to those to whom they are addressed and shall take effect upon such notification.

CHAPTER 3
THE UNION'S ADVISORY BODIES

Article 300

1. The European Parliament, the Council and the Commission shall be assisted by an Economic and Social Committee and a Committee of the Regions, exercising advisory functions.

2. The Economic and Social Committee shall consist of representatives of organisations of employers, of the employed, and of other parties representative of civil society, notably in socio-economic, civic, professional and cultural areas.

3. The Committee of the Regions shall consist of representatives of regional and local bodies who either hold a regional or local authority electoral mandate or are politically accountable to an elected assembly.

4. The members of the Economic and Social Committee and of the Committee of the Regions shall not be bound by any mandatory instructions. They shall be completely independent in the performance of their duties, in the Union's general interest.

5. The rules referred to in paragraphs 2 and 3 governing the nature of the composition of the Committees shall be reviewed at regular intervals by the Council to take account of economic, social and demographic developments within the Union. The Council, on a proposal from the Commission, shall adopt decisions to that end.

SECTION 1
THE ECONOMIC AND SOCIAL COMMITTEE

Article 301

(ex Article 258 TEC)

The number of members of the Economic and Social Committee shall not exceed 350.

The Council, acting unanimously on a proposal from the Commission, shall adopt a decision determining the Committee's composition.

The Council shall determine the allowances of members of the Committee.

Article 302

(ex Article 259 TEC)

1. The members of the Committee shall be appointed for five years The Council shall adopt the list of members drawn up in accordance with

the proposals made by each Member State. The term of office of the members of the Committee shall be renewable.

2. The Council shall act after consulting the Commission. It may obtain the opinion of European bodies which are representative of the various economic and social sectors and of civil society to which the Union's activities are of concern.

[...]

PART SEVEN
GENERAL AND FINAL PROVISIONS

Article 340

(ex Article 288 TEC)

The contractual liability of the Union shall be governed by the law applicable to the contract in question.

In the case of non-contractual liability, the Union shall, in accordance with the general principles common to the laws of the Member States, make good any damage caused by its institutions or by its servants in the performance of their duties.

Notwithstanding the second paragraph, the European Central Bank shall, in accordance with the general principles common to the laws of the Member States, make good any damage caused by it or by its servants in the performance of their duties.

The personal liability of its servants towards the Union shall be governed by the provisions laid down in their Staff Regulations or in the Conditions of Employment applicable to them.

[...]

Article 352

(ex Article 308 TEC)

1. If action by the Union should prove necessary, within the framework of the policies defined in the Treaties, to attain one of the objectives set out in the Treaties, and the Treaties have not provided the necessary powers, the Council, acting unanimously on a proposal from the Commission and after obtaining the consent of the European Parliament, shall adopt the appropriate measures. Where the measures in question are adopted by the Council in accordance with a special legislative procedure, it shall also act unanimously on a proposal from the Commission and after obtaining the consent of the European Parliament.

2. Using the procedure for monitoring the subsidiarity principle referred to in Article 5(3) of the Treaty on European Union, the

Commission shall draw national Parliaments' attention to proposals based on this Article.

3. Measures based on this Article shall not entail harmonisation of Member States' laws or regulations in cases where the Treaties exclude such harmonisation.

4. This Article cannot serve as a basis for attaining objectives pertaining to the common foreign and security policy and any acts adopted pursuant to this Article shall respect the limits set out in Article 40, second paragraph, of the Treaty on European Union.

PART 3: DIRECTIVE 2004/38/EC

DIRECTIVE 2004/38/EC OF THE EUROPEAN PARLIAMENT AND OF THE COUNCIL of 29 April 2004 on the right of citizens of the Union and their family members to move and reside freely within the territory of the Member States amending Regulation (EEC) No 1612/68 and repealing Directives 64/221/EEC, 68/360/EEC, 72/194/EEC, 73/148/EEC, 75/34/EEC, 75/35/EEC, 90/364/EEC, 90/365/EEC and 93/96/EEC

[. . .]

CHAPTER I

General provisions

Article 1

Subject

This Directive lays down:

(a) the conditions governing the exercise of the right of free movement and residence within the territory of the Member States by Union citizens and their family members;

(b) the right of permanent residence in the territory of the Member States for Union citizens and their family members;

(c) the limits placed on the rights set out in (a) and (b) on grounds of public policy, public security or public health.

Article 2

Definitions

For the purposes of this Directive:

1) "Union citizen" means any person having the nationality of a Member State;

2) "Family member" means:

(a) the spouse;

(b) the partner with whom the Union citizen has contracted a registered partnership, on the basis of the legislation of a Member State, if the legislation of the host Member State treats registered partnerships as equivalent to marriage and in accordance with the conditions laid down in the relevant legislation of the host Member State;

(c) the direct descendants who are under the age of 21 or are dependants and those of the spouse or partner as defined in point (b);

(d) the dependent direct relatives in the ascending line and those of the spouse or partner as defined in point (b);

3) "Host Member State" means the Member State to which a Union citizen moves in order to exercise his/her right of free movement and residence.

Article 3

Beneficiaries

1. This Directive shall apply to all Union citizens who move to or reside in a Member State other than that of which they are a national, and to their family members as defined in point 2 of Article 2 who accompany or join them.

2. Without prejudice to any right to free movement and residence the persons concerned may have in their own right, the host Member State shall, in accordance with its national legislation, facilitate entry and residence for the following persons:

(a) any other family members, irrespective of their nationality, not falling under the definition in point 2 of Article 2 who, in the country from which they have come, are dependents or members of the household of the Union citizen having the primary right of residence, or where serious health grounds strictly require the personal care of the family member by the Union citizen;

(b) the partner with whom the Union citizen has a durable relationship, duly attested.

The host Member State shall undertake an extensive examination of the personal circumstances and shall justify any denial of entry or residence to these people.

CHAPTER II

Right of exit and entry

Article 4

Right of exit

1. Without prejudice to the provisions on travel documents applicable to national border controls, all Union citizens with a valid identity card or passport and their family members who are not nationals of a Member State and who hold a valid passport shall have the right to leave the territory of a Member State to travel to another Member State.

2. No exit visa or equivalent formality may be imposed on the persons to whom paragraph 1 applies.

3. Member States shall, acting in accordance with their laws, issue to their own nationals, and renew, an identity card or passport stating their nationality.

4. The passport shall be valid at least for all Member States and for countries through which the holder must pass when travelling between Member States. Where the law of a Member State does not provide for identity cards to be issued, the period of validity of any passport on being issued or renewed shall be not less than five years.

Article 5

Right of entry

1. Without prejudice to the provisions on travel documents applicable to national border controls, Member States shall grant Union citizens leave to enter their territory with a valid identity card or passport and shall grant family members who are not nationals of a Member State leave to enter their territory with a valid passport.

No entry visa or equivalent formality may be imposed on Union citizens.

2. Family members who are not nationals of a Member State shall only be required to have an entry visa in accordance with Regulation (EC) No 539/2001 or, where appropriate, with national law. For the purposes of this Directive, possession of the valid residence card referred to in Article 10 shall exempt such family members from the visa requirement.

Member States shall grant such persons every facility to obtain the necessary visas. Such visas shall be issued free of charge as soon as possible and on the basis of an accelerated procedure.

3. The host Member State shall not place an entry or exit stamp in the passport of family members who are not nationals of a Member State provided that they present the residence card provided for in Article 10.

4. Where a Union citizen, or a family member who is not a national of a Member State, does not have the necessary travel documents or, if required, the necessary visas, the Member State concerned shall, before turning them back, give such persons every reasonable opportunity to obtain the necessary documents or have them brought to them within a reasonable period of time or to corroborate or prove by other means that they are covered by the right of free movement and residence.

5. The Member State may require the person concerned to report his/her presence within its territory within a reasonable and non-discriminatory period of time. Failure to comply with this requirement may make the person concerned liable to proportionate and non-discriminatory sanctions.

CHAPTER III

Right of residence

Article 6

Right of residence for up to three months

1. Union citizens shall have the right of residence on the territory of another Member State for a period of up to three months without any conditions or any formalities other than the requirement to hold a valid identity card or passport.

2. The provisions of paragraph 1 shall also apply to family members in possession of a valid passport who are not nationals of a Member State, accompanying or joining the Union citizen.

Article 7

Right of residence for more than three months

1. All Union citizens shall have the right of residence on the territory of another Member State for a period of longer than three months if they:

(a) are workers or self-employed persons in the host Member State; or

(b) have sufficient resources for themselves and their family members not to become a burden on the social assistance system of the host Member State during their period of residence and have comprehensive sickness insurance cover in the host Member State; or

(c) — are enrolled at a private or public establishment, accredited or financed by the host Member State on the basis of its legislation or administrative practice, for the principal purpose of following a course of study, including vocational training; and

— have comprehensive sickness insurance cover in the host Member State and assure the relevant national authority, by means of a declaration or by such equivalent means as they may choose, that they have sufficient resources for themselves and their family members not to become a burden on the social assistance system of the host Member State during their period of residence; or

(d) are family members accompanying or joining a Union citizen who satisfies the conditions referred to in points (a), (b) or (c).

2. The right of residence provided for in paragraph 1 shall extend to family members who are not nationals of a Member State, accompanying or joining the Union citizen in the host Member State, provided that such Union citizen satisfies the conditions referred to in paragraph 1(a), (b) or (c).

3. For the purposes of paragraph 1(a), a Union citizen who is no longer a worker or self-employed person shall retain the status of worker or self-employed person in the following circumstances:

(a) he/she is temporarily unable to work as the result of an illness or accident;

(b) he/she is in duly recorded involuntary unemployment after having been employed for more than one year and has registered as a job-seeker with the relevant employment office;

(c) he/she is in duly recorded involuntary unemployment after completing a fixed-term employment contract of less than a year or after having become involuntarily unemployed during the first twelve months and has registered as a job-seeker with the relevant employment office. In this case, the status of worker shall be retained for no less than six months;

(d) he/she embarks on vocational training. Unless he/she is involuntarily unemployed, the retention of the status of worker shall require the training to be related to the previous employment.

4. By way of derogation from paragraphs 1(d) and 2 above, only the spouse, the registered partner provided for in Article 2(2)(b) and dependent children shall have the right of residence as family members of a Union citizen meeting the conditions under 1(c) above. Article 3(2) shall apply to his/her dependent direct relatives in the ascending lines and those of his/her spouse or registered partner.

Article 8

Administrative formalities for Union citizens

1. Without prejudice to Article 5(5), for periods of residence longer than three months, the host Member State may require Union citizens to register with the relevant authorities.

2. The deadline for registration may not be less than three months from the date of arrival. A registration certificate shall be issued immediately, stating the name and address of the person registering and the date of the registration. Failure to comply with the registration requirement may render the person concerned liable to proportionate and non-discriminatory sanctions.

3. For the registration certificate to be issued, Member States may only require that

— Union citizens to whom point (a) of Article 7(1) applies present a valid identity card or passport, a confirmation of engagement from the employer or a certificate of employment, or proof that they are self-employed persons;

— Union citizens to whom point (b) of Article 7(1) applies present a valid identity card or passport and provide proof that they satisfy the conditions laid down therein;

— Union citizens to whom point (c) of Article 7(1) applies present a valid identity card or passport, provide proof of enrolment at an accredited establishment and of comprehensive sickness insurance cover and the declaration or equivalent means referred to in point (c) of Article 7(1). Member States may not require this declaration to refer to any specific amount of resources.

4. Member States may not lay down a fixed amount which they regard as "sufficient resources" but they must take into account the personal situation of the person concerned. In all cases this amount shall not be higher than the threshold below which nationals of the host Member State become eligible for social assistance, or, where this criterion is not applicable, higher than the minimum social security pension paid by the host Member State.

5. For the registration certificate to be issued to family members of Union citizens, who are themselves Union citizens, Member States may require the following documents to be presented:

(a) a valid identity card or passport;

(b) a document attesting to the existence of a family relationship or of a registered partnership;

(c) where appropriate, the registration certificate of the Union citizen whom they are accompanying or joining;

(d) in cases falling under points (c) and (d) of Article 2(2), documentary evidence that the conditions laid down therein are met;

(e) in cases falling under Article 3(2)(a), a document issued by the relevant authority in the country of origin or country from which they are arriving certifying that they are dependants or members of the household of the Union citizen, or proof of the existence of serious health grounds which strictly require the personal care of the family member by the Union citizen;

(f) in cases falling under Article 3(2)(b), proof of the existence of a durable relationship with the Union citizen.

Article 9

Administrative formalities for family members who are not nationals of a Member State

1. Member States shall issue a residence card to family members of a Union citizen who are not nationals of a Member State, where the planned period of residence is for more than three months.

2. The deadline for submitting the residence card application may not be less than three months from the date of arrival.

3. Failure to comply with the requirement to apply for a residence card may make the person concerned liable to proportionate and non-discriminatory sanctions.

Article 10

Issue of residence cards

1. The right of residence of family members of a Union citizen who are not nationals of a Member State shall be evidenced by the issuing of a document called "Residence card of a family member of a Union citizen" no later than six months from the date on which they submit the application. A certificate of application for the residence card shall be issued immediately.

2. For the residence card to be issued, Member States shall require presentation of the following documents:

(a) a valid passport;

(b) a document attesting to the existence of a family relationship or of a registered partnership;

(c) the registration certificate or, in the absence of a registration system, any other proof of residence in the host Member State of the Union citizen whom they are accompanying or joining;

(d) in cases falling under points (c) and (d) of Article 2(2), documentary evidence that the conditions laid down therein are met;

(e) in cases falling under Article 3(2)(a), a document issued by the relevant authority in the country of origin or country from which they are arriving certifying that they are dependants or members of the household of the Union citizen, or proof of the existence of serious health grounds which strictly require the personal care of the family member by the Union citizen;

(f) in cases falling under Article 3(2)(b), proof of the existence of a durable relationship with the Union citizen.

Article 11

Validity of the residence card

1. The residence card provided for by Article 10(1) shall be valid for five years from the date of issue or for the envisaged period of residence of the Union citizen, if this period is less than five years.

2. The validity of the residence card shall not be affected by temporary absences not exceeding six months a year, or by absences of a longer duration for compulsory military service or by one absence of a

maximum of twelve consecutive months for important reasons such as pregnancy and childbirth, serious illness, study or vocational training, or a posting in another Member State or a third country.

Article 12

Retention of the right of residence by family members in the event of death or departure of the Union citizen

1. Without prejudice to the second subparagraph, the Union citizen's death or departure from the host Member State shall not affect the right of residence of his/her family members who are nationals of a Member State.

Before acquiring the right of permanent residence, the persons concerned must meet the conditions laid down in points (a), (b), (c) or (d) of Article 7(1).

2. Without prejudice to the second subparagraph, the Union citizen's death shall not entail loss of the right of residence of his/her family members who are not nationals of a Member State and who have been residing in the host Member State as family members for at least one year before the Union citizen's death.

Before acquiring the right of permanent residence, the right of residence of the persons concerned shall remain subject to the requirement that they are able to show that they are workers or self-employed persons or that they have sufficient resources for themselves and their family members not to become a burden on the social assistance system of the host Member State during their period of residence and have comprehensive sickness insurance cover in the host Member State, or that they are members of the family, already constituted in the host Member State, of a person satisfying these requirements. "Sufficient resources" shall be as defined in Article 8(4).

Such family members shall retain their right of residence exclusively on a personal basis.

3. The Union citizen's departure from the host Member State or his/her death shall not entail loss of the right of residence of his/her children or of the parent who has actual custody of the children, irrespective of nationality, if the children reside in the host Member State and are enrolled at an educational establishment, for the purpose of studying there, until the completion of their studies.

Article 13

Retention of the right of residence by family members in the event of divorce, annulment of marriage or termination of registered partnership

1. Without prejudice to the second subparagraph, divorce, annulment of the Union citizen's marriage or termination of his/her registered partnership, as referred to in point 2(b) of Article 2 shall not

affect the right of residence of his/her family members who are nationals of a Member State.

Before acquiring the right of permanent residence, the persons concerned must meet the conditions laid down in points (a), (b), (c) or (d) of Article 7(1).

2. Without prejudice to the second subparagraph, divorce, annulment of marriage or termination of the registered partnership referred to in point 2(b) of Article 2 shall not entail loss of the right of residence of a Union citizen's family members who are not nationals of a Member State where:

(a) prior to initiation of the divorce or annulment proceedings or termination of the registered partnership referred to in point 2(b) of Article 2, the marriage or registered partnership has lasted at least three years, including one year in the host Member State; or

(b) by agreement between the spouses or the partners referred to in point 2(b) of Article 2 or by court order, the spouse or partner who is not a national of a Member State has custody of the Union citizen's children; or

(c) this is warranted by particularly difficult circumstances, such as having been a victim of domestic violence while the marriage or registered partnership was subsisting; or

(d) by agreement between the spouses or partners referred to in point 2(b) of Article 2 or by court order, the spouse or partner who is not a national of a Member State has the right of access to a minor child, provided that the court has ruled that such access must be in the host Member State, and for as long as is required.

Before acquiring the right of permanent residence, the right of residence of the persons concerned shall remain subject to the requirement that they are able to show that they are workers or self-employed persons or that they have sufficient resources for themselves and their family members not to become a burden on the social assistance system of the host Member State during their period of residence and have comprehensive sickness insurance cover in the host Member State, or that they are members of the family, already constituted in the host Member State, of a person satisfying these requirements. "Sufficient resources" shall be as defined in Article 8(4).

Such family members shall retain their right of residence exclusively on personal basis.

Article 14

Retention of the right of residence

1. Union citizens and their family members shall have the right of residence provided for in Article 6, as long as they do not become an unreasonable burden on the social assistance system of the host Member State.

2. Union citizens and their family members shall have the right of residence provided for in Articles 7, 12 and 13 as long as they meet the conditions set out therein.

In specific cases where there is a reasonable doubt as to whether a Union citizen or his/her family members satisfies the conditions set out in Articles 7, 12 and 13, Member States may verify if these conditions are fulfilled. This verification shall not be carried out systematically.

3. An expulsion measure shall not be the automatic consequence of a Union citizen's or his or her family member's recourse to the social assistance system of the host Member State.

4. By way of derogation from paragraphs 1 and 2 and without prejudice to the provisions of Chapter VI, an expulsion measure may in no case be adopted against Union citizens or their family members if:

(a) the Union citizens are workers or self-employed persons, or

(b) the Union citizens entered the territory of the host Member State in order to seek employment. In this case, the Union citizens and their family members may not be expelled for as long as the Union citizens can provide evidence that they are continuing to seek employment and that they have a genuine chance of being engaged.

Article 15

Procedural safeguards

1. The procedures provided for by Articles 30 and 31 shall apply by analogy to all decisions restricting free movement of Union citizens and their family members on grounds other than public policy, public security or public health.

2. Expiry of the identity card or passport on the basis of which the person concerned entered the host Member State and was issued with a registration certificate or residence card shall not constitute a ground for expulsion from the host Member State.

3. The host Member State may not impose a ban on entry in the context of an expulsion decision to which paragraph 1 applies.

CHAPTER IV

Right of permanent residence

Section I

Eligibility

Article 16

General rule for Union citizens and their family members

1. Union citizens who have resided legally for a continuous period of five years in the host Member State shall have the right of permanent residence there. This right shall not be subject to the conditions provided for in Chapter III.

2. Paragraph 1 shall apply also to family members who are not nationals of a Member State and have legally resided with the Union citizen in the host Member State for a continuous period of five years.

3. Continuity of residence shall not be affected by temporary absences not exceeding a total of six months a year, or by absences of a longer duration for compulsory military service, or by one absence of a maximum of twelve consecutive months for important reasons such as pregnancy and childbirth, serious illness, study or vocational training, or a posting in another Member State or a third country.

4. Once acquired, the right of permanent residence shall be lost only through absence from the host Member State for a period exceeding two consecutive years.

Article 17

Exemptions for persons no longer working in the host Member State and their family members

1. By way of derogation from Article 16, the right of permanent residence in the host Member State shall be enjoyed before completion of a continuous period of five years of residence by:

(a) workers or self-employed persons who, at the time they stop working, have reached the age laid down by the law of that Member State for entitlement to an old age pension or workers who cease paid employment to take early retirement, provided that they have been working in that Member State for at least the preceding twelve months and have resided there continuously for more than three years.

If the law of the host Member State does not grant the right to an old age pension to certain categories of self-employed persons, the age condition shall be deemed to have been met once the person concerned has reached the age of 60;

(b) workers or self-employed persons who have resided continuously in the host Member State for more than two years and stop working there as a result of permanent incapacity to work.

If such incapacity is the result of an accident at work or an occupational disease entitling the person concerned to a benefit payable in full or in part by an institution in the host Member State, no condition shall be imposed as to length of residence;

(c) workers or self-employed persons who, after three years of continuous employment and residence in the host Member State, work in an employed or self-employed capacity in another Member State, while retaining their place of residence in the host Member State, to which they return, as a rule, each day or at least once a week.

For the purposes of entitlement to the rights referred to in points (a) and (b), periods of employment spent in the Member State in which the person concerned is working shall be regarded as having been spent in the host Member State.

Periods of involuntary unemployment duly recorded by the relevant employment office, periods not worked for reasons not of the person's own making and absences from work or cessation of work due to illness or accident shall be regarded as periods of employment.

2. The conditions as to length of residence and employment laid down in point (a) of paragraph 1 and the condition as to length of residence laid down in point (b) of paragraph 1 shall not apply if the worker's or the self-employed person's spouse or partner as referred to in point 2(b) of Article 2 is a national of the host Member State or has lost the nationality of that Member State by marriage to that worker or self-employed person.

3. Irrespective of nationality, the family members of a worker or a self-employed person who are residing with him in the territory of the host Member State shall have the right of permanent residence in that Member State, if the worker or self-employed person has acquired himself the right of permanent residence in that Member State on the basis of paragraph 1.

4. If, however, the worker or self-employed person dies while still working but before acquiring permanent residence status in the host Member State on the basis of paragraph 1, his family members who are residing with him in the host Member State shall acquire the right of permanent residence there, on condition that:

(a) the worker or self-employed person had, at the time of death, resided continuously on the territory of that Member State for two years; or

(b) the death resulted from an accident at work or an occupational disease; or

(c) the surviving spouse lost the nationality of that Member State following marriage to the worker or self-employed person.

Article 18

Acquisition of the right of permanent residence by certain family members who are not nationals of a Member State

Without prejudice to Article 17, the family members of a Union citizen to whom Articles 12(2) and 13(2) apply, who satisfy the conditions laid down therein, shall acquire the right of permanent residence after residing legally for a period of five consecutive years in the host Member State.

Section II

Administrative formalities

Article 19

Document certifying permanent residence for Union citizens

1. Upon application Member States shall issue Union citizens entitled to permanent residence, after having verified duration of residence, with a document certifying permanent residence.

2. The document certifying permanent residence shall be issued as soon as possible.

Article 20

Permanent residence card for family members who are not nationals of a Member State

1. Member States shall issue family members who are not nationals of a Member State entitled to permanent residence with a permanent residence card within six months of the submission of the application. The permanent residence card shall be renewable automatically every ten years.

2. The application for a permanent residence card shall be submitted before the residence card expires. Failure to comply with the requirement to apply for a permanent residence card may render the person concerned liable to proportionate and non-discriminatory sanctions.

3. Interruption in residence not exceeding two consecutive years shall not affect the validity of the permanent residence card.

Article 21

Continuity of residence

For the purposes of this Directive, continuity of residence may be attested by any means of proof in use in the host Member State. Continuity of residence is broken by any expulsion decision duly enforced against the person concerned.

CHAPTER V

Provisions common to the right of residence and the right of permanent residence

Article 22

Territorial scope

The right of residence and the right of permanent residence shall cover the whole territory of the host Member State. Member States may impose territorial restrictions on the right of residence and the right of permanent residence only where the same restrictions apply to their-own nationals.

Article 23

Related rights

Irrespective of nationality, the family members of a Union citizen who have the right of residence or the right of permanent residence in a Member State shall be entitled to take up employment or self-employment there.

Article 24

Equal treatment

1. Subject to such specific provisions as are expressly provided for in the Treaty and secondary law, all Union citizens residing on the basis of this Directive in the territory of the host Member State shall enjoy equal treatment with the nationals of that Member State within the scope of the Treaty. The benefit of this right shall be extended to family members who are not nationals of a Member State and who have the right of residence or permanent residence.

2. By way of derogation from paragraph 1, the host Member State shall not be obliged to confer entitlement to social assistance during the first three months of residence or, where appropriate, the longer period provided for in Article 14(4)(b), nor shall it be obliged, prior to acquisition of the right of permanent residence, to grant maintenance aid for studies, including vocational training, consisting in student grants or student loans to persons other than workers, self-employed persons, persons who retain such status and members of their families.

Article 25

General provisions concerning residence documents

1. Possession of a registration certificate as referred to in Article 8, of a document certifying permanent residence, of a certificate attesting submission of an application for a family member residence card, of a residence card or of a permanent residence card, may under no circumstances be made a precondition for the exercise of a right or the

completion of an administrative formality, as entitlement to rights may be attested by any other means of proof.

2. All documents mentioned in paragraph 1 shall be issued free of charge or for a charge not exceeding that imposed on nationals for the issuing of similar documents.

Article 26

Checks

Member States may carry out checks on compliance with any requirement deriving from their national legislation for non-nationals always to carry their registration certificate or residence card, provided that the same requirement applies to their own nationals as regards their identity card. In the event of failure to comply with this requirement, Member States may impose the same sanctions as those imposed on their own nationals for failure to carry their identity card.

CHAPTER VI

Restrictions on the right of entry and the right of residence on grounds of public policy, public security or public health

Article 27

General principles

1. Subject to the provisions of this Chapter, Member States may restrict the freedom of movement and residence of Union citizens and their family members, irrespective of nationality, on grounds of public policy, public security or public health. These grounds shall not be invoked to serve economic ends.

2. Measures taken on grounds of public policy or public security shall comply with the principle of proportionality and shall be based exclusively on the personal conduct of the individual concerned. Previous criminal convictions shall not in themselves constitute grounds for taking such measures.

The personal conduct of the individual concerned must represent a genuine, present and sufficiently serious threat affecting one of the fundamental interests of society. Justifications that are isolated from the particulars of the case or that rely on considerations of general prevention shall not be accepted.

3. In order to ascertain whether the person concerned represents a danger for public policy or public security, when issuing the registration certificate or, in the absence of a registration system, not later than three months from the date of arrival of the person concerned on its territory or from the date of reporting his/her presence within the territory, as provided for in Article 5(5), or when issuing the residence card, the host Member

State may, should it consider this essential, request the Member State of origin and, if need be, other Member States to provide information concerning any previous police record the person concerned may have. Such enquiries shall not be made as a matter of routine. The Member State consulted shall give its reply within two months.

4. The Member State which issued the passport or identity card shall allow the holder of the document who has been expelled on grounds of public policy, public security, or public health from another Member State to re-enter its territory without any formality even if the document is no longer valid or the nationality of the holder is in dispute.

Article 28

Protection against expulsion

1. Before taking an expulsion decision on grounds of public policy or public security, the host Member State shall take account of considerations such as how long the individual concerned has resided on its territory, his/her age, state of health, family and economic situation, social and cultural integration into the host Member State and the extent of his/her links with the country of origin.

2. The host Member State may not take an expulsion decision against Union citizens or their family members, irrespective of nationality, who have the right of permanent residence on its territory, except on serious grounds of public policy or public security.

3. An expulsion decision may not be taken against Union citizens, except if the decision is based on imperative grounds of public security, as defined by Member States, if they:

(a) have resided in the host Member State for the previous ten years; or

(b) are a minor, except if the expulsion is necessary for the best interests of the child, as provided for in the United Nations Convention on the Rights of the Child of 20 November 1989.

Article 29

Public health

1. The only diseases justifying measures restricting freedom of movement shall be the diseases with epidemic potential as defined by the relevant instruments of the World Health Organisation and other infectious diseases or contagious parasitic diseases if they are the subject of protection provisions applying to nationals of the host Member State.

2. Diseases occurring after a three-month period from the date of arrival shall not constitute grounds for expulsion from the territory.

3. Where there are serious indications that it is necessary, Member States may, within three months of the date of arrival, require persons entitled to the right of residence to undergo, free of charge, a medical examination to certify that they are not suffering from any of the conditions referred to in paragraph 1. Such medical examinations may not be required as a matter of routine.

Article 30

Notification of decisions

1. The persons concerned shall be notified in writing of any decision taken under Article 27(1), in such a way that they are able to comprehend its content and the implications for them.

2. The persons concerned shall be informed, precisely and in full, of the public policy, public security or public health grounds on which the decision taken in their case is based, unless this is contrary to the interests of State security.

3. The notification shall specify the court or administrative authority with which the person concerned may lodge an appeal, the time limit for the appeal and, where applicable, the time allowed for the person to leave the territory of the Member State. Save in duly substantiated cases of urgency, the time allowed to leave the territory shall be not less than one month from the date of notification.

Article 31

Procedural safeguards

1. The persons concerned shall have access to judicial and, where appropriate, administrative redress procedures in the host Member State to appeal against or seek review of any decision taken against them on the grounds of public policy, public security or public health.

2. Where the application for appeal against or judicial review of the expulsion decision is accompanied by an application for an interim order to suspend enforcement of that decision, actual removal from the territory may not take place until such time as the decision on the interim order has been taken, except:

— where the expulsion decision is based on a previous judicial decision; or

— where the persons concerned have had previous access to judicial review; or

— where the expulsion decision is based on imperative grounds of public security under Article 28(3).

3. The redress procedures shall allow for an examination of the legality of the decision, as well as of the facts and circumstances on which

the proposed measure is based. They shall ensure that the decision is not disproportionate, particularly in view of the requirements laid down in Article 28.

4. Member States may exclude the individual concerned from their territory pending the redress procedure, but they may not prevent the individual from submitting his/her defence in person, except when his/her appearance may cause serious troubles to public policy or public security or when the appeal or judicial review concerns a denial of entry to the territory.

Article 32

Duration of exclusion orders

1. Persons excluded on grounds of public policy or public security may submit an application for lifting of the exclusion order after a reasonable period, depending on the circumstances, and in any event after three years from enforcement of the final exclusion order which has been validly adopted in accordance with Community law, by putting forward arguments to establish that there has been a material change in the circumstances which justified the decision ordering their exclusion.

The Member State concerned shall reach a decision on this application within six months of its submission.

2. The persons referred to in paragraph 1 shall have no right of entry to the territory of the Member State concerned while their application is being considered.

Article 33

Expulsion as a penalty or legal consequence

1. Expulsion orders may not be issued by the host Member State as a penalty or legal consequence of a custodial penalty, unless they conform to the requirements of Articles 27, 28 and 29.

2. If an expulsion order, as provided for in paragraph 1, is enforced more than two years after it was issued, the Member State shall check that the individual concerned is currently and genuinely a threat to public policy or public security and shall assess whether there has been any material change in the circumstances since the expulsion order was issued.

CHAPTER VII

Final provisions

Article 34

Publicity

Member States shall disseminate information concerning the rights and obligations of Union citizens and their family members on the subjects covered by this Directive, particularly by means of awareness-raising campaigns conducted through national and local media and other means of communication.

Article 35

Abuse of rights

Member States may adopt the necessary measures to refuse, terminate or withdraw any right conferred by this Directive in the case of abuse of rights or fraud, such as marriages of convenience. Any such measure shall be proportionate and subject to the procedural safeguards provided for in Articles 30 and 31.

Article 36

Sanctions

Member States shall lay down provisions on the sanctions applicable to breaches of national rules adopted for the implementation of this Directive and shall take the measures required for their application. The sanctions laid down shall be effective and proportionate. Member States shall notify the Commission of these provisions not later than ([15]) and as promptly as possible in the case of any subsequent changes.

Article 37

More favourable national provisions

The provisions of this Directive shall not affect any laws, regulations or administrative provisions laid down by a Member State which would be more favourable to the persons covered by this Directive.

[...]

PART 4: REGULATION NO. 1612/68/EEC

REGULATION (EEC) No 1612/68 OF THE COUNCIL of 15 October 1968 on freedom of movement for workers within the Community

[...]

Article 1

1. Any national of a Member State, shall, irrespective of his place of residence, have the right to take up an activity as an employed person, and to pursue such activity, within the territory of another Member State in accordance with the provisions laid down by law, regulation or administrative action governing the employment of nationals of that State.

2. He shall, in particular, have the right to take up available employment in the territory of another Member State with the same priority as nationals of that State.

Article 2

Any national of a Member State and any employer pursuing an activity in the territory of a Member State may exchange their applications for and offers of employment, and may conclude and perform contracts of employment in accordance with the provisions in force laid down by law, regulation or administrative action, without any discrimination resulting therefrom.

Article 3

1. Under this Regulation, provisions laid down by law, regulation or administrative action or administrative practices of a Member State shall not apply:—where they limit application for and offers of employment, or the right of foreign nationals to take up and pursue employment or subject these to conditions not applicable in respect of their own nationals; or

— where, though applicable irrespective of nationality, their exclusive or principal aim or effect is to keep nationals of other Member States away from the employment offered.

This provision shall not apply to conditions relating to linguistic knowledge required by reason of the nature of the post to be filled.

2. There shall be included in particular among the provisions or practices of a Member State referred to in the first subparagraph of paragraph 1 those which:

(a) prescribe a special recruitment procedure for foreign nationals;

(b) limit or restrict the advertising of vacancies in the press or through any other medium or subject it to conditions other than those applicable in respect of employers pursuing their activities in the territory of that Member State;

(c) subject eligibility for employment to conditions of registration with employment offices or impede recruitment of individual workers, where persons who do not reside in the territory of that State are concerned.

Article 4

1. Provisions laid down by law, regulation or administrative action of the Member States which restrict by number or percentage the employment of foreign nationals in any undertaking, branch of activity or region, or at a national level, shall not apply to nationals of the other Member States.

2. When in a Member State the granting of any benefit to undertakings is subject to a minimum percentage of national workers being employed, nationals of the other Member States shall be counted as national workers, subject to the provisions of the Council Directive of 15

October 1963.2 1 OJ No L 257, 19.10.1968, p. 1. 2 OJ No 159, 2.11.1963, p. 2661/63.

Article 5

A national of a Member State who seeks employment in the territory of another Member State shall receive the same assistance there as that afforded by the employment offices in that State to their own nationals seeking employment.

Article 6

1. The engagement and recruitment of a national of one Member State for a post in another Member State shall not depend on medical, vocational or other criteria which are discriminatory on grounds of nationality by comparison with those applied to nationals of the other Member State who wish to pursue the same activity.

2. Nevertheless, a national who holds an offer in his name from an employer in a Member State other than that of which he is a national may have to undergo a vocational test, if the employer expressly requests this when making his offer of employment.

TITLE II. Employment and equality of treatment

Article 7

1. A worker who is a national of a Member State may not, in the territory of another Member State, be treated differently from national workers by reason of his nationality in respect of any conditions of employment and work, in particular as regards remuneration, dismissal, and should he become unemployed, reinstatement or re-employment;

2. He shall enjoy the same social and tax advantages as national workers.

3. He shall also, by virtue of the same right and under the same conditions as national workers, have access to training in vocational schools and retraining centres.

4. Any clause of a collective or individual agreement or of any other collective regulation concerning eligibility for employment, employment, remuneration and other conditions of work or dismissal shall be null and void in so far as it lays down or authorises discriminatory conditions in respect of workers who are nationals of the other Member States.

Article 8

1. A worker who is a national of a Member State and who is employed in the territory of another Member State shall enjoy equality of treatment as regards membership of trade unions and the exercise of rights attaching thereto, including the right to vote; he may be excluded from taking part in the management of bodies governed by public law and from

holding an office governed by public law. Furthermore, he shall have the right of eligibility for workers' representative bodies in the undertaking. The provisions of this Article shall not affect laws or regulations in certain Member States which grant more extensive rights to workers coming from the other Member States.

2. This Article shall be reviewed by the Council on the basis of a proposal from the Commission which shall be submitted within not more than two years.

Article 9

1. A worker who is a national of a Member State and who is employed in the territory of another Member State shall enjoy all the rights and benefits accorded to national workers in matters of housing, including ownership of the housing he needs.

2. Such worker may, with the same right as nationals, put his name down on the housing lists in the region in which he is employed, where such lists exist; he shall enjoy the resultant benefits and priorities.

If his family has remained in the country whence he came, they shall be considered for this purpose as residing in the said region, where national workers benefit from a similar presumption.

TITLE III. Workers' families

Article 10

1. The following shall, irrespective of their nationality, have the right to install themselves with a worker who is a national of one Member State and who is employed in the territory of another Member State: (a) his spouse and their descendants who are under the age of 21 years or are dependents; (b) dependent relatives in the ascending line of the worker and his spouse.

2. Member States shall facilitate the admission of any member of the family not coming within the provisions of paragraph 1 if dependent on the worker referred to above or living under his roof in the country whence he comes.

3. For the purposes of paragraphs 1 and 2, the worker must have available for his family housing considered as normal for national workers in the region where he is employed; this provision, however must not give rise to discrimination between national workers and workers from the other Member States.

Article 11

Where a national of a Member State is pursuing an activity as an employed or self-employed person in the territory of another Member State, his spouse and those of the children who are under the age of 21 years or dependent on him shall have the right to take up any activity as an employed person throughout the territory of that same State, even if they are not nationals of any Member State.

Article 12

The children of a national of a Member State who is or has been employed in the territory of another Member State shall be admitted to that State's general educational, apprenticeship and vocational training courses under the same conditions as the nationals of that State, if such children are residing in its territory.

Member States shall encourage all efforts to enable such children to attend these courses under the best possible conditions.

[. . .]

INDEX

References are to Pages

ADMINISTRATIVE LAW
Enforcement actions targeting administrative practices, 82
Supremacy principle, Member State conflicts, 124

BREXIT
Generally, 367 et seq.
Article 50 of Treaty on European Union, 26
European Economic Area agreement options, 392
Intergovernmentalist theory of European integration and, 16
Negotiability of withdrawal rights, 371, 374
Notification of withdrawal, 367, 373, 382
Options of withdrawing states, 392
TFEU Article 50, 373

CAPITAL
Free movement of capital. *See* Internal Market, this index

CHOICE OF LAW
Companies, this index

CIVIL RIGHTS
EU vs U.S. terminology, 136
State liability doctrine, 141
Supremacy doctrine tensions, 130, 133

CIVIL SERVICE TRIBUNAL, 40

COLLECTIVE ACTION PROBLEMS, 61

COMMISSION
European Commission, this index

COMMITTEE OF THE REGIONS, 42

COMMON CURRENCY
Monetary Union, this index

COMPANIES
Generally, 274 et seq.
Choice of law issues
    Generally, 275 et seq.
    Board composition requirements, 294
    Free movement of workers, 299
    Incorporation fees, 296
    Indeterminacy in corporate law, 297
    Limited liability companies, 284
    Member State connections, 279
    Real entity theory, 280
    Real seat doctrine, 276, 289
European Company or Societas Europaea option, 298
Fiction and aggregate theories compared, 281
Freedom of establishment, 274 et seq.
Incorporation fees, choice of law, 296
Indeterminacy in corporate law, 297
Limited liability companies, 284
Member State connections, 279
Merger directive, 298
Mobility of corporations, 274
Privatization of utilities, 319
Real seat doctrine, 289
Rights and duties, 280
Taxation, 274

COMPETENCE ISSUES
European Parliament, 151
Exclusive and shared legislative competence, 151, 384

CONSTITUTIONAL LAW
International law in national constitutions, 96
Supremacy principle, Member State constitution conflicts, 124
Treaties as substitute for EU constitution, 3, 25
Treaty Establishing a Constitution for Europe, proposal, 24

COPENHAGEN CRITERIA
EU membership, 27

COUNCIL OF EUROPE
European Council distinguished, 34
Historical background, 13

COURT OF JUSTICE
Generally, 53 et seq.
See also Judiciary, this index
Acte clair doctrine, 73
Advisory opinions, 68, 70
Advocates-General, roles of, 54
Appointments, 53
Composition, 53
Constituent courts, 39, 53
Cultural diversity of judges, 53
Dynamic interpretation, 58
Enforcement Actions, this index
European integration risks, 61
Interpretation of treaties, 63
Interpretative methodology, 57

Jurisdiction
    Generally, 39, 55
    Necessity rule, 67
    Private parties' litigation, 63
    TFEU mandate, 72, 75
Legal diversity of judges, 53
Legislative history, arguments based on the, 59
Member States
    Referrals
        Generally, 55, 66
        Limitations on referral duty, 72
    Treaty validity and interpretation rulings, review of, 64
Necessity rule, 67
Powerfulness of court, 59
Precedent, 72
Preliminary rulings procedure, 63 et seq.
Procedural law, 54
Relevance issues, 67
Systematic arguments, 58
Teleological reasoning, 57
Treaty validity and interpretation rulings, 63

CUSTOMS LAWS
Internal Market, this index

DIRECT EFFECT DOCTRINE
Generally, 95 et seq.
Directives, effect of, 103 et seq.
Individuals vs Member States as subject of EU norms, 95
Interpretive requirements for Member States, 113
Laws and Legislative Process, this index
Monism/dualism distinction, 95
Quasi-horizontal effect, 110
Regulations, effect of, 102
Sufficient precision requirement of directives, 106
Supremacy principle relationship, 45, 121
Transformation of Europe, 102
Treaty provisions, interpretation by Member States, 98
Unconditional effect of directives, 106
Vertical direct effect of directives, 105

DISCRIMINATION
Direct and indirect discrimination, 183
Employment law, 119
Internal Market, this index
Reverse discrimination, supremacy doctrine issues, 128
Tax regimes, 180

DUAL CITIZEN ISSUES, 260

DUALISM/MONISM DISTINCTION, 95

ECONOMIC AND SOCIAL COMMITTEE, 42

EMPLOYMENT LAW
Discrimination, 119
Framework Agreement, 115
Free movement of workers. *See* Internal Market, this index

ENFORCEMENT ACTIONS
Generally, 77 et seq.
See also State Liability Doctrine, this index
Administrative practices subject to, 82
Burden of proof of infringement, 81
Compliance duties of Member States, 77
Defenses, 88 et seq.
European Commission role, 77
Expulsion from the EU, 394
Force majeure defense, 88
Formal stage, 78
Infringement, 81
Internal difficulties defense, 89
Lump sum and penalty payments sanctions, 395
Member State courts as subjects of, 84
Reasoned opinions in support, 78
Reciprocity defense, 89
TFEU mandate, 77

ESTABLISHMENT, FREEDOM OF
Internal Market, this index

EUROPEAN ATOMIC ENERGY COMMUNITY (EURATOM), 25

EUROPEAN CENTRAL BANK (ECB), 40, 358

EUROPEAN COAL AND STEEL COMMUNITY (ECSC)
European Economic Community compared, 22
Founding of, 17
Treaty, 18

EUROPEAN COMMISSION
Generally, 36
Enforcement action role, 77
Membership, 37
Reasoned opinions in support of enforcements, 78
Responsibilities, 37

EUROPEAN COMMUNITY (EC)
European Economic Community and, 3, 23

EUROPEAN CONVENTION ON HUMAN RIGHTS, 14

EUROPEAN COUNCIL
Generally, 33
Council of Europe distinguished, 34
Legislative approvals, 157

EUROPEAN ECONOMIC AREA (EEA) AGREEMENT
Dispute resolution, 387
EU law harmonization, 393
Market access of non-EU states, 392
Updates modifying, 392

Withdrawing state options, 392

EUROPEAN ECONOMIC COMMUNITY (EEC)
Common market creation of, 101
Economic Community and, 3, 23
ECSC compared, 22
Historical background, 22
TFEU supersession of, 99
Treaty, 21
Withdrawal rights, 367

EUROPEAN INTEGRATION
Alternatives to EU, 15
Churchill speech, 6
Collective action problems, 61
Court of Justice role risks, 61
Historical background, 4
Legislative process, centralist tendency tensions, 154
Monetary Union, this index
Neofunctionalism theories, 15, 16
Sovereignty tensions, 5

EUROPEAN PARLIAMENT
Autonomy of Member States, 43
Competence issues, 151, 384
Legislative approvals, 157
Proportionality of representation, 35

EUROZONE
Monetary Union, this index

EXCHANGE RATE MECHANISM (ERM)
Generally, 347
Monetary union, 349
See also Monetary Union, this index

EXPORTS AND IMPORTS
Internal Market, this index

FINANCE
European Central Bank, 40, 358
Free movement of capital. *See* Internal Market, this index
Monetary Union, this index

FOUR FREEDOMS PRINCIPLE, 9, 12

FUNDAMENTAL FREEDOMS
Generally, 257 et seq.
See also Internal Market, this index
Act of state violations, 327
Assembly, laws affecting right of, 333
Boycotts violating free movement of goods, 328
Common problems, 327 et seq.
Failure to act violations, 327
Free movement of goods as component, 175
Interstate element, freedom to provide services, 305
Margin of discretion in enforcement, free movement of goods, 332
Private party obstacles impeding
    Private party liabilities, 339
    State liabilities, 327
Residence Rights, this index
Services, interstate element of freedom to provide, 305
State inaction violative of, 327
Supremacy doctrine and, 127
Violations
    Private party liabilities, 339
    State liabilities, 327

FUNDAMENTAL RIGHTS
EU vs U.S. terminology, 136

HISTORICAL BACKGROUND
Generally, 3 et seq.
Admission to EU, procedure, 27
Amsterdam, Treaty of, 24
Briand memorandum, 4
Brussels Treaty, 13
Churchill speech, 6
Common market, EEC creation of, 101
Copenhagen criteria for membership, 27
Council of Europe, 13
Development of EEC/EC/EU membership, 25
European Convention on Human Rights adoption, 14
European Economic Community, this index
Founding of the European communities, 17 et seq.
Internal market, 169
League of Nations failure, 7
Leaving the EU, 367
Lisbon, Treaty of, 24
Maastricht, Treaty of, 23
Monetary union, 349
Nice, Treaty of, 24
North Atlantic Treaty Organization formation, 13
Organisation for Economic Co-operation and Development formation, 13
Organisation for European Economic Co-operation formation, 12
Rome Treaties, 21
Single European Act, 23
State liability doctrine, 138
Statute of the Council of Europe, 14
Supremacy principle, 123
UK role in EU development, 10
World War II effects, 6

HUMAN DIGNITY
Treaty protection, 312

HUMAN RIGHTS
EU vs U.S. terminology, 136
European Convention on Human Rights adoption, 14
Treaty protection, 313

IMMIGRATION
Free movement of workers. *See* Internal Market, this index

IMPORTS AND EXPORTS
Internal Market, this index

INSTITUTIONAL STRUCTURE OF EU, 33

INTEGRATION
European Integration, this index

INTERGOVERNMENTALISM, 15

INTERNAL MARKET
    Generally, 169 et seq.
    See also Fundamental Freedoms, this index
Boycotts, 328, 343
Burdens amounting to customs duties, 171
Capital. Free movement of capital, below
Choice of law issues
    Companies, this index
    Free movement of workers, 299
Civil service employment, 239
Country of origin labels, 193
Customs union, 171 et seq.
Discrimination prohibitions
    Direct and indirect discrimination, 183
    Free movement of capital, 325
    Free movement of goods, 180
    Free movement of workers, 245
    Freedom of establishment, 273
    Freedom to provide services, 305
    Tax regimes, 180
Dual citizen issues, 260
Employment. Free movement of workers, below
European Coal and Steel Community Treaty, 18
European Economic Area, non-EU states access, 392
Family members of workers, 258 et seq.
Financial services, freedom to provide, 305
Free movement of capital
    Generally, 317 et seq.
    Discrimination prohibitions, 325
    Freedom of establishment distinguished, 319
    Gold and silver coins as capital or goods, 318
    Privatization of utilities, 319
    Restriction justifications, 325
    Scope of protection, 317
Free movement of goods
    Generally, 171 et seq.
    Boycotts violating, 328
    Burdens amounting to customs duties, 171
    Country of origin labels, 193
    Cross-border determinations, 172
    Customs union, 171 et seq.
    Direct and indirect discrimination, 183
    Discriminatory tax regimes, 180
    Fundamental freedoms, 175
    Gold and silver coins as capital or goods, 318
    Inspection fees, 176
    Mandatory requirements doctrine, 199 et seq.
    Margin of discretion in enforcement, 332
    Political demonstrations impeding, 333
    Protective effect issues, 186
    Quantitative restrictions on free movement of goods, below
    Restrictions, 199
    Service-related fees, 179
Free movement of workers
    Generally, 227 et seq.
    Choice of law issues, corporate employers, 299
    Civil service employment, 239
    Directive 2004/38/EC, 257
    Discrimination prohibitions, 245
    Dual citizen issues, 260
    Eligibility for employment, 267
    Employers' rights, 249
    Equal treatment in employment, 267
    Family member protections, 258 et seq.
    Freedom to provide services distinguished, 301
    Functional vs institutional interpretations, 239, 244
    Gainful employment qualification, 228
    Low-income workers, 230
    Make-work social programs, 234, 236
    Management employees, 250
    Mandatory requirements doctrine, 249
    Military service, 242
    Public service exception, 239
    Regulation 1612/68/EEC, 267
    Residence Rights, this index
    Restriction justifications, 249
    Scope of protection, 227
    Secondary legislation, 257 et seq.
    Students receiving financial aid, 231
    Teachers, 242
    Unemployment compensation laws, 246
Freedom of establishment
    Generally, 273 et seq.
    See also Companies, this index
    Discrimination prohibition, 273
    Free movement of capital distinguished, 319
    Freedom to provide services distinguished, 301
    Justifications for interference, 273
    Self-employment, 273
Freedom to provide services
    Generally, 301 et seq.
    Discrimination prohibition, 305
    Financial services, 305
    Free movement of workers distinguished, 301
    Freedom of establishment distinguished, 301

Interstate element, 305
Justifications for restrictions, 308
Personal scope of protection, 304
Professional persons, 302
Scope of protection, 301
Historical background, 169
Immigration. Free movement of workers, above
Inspection fees, free movement of goods, 176
Interstate element, freedom to provide services, 305
Investments. Free movement of capital, above
Justifications for restrictions
    Free movement of capital, 325
    Free movement of workers, 249
    Freedom of establishment, 273
    Freedom to provide services, 308
    Quantitative restrictions on free movement of goods, below
Labor. Free movement of workers, above
Management employees, free movement of, 250
Mandatory requirements doctrine
    Free movement of goods, 199 et seq.
    Free movement of workers, 249
    Quantitative restrictions, 200 et seq.
Margin of discretion in enforcement, 332
Military service, free movement of workers, 242
Monetary Union, this index
Payments. Free movement of capital, above
Political demonstrations impeding free movement of goods, 333
Privatization of utilities, free movement of capital issues, 319
Professional persons, freedom to provide services, 302
Protective effect issues in free movement of goods, 186
Public health and policy issues.
    Justifications for restrictions, above
Public service exception to free movement of workers, 239
Quantitative restrictions on free movement of goods
    Generally, 191
    Country of origin labels, 193
    Equivalent effects, 193
    Justifications, 199
    Proportionality requirement, 201
    Public policy considerations, 205, 217
    Without distinction principle, 201 et seq.
Requirements. Mandatory requirements, above
Residence Rights, this index
Restrictions
    Justifications for restrictions, above
    Quantitative restrictions on free movement of goods, above
Sales. Free movement of goods, above
Scope of protection
    Free movement of capital, 317
    Free movement of workers, 227
    Freedom to provide services, 301, 304
Security issues. Justifications for restrictions, above
Self-employment. Freedom of establishment, above
Services
    Fees, service-related impeding free movement of goods, 179
    Freedom to provide services, above
Students receiving financial aid, free movement of workers, 231
Teachers, free movement of workers, 242
TFEU mandate, 169
Unemployment compensation laws, free movement of workers, 246

INVESTMENTS
Free movement of capital. *See* Internal Market, this index

JUDICIARY
    Generally, 51 et seq.
    See also Court of Justice, this index
Civil Service Tribunal, 40
Court of Auditors, 42
Enforcement Actions, this index
Institutional structure of EU, 33
Precedent, 72
Preliminary rulings, 63 et seq.
State liability for court decisions, 143
Supremacy Doctrine, this index

JURISDICTION
Court of Justice, this index

LAWS AND LEGISLATIVE PROCESSES
    Generally, 33 et seq., 151 et seq.
    See also European Commission, this index; European Parliament, this index
Administrative Law, this index
Approvals by parliament and council, 157
Autonomy of Member States, 43
Centralist tendency tensions, 154
Characteristics of EU law, 93 et seq.
Committee of the Regions, 42
Competence, exclusive and shared, 151, 384
Conciliation Committee, 156
Decisions, effect of, 48
Directives
    Effect of
        Generally, 46
        Direct effect principle, 103 et seq.
        Interpretive requirements for Member States, 113
Economic and Social Committee, 42
Enforcement Actions, this index

EU law vs Member State law, tensions, 45
Framework, legal, 45 et seq.
Harmonizing measures, 166
Implied powers of EU legislators, 153
Institutional structure of EU, 33
Legislative history, court arguments based on the, 59
Necessity to achieve objectives of treaty, 154
Opinions
    Effect of, 48
    Reasoned opinions in support of enforcement, 78
Primary vs secondary EU law, 45
Procedural requisites, 54, 154 et seq.
Proportionality principle, 154
Recommendations, effect of, 48
Regulations, effect of
    Generally, 46
    Direct effect principle, 102
Subsidiary principle, 153
Supremacy Doctrine, this index

LEAVING THE EU
    Generally, 353, 367 et seq.
    See also Brexit, this index
British rebate, 372
EU international treaties effects, 383
European Convention proposal, 369
Expulsion, 394
Historical background, 367
International agreements following withdrawal, 389
Lisbon Treaty withdrawal rights, 367
Lump sum and penalty payments sanctions, 395
Negotiability of withdrawal rights, 371, 374
Notifications of withdrawal, 373, 382
Options of withdrawn state, 392
TFEU Article 50, 373

LIABILITY DOCTRINE
State Liability Doctrine, this index

MAASTRICHT, TREATY OF, 23

MANDATORY REQUIREMENTS DOCTRINE
Internal Market, this index

MARKETS
Internal Market, this index

MEMBER STATES' SOVEREIGNTY
    See also Supremacy Doctrine, this index
Brexit, this index
European integration tensions, 5
Leaving the EU, this index
United Kingdom concerns, 14
U.S. federalism parallels, 43

MONETARY UNION
    Generally, 347
Asymmetrical economy shocks, 354
British rebate, 372
Convergence criteria for membership, 348
Economic challenges, 349
Economic perspective, 353
Exchange Rate Mechanism, 347
Expulsions from Eurozone, 347, 351
Financial crisis of 2008 impacts, 349
Historical background, 347, 349
Inflation concerns, 41, 348
Joining the Eurozone, 350
Leaving the EU effects, 353, 367 et seq.
Leaving the Eurozone, 351
Monetary policy, 358
Payment issues, 355
Political opposition to a common currency, 348
Stability and Growth Pact, 348
State of economic and fiscal integration, 358
Withdrawals from Eurozone, 347

MONISM/DUALISM DISTINCTION, 95

NECESSITY RULE
Court of Justice jurisdiction, 67

NEOFUNCTIONALISM
Theories of European integration, 15, 16

NICE, TREATY OF, 24

NON-DISCRIMINATION PRINCIPLE
Discrimination, this index

NORWAY
EU membership issues, 25

ORGANISATION FOR ECONOMIC CO-OPERATION AND DEVELOPMENT (OECD)
Formation, 13
Tax policy, 274

ORGANISATION FOR EUROPEAN ECONOMIC CO-OPERATION, 12

PARLIAMENT
European Parliament, this index

PAYMENTS
Internal Market, this index
Monetary Union, this index

RESIDENCE RIGHTS
    Generally, 260 et seq.
Entry restrictions, 265
Equal treatment, 266
Family members, 262
Illegal immigrants, 262
Lawful resident qualifications, 262
Permanent residence, 264
Public policy restrictions, 265
Three month rule, 261

ROME TREATIES, 21

SINGLE EUROPEAN ACT, 23

SOVEREIGNTY
Member States' Sovereignty, this index

STABILITY AND GROWTH PACT
Monetary union, 348

STATE LIABILITY DOCTRINE
　　Generally, 137 et seq.
　　See also Enforcement Actions, this index
Causation issues, 141
Civil rights, 141
Conditions governing, 147
Court decisions, state liability for, 143
Expulsion from the EU, 394
Historical background, 138
Individual claims, 395
Lump sum and penalty payments, 395
Preconditions, 141
Private party claims, 395
Res judicata, 149

STATUTE OF THE COUNCIL OF EUROPE, 14

SUBSIDIARY PRINCIPLE, 153

SUPREMACY DOCTRINE
　　Generally, 121 et seq.
Administrative law of Member States conflicts, 124
Civil rights issues tensions, 130, 133
Conflicts, effects of, 121, 127
Courts of Member States opposition, 129
Cross-border issues vs purely domestic issues, 128
Direct effect doctrine relationship, 45, 121
Foundational opinions, 123
Fundamental freedoms and, 127
Historical background, 123
Judicial decisions of Member States conflicts, 125
Member State courts opposition, 125, 129
Primacy in application, primacy in validity distinguished, 121
Priority in application, 127
Reverse discrimination issues, 128

TAXATION
Companies, 274
Discriminatory tax regimes, 180
Internal Market, this index
OECD tax policy, 274

TELEOLOGICAL REASONING, 57

TRADE
Internal Market, this index

TREATIES
Different types of, 386
Exclusive and shared legislative competence, 384
Member States interpretations of treaty provisions, 98
Neighborhood treaties, 388

Norway-EU treaties, 391
Switzerland-EU treaties, 391

TREATY ON THE FUNCTIONING OF THE EUROPEAN UNION (TFEU)
Constitution of EU, effect as, 25
EEC superseded by, 99
Enforcement Actions, this index
Internal market mandate, 169
Leaving the EU provision, 373

TURKEY
EU membership issues, 29

UNITED KINGDOM
Brexit, this index
EU development, UK role, 10
Sovereignty concerns, 14

WITHDRAWAL RIGHTS
European Economic Community, 367
Leaving the EU, this index
Monetary Union, this index